UK POLITICS

Edited by
Alan Convery

1 Oliver's Yard
55 City Road
London EC1Y 1SP

2455 Teller Road
Thousand Oaks
California 91320

Unit No 323-333, Third Floor, F-Block
International Trade Tower
Nehru Place, New Delhi – 110 019

8 Marina View Suite 43-053
Asia Square Tower 1
Singapore 018960

Editor: Andrew Malvern
Development editor: Jessica Moran
Editorial assistant: Clara Landgren
Production editor: Imogen Roome
Copyeditor: Sarah Bury
Proofreader: Neil Dowden
Typeset by: C&M Digitals (P) Ltd, Chennai, India
Printed in the UK by Bell & Bain Ltd, Glasgow
BB0347467

Library of Congress Control Number: 2024944283

British Library Cataloguing in Publication data

A catalogue record for this book is available from the British Library

ISBN 978-1-5296-3008-4
ISBN 978-1-5296-3007-7 (pbk)

UK
POLITICS

Brief Contents

Extended Contents

About the Editor

Alan Convery is Senior Lecturer in Politics at the University of Edinburgh. His research focuses on UK and Scottish politics and conservatism and the Conservative Party. He is the author of *The Territorial Conservative Party: Devolution and Party Change in Scotland and Wales* (2016). He was Deputy Editor (2015–2018) and Lead Editor (2018–2021) of the *British Journal of Politics and International Relations*. At Edinburgh, he organises the Introduction to British Politics course and received the Chancellor's Award for Teaching in 2019.

About the Contributors

Sarah Childs is Professor of Politics and Gender at the University of Edinburgh.

Marc Geddes is Senior Lecturer in Politics at the University of Edinburgh.

Joe Greenwood-Hau is Lecturer in Politics at the University of Edinburgh.

Ailsa Henderson is Professor of Political Science at the University of Edinburgh.

Victoria Honeyman is Professor of British Politics at the University of Leeds.

Richard Wyn Jones is Professor of Politics at Cardiff University.

Daniel Kenealy is Senior Lecturer in Public Policy at the University of Edinburgh.

Meryl Kenny is Professor of Gender and Politics at the University of Edinburgh.

Harshan Kumarasingham is Reader in Politics and History at the University of Edinburgh.

Jac Larner is Lecturer in Politics at Cardiff University.

Clare Llewellyn is Lecturer in Governance, Technology and Data at the University of Edinburgh.

Benjamin Martill is Senior Lecturer in Politics and International Relations at the University of Edinburgh.

Nasar Meer is Professor of Social and Political Sciences at the University of Glasgow.

Richard Parry is Honorary Fellow in the School of Social and Political Science at the University of Edinburgh.

Timothy Peace is Senior Lecturer in Politics at the University of Glasgow.

Karl Pike is Senior Lecturer in Public Policy at Queen Mary University of London.

Cristian Vaccari is Professor of Future Governance, Public Policy and Technology at the University of Edinburgh.

Asanga Welikala is Senior Lecturer in Public Law at the University of Edinburgh.

Ben Wellings is Associate Professor of Politics and International Relations at Monash University.

Lisa Claire Whitten is a Research Fellow at Queen's University Belfast.

Preface

Students are not underserved by UK politics textbooks. Old editions prop up the monitor in my office. Why then do we need another one? This idea of this textbook is to view UK politics from a different angle. We try to present an account that is more territorial, critical and expansive. We start from the premise that the UK is now in part a 'Post-Westminster' polity: more decentralised, contested and diverse. We use this theoretical debate to frame a series of provocative questions about the nature of UK politics today and how we should study it. We present the institutions of the Westminster Model Narrative as still relevant, but in need of interpretation through a different lens.

This textbook brings together some of the leading scholars in the discipline and tasks them with presenting the latest research in an engaging and accessible way. The idea is to provide a clear bridge between research and teaching, giving students a 'way in' to cutting-edge work via clear explanations and engagingly pitched essential knowledge.

In taking diversity seriously, we engage up front with contemporary questions of representation and identity. Sarah Childs draws on her own cutting-edge research to try to break out of arid debates about percentages and try to get students to think about representation in new ways. This chapter provides the tools students need to engage with big debates about gender, race and ethnicity, and class in the following chapters. These authors, who are all at the forefront of their respective fields, give students the rich conceptual and empirical material needed to frame debates about inequality, diversity and access to power in the modern UK.

In taking territory seriously, we present a chapter on each of the four nations of the UK. We do not put Northern Ireland in the 'too hard' basket and instead have Lisa Clare Whitten provide an accessible introduction that gives students the tools to talk about devolution in the round. We also include a separate chapter on England by Ben Wellings that encourages students to think about the idea of Anglo-British institutions and make sense of the discussion of the rise of English identity.

Structure and content

The book is structured in five broad sections: (I) introduction, (II) representation, (III) central institutions, (IV) beyond the centre and (V) big issues. Convery's introductory chapter sets the stage for a refocusing of our attention. It asks whether the UK is a 'Post-Westminster' Polity. Using the Westminster Model Narrative as a starting point, it examines how far the UK has moved beyond the centralised and majoritarian descriptions of the past. Signposting the themes in the subsequent chapters throughout, it poses a series of provocative questions about the study and practice of UK politics.

Sarah Childs' chapter then suggests that students approach representation in a different way. She makes explicit the implicit tendency towards the trusteeship model in UK politics. Dispensing with the zero-sum discussions, Childs proposes a framework for interrogating the quality of representation and asking questions about the messy reality of democratic politics. That framework sets the context for students' engagement with the subsequent chapters on how we should study major divides in UK politics.

Meryl Kenny's chapter on gender introduces students to the possibilities of applying a gendered lens to the study of politics. She outlines the state of play when it comes to women's representation and uses the latest research to home in on candidate selection and parliamentary culture as key sites of gendered power relations. Her chapter is both an accessible state of the art and a challenge to students to think more expansively about what politics is and what political science is.

Peace and Meer's chapter on race and ethnicity provides students with the tools to discuss a topic that has been increasingly on the media and political agenda. Drawing on Meer's work on definitions and identity, it explores what we mean by social categories and their consequences. The evolution of ethnic minority representation in the UK gives students the empirical context to make sense of patterns of recruitment, discrimination and breakthroughs. Peace's research on ethnic minority voting behaviour gives a deeper dive into the latest questions and puzzles.

Joe Greenwood-Hau then draws students' attention to the idea of social class. He asks a series of questions about the nature of this category and students' relationship with it. Should we care if there is a lack of working-class representation in UK legislatures? Drawing on his own work, Greenwood-Hau shows the major changes in the evolution of the UK's political elites and our attitudes to them (bringing in major questions of authenticity, performance and what makes a good representative).

The textbook then moves on to examine the two major UK statewide parties. Alan Convery's chapter on the Conservative Party tries to make sense of the tumultuous 2019–2024 Parliament and the journey from Johnson to Sunak. It provides a framework for analysing the ideological fault-lines in the party and the big questions about the battle for its future. Karl Pike's chapter on Labour likewise tries to make sense of the major shift from Corbyn to Starmer and the underlying ideological and policy changes. Setting the current leadership in the wider context of debates about the party's purpose, it gives students the tools to explain the Starmer project and the 2024 election victory.

Finally, in this section Ailsa Henderson provides an essential one-chapter primer on the new electoral politics of a devolved UK. She shows how national identity, new divides and electoral shocks have up-ended old assumptions about electoral behaviour, necessitating new methods and a new approach. It is an explicitly multi-level perspective on public opinion and behaviour.

Moving on to central institutions, this section presents students with essential knowledge of the core wiring of the UK but with a critical edge and a grounding in the latest work with an eye to further questioning the Westminster Model Narrative. Convery and Welikala's chapter on the constitution combines public law and political science perspectives. It places devolution, judicialisation and parliamentary sovereignty in context and outlines the contours of the key contemporary debates.

Marc Geddes' chapter on Parliament makes a compelling revisionist case for looking again at the legislative clichés about weak MPs and over-mighty ministers. Drawing on the latest research (including his own work), he shows students the diverse methods and innovations in parliamentary studies. He brings Westminster perspectives into conversation with works on the devolved legislatures, noting the uneven impact of parliamentary reform and the options for future changes.

Richard Parry continues this questioning of the powerful Westminster executive in a chapter that introduces students to the latest conceptual thinking about the centre of government, from the core executive to court politics. It outlines the key governing challenges facing White-hall and draws on lively contemporary examples from the Covid Inquiry to ministerial resig-nations to bring the academic debates to life. The relationship between ministers and the civil service is a live topic.

The book then moves to consider the territorial aspect of UK politics. Each UK nation is considered in a separate chapter. Ben Wellings begins by looking at England – a major departure from the Westminster Narrative presentation of UK politics. Why is there a need for a separate chapter about the biggest part of the UK? Wellings confronts the squeamishness about talking about Englishness and unpacks the major debates about identity, governance and empire.

In their chapter about Scotland, Alan Convery and Ailsa Henderson place debates about independence in context and examine the ambiguous nature of devolution. Scotland already had a great deal of autonomy within the union and the creation of the Scottish Parliament extended a long-standing trend. The chapter examines the Scottish National Party (SNP), a major party at the UK level since 2015, and explains the reasons for its success. It also looks at policy divergence in Scotland since 1999: public policy in the UK operates in increasingly dif-ferent ways, with implications for democratic satisfaction and support for the union.

Jac Larner and Richard Wyn Jones consider Wales. They break down the complicated story of the evolution of Welsh devolution and place the current debates about the Welsh Parliament reforms in context. They examine public opinion in Wales and explain the extraordinary suc-cess of the Welsh Labour Party in elections over 100 years. The Welsh Government now con-fronts major public policy challenges and a tricky relationship with the UK Government in the UK's messy devolution framework.

Lisa Claire Whitten's chapter on Northern Ireland tries to move it firmly from the 'too hard' basket and into the mainstream of discussions about UK politics. She gives students the tools to understand the complicated history of divisions in Northern Ireland and shows how this maps on to public opinion and the party system. Her primer on the Belfast Agreement helps students to understand the place of Northern Ireland in the UK and why it became such a massive issue during the implementation of Brexit. Whitten ends by reflecting on deeper changes that will shape Northern Ireland politics in the years to come.

The final section of the textbook examines big issues in UK politics. Daniel Kenealy's chapter on public policy looks at the major policy theories from a UK angle and applies them to recent case studies and examples. He examines how governments have tried to manage complexity and the devolved nature of more policy areas. He also outlines the importance of institutions (especially the Treasury) and path dependency in policy decisions.

In their chapter on the media and social media, Clare Llewellyn and Christian Vaccari take a hot topic beyond the realm of opinions and hunches and into the latest research. They look at the media landscape in the UK and ask about the continuing role of the old media in news-papers and television. They then examine the impact of social media on UK politics and how parties have tried to engage with voters in new ways. Drawing on the latest research about Twitter/X, they bring a contested topic to life.

In confronting Brexit, Benjamin Martill considers how the UK got here. He distils the debates and the sudden changes of recent years in an accessible narrative. He links the discussion to wider issues about how states negotiate and the options open to the UK. Brexit is a political, economic and ideological question that will continue to shape UK politics.

Relatedly, Victoria Honeyman then considers the wider issue of UK foreign policy. As a declining power in the twentieth century, the UK faced major questions about its role in the world and the foreign policy it could afford to pay for. Recent foreign policy fiascos, like the Iraq War, still weigh heavily on the UK's thinking. The extent of security and defence co-operation after Brexit is still an open question.

Finally, Harshan Kumarasingham argues that the study of UK politics needs to involve some consideration of the impact of UK politics beyond the UK. He examines the impact of the British Empire at home and abroad, introducing students to the major debates about its legacy. He presents the concept of 'Eastminster' to capture the ways in which Westminster Model ideas were exported and adapted elsewhere. It is a neat coda to the initial consideration of the idea of a Post-Westminster Model Narrative.

How to use this book

Each chapter begins with a summary of its key messages. It then presents a 'What do I need to know?' box as a reminder for students of some of the assumed background knowledge and concepts they should be aware of. 'Case Study' boxes bring the themes to life and show some of the big debates in action. 'Reflective questions' provide a jumping-off point for tutorial discussions or further investigation. 'Research in Focus' boxes introduce students to some of the most interesting work in the field, bridging the gap between textbook and scholarship. These boxes demonstrate research-led teaching in action.

The chapters make connections but they are also very suitable for use on their own. Lecturers can therefore easily adopt a mix and match approach, assigning chapters that are most relevant to the topics at hand and leaving others for further reading. The recommended reading sections are further designed to bridge the gap between the textbook and the academic literature, encouraging students to explore further in their independent reading.

Part I

Introduction

Image 1   A row of cottages in Bibury, Cotswolds, England. Politics happens throughout the United Kingdom and impacts people in very different ways based on their geography, family, religion, wealth, gender, ethnicity, sexuality, and more. Politics is not the sole preserve of Westminster, but happens everywhere from countryside villages to urban centres. Photo by David Iliff. License: CC BY-SA 3.0.

Chapter 1

The post-Westminster polity?

Alan Convery

What will this chapter tell me?

- This chapter outlines the most influential way of looking at UK politics: a set of ideas that scholars have labelled the Westminster Model. Because it is neither as precise nor stable as a model, this chapter suggests we view it as a narrative – a story that seeks to explain the world.
- This chapter examines the ways in which this Westminster Model Narrative fails to capture recent changes in UK politics. However, it still exerts a strong influence because it is generally the prism through which UK political elites view their roles.
- Instead, this chapter uses the Westminster Model Narrative as a starting point to suggest some of the ways in which we might view the UK as a 'Post-Westminster Model' polity.
- A Post-Westminster Model Narrative retains many of the core institutional features of the Westminster Model but it is much more decentralised, critical and contingent.

What do I need to know?

- The UK is a plurinational state of four parts: England, Scotland, Wales and Northern Ireland.
- 'Westminster' is a place: it refers to the area in London where the UK Parliament is located (in the Palace of Westminster). However, it is also used as political and academic shorthand for central UK Government ('the Government at Westminster') and a style of politics or institutions ('a Westminster-style system'). Similarly, 'Whitehall' (an area in London) is used as shorthand for the central UK Government departments.
- The UK was sometimes viewed as a centralised and unitary state. However, even before major decentralisation reforms in 1999, it tolerated a great deal of sub-state policy variation.

Introduction

This textbook aims to broaden what we view as *UK* and what we view as *politics*. In so doing, we want to disrupt some of the existing narratives about UK politics and suggest how we may study it in a more critical, territorial and expansive way. As a way into some of the key themes of the book, this chapter uses the ideas contained in the traditional Westminster Model to structure a series of questions about UK politics today. It examines some background assumptions about the study and practice of UK politics through the themes of representation, ideology, governing and identity.

The Westminster Model is both a descriptive list of attributes and a set of normative assumptions about the best way to govern. There is not a single standardised definition; rather, there are multiple ideas about the Westminster Model and about whether it is an ideal type set of arrangements that the UK originated and other countries emulated. Definitions typically contain some elements that students might already be familiar with (such as Parliament and the First-Past-the-Post electoral system) and some less well-known doctrines (such as ministerial responsibility and institutionalised opposition).

The chapter reveals how some of the core preoccupations of the Westminster Model remain relevant for students of UK politics (Flinders et al. 2021). UK political elites – politicians, civil servants, commentators – often describe their roles in these terms and students should be alert to stories or justifications that are refracted through a Westminster Model lens. Why is politics sometimes described in particular ways and to emphasise – and valorise – particular practices? However, this chapter's interrogation of the Westminster Model also reveals a polity that is in many ways 'post-Westminster'. That means we need both new tools to study 'Westminster' and to pay more attention to people and processes outside it.

What is the Westminster Model or Narrative?

The most influential way of explaining UK politics is a set of ideas known as the Westminster Model (Gamble 1990; Kerr and Kettell 2006; McAnulla 2006; Hall 2011). As the name suggests, this explanation revolves around what happens at the centre of UK Government in London. It is commonly referred to as a 'model', which suggests that it provides a coherent account of how politics works, perhaps with some testable propositions. It is more a disparate jumble of institutions, ideas and rules about how things ought to work. It describes a certain mode of working and provides a justification for the power relationships within it. It might therefore more accurately be characterised as the Westminster 'narrative' (Hall 2011: 43), mindset or philosophy. This narrative tells a story about UK politics from a central perspective, providing a creation myth, an idealised way of working and a justification for why power lies – and should lie – in certain places.

There is no single agreed account of what the Westminster Model covers and there have been several attempts to define it (e.g. Lijphart 1999). Figure 1.1 distils some of the central

```
┌─────────────────────────────────────────┐
│ Representation                            │
│ First-Past-the-Post electoral system      │
│ Parliamentary system                      │
│ Two-party system                          │
│ Institutionalised opposition              │
│ Strong party discipline                   │
│                                           │
│ Ideology                                  │
│ Parliamentary sovereignty                 │
│ Absence of judicial review                │
│ Unitary state                             │
│ Adversarial political culture             │
│ Constitutional flexibility                │
│                                           │
│ Governing                                 │
│ Single-party majority government          │
│ Neutral civil service                     │
│ Cabinet government                        │
│ Executive dominance                       │
│ Individual ministerial responsibility     │
│ Centralised government                    │
│ Executive drawn from the legislature      │
│ Collective cabinet responsibility         │
└─────────────────────────────────────────┘
```

Figure 1.1   Ideas associated with the Westminster Model

Source: Lijphart (1999: 10–21); Russell and Serban (2021: 752)

components. There is also a lively academic debate about whether it is a concept that has been 'stretched beyond repair' (Russell and Serban 2021) or remains 'stretched but not snapped' (Flinders et al. 2021). The Westminster Model functions firstly as a description of UK politics. It describes some of the central features and how they relate to one another. In the middle of the twentieth century, it also provided the prism through which UK politics was studied.

The description of UK politics that the Westminster Model Narrative offers is not entirely wrong. You can recognise elements of this account that still ring true today. UK Government is still highly centralised, especially in England (Institute for Public Policy Research (IPPR) 2019; Carrascal-Incera et al. 2020), and the executive does tend to get its way in Parliament. There is a strong argument that UK Government elites are still influenced by a tendency to want to hoard power at the centre (Flinders 2010: 22; Diamond 2013: 21; Ward 2020; Kenny and Casey 2021). Some scholars have also argued that Brexit has resulted in a re-assertion of Westminster Model assumptions because the UK Government attempted to keep returning powers at the centre, rather than devolve them to other legislatures in the UK (Baldini et al. 2022; Dudley and Gamble 2023).

Nevertheless, the overall account is too simplistic and incomplete to be a convincing guide to how the UK's political system works. It fails to take into consideration, for example: the policy impact of Parliament (Russell and Cowley 2016); long-standing features of the UK's territorial politics or the devolution reforms after 1999 (Bogdanor 1999; Mitchell 2009; Flinders 2010); the challenges to the idea of untrammelled parliamentary sovereignty from EU membership, devolution or critical scholars (Loughlin and Tierney 2018); or the dispersal of power and functions from Westminster to arm's-length bodies and quangos (Matthews 2013).

However, crucially, the Westminster Model also has a prescriptive or normative quality. It describes how the system *ought* to work (Rhodes 2011: 306–307; Diamond 2013: 43–45). The Westminster Model emphasises the power of elites at the centre. There is a strong tendency to want to protect the centre of government from being forced to react to public opinion (Richards 2014). Instead, it should be insulated between elections so that it can take difficult and necessary decisions in the national interest. Strong government is sustained by adherence to the concept of parliamentary sovereignty (which often in practice means the sovereignty of the executive) and an electoral system that tends towards single-party majority governments. Local government is not a prominent feature and there is no strong role for the courts. There is also no discussion of how access to the levers of power described here might be affected by class, race or gender or other inequalities in society (Marsh et al. 2003; Akram 2024). It is therefore not a neutral description of UK politics.

Even so, it is important for students to recognise the Westminster Model Narrative because it tends to be the implicit mental model of how UK Government works that UK elites use:

> the Westminster Model presents a false picture of how the British political system
> works. The key features – parliamentary sovereignty, ministerial responsibility
> and collective responsibility – do not function as the model suggests. However,
> unsurprisingly, it is the view of democracy shared by actors in the core executive
> … it legitimises their authority and power. As such it affects how the system works.
> It shaped the process of constitutional and organisational reform and continues to
> maintain elite rule. (Marsh et al. 2003: 247)

When English or British politicians talk about how government works, they tend to reach for explanations that implicitly draw on a Westminster Model Narrative (Richards and Smith

2002: 48; Rhodes 2011). Much political and journalistic commentary on UK politics also tends to describe the system using Westminster Model assumptions. There is not a blanket adherence to a description outlined in academic books, but as students of politics it is often useful to label a particular way of describing institutions so that we can question the assumptions behind it. In 2011, the Government published the *Cabinet Manual*, a distilled version of various conventions and assumptions in the Cabinet Office, as a guide to UK Government.

Westminster Model Narrative	Post-Westminster Model Narrative
Representation	
• Unified political nation represented in Parliament • First-Past-the-Post transmits the will of the UK electorate • Centralised statewide parties aggregate interests in UK party system • Trusteeship model of representation where the characteristics of representatives do not matter • Institutions open to all via democratic means	• Greater recognition of plurinational UK and contested meanings of Britishness • Multiple UK *electorates* with competing priorities and multi-level electoral behaviour • Multi-level statewide parties and different party systems • Contested understanding of representation and critical attention to *who* represents • Critical understanding of political institutions as sites that can reflect or reproduce unequal distributions of power
Ideology	
• Adherence to parliamentary sovereignty as a governing ideology, creation myth and symbol of national distinctiveness • Judicial restraint and weak judicial review, anonymous courts • Unitary understanding of the nature of the UK • Export of Westminster practices	• Contested sovereignty claims (which nation?), popular sovereignty via referendums, post-sovereign understandings of political power • Greater judicial intervention and controversy • Post-unitary understanding – a union state/state of unions • Multiple Westminsters – and Eastminster
Governing	
• Strong executive as legitimate locus of political power – centralisation is democratic and good for policy making • Executive dominance of weak Parliament via absolute majorities and strong party discipline • Ministerial accountability to Parliament • National pluralism recognised via Westminster • Weak local government and no interest in meso-level government for England	• Contested understanding of the wisdom of strong executive and critical view of whether executive is in control (government to governance) • Greater recognition of Parliament as a check on executive and erosion of party discipline • Critical view of accountability (delegation, arm's-length bodies, parties protect their ministers) • Devolved government, intergovernmental relations, multi-level policy making • Meso-level English governance via metro mayors and devolution
Identity	
• Unified national identity with Englishness masked under Anglo-British attitudes and institutions • Homogeneous and unquestioned white Britishness	• Contested multiple national identities with new recognition of Englishness and England as a political unit beyond Westminster • Recognition of diversity and attention to the effects of, for example, gender, race, class, disability and their interactions on political outcomes and access to power

Figure 1.2   Westminster and Post-Westminster Narratives of UK politics

The outline it gives draws heavily on Westminster Model ideas (Cabinet Office 2011: 2–4). The *Ministerial Code* (Cabinet Office 2022) and the UK Parliament also use this frame to structure their descriptions (Flinders et al. 2021: 358–359). Politicians and civil servants therefore operate in a world in which they view their roles in the system through a (more or less) Westminster Model Narrative prism (Rhodes 2011: 306).

This textbook attempts to disrupt the Westminster Model Narrative and to draw attention to aspects that it ignores or downplays. In the left-hand column of Figure 1.2, we suggest an expanded set of ideas that might constitute the Westminster Model Narrative. In the right-hand column in Figure 1.2, we suggest the elements that might make up a Post-Westminster Narrative. The gravitational pull of elements like parliamentary sovereignty and First-Past-the-Post are still there, but we need to view them critically and in light of recent developments. The next section of this chapter examines representation, government, ideology and identity in turn. It suggests how we might view UK politics through a Post-Westminster lens. The aim is not to use the Westminster Model Narrative as a 'straw man'; we do not suggest that it is subscribed to in its entirety or that it ever accurately reflected how UK politics was studied and practised. Instead, we use it here as a jumping-off point to structure some initial thoughts about continuity and change in UK politics.

The idea is not to provide a coherent new account, but rather to focus students' attention on the ways in which the study and practice of UK politics has moved beyond the Westminster Model Narrative (Marsh et al. 2003). The intention is not to be prescriptive; rather, we want to be provocative. A central open question is: what is UK politics like now and how should we study it? The authors in this volume do not all agree on the answer to that question, but we hope to provide students with the tools to make up their own mind.

Representation

The Westminster Model Narrative suggests a unified political nation represented in Parliament. The wishes of the electorate are transmitted via the majoritarian First-Past-the-Post electoral system and there is a reverence for an MP's strong and individual constituency link. That MP's representative duty tends to be framed in terms of a trusteeship model: an MP should not slavishly follow their constituents' opinions; rather, they do their best work when they trust their own judgement. Centralised statewide parties provide the means for recruiting candidates, forming governments, and representing territorial interests at the parliamentary centre.

Viewing UK politics through the lens of a Post-Westminster Narrative, in contrast, draws our attention to a much messier and more contested picture. The idea of a single UK political nation is much more difficult to sustain in the 2020s and some scholars would argue that it never existed at all. The UK is a multi-national state of four parts: England, Scotland, Wales and Northern Ireland. Northern Ireland has always had a different party system (see Whitten, in this volume) and had a devolved government from 1921 to 1972. In Scotland and Wales, electoral behaviour has been diverging from England since the 1970s (Miller 1981; Griffiths et al. 2023; Larner and Wyn Jones, in this volume). In the 2016 referendum on EU membership, England and Wales voted to leave and Scotland and Northern Ireland voted to remain (Henderson et al. 2021). After the 2019 UK general election, the third-largest party in the House of Commons was the Scottish National Party, which is not a statewide party and only fields candidates in one part of the UK. As Ailsa Henderson argues in Chapter 8, there is no such thing as a UK electorate.

The study of elections in the UK is now therefore a multi-level exercise. Talking about people like the 'typical British voter' occludes major differences in behaviour and outlook across the UK. When we talk about British elections, we are sometimes in danger of describing an imaginary place or we say 'UK' when we actually mean 'England' (Henderson et al. 2017: 632). Instead, a Post-Westminster Narrative seeks to disaggregate the multiple political nations in the UK and pay attention to where they converge and diverge. For instance, Scottish voters behave differently at the ballot box, but many of their underlying political attitudes are in fact very similar to voters in England (Henderson 2014a).

The First-Past-the-Post (FPTP) electoral system still generates majority governments from minority shares of the vote at the UK level. The idea of a strong majority government that can be removed at periodic elections is a central feature of the Westminster Model Narrative. Strong central authority is tempered with strong electoral accountability: there is little prospect of a defeated governing party clinging on to power through a rejigged coalition arrangement. However, FPTP at Westminster and in English and Welsh local government is no longer the only game in town in terms of electoral systems. Scottish local government and the Northern Ireland Assembly use the Single Transferable Vote (STV) system. The Scottish Parliament, Welsh Parliament and London Assembly use a form of Mixed Member Proportional (MMP) electoral systems. The Welsh Parliament plans to move towards a different proportional system and Welsh local authorities can choose to switch to STV if they wish.

Within and beyond England, the UK's political parties confront a much more volatile electorate. The Westminster Model Narrative's focus on the idea of a two-party system masks a great deal of churn underneath the surface. Voters switch their vote to a different party in greater numbers between elections. Voters react more strongly to shocks (like Brexit) because they are less and less attached to the established parties and more likely to vote for other parties (Fieldhouse et al. 2020). Vote switching peaked in the 2015 general election when there was a collapse in support for the Liberal Democrats, a big rise in support for the SNP in Scotland and the rise of smaller parties like UKIP in England (Fieldhouse et al. 2023: 539). The Brexit shock has had a wider sorting effect and started to shift the traditional bases of support for the two parties in England that tend to alternate in government at Westminster. As Fieldhouse et al. (2023: 541) summarise: 'Labour [is] losing a substantial proportion of its support among its traditional heartlands, especially more socially conservative, older, working-class voters—while gaining support among younger, highly educated, and socially liberal voters. The Conservatives increased their support in those groups that deserted Labour.' This shift underlines a wider trend in England of urban areas leaning Labour and rural areas and towns leaning Conservative (Jennings and Stoker 2017; Furlong and Jennings 2024).

The Westminster Model Narrative in the 2020s also confronts different ways of understanding the concept of representation. The trusteeship model of MPs' behaviour tends to be invoked selectively and does not quite capture the multi-faceted nature of the role. In Chapter 2, Sarah Childs argues that we need to engage more deeply and critically with the question of what makes a 'good' representative. It is not a zero-sum game among different groups, but rather a messy question of evaluating the quality of representation. The MP's role itself has also changed markedly in the latter half of the twentieth century. As Marc Geddes outlines (in this volume), MPs need to be adept at playing different roles, moving from constituency champion to policy wonk, debater, fundraiser and (for some of them) government minister. We can also broaden the conversation to include discussions of the practical barriers to becoming an MP (Hardman 2018), the type of people who go into politics (Weinberg 2020) and MPs' mental health (Flinders et al. 2020). The changing media landscape and social media also affects how we view the representative process (Llewellyn and Vaccari, in this volume).

Given the uneven access to political power across different groups in the UK, scholars have also increasingly focused on the institutions described in the Westminster Model as sites that might reflect and reproduce wider inequalities. As the chapters in this volume describe, we can observe how different groups experience institutions and how patterns of access have changed over time in terms of gender (Kenny, in this volume), race and ethnicity (Peace and Meer, in this volume) and social class (Greenwood-Hau, in this volume). Moreover, Kenny (in this volume) argues that gender is not just a substantive area of study, but also an analytical lens for understanding institutional power relations – and that the impetus for changing this system should be on institutions, not those affected by them. Other scholars would also draw our attention to the argument that these (and other) characteristics might intersect to contribute to the further marginalisation of different people (Smooth 2011; Celis and Childs 2020; Siow 2023a). The political institutions at the heart of the Westminster Model Narrative are not therefore neutral: Parliament, central government and the civil service are workplaces that are affected by the rest of everyday life in the UK.

Ideology

The Westminster Model Narrative conceals some underlying ideological assumptions about the legitimate exercise of power. The concept of parliamentary sovereignty is a cornerstone of the UK's constitutional arrangements. The idea that Parliament can make or unmake any law provides a public law concept to understand the constitution, a guide to where power lies and a heritage or culture to be defended. It is a part of the overall tendency of the Westminster Model Narrative to prefer strong central government. Although in theory Parliament is sovereign, the executive with its reliable majority ends up being sovereign in practice.

However, as Convery and Welikala (in this volume) show, parliamentary sovereignty has come under pressure on several fronts. It is often predicated on a unitary understanding of the nature of the UK that supposes that the English concept of parliamentary sovereignty simply expanded its territorial reach each time a new state joined. Such an understanding is not universally accepted (MacCormick 1999; Keating 2021). It has also come under greater pressure since the creation of the devolved legislatures in 1999. The UK Parliament can of course theoretically abolish these institutions, but its ability to do so in practice is constrained by political considerations and, in the case of Scotland, a declaration in the Scotland Act 2016 that such a move would require a referendum.

Referendums have provided another key challenge to the idea of parliamentary sovereignty. The 2014 referendum on Scottish independence explicitly recognised the sovereignty of the Scottish people to decide on the question of secession. The Belfast Agreement in Northern Ireland also recognises its right to secede from the UK (see Whitten, in this volume). There have been UK-wide referendums on EC membership (1975), changing the electoral system (2011) and EU membership (2016). As Ben Martill explains (in this volume), this latter referendum set up a showdown between parliamentary and popular sovereignty in 2018 and 2019 about how the UK should leave the EU (Russell and James 2023).

A Post-Westminster Narrative would therefore have to contend with multiple competing sovereignty claims that are not easily reconciled. Parliamentary sovereignty remains the key organising feature of the UK's constitutional arrangements, but it is more contested than ever and is no longer capable of uniting the UK's multi-national state under a common sense of Britishness. Keating (2021) and Kenny (2024) discuss how the UK is now a 'fractured union'. The clash between parliamentary and popular sovereignty also poses new questions about the UK's tendency to emphasise a trusteeship model of representation.

The Westminster Model Narrative has almost nothing to say about the judiciary except to imply that its role is subordinate to supreme parliamentary authority. However, the courts are more involved in constitutional questions and controversial matters than ever before in the UK. The UK Supreme Court was established in 2005 and has gradually become a constitutional court in the way that other countries would recognise but which goes against the grain of the Westminster Model Narrative. Again, the 2016 referendum on EU membership set off a series of unintended consequences for parliamentary sovereignty and the UK constitution (Ewing 2017; Gordon 2019). There were two blockbuster constitutional cases in the Supreme Court that established that the executive required parliamentary approval to begin the process of exiting the European Union (Elliott 2017) and that the executive could not prorogue Parliament to prevent it debating issues (Elliott 2020).

The export of this political system elsewhere via the British Empire also means that there are multiple Westminster Models (Flinders et al. 2021). For Harshan Kumarasingham (in this volume), there also exists a version of 'Eastminster' that incorporates a tendency towards majoritarianism and a strong executive but with fewer minority rights and a more interventionist head of state (Kumarasingham 2016). Any pre- or post-Westminster narrative also bears the mark of the UK's imperial legacy, an inheritance that shaped both coloniser and colonised. There are further debates about echoes of Empire in the UK's foreign policy (see Honeyman, in this volume).

Governing

As David Judge argues, the English and then UK system has always had a tendency towards a strong central executive (Judge 1993). This feature is also a key bias of the Westminster Model Narrative. The uncodified constitution places a great deal of power in the hands of a government and a Prime Minister with a reliable parliamentary majority. It suggests that the Cabinet is the principal decision-making body in the UK with Parliament playing a peripheral role in the policy process. The Westminster Model Narrative also mentions nothing about local government or meso-level tiers of government beyond the centre. Local government has traditionally been weak and controlled by the centre (King 2007: 151). However, while it is still the case that UK central governments can achieve a great deal, the notion of the strong UK executive has come under greater scrutiny.

As Richard Parry (in this volume) points out, UK central government faces major challenges of organisation and performance. A major policy problem is the lack of economic growth. The Prime Minister's Office is enmeshed within a 'core executive' of key decision-makers that varies depending on the issue or the cast of politicians and civil servants involved (Dunleavy and Rhodes 1990; Rhodes 2011). It often includes the UK's all-powerful Treasury, an unusual finance *and* economics ministry with considerable sway over government policy. Daniel Kenealy (in this volume) argues that we need to ditch the idea of the all-powerful Prime Minister whose decisions cascade through the system and then into action. The Prime Minister's Office is underpowered and lacks the bandwidth to be on top of every issue (Diamond 2013; Harris and Rutter 2014; Urban et al. 2024). Prime Ministers must negotiate, coordinate and exchange resources to get things done. Their impact depends on a complex interplay of personal and electoral factors (Blick and Jones 2010; Byrne and Theakston 2019).

The strong executive narrative also needs to contend with revisionist scholarship on the policy power of Parliament. The dominant view of Parliament in the latter half of the twentieth century and in the Westminster Model Narrative was that it was a peripheral player in the policy process (Flinders and Kelso 2011). Executive control over the agenda and strong party discipline ensured that the government got its way and did not need to pay too much attention to MPs' views. Journalists and academics bemoaned the tendency of MPs to vote with the government and lamented the loss a bygone golden age of parliamentary influence. However, as Marc Geddes argues (in this volume), this view of parliamentary decline needs to be qualified. An executive at Westminster with a majority is in a strong position in relation to Parliament but that does not mean that Parliament does not matter. Simply counting the number of times the government is defeated in Parliament is a misleading guide to its influence. Instead, deeper analysis of parliamentary votes and interviews with MPs, civil servants and ministers reveals a more complicated picture (Russell and Cowley 2016). We need to pay attention to anticipated reactions and the process before legislation is introduced: governments generally do not bring forward bills that are unpopular with MPs. Informal discussions before draft legislation is produced influence the policy process. Governments will also respond to parliamentary pressure for amendments to legislation in both the Commons and the Lords (Russell et al. 2016).

Moreover, recent parliamentary reforms have increased the power of backbench MPs to hold the government to account. The chairs of select committees in the House of Commons, for example, are now elected and have taken the enhanced role seriously. The devolved legislatures were designed to be at the forefront of parliamentary reform and committee empowerment but have found themselves behind the curve as Westminster has reformed itself (Mitchell 2009). The changes in our understanding of Parliament's position prompted one academic to ask whether the House of Commons has become too powerful (Norton 2019).

The changing nature of governance has sparked an academic debate about how far the UK Government has been 'hollowed out'. Rhodes argues that ministers at the centre are pulling rubber levers. Power has been dispersed downwards through devolution, upwards through international organisations, and sideways to agencies and other delivery bodies (Bevir and Rhodes 2003). For others, the strong UK executive of the traditional Westminster narrative remains down but not out. Central government has been undermined by fragmentation, complexity and some decentralisation. However, in any policy discussion it remains the most important actor with the most powerful resources, including budget-setting, legislation and regulation (Marsh et al. 2003; Bell and Hindmoor 2012). Moreover, the UK's devolution reforms were carried out within the parameters of the Westminster Model mindset (Marsh and Hall 2007). Parliament retains the ability to overrule the devolved legislatures and did so during the implementation of Brexit (Keating 2022).

A Post-Westminster Model Narrative also draws our attention to the never-quite-unitary nature of the UK – and the ways in which its constitution has become more decentralised in recent years. The Scottish Office and the Welsh Office gradually gained more functions over the course of the twentieth century (Mitchell 2014), giving a distinctive territorial dimension to public policy. The devolution reforms of the Labour Governments (1997–2010) cemented this trend through the creation of the Scottish Parliament, Welsh Assembly, Northern Ireland Assembly, and the London Assembly and Mayor.

The Conservative-led governments after 2010 built on this legacy and started to experiment with devolution of power *within* England through the creation of combined authorities and metro mayors (Sandford 2023a). However, as with the late 1990s devolution arrangements, these new tiers of government occupy an ambiguous position in the Westminster Model Narrative. On the one hand, they have significant powers over transport, housing and economic development. However, they also lack any entrenched constitutional protection and rely on central government for their powers and most funding. The process has been top-down and uneven, resembling a contractual process in which central government decides the circumstances under which it will outsource the delivery of certain policy areas to local government and then monitor implementation (Sandford 2016). Devolution in England has therefore been designed specifically not to significantly alter the balance of power between central and local government (Ayres et al. 2017).

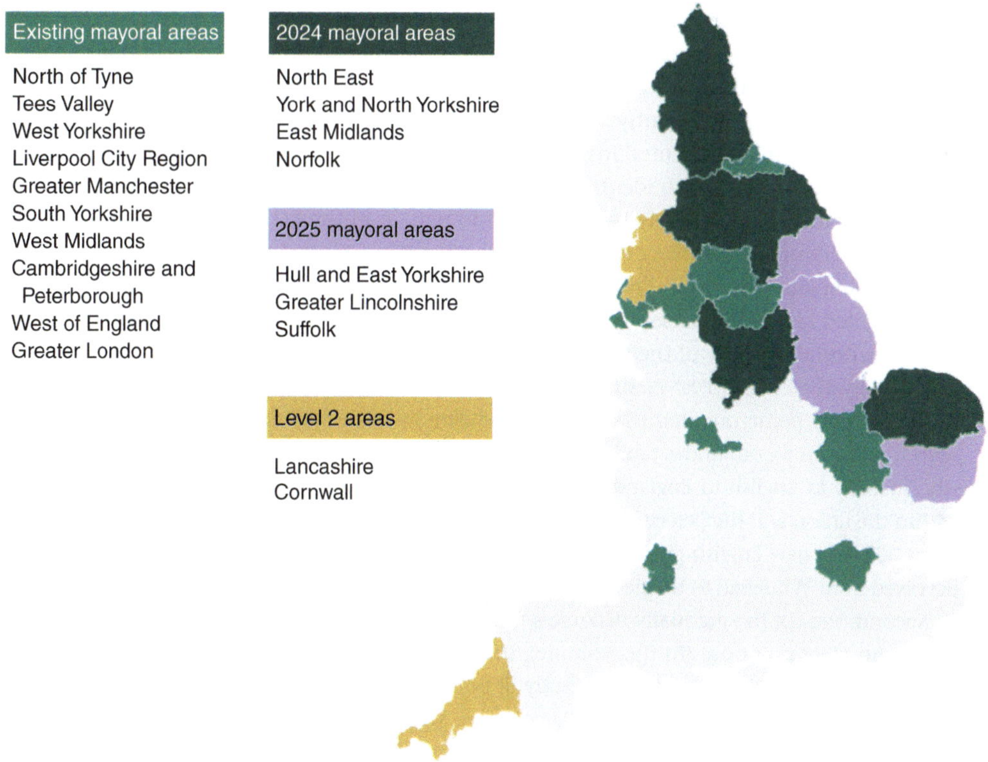

Existing mayoral areas	2024 mayoral areas
North of Tyne	North East
Tees Valley	York and North Yorkshire
West Yorkshire	East Midlands
Liverpool City Region	Norfolk
Greater Manchester	
South Yorkshire	**2025 mayoral areas**
West Midlands	
Cambridgeshire and	Hull and East Yorkshire
Peterborough	Greater Lincolnshire
West of England	Suffolk
Greater London	

Level 2 areas

Lancashire
Cornwall

Figure 1.3   English devolution: current and future

Source: House of Commons Library (https://commonslibrary.parliament.uk/english-devolution-deals-in-the-2023-autumn-statement/)

The Government at Westminster is still an important actor in the UK political system (perhaps even the most important actor – Marsh et al. 2003). However, it now interacts with increasingly powerful sub-state institutions, a UK Parliament that influences policy much more than the hoary caricatures suggest, and a series of governing problems that are becoming more difficult to manage. It carries out these functions in a UK that is increasingly fragmented, as we will now explore.

Identity

The Westminster Model Narrative's underlying assumption is that the multi-national nature of the UK is expressed through central institutions in London. There is an overarching British identity that unites the polity. The institutions at the centre are Anglo-British: they function in specifically English or in 'federal' UK-wide modes, but this distinction is never made explicitly. Englishness and England tend to be hidden in the Westminster Model Narrative.

A Post-Westminster Model Narrative, in contrast, confronts a much more complicated picture of identity and the institutions onto which it maps. First, the UK's multiple national identities have become more explicit and more important in recent years. In particular, the vote to leave the European Union in 2016 underlined fundamental differences in outlook shaped by national identity (Henderson and Wyn Jones 2023: 8). Understandings of Britishness are complicated and work differently in different parts of the UK. British identifiers in Scotland and Wales tend to like the central institutions of the UK state and are more likely to have voted for Brexit. In contrast, British identifiers in England tend to have a much more cosmopolitan set of views and are more likely to have voted to remain in the EU in 2016 (Henderson et al. 2021). Identifying as Scottish or Welsh in Scotland or Wales tended to increase your likelihood of voting Remain. Citizens in England who identified as English, in contrast, were more likely to have voted Leave (Henderson and Wyn Jones 2021). There is also an ambivalent attachment to the territorial integrity of the UK state in all areas.

Crucially, therefore, a Post-Westminster Narrative must take England and Englishness seriously. As Ben Wellings points out (in this volume), the tendency to elide Englishness and Britishness creates serious problems for our understanding of UK politics. There has been a rise in the number of people who identify as English in England and we know that they tend to resent the power of Scotland within the union and the perceived level of public spending outside England (Henderson and Wyn Jones 2021). A new English politics of the meso-level also requires our attention as more power is devolved from Whitehall to the new combined authorities (however tentatively).

Second, the UK has gradually become a much more ethnically diverse society since 1945. As Peace and Meer point out (in this volume), that shift has had major consequences for political representation, public policy and the study of politics. It is also linked in part to a legacy of the British Empire (Kumarasingham, in this volume). Migration in the postwar period from countries that were formerly part of the British Empire fundamentally changed the make-up of the UK and UK politics. Part of this change is often symbolised by the arrival of the *SS Empire Windrush*, but the UK had always been a migrant nation. This shift requires students of UK politics to confront questions about, for instance, whether ethnic minority candidates are penalised for providing substantive representation for minority groups (Martin and Blinder 2021) and the sort of expectations they feel about the representative role (Sobolewska et al. 2018). More broadly, Akram (2024) argues that the whole discipline of UK politics has neglected questions of race and racism: 'The overall effect of this position is that the discipline has been unwilling or indeed unable to respond to Grenfell, to the Windrush scandal, to the Black Lives Matter Movement, or the Sewell Report' (Akram 2024: 2).

The expansion of higher education has also opened another divide in the electorate: between graduates and non-graduates. Levels of education have become a major predicter of values and voting intention (Sobolewska and Ford 2020: 22). Sobolewska and Ford (2020) call the new political context 'Brexitland'. They make a distinction between voters who prioritise their in-group identity (ethnocentrism) and voters who are much more open to a range of identities and may view diversity in society as a positive good to be promoted and extended. On the one hand, there are what they term 'identity conservatives': 'white voters with lower levels of formal education who most frequently hold ethnocentric worldviews, making them more strongly attached to in-group identities ... and more threatened by out-groups such as migrants and minorities' (Sobolewska and Ford 2020: 22). On the other hand, there are 'two 'identity liberal' groups – university graduates and ethnic minorities – who for different reasons reject ethnocentrism' (Sobolewska and Ford 2020: 22). Thus: 'The conflict between these groups runs right through the heart of the electorate, and the activation of this conflict is a major source of the political upheavals and volatility of the past decade' (Sobolewska and Ford 2020: 22).

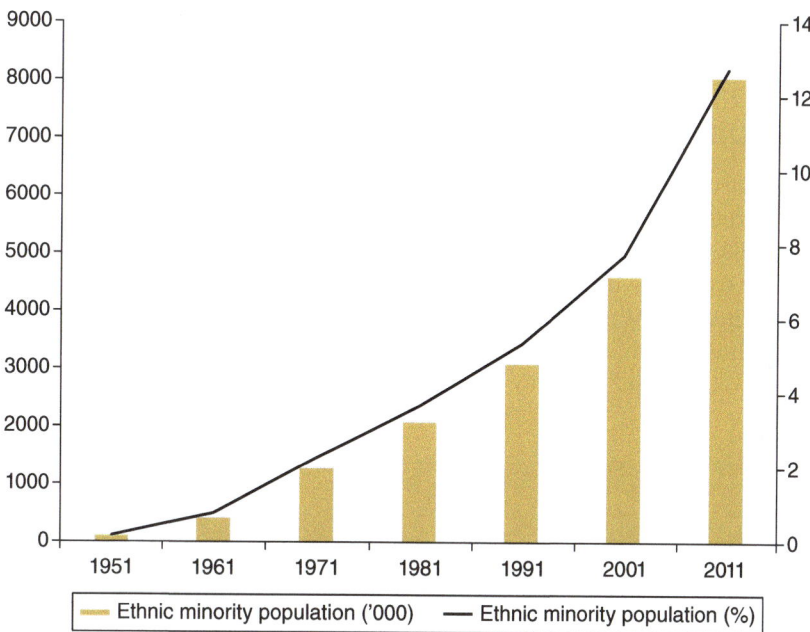

Figure 1.4 Ethnic group distribution (high-level categories), 2011 and 2021, England and Wales

Source: Office for National Statistics (2022) https://www.ons.gov.uk/peoplepopulationandcommunity/cultural identity/ethnicity/bulletins/ethnicgroupenglandandwales/census2021#:~:text=The%20largest%20increases%20 were%20seen,%25%2C%20564%2C000%20in%202011).

The Leave/Remain identities that emerged after the referendum in 2016 were not created on that date; rather, they reflected much deeper trends in the electorate. Students should be aware of these long-term transformations. The shift from a mostly white school-leaver electorate to a much more graduate and ethnically diverse electorate is a powerful driver of surface-level political conflict (Sobolewska and Ford 2020).

These long-term trends have changed the profile of voters for the two main parties. Broadly, the Conservatives draw much of their support from older voters and those who own their own home outright (Convery, Chapter 6 in this volume). The Labour Party now draws much of its support from younger voters and is especially ahead among those who rent their home (Pike, in this volume). The changed electoral context creates strategic dilemmas and opportunities for the parties. There are also gender gaps that increase with age (Sanders and Shorrocks 2019). In the 2019 general election, women were more likely than men to vote Labour and men were more likely than women to vote Conservative (Campbell and Shorrocks 2021). These effects are more pronounced among younger voters.

Finally, therefore, in that context, the study of UK politics in a Post-Westminster sense pays much more attention to the diversity of the UK. It asks questions about why certain groups are over- or under-represented in Parliament and Government (Childs, in this volume).

It asks what a gender (Kenny, in this volume), race and ethnicity (Peace and Meer, in this volume) or class (Greenwood-Hau, in this volume) lens can tell us about the distribution of power in UK politics. It now pays much more attention to the inequalities in UK society that affect how politics is conducted and discussed.

Conclusion

This chapter has used the Westminster Model Narrative as a starting point to explore the ways in which the study and practice of UK politics has evolved. It has tried to disrupt the narrative and critically engage with its explicit (and implicit) assumptions. As a starting point, we have suggested trying to view UK politics through a 'Post-Westminster Model' Narrative lens. The central institutions of the Westminster Model Narrative and many of its assumptions and modes of operating remain intact. However, they now sit on much shakier foundations and in some cases provide a polite fiction to paper over anomalies and incongruities.

Summary

- The Westminster Model Narrative is the traditional lens through which UK politics has been viewed.
- It presents an inaccurate account of how UK politics works but it is important to be aware of it because it still influences how UK politics is conducted and discussed.
- Using the assumptions in the Westminster Model Narrative as a starting framework, we can construct a Post-Westminster Model Narrative that tries to grapple with recent changes in UK politics, society and the constitution.
- Some central features of the Westminster Model Narrative remain in place (especially the tendency towards a strong executive), but what emerges elsewhere is a much more decentralised, contested and diverse polity.
- Trying to make sense of this mixture of old and new is part of the joy of studying UK politics – and is the task this book sets itself.

Recommended and further reading

- Hall's (2011) *Political Traditions and UK Politics* (Basingstoke: Palgrave) is an excellent introduction to the Westminster Model, the British Political Tradition, and other alternatives.
- For a suggestion of an Asymmetric Power Model to replace the Westminster Model, see Marsh, D., Richards, D. and Smith, M. (2003) 'Unequal plurality: towards an Asymmetric Power Model of British politics', *Government and Opposition*, 38(3): 306–332. They argue that the centre of UK Government remains the most important actor in the system, even if it has been challenged on several fronts.
- Bevir and Rhodes' (2003) *Interpreting British Governance* (London: Routledge) suggests that there are multiple competing narratives that operate alongside the Westminster Model Narrative. They argue for an interpretivist lens on UK politics that concentrates on understanding political practices by examining actors' beliefs.
- For a robust challenge to the discipline of British politics on the question of ignoring race and racism, see Akram, S. (2024) 'Dear British politics—where is the race and racism?', *British Politics*, 19(1): 1–24. Akram argues that these topics are hidden because the discipline does not talk about them enough.

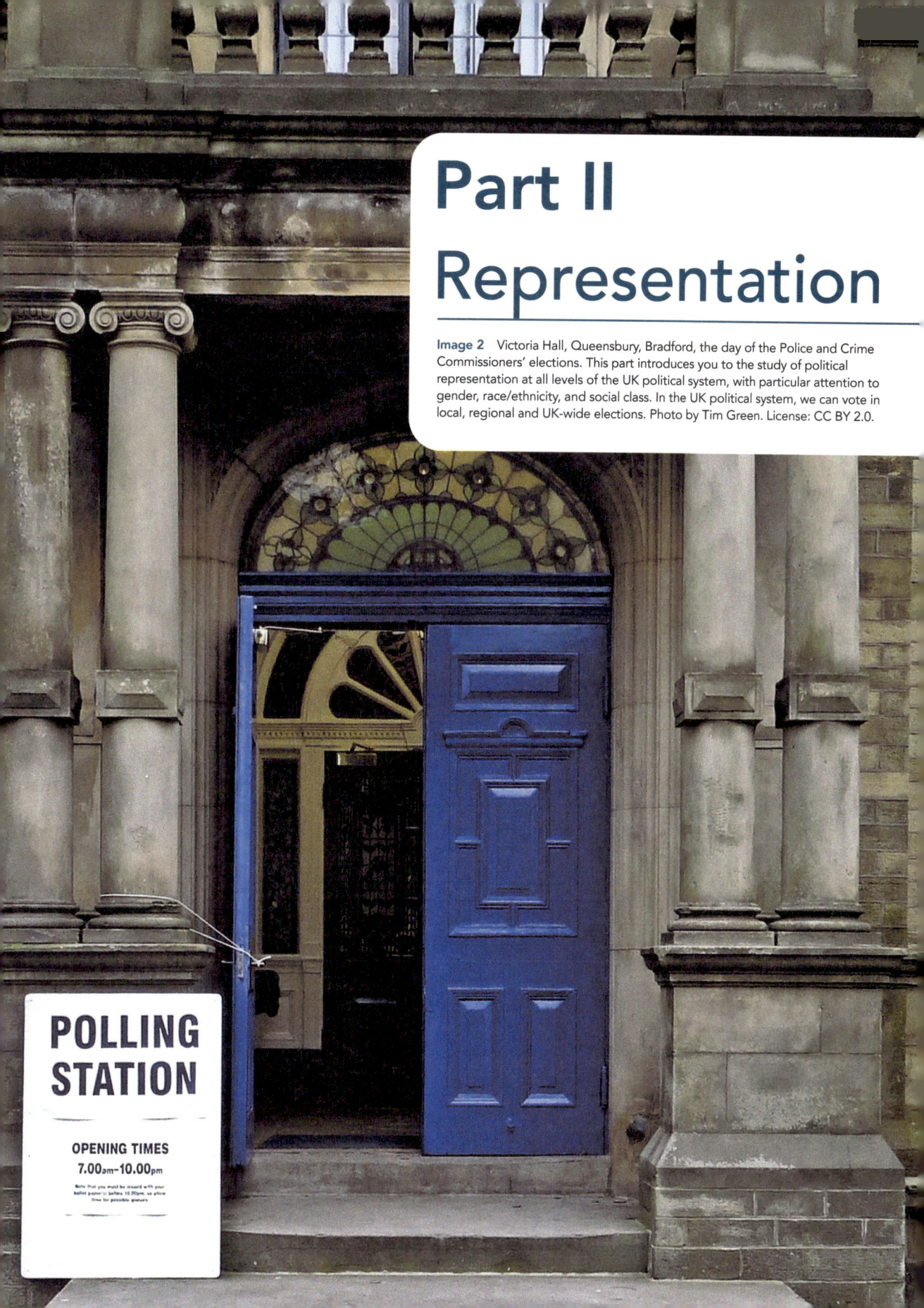

Part II

Representation

Image 2 Victoria Hall, Queensbury, Bradford, the day of the Police and Crime Commissioners' elections. This part introduces you to the study of political representation at all levels of the UK political system, with particular attention to gender, race/ethnicity, and social class. In the UK political system, we can vote in local, regional and UK-wide elections. Photo by Tim Green. License: CC BY 2.0.

POLLING STATION

OPENING TIMES
7.00am–10.00pm

Note that you must be issued with your ballot paper(s) before 10.00pm, so allow time for possible queues

Chapter 2

Concepts of political representation

Sarah Childs

What will this chapter tell me?

- Traditionally, UK elites subscribe to a trustee model of representation: representatives should trust their judgement, rather than act as a delegate, straightforwardly advancing the views of those they represent.
- This chapter asks students to think in a more sophisticated way about representation, and particularly the nature of the relationship between the represented and elected representatives.
- Students are introduced to a fundamental question at the heart of representation: whether it matters if representatives do not share the same characteristics as the people they are representing. This is the distinction between descriptive and other concepts of representation, notably symbolic and substantive.
- This chapter argues that the composition of our parliaments matter: political institutions should reflect those they represent.
- Students will understand, however, that simplistic claims about the relationship between the 'who' and 'what' of representation are inadequate and that compelling accounts of representation (in the UK and elsewhere) require deeper and more critical engagement with the theory and practice of representation.
- Eight essential questions are suggested to frame students engagement with the concept of representation and to start to evaluate the quality of representation in practice.
- Political representation is better understood as a practice that takes place within particular polititical systems and is mediated by many contextual factors – societal, structural, as well as institutional.

What do I need to know?

- The UK is a representative democracy. It elects representatives to legislatures, councils, assemblies, parliaments at various levels to represent political interests, deliberate and make decisions.
- The expansion of directly elected mayors in recent years begs questions of the representative relationship between the represented and a single elected representative.
- The concept of representation is essentially contested, meaning there is no absolute agreement about its meaning.
- Theories of representation have traditionally focused on the representation of 'political ideas', but much debate today focuses on 'political presence', and, crucially, the relationship between the two.
- Theoretical debates regarding representation inform judgements about the differences between, and the efficacy of, a country's electoral and party systems, elected political institutions, political parties and political actors.

Representative democracy in troubled times

It is not always easy to make the case for representative democracy, and its institutions and actors; electoral politics is currently neither popular nor fashionable. Against a backdrop of the UK's recent political history, it seems harder still. Crudely put, the Brexit turbulence at Westminster delivered unstable governments with a revolving door of five Conservative Prime Ministers in fewer than ten years (see Martill, in this volume; Bale 2023); a UK Parliament at odds with the public interest as registered in the 2016 European Union Referendum and unable to cohere around an agreeable Brexit (see Geddes, this volume; Russell and James 2023); and the UK Government in conflict with all three of the UK's devolved institutions, which voted against its Brexit Withdrawal Bill. Dissatisfaction with formal politics among the masses (Henderson, this volume; see also https://trustgov.net/recent-papers) is matched at the elite level by an emergent group of elected and would-be politicians championing populist politics against the 'corrupt elite' (Mudde and Rovira Kaltwasser 2017). If the populist offers a critique of parliamentarianism and favours the greater use of referendums and strong executives to enact the 'will of the people' (Weale 2018), progressive post-representative politics looks instead towards 'bottom-up' democratic demands – direct action, flash protests, Twitter-led mobilisations and 'swarms' – to which 'parties of governance' respond (Tormey 2015). Both critiques seem to suggest that the policies enacted by elected representatives are at some distance from and failing to meet the 'interests' of the people; that there is, in short, a failure of representation.

Defenders of representative democracy unpersuaded by these alternatives can return to and reclaim its essential character: that it addresses in large, populous, countries: (i) the inability of 'the people' to meet together and take political decisions, and (ii) the inability of complex political issues to be resolved by simple answers. Admittedly, technology now allows millions to vote all at once, but for most people, politics is not an activity they want to undertake on a daily or weekly basis. In any case, without significant societal transformation, a healthy scepticism of tech's participatory potential is merited. Like slaves enabling the political activities of Athenian citizens, women and minoritised people's domestic and paid work renders them less free (not least time and money) to engage in politics, even as their labour provides for the participation of those already with power and resources (Lovenduski 2019). And even if equality of participation can be achieved, direct politics remains vulnerable to arguments that stress the value of the very indirectness of representative democracy. In other words, representation allows for difficult decisions to be taken by elected representatives with a temporal gap between this and the next election (accountability moment), and thus providing for the the possibility for the represented to judge outcomes and effects in a considered, thoughtful fashion. Elected representatives are, in sum, better positioned by the nature of representative politics to deliberate and debate more extensively than any 'flash' democracy or direct popular vote allows.

Rather than walking away from representative democracy, a renewed attention to political representation – in theory and in practice – enables the imagining of a better representative politics. Such an approach rejects any simple definition of representation, or the choice between alternative types of representation (or typologies of representation), in favour of understanding representation 'in the round' (Celis and Childs 2020). This approach asks a series of questions that reflect feminist and constructivist scholars' critical engagement with traditional theoretical and empirical representation literatures. These have problematised the concept of interests (too easily assumed to be fixed and known, as if they can simply be handed over by the represented to the representatives who then act on them), critiqued the limitations of party representation (which fail to acknowledge that some political interests are not reflected in what parties talk about or put into their party manifestos), and expand the identity of the representative, beyond the elected, offering better links between the represented, civil society, public life and elected repesentatives. Together, these interventions speak to what has been termed the 'representational' and 'institutional' turns in democratic theory, and underpin the case for the re-design of democracies, and within this, the workings of political institutions, including parliaments (Saward 2021). Discussed towards the end of this chapter, eight questions are posed to guide students' enquiries: the *why* of representation; *who* – and *which* – are represented? (which groups and which members of these groups); *where, how* and *when* representation takes place?; to *whom* are representatives accountable; and *how* effective is the (acclaimed) representation? (Dovi 2007, 2010; Celis et al. 2008; Lovenduski and Gaudagnini 2010).

Representation in UK politics: The traditional take

> Certainly, gentlemen, it ought to be the happiness and glory of a representative to live in the strictest union, the closest correspondence, and the most unreserved communication with his constituents. Their wishes ought to have great weight with him; their opinion, high respect; their business, unremitted attention. It is his duty to sacrifice his repose, his pleasures, his satisfactions, to theirs; and above all, ever, and in all cases, to prefer their interest to his own. But his unbiassed opinion, his mature judgment, his enlightened conscience, he ought not to sacrifice to you, to any man, or to any set of men living. ... Your representative owes you, not his industry only, but his judgment; and he betrays, instead of serving you, if he sacrifices it to your opinion. (Edmund Burke, 1774)

Many a textbook and teacher, alongside a good few political commentators, will reference Edmund Burke's famous 'Speech to the Electors of Bristol', delivered in 1774. Historically part of common parlance, it still has some popular purchase today. In essence, Burke's account renders the elected representative a *trustee*. Unlike the delegate, a trustee is not to be constrained by any mandate or instruction handed down by their electors but rather should – and must – be free to deploy their judgement. In its apparent simplicity the trustee model has intuitive appeal, especially when analogies are made to others whose judgements we readily accept. It is, for example, a doctor's knowledge and experience that we seek, not that they treat us according to what we consider our particular ailment or condition, even if most of us will have already searched the internet.

Fleeting references to Burke miss key political dynamics underpinning his intervention, and which render representation in the UK much more complex than the single opposition between trustee and delegate suggests. His was, moreover, an aristocratic, elitist perspective, dismissive of the masses and political equality. For Burke, as David Judge (1999) identifies: (i) representation was to be of particular geographical constituencies – a spatial dimension of representation; (ii) the purpose of representation was to constitute a deliberative body; and (iii) Parliament was to play a leading role in decision-making. In other words, constituency interests brought to Parliament by MPs would, through debate in Parliament, realise and be ruled upon in the national interest. In Burke's words, once again:

> Parliament is a deliberative assembly of one nation, with one interest, that of the whole – where not local prejudices ought to guide, but the general good, resulting from the general reason of the whole. You chose a member, indeed; but when you have chosen him, he is not a member of Bristol, but he is a member of Parliament.

Burke's account is clear (and influential) but it does not quite capture the complexities and dilemmas of representative democracy in the UK in the 2020s. Each one of Burke's assumptions invites critical reflection: while beyond the scope of this chapter, but discussed in Chapters 10 and 11, respectively, these include the relationship between parliaments and governments. Their relative roles in decision-making are critical to debates over conceptions of parliamentary systems and parliament types, and to the theories and practices of executive–legislative relations. Where executives dominate and legislatures are more reactive, for example, and parliamentarians follow the instructions of their Whips, to what extent are MPs really acting as trustees and not simply 'lobby fodder', acting in line with their parties? Turning to 'constituency interests', how should these be conceived? There *may* be constituencies with a 'singular' interest meriting representation and easily articulated in a parliament. For example, in a fishing or farming community, an objectively identifiable shared interest might make sense. Even so, this might be contested by those involved in other, smaller productive activities and/or those whose labour is exploited to maximise the outputs/profits from the dominant interest. In many parts of the UK, and especially in heterogeneous town and city constituencies, such as Vauxhall in London, Edinburgh Central in Scotland, or Swansea East in Wales, it makes more sense to talk of multiple interests, some of which may very well compete over, *inter alia*, resources, investment, space, and labour. Similarly, it is not always clear how to reconcile the apparent interests of a constituency when this will be disadvantaged by a policy that brings overall benefits to a country. Such dilemmas are frequently associated in contemporary UK politics with the beloved, local hospital threatened by closure; the pleasing area of green land about to be despoiled by a new high-speed train line; or, as in summer 2023, when the UK Government sought moorage for refugee barges in popular, and not so popular, ports; or when the shift away from fossil fuels to renewables will, in the absence of compensatory measures, harm constituencies dominated by North Sea oil production, notably the North East of Scotland. In such circumstances, the local MP may very well vote in favour of their constituency's objective interest (Cowley 2002, 2005), in part fearful of their own electoral standing.

To these concerns, it is necessary to add that Burke's account misses – because it predates – the central role of party politics, which has been dominant in British politics since the late nineteenth century. At elections, most voters choose for and among representatives of political parties (see Henderson, in this volume). The UK, Scottish and Welsh Parliaments are consequently better conceived as institutions comprised of party representatives, and much less the individual representative from constituency A or B, even as constituency A returns a Conservative MP and constituency B a Labour one. As already noted, party cohesion – where MPs vote along party lines – is both expected by voters (you vote for the party you support, or at least for the candidate from the party best placed to defeat your least preferred party candidate) and is logically coherent (MPs from the same party usually share views, which is why they are members of party A and not a member of party B in the first place). Understanding political representation is, in this depiction, as much as, if not more, about the politics of ideas (Phillips 1995) than it is about geographic representation or notions of trusteeship indicated by the Burkean tradition.

The concept of representation

To better understand, and to be in a position to evaluate the quality of, representation provided by electoral politics in the UK, the public, and especially students of politics, must be able to uncover and then critically evalute the way in which representation is deployed by elected representatives and in popular conversation, and moreover how it is practised by MPs and other office holders. Political theory provides us with different ways of thinking about – and making judgements on – what passes as political representation on the ground. Pitkin's classic study is a very good place to start, as she analyses the meaning of representation, and offers up a typology that can then be applied to the representative politics around us.

Pitkin and the four dimensions of representation

Hanna F. Piktin's *The Concept of Representation* (1967) is widely acknowledged as the pre-eminent study that, nearly half a century on, continues to influence theoretical and empirical work on political representation. Drawing on the word's etymological origins, Pitkin defines representation as *making present again*. Straightaway she acknowledges that this simple rendition is insufficient:

> Except in its earliest [Roman] use ... this has always meant more than a literal bringing into presence, as one might bring a book into the room. (Pitkin 1967: 8)

Pitkin clarifies further. Representation refers to:

> The making present *in some sense* of something which is nevertheless *not* present literally or in fact. (Pitkin 1967: 8–9, emphasis in the original)

Yet to state that 'something is simultaneously both present and not present' is paradoxical, and begs additional questions, namely, in what sense can the 'something' be considered present when 'in fact it is not', and 'who is [doing the] considering' (Pitkin 1967: 9)? Choosing to explore the concept of representation through looking at its ordinary usage – considering the family of words on the root 'represent' and its close synonyms – Pitkin develops a four-part typology of representation:

1   Formalistic representation.
2   'Standing for': descriptive representation.
3   'Standing for': symbolic representation.
4   Representing as 'acting for'.

Formalistic representation refers to the formal bestowing of authority (the right) onto a person to act for others. In the UK, elections confer the status of representative onto an individual, and provides them with the authority to act in our place. Pitkin distinguishes between authorisation and accountability formalistic representation. In its *authorisation* form, the represented become responsible for the consequences of the representatives' actions, *as if they had done them themselves* (Pitkin 1967: 38–39, 42–43, emphasis added). That said, and problematically, this assumes that 'as long as he has been authorised *anything* that a man does is representing' (Pitkin 1967: 39, emphasis added). For the same reason, Pitkin rejects formalistic representation's *accountability* form – where the representative is 'to be held to account ... for what he does' (Pitkin 1967: 55). Once again, there is no guarantee that the representative will act *for* the represented; that they might be removed from office at the end of their term cannot guarantee the quality of representation *as it occurs*. Applied to the UK, the represented may have voted for their MP but who then acts in a way that the voter does not want them to, nor would have assumed that they would have acted. Such voters are left waiting for the next election, some years ahead, to be able to vote against the said MP.

'Standing for': descriptive representation refers to a notion of correspondence or connection between a representative's characteristics and the represented (Pitkin 1967: 61). In multicultural states such as the UK, looking in on a parliament and finding it full of white, elite men jars precisely because its composition is skewed relative to the social characteristics of the wider population. Descriptive representation is particularly troubling for Pitkin. First, because she considers the idea of reflection misleading. Representative art is 'never a replica', neither is a map absolutely accurate – some depict 'land', others 'topography' or 'economic trade regions'; mirrors reflect 'only visual features' (Pitkin 1967: 66–72). In political representation, the characteristics warranting representation are, in Pitkin's view, not always self-evident nor constant (1967: 87). In the UK, these characteristics include sex/gender, class, race and ethnicity, sexuality and disability, but young people may also want to make the case for descriptive representation, not least against the backdrop of claims of intergenerational injustice. Piktin also asks: should it be 'the one who is typical and average in every conceivable respect, including intelligence, public spiritedness, and experience' (Pitkin 1967: 76)? Is there a sound basis for the observable increases in the election of degree-educated politicians? Second, Pitkin asserts that there is 'no simple correlation' between a representative's characteristics and their actions (Pitkin 1967: 89). We should take care, then, in assuming that one's identity determines political attitudes and behaviour in any simple way. Third, one can 'only be held to account for what he has done' and 'not for what he is'. The use of the masculine here follows Pitkin. Consequently, neither representation as 'acting for' nor representation as accountability is possible within descriptive representation (Pitkin 1967: 90). Finally, Pitkin worries that descriptive representation 'almost inevitably' means that there is a concentration on the composition of our political institutions (who is present), rather than its activities (what they do) (Pitkin 1967: 226). Pitkin's critique here is strong, but there has been, as the presence theories discussed below suggest, more to be said about this conception.

'Standing for': symbolic representation. Symbols represent something or someone because they 'stand for' and 'evoke' their referent – the flag representing the nation, for example. Yet symbols can be arbitrary, lacking any obvious connection to the represented (Pitkin 1967: 97). This means that it is 'peoples' attitudes and beliefs' that determine the quality of the representation (Pitkin 1967: 100). To be sure, some flags depict a 'national' plant, topographical feature, or animal, but others lack any obvious such association. It is the public's belief in a political representative or a representation that constitutes the criterion of symbolic representation in politics. This, however, renders the basis for symbolic representation 'emotional, affective, irrational psychological responses' (Pitkin cited in Squires 1995: 16). Without a rational criterion for judging acting for representation, Pitkin is fearful that the represented can be manipulated by representatives into erroneously *feeling* represented. Her caution here is a good reminder that scholars of representation should be concerned about how the quality of representation is ajudged.

Representing as 'acting for'. In everyday language, representatives are said to act 'on behalf of others', 'in their place' and 'in their interest' (Pitkin 1967: 17). The relationship between the represented and the representative is such that the former is 'logically prior'; the representative must be 'responsive to' the represented 'rather than the other way around' (Pitkin 1967: 140).

This implies that 'normally' the wishes of the represented and the action of the representative will converge. When this does not occur, the representative should provide an explanation for their actions (Pitkin 1967: 163–165). Moving from the individual to the systemic level, the *representative system* must look after the public interest and be responsive to public opinion, except insofar as non-responsiveness can be justified in terms of the public interest (Pitkin 1967: 224, emphasis added). Here, the non-responsiveness qualification is important because, once again, the influence of Burkean ideas of trusteeship, as well as tension between individuals, constituents and the nation, and the politics of ideas are (potentially) in play.

Of her four dimensions, the true meaning of representation for Pitkin is 'acting for' representation. This conception has proved hugely influential in studies of what are commonly referred to as substantive representation. This is where scholars empirically examine whether the acts of the elected representative marry the stated interests of the represented. Is there congrugency in mass and elite attitudes? Pitkin's privileging of this one dimension downplays the others, not only as alternative conceptions, but also for how they may, each and together, mediate representation as 'acting for'. Indeed, in contemporary debates, to which the chapter now turns, 'acting for' representation is commonly linked to 'standing for' descriptive, and increasingly to standing for, symbolic representation. Chapters 3 and 4, respectively, provide comprehensive consideration of how Pitkin's four dimensions speak to questions of identity and political representation. Oftentimes, these dimensions work together to enhance or limit – mediate – the political representation of historically excluded and/or marginalised groups.

Research in Focus

Increasing the cost of female representation?

It is nearly a decade ago that British politics was rocked by the murder of Jo Cox, MP in 2016. Five years later, in 2021, a second MP, David Amess, was killed. Seemingly, week after week, social media and in-person harassment, abuse and intimidation (HAI) are reported. HAI is experienced by both women and men, but women are targeted because of their sex/gender and to limit their political pariticpation. Black and minority ethnic women MPs are particularly subject to HAI, with Diane Abbott MP, for example, being in receipt of unprecedented violence.

In their award-winning article, Sofia Collignon and Wolfgang Rüdig (2021) investigate the damaging effects of HAI on representation: how it constrains not just who stands for political office, but also how they campaign, and in turn how this reduces their electoral success. Using Representative Audit of Britain (RAB) data, Collignon and Rüdig (2021) establish:

- In 2019, 49% of parliamentary candidates suffered some form of HAI while campaigning – a rise of 11 percentage points compared with 2017.
- In 2019, 44% of men and 58% of women were abused in some form, compared with 35% and 45% two years previously. The increases are larger for women than for men – some 13 percentage points for women.
- Women candidates are significantly more likely to modify their campaign behaviour, avoiding canvassing and social media.
- Candidates who avoid canvassing reduce their vote share by about 20%.

Over and above the direct harmful effects on individual politicians are wider, damaging effects on representative democracy. Those working to diversify the political class – whether in parties, civil society and/or international organisations, such as The Inter-Parliamentary Union or Commonwealth Parliamentarians Association, are increasingly concerned that the prevalence of HAI will reduce the supply pool of people willing to put themselves forward for political office, and that this reduction will disproportionately affect candidates from atypical backgrounds. In the UK, minority ethnic women and women who campaign on policies linked to 'redistribution and equality', 'left' politics more generally and 'Brexit' are most likely to be affected, and thus have their right to participate in politics challenged, and political equality undermined.

Reflective questions

1   Does the prevalence of HAI affect your understanding of descriptive representation?
2   How might HAI mediate the relationship between descriptive and substantive, and descriptive and symbolic representation?

Source: Collignon and Rüdig (2021)

The politics of presence critique: Attending to the 'who' of representation

Pitkin's typology had a signficant hold on the theoretical and empirical scholarship on representation from the late 1960s until the mid-1990s. Her influence was such that she effectively rendered descriptive representation as unimportant for a whole generation (Childs and Lovenduski 2013: 491). This changed as feminist scholars turned their attention to the identity of elected representatives, and whether they really could stand and act for women (see Kenny, in this volume). At the heart of this focus was a challenge to Pitkin's dismissiveness of descriptive representation. It is a simple question posed pithily by Jane Mansbridge in 1999: 'Should Blacks represent Blacks and women represent women?' In other words, do certain groups with similar characteristics have to be *present* for them to be represented effectively? The question is concise but the answer is complicated, and students of politics need to take some time to work through the attendant arguments.

The politics of presence literature is marked by a shared critique that ideas are regarded as distinct from identity, and by a dissatisfaction that the identities of our elected representatives have for too long not been considered of political concern, or rather, *some* identities have not been deemed to matter. Political parties have sought to represent class identity in the UK from the emergence of parties in the nineteenth century. Presence theories are most associated with the pioneering work of Anne Phillips (1995), and include Jane Mansbridge (1999), Suzanne Dovi (2007), Melissa Williams (1998) and Iris Marion Young (2002). Their collective significance on the discipline of political science is such that 'after Phillips', 'no one' can regard descriptive representation as 'unimportant' (Childs and Lovenduski 2013: 491), whatever Pitkin might (or was perceived to) have suggested. Presence theory is, then, a clear example of the influence of feminist research on mainstream political science.

Taken together, presence theory makes the case for the political presence of descriptive representatives in respect of gender, race, and other historically excluded, oppressed and marginalised groups (as discussed further below), even as Phillips speaks of the coming together of the politics of ideas and the politics of presence. Phillips' normative case for the politics of presence is argued on four grounds – the specific basis for women's representation is discussed in Chapter 3, with race and ethnicity addressed in Chapter 4.

1   Symbolic representation.
2   Party representation's limitations and exclusions.
3   Disadvantaged groups' need for aggressive advocates.
4   The transformation of the political agenda.

Symbolic representation. Unlike Pitkin, who queried the relationship between the symbol and that or to whom it refers, it is now precisely the presence of the formerly excluded that demonstrates their political equality. The inclusion of the previously excluded or under-represented furthermore adds legitimacy to political institutions, as higher numbers identify with them, and hence electoral politics more widely, because they see others like them present as elected representatives. Symbolism therefore matters for perceptions of the overall legitimacy of the political system.

The limitations and exclusions of party representation. Party politics is here characterised as: (i) offering only a limited choice to the electorate in terms of the total number of political parties; (ii) each party putting only a limited agenda before voters and acting on these when in power; and (iii) presenting agendas that prioritise the interests of party leaders and elites. With these interests frequently 'frozen' at the time of parties' establishment, which for many mainstream European political parties was over a century ago, parties' foci are skewed to what we usually think of as aristocratic, business, agrarian or workers' interests, but which we might better term ethnic majority, men's interests (Celis and Childs 2020). To all this, as Phillips stated, a party position on policy A or B may well be a poor indicator of a party's position on sexual or racial equality (Phillips 1995: 41–42). At the same time, and even where party cohesion is strong, representatives still have some room to act independently, which is why it matters that they are not homogeneous in their composition. It is, then, possible – even within strong party sytems – for representatives to bring new issues to the table, and thereafter for descriptive representatives to act for those they are descriptive representatives of. At the same time, Phillips' now famous 'hitting the target' metaphor should be borne in mind: women are shooting in the dark but they 'are far more likely to reach its target than when those shooting are predominantly male, but still open to all kinds of accident' (1995: 84).

Aggressive advocacy. This is not a claim that no one ever acts on behalf of others – evidently, they do. For example, elite men MPs had to pass laws for working-class and women's suffrage in the UK and elsewhere – but rather, that the presence of the previously excluded may be necessary to ensure the assertive articulation of the group's concerns.

Political agenda transformation. Building on the aggressive advocacy argument, this looks to the broadening of the political agenda. It focuses on the realm of preferences not yet formulated, articulated or legitimated on the political agenda, and therefore outside party packaging (Phillips 1995: 44). Put simply, and for example, if 'disability interests', were known, then arguably able-bodied men would be able to articulate and act upon them in parliaments. Where interests need to be 'worked through', then descriptive representatives are necessary to interest identification (a point developed more below, in respect of creative representation) (see Evans and Reher 2024). Minority group representation is not just about presence and representation, therefore: it is also, crucially, about identifying and mobilising around interests that may not otherwise be articulated. In Phillips' own words:

> If, however, the interests [of women] are varied, unstable, perhaps still in the process of formation, it will be far more difficult to separate out what is to be represented from who is to do the representation. (Phillips 1998: 235)

Concerned, like Phillips, with the political representation of *disadvantaged* groups, Jane Mansbridge (1999) identifies four contexts necessitating descriptive representation. It is because of these that Blacks should represent Blacks and women represent women, as her classic article title frames it:

1   Mistrust between disadvantaged and advantaged groups.
2   Uncrystallised, not fully articulated, interests.
3   Where the social meaning of 'ability to rule' has been seriously questioned for members of disadvantaged groups.
4   Past discrimination against disadvantaged groups.

Again, similar to Phillips, Mansbridge distinguishes between substantive and non-substantive reasons for political presence. Of her four functions of representation, only the first two engender substantive representation: communication and innovative thinking. The third and fourth – creating a social meaning of 'ability to rule' and increasing the polity's *de facto* legitimacy – provide non-substantive, albeit significant, goods. In her oft-cited words:

> Although a representative need not have shared personally the experiences of the represented to facilitate communication and bring subtlety to a deliberation, the open-ended quality of deliberation gives informational and communicative advantages to representatives who are existentially close to the issues. (Mansbridge 1999: 635–636)

Accordingly, and as issues arise, descriptive representatives are more likely than the non-descriptive representative to 'react more or less the way' the represented would have, were they present (Mansbridge 1999: 644).

As currently presented, these arguments might seem disconnected from representative politics on the ground – representative institutions, processes and actors. Importantly, Phillips addresses how her ideas might support different real-world interventions. For example, and as discussed further in Chapter 3, regarding women, quotas are one way in which the politics of presence and ideas can be brought together. More precisely, quotas, whether for women or other historically under-represented groups – augment existing electoral systems by providing for (when voluntary) or by guaranteeing (when prescriptive) members of particular groups are formally present in a parliament, assembly or council chamber. In the UK case, party sex/gender quotas at Westminster have taken the form of All Women Shortlists, where party selectorates choose among party aspirant candidates who are all women. There have been fewer calls for minority ethnic quotas over the last decade (see more broadly Chapter 4), and recently discussions are becoming more common about what might be necessary to halt the decline in working-class representation, and provide for the inclusion of people with disabilities (Evans and Reher 2024). Another approach might be to consider what difference different electoral systems make to descriptive representation; systems of proportional representation are frequently associated with more diverse representatives, but at least in part this is due to the ways in which quotas work in tandem with either multi-member constituencies and party lists (Hughes et al. 2019).

Anti-identity, essentialist and reductivism (counter)criticism

Presence literatures have undoubtedly transformed the study of political representation within and beyond academia. There is high-profile attention, for example, to 'counting' the numbers of women in parliaments by international organisations, notably The Inter-Parliamentary Union and the Commonwealth Parliamentarians Association, as well as growing attention given to the political presence of ethnic minorities, different sexualities, people with disability and younger people. Yet if during the 2000s gender and politics scholars were confident that presence arguments were becoming widely accepted, the rise of anti-identity politics means that this can no longer be taken for granted. Some criticism is disingenuous, when opponents fail to acknowledge that their's is a case of identity too. The call for the representation of MPs who are non-graduates and who come from manual labour is about the social characteristic of class. Other times, it is distinctly anti-women, as when *middle-class* women's descriptive representation is blamed for reducing working-class *men's* presence, when it is elite, majority ethnic men who over-populate our parliaments relative to their percentage in the population (Hughes 2011). Feminists are equally suspicious of accepting the public's lack of concern for women's political presence, as if its redress is thereby unimportant (see Campbell and Cowley 2014). And if Phillips' (1995) rationale for excluding class is less than compelling, as she admits, contending that the politics of ideas and party politics is about representing working-class interests, then presence arguments can extend to more explicitly include class identities. As our elected representatives have become less and less representative of working people through professionalisation, both the normative case for and interventions to deliver working-class presence are persuasive, for example, via additional funds for poorer candidates, bespoke training and/or selecting by lot (sortition) or, as suggested above, using quotas (Childs and Cowley 2011; Heath 2015; Evans and Tilly 2017; Hardman 2018).

For those convinced that characteristics and identities meriting representation are difficult to discern, or that descriptive representation is essentialist or reductionist, a closer reading of presence theories reveal sophisticated justifications that are less easily dismissed. Mansbridge (1999), for example, presents three questions to identify groups warranting descriptive representation (see also Young 1990). A group 'appears to be a good candidate for affirmative selective representation' when the answer to the first suggests discrimination and the suppression of interests, and answers to the second and third questions are positive (Mansbridge 1999: 639).

1   What are the features of the existing electoral process that have resulted in lower proportions of certain descriptive groups in the legislature rather than in the population?
2   Do members of that group consider themselves able adequately to represent themselves?
3   Is there any evidence that dominant groups in the society have ever intentionally made it difficult or illegal for members of that group to represent themselves?

Iris Marion Young (2002) develops the concept of 'social perspective' in her response to criticism of group representation. This 'consists in a set of questions, kinds of experience and assumptions with which reasoning begins' and derives from group members being 'similarly positioned' and 'attuned to particular kinds of social meanings' and shared affinity (Young 2002: 123, 136–137). Representation is conceptualised as a 'differentiated relationship among political actors engaged in a process extending over space and time' (ibid.). Here, the representative 'speaks for' the represented even though they cannot 'speak as' they would (Young 2002: 127). Descriptive representation is also about more than a single representative speaking for a group, because of intra-group differences (Young 2002: 123).

Suzanne Dovi's *The Good Representative* (2007; see also Dovi 2002) delves deeper still into the quality of representation provided by descriptive representation, contrasting *preferable and non-preferable descriptive representatives*. The latter 'fail to further, and can even undermine, the best interest' of those they represent (Dovi 2002: 742); they do not share 'policy preferences' or 'values' with those they represent (Dovi 2002: 737–738). In a highly quoted statement, Dovi argues that the African American representative 'who grew up in a primarily white neighborhood, attended primarily white private schools, has a white spouse, *and has shown no demonstrable interest in the problems of other African Americans*' (Dovi 2002: 737, emphasis added) is unlikely to be judged a preferable descriptive representative. They lack the experiences and relationships to 'achieve mutual recognition' with the represented. For these reasons, and referencing Pitkin, Dovi reminds us to look at what descriptive representatives *do* as well as who they *are*. The preferable descriptive representative experiences a sense of belonging to, has strong mutual relationships with, and share aims with others in the group – they want to see their 'social, economic, and political status' improved – and experience a 'reciprocated sense of having [their] … fate linked' (Dovi 2002: 736–737). In acknowledgement of group heterogeneity, and 'different conceptions of what is necessary' to achieve their aims, the preferable descriptive representative should be judged by whom they know and interact with. Specifically, they should have 'strong mutual relationships with dispossessed subgroups of historically disadvantaged groups' (Dovi 2002: 729).

Dovi (2002: 733) is attentive to the risks of questioning the 'authenticity' of some descriptive representatives. She also acknowledges that it is usually not members of historically disadvantaged groups who select descripitive representatives. One way to address these two points is to return to Pitkin's formalistic representation; voters are able to vote against any representative whom they consider has not represented them well. And, it should be noted that in the UK's single-member Parliament constituencies, a representative will be only ever descriptively representative of some of the represented, even if we work with the classic identities of sex/gender, race and ethnicity, class, sexuality and disability. If this first approach is not sufficient, as it might not be, party selectorates can look to whether particular aspirant candidates meet Dovi's standards for being a preferable descriptive representative, by assessing what they 'do', not least in respect of with 'whom' they meet. For example, does the aspirant candidate or MP meet only with elite groups rather than 'dispossesed sub groups'? Do they raise the former's interests while ignoring the latter's? Orly Siow provides an important new schema by which to make such judgements (see Table 2.1). Some representatives – whether descriptive or not – might well be speaking on behalf of a group, yet others might well speak about, or against, a group, counterbalancing from the group's perspective desirable representations with ones that instrumentalise, essentialise, stereotype and actually disempower them (see also Joly and Wadia 2017).

Table 2.1   Siow's facets of substantive representation

Substantive representation includes: Speaking on behalf of		Substantive representation excludes: Speaking against/about	
1	Constitutes the group in a way that is not negative or hostile	1	Constitutes the group in a way that is negative or hostile
2	Constitutes the group as an end in itself	2	Constitutes the group solely as a means to an end (instrumentalising)
3	Constitutes the group in relation to the structural factors which positions it as vulnerable	3	Constitutes problems as solely within racialised community (stigmatising)
4	Constitutes the group's heterogeneity, and in relation to a wide range of issues	4	Constitutes the group as homogeneous or in relation to limited range of issues (homogenising)
5	Constitutes the group on its own terms, including relevant civil society	5	Constitutes the group relying on stereotypes
6	Maintains agency	6	Fails to maintain agency
7	Makes an explicit request	7	Does not make an explicit request
8	Constitutes both the problem and the solution intersectionally	8	Constitutes either the problem or the solution in relation to single axis or structure

Source: Siow (2023b: 4)

Democratic theory and representative politics

Michael Saward's *The Representative Claim* (Saward 2006, 2010) offers another strong challenge to Pitkinian conceptions of representation as 'acting for'. In his highly influential book, Saward centres and extends arguments first introduced by Phillips and Mansbridge regarding uncrystal-lised interests (see also Disch 2011, 2021). In everyday words: a group's interest should not be thought of as a shopping list of political needs and wants handed over to elected representatives in a uni-directional, linear fashion, but reflect claims made about the represented as part of the representative process. This is an active, creative understanding of representation also referred to as a constructivist approach. Avoiding universal or essentialist claims about what is in the interests of any particular group, the 'interests' of a constituency are 'read in' more than 'read off': representatives and the represented are engaged in a process of making, receiving and reading back claims. Nor is representation for Saward something that only elected representatives can or should do; representation is a process of claim-making rather than a fact established by institutional election or selection' (Saward 2010: 44). As he specifies:

> A MAKER of representations (M) puts forward a SUBJECT (S) which stands for an OBJECT (O) which is related to a REFERENT (R) and is offered to an AUDIENCE (A). (Saward 2010: 36)

Saward provides examples, two of which, one elected and one other, I reproduce here (2010: 37):

> The MP (maker) offers himself or herself (subject) as the embodiment of constituency interests (object) to that constituency (audience). The referent is the actual, flesh and blood people of the constituency. The object involves a selective portrayal of constituency interests.

Anti-globalization demonstrators (makers) set up themselves and their movements (subjects) as representatives of the oppressed and marginalized (object) to Western governments (audience).

That the represented have agency to contest – to hold to account – representatives for 'the representations offered to them' is a crucial intervention made by creative theorists of representation (Saward 2006, 2010; Severs et al. 2016). It is this very possibility that enables us to establish how representatives define particular societal problems and representable groups or constituencies, what questions representatives raise, what solutions they consider, what voices they listen to (Severs et al. 2016: 351–352), and which claims are accepted by the represented and which rejections are responded to by representatives. All this matters because a commitment to intersectionality demands attention to the relative power between claim makers and those they claim to represent, and within the latter, between differently positioned subgroups. Without this, Saward's 'economy of claims' metaphor hides the likelihood that representations made to and by the resource-rich dominate, leaving the resource-poor unable to contest ('read back') against those making claims in their name. Are the Muslim women Marine Le Pen claims to represent positioned to challenge her views of the veil, for example (Celis and Childs 2020: introductory essay). As presence theorists remind us, as in the discussion above of Dovi's preferable descriptive representatives, it is important to determine *which* women and men, or *which* minority ethnic people and not others, are being represented, and by whom (Siow 2023a, 2023b).

Michael Saward's most recent book *Democratic Design* (2021) presents a framework to democratise democracies and talks of the re-design of formal political institutions. The new plan should enact core and optional democratic principles to meet the democratic deficit of the particular case. In many ways, this contribution is a return to earlier democratic theorising, which rejects the opposition between representative and participatory models of democracy, and instead seeks greater institutional and institutionalised connections between society and electoral politics. In this, there should be 'many avenues and institutions' (Young 2002: 8), and a circularity between representative institutions and society over time (Urbinati 2006: 24). In Mansbridge's terms, *recursive representation* refers to 'iterative and interactive communication' between citizens and their representatives, with both learning from one another and inciting each other to action (Mansbridge 2019: 312, 307). Lisa Disch (2011) talks of *reflexive* political institutions 'interlocking' with other sites of contestation to engender dissent and secure accountability between representatives and the represented. In all this, the represented through participation are better able to determine what they think, prefer or find the most compelling and strongest argument; that is, what is in their and others' interests (Disch 2011: 4; Hamilton 2014: 149; Warren 2019: 48; for a fuller discussion see Celis and Childs 2020: 110–121). Finally, and to be clear, these accounts maintain the emphasis on representation's indirectness and an eschewal of delegation as instruction (Hamilton 2014: 115–116).

Studying political representation: Eight essential questions

Changing conceptions of representation is a story of the contextually specific times and concerns of those writing about and engaging in representation (Childs and Lovenduski 2013: 489).

In unequal political and societal contexts, there is a good case to be made for the centrality of political representation, and the core institutions, actors and processes of representative democracy. Elected representatives in Parliaments can give and take away political rights, and can reproduce or redress social, cultural and economic inequalities. As Lawrence Hamilton contends:

> Our individual freedom is determined to a significant degree by the material conditions and power of the groups or classes that we find ourselves (or in some cases choose) to be members, and that the power of each group is determined itself by the power of its representatives, which given the nature of power relations is itself heavily determined by the nature and relative access they have to their polity's formal political representatives. (Hamilton 2014: 14)

What, then, constitutes 'good' political representation? Strongly influenced by presence, creative and institutionalist literatures, in *Feminist Political Representation*, Karen Celis and I (2020) contend that representation should be considered not in its discrete dimensions but 'in the round'. This means attending to the processes of representation as well as substantive outcomes, and all the time being attuned to the associated affects and emotions prompted through these representations. Ours is a book about women's political representation, but we are confident it speaks to others previously shut out of, or pushed to the margins of, elected political institutions. Whether representative processes and outcomes are judged good for the represented:

> Requires us to establish not only whether women agree with the claims and acts made in their name, or the extent to which they are able to engage in counter-claim-making, but also how they feel about their representation. Representatives making the 'right' claims might still be judged to have the 'wrong' ideological profile in the eyes of the represented or have made the 'wrong' arguments. (Celis and Childs 2020: 73)

The following eight questions can guide the judgement of the overall quality of political representation provided by electoral politics (following Childs and Lovenduski 2013). These are demanding questions. They involve working through substantial theoretical debates, and when applied to the real world of politics will necessitate considerable quantitative and qualitative data analysis. They will not offer easy or quick answers. But this is not the primary concern. For what matters is less a simple 'dictionary' definition of a complex and contested political concept than the appreciation of the 'work' the concept of representation can do and does in our politics, to the betterment or detriment of the represented.

1   *Why should X be represented?* Presence arguments look to the representation of previously excluded or marginalised groups, and identify substantive and non-substantive reasons. This begs additional questions regarding identifying groups and group interests.
2   *Who are the representatives of X?* This refers to the composition of a parliament but also includes other 'claim makers'. In the former, this involves the counting of different types of elected representatives, including descriptive ones, preferable and other, a focus on the myriad factors accounting for change/statis in composition and among claims makers over time, and to what interventions might be adopted to deliver fair descriptive representation in elected forums.
3   *Which members of X are represented?* Adopting an intersectional approach, this question homes in on intra-group differences – and potential differences in the interests within a

group – and is sensitive to charges that simple 'counts' may miss the ongoing dominance of elite representatives even as some under-representations are redressed. For example, it draws attention to a majority ethnic, professional class of politicians as well as ideological differences held by members of a group.

4   *Where does the representation of X occur?* Most studies of political representation emphasise the role of elected legislatures and assemblies, even as these are just one, albeit central, site of representation. Other institutions, only some of which are elected, include: government and public bodies, political parties, economic organisations such as trade unions, profession and employer organisations, firms, non-governmental organisations (NGOs), social movements, the media. How these different arenas and institutions – the rules and processes – shape and interact with each other are important questions for research.

5   *How is the substantive representation of X done?* What are the processes through which a group's claims are formulated, refined and advanced? How, if at all, do representatives' claim and act for a group. Answering these questions empirically involves addressing methodological questions and research project design ones. Studies include, *inter alia,* roll-call analysis, discourse and framing analysis, process-tracing and policy case studies.

6   *When does representation take place?* This question calls attention to timing: (i) juxtaposition, examples of which include connection to other issues, proximity to election years, phases of the world and national economies, the public opinion cycle, and timetable of decision processes; and (ii) sequencing, for example, whether an attempt to act on a particular issue is followed by victory or defeat, or whether a claim is an obvious extension of a previously stated policy.

7   *To whom are representatives accountable?* If Pitkin's criticism of formal representation draws attention to the inability to hold representatives to account for what they do while they are doing it, Saward's 'reading back' also emphasises the fundamental importance of the represented's response to representative claims. Taking accountability seriously means examining how the represented can hold their elected (and non-elected) representatives to account, especially beyond, or more precisely in addition to free and fair elections, given the dominance of party politics and the constraints of any one electoral system.

8   *How effective is the (claimed) representation?* Good representation exists along a continuum from 'non-representation to representation' (Celis 2008: 82). It requires presence, but this is a necessary and not sufficient condition. Celis and Childs (2020) look to a procedural definition, one that institutionalises representative processes that engender new relationships between members of parliaments and those they represent, in ways attendant to debates over the content of group interests, and all the time conceiving of political representation in the round.

Summary

- This chapter has explored traditional and contemporary theories of political representation.
- It challenges those who disregard descriptive representation as an important dimension of representation.
- In making the case for more diverse parliaments, ideas of good representation are undersood in the round, rather than lying with any one dimension.

- Links between descriptive, substantive and symbolic representation are complicated rather than certain.
- Representation speaks to questions of democratic design, electoral systems and political institutions.

Recommended and further reading

- Celis, K. and Childs, S. (2020) 'An essay on women's political representation', in *Feminist Democratic Representation*. Oxford and New York: Oxford University Press. This introductory chapter presents a series of vignettes – sex work/prostitution, the veil, abortion, Marine Le Pen – that illuminate contemporary issues through a representational lens.
- Phillips, A. (1995) *The Politics of Presence*. Oxford: Clarendon Press. Phillips' monograph transformed how the concept of representation has been studied. It is a must-read for all students of political representation.
- Siow, O. (2023) 'What constitutes substantive representation, and where should we evaluate it?', *Political Studies Review*, 21(3): 532–538. Siow's work reflects on theoretical and methodological issues of studying substantive representation.

- Dovi, S. (2002) 'Preferable descriptive representatives: Will just any woman, Black, or Latino do?', *American Political Science Review*, 96(4): 729–743. This classic article questions simplistic claims about descriptive and substantive representation, outlining the basis for determining whom are preferable.
- Lovenduski, J. (2019) 'Feminist reflections on representative democracy', *The Political Quarterly*, 90(S1): 18–35. Lovenduski makes a strong argument that representative democracy has failed to deliver equality for women, even as she maintains feminists should continue to support it.
- Saward, M. (2006) 'The representative claim', *Contemporary Political Theory*, 5(3): 297–318. Saward offers a creative theory of representation that challenges traditional assumptions about who is a representative and what they do.

Chapter 3

Gender and politics in the UK

Meryl Kenny

What will this chapter tell me?

- This chapter will further develop and deepen your understanding of representation by engaging with feminist approaches (building on Childs, in this volume).
- It will help you to identify and critically evaluate patterns of women's political participation and representation across the UK, and the form and effectiveness of different strategies to achieve equal representation.
- It will outline the complex and contingent relationship between descriptive and substantive representation, and its critiques.
- This chapter will evaluate parliaments as gendered institutions, and consider the resultant implications for gender- and diversity-sensitive parliamentary reform.
- It will begin to show you how to apply gendered approaches to the study of political institutions, parties, and politics more generally.

What do I need to know?

- Gender – understood here as a structure of power – is both a subject of substantive research and an analytical approach to the study of politics. The contents of this chapter are therefore closely intertwined with others in this textbook – in particular, chapters focusing on representation; race, ethnicity and politics; Parliament; and political parties – and we advise you to read this chapter in conjunction with the above.
- There are differences between political institutions and political parties across different levels of the United Kingdom, in part because of their historical context.
- You should have some awareness of key debates about the nature of British politics, particularly with regards to representation.

Introduction

The traditional start to an introductory political science course might begin with Laswell's (1936) famous encapsulation of politics as the study of 'who gets what, when, where and how'. Feminist political scientists have taken and transformed these conventional preoccupations, focusing squarely on the problem of women's historical and continuing exclusion from political power. The study of women, gender and politics has become a thriving international sub-field of political science, with governments, parliaments and parties also put under increasing pressure to take action to remedy the under-representation of women and other marginalised groups. Interest in women's political representation in the UK in particular has flourished in recent decades, due to a variety of factors, including increases in women's numbers in the UK political science profession; gains in women's representation in political institutions from the 1990s onwards; and wider processes of institutional and constitutional restructuring that have opened up new opportunities for women to advance claims for political inclusion.

This chapter places these developments in context, asking how much has changed for women and for gender equality in UK politics over time. It focuses on institutional politics, and parliamentary politics, specifically, as a key site of representation and change. It examines different dimensions of representation and power over time and across political levels, focusing on opportunities for change, but also highlighting ongoing continuities and resistances.

This chapter begins by introducing you to feminist theories of representation and political institutions. It then turns to assess trends in women's descriptive (or numerical) representation, highlighting patterns in women's diverse recruitment, representation and leadership across the four nations of the UK. It moves on to explore the dynamics of women's substantive representation, asking how women's different needs, policy preferences and political interests have been studied and represented over time. It finally turns to the question of institutional change, asking to what extent political institutions in the UK have been 're-gendered' in more equitable and just directions.

Feminist theories of representation

In Chapter 2, Childs suggests that representational dynamics cannot be captured by a simple dictionary definition, but instead require the researcher to undertake a more holistic and contextual consideration of the why, who, where, how and when of political representation (see also Childs and Lovenduski 2013). A feminist answer to these questions begins with the 'why'. The first, and simplest, answer to the question of 'why should women be represented' rests on the grounds of justice – that it is unfair and unjust for men from majority groups to dominate political institutions and decision-making, particularly in modern, representative democracies. Pragmatic arguments for women's political representation stress the political advantages of promoting women's representation, for example in terms of attracting women's votes or improving a political party's image. Difference arguments, meanwhile, suggest that women and other marginalised groups bring a different set of interests and approaches to politics, which will change it for the better – an outcome which is of benefit to all.

While political representation has multiple dimensions – formalistic, symbolic, descriptive and substantive (cf. Pitkin 1967) – feminist research has traditionally focused on the latter two dimensions, and the ways in which these might be inter-linked (Phillips 1995; Young 2002). Specifically, scholars have asked whether an increase in the number of female representatives (*descriptive representation*) might result in an increase in attention to women's policy concerns (*substantive representation*) (see also Childs, in this volume; Geddes, in this volume). Number-based theories of representation have often revolved around the idea of *critical mass* (cf. Dahlerup 1988; see also Kanter 1977) – assuming that once women move from a small to a large minority in Parliament, a 'tipping point' will be reached that will start to transform politics. While 'critical mass' has become a popular argument for increasing women's political presence – deployed by politicians, international organisations and women's groups – this understanding misrepresents the more nuanced arguments made by its originators, who in fact suggested that critical acts and actors might be more important than overall numbers in ensuring change (Dahlerup 2006). This in turn shifts the question from 'what women do' to 'what *specific actors* do', opening up the possibility that representatives acting for (or claiming to act for) women may not always or necessarily be women (Childs and Krook 2008: 734).

Indeed, most feminist political scientists understand the link between these two dimensions of representation to be complex and contingent – while possible, there are no guarantees that women representatives will 'make a difference' to policy outcomes and ways of working within political institutions. Different identities and experiences, partisan loyalties and institutional environments all play roles in enabling or constraining the inclination and capacity to 'act for' women (Mackay 2004). Indeed, Anne Phillips memorably equates increasing women's political presence to a 'shot in the dark': 'far more likely to reach its target than when those shooting are predominantly male, but still open to all kinds of accident' (1995: 83). Intersectional approaches to studying representation further highlight how differences among women complicate our understandings of group interests and the representation of those interests (Smooth 2011; Severs et al. 2016; Montoya et al. 2022), while studies of men and masculinities also point to the diversities and inequalities among men in politics (Bjarnegård and Murray 2018; Murray 2024). 'One-at-a-time', single-axis approaches (e.g. looking at representation in terms of gender *or* race) are therefore seen to be overly simplistic (cf. Smooth 2011); rather, the argument is that gender interacts with race, sexuality, class, disability and other structures of power to shape representational practices and outcomes.

Studies of political representation in the UK and beyond have therefore increasingly moved towards more intersectional, institutionally focused and 'whole-system' approaches to studying political representation (see, for example, Lovenduski 2005a; Mackay 2008; Celis and Childs 2020; Siow 2023b). The ability of particular parliamentarians to make a difference, for example, is significantly constrained in Westminster systems, where the government initiates almost all legislation (see Geddes, in this volume). Multi-level polities like the UK add additional complexity, given the constraints and interdependencies between different levels (see Part IV, in this volume). And alternative institutionalised channels may be equally or more important to parliamentary ones in advancing representative claims and activities – for example, through government bodies or social movements (Weldon 2002; Lovenduski 2005b). The argument, then, is that focusing on the narrow question of whether women 'act for' women cannot capture the full picture. Rather, there is a need to develop research designs that can address complexity, thinking about differences among and between women and men within their wider political and institutional contexts.

Gendering political institutions

Central to these approaches is an understanding that institutions play a central role in constructing gender. Gender is not a synonym for women (Carver 1996); rather, it is understood here as a social structure, a 'constitutive element of social relations based upon perceived differences' between women and men that is also a 'primary means of signifying relationships of power' (Scott 1986: 1067). In other words, gender legitimises and constructs particular social and political relationships, while institutions and structures also shape gender relations: 'politics constructs gender and gender constructs politics' (Scott 1986: 1070). Gender relations, then, are power relations – gender makes 'distinctions between different categories of people, valorizes some over others, and organises access to rights, responsibilities, authority, and life options along the lines demarcating these groups' (Cohn 2013: 4).

To say that a political institution is 'gendered' therefore means that constructions of masculinity and femininity are intertwined in institutional cultures or 'logics'. Political institutions rely on particular ideas about gender to function, but they are also producers of ideas about 'appropriate' masculinities and femininities (Chappell 2006). Prevailing assumptions around

what makes a 'good' political leader, for example, are often biased towards stereotypically masculine traits, including competitiveness, assertiveness and adversarial styles of debate (Lovenduski 2005a, 2014a). In the context of these organisational norms, women parliamentarians
are subject to a 'double bind' (cf. Jamieson 1995), and can be penalised either because they
do not fulfil masculinised leadership expectations, or because, in attempting to do so, they
violate expectations around 'appropriate' feminine behaviour. Institutions are also shaped by –
and reproduce – other intersecting categories of race, ethnicity, class, disability, sexuality, and
so on (see Peace and Meer, in this volume; Greenwood-Hau, in this volume). Understanding
institutions in this way means that – for the readers of this textbook, as you continue to learn
more about UK politics – gender remains a relevant category of analysis, even in contexts where
women are not present.

In the UK Parliament, for example, norms of behaviour have been established, over centuries of repetition and in the context of the historic and continuing relative exclusion of women
and other marginalised groups, which are imbued with assumptions about gender, race, class
and ableism (Lovenduski 2005a). Westminster's 'gender regime' – that is, the pattern of gender
arrangements within Parliament – is well summarised in the reflections of a female Labour MP,
cited in Nirmal Puwar's (2004) analysis of racialised and gendered institutional cultures in the UK:

> … it's a cross really between a cathedral and a public boys' school and that's still the
> ethos that pervades the place. … It's the whole history of Parliament. It was a place
> where gentlemen with a gentlemen's profession came after they had a good lunch and
> really in lots of ways that kind of ethos hasn't changed. We still have people dressed
> up in eighteenth-century costumes and stockings and buckle shoes. I mean, it's a
> bizarre institution. (Puwar 2004: 38)

Within this context, white women, men and women of colour, working-class, disabled and
other 'non-standard' MPs at Westminster have been treated as 'space invaders' (Puwar 2004).
This disruption is embodied in a notable quote from Winston Churchill, who reportedly told
Nancy Astor, the first woman to take her seat in the House of Commons, that her presence
there was 'as embarrassing as if she burst into my bathroom when I had nothing with which to
defend myself, not even a sponge' (Churchill Archives Centre n.d.).

Of course, the House is not the same as it was in Churchill's day, but even as women's
parliamentary presence has increased over time, many manifestations of this traditional gender regime have continued, reflected in examples such as: allegations and investigations of
sexual harassment and abuse; the opprobrium faced by women MPs bringing children onto
the parliamentary estate and the absence (until 2010) of a parliamentary nursery; formal and
informal requirements for masculine dress; the privileging of Oxford Union-style debates; and
the reported experiences of white women and MPs of colour asked to justify their presence in
Member-only areas (Lovenduski 2014a; Childs 2016).

Nonetheless, while gendered institutions can act as central obstacles to numerical and substantive change, there is also always the possibility that they can be 're-gendered' in more equitable directions (Beckwith 2005). For example, institutional and constitutional restructuring in
Scotland and Wales in the 1990s opened up new opportunities for women to mobilise around
issues of political representation and to play a central role (albeit in different ways) in designing
new institutions. As a result of these efforts, debates over devolution – especially in Scotland
and to a lesser extent in Wales – saw the successful integration of gender perspectives, with

women's representation seen as a symbolic 'shorthand' for a 'new' and more inclusive democratic politics in the devolved polities (Mackay et al. 2002). There was, therefore, an explicit aspiration in Scotland and Wales to create a new set of devolved institutions that would disrupt and depart from the traditional (masculinised) Westminster political model: including new electoral systems intended to promote multi-party politics and more diverse representation; symbolic and practical recognition of caring responsibilities (e.g. through family-friendly sitting hours); and commitments to the promotion of equal opportunities and 'mainstreaming' of gender equality (Mackay and McAllister 2012). Yet scholars suggest that these new rules and practices have only been partly institutionalised, with Westminster legacies continuing to play a powerful role in limiting the potential for transformative change (see, for example, Bradbury and Mitchell 2001; Cairney 2011; Mackay 2014).

Opportunities for re-gendering political institutions in Northern Ireland, in contrast, have been more limited. Equality of representation in the post-Good Friday Agreement institutions was framed exclusively around ethno-nationalism, constraining the emergence of the more pluralist coalitions seen particularly in Scotland (Mackay et al. 2002). Institutions were also not completely created *de novo* in Northern Ireland, where there was already a history of devolved governance; rather, the Northern Ireland Assembly was a rebooted (albeit radically revamped) version of the old parliament at Stormont (Thomson 2019; Whitten, in this volume). As a result, the Assembly has been very much constrained by 'past understandings of politics', including the continuing presence of key political actors, which has meant that women and gender equality issues in particular have struggled to be included (Thomson 2019). The suspension of the Assembly through much of the 2000s has further limited progress.

We will explore these tensions between the 'old' and the 'new' in further depth in the following sections, investigating the uneven progress for women as political actors, and gender equality as an issue, in UK politics over time and across different dimensions of political representation.

Descriptive representation

UK politics offers a fascinating multi-level arena through which to study the dynamics of women's political representation. Women have occupied prominent political positions as Prime Ministers (Liz Truss, Theresa May, Margaret Thatcher) and as First Ministers in Scotland (Nicola Sturgeon), Northern Ireland (Michelle O'Neill, Arlene Foster) and Wales (Eluned Morgan). While women were less than a third of Rishi Sunak's cabinet, at the time of writing they make up 46% of those attending Keir Starmer's new cabinet (including the first female Chancellor of the Exchequer Rachel Reeves) and occupy a majority of cabinet posts in Scotland and Wales. At time of writing, women are 40% of Westminster MPs and 46% of Members of the Scottish Parliament (MSPs) (Figure 3.1). The Senedd has been the most consistent performer on women's representation over time, never dropping below 40% (43% of Members of the Senedd elected in 2021 are women). Wales achieved gender parity after the 2003 elections, and a majority-female parliament for a brief period after a by-election in 2006. The Northern Ireland Assembly has historically had the lowest proportion of women among UK parliaments, but these numbers have recently increased, rising to 36% in the 2022 elections.

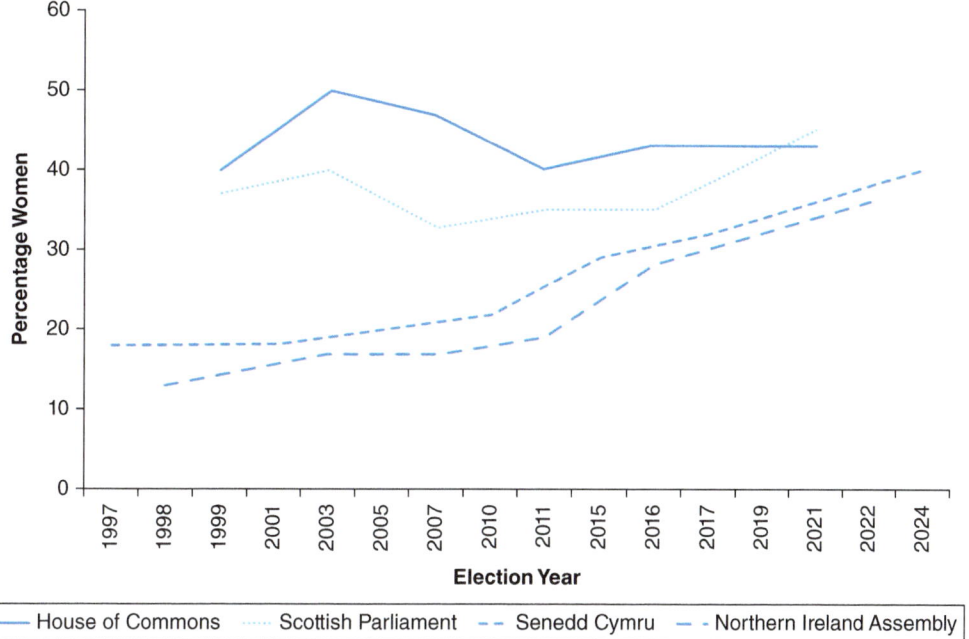

Figure 3.1 Female membership of parliaments in the UK following elections, 1997–2024

Source: House of Commons Library. Contains Parliamentary information licensed under the Open Parliament License v3.0

While still presently short of equal representation, these achievements represent a significant break with the past. Through the late 1980s, women's representation in the UK Parliament had always been below 5%, and didn't rise above 10% until the 1997 General Election. However, progress since this time has not been straightforward – with Figure 3.1 highlighting increases in women's representation, but also patterns of stagnation and setbacks over time. Focusing on headline figures of women parliamentarians also obscures intersectional inequalities (see Peace and Meer, in this volume). Until 2010, Diane Abbott, Dawn Butler and Oona King were the only women of colour elected to Westminster. In the 2024 General Election, 50 women from an ethnic minority background were elected to the House of Commons, more than half of all ethnic minority MPs (56%). Yet it took until 2021 for the first women of colour to be elected to the Scottish Parliament (Kaukab Stewart and Pam Gosal) and to the Welsh Senedd (Natasha Asghar). Stewart's appointment as Minister of Culture, Europe and International Development in February 2024 and subsequently as Minister for Equalities in May of the same year also makes her the first woman of colour to hold a (junior) ministerial post in the Scottish Government. There are no women (or men) of colour in the current Northern Ireland Assembly – Anna Lo previously represented the Alliance Party from 2007 to 2016, becoming the first Chinese-born member of a UK legislature.

What explains these patterns? The causes of women's political under-representation (and men's political over-representation) are well studied, with scholars focusing on the interplay between candidate supply and party demand, investigating who comes forward to run for office and what obstacles are placed in their paths (Norris and Lovenduski 1995). Those who advocate supply-side explanations for women's numerical under-representation suggest that the representational inequalities evident in most legislatures simply reflect the supply of candidates aspiring to a political career. This line of argument is sometimes used by political parties, who claim that they would like to select more women, but that not enough are coming forward.

In the UK, however, research points to the ongoing and limiting power of party demand in shaping representative outcomes (see, for example, Lovenduski 2005a; Kenny 2013; Ashe 2019; Butler et al. 2024). While the electoral system sets the general 'rules of the game', political access in the UK is controlled by party 'gatekeepers'. In order to achieve elected office, then, prospective female candidates must not only decide that they want to stand, but must also be selected by a political party. Studies of gender and political recruitment highlight that this process is not neutral or free from bias. Instead, it is shaped by both formal and informal internal party rules, practices and often hidden power relationships, which favour particular types of candidates over others, resulting in political institutions that are unrepresentative of the wider electorate (see Geddes, in this volume, for a discussion of wider representational trends in the UK Parliament).

Just as Parliament is a gendered institution, then, parties can also be understood as gendered organisations. Indeed, as Lovenduski (2005a: 56) memorably states: 'If parliament is the warehouse of traditional masculinity in British politics, political parties are its major distributors.' Founded and historically populated and led by men from majority groups, the organisations, rules and practices of political parties have been historically built around traditional (and usually unacknowledged) conceptions of gender roles. In the UK Labour Party, for example, women members were largely integrated through women's sections, cut off from the party's main decision-making processes and set up after the party's 1918 constitution (Perrigo 1996). While the party presented itself as a mass-membership party, it was run by an alliance of parliamentary and trade union elites, both overwhelmingly male-dominated (Perrigo 1996; see also Pike, in this volume). The archetypal model of the party member, then, was the male unionised worker, with women seen as subordinate wives and mothers rather than actors with political agency (Perrigo 1996; Lovenduski 2005a).

While British parties have changed significantly over time, studies suggest that gender continues to shape the decisions of party selectors, in both direct and indirect ways and in interaction with other axes of inequality. For example, Laura Shepherd-Robinson and Joni Lovenduski's (2002) Fawcett Society report following the 2001 UK General Election found that gender bias was well entrenched in UK politics, with incidences of direct and indirect discrimination widespread across all of the main British parties. This ranged from gendered assumptions about women's traditional roles (e.g. *what are you going to do about your children*) to explicit sexual harassment (*let's go away for the weekend to talk about how I can help you get selected*) (Lovenduski 2005a: 71). Similarly, Durose et al.'s (2013) interviews with representatives and candidates from under-represented groups in the run up the 2010 General Election highlighted evidence of local party selectorate hostility towards diverse candidates who didn't confirm to the 'archetypal' model of a prospective candidate, with Black and minority ethnic women in particular facing a 'double whammy' of discrimination.

These findings, in turn, have implications for equality strategies, putting the pressure for change on political parties (rather than prospective women candidates) and highlighting the need for concrete measures to ensure that women are selected and elected. British parties have tended to focus on three main strategies for improving women's political presence (see Box 3.1; cf. Lovenduski 2005a).

Box 3.1   Party strategies to promote women's representation

Equality rhetoric entails the public acceptance of claims for women's representation, for example in party platforms, manifestos and speeches. Equality rhetoric can legitimise women's political presence and open up possibilities for action. Most political parties in the UK have made at least a rhetorical commitment to increasing women's representation. An example of this is the shift in UK Conservative Party rhetoric after David Cameron's election as party leader, where he announced plans to tackle women's under-representation by stating that 'the sound of Modern Britain is a complex harmony, not a male voice choir' (Cameron, 2005).

Equality promotion, or positive action, attempts to bring women into politics through measures such as training, financial assistance, mentoring and other initiatives. In the UK, this kind of work takes place through both partisan (e.g. the Conservative group Women2Win, Labour's Jo Cox Women in Leadership Programme) and non-partisan organisations (e.g. Elect Her). Elect Her, for example, seeks to connect prospective candidates with political role models, equip women with essential skills, including around public speaking and campaigning, and support candidates from under-represented backgrounds with the personal expenses of standing for office.

Equality guarantees, or positive discrimination, encapsulate strategies such as party or legislative quotas to secure places for aspiring women candidates. Examples of gender quota measures used in the context of different electoral systems in the UK include 'all-women shortlists', where only women are allowed to stand in particular constituencies for a particular party, 'twinning', where paired constituencies select one man and one woman, and 'zipping', where parties alternate men and women on their candidate lists (with the latter used by some parties in Scottish and Welsh elections under the more proportional Additional Member System (AMS), and formerly in elections to the European Parliament under closed PR lists in Scotland, Wales and England).

In the UK, gains made for women's representation from 1997 onwards and in the devolved institutions largely reflects the use of the third category of strategies, in the form of voluntary quotas implemented by some parties. Women's political presence therefore varies considerably not only across the UK's parliaments, but also across different political parties (see Figures 3.2, 3.3 and 3.4). The introduction of gender quotas was jumpstarted by the UK Labour Party and was deeply intertwined with internal debates around party modernisation and reform after the party's four successive electoral defeats from 1979 to 1992. Women activists within the Labour Party were able to take advantage of these developments, strategically linking Labour's electoral failures to the party's 'old-fashioned' masculinised culture and to the gender gap in Labour's electoral support (Hewitt and Mattinson 1989; Short 1996; Eagle and Lovenduski 1998), and coupling arguments for gender quotas with broader calls for party modernisation. This strategy was crucial in ensuring that the party's policy of implementing all-women shortlists in half of all winnable seats was supported by the party's annual conference in 1993 (for a fuller account of this history, see Lovenduski 2005a). Figure 3.2 shows the clear impact of these measures from 1997 onwards. After legal challenge, the Sex Discrimination Candidates (Electoral Candidates) Bill was introduced in 2001, gaining Royal Assent in 2002 and permitting parties to take action to reduce inequality in the numbers of women and men candidates (subsequently extended until 2030 under the Equality Act 2010).

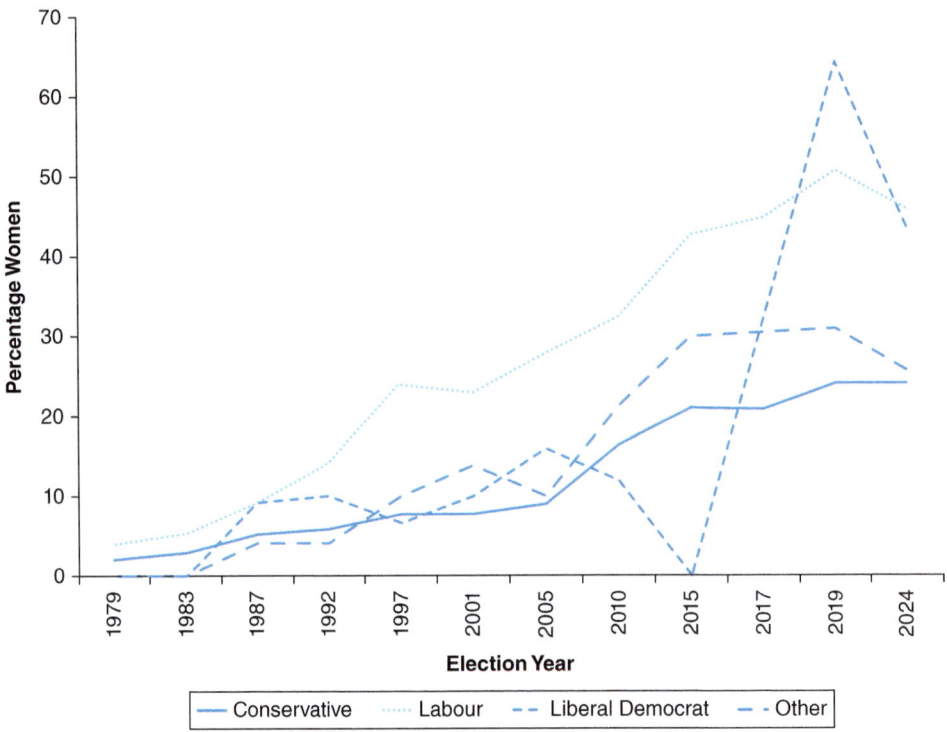

Figure 3.2 Proportion of women Members of Parliament by party following elections, 1979–2024

Source: House of Commons Library. Contains Parliamentary information licensed under the Open Parliament License v3.0

Comparative evidence suggests that the adoption of quota-type measures by one political party may lead to a 'contagion' effect in which other parties respond by actively promoting women in order to compete (Matland and Studlar 1996). The Scottish and Welsh Labour Party's use of gender quotas, including through the 'twinning' mechanism aimed at ensuring gender balance in constituency selections, delivered high levels of women MSPs in the first elections to the devolved parliaments. Their main electoral rivals also implemented formal (Plaid Cymru in Wales) and informal (the SNP in Scotland) measures to promote gender balance among candidates in the 1999 devolved elections.

In Scotland, however, from 2003 to 2016, there was little obvious contagion among Scottish political parties in terms of the adoption and implementation of gender quota measures (see Figure 3.3; see also Kenny and Mackay 2014, 2020). During this period, only Scottish Labour consistently implemented gender quotas, which, post-1999, largely focused on 'low cost' quota measures aimed at the regional lists, while the SNP adopted no formal quota measures until 2016. Trends from 2016 onwards, however, suggest that women's representation has been 'catching on' again in a wider range of Scottish parties (Figure 3.3). Key to this shift has been the impact of the 2014 Scottish independence referendum on both elite-level representation and grassroots women's mobilisation, and the SNP's adoption of strong gender quotas for the first time in the form of all-women shortlists for constituency seats and favourable placement for women candidates on the regional lists (Belknap and Kenny 2023).

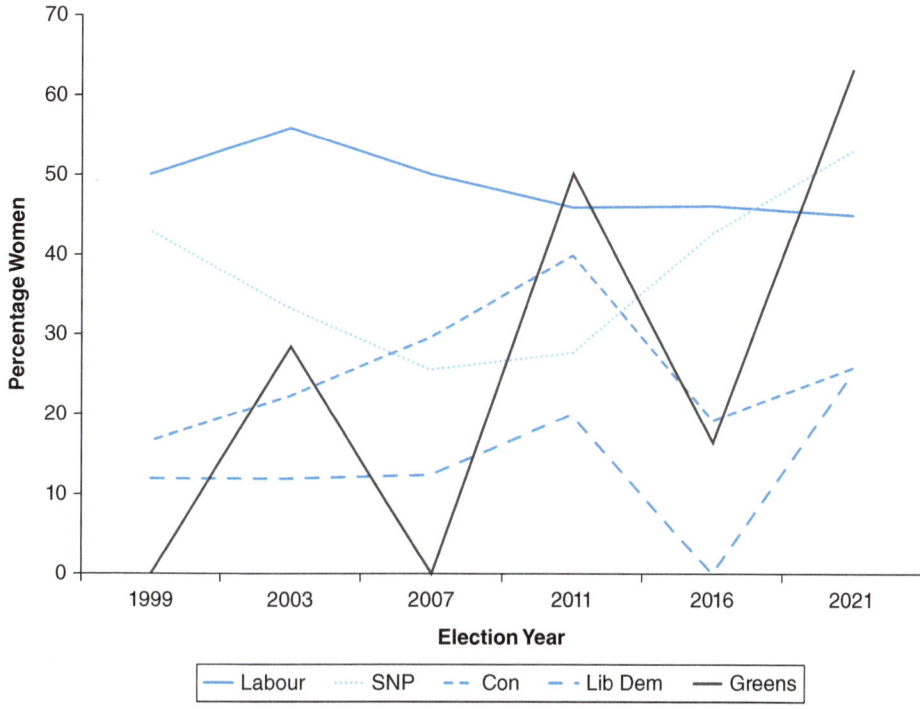

Figure 3.3 Proportion of women Members of the Scottish Parliament by party following elections, 1999–2021

Source: Belknap and Kenny (2023)

In Wales, there has also been significant variation in women's representation across political parties and over time (see Figure 3.4). Labour has consistently achieved gender parity or better in the Senedd since devolution. Plaid Cymru, meanwhile, saw a downward trend in women's representation, with the party moving away from the gender quota measures implemented in 1999 before implementing a revised strategy for regional list placement from the 2016 elections (Stirbu et al. 2018). The Welsh Liberal Democrats have had a gender-balanced parliamentary group or better for most of the period since 1999, albeit in the context of small numbers. From 2016 these numbers should be read in context – the party has only had one representative total in the Senedd during this period (Kirsty Williams in the fifth Senedd and Jane Dodds in the sixth Senedd).

As Figures 3.2–3.4 highlight, the Conservative Party and its Scottish and Welsh branches have remained largely 'immune' to quota contagion effects. The party has tended to adopt a more laissez-faire attitude to women's representation in keeping with its ideological foundations and decentralised approach to candidate selection, one centred around supply-side encouragement, and citing the party's history of female leaders. High-profile efforts by former leader David Cameron to modernise the candidate selection process between 2005 and 2010 stopped short of adopting strong gender quotas. Building on Cameron's rhetorical commitments to increase the party's number of women, BAME and disabled MPs, a gender-balanced Priority List of candidates for Westminster elections was created, alongside

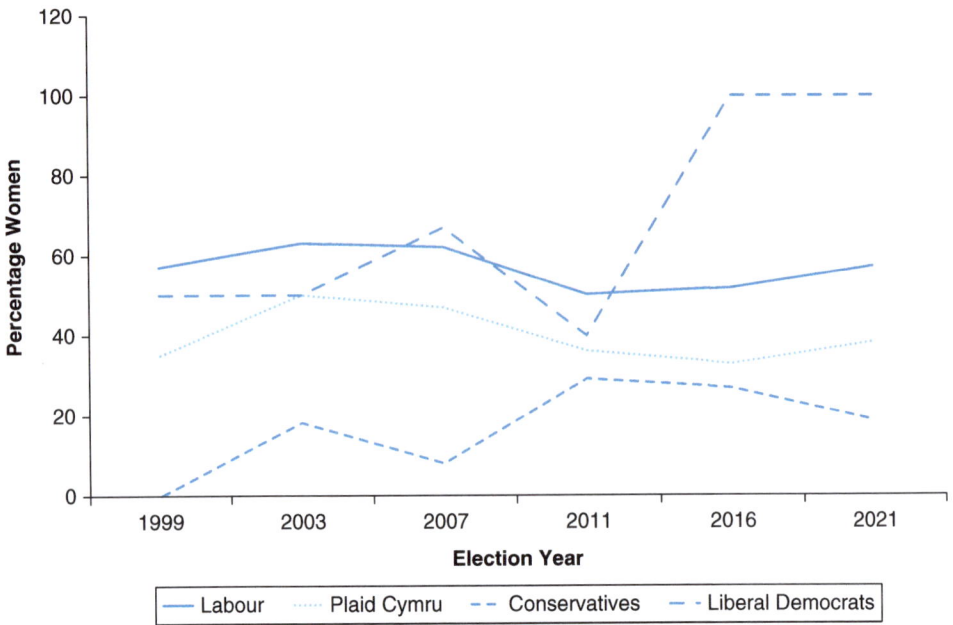

Figure 3.4 Proportion of women Members of the Senedd by party following elections, 1999–2021

Sources: Stirbu et al. (2018); Welsh Parliament (2021)

other reforms to selection meetings and processes (Childs and Webb 2012). This 'A-list' generated significant hostility, particularly from local party associations, and was quietly dropped before the 2015 election. While the party had seen gains in the overall number of Conservative women at Westminster, Holyrood and Cardiff, its landslide defeat in the 2024 General Election saw only 29 Conservative women MPs elected to the House of Commons (a significant drop from the 87 elected in 2019). Indeed, more Labour women MPs were elected in 2024 (190) than all Tory MPs combined (121). At time of writing, of all the main parties, the Conservatives have the lowest proportion of women in the UK Parliament (24%) and the Senedd (19%), and in Scotland they hold the second-to-last spot on women's representation (29%) after the Scottish Liberal Democrats.

Trends in women's descriptive representation over time and across the UK, then, show that gains cannot be taken for granted, and that progress has often been uneven. Moreover, the continuing asymmetries across parties in terms of their performance on women's representation raises questions as to whether this pressing issue should be taken out of the hands of political parties (Childs and Evans 2012; Belknap and Kenny 2023). While voluntary party gender quotas apply only to those parties that have chosen to implement them, the introduction of legislative quotas would apply to all parties. Repeated calls have been made by academics, campaigners and other bodies at the devolved and UK level for the need to go beyond parties and implement legislative gender quotas to ensure real change – including, for example, through the Scottish Women 5050 campaign, the House of Commons Speaker's Conference on Parliamentary Representation, and the UN Committee on the Elimination of Discrimination Against Women, which called on the UK to consider more prescriptive measures to address the under-representation of women in political life. Yet these calls have gained little purchase, particularly in the context of 14 years of Conservative government at Westminster. It remains to be seen whether a Starmer government will be more receptive. Meanwhile, in the devolved institutions, and at time of writing, recent plans to advance a gender quota law for the Senedd have been dropped by the Welsh Government, after facing questions and uncertainties over legislative competence (see, for example, BBC News 2024).

Substantive representation

As the numbers of women representatives have increased across the UK, there has been significant theoretical and empirical interest in what difference women's political presence might make to institutional dynamics and outcomes. A key puzzle for gender politics scholars is the relationship between 'representativeness' and 'representation' – that is, between descriptive and substantive representation. As already highlighted, empirical studies of this relationship take place against a backdrop of complex theorising about political representation, gender and intersectionality. A large body of work has explored the contingent and complex dynamics of the politics of presence in UK political institutions, including the House of Commons and the devolved legislatures. None of this work would claim that numbers alone can deliver the substantive representation of women (SRW), with most scholars agreeing that SRW is 'probabilistic' rather than 'deterministic' (Mackay 2004). Data has been gathered through multiple methods encompassing quantitative analysis of legislative behaviour, textual analysis of parliamentary and legislative debates, surveys of attitudes and values, and in-depth interviews with politicians.

Some studies point to differences in attitudes and some policy priorities between male and female representatives, but find that these are mediated (and sometimes superseded) by party loyalty (Norris and Lovenduski 1995; Norris 1996; Lovenduski and Norris 2003). Interviews with women politicians at Westminster suggest that they are more likely to see the articulation of women's concerns as part of their representative functions (Childs 2004b), but this is not universal and does not necessarily translate into policy outcomes (see, for example, Cowley and Childs 2003). In Scotland and Wales, studies suggest that men and women are more 'equally at home' in the new devolved institutions, and that devolution has 'made a difference' to SRW (see the box Research in Focus: Substantive representation in practice). Interview data from the early years of the Scottish Parliament, for example, found that both women and men MSPs felt that the priority given to certain issues had changed as a result of women's increased political presence (Mackay et al. 2003). Paul Chaney's (2006) analysis of plenary debates in the first term of the then National Assembly for Wales, meanwhile, found that while women parliamentarians were more likely than their male colleagues to engage in and initiate debate on 'women's issues', it also mattered who these women were. Chaney points in particular to the disproportionate influence of 'equality champions' or 'strategic insiders' – women parliamentarians who drew on previous experiences in women's movement activism and gender equality knowledge to promote substantive outcomes in the new institution.

Research in Focus

Substantive representation in practice – domestic abuse policy in Scotland

Has devolution made a difference to the substantive representation of women? Research on domestic violence policy in Scotland suggests that the mutually reinforcing relationship between a more gender-balanced politics and constitutional change has resulted in positive gender equality outcomes (Mackay 2010). Gender-based violence is a classic 'women's issue', affecting women across different identities and backgrounds. Policy developments to address domestic violence (termed 'domestic abuse' in Scotland) were a key early achievement of the first Scottish Parliament and Scottish Executive, and also serve as a continuing example of a differentiated and distinctive approach from the rest of the UK.

Strong political leadership provided by women ministers and parliamentarians, many with established relationships with women's movement organisations and explicitly feminist credentials, together with some key male allies, played a key role in progressing this agenda (Mackay 2010). Women's Aid and other anti-violence women's organisations also made use of the enhanced parliamentary and executive opportunities in the new institution to lobby political actors, give evidence to parliamentary committees and participate in the Scottish Partnership on Domestic Abuse established by the former Scottish Office. Together, they exerted significant influence over the *National Strategy to Address Domestic Abuse in Scotland* (Scottish Executive 2000), including the incorporation of a gendered framing of domestic abuse which recognised the relationship between domestic abuse and broader gender inequality (McCabe 2024).

Significant and sustained gains have been achieved in service provision, protection and prevention since these early years (Burman and Johnson 2015; Kenny and Mackay 2020). This includes the Domestic Abuse (Scotland) Act (2018), which addresses psychological abuse and coercive and controlling behaviour alongside physical abuse, and has been commended by experts as the 'gold standard' of domestic violence prevention (BBC News 2018). Scotland's current national strategy *Equally Safe* (Scottish Government 2016) positions the elimination of gender inequality as a central goal, with violence against women and girls seen to be rooted in unequal gendered power relationships.

Nonetheless, while there has been considerable progress in tackling gender-based violence, inequalities and shortfalls in institutionalisation and implementation persist. Fiona Mackay (2010), for example, questions whether domestic abuse has been fully institutionalised or routinised as a mainstream policy area, pointing to the example of the Scottish Labour Party 'forgetting' about domestic abuse in the run-up to the second Scottish Parliament elections when heralding its policy achievements. Meanwhile, Leah McCabe's (2024) research points to ongoing contestations between gender frames and intersectional perspectives in Scottish domestic abuse policy, tensions which run the risk of excluding marginalised survivors. Services for minority ethnic women remain under-resourced, with less attention paid towards forms of violence such as forced marriage and female genital mutilation (Burman and Johnson 2015). Thus, while domestic abuse is arguably a case of successful feminist constitutional activism (Mackay 2010), asking the question of 'success for whom' remains important, as is the continued presence of feminist actors in multiple arenas to keep gender equality issues from falling off the agenda.

While much of the work on SRW in the UK has focused on how positive gender change can happen, it is also important to consider cases where it doesn't happen. Jennifer Thomson's (2019) study of abortion law in Northern Ireland, for example, draws on textual analysis of political debates and interviews with key actors to ask how this issue has been addressed at Westminster and at Stormont. In Northern Ireland, as already highlighted, power-sharing structures have privileged ethno-nationalism at the expense of other identities, inhibiting opportunities for women's substantive representation. Progress on abortion rights has been particularly resistant to change, falling through the gaps of sub-national and central governance within the UK, with no institution 'owning' the issue (Thomson 2019). Thomson's research points to the difficulties of forming communities of women Members of the Legislative Assembly (MLAs) across parties on this issue within this inhospitable political and institutional context, while also highlighting the crucial role of conservative 'critical actors' working to maintain the status quo of restrictive abortion laws across party and ethno-national boundaries (see also Thomson 2018). Yet, changing attitudes at Westminster and pressure from opposition backbenchers, coupled with a series of political crises (Brexit, the suspension of the Northern Ireland Assembly from 2017), put the issue of abortion back onto Westminster's political agenda after the 2017 General Election, ultimately leading to the decriminalisation of abortion in Northern Ireland in 2019 (Thomson 2022).

Research on women's substantive representation in the UK is ongoing, but a number of challenges remain in the field. The first is the intersectional imperative – too few studies consider representative claims through the perspective of multiple power structures. A notable exception here is Orlanda Siow's (2023a) analysis of the representation of minoritised women in parliamentary debates. Siow finds that racially minoritised women are mentioned extremely rarely in UK parliamentary debates, and that they are more likely to be mentioned by minoritised women than MPs from other groups (including white women and minoritised men). Siow argues that it is crucially important to parse out the differences between speaking 'on behalf of' versus speaking 'about' or even 'against' a particular group. However, silence on race/gender does not mean that SRW is not occurring; indeed, in some cases, she argues, it may be more 'expedient to act *for* without speaking *about*' (Siow 2023a: 341).

There is also a need to employ gendered analytical frameworks that examine both men and women as political actors. While feminist political scientists have historically focused on the experiences of women politicians, new research agendas draw on wider inter-disciplinary work on men and masculinities seek to better understand the nature of male dominance in politics, and to investigate *how* men represent *which* men (see, for example, Bjarnegård and Murray 2018; Murray 2024). Work on substantive representation in the UK has also been slow to move beyond the near-exclusive focus on parliaments and legislatures to study the multiple sites and actors involved in interest representation and policy making, including executives, bureaucracies and extra-institutional spaces such as civil society (for one exception see Annesley and Gains 2010). And much of the research to date on substantive representation has focused on left-of-centre parties across the UK, in particular the Labour Party. More research is needed to further explore the theoretical and empirical challenges posed by conservative and/or anti-feminist representatives who claim to 'act for' women, building on but also expanding and updating existing work on gender and conservative parties and actors in the UK (Childs and Webb 2012; see also Thomson 2019).

Gender-sensitising political institutions

While much of the scholarship on gender and representation in the UK continues to focus on obstacles to women's descriptive representation, or on evaluating similarities and differences in behaviour once elected representatives are present, more recent work shifts the focus towards parliaments themselves and the work that gender does therein (Childs and Kenny 2025). The increasing scholarly interest in parliaments as institutions has been matched by practitioner interest in gender- and diversity-sensitive parliamentary reform.

The concept of a 'gender-sensitive parliament' (GSP) dates to 2001 – and a special study group of the Commonwealth Parliamentary Association (CPA) – but was particularly taken forward by the Inter-Parliamentary Union (IPU) in the 2010s (Box 3.3) and has subsequently been advanced by a range of international organisations. Building on these foundations, a gender-sensitive parliament can be defined as one that:

> values and prioritises gender equality as a social, economic and political objective and reorients and transforms a parliament's institutional culture, processes and practices, and outputs towards these objectives. (Childs and Palmieri 2023: 177)

Box 3.2   IPU criteria for a gender-sensitive parliament

A gender-sensitive parliament is one that:

1   Promotes and achieves equality in numbers of women and men across all of its bodies and internal structures.
2   Develops a gender equality policy framework suited to its own national parliamentary context.
3   Mainstreams gender equality throughout all of its work.
4   Fosters an internal culture that respects women's rights, promotes gender equality and responds to the needs and realities of MPs – men and women – to balance work and family responsibilities.
5   Acknowledges and builds on the contribution made by its men members who pursue and advocate for gender equality.
6   Encourages political parties to take a proactive role in the promotion and achievement of gender equality.
7   Equips its parliamentary staff with the capacity and resources to promote gender equality, actively encourages the recruitment and retention of women to senior positions, and ensures that gender equality is mainstreamed throughout the work of the parliamentary administration.

Source: Inter-Parliamentary Union (2012)

At the core of GSP approaches is a recognition that parliament *as an institution* is responsible for realising equal representation and gender equality, not individual women parliamentarians. GSP work encourages parliaments to reflect on – and change – their processes, infrastructure and culture through either self-assessments or independently conducted audits. It is, therefore, aimed not just at ensuring that women share opportunities for numerical and substantive participation within parliaments once elected, but also that gender equality is prioritised and mainstreamed across parliamentary work and outcomes. While initially practitioner-led, increasingly practitioners and academics have worked together in carrying out GSP work – for example, in consultant or advisory roles. This kind work has been facilitated by long-established feminist academic commitments to 'real-world' impact; feminist political scientists seek not only to recognise and understand gendered inequalities in public and political life, but also to change and transform them (Campbell and Childs 2013; Kenny and Mackay 2017).

The concept of a 'gender-sensitive parliament' has become an international democratic standard, evidenced, for example, in the 2022 Kigali Declaration at the 145th IPU Assembly in Rwanda, where IPU member parliaments recommitted to the GSP agenda. It has also proved influential in the UK, not least because of the efforts of UK gender politics scholars, working within and/or in partnership with parliaments, and drawing on international research and best practice. Yet, while there have been notable successes in gender and diversity sensitising efforts at both UK and devolved level (see Case Study 3.1), experiences to date highlight the crucial importance of political and institutional leadership in advancing the GSP agenda, and raise questions as to the extent to which GSP work has been institutionalised (or not) over the medium- to long-haul.

Case Study 3.1

Gender-sensitising parliaments in the UK

The Good Parliament report, launched in the UK Parliament in 2016 by gender politics academic Professor Sarah Childs, set out a comprehensive agenda to improve representation and inclusion in the House of Commons (Childs 2016). Informed by the IPU's GSP framework, Childs' report took a broader intersectional approach to documenting and rectifying Parliament's 'diversity insensitivities'. Having invited herself into the Parliament, the then Speaker, the Rt Hon John Bercow MP, actively supported her independent report and set up a group of MPs through the Commons Reference Group on Representation and Inclusion to lead this agenda. The report encompassed 43 wide-ranging recommendations, each attached to a named, responsible decision-maker, in an effort to hold Parliament as an institution as well as individual members to account for its implementation. These included recommendations around improving equality of participation, parliamentary infrastructure and Commons culture, for example:

- Systematic diversity monitoring of parliamentary activities and select committee witnesses (Recs. 2, 28)
- Measures aimed at enhancing the supply of, and demand for, diverse parliamentary candidates, including the potential introduction of statutory sex/gender quotas (Recs. 6–9, 43)
- A 'House Statement' on maternity, paternity, parental, adoption and caring leave (Rec. 12)
- Establishing the Women and Equalities Committee as a permanent select committee of the House (Rec. 25)
- Abolishing the '10 year dead rule' to enable more diverse artwork in the palace of Westminster (Recs. 40, 42)

(Continued)

At time of writing, 18 of *The Good Parliament* report's recommendations have been implemented in part or in full. One of the key successes of the report was the introduction of proxy voting for 'baby leave', whereby Members on maternity, paternity or shared parental leave can arrange for their vote to be cast by another MP. The Commons Reference Group, however, ceased meeting from autumn 2018 – the result of a combination of Brexit politics and the fallout over the handout of bullying and harassment allegations in Parliament.

The GSP agenda has subsequently been taken forward through the *UK Gender-Sensitive Parliament Audit 2018* (itself one of Childs' recommendations; see UK Parliament 2018) and the Women and Equalities Committee's subsequent inquiry and 2022 report on a gender-sensitive House of Commons (House of Commons Women and Equalities Committee 2022). The latter report, among other recommendations, recommended that the House of Commons Commission conduct a review of the implementation of *The Good Parliament* and the 2018 gender-sensitive audit, accompanied by annual reporting on progress. A subsequent 2023 report from the Women in Parliament All-Party Parliamentary Group audited these previous reports and once again called for a body to be established to lead and advance the GSP agenda and oversee future audits (APPG on Women in Parliament 2023). Thus, while progress has been made on gender-sensitising reforms at Westminster, ongoing GSP work has been conducted within a context of reduced remit and reach over time, in which overall responsibility for and the role of independent expertise in advancing the GSP agenda has not been fully institutionalised.

GSP work has also been taken forward in other parts of the UK, most notably in the Scottish Parliament's gender-sensitive audit of its rules, practices and culture, launched by the Presiding Officer Alison Johnstone MSP in 2022. While the audit highlighted Holyrood's strong record to date on women's representation and gender equality, it also pointed to fluctuations over time in women's participation and representation, the persistence of intersectional inequalities, and an *ad hoc* rather than institutionalised approach to the mainstreaming of equalities. Responding to the findings of the audit, a GSP board chaired by the Presiding Officer and made up of cross-party MSPs and academic experts published *A Parliament for All*, outlining 34 recommendations focused on participation, representation, parliamentary culture and gender equality mainstreaming (Scottish Parliament 2023). As with *The Good Parliament* (Childs 2016), each recommendation is linked to specific individuals, groups or bodies, identifying who is responsible and accountable for implementation. The recommended reforms include:

- A rule that there should be no single-sex parliamentary committees (Rec. 19)
- Rule changes to guarantee women's representation on key bodies and groups, including committees, the Parliamentary Bureau and the Scottish Parliamentary Corporate Body (Recs. 18–21)
- The establishment of a forum for women MSPs to discuss issues of mutual interest (Rec. 29)
- A review of the Parliament's sitting time data to determine what changes need to be made to limit unpredictability and maximise inclusion and wellbeing (Recs. 15–17)
- The permanent introduction of a proxy voting scheme covering parental leave, illness and caring/bereavement leave (Rec. 22)

Crucially, the first and overarching recommendation of *A Parliament for All* is the creation and resourcing of a Scottish Parliament GSP Advisory Group, composed of cross-party representatives, academics and other external experts. Reflecting international best practice, the Group has been tasked by the Presiding Officer to oversee the delivery of the report's recommendations and Parliament's progress towards gender sensitivity. At the time of writing, it is still early days to evaluate the longer-term impact of this group and the wider GSP agenda, but progress on the report's recommendations continues, including the commissioning of an estates' disability audit, new intersectional data collection and monitoring, gender-sensitive legislative scrutiny guidance, outreach efforts and the creation of a women's caucus.

Reflective questions

1   How might institutional gender and diversity insensitivities vary (or not) across the UK? Think about the features and experiences of different parliaments as well as different dimensions of gender sensitivity.
2   What do you think are the strengths and weaknesses of GSP approaches?

Conclusion

These days, it would probably be hard to find a UK politics course or module that doesn't incorporate women's representation or gender equality to some degree. As this chapter argues, processes of political 'feminisation' – that is, the political integration of women and women's concerns – have transformed the context within which parties and parliaments operate, and are therefore a centrally important research area in UK politics. But, after reading this chapter, you will also know that studying gender and politics is about more than counting different groups of women (though this is still important); it is also about illuminating gender power relations, gendered institutions and their gendered effects. Gendered approaches are therefore essential to the study of *all* areas of UK politics.

Summary

- This chapter introduced feminist theories of representation and gendered institutions. Through this discussion, you should have a better understanding of the institutional 'turn' in studies of gender and political representation in the UK, the relationship between gender and other structures of power, and how to begin to conceptualise and research the gendered dynamics of political institutions.
- It gave you a comprehensive overview of women's diverse political participation and representation, and strategies for increasing women's political presence across the UK. The chapter highlights improvements in the number and diversity of women representatives over time and the partial 'contagion' of gender quotas across different party systems. However, it also contends that progress has been asymmetrical and that significant gaps remain in terms of promoting women's diverse representation.
- It introduced debates over the complex and contingent relationship between women's political presence and the substantive representation of women's interests (SRW), through a range of case studies that investigate the who, where, why and how of SRW in the UK.
- It identified efforts to 're-gender' political institutions in the UK, drawing on international debates and focusing in particular on gender- and diversity-sensitising parliamentary reform. This, in turn, points to both the promise and limits of institutionalising gender equality reforms within existing institutions, with resultant implications for change strategies.

Recommended and further reading

- For *the* classic (and to date, still the most comprehensive) study of political recruitment in the UK, read Pippa Norris and Joni Lovenduski (1995) *Political Recruitment: Gender, Race and Class in the British Parliament*. Cambridge: Cambridge University Press, lauded as one of the best books ever published on British politics (*The Guardian* 2017).
- If you want to delve deeper into the question of what makes a parliament 'gender-sensitive', read Sarah Childs (2016) *The Good Parliament*. University of Bristol. Available at: https://commonslibrary.parliament.uk/research-briefings/cdp-2016-0201/, in conjunction with the Scottish Parliament's new (2023) report *A Parliament for All: Report of the Parliament's Gender Sensitive Audit*. Available at: www.parliament.scot/about/news/news-listing/a-parliament-for-all-reforms.
- While the relationship between gender and voting behaviour is beyond the scope of this chapter, you may want to further explore this by reading Rosie Campbell and Rosalind Shorrocks' analysis of the gender gap and the vote in the 2019 British elections, which points to a (contingent) 'modern gender gap': Campbell, R. and Shorrocks, R. (2021) 'Finally rising with the tide? Gender and the vote in the 2019 British Elections', *Journal of Elections, Public Opinion and Parties*, 31(4): 488–507.
- Elizabeth Evans and Stefanie Reher's (2024) *Disability and Political Representation*. Oxford: Oxford University Press will allow you to build on what you've learned so far about intersectionality and representation, offering the first systematic study of the political representation of disabled people in the UK, while also placing the UK within its international context.

Chapter 4

Race, ethnicity and UK politics

Timothy Peace and Nasar Meer

What will this chapter tell me?

- We need to treat the category of 'race' carefully and critically: it is an unstable and socially constructed concept.
- Migration in the postwar period from countries that were formerly part of the British Empire fundamentally changed the make-up of Britain and British politics. This is often symbolised by the arrival of the SS *Empire Windrush*, although the UK had always been a migrant nation.
- Despite initial barriers, ethnic minority representation has gradually increased at the local government and then the UK Parliament level. Initially, the Labour Party elected the most ethnic minority representatives. That association persists and Labour still attracts majority support from ethnic minority voters.
- Two general elections stand out as watershed moments. In 1987 the first ethnic minority MPs were elected in the postwar period. In 2010 the number of ethnic minority MPs almost doubled from 15 to 27 and included several from the Conservative Party.
- All four Great Offices of State, including that of Prime Minister, as well as the First Ministers of Scotland and Wales, have been held by someone from an ethnic minority background.
- Trying to attract the support of certain ethnic communities has been embedded in British electoral campaigning for many years.
- While important progress has been made in terms of how parties engage with ethnic minorities, there remain significant disparities in the levels of electoral registration.
- Minority candidates have faced an 'ethnic penalty' from the electorate although its impact is now more negligible.
- It is unclear whether increased descriptive minority representation translates into substantive policy outcomes that benefit ethnic minorities.

What do I need to know?

- The UK became a much more ethnically diverse society after the 1950s. Race and 'race relations' became key issues in British politics from this moment on.
- The representation of ethnic minorities in elected positions was part of a long struggle to impose upon political parties the need to provide opportunities for all.
- Candidate selection procedures for parties are a key area of study for those interested in minority representation.
- The Labour Party was traditionally the party that was most supported by ethnic minority voters. This attachment still persists but to a much lesser extent.
- In the 2021 England and Wales Census, 81.7% (48.7 million) of usual residents identified their ethnic group within the 'White' category with 'Asian, or Asian British' at 9.6% (5.4 million), 'Black, Black British, Caribbean or African' at 4.2% (2.4 million) and 'Mixed or Multiple ethnic groups' at 3.0% (1.7 million).

Introduction

How and in what ways do race and ethnicity feature in UK politics? This chapter will help readers to understand what role these issues play in the institutions of political life (such as the Westminster and devolved Parliaments), the systems that reproduce these issues (such as the electoral process and party politics) and the changing dynamics of social relations (such as shifts in identities and values). It will discuss the relationships between categories of analysis and the political *participation* of racial and ethnic minorities, especially in achieving political *representation*, and consider how this has changed over time. The chapter will begin with how we use racial and ethnic categories to describe differences among and across populations, before tracing their salience in political mobilisation. It will show how these have neither been linear nor stable, but that political participation has been at their core. Following this, the chapter will consider the development of a so called 'ethnic vote' in electoral campaigning, and whether this focus has obscured lower levels of electoral registration among ethnic and racial groups. The chapter will then discuss the relationship between an increased presence in electoral politics for minorities, and the party-political pathways to improved political representation.

Race and ethnicity in society and politics

The political representation of ethnic and racial minorities in Britain occupies an important place in public debates on society-wide representativeness, inclusion and the quality of democracy (Akhtar and Peace 2019). As we have seen in the discussion of gender (Kenny, in this volume), the relationship between *holding* and *exercising* political rights is not straightforward and often subject to intended and unintended obstacles. In this chapter, we will discuss how 'barriers and prejudices' concerning racial and ethnic status in particular can 'make it difficult for historically disadvantaged groups to participate effectively in the political process' (Kymlicka 1995: 141). To do so requires us to grasp how inequalities in social status – and how minorities may respond to these – play a role in formal political participation. The first challenge is to ensure we think critically about how we use racial and ethnic categories to describe differences among and across populations. We know, for example, that these categories have changed across the social and political contexts in which they are found, and do not refer to anything such as fixed group tendencies in any given society. In his study of what the idea of race means, Omi (2001: 244) concluded that its expression 'has been and probably always will be fluid and subject to multiple determinations. Race cannot be seen simply as an objective fact, nor treated as an independent variable.' There are here two important issues to keep uppermost in mind. First, many academics tend to treat these categories, and race in particular, as dynamic (changing) and contested (challenged) to indicate that we are using a socially constructed category to study society and politics (so we are not simply reporting on the world as it has always been). The history of racial categories in particular renders it an exceptionally problematic idea that cannot be treated as self-evidently real in the world, but rather reflects how minority groups negotiate its formal and informal use (Meer 2022). In this respect, race is a verb rather than a noun: we imbue something with the characteristics of race in the action of describing it.

Second, the meaning of ethnicity partly attends to the problem of categories of race because it prioritises self-definition. People consciously identify as a member of a certain group, typically a linguistic community or territory, or real or imagined ancestry (including religion), or membership of a perceived group with other distinguishing cultural characteristics (Meer 2019). In many countries, ideas of race and ethnicity remain a fixture in the popular discussion, or a basis for social action, a foundation of government policy and often a justification for distinctive treatment of one group over another. Where too much emphasis is placed on the internal strategies, hopes and aspirations of racial and ethnic group members, and too little on the external structural, institutional and systemic dynamics, it can make the very fact of 'difference' an explanatory variable. To guard against this, we must place the use of these categories in their historical context. The concept of 'political blackness' meant that 'black' in the UK context signified any person of colour who wished to identify with this term. The use of the term 'black' for all ethnic minorities was critiqued by Tariq Modood, among others, and this fell out of favour from the mid-1990s onwards. The term 'Asian' in the British context usually denotes someone of South Asian heritage, i.e. from today's nations of India, Pakistan and Bangladesh. This is reflected in official documentation, such as the census, where the categories 'Asian' and 'Asian British' are used. The term 'immigrant' was commonly used until the 1970s to denote anyone who was not white irrespective of whether they had migrated to the UK or had actually been born there. More recently, acronyms such as BAME (Black, Asian and Minority Ethnic) have been preferred, despite resistance from some of those to whom the term applies (Fakim and Macaulay 2020). This terminology needs to be borne in mind but for the sake of simplicity we have used the terms 'ethnic minority' or 'racial and ethnic minorities' to denote the actors we are describing.

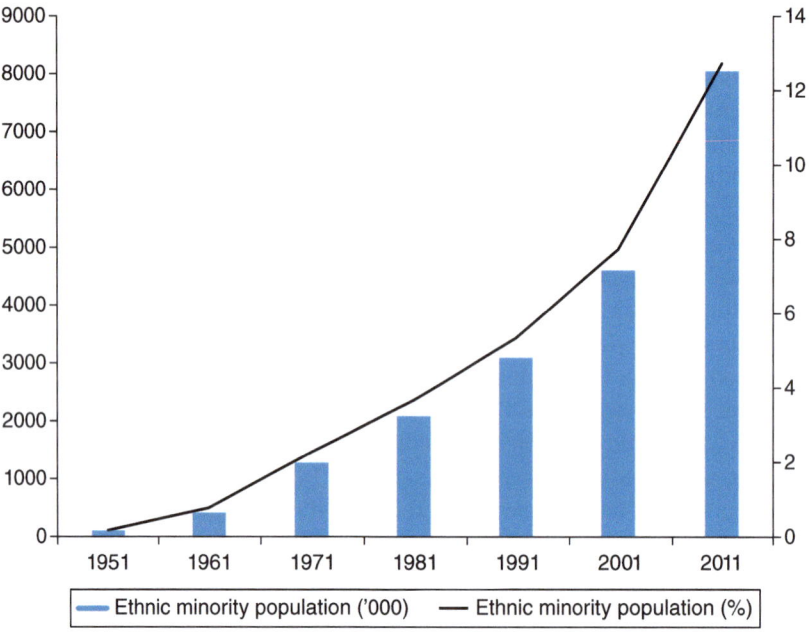

Figure 4.1   Ethnic group distribution (high-level categories), 1951–2011, England and Wales

Source: Office for National Statistics (2022) https://www.ons.gov.uk/peoplepopulationandcommunity/culturalidentity/ethnicity/bulletins/ethnicgroupenglandandwales/census2021#:~:text=The%20largest%20increases%20were%20seen,%25%2C%20564%2C000%20in%202011).

Political participation and representation

The arrival of the SS *Empire Windrush* in June 1948, a ship carrying passengers from the Caribbean who would go on to make Britain their home, is often seen as a key moment in the development and importance of the UK as a multi-racial and multi-ethnic polity. As has been noted by Back et al. (2022), the idea that 'multicultural Britain emerged from the arrival of the *SS Windrush* in 1948 has been subjected to critique both as a historical narrative that simplifies the many centuries of migrant history and black presence in the United Kingdom'. Nevertheless, it provides an important starting point for thinking about the impact of race and ethnicity in UK politics. The 1948 Nationality Act gave people living in Britain's former colonies the right of entry and settlement on the British mainland and many came to the UK in order to fulfil labour shortages during the 1950s and 1960s. In the postwar period, migration from these countries of the 'New Commonwealth' fundamentally changed the make-up of Britain and, by extension, British politics. These migrants 'made claims of belonging that fundamentally shaped the politics of race in postwar British society in ways that subsequently transformed notions of citizenship and ideas about what it meant to be British' (Perry 2015: 4). In those early years of settlement, race and 'race relations' became a key issue in British politics and in academia the study of race was developed by scholars such as Michael Banton, Ruth Glass, Shelia Patterson, John Rex and Robert Moore, among others (see Meer and Nayak 2013, for an overview and retrospective). The issue of race in Britain in this postwar period was most often framed in negative terms. Hostility to these new populations led successive governments to restrict further migration through a series of legislative measures, starting with the Commonwealth Immigrants Act of 1962.

Research in Focus

Racial justice

What can we learn from successes and failures in the pursuit of racial justice in the UK and elsewhere in the Global North? One recent view is that we are motivated by a 'cruel optimism' which normalises social and political outcomes that sustain racial injustice, despite successive governments wielding the means to address it. In *The Cruel Optimism of Racial Justice* (2022), Nasar Meer argues that an image of a better or available good life creates an impasse that does not easily allow us to detach from what is not working. Researchers, activists and policy-makers committed to the pursuit of racial justice often make a difficult peace with this impasse; something that comes not in a single event or episode that typically characterises a trauma, but which is something more akin to an undulating pain and discomfort.

Some people will recognise in themselves how we have routinely arrived at this impasse, and have perhaps even clung, in different ways, to the cruel optimism that racism in our societies can lessen, because some attitudes are evidently less hostile. This is not naivety. It is instead to hold that what is morally unjust should not prosper in our societies, and researchers, activists and minoritised groups continually identify the drivers of these outcomes but have grown accustomed to persevering despite strong resistance to change. It is argued that by looking at numerous examples across anti-racist movements and key developments in nationhood/nationalism, institutional racism, migration, white supremacy and the disparities of Covid-19, it becomes apparent that societies have grown accustomed to a 'crisis ordinariness'.

Recognising this cruel optimism, it is argued, will better equip us to move on from a perpetual crisis to a turning point. In order to do so, *The Cruel Optimism of Racial Justice* invites us to re-examine racial justice outside the realm of ideal theory and re-inscribe it with

(Continued)

sociological content. Doing so shows us how racial injustice is often co-constituted across different social domains and ancillary social spheres, from education to the criminal justice system, from housing to public discourse.

Yet, the impact of racial injustice is presently asymmetrical in landing disproportionately on racialised minorities who can see as self-evident these inequalities as they manifest across social systems. A fundamental rebalancing of this is only possible when the beneficiaries of the social production of moral indifference recognise that this is their load to bear as well. As a society, Meer insists, we must reckon with the social and, of course, moral cost of racial injustice, but also support the necessary imagination that takes us through and beyond understandable despair. If this is the same motive that binds us into a cruel optimism presently, this need not be our future too.

Source: Meer (2022)

In electoral politics, the issue of race was present from the 1960s onwards and was often weaponised in order to score political points. In every general election the 'race card' was played by politicians to undermine the presence of ethnic minorities as British citizens (Anwar 2001). During the general election of 1964, the electoral contest in Smethwick, near Birmingham, was the scene of an overtly racist anti-immigrant campaign by the Conservative Party's candidate, Peter Griffiths. Although events in Smethwick came to national prominence, such rhetoric was not unusual from both politicians and the general public during this time. Widespread discrimination faced by people of colour led to the passing of the Race Relations Act in 1965, the first legislation in the United Kingdom to address racial discrimination, which was further strengthened in 1968. It directly led to another key episode in the history of race and politics in the UK – the so-called 'Rivers of Blood speech' made by Conservative MP Enoch Powell in April 1968 in Birmingham. In this now notorious address, Powell 'warned that, with continued large-scale immigration of non-white people into the country, Britain would face inevitable racial violence and eventual national disintegration' (Schofield 2013: 208). The speech split the nation and would go on to have important repercussions in the subsequent general election of 1970 and for many years to come.

Despite the evident racism and discrimination faced by racial and ethnic minorities in Britain at this time, their involvement in both local and national politics was significant. This was aided by the fact that most had the right to vote and stand for election as either British or Commonwealth citizens. One pioneer in terms of representation was Dhani Prem, originally from India, who was elected as the first councillor of South Asian origin in Birmingham in 1946. Another important figure was Dr David Pitt (later to become Baron Pitt of Hampstead), who made history in 1959 as the first person of African descent to be a parliamentary candidate. He was subsequently elected as a member for Hackney for the London County Council (LCC) in 1961 and is considered as one of the first black people to serve in a local government position (Ventre 2023). By the end of the 1960s he had been joined by others, such as Basil Lewis, originally from Jamaica, elected as a Conservative Councillor for Haringey Borough Council in London in 1968. Bashir Maan in Glasgow is regarded as the UK's first Muslim councillor when he was elected for Labour in 1970 and one of the first ethnic minority elected representatives in Scotland. These pioneers were followed by others throughout the 1970s when ethnic minority political participation became more visible and routine, especially in areas of the UK which had sizeable minority communities. In 1970 it was reported that eight candidates from ethnic minorities stood for the general election that year, including David Pitt, who at that time was vice-chairman of the Greater London Council. His candidacy attracted much national publicity but his failure to win the safe Labour seat of Clapham indicated that 'the electorate was not ready to accept a West Indian to represent them in Parliament' (Deakin and Bourne 1970: 411). Indeed, it was not for another 17 years that the UK would see the first ethnic minority MPs elected in the postwar era, but in the intervening period inroads were being made in local government.

Ethnic minority representation in local government from the 1970s onwards was overwhelmingly dominated by the Labour Party and this has continued to be the case well into the twenty-first century. However, the representation of ethnic minorities in elected positions was part of a long struggle to impose upon political parties the need to provide opportunities for all. This began with the creation of the Labour Party Race and Action Group (LPRAG) in 1975. A more important development was the creation of unofficial 'Black Sections' in the Labour Party from 1983 onwards. Within the national Labour Party, a group or caucus of its 'black' members insisted that only by organising and mobilising a 'black' constituency within it could they orient the party towards more substantively addressing matters of ethnic minority parliamentary representation. Within the Labour Party, this constituency (or smaller groups of constituencies) became known as the Labour Party Black Sections (LPBS), which sought a constitutional status within the party on a par with already existing Women and Youth sections (Shukra 1998). Although unsuccessful in terms of gaining official recognition in the party, the LPBS movement was indirectly responsible for the election of increased numbers of 'black' Labour councillors and eventually the first ethnic minority MPs in the postwar period. The vice chair of LPBS was Linda Bellos, who was first elected as a Labour councillor for Lambeth Council in 1985 and subsequently led that council from 1986 to 1988. In the same period, Merle Amory became the leader of Brent Council, the first black woman to reach a leadership position within a British local authority. It was the general election of 1987, however, that was seen as a true watershed moment for ethnic minority representation when Diane Abbott, Paul Boateng, Bernie Grant and Keith Vaz were elected to the House of Commons, all of whom had been involved in the LPBS movement.

In subsequent years, the number of MPs from minority ethnic groups rose slightly after each general election. From four in 1987 to six in 1992, then from nine in 1997 to 12 in 2001. With the exception of Nirj Deva, who represented the Conservatives between 1992 and 1997, all of these parliamentarians were Labour politicians. This reflected the ongoing association between the Labour Party and the ethnic minority electorate given that, with the possible exception of Mohammed Sarwar in Glasgow Govan (the first Muslim MP), these parliamentarians all represented constituencies with a significant ethnic minority electorate. While other parties may have been fielding minority candidates, they were clearly not placing them in winnable seats. Indeed, it has been demonstrated that parties often placed minority candidates in 'unwinnable' seats in areas of high anti-immigrant public opinion (English 2019). A breakthrough occurred in 2010 when the number of ethnic minority MPs almost doubled from 15 to 27, including 11 elected for the Conservatives (from a total of 138 minority candidates standing for election). While still representing just 4% of the total number of MPs, the shift was significant as it indicated that ethnic minority MPs could be selected and go on to win in a variety of constituencies. The trend continued in 2015 with a total of 42 ethnic minority MPs (including the first for the Scottish National Party) and this was confirmed again two years later in 2017 when the total number rose to 53. In 2019 a symbolic barrier was passed when 10% of all elected MPs (66 in total) were from a Black, Asian and Minority Ethnic (BAME) background. For the first time, the House of Commons started to resemble more closely the ethnic make-up of the UK electorate. At the time of writing there are 90 MPs from an ethnic minority background who were elected during the General Election of 2024. That represents 14% of the total with 10% of all male MPs and 19% of all female MPs. These steadily increasing figures have also been reflected in the number of government ministers from a minority background. In 2002, Paul Boateng became Britain's first black cabinet minister and by 2022 all of the four Great Offices of State (Prime Minister, Chancellor of the Exchequer, Home Secretary and Foreign Secretary) had been held by someone with a minority ethnic background. The rapid rise of Rishi Sunak, who became Prime Minister in October 2022, indicated that minorities in the UK could reach the very top of UK politics.

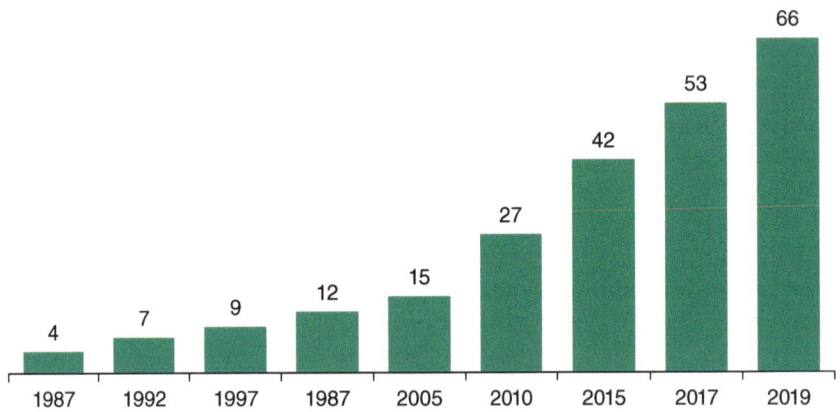

Figure 4.2   Number of MPs from minority ethnic groups elected at general elections

Source: House of Commons (2023). Contains Parliamentary information licensed under the Open Parliament Licence v3.0

In the devolved parliaments and governments, the success of minority representation has been less marked but also reflects different demographics compared to England. In the Scottish Parliament, the representation of ethnic minority MSPs increased significantly in 2021 from two to six, and included the first women of colour to be elected to Holyrood (see also Kenny, in this volume). Earlier that year Anas Sarwar became the first person of colour and first Muslim to lead a major political party in Scotland, and indeed anywhere in the UK. Then, in March 2023, Humza Yousaf, who is also a Scottish Muslim of South-Asian heritage, superseded this achievement by becoming the First Minister of Scotland. Since 2021 the Welsh Parliament has three members from a minority ethnic background, including one woman, and in March 2024 Vaughan Gething won the Welsh Labour leadership election and subsequently became First Minister of Wales. The son of a Welsh father and Zambian mother therefore became the first Black leader of a national government anywhere in Europe. However, the Northern Ireland Assembly lags behind in this respect as there are, at the time of writing, no members of the legislative assembly (MLAs) from minority ethnic groups, despite making up around 4% of the population (not dissimilar to Scotland and Wales). According to one report, 'mainstream preoccupation with the traditional

Green and Orange divide has left little political attention available for other important matters in Northern Ireland, with many minority ethnic communities feeling overlooked by politicians and policy makers as a result' (House of Commons 2022: 3).

In UK local government, diversity has slowly but steadily increased, and it was estimated in 2020 that 7% of local councillors in the United Kingdom are of ethnic minority background. The diversity now seen in the UK Parliament is not quite replicated at the local level because most ethnic minority councillors represent the Labour Party, the numbers of ethnic minority councillors are higher in ethnically diverse areas and most ethnic minority councillors are of South Asian background, whereas people of black background are less well represented (Sobolewska and Begum 2020). Sadiq Khan, a Londoner from a British Pakistani family, became Mayor of London in 2016 and was re-elected in both 2021 and 2024. In his resignation speech in April 2024, Humza Yousaf reflected on these achievements for ethnic minority politicians in the UK:

> People who looked like me were not in positions of political influence, let alone leading governments when I was younger. But we now live in a UK that has a British-Hindu prime minister, a Muslim mayor of London, a black Welsh first minister and for a little while longer, a Scots Asian first minister of this country. So for those who decry that multiculturalism has failed across the UK, I would suggest that the evidence is quite to the contrary, and that is something we should all celebrate. (Yousaf 2024)

Electoral participation and the 'ethnic vote'

While representation at different levels of government is important, for most ethnic minority Britons, their engagement with politics will mostly consist of voting at elections. By the mid-1970s, political parties were more aware of the potential of a minority vote and the importance of attracting it. As Muhammad Anwar (1975: 378) explained: 'In 1964 no party thought the immigrant vote worth bidding for with the concomitant risk of losing native support. Ten years later, in 1974, all three main political parties did their best to win immigrant support in general, but [South] Asian votes in particular.' The notion of trying to attract the support of certain ethnic communities became embedded in British electoral campaigning, especially in those parts of the country where it was deemed that an 'ethnic vote' could potentially determine the outcome of a result. By this time social scientists, too, were analysing the importance of an 'ethnic vote' in towns such as Rochdale (Anwar 1973) and Bradford (Le Lohé 1975). After the 1974 general election, parties paid even closer attention to the potential of an ethnic minority electorate in the wake of a report published by the Race Relations Board. This report 'suggested that Labour owed its victory to the support of ethnic minority electorates in certain electorally marginal areas' and 'helped to shape the perception that minority electorates might need to be considered as such by party strategists' (Garbaye 2005: 52). The Labour Party Race and Action Group (LPRAG) was created in 1975 as a pressure group to educate and advise the party on matters of race equality and the Conservative Party set up an Ethnic Minority Unit in its Central Office's Department of Community Affairs in 1976 (Anwar 2001). Academic research into politics and ethnicity in the UK was also starting to thrive with the foundation of the Centre for Research in Ethnic Relations (CRER) in Bristol in 1970 before it moved to Aston University in 1978 and finally to the University of Warwick in 1984 (before eventually closing in 2011). This research has been a feature of UK social and political studies since the 1960s, with Nicholas

Deakin's *Colour and the British Electorate, 1964* (1965) hailed as one of the first studies of its kind. It was followed by *Colour and Citizenship* (1969), an influential report authored by Jim Rose and Nicholas Deakin. Both were involved with the creation of the Runnymede Trust in 1968 and formed part of a pioneering generation of scholars, including the likes of Muhammad Anwar, Zig Layton-Henry and Michel Julian Le Lohé, who took race, and its impact on British politics, seriously. The development of interest in this area of political science was no doubt influenced by the role of research coming out of the USA, and American scholars such as Anthony Messina and Donley T. Studlar brought their expertise to bear on the UK situation in light of events across the Atlantic.

From the research that was carried out from the late 1960s onwards, it was clear that the Labour Party was, overwhelmingly, the party that was favoured by most minority voters come election time. This is explained via several factors. Labour Party policies, particularly on immigration, were seen as less hostile to migrant and migrant-origin populations. The Labour Party was the natural ally of ethnic minority concerns, particularly campaigns concerning racism. Labour governments had brought in anti-discrimination legislation, such as the Race Relations Acts of 1965, 1968 and 1976. Grassroots solidarity on local, or indeed national, campaigns against racism was often shaped by Labour supporters or others on the left. Most ethnic minorities were also part of the working class and could therefore already be expected to favour the Labour Party, irrespective of issues related to race. Likewise, minority communities tended to be concentrated in large urban areas where Labour was historically strong. At the 1979 general election, 86% of South Asians and 90% of Afro-Caribbeans were estimated to have voted for the Labour Party, and over subsequent years analysis showed that solid support for Labour among Afro-Caribbean voters remained high, while South Asians started to move towards other political parties (Anwar 2001).

Recognising the disparity in support from minority supporters, the Conservative Party responded in the 1983 general election with a memorable campaign poster featuring a black man with the slogan 'Labour says he's Black. Tories say he's British'. Advocating a colour-blind approach that remained for the next 20 years, the poster told voters that: 'The Conservatives believe that everyone wants to work hard and be rewarded for it. Those rewards will only come about by creating a mood of equal opportunity for everyone in Britain, regardless of their race, creed or colour.' Such statements were somewhat undermined by legislation passed by the Conservative government at that time, most notably the British Nationality Act 1981, which created a new definition of British citizenship and 'effectively announced Britain as postcolonial by drawing a geographical boundary around Britain as distinct from its colonies and the Commonwealth' (El-Enany 2020: 74). For some time, then, Labour remained the 'natural' choice for many such voters, leading Anthony Messina (1989: 151) to conclude that 'Labour is the party of, if not unambiguously for, non-whites'. The Labour Party was not only more successful in its appeals to ethnic minority voters, it was also more proactive in terms of encouraging minority participation (including beyond voting) and allowing opportunities to represent the party for elected office.

It took other parties in the UK a long time to catch up and this explains why the numbers of ethnic minority MPs outside Labour did not increase until 2010. In 2015, it was widely reported that votes from minority ethnic communities helped put David Cameron back into Downing Street (Wintour 2015). Although later research qualified this estimation (Martin 2019), it was acknowledged that the voting patterns of minority communities had changed dramatically. During the referendum on UK membership of the European Union in 2016, the Leave side received approximately one third of the votes of ethnic minorities, leading researchers to question the continued existence of an ethnic bloc vote (Martin and Sobolewska 2023). Yet while important progress has been made in terms of how parties engage with ethnic minorities, there remain significant disparities in the levels of electoral registration. Sobolewska and Barcalay (2021), for example, note that the percentage gap in UK-level electoral registration is as wide as 25% for Black African minorities compared to their white counterparts. If a section of the population is under-represented on the electoral register, the level of turnout will not offer a reliable account of formal political participation. Some of the reasons for this are long established and include factors such as concerns over anonymity and confidentiality, fear of harassment, administrative inefficiency and anxieties over residence status (Laniyonu 2018; Galandini and Fieldhouse 2019). There is also the issue of housing tenure, since disproportionately high levels of black African and black Caribbean minorities reside in social or rented housing which can lead to frequent movement and thus a requirement to continually re-register (although, conversely, there are disproportionately high levels of home ownership among some South Asian communities).

Figure 4.3 illustrates the diversity within the South Asian category through plotting the vote shares for the Labour and Conservative parties over three general elections since 2010, showing notable differences between British Indian and British Pakistani votes (Martin and Khan 2019). A key point is that where research has sought to ascertain why ethnic minorities are, to a disproportionate extent, not being registered, it has rarely been reported that this stems from a lack of desire to participate in politics (House of Commons Library 2019). While it is clear that ethnic minorities share similar concerns with the wider electorate on matters such as education, health care, crime, unemployment and so forth, they also have specific concerns about the operation of racial discrimination in these very areas, as well as the impact of immigration policies, and, of course, transnational and international issues (Saggar, 2004; Martin, 2017). Studies have highlighted experiences of discrimination and frustration resulting from the failure to represent issues of concern or to allow equal access to positions of power, or to promote and support minority candidates, an issue that we consider next.

Political party candidacy

The changing levels of ethnic minority electoral registration illustrate the progress that has been made since the early 1960s, albeit in varying degrees across and within different communities. Over the last 60 years, an important body of scholarship has built up on the political participation of racial and ethnic minorities (including religious minorities) and this has included a range of different aspects. Perhaps one of the most recurrent is how categories of race and ethnicity have played a role in party candidacy. This aspect has been studied both from the perspective of candidates themselves, including their motivation for seeking to hold public office, as well as the political parties and how the selection of minority candidates might play out as part of a wider electoral strategy (Akhtar and Peace 2019). A further area of research has been the study of how such candidates have been received by the wider electorate and whether there is an 'ethnic penalty' for selecting somebody perceived as different or, conversely, if candidates are better received, particularly if they are viewed as representing a particular community.

Due to the First-Past-the-Post electoral system, debates about ethnic minority representation tended to focus on those areas of the country where there are sizeable populations of ethnic

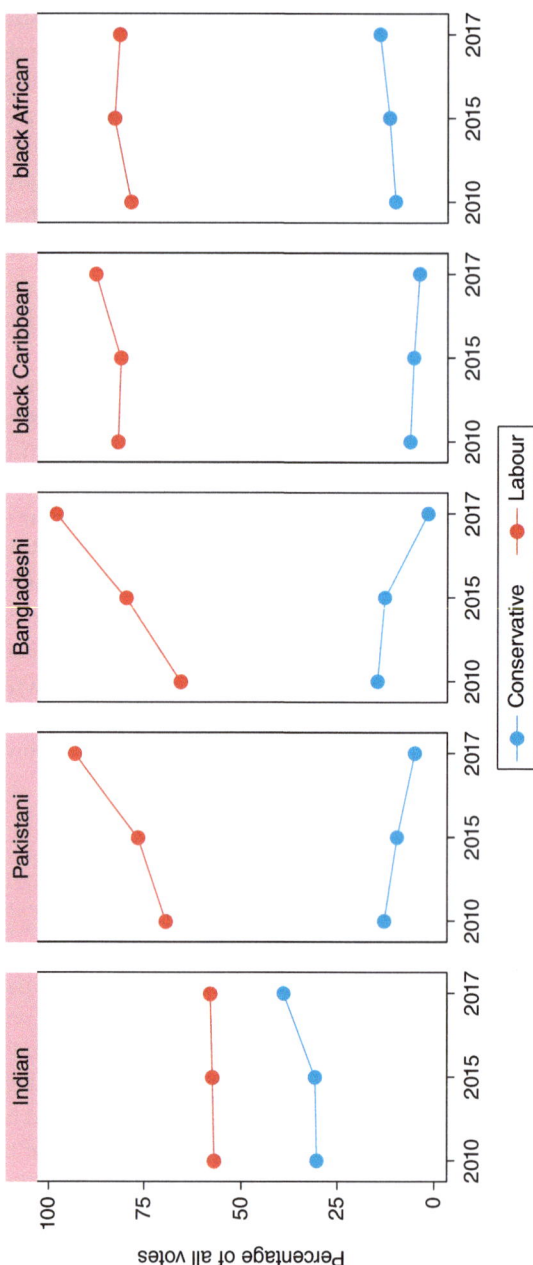

Figure 4.3 Labour and Conservative vote shares among different minority groups in 2010, 2015 and 2017

Source: Printed with permission of The Runnymede Trust

minority origin (Saggar and Geddes 2000). The creation of cohesive 'ethnic communities' in the early years of settlement forced political parties to reckon early with how this might play out in the electoral arena given that many migrants held voting rights on arrival. Residential concentration combined with a majoritarian electoral system meant that ethnic minorities could 'use group mobilisation in particular localities to their advantage' (Bloemraad and Schönwälder 2013). In many neighbouring European countries, despite similar waves of postcolonial migration, this issue did not become apparent until much later. As many scholars have shown, in the UK, from 'the very earliest stages of the migration processes that evolved through the 1950s and 1960s as groups of migrants from the colonies or ex-colonies came and settled, the emerging minority communities were involved in various forms of political action, both locally and nationally' (Back et al. 2022: 18). While this political action was largely concentrated around grassroots activism and social movement campaigns, there was also a desire to participate in forms of electoral politics. This happened despite the barriers and hostility faced by potential candidates of colour who wished to run for office.

Parties themselves were not immediately interested in offering equal opportunities for all potential candidates for fear of negative reactions from the electorate. As Saggar (2013: 72) explains, 'in the context of the polarized politics of post-war Commonwealth immigration, the concern was that white electorates at constituency level would, other things being equal, hold back support for minority candidates'. However, the endorsement (or lack of) from an established political party did not hold back individuals from putting themselves up for election. Some of the first research into the phenomenon of Pakistanis participating in local elections in Bradford shows that they were prepared to stand as independent candidates (Spiers and Le Lohé 1964). This very early study of local politics and what at the time were dubbed 'racial issues' offers a glimpse into how political parties were beginning to adapt to the new situation whereby 'immigrants' now formed an important section of the electorate. We learn, for example, that both the Labour Party and the Conservative Party were printing pamphlets in community languages (in this case Bengali and Urdu) and that the former had already included a Pakistani on a panel of eligible candidates in 1962. Another important finding was that the decision to stand as a candidate for the local city council was rooted in a desire to have a community representative and to be able to lead that community. This is a theme that subsequent research on local political participation among minority communities, particularly South Asian communities, would return to over the years (Akhtar 2013). The difficulties experienced by potential minority candidates at this time are highlighted by the study of a local election campaign in Rochdale in 1968 that took place immediately following the notorious 'Rivers of Blood' speech. Munir Ahmed Akhtar had been selected as a candidate for the Liberal Party, but his experience demonstrated why at this time it was still relatively rare for non-white candidates to get selected. The fact that Mr Akhtar came from Pakistan became 'the most important factor in the campaign' and some of the electors surveyed mentioned voting for the rival Conservative candidate as a means to 'keep the Pakistani out', indicating racism as a reason for changing their vote (Le Lohé and Goldman 1969). This example also highlighted the bind that the local Liberal Party found itself in as a result of choosing a non-white candidate, an action that they were subsequently forced to justify. The authors of this study claim that they 'never resolved whether they were simply supporting a Liberal candidate who just happened to be coloured, whether they were striking a blow for racial equality by putting up a coloured candidate, or whether they saw an electoral advantage in putting up such a candidate in a ward where one-sixth of the electorate were coloured' (Le Lohé and Goldman 1969: 440).

From the 1970s onwards, the practice of fielding ethnic minority candidates became more prominent but was still largely confined to local elections and was more likely to happen almost exclusively in areas that were viewed as having significant ethnic minority populations. This practice, sometimes referred to as 'colour coding', became a key modus operandi, especially by the Labour Party, when it was deemed electorally expedient. It was later also criticised as leading to the racialisation of the issue of minority participation and representation (Saggar and Geddes 2000). At that time more attention was devoted to the voting intentions and preferences of minority communities as a whole. However, the general lack of candidates for parliamentary elections from a minority background was remarked upon and efforts to change this were part of a 'lively debate about descriptive and substantive representation that occurred during the 1970s and 1980s, particularly within the Labour Party' (Chaney 2015: 164). This debate was most pronounced in Labour, as it was recognised that the party had received solid support from the ethnic minority electorate. Research in the early 1980s among the selectors for the party indicated that there was still much hesitancy to select non-white candidates as it was seen as a potential electoral liability, despite publicly disavowing any prejudice (Bochel and Denver 1983). This prediction was borne out in the 1983 general election when the 18 ethnic minority candidates (seven of whom represented Labour) were placed in mostly unwinnable seats, although often in constituencies that had a sizeable ethnic minority population, such as Birmingham and the London boroughs of Brent, Ealing and Newham. An analysis of their performance showed that 'the black or Asian candidates attracted fewer votes than could have been expected', although the ethnic penalty was not as severe as some may have predicted and that there was therefore 'no justification whatever for assertions that an ethnic minority candidate will lose the seat' (Le Lohé 1983: 105, 108). It is perhaps unsurprising that initiatives such as the LPBS movement originated at this time in order to push for more opportunities for ethnic minority candidates.

Following on from the election of four ethnic minority MPs in 1987, the drive to select more candidates from diverse backgrounds continued, and this was also reflected in academic research on the topic. Scholars such as Les Back, Andrew Geddes, Shamit Saggar and John Solomos studied the increasing diversity present in local politics and the dynamics around candidate selection. By the early 1990s it was noted that efforts to increase diversity of representation were slowly succeeding with growing numbers of local councillors from South Asian and Afro-Caribbean backgrounds, 85% of whom represented Labour, with more than half elected in the London area (Geddes 1993). However, only 6% were women, indicating a significant gender disparity and difficulty for ethnic minority women to get selected. It was also noted that among ethnic minorities it was men of South Asian origin who were the most likely to be councillors. There are multi-factor reasons for this. It has been argued that such under-representation reflects differences in political interest and ambition that are shaped by gendered cultural expectations (Dancygier 2018), but which should not be understood apart from the function of wider societal expectations (Kage et al. 2019). It is impossible to satisfactorily explain such differentials independently of either the intersectional inequalities encountered by minority women or the broader strategic focus on improving gendered inequalities that has overlooked the specificities of these intersectional inequalities. While a decade later, by 1997, there were still just nine ethnic minority MPs (from a total of 39 candidates), the election of these representatives was quite an achievement given that it had 'occurred despite numerous limitations placed by parties, however unknowingly or otherwise, on the ambitions of minority political activists-cum-candidates' (Saggar and Geddes 2000: 31).

Indeed, the issue of candidate selection among ethnic minorities rose up the political agenda, including a significant increase in the salience of ethnic minority representation in parties' election programmes (Chaney 2015). Minority representation was no longer just a matter for the Labour Party, the issue also moved beyond the borders of England to the rest of the UK. In 2007, Bashir Ahmad became the first non-white Member of the Scottish Parliament. He had founded Scots Asians for Independence in the mid-1990s and was the SNP's first South Asian councillor in 2003. Also in 2007, Mohammad Asghar was elected to the Senedd for Plaid Cymru before later defecting to the Conservatives. Research on the topic also became more sophisticated, driven by a significant increase in minority candidates (and eventually MPs) between the 2005 and 2010 general elections. Increasing the number of minority candidates became an imperative for the Conservative Party under the leadership of David Cameron, who had promised to transform the party by making it more diverse and representative. This included the creation of an 'A-list' of candidates, 50% of whom would be women and 10% from ethnic minority backgrounds who were to be placed in selection contests for 'winnable seats', despite the entrenched local-level Conservative prejudices against the adoption of more diverse candidates (Dorey 2007).

The effect of the A-list was mixed in terms of the number of candidates who were selected and elected for the Conservatives in the 2010 election. Forty-three were from an ethnic minority background, which was actually only two more than the number the party fielded in 2005. The key difference this time around was the placing of more minority candidates in constituencies where the party had a good chance of winning, which led to the election of 11 MPs (up from a total of two). Nevertheless, it was observed that the A-list benefitted female candidates more than ethnic minorities as only two of the A-list MPs came from minority ethnic backgrounds compared with seven non-A-list MPs (Hill 2013). The results of the 2010 election were a watershed because the traditional pattern of minority MPs only representing the Labour Party in seats with high minority populations had been disrupted. This was also a result of strategies by the Labour Party itself which made a more concerted effort to place candidates in a more diverse range of seats, including in constituencies where no minority candidate had stood previously. Indeed, the combined strategies of fielding minority candidates in 'non-minority' seats, selecting local minority candidates, centralising the selection process and, in some cases, bringing in minority candidates from outside the party, all contributed to the increased success of minority candidates in 2010 (Sobolewska 2013). The perceived ethnic penalty faced by minority candidates was shown to still exist, but with a more negligeable impact. In a controlled analysis of the 2010 general election results, Stegmaier et al. (2013) showed that while the presence of a BAME challenger helped the incumbent party, on average that gain was just over 2 percentage points, and in the case of Labour the candidate being from a minority did not have a statistically significant impact on individual vote choice.

The results in 2010 spurred increased research into the political participation of ethnic minorities and this was also boosted by the 2010 Ethnic Minority British Election Study (EMBES), the first of its kind in the UK (Heath et al. 2013). The availability of such data allowed for a number of interesting studies regarding minority candidates and their effects on voting patterns. One significant finding was that ethnic minority voter responses to candidate ethnicity differed by ethnic group. While there were no candidate ethnicity effects of any kind for Indians, black Caribbeans or black Africans, Pakistani and Bangladeshi Muslim voters were significantly more likely to vote for ethnic minority candidates overall (Fisher et al. 2015). The same study showed that white British voters, on average, were less willing to vote for ethnic minority candidates, especially Muslim candidates. A follow-up study, also using EMBES, confirmed these results and suggested that most ethnic minority candidates did not actually mobilise ethnic minority voters, although the notable exception was the fact that Pakistanis were more likely to vote when there is a Pakistani candidate (Martin 2016).

These results thereby showed the limited effects of 'colour coding' when applied to all minorities. If minority candidates don't necessarily mobilise voters who look like them, it creates a distinct question for proponents of descriptive representation, although it may also encourage parties to field minority candidates outside what are perceived as 'minority areas'. Further research using survey data from ethnic minority and white candidates at the 2015 UK general election queried the notion that we should expect a link between descriptive and substantive representation of ethnic minorities (on which see Childs, in this volume). The authors found that intrinsic mechanisms for why ethnic minority candidates would want, or be able, to represent ethnic minorities in Parliament received empirical support. That is, ethnic minority candidates and voters had a unique sense of linked fate and that these ethnic minority candidates felt a responsibility to represent ethnic minority interests (Sobolewska et al. 2018).

Conclusion

The participation and representation of ethnic and racial minorities occupies an important place in debates around political participation in general. Progress has been made in encouraging ethnic minority voter registration and ethnic minority voter participation, as well as incrementally improving and expanding the proportion of minority representatives holding elected office. Significant disparities remain, however, and the challenge for political parties is not only how to appeal to all sections of society, including ethnic and racial minorities, but specifically to ensure that ethnic minorities participate, and that minority candidates are selected and elected. As research has developed in this area, it has become evident that even though opportunities for selection and election have increased, ethnic minority candidates still face several distinct types of penalties, especially if they seek to represent minority group interests substantively. Empirical research over the past 25 years shows the impact of public opinion on patterns of minority candidacy in British elections and that 'we can expect ethnic minority candidates to be systematically disadvantaged when public opinion is at its most restrictive' (English 2022: 301). In the run-up to the 2017 general election, the Conditional Ethnic Penalty Hypothesis was tested using data from the British Election Study Internet Panel (BESIP). The results revealed that ethnic minority candidates are still penalised but that pro-minority policy positions incur a greater penalty than a candidate's ethnic background itself.

The results of the 2024 general election provide an important opportunity to 'take stock' of progress across the range of key areas surveyed above. A total of 90 MPs from minority ethnic groups, up from 66 MPs in 2019, means that 14% of MPs in the House of Commons are now from a minority ethnic background. This includes Labour MP, Diane Abbott, who was first elected in 1987 and has become a symbol of the struggle of minorities to achieve representation in British politics. The 2024 election was also the first time that official voter identification was be required to cast a ballot in the UK. In the immediate aftermath of the election it was reported that more than 400,000 people may have been prevented from voting because they lacked the necessary ID, with those from minority ethnic communities more than twice as likely to have experienced this (Walker 2024). This suggests that the fight for equality continues and the patterns of participation and representation established in this chapter, therefore, will remain a key means of gauging the quality of our democracy more broadly.

Summary

- Ethnic minorities have been participating significantly in British politics since the 1950s and 1960s.
- There is an ongoing association between the Labour Party and the ethnic minority electorate.
- Political parties try to court an 'ethnic vote'.

Recommended and further reading

- Akhtar, P. and Peace, T. (2019) 'Ethnic minorities in British politics: Candidate selection and clan politics in the Labour Party', *Journal of Ethnic and Migration Studies*, 45(11): 1902–1918. This article looks at how the Labour Party's candidate selection process is influenced by strategic party membership and nomination in areas with a significant British Pakistani community. It focuses on the cases of Bradford and Birmingham with respect to the nominations for prospective candidates at both parliamentary and local council level.
- Martin, N.S. and Sobolewska, M. (2023) 'The end of the ethnic bloc vote? Ethnic minority leavers after the Brexit referendum', *PS: Political Science & Politics*, 56(4): 566–571. This article looks at the importance of the ethnic vote both during and after the referendum on membership of the European Union. It shows that the referendum marked the biggest departure from the traditional ethnic minorities bloc vote since 2005 and explains why some ethnic minorities voted to leave the EU despite the association of this vote with white ethnocentrism.
- Sanders, D., Heath, A., Fisher, S. and Sobolewska, M. (2014) 'The calculus of ethnic minority voting in Britain', *Political Studies*, 62(2): 230–251. Using data from the 2010 UK General Election, the article shows that there is a distinctive calculus of party choice among Britain's overwhelmingly Labour-supporting ethnic minorities. The findings reflect the history of Labour and Conservative governments in the UK, showing that Labour is the only party that, in power, has legislated actively to promote ethnic minority rights and interests.

Chapter 5
Class and politics in the UK

Joe Greenwood-Hau

What will this chapter tell me?

- This chapter outlines the importance of class, in the UK, for voting, non-electoral political participation, who gets elected to legislatures, and how well different classes (and particularly the working class) are represented.
- The impact of class on politics in the UK depends partly on how we understand and measure it. The observed decline in the alignment between classes and parties is partly contingent on how we measure class.
- The declining representation of working-class people at Westminster, and the similar lack of representation at the devolved legislatures, has further driven class–party dealignment, fuelling working-class disengagement and support for other parties.
- Despite declining descriptive and substantive representation of working-class voters, many politicians are keen to highlight their working-class credentials in order to appeal to those voters by offering symbolic representation.

What do I need to know?

- Class can be measured in different ways but the most widely used in the UK is the National Statistics Socio-economic classification (NS-SEC).
- The 'frozen' system of working-class Labour voting and middle-class Conservative voting has been gradually 'unfrozen' since the Second World War.
- There has been a dramatic decline in the number of people being elected as MPs from working-class occupations, and this has not clearly been counterbalanced by working-class representation in the devolved legislatures.

Introduction

Class is everywhere in UK politics, from Margaret Thatcher's bouffant hair, handbag and received pronunciation to *Sir* Keir Starmer's toolmaker dad and nurse mum, and Rishi Sunak's multi-millionaire wife. And yet, its meaning, implications and importance remain contested. In 1990, John Major became the third prime minister since the Second World War not to have been educated at the University of Oxford, and declared the goal of turning the UK into a 'classless society' (Major 1993). In 2019, the Workers Party of Britain was founded by George Galloway, who went on to be elected as the party's sole MP more on the basis of his foreign policy positions than his advocacy for the working class. Since Major's declaration, the UK has seen seven different prime ministers, four of whom were privately educated, two at Eton College, and six of whom attended Oxford.

In the above there are references to dress, speech, occupation, wealth, and both private and university education. This indicates one of the problems with talking about class in the UK: we often mean different things when we use the word. Indeed, people can draw conclusions about the classes of others, including politicians, on the basis of visible characteristics, such as how they dress or speak, even if those characteristics themselves do not actually constitute class. This categorisation of people's classes, whether accurate or not, comes with other assumptions, including about how 'easy' or 'difficult' their lives have been and whether they are 'like me'. This may be why, as we will see, many politicians are keen to signal their (humble) class origins.

Before getting onto how politicians present themselves in the UK, this chapter will consider what we mean by class, with reference to three overarching conceptualisations drawing on the work of Karl Marx, Max Weber and Pierre Bourdieu. We also consider whether class is more about where you came from or your current position. These different conceptualisations help us to understand what we think really matters when we talk about class: economic position, social status, or stocks of economic, social and cultural resources. This allows us to move onto considering whether and how class matters for public participation in UK politics. Here, we start by observing the classic class–party alignment in the UK before considering its decline since before the end of the postwar consensus. The chapter then outlines the importance of class for other forms of political participation, focusing on the prominent recent example of Just Stop Oil protests.

Shifting from public participation to politicians, the next section of the chapter considers the class backgrounds of elected representatives in the UK. We start by observing the declining number of Westminster MPs who come from working-class occupations. We then turn to the class make-up of the Scottish Parliament, the Senedd Cymru and the Northern Ireland Assembly, observing that there is a scarcity of information about the class-backgrounds of their members but little evidence that they are more representative in that regard. Beyond their preceding education and occupations, we also consider how politicians talk about their backgrounds, and particularly their emphasis on humble origins. This leads us to consider the implications of class representation, and what public preferences are in this regard. Finally, the chapter suggests that symbolic representation of class may now be as important as its descriptive representation among elected politicians. This means that, while actual representation of working-class voters in the UK has declined, some politicians have sought to address such voters' concerns in the ways that they present themselves.

What do we mean by class?

Our understanding of class can draw on one (or more) of at least three different approaches to the concept. Commonly, when we talk about people's classes we are talking about their jobs or things that stem from jobs, such as their incomes. As such, we are focusing on indicators of their economic positions. This is crucial to the first understanding of class that we consider, with its roots in the work of Karl Marx. This approach distinguishes between two fundamental classes: the bourgeoisie or capitalist class, who own companies and the facilities where work is done (referred to as the means of production); and the proletariat or working class, who work in the companies and facilities owned by the bourgeoisie, and whose work produces the profits that the bourgeoisie make from the means of production (Marx and Engels 1948; Wright 1997). People with this understanding of class are concerned about the exploitation of workers by capitalists, and focus on things such as the impact of the gig economy on job security, levels of pay and wellbeing (e.g. Wood 2020).

The second common approach to class, based on the work of Max Weber, differentiates between class and status (Weber 2010). In this approach, class is based on economic position, not only in terms of job conditions and income, but also wealth. By contrast, status is based on prestige, which is to say the respect given to someone by others because of their social position. This approach has been very influential in the UK, contributing to the work of John Goldthorpe (Evans 1992), which itself shaped the National Statistics Socio-economic classification (NS-SEC). The NS-SEC places every occupation in the UK into different categories, which are then grouped into wider ones. The three broadest categories are higher occupations, intermediate occupations and lower occupations (Pevalin and Rose 2002; Drever et al. 2004; Social Mobility Commission 2021), which are often treated as representing middle-class, skilled working-class and unskilled working-class occupations. The NS-SEC is now one of the most widely used categorisations in the UK and, because it is used by the Office for National Statistics, informs much government and academic analysis of class.

Box 5.1   What is your class in the NS-SEC?

There is an eight-category version of the NS-SEC that can be mapped onto the three overarching categories as follows:

Higher occupations

- Higher managerial, administrative and professional occupations
    - Examples: chief executive, senior military officer, doctor, lecturer
- Lower managerial, administrative and professional occupations
    - Examples: journalist or editor, musician, nurse or paramedic, school teacher

Intermediate occupations

- Intermediate occupations
    - Examples: call centre agent, graphic designer, nursery nurse, police officer, secretary
- Small employers and own-account workers
    - Examples: farmer, hotel manager, product designer, roofer, taxi driver

Lower occupations

- Lower supervisory and technical occupations
    - Examples: baker, electrician, gardener, mechanic, plumber, train driver
- Semi-routine occupations
    - Examples: dental nurse, farm worker, postal worker, security guard, sales assistant
- Routine occupations
    - Examples: bar staff, building labourer, butcher, cleaner, lorry driver, waiter or waitress
- Never worked and long-term unemployed

Note that full-time students have a separate category from any of the above. So, if you work, which category would you be in based on your job? What about if you categorised yourself using your parents' occupations (this is commonly done for children and teenagers)?

Often when we talk about class, however, we are not focusing only on people's occupations or statuses. We can talk about how much money people have, but we can also talk about who they know, how they speak and dress, and their pastimes and consumption habits as indicators of class. For example, without knowing anything about their occupation, we might be comfortable describing someone who has a degree, reads *The Guardian*, enjoys going to watch ballet and goes on skiing holidays in the Alps as middle class. Indeed, we might not even need that information; sometimes we attribute a class to someone as soon as they start talking, simply because of their accent. In these examples, we are (whether we know it or not), using the third approach to class, based on the work of Pierre Bourdieu. He wrote about stocks of economic, social and cultural resources (or capital) as being crucial in defining people's class positions (Bourdieu 1984, 1986). This approach was famously used to create the BBC's Great British Class Calculator (BBC News 2013; Savage et al. 2013), and propose a new seven-class categorisation, which sparked much debate about what class means in the contemporary UK (e.g. Mills 2013). This reminds us that class itself is a (politically) contested subject, so our understanding of it has implications for how we understand its relationship with politics. Indeed, the debate about what class is remains unresolved, so we should be careful to consider what people (including ourselves) mean when talking about class in relation to politics.

Adding further complexity to our understanding is whether we are concerned with where people come from or where they are now. In other words, is the class that someone grew up in more or less important than their class once they have grown up and have a job? This matters not only because people's experiences when they are growing up shape them politically (Dinas 2013; Grasso et al. 2019), but also because those experiences matter for their (class) identities. Someone who grew up in a mining community in South Wales during the miners' strike of the mid-1980s might feel working class for the rest of their life, even if they go on to get a degree and a professional job. Even if they recognise their newfound middle-class position, they might still feel partly working class or have their political views shaped by their experiences when growing up. Indeed, both childhood and adult class had implications for, for instance, how people voted in the 2016 Brexit referendum. In that case, both working-class backgrounds and current working-class positions reduced the likelihood of having supported Remain (McNeil and Haberstroh 2022). Thus, however we understand and measure it, class can have important implications for political participation and elections.

Political participation and class

There was a period running from the beginning of the twentieth century until well into its second half, in which many countries, including the UK, were seen to have 'frozen' party systems organised around a number of cleavages, including class (Lipset and Rokkan 1967). During this period, there was minimal movement of people between classes during their lives, and most people inherited both their class position and their party identity from their parents. Thus, there were two reinforcing processes at work that, in the UK, sustained the strength of the alignments between working-class voters and the Labour Party, and middle-class voters and the Conservative Party. First, the parties sought to serve the interests of the classes from which they gained their support. Second, in addition to having the interests of their classes reflected by the parties, people often felt a strong sense that being a Labour or Conservative supporter was part of who they were.

This era saw the establishment of stereotypes about Conservative and Labour voters that still cast shadows over UK politics today. On the one hand, we had the Home Counties-dwelling, Church of England-attending, suit-wearing suburban commuter, reading a copy of the *Daily Telegraph* while eating marmalade on toast at the kitchen table before leaving for their salaried white-collar job. This middle-class caricature would naturally have been a Conservative voter. By contrast, we also had the resident of the industrial heartlands of Northern England, trudging from their terraced house to the local mine, steelworks or docks, tin lunchbox in hand, cloth cap on head and copy of the *Daily Mirror* (or *Morning Star*) tucked under their arm. This working-class caricature? A Labour voter, of course.

The latter stereotype also reflects the roots of the Labour Party in the trade union movement that centred on industrial areas. Labour was explicitly intended to be a party of the working class so we could substitute Northern England with the industrial areas of Scotland's Central Belt or of South Wales. And here we also see signs of the other cleavages that overlayed the class one. While highly populated, industrialised, urban areas tended to vote Labour, more sparsely populated rural areas were apt to opt for the Conservatives. In the postwar period, however, this class–party alignment gradually 'unfroze'. This process of dealignment was partly the consequence of a gradually growing number of people gaining higher levels of education and moving into higher occupational classes over the course of their lives. That is to say, dealignment was partly a result of growing social mobility (Young 1994; Eyles et al. 2022), which meant that people who would previously have inherited their parents' class positions instead attained different ones. Thus, people's preferred policies and parties differed from those of their parents and, at the same time, the sizes of different social classes changed over time (Best 2011).

Class–party dealignment was also driven by a wider trend, not only in the UK, in which party identity became progressively less widespread and less strongly felt among voters. Within this, the specific alignment between being working class and identifying with the Labour Party, and being middle class and identifying with the Conservative Party, was eroded (Denver and Garnett 2021). This meant that, by the time of her election as Prime Minister in 1979, Margaret Thatcher could gain votes among the 'aspirational working class', embodied in archetypes such as 'Essex man'. By 1997, Tony Blair's movement of New Labour to the centre allowed him to build a new electoral coalition. This drew together support not only from the party's traditional industrial heartlands, but also from aspirational working-class voters, now embodied in the idea of 'Mondeo man' (a reference to the mid-range Ford car that they hoped to own), and from middle-class voters.

Key debate   The problem with social mobility

As well as being only one possible driver of party dealignment, social mobility itself is a problematic idea. On a basic level, it is simply a description of people changing their social positions by moving between classes, either over their lifetimes or in comparison to their parents. It is also associated with the idea of meritocracy, which is to say a social system in which people's social positions are based on their skills, abilities and work rather than on advantages or disadvantages stemming from their backgrounds (e.g. the class they grew up in, their gender, their ethnicity or some combination of those).

Social mobility is treated as desirable by most politicians and political parties in the UK, and a Social Mobility Commission has been created to monitor how easy or difficult it is for people to change their social positions based on their merits. But others are critical of the idea and argue that there can never be a truly meritocratic system if social inequality exists. This is because people will use the advantages that they have to ensure better outcomes for themselves and their children. Indeed, the sociologist who coined the word 'meritocracy' did so satirically when writing about how education can be used to marginalise groups who, for a range of reasons other than merit, do not excel in educational environments (Young 1994).

What has been your experience of social mobility? Are your parents in different classes from their parents, and do you think you will be in a different class from them? Whatever class you end up being in, to what extent do you think that will be because of your skills, abilities, and work compared to the advantages or disadvantages you have been given by your background?

Both Thatcher and Blair, then, strategically positioned their parties to try to win elections by building new coalitions of voters. Far from being only a reflection or consequence of class–party dealignment, this process of party positioning has also been a driver of that dealignment. Indeed, there has been debate about whether the key driver of party dealignment has been the changing sizes of classes, the social mobility and psychological de-attachment of people, or the movement and electoral coalition building of parties themselves (Best 2011; Heath 2015; Evans 2017). In other words, by appealing to people in classes outside their established support bases, the parties indicated to the electorate that they were no longer prioritising the interests of one class or another. We also saw this in the 2019 general election and, following that, the electoral dilemma facing the Conservative Party (see also Convery, Chapter 6 in this volume). By deploying cultural issues linked to Brexit, and the idea of 'levelling up', Boris Johnson's Conservatives successfully won support from traditional Labour voters in 'Red Wall' seats in 2019. However, they then had to balance the (class) interests of those seats and voters with the interests of traditional Conservative voters in rural and southern England, which proved challenging.

The process of class dealignment also meant that more attention could be paid to other voting cleavages in the population. It is notable that the caricatures outlined at the beginning of this section implicitly paint pictures of voters who are male and white. Yet, though it took some time to emerge, a gender gap in voting was observed in both the 2017 and 2019 general elections, with a higher proportion of women than men voting Labour and a higher proportion of men than women voting Conservative (Campbell and Shorrocks 2021). At the same time, the well-established tendency for ethnic minority voters to support Labour seems to persist (Martin and Sobolewska 2023). This is despite the electoral realignment that followed the 2016 referendum on the UK's membership of the European Union, whereas the gender gap in voting emerged in part because of that realignment. Specifically, the tendency of younger women to favour Labour in 2017 and 2019 was partly shaped by their greater likelihood of having supported Remain in 2016.

The realignment of the UK electorate after the Brexit referendum sustained a debate about what drove support for 'Leave' and the politicians and parties that campaigned for it. Some explanations focused on economic drivers, such as the marginalisation of communities by globalisation or the security afforded by property wealth. Others focused instead on shifting social and political values as key drivers of political realignment, while yet others tried to reconcile economic and cultural accounts. All of these drivers have some relationship with class, whether in terms of the job opportunities in one's local community (Colantone and Stanig 2018), the changing possibility of owning one's home in different occupations (Adler and Ansell 2020), reaction against liberal values that have been facilitated by growing economic security in the West (Inglehart and Norris 2016), or a sense of declining economic and social status relative to others (Gidron and Hall 2017). Those accounts can all also be refracted through the idea that the Brexit referendum acted as an 'electoral shock' (Fieldhouse et al. 2020) that catalysed an realignment with implications for the 2019 general election and beyond.

The idea of electoral shocks prompting voter realignment has also been evident in Scotland. In 2007, the Scottish National Party (SNP) grew to become the largest party in the Scottish Parliament, before gaining a majority in 2011 and then calling the 2014 referendum on independence from the UK. The referendum solidified pro-independence and pro-union identities in Scotland, as well as the SNP's position as the pre-eminent pro-independence party, which they capitalised on in the 2015 general election by winning all but three of Scotland's Westminster seats. The basis for this dramatic realignment was, in part, the SNP's successful campaign to win over traditionally Labour-supporting working-class voters. Thus, one of the most significant electoral shifts in the UK over the last decade has its roots, in part, in the process of class dealignment. Labour's electoral health in Scotland, then, is contingent, in part at least, on sustaining their working-class voter base in the country.

All of the above indicates the complexity of identifying and measuring the impact of class on voting, not least because of the debates about how to measure it that we encountered earlier in this chapter. When class is measured using a greater number of categories, a more complex but continuing class-voting pattern can be observed (Evans 2017). At the same time, as classes with strong party attachments decline in size, while classes with mixed voting habits increase in size, the link between class and voting appears weaker (Best 2011). This highlights the importance of the 'demand side' of the equation, which is to say the prevailing preferences in the population. On the other side, the examples of Margaret Thatcher's Conservatives, Tony Blair's New Labour, and the SNP and the 2014 Scottish independence referendum indicate the importance of the 'supply side' of the equation. This is also reflected in the realignment of voters after the 2016 Brexit referendum, and the example of the electoral coalition built by Boris Johnson's Conservatives in 2019. As noted previously, there is debate about whether it is 'demand side' changes in the population or 'supply side' changes in party position and presentation that have been key in class–party dealignment. Nevertheless, the 2019 general election still saw seats with higher numbers of manual workers returning higher vote shares for Labour, while seats with higher numbers of professionals and managers tended to have higher Conservative (and Liberal Democrat) vote shares (Denver 2020: 22).

Beyond the ballot box, the vast array of political acts that people choose to participate in, or not to participate in, between elections are also shaped by class. From signing petitions or reposting political content on social media to joining marches or taking more dramatic direct actions, there are numerous ways in which people can express their political views and try to influence politicians. Here, people's economic, social and cultural resources (or capital) are relevant, since they facilitate political participation. Those resources are also likely to be shaped by class, which also means that class has an impact on political participation more widely. For instance, the higher incomes of middle-class people means that they are more likely than working-class people to be able to donate, and donate generously, to the causes that they support (Schlozman et al. 2020: 87). Similarly, people who are part of social networks that are politically active in particular ways are likely to be asked to get involved in those ways. If these networks are organised, at least partly, around class, then political acts can become associated with class. This is the case with industrial action, such as the

UK rail strikes that began in 2022. Indeed, the explicitly working-class leadership of Mick Lynch, the General Secretary of the National Union of Rail, Maritime and Transport Workers, has inspired staunch support and opposition, and even grudging respect from some of his opponents. Since union membership is associated with other forms of political activity (Trentini 2022), we can see a link from class-based networks to political participation more widely.

Continuing the idea that social networks and organisations with links to classes can sustain particular kinds of political activity, we can consider the actions of Just Stop Oil. Aiming to highlight and prompt a more radical response to the climate crisis, this organisation has gained a great deal of attention since its formation in 2022 by engaging in numerous provocative direct actions. Although they have focused on a range of targets, a number of Just Stop Oil's actions have centred on events and venues with middle-class associations, such as the Chelsea Flower Show, the Proms, Wimbledon and the National Gallery. This has been seized upon by their opponents to paint them as 'posh', 'upper middle-class' beneficiaries of 'class privilege' (O'Neill 2023). References to their accents and names, as well as the venues and events that they target, indicate the importance of cultural indicators in narratives around class in the UK.

The actions of Just Stop Oil protesters, and their links with class and class symbols, also highlight the importance of 'postmaterial values' that drive concern about issues such as the environment, as opposed to more material values relating to economic security (Inglehart 2015). This distinction became more important as the growing material affluence of Western societies enabled people to become more concerned about issues beyond their own material wellbeing. Recent generations in the UK have grown up in a context of material security not enjoyed by previous generations, albeit hampered by economic instability and hardship since the 2008 financial crash. This relative material security has meant that they have been able to focus some of their political energy on 'postmaterial' issues, such as marriage equality, gender identity and the environment. Thus, we can observe a divide between younger, more highly educated, often middle-class 'identity liberals' and older, less educated, often working-class 'identity conservatives' (Sobolewska and Ford 2020). We see this not only in the conflict between Just Stop Oil protesters and the archetypal 'white van man' frustrated in his attempts to get to work, but also in the electoral realignment around Brexit that we considered previously.

As with the class–voting relationship, the above examples of political activity outside the ballot box illustrate the importance of how we understand class. The implications of income for donating, social networks for recruitment, and cultural signals for presentation of political acts indicates the possible usefulness of Bourdieu's idea of class position being based on stocks of economic, social, and cultural resources. But we can also say that those resources have their roots in occupation-based categorisations of class, such as NS-SEC. Either way, class has a role in facilitating or inhibiting political participation, and in how people react to those who undertake political activities. It also has implications for who moves beyond voting and grassroots political activity to enter electoral politics, as well as how the public perceives and reacts to them.

Politicians and class

Just as there were stereotypes about the kinds of people who vote for different parties, there were also established images of the kinds of people who became MPs for those parties. On the Conservative side, we had the terribly well-spoken, stiff-upper-lipped, wealthy (perhaps aristocratic), public school educated gentleman. Here, we might think of former Prime Minister Harold Macmillan. On the Labour side, we had the tub-thumping union organiser and former manual labourer, with a strong regional accent and an explicit disdain for the anachronistic practices of the House of Commons. This was exemplified, perhaps, by former Bolsover MP Dennis Skinner. Of course, these images are complicated by the fact that most post-Second World War prime ministers of both parties have attended elite universities, and all but one of those went to Oxford. Thus, while MPs overall had varied class backgrounds, the upper echelons of UK politics have generally been the preserve of highly educated professionals (Bukodi et al. 2024).

We can see the continuation of this tendency, and the complexity of the role of class in politics, when we consider the Prime Minister and his predecessor. Keir Starmer's father was a toolmaker, his mother was a nurse, and he was educated at a state-funded grammar school (that became private during his time there) before studying law at the University of Leeds. He went on to postgraduate studies at Oxford before becoming a barrister and, later, Director of Public Prosecutions. By comparison, Rishi Sunak's father is a general practitioner, his mother was a pharmacist, and he was educated at a preparatory school and the elite public school Winchester College. He went onto study philosophy, politics and economics at Oxford University before pursuing a career in investment banking. Thus, while Starmer has more humble class and educational origins than Sunak, they both ultimately studied at prestigious universities and pursued well-paid, white-collar careers.

How they have talked about their backgrounds (particularly during the 2024 general election campaign), however, indicates that politicians are concerned not to appear 'too' middle class. Starmer has emphasised his parents' occupations, including the fact that his mum worked for the National Health Service (NHS). Sunak, by contrast, sought to disarm concern about his private education by focusing on his parents' own efforts to achieve their positions (and his dad's work for the NHS), and their emphasis on the importance of educational achievement. In both cases, part of the point of these statements was to indicate the importance of hard work, with the implication that both Starmer and Sunak earned their positions. This hints at a theme that we return to below: being seen as too comfortable and middle class can be electorally problematic in the UK, where voters often want working-class candidates or, at least, candidates who have had to work hard. These electoral preferences persist despite a clear decline in the parliamentary representation of working-class people from the late twentieth century onwards.

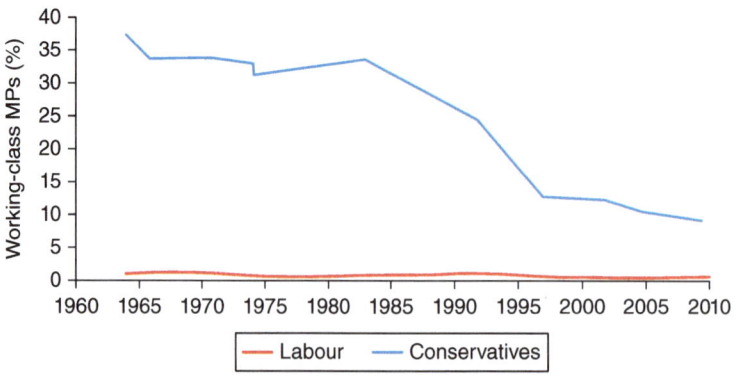

Figure 5.1 Working-class MPs in Britain, 1964–2010

Source: Heath (2015). Printed with permission

Following the 1964 General Election, one in five Members of Parliament had working-class occupational backgrounds, with the figure approaching twice that among Labour MPs (Heath 2015: 182). By 2010, the figure among all MPs had fallen to one in 20, and it stood at one in ten among Labour MPs (Figure 5.1). At the 2019 General Election, the number of MPs who had held manual occupations immediately prior to their election stood at zero (Butler et al. 2021: 411). Labour did manage to have one in ten of its MPs elected from positions as trade union officials, which can be a stepping stone for manual workers, but some of them had white-collar occupations previously as well. Given that slightly fewer than one in three adults in the UK are employed in routine or manual occupations (Kirk-Wade 2023), the lack of MPs with recent experience of such jobs is a dramatic gap in representation.

At the UK's devolved legislatures, the picture differs slightly but there is little evidence of substantial working-class representation. The Scottish Parliament's report on the backgrounds of its members elected in 2021 includes information on gender and ethnicity but not about their previous occupations (Appleby-Donald et al. 2023). Further, it has been observed that while there was a hope that the Scottish Parliament would broaden the backgrounds of elected representatives, 'we have not really seen a major divergence in social backgrounds between MSPs and MPs' (Keating and Cairney 2020: n.p.). Similarly, after the 2021 elections to the Senedd Cymru, it was observed that there is little information available on members' occupational backgrounds but that many were elected 'from "politics facilitating professions" such as law, journalism and education' (Thomas et al. 2021: n.p.). Finally, there is information available about the representation of women and ethnic minorities in the Northern Ireland Assembly, but no such information about the occupational backgrounds of the Members of the Legislative Assembly (Howe 2022). This creates the strange scenario in which class is commonly understood to be an important feature of the UK's political terrain, but evidence about how it is reflected among those elected to represent the population is not routinely gathered.

Part of the problem here, again, is that what we mean by class can be nebulous. Consideration of the class of elected representatives usually focuses on their previous occupations, but it can also focus on education (Cracknell and Tunnicliffe 2022: 19–22). This is because, although it is a distinct concept, education is related to class. When someone moves between classes, which is to say is socially mobile, it is often because of education. Similarly, when someone remains in the same class as the one that they grew up in, it is often because they received an education (or lack thereof) that helped them to stay in that class (or limited them to doing so). Finally, in the caricatures of Harold Macmillan and Dennis Skinner offered at the beginning of this section, there were references to speech and manner as reflections of class. While such things are seldom measured when considering the backgrounds of elected representatives, they can be important signals of class.

Indeed, the ready accessibility, and perhaps intentional sending, of signals about politicians' backgrounds is part of what sustains the importance of class in UK politics. The nature of these signals has changed over time, perhaps in line with changing representation of class in the UK's elected legislatures. Following the many apparently upper-class prime ministers that preceded her, Margaret Thatcher spoke with a distinctive form of received pronunciation and, as we can see in Figure 5.2, deployed her famed suit dress, handbag and bouffant hair to reflect her middle-class status. We also saw the importance of politicians' class backgrounds, and symbols associated with class, play out in the summer of 2022. At that time, then Deputy Prime Minister and Conservative MP Dominic Raab criticised Labour MP and Deputy Leader Angela Rayner for attending the opera at Glyndebourne. The implication of Raab's criticism was that

Figure 5.2 Margaret Thatcher meets Prime Minister Lubbers and Foreign Minister Van den Broek of the Netherlands at Catshuis in September 1983

Source: https://commons.wikimedia.org/w/index.php?curid=65624964

Rayner, famously an MP with a working-class background, had betrayed her roots by becoming a 'champagne socialist'. Her response, shown in Figure 5.3, asserted both the importance of her class origins and the idea that they should not constrain the activities that she participates in, making Raab's criticisms of her an issue of 'Tory snobbery' (Moore 2022). In these examples, we can see the importance of the ideas that we encountered earlier about whether it is your background or current position that is more important in defining your class. This can be a challenge for MPs with working-class backgrounds who are elected to a uniquely privileged and very well-paid white-collar position, and thus lose something of their claim to be working class. At the same time, their class origins mean that they have had very different backgrounds from many of their MP colleagues, and may experience the 'imposter syndrome' reported by many upwardly mobile people (Savage 2015: 211; Greening 2023).

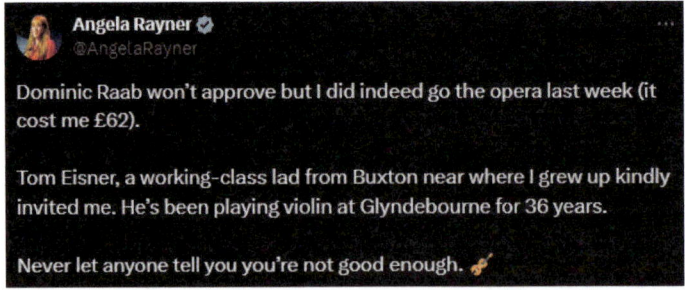

Figure 5.3 Angela Rayner's tweet in response to Dominic Raab's criticism of her attendance at the opera at Glyndebourne

Credit: Angela Rayner/X

These examples also demonstrate the prominence of Bourdieu's idea that cultural habits and tastes indicate people's class positions. Without knowing MPs' occupational backgrounds, people can use how they speak and dress, and what they do in their spare time, as indicators of their classes. This is additionally important because class can also have implications for how people communicate and express themselves, which is crucial in a political career. Whereas middle-class culture is associated with restraint, propriety and calculation, working-class culture is associated with being 'the true "nice guy", blunt, straightforward, unbending, honest, genuine' (Bourdieu 1984: 199). This may be part of the reason why, despite declining representation of working-class people, many MPs are keen to emphasise their working-class roots.

Class and political representation

The decline in working-class representation at Westminster, and the similar under-representation of working-class voters at Holyrood, Cardiff Bay and Stormont, has left a sizeable portion of the population with few people in positions of political power who share their experiences of working life (at least, recently). The fact that this is known, and apparent, can lead to a sense that politics does not, and cannot, prioritise the needs of working-class people. In other words, working-class people might be concerned that their interests are not being reflected in policy decisions, meaning that they are not being substantively represented (Pitkin 1967). Beyond this, working-class people might also be aggrieved that there are so few people like them in the upper echelons of political power, which is to say that they are not being descriptively represented (again, see Pitkin 1967).

This low and declining representation can result in at least two responses: disengagement or radicalisation (Gest 2016). In the first, the fact that the political system is seen not to be acting in the interests of working-class people, and to be populated by middle-class politicians, prompts resignation and a sense that 'politics isn't for people like me, so why bother'. This can result in, for instance, the decision not to vote. Consequently, it is not only the case that working-class politicians attract working-class votes (Heath 2015), but also that the lack of working-class representation drives greater working-class abstention from voting (Heath 2018). By contrast, in the second response, the lack of substantive and descriptive representation prompts anger and a desire to challenge the status quo. This points towards voting for radical, populist, and often right-wing challenger parties. The result has been some white working-class people supporting the British National Party (BNP) and, later, the United Kingdom Independence Party (UKIP) and its successor parties.

The idea of working-class people channelling frustration with their lack of representation into support for right-wing populist parties dovetails with the idea that such parties, and causes such as Brexit, appeal to 'left behind' communities and individuals (Colantone and Stanig 2018). It also fits with a key feature of a common definition of populism: that it 'considers society to be ultimately separated into two homogeneous and antagonistic groups, "the pure people" versus "the corrupt elite"' (Mudde 2004: 543). In a context, such as the UK, in which a significant portion of the electorate can see very few politicians who look like them, it is easy to sustain the idea of a detached, distant political elite with little understanding of what life is like for 'ordinary' people, and who therefore act in the interests of elites rather than the population at large. This characterisation of the situation does not need to tell the whole story. That it tells part of the story, and is believable, is enough to motivate people. Thus, part of what drives support for right-wing populists among white working-class men is the sense that their status is in decline (Gidron and Hall 2017). In other words, the feeling that societal changes have altered their social standing leads to anger with incumbent political elites, who allowed or supported those changes, fuelling support for right-wing populist parties.

We can also see the role of class in the connection between the closure of local community pubs and support for the right-wing populist parties in the UK (Bolet 2021). Often key centres of social life, and symbols of the economic state of local areas, the closure of such pubs offers a signal of the decline of working-class communities. Again, this can fuel resentment and anger with incumbent policy makers who have not averted, or have contributed to, the demise of such communities. Such closures, then, can be symbols of the neglect of working-class areas by politicians who appear to have little understanding of the lives of the people who live in them. The importance of such symbols, and of the sense of neglect and under-representation, helps explain why politicians are often keen to emphasise their working-class credentials, even when they are highly educated professionals. It is an attempt to re-establish a connection with the electorate by appearing to be 'normal' and understand the challenges that they face in their daily lives.

Politicians also burnish their working-class credentials because there is evidence that many in the electorate would like to vote for working-class representatives. Indeed, voters in the UK are no less likely to vote for candidates with working-class than middle-class occupations and are more likely to see working-class candidates as able to understand the problems facing people like them (Carnes and Lupu 2016). Thus, voter aversion to working-class candidates does not explain their under-representation in the UK's elected legislatures. Quite the opposite, in fact, when we consider the class backgrounds of candidates rather than their current classes. Candidates with working-class, or lower-middle-class, backgrounds are preferred to those with upper-middle-class backgrounds, and this is largely the result of working-class voters choosing working-class candidates (Vivyan et al. 2020).

There are many prominent examples of politicians addressing these preferences by highlighting their working-class statuses or roots. We have already considered Keir Starmer talking about his dad being a toolmaker and his mum being a nurse, as well as Rishi Sunak defending his middle-class background with reference to his parents' emphasis on education and hard work. To these examples, we could add Mayor of London Sadiq Khan and former Health Secretary Sajid Javid, both of whom have highlighted that their dads were bus drivers. Additionally, there is the Conservative Party's past emphasis on the presence of an ex-coal miner Patrick McLoughlin (now Baron McLoughlin) in the cabinet, as well as the famously straight-talking styles of former Labour Deputy Prime Minister John Prescott (later Baron Prescott), Labour MP Jess Phillips and Reform UK MP (former coal miner, Labour councillor and Conservative MP) Lee Anderson. In each of these cases, the working-class credentials of the MPs can be both an electoral asset to them and a means by which to show working-class voters that they are still being represented.

In other cases, there are also politicians with middle-class backgrounds who behave in ways that signal their affinity with working-class people. Like Keir Starmer, former First Minister of Scotland Nicola Sturgeon can claim working-class roots, with a father who worked as an electrician and a mother who worked as a dental nurse, but she went on to study law at the University of Glasgow and then to a career as a solicitor. As a politician, however, she deployed a direct style of communication and had a talent for meeting voters on their own turf, often in a more easy-going manner than some politicians could muster. As an example, one SNP MP reported that:

> She [Nicola Sturgeon] came to open my office and there's a pub across the road, it was about three in the afternoon on a Friday so there was quite a few folk outside the pub and they'd sort of twigged something was going on so they were looking out: 'Who's that,' 'That's Nicola Sturgeon, Nicola come and have a drink.' She'd go 'Okay then' and off she went into this old man's pub. Up and down the bar, said hello to everybody. (Anonymised interview with the author, 2016)

Here we can see an example of the idea that we encountered earlier of the pub, and specifically the 'old man's pub', as a site of working-class social life. It is also an example of a politician deploying the 'straightforward … honest, genuine' style that Bourdieu associated with working-class culture.

That style is also exemplified by the leading light of UK right-wing populism, Nigel Farage. A privately educated former City of London trader, and son of a City of London stockbroker, Farage is not a man who can lay great claim to having working-class roots. Nonetheless, he is famously associated with a straight-talking style, a taste for Rothmans cigarettes and for being photographed in pubs with a pint in hand. These symbols of working-class culture help him appeal to voters with whom he shares little in terms of class position or background. This illustrates the importance of symbolic representation (Pitkin 1967), in which politicians claim an affinity with and ability to speak for groups that they neither descriptively nor substantively represent. In this way, working-class people who are under-represented can nonetheless feel that there are people speaking like or for them in politics. Whether such symbolic representation can act as a sufficient substitute for having elected representatives who were recently working class, or who pursue a more clearly class-based policy agenda, remains to be seen.

Summary

- There has been a decline in traditional class-based voting in the UK, but class still matters for voting (and non-voting) as well as other types of political participation.
- There has been a clear and sizeable decline in working-class representation at Westminster, with the picture little different at Holyrood, Cardiff Bay and Stormont.
- Declining substantive and descriptive representation have driven working-class abstention from the ballot box as well as switching to right-wing populist parties.
- Class remains symbolically important in UK politics, with many politicians choosing to emphasise their working-class credentials in order to win votes.

Recommended and further reading

Geoffrey Evans is the leading expert on class and politics in the United Kingdom: see his work with James Tilley on the political exclusion of the British working class (Evans and Tilley 2017) and with Matthew Hepplewhite on growing class- and education-based inequality in electoral participation in the UK and beyond (Evans and Hepplewhite 2022). See also his work with Erzébet Bukodi, John Goldthorpe and Matthew Hepplewhite on the class and educational make-up of UK cabinets since 1945 (Bukodi et al. 2024). Looking beyond the cabinet, for a detailed account of the backgrounds of MPs following the 2019 general election, including their previous occupations and education, see Butler, Campbell and Hudson (2021). On the consequences of declining descriptive and substantive representation of working-class voters, see work by Heath (2015, 2018), and on voters' preferences for working-class candidates, see Carnes and Lupu (2016) and Vivyan, Wagner, Glinitzer and Eberl (2020).

Chapter 6

The Conservative Party

Alan Convery

What will this chapter tell me?

- This chapter outlines the principal ideological fault-lines in the UK Conservative Party. Like many other mainstream parties of the centre-right, it contains a mixture of conservatism and (free market) liberalism.
- The disquiet in the Conservative Party at the end of the 2019 Parliament reflects a particularly acute case of the party being pulled in different directions. The party is suffering from an identity crisis.
- It discusses the recent history of the party from Thatcher to Sunak, tracing the strategies of different leaders and how they have tried to find a successful electoral and governing code.
- This chapter looks at how the threat of UKIP and the implementation of Brexit have posed dilemmas for the party. The 2019 triumph of Boris Johnson concealed some worrying longer-term trends that will exercise the party in the years to come.

What do I need to know?

- The First-Past-the-Post electoral system severely punishes smaller parties or breakaway attempts. The two main UK political parties are therefore broad churches.
- The Conservative Party is the UK's main centre-right political party.
- The party governed the UK for most of the twentieth century and has a reputation for being highly adaptable and pragmatic.

Introduction

In December 2019, the Conservative Party was basking in the glow of electoral success. Under the leadership of Boris Johnson, the party had just won its largest majority since 1983. Johnson removed MPs who did not agree with his Brexit policy, united the party around a Get Brexit Done slogan, and broke new ground for the Conservatives in seats that were previously considered solidly Labour. The Labour Party, on the other hand, suffered its worst result since 1935 and was reduced to just 202 MPs. It seemed like Johnson had hit on a winning electoral formula and that the Conservatives might govern for a decade or more (Hayton 2021).

However, in the space of a few years, that victory turned to ash. Having received an initial vaccine bounce, the Conservatives' poll ratings were badly hit by revelations about lockdown parties in Downing Street. Johnson's management style began to grate with even his closest colleagues. In less than three years, Boris Johnson was replaced as Prime Minister by Liz Truss, following a rebellion by his ministers. She then resigned amid a crisis after just 44 days in office, making her the UK's shortest-serving Prime Minister. Faith in the Conservatives' reputation for governing competence was severely eroded by her tumultuous tenure, resulting in a sterling crisis, sharp increases in borrowing costs and a humiliating climbdown from almost all her economic plans. She was then succeeded by Rishi Sunak in October 2022. The Conservatives' popularity never recovered. The Conservatives' suffered their worst-ever result at the 2024 general election. What went so wrong so quickly for the Conservatives? This chapter tries to pick out some consistent themes and trends among this period of turmoil for the Conservative Party.

It begins by discussing the ideological fault-lines in the party, noting the distinctive pulls of conservatism, economic liberalism and pragmatism. It then discusses the impact of the leadership of Margaret Thatcher on the party's strategy and ideology. We cannot understand the modern Conservative Party without discussing the stamp she placed on it. Conservative mythologising about the Thatcher era remains hugely significant today and she acts as both a heroine and a yardstick for Conservative MPs. The chapter then turns to the transition from opposition in 1997 to David Cameron's modernisation programme and the Coalition Government. It examines the impact of austerity and the debates it has generated in the party. It considers why the Conservative Party finds European Union membership such a difficult issue to deal with and the road to the Bloomberg Speech and 2016 referendum.

That referendum result opened new opportunities for the Conservative Party electorally (and sparked a highly significant debate about Red and Blue Walls) but unleashed internal chaos that was only brought under control by Johnson in 2019. Finally, this chapter considers where this journey has left the Conservatives. Having been buffeted by Brexit, a pandemic and three Prime Ministers since 2019, its ideological debates are as fierce as any since 1997.

Ideology: What do Conservatives believe?

This chapter looks at Conservative ideology through three lenses: conservatism, market liberalism (or neoliberalism) and pragmatism. It might be thought that the political philosophy of conservatism unites the UK Conservative Party. However, paying attention to conservatism only takes us some of the way in understanding its ideology. Self-identifying conservatives do not all agree about what conservatism means – and they do not agree about how we should apply its principles to twenty-first-century problems.

What is conservatism? For Girvan, conservatism is 'an attempt to justify what exists and to challenge advocates for change' (Girvan 1994: 4). According to Green (2002: 281), there are therefore three fundamental elements to conservatism: imperfection, traditionalism and organicism. For conservatives, there is no ideal form of society. Human knowledge is too imperfect and incomplete to plan a complete redesign of society. Instead, we can only hope to make incremental improvements based on our experience. Grand visions are treated with suspicion; practical knowledge accumulated from real-world experience tends to be valued more.

Conservatives also value traditions. Established ways of working and their associated rituals may seem archaic or ripe to be streamlined and modernised. However, for conservatives, institutions and traditions contain a wisdom that may be invisible to the naked eye. Sweeping away traditions risks discarding the important lessons of the past that they contain. Like rocks gradually eroded by the sea over hundreds of years, institutions bear the mark of previous mistakes and accumulated knowledge about human behaviour. The worst-case scenario for conservatives is to start a conversation about reform with a blank piece of paper.

It follows, therefore, that change should ideally be organic and follow the grain of inherited practices. Wholesale revolutions are to be avoided: incremental reform is the preferred option. That does not mean that no change should be permitted. Rather, the burden of proof for changes rests with advocates for change. Ideally, such change would be reversible in light of experience (O'Hara 2011).

Parties very rarely line up exactly behind abstract ideologies. The Conservative Party draws on some philosophical conservatism but is not totally driven by it. Reasonable people also disagree about how conservatives should approach certain issues. For example, should we view Brexit as a conservative reform or a revolutionary one? It caused a lot of upheaval, but some Conservatives viewed it as a return to the past, rather than a rupture with established ways of working.

However, conservatism is not the only ideology that motivates Conservatives in the UK. There is also a strong strain of economic liberalism in the party: the belief in the superiority of free markets. Conservatives have been traditionally viewed as the party of the UK's business interests and have been more sceptical about using the power of the state to support industries or solve policy problems. This ideology has become much more prominent in the party since the leadership of Margaret Thatcher in the 1970s and 1980s. The Conservative MPs who entered Parliament after she became Prime Minister were generally much more in favour of free-market policy solutions than those who came before (Heppell 2002; Bale, Cheung et al. 2020). Contemporary conservatism in the UK is therefore closely associated with a desire for a smaller state, cutting taxes and encouraging enterprise.

However, there is still a tension in the Conservative Party between conservatism and economic liberalism. This dilemma was again demonstrated most clearly in the ambiguous case for Brexit. Was the purpose of Brexit to allow the UK to free itself from EU regulations and be a 'free-trading, deregulated, off-shore Britain' (Hannan 2016a: 141)? Or was the purpose of Brexit to restore national sovereignty, increase health spending and reduce immigration? This philosophical debate remains unresolved in the Conservative Party.

Some Conservatives think that the party has gone too far in the free-market direction. Nick Timothy, Theresa May's former chief of staff, thinks that the right in the UK has become 'attached to market fundamentalism' (Timothy 2020: 39). He argues that some aspects of life are too important to be left to markets and that Conservatives should emphasise ideas about community, solidarity and the nation state. This mode of thinking is sometimes labelled 'One Nation' conservatism, but the meaning of this term is disputed (Seawright 2011). It is often used as shorthand for the economic left of the party. Others think that the Conservative Party needs to focus more on economic liberalism. The Conservative MPs Kwasi Kwarteng, Priti Patel, Dominic Raab, Chris Skidmore and Liz Truss wrote in 2012 that: 'We should focus on trying to make it easier for firms to recruit people and ensuring the tax burden is less onerous' (Kwarteng et al. 2012: 3). Their book proposed that the UK should be 'unembarrassed about its support for business, the profit motive and the individual drive of the wealth creator' (Kwarteng et al. 2012: 4).

In some policy areas, conservatism and economic liberalism can rub along quite happily. However, in other areas, the Conservative Party is pulled in different directions. For example, in the case of immigration, there is a clear economically liberal case for increased immigration to drive growth and provide businesses with new workers. These arguments clash with more conservative arguments that emphasise control or reducing immigration to allow communities more time to integrate past arrivals.

A final strand of UK Conservative thinking is pragmatism. The Conservative Party was in government in the UK for most of the twentieth century. It did not achieve this 'Conservative Century' (Seldon and Ball 1994) by sticking rigidly to the same ideology. Instead, the Conservative Party has been viewed in political science as one of the ultimate office-seeking parties. Observers have noted 'the party's quite remarkable facility for adaptation and, closely allied to this, its appetite for power, often indeed its readiness to subordinate all other considerations to that one objective' (Ramsden 1998: 495). Thus, having lost the 1945 General Election to the Labour Party, the Conservatives accepted many of the changes it introduced, including the National Health Service. From the 1950s most Conservatives accepted that 'the state sector was to be administered, not dismantled' (Gamble 1974: 63). A key question for contemporary students of the Conservative Party is the extent to which that ideological pragmatism still holds.

Case Study 6.1

The relationship between the Conservative Party and UKIP

The 'revolt on the right' (Ford and Goodwin 2014) is one of the most significant factors influencing the strategy of the Conservative leadership since 2005. The United Kingdom Independence Party (UKIP) was formed in the early 1990s initially to oppose the UK's signing of the Maastricht Treaty on further European integration (Goodwin and Milazzo 2015: 21). It did not have much impact initially. In the 1997 General Election, the Conservatives' prospects were more damaged by another Eurosceptic Party called the Referendum Party, funded by James Goldsmith (McAllister and Studlar 2000).

However, over the course of the 2000s, the Conservative Party began to perceive UKIP as much more of an ideological and electoral threat. Initially, it tended not to perform well at UK Parliament elections. The First-Past-the-Post electoral system is very unforgiving for smaller parties whose vote share is spread widely. But UKIP did start to perform well in elections to the European Parliament, beginning in 2004 when they won 2.6 million votes (16%) and nine MEPs (Ford and Goodwin 2014: 48).

Conservatives worried that splitting the votes on the right of UK politics might lose them seats. As Conservative MPs became more Eurosceptic over time, there was also greater sympathy for UKIP's message about a referendum on EU membership (Crowson 2007; Lynch and Whitaker 2013). That pressure gradually increased as UKIP's electoral performance improved after 2005 in particular. The internal Conservative demands on David Cameron to adopt a more Eurosceptic position in part stemmed from perceptions about the UKIP threat (Bale 2022).

Even so, as Tim Bale (2018) also argues, we should be careful about assuming that UKIP was solely responsible for the Conservatives' moves towards a more populist Eurosceptic position. In fact, Conservative leaders from Hague in the late 1990s had already been moving the party towards those issues. The problem was that under Cameron, they briefly abandoned that position, creating space for UKIP to fill. Thus:

> The first 8 years of the 13 years that the Tories spent in opposition after 1997 primed the electorate perfectly for populist Euroscepticism, while the following year and a half – the first flush of David Cameron's attempt to modernise the party by moving away from it – alienated those voters who had previously welcomed what he now seemed so keen to reject, thereby rendering them highly receptive to UKIP's message that it was now very much the party for them. (Bale 2018: 265)

Reflective questions

1   How should centre-right parties react to challenges from smaller parties?
2   How electorally threatening for the Conservatives was UKIP?
3   Was the rise of UKIP about more than just European issues?

How much did the Conservatives change under Thatcher?

However, by the 1970s some Conservatives began to question the party's accommodation with the changes that the Labour Government made after 1945. The UK was going through tough economic times and had to apply for a loan from the International Monetary Fund in 1976. There were problems with economic growth, strikes and inflation. The experience of some Conservatives in Edward Heath's Government (1970–1974) convinced them that they needed a change of direction. Instead of focusing on more conservative themes about working together with institutions like trade unions or focusing on full employment as an expression of social obligations, these thinkers (like Keith Joseph) emphasised the need for the state to remove itself from economic management so that the free market could flourish. The idea was that the state was overloaded and was allocating resources inefficiently (King 1975).

The Conservatives therefore took a much stronger pivot towards economic liberalism under the leadership of Margaret Thatcher from 1975 (E.J. Evans 2019). She was also much more critical of traditional institutions like the civil service and the universities than her predecessors. However, we should not assume that her impact was as immediate or wide-ranging as her critics and cheerleaders suppose. As Kenneth Clarke observed: 'The truth was that she was more pragmatic, and less ideological, than either the right or the left have made her out' (Clarke 2016: 227). One of the keys to understanding the contemporary Conservative Party is to note that its elites tend to misremember or mythologise what Thatcher achieved in office and how she went about it.

In the first instance, we must remember that Thatcher's changes to the Conservative Party and the UK were slow-burning ones. In 1975, she was not expected to win the leadership and she encountered a great deal of hostility and scepticism in the party, both because of her right-wing economic views and her gender (Campbell 2001: 280–286). Initially, she had to proceed cautiously and retain shadow cabinet and then cabinet ministers who strongly disagreed with her economic plans (Campbell 2003: 7–8). Far from approaching every issue with uncompromising zeal, she in fact dodged an initial confrontation with the UK's mineworkers and reformed trade union legislation in small chunks as the 1980s went on and as circumstances allowed (Dorey 1993). The significant tax cuts for which her government is lauded by some Conservatives came much later in her premiership, mainly during Nigel Lawson's budget in 1986.

She thus gradually consolidated her grip on power throughout the course of the 1980s. She judged when the circumstances were right to take on the UK's mineworkers or offer significant tax cuts. Indeed, the principal economic concern of her first government was tackling inflation, rather than cutting the state or taxes. However, she is mainly remembered at the height of her powers in the late 1980s. Moreover, impressions of Thatcher are coloured by her personal style (Bale 2014). As Jackson and Sunders (2012: 1) summarise: 'Margaret Thatcher was one of the most controversial figures in modern British history. No Prime Minister since Gladstone aroused such powerful emotions, or stirred such equal measures and hatred and veneration.'

The Thatcher Governments' effects on the UK are the subject of fierce debate. For her supporters, she kickstarted an economic renaissance in the UK that restored its national pride and place in the world; for her detractors, she presided over rapid deindustrialisation that left millions unemployed and had permanent scarring effects on the social fabric of the UK that are still visible today.

One of the key legacies of Thatcher's time in office is also territorial (Stewart 2009; Torrance 2009). The numbers of Conservative MPs in Scotland and Wales gradually declined over the

1980s and 1990s until there were none left at the 1997 General Election. The acceleration of deindustrialisation under Thatcher had a disproportionate impact on those areas with heavy industry. In addition to some of the north of England and the midlands, that included Scotland and Wales especially. The impression of a remote government imposing controversial policies with declining support was a toxic combination for the Conservative Party (Convery 2016; Blaxland 2024; see also the chapters on Scotland and Wales in this volume). However, even in the case of Scotland, it should be borne in mind that public spending was higher in Scotland in 1990 than it was in 1979.

Her impact on the Conservative Party is less debatable. We know that Conservative MPs elected after her leadership were much more likely to have economically liberal views than their predecessors. She also had a profound impact on how the Conservative Party thought about European issues (Fontana and Parsons 2015). However, as Liz Truss's approach demonstrates, some of the celebration of Thatcher's achievements is based on a simplified and exaggerated version of her policies and approach. The Conservative mythologising and misremembering of Thatcher have profound consequences.

From Thatcher to Cameron

Thatcher was succeeded by John Major in 1990. The manner of her departure cast a shadow over the party for many years afterwards. She was forced to resign after a leadership challenge. She won a ballot of MPs but not by a convincing enough margin to quash the idea that support for her was waning (Cowley 1996). The Conservatives' defeat at the 1997 General Election was their worst result in over a century. It marked the beginning of a long period in opposition.

Instead of opting for the more experienced (and more well-liked) Kenneth Clarke in the 1997 leadership election, the Conservatives instead chose William Hague (Heppell and Hill 2008). Clarke's views on Europe were a major sticking point: unlike Mrs Thatcher (and increasing numbers of Conservative MPs) he held very pro-European views. At this point, he also supported the UK joining the single European currency. Hague prioritised traditional Conservative issues and made keeping the pound a central part of the Conservatives' pitch to the electorate in 2001. The Conservatives were defeated again, by a similar margin to 1997. They then once again rejected Kenneth Clarke in favour of Iain Duncan Smith in the 2001 leadership election (Heppell and Hill 2010). MPs became so concerned about his leadership skills that they removed him as leader in a confidence vote in 2003. Sensing that they needed some stability and a leader who could take the fight to Tony Blair, Conservative MPs rallied around the former cabinet minister Michael Howard. He was installed as leader without a contest.

Although Howard certainly improved the situation and provided robust parliamentary opposition to Tony Blair, few Conservative MPs expected him to be able to defeat Labour at the 2005 General Election (Garnett 2012). Instead, Howard steadied the ship and laid some of the groundwork in terms of modernisation that could help his successor. The Conservatives were once again defeated in 2005, but made much more progress than in 2001.

Having endured three successive election defeats, the Conservative Party in 2005 was in much more of a mood to hear some hard truths about what had gone wrong and the sort of changes that might be required to form a government again. David Davis started off as the favourite to win the leadership election but ended up being defeated by the younger and more inexperienced David Cameron. Cameron ran on an explicitly modernising pitch that promised to make the party look and sound more like modern Britain. He won convincingly and started to implement his vision of a more modern form of conservatism (Denham and Dorey 2006).

David Cameron wanted to get the Conservatives out of the rut they had been stuck in since 1997 (Bale 2012: 283–287). His analysis of the situation was that the party had been too focused on issues like Europe and tax cuts, which did not resonate with voters. Instead, the party needed to start talking about more traditional Labour issues, such as the National Health Service and improving schools. He also tried to emphasise concerns about the environment, childcare and wellbeing. He wanted the list of Conservative candidates to be more diverse. He apologised for the Conservative Party's role in introducing 'Section 28', a law that banned the promotion of homosexuality in schools. The idea was to move the Conservatives on to unexpected areas so that they earned the right to be heard.

There is a debate about the extent to which Cameron modernised the Conservative Party. It is certainly true that he ditched some policies that were popular among MPs, including support for new grammar schools and the 'Patient's Passport', which would allow people to spend NHS money on private operations. However, on the market liberal dimension, there is much less evidence that Cameron changed the Conservative Party's stance (Hayton 2012). Hayton (2018) judges that Cameron's modernisation was a failure. It essentially repackaged Thatcherite economic solutions with more liberal social policies (Kerr and Hayton 2015).

Cameron was the party's most popular post-1997 leader and he brought them closest to contending for government. The party also benefitted from the Labour Party's difficulties under Gordon Brown and the impact of the global financial crisis after 2008. However, at the 2010 General Election, the Conservatives did not quite make it over the line into the territory of a parliamentary majority. Instead, Cameron made an offer to the Liberal Democrats to form a Coalition Government.

The Conservatives and the Coalition Government (2010–2015)

The formation of the Coalition Government could be seen as one of the successes of Cameron's programme of modernisation. He had moved the party on so far from Howard in 2005 that it was possible to make a deal with a party that was more associated with the left of UK politics. However, Cameron's critics in the Conservative Party viewed his failure to win a majority against a fading Labour Party as a major weakness. Some MPs were also suspicious that

Cameron preferred to work with the Liberal Democrats than with the right of the Conservative Party, who had long been critical of his political approach (Bale 2016: 361).

For Beech (2011), the Coalition worked because it emerged from a 'tale of two liberalisms'. Thus, Cameron had moved his economically liberal party towards social liberalism on issues such as gay rights. On the other side, Nick Clegg's leadership of the Liberal Democrats had emphasised much more the party's economically liberal roots, rather than its social democratic side. Moreover, the Coalition's central economic policy was dictated by a commitment to economic liberalism. Both parties agreed that the deficit (the amount that the government borrows each year to make up the shortfall between spending and tax receipts) was too high and needed to be reduced at a quicker pace.

There is a fierce debate about the wisdom of the focus on austerity during the Coalition Government. On the one hand, Cameron and his supporters argue that it was a necessary response to the UK's economic problems in the 2010s. The UK was borrowing too much and had to focus on reducing the size of the state to help it live within its means. They also point to the economic growth during the 2010s and the UK's relatively low levels of unemployment. The higher spending of the post-2016 era, they argue, was only made possible by the disciplined approach to the public finances taken under the Coalition.

However, there are nowadays few defenders of austerity beyond those close to Cameron, even in the Conservative Party. At the time, Boris Johnson himself was not a fan of what he called a 'hair shirt agenda' (Elliott 2013). The alternative argument posits that the misguided focus on austerity resulted in the severe weakening of public services and worse outcomes for the poorest people in the UK (Blyth 2013). It compounded other chronic problems in the UK economy of low public and private investment. It was a solidly Thatcherite policy prescription from the Conservatives that repeated the same mistakes of the 1980s in focusing on short-term wins and neglecting the UK's long-term productivity problems.

This period also therefore set the stage for future debates in the Conservative Party between its more liberal and conservative wings. For some thinkers on the UK right, the economic policies the Conservatives pursued in the Coalition neglected the importance of community and prioritised a 'market fundamentalism' that eroded the sorts of institutions that conservatives ought to care about (e.g. Timothy 2020). Some researchers have also proposed that there is a link between the areas most affected by austerity and the likelihood of them voting for Brexit in 2016 (Fetzer 2019).

Reheated Thatcherism also had wider implications. The English language, a flexible labour market and UK's preponderance of low-skill, lower-wage employment, particularly in the hospitality sector, had always made it an attractive destination for immigration. The UK's relatively stronger economic performance and recovery compared with the European Union after 2010 added to its attractiveness and resulted in a historically significant inflow of migrants, particularly from Eastern Europe (Evans and Menon 2017: 14; Sobolewska and Ford 2020). The Conservative Party has therefore found itself in the position of trying to take a rhetorically tough line on immigration at the same time as in government presiding over record levels of immigration.

Referendum promise and Brexit

Initially, Cameron wanted the Conservative Party to 'stop banging on about Europe'. His strategy instead involved talking about issues that might persuade voters that the Conservatives cared about their daily lives. However, the European Question came to define Cameron's premiership and prematurely end it. How did his position move from de-emphasising Europe to promising the 2016 referendum?

The European issue had been a problem for Conservative leaders since the beginning of the UK's membership but the pressures in the party started to heat up in the 1990s, particularly after Thatcher's resignation and the negotiations over the Maastricht Treaty in 1992. Although Cameron de-emphasised the issue, for some of his MPs it remained one of the central motivations for their political career. Cameron also had to make sense of the inheritance of hardening party policy positions on the European issue from his predecessors after 1997. In various manifestos, the party promised that it could obtain a new deal for the UK inside the EU that involved the benefits of economic integration without the political integration that Conservatives did not like. Thus, the pressure for some sort of renegotiation or recalibration of the UK's membership was a longstanding feature of post-1997 Conservative debates (Glencross 2023).

The pace of European integration had also continued under the Labour Governments (1997–2010) which signed up to the Nice, Amsterdam and Lisbon Treaties. The last of these treaties was the most significant one in terms of Conservative European debates. Under pressure from his MPs, Cameron promised a referendum on whether to ratify the treaty. The idea of some sort of referendum was therefore also a key part of the Conservative policy offer before Cameron made his in–out referendum promise in 2013.

Unfortunately for the Conservatives, the Labour Government ratified the treaty before the Coalition Government entered office in 2010. Cameron concluded, therefore, that there was no point in having a referendum on a treaty that had already come into force. There was no option to unravel it. That position irritated many Conservative MPs, who felt that Cameron had reneged on a 'cast-iron' promise. Cameron's commitment to Eurosceptic policies was called into question. Having conceded the principle of a referendum, however, the issue did not go away. The Eurosceptic MEP Daniel Hannan reflected at the time that 'he had just lost his last opportunity to hold a referendum on something other than membership of the EU' (Hannan 2016a: 36).

During the Coalition Government, Cameron faced increasing internal dissent on the European issue (Lynch and Whitaker 2013). The biggest rebellion occurred in 2011 on a backbench motion about whether the Government should support an in–out referendum. Cameron therefore faced a strategic dilemma. He was instinctively a Eurosceptic and felt that John Major's line on the euro in the late 1990s was too soft, for instance (Elliott and Hanning 2012: 183). However, it did not define his politics and he did not feel as strongly about the issue as some of his rebellious MPs. He faced a choice between continuing to placate his MPs with more concessions or giving in and promising a referendum on the UK's EU membership. This was the most consequential decision Cameron took in his entire political career.

George Osborne advised against going down the referendum route (Fall 2021: 254–255). On the other hand, William Hague thought it was the only way forward (Shipman 2017: 3). In the end, Cameron thought that the Conservative Party had become so Eurosceptic that a referendum was inevitable. If he did not promise it, one of his successors would. Therefore: 'I was increasingly convinced that an in/out referendum would be held in the not too distant future, quite probably by a successor Conservative government that might well recommend leaving' (Cameron 2019: 401). Cameron promised an in–out referendum on the UK's EU membership at a speech at the

Bloomberg headquarters in London in January 2013. However, even this concession did not quell the Eurosceptic rebellions (Lynch 2015). The Conservatives returned to office in 2015 with a small majority and Cameron set about trying to negotiate a new deal for the UK in the EU that would be put to a referendum in 2016 (for the full detail, see Martill, in this volume).

May

Cameron announced his intention to resign as Prime Minister on the morning after the referendum in June 2016. In the subsequent Conservative Party leadership election, Boris Johnson withdrew and the final two candidates were Andrea Leadsom and Theresa May. Leadsom also then withdrew from the election, leaving May to be elected without a vote of the party membership.

May's first speech as Prime Minister outside Number 10 Downing Street is noteworthy in terms of the splits and debates in the Conservative Party after Thatcher. May explicitly tried to position herself as a different sort of leader (Seldon 2019: 45–47). She spoke about the 'burning injustices' in society. The speech was written for her by Nick Timothy, one of her joint chiefs of staff, and, as we have seen, someone from the conservative wing of the party who thought the adherence to Thatcherite policy prescriptions had gone too far. However, while May rhetorically set out to do something different, she was constrained both by the bandwidth-sucking enormity of delivering Brexit and by the fact that her Chancellor of the Exchequer, Philip Hammond, was much more of an economic liberal on questions of taxation and spending (Seldon 2019: 467).

May was conscious of having been a Remainer during the Brexit debates and wanted to demonstrate her commitment to delivering on the result of the referendum (Shipman 2018: 3). May resigned in June 2019, after her Brexit deal was rejected by Parliament three times (on which see Geddes, in this volume; Martill, in this volume).

Johnson – what sort of Prime Minister was he?

In the 2019 Conservative Party leadership election, Boris Johnson was once again a candidate. The election was dominated by debates about May's failure to deliver Brexit and how the question might be resolved in future (Jeffery et al. 2020). Johnson campaigned for Brexit in 2016 and pitched himself as the candidate who could deliver a version of it that was true to the spirit of the original Leave campaign. The final two candidates in the election were Johnson and the former Health Secretary Jeremy Hunt. The membership (which we know from other research is overwhelmingly pro-Brexit; see Bale 2019) decisively backed Johnson. He won 66.4% of the members' vote to Hunt's 33.6%.

Johnson's first speech as Prime Minister prioritised the delivery of Brexit. However, he also hinted at a more post-Thatcherite turn for the Conservative Party. In the end, he concluded that it would be impossible to deliver Brexit when the composition of Parliament (and the parliamentary Conservative Party) was so divided. He therefore tried to engineer a general election. Eventually, the other parties agreed and an election was called in November 2019. The Conservatives' 'Get Brexit Done' election slogan defined the campaign – and had some success (Ford et al. 2021: 243–244). The manifesto also doubled-down on ideas about a different sort of conservatism. Instead of fiscal prudence and tax cuts, it instead emphasised more doctors, nurses and hospitals. It also promised to 'level up' parts of the UK that had fallen economically further behind that the prosperous southeast.

Red Walls, Blue Walls and a new conservatism?

Sobolewska and Ford (2020) argue that the 2016 EU referendum was not so much a moment of creation as a moment of awakening: it revealed, rather than created, divides that had been present in the electorate for a long time and were widening. Previous research had also demonstrated that the United Kingdom Independence Party (UKIP) drew much of its support from traditional Labour voters, as well as former Conservatives concerned about EU membership (Sobolewska and Ford 2020: 192–197). That is in part an outcome of the decline of working-class attachment to traditional centre-left or social democratic parties, a widely documented shift across rich Western democracies (Rennwald 2020). The Conservative Party therefore spotted an opportunity after 2016: could all the people who voted Brexit be persuaded to vote Conservative?

Herein lies the origins of the idea of the 'Red Wall' and the potential for the Conservative Party to tap into a new group of voters outside its traditional heartlands. The term was coined by the political analyst James Kangasooriam to describe a group of seats long held by the Labour Party whose demographic profile (and proportion of Leave supporters) suggested they might be vulnerable to a challenge from the Conservatives (Ford et al. 2021: 195). It has since become a catch-all term for those seats, a set of ideas, and an imagined part of England that has felt economically 'left behind' and overlooked by a political class of graduate social liberals.

Theresa May had tried in 2017 to win over some of these voters and had some success. The Conservative vote share among C2DE voters increased by 12% (Cowley and Kavanagh 2018: 422). However, she failed to secure enough Labour seats outside the southeast to compensate for Conservative losses in more traditional Tory seats, such as Kensington and Chelsea. Attracting Brexit voters in 2017 meant repelling more socially liberal Remainers elsewhere (Cowley and Kavanagh 2018: 427). Johnson executed the strategy much more successfully in 2019. He won a swathe of seats in the northern half of England that were traditionally held by the Labour Party. In Redcar, for instance, a seat held by Labour for all but five years since its creation in 1974, the Conservatives overturned a Labour majority of 9,485 and secured a Conservative one of 3,527.

The parliamentary Conservative Party in 2019 therefore included for the first time a group of MPs from what had become non-traditional Conservative seats. Some of them formed a parliamentary grouping called the Northern Research Group. One of the interesting questions for observers of the party is therefore whether this group of new MPs has had any effect on the overall ideology of the Conservative Party. Have they pressured the party to move on further along the post-Thatcher agenda set out first by May and then seemingly embraced by Johnson?

At first, it was difficult to tell. Johnson appeared to prefer a broad coalition in the Conservative Party and to try to please all wings (Hayton 2021). His initial spending plans suggested a modest increase in public spending for departments most affected by the austerity years. However, very soon after the election, the Johnson Government had to deal with the Covid pandemic, requiring a massive increase in public spending on healthcare and on the furlough scheme. It is therefore difficult to come to a precise conclusion about the impact of the new MPs. However, we know that the next leader of the Conservative Party and Prime Minister pitched herself much more decisively as an economic liberal in the mould of Margaret Thatcher.

From Johnson to Sunak (via Truss): Back to economic liberalism?

Johnson was eventually forced to resign after MPs tired of his chaotic style and a series of scandals, most notably 'Partygate', the allegations about lockdown-breaking and alcohol-fuelled gatherings in Downing Street during the Covid crisis. The Conservative Party therefore organised its third leadership election in three years. Unlike the previous election, the debate in this contest centred on the idea of economic growth and recovery. However, views on Europe still played an important role in Conservative MPs' decisions (Jeffery et al. 2023). The final two candidates were Liz Truss and Rishi Sunak. Liz Truss's analysis of the problems facing the UK was that taxes were too high, regulations were too restrictive, and that economic policy had been dominated for too long by a cautious consensus (characterised by the 'abacus economics' attitude of civil servants in the Treasury). While she wanted tax cuts to stimulate growth, Sunak warned of the danger of cutting taxes because of the effects on inflation.

Liz Truss decisively won the 2022 Conservative leadership election (57.4% of members to 42.6%) and became Prime Minister on 6 September. At the heart of her economic plan was a bold budget to cut taxes and jolt the UK out of what she saw as its trajectory of decline. The Chancellor of the Exchequer, Kwasi Kwarteng, announced the deepest tax cuts since the 1980s (Adam et al. 2022). However, Truss's desire to move quickly and her distrust of the civil service meant that the 2022 budget deviated from the traditional processes for fiscal policy making in the UK. One of her first acts as Prime Minister was to dismiss the most senior civil servant in the Treasury (Sir Tom Scholar). The budget was also not accompanied by the usual analysis and set of forecasts by the independent Office for Budget Responsibility (set up by George Osborne in 2010 when he was Chancellor of the Exchequer).

The tax cuts in the budget were to be paid for not by spending cuts, but by additional borrowing from financial institutions. Those institutions had to make a judgement about the government's attitude to fiscal policy and the likely impact of further borrowing on the UK's ability to pay. Unfortunately for the Prime Minister, they took a dim view of both the process and the substance of the budget. The abrupt dismissal of an experienced senior official and the circumventing of the usual processes (however tiresome the Prime Minister considered them) raised eyebrows. In the end, financial institutions judged that the budget was a reckless move and signalled that they considered that lending money to the UK was now riskier than it was before. They therefore decided to charge the UK more interest to borrow money. Other investors agreed: the value of the pound against the dollar fell to an all-time low.

Truss dismissed Kwarteng on 14 October 2022 and replaced him with Jeremy Hunt. He promptly reversed all but one of the measures in Kwarteng's budget. The financial markets calmed and the pound recovered. However, Liz Truss announced on 20 October that she would resign as Prime Minister. The Conservative Party was on the cusp of its fourth leadership election since 2016. In the end, MPs decided to rally around Rishi Sunak, the second-placed candidate from the election just a few months earlier. He was elected unopposed as Leader of the Conservative Party and the King appointed him as Prime Minister on 25 October 2022.

Ideologically unmoored?

All governments are battered by crises and unexpected events. However, the Conservative Party's period in office in 2010–2024 was particularly eventful (including a pandemic, leaving the EU, an energy price shock and a sterling crisis), resulting in several abrupt changes in direction. The party is going through a period of ideological unsettlement. The battle for its future has just begun.

In 2010, the Conservative strategy under Cameron was to continue with the basic tenets of Thatcherism (competition, low tax, pro-business) but blend them with a more relaxed attitude to social issues and an understanding of the importance of the core issues of health and education. Thus, the Coalition Government pursued an orthodox mix of liberal economic policies to reduce the size of the state, cut taxes and tried to return the UK to the economic trajectory it had been on since the 1990s. At the time, there was little internal dissent on these economic measures (Thatcherism was the natural instinct for most of the party's MPs). However, there was disquiet about social liberalism (fewer than half of Conservative MPs backed gay marriage in 2012), the idea that Cameron was an out-of-touch elite politician, and, most especially, the European Question.

May's first speech as Prime Minister hinted at a different economic direction, but she had little opportunity to pursue it in office. However, the Brexit coalition had a strong impact on the party's thinking about where its votes would come from. Johnson therefore proposed a different sort of conservatism from Cameron: one that emphasised traditional themes of patriotism and sovereignty, and was not at all embarrassed about promising to spend more money on things that voters cared about. Austerity was out and levelling up was in.

The Truss interlude snapped the party right back to its Thatcherite roots (and then some), promising speedier and deeper tax cuts than at any time in the 1980s. The prescription of tax cuts as a cure for the UK economy's sluggish growth relies on a caricatured interpretation of what Thatcher did in the 1980s. Nevertheless, it still exerts a powerful hold on the Conservative imagination, as demonstrated by Truss's nomination and leadership campaign victory. Sunak had similar instincts to Truss on the overall desirability of returning the UK to a set of 1990s orthodoxies about lower taxes, restrained spending and competitiveness. However, in difficult economic circumstances he moved cautiously, prompting calls from some MPs for deeper tax cuts and more deregulation to take advantage of Brexit freedoms.

Having been yanked in different directions by different leaders, the party finds itself in a period of ideological unsettlement. As it has seen its poll ratings decline, the arguments have become more intense. There are some deeper trends that the party will need to consider. Johnson's new coalition of voters in the 2019 election hints at a possible future for the Conservative Party. It is doing less and less well among younger sections of the electorate and among people who do not own their own home outright. It is also performing poorly among graduate voters. It is attracting a higher share of votes from those with no qualifications. These changes are the product of the party's choices and of longer-term shifts in the make-up of the UK electorate (Sobolewska and Ford 2020). It means, for example, that seats in and around London that were traditionally Conservative are becoming more of a challenge for the party to hold on to.

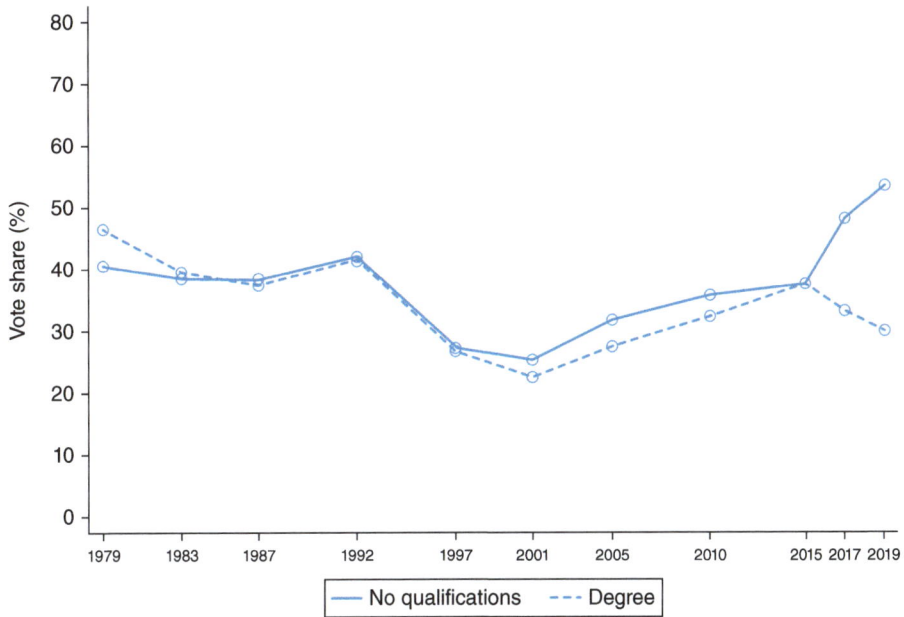

Figure 6.1 Conservative vote share by educational attainment, British Election Study (BES) data, 1979–2019

Source: Ford et al. (2021: 531). Reprinted with permission

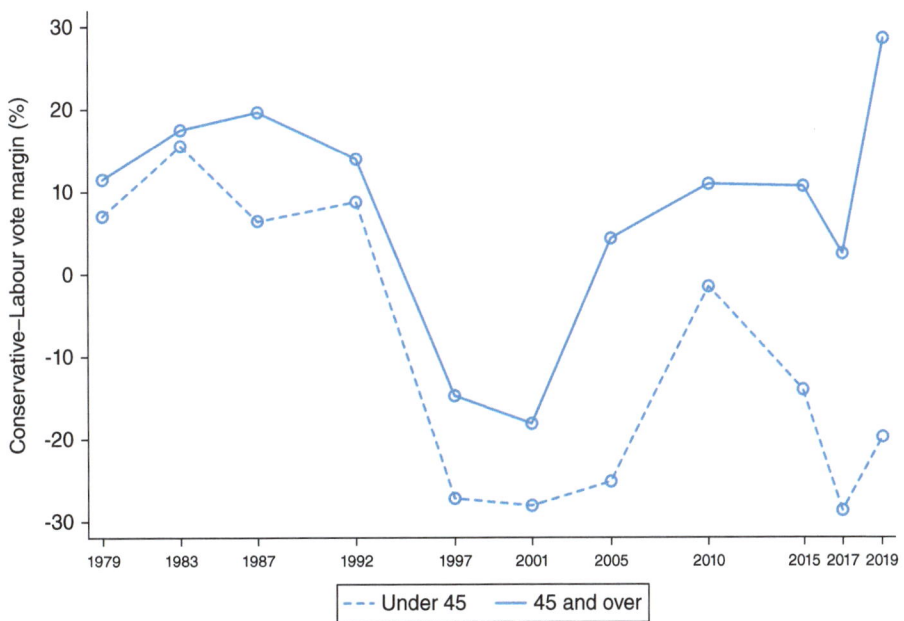

Figure 6.2 Conservative–Labour vote margin by age, BES 1979–2019

Source: Ford et al. (2021: 532). Reprinted with permission

These shifts pull the party in different directions. Should they double down on trying to keep hold of the Red Wall seats they won in 2019? Or do they need another dose of Cameron moderation to shore up seats in the southeast? The Conservatives in 2024 are definitely no longer Cameron's party (although he made a return as Foreign Secretary and was responsible for some candidate selection changes that profoundly shaped its diversity). However, nor are they definitively a party that has shifted towards Johnson's working-class Conservatism vision or Truss's reheated Thatcherism. The party finds itself stranded and exhausted somewhere in the middle. Its room for manoeuvre is constrained by a tricky set of economic circumstances and the general degenerative tendencies that accompany a party that has been in office for an extended period.

Research in Focus

Sex, gender and the Conservative Party

One of the aims of David Cameron's modernisation of the Conservative Party was to attract and select more women candidates. He wanted the party to reflect the modern UK. In this way, it is possible for parties to use issues like candidate selection as a symbol to signal changes in emphasis to the electorate. In *Sex, Gender and the Conservative Party: From Iron Lady to Kitten Heels* (2012), Childs and Webb investigate the extent to which the Conservative Party became 'feminised': that is, did it integrate women and their concerns? Childs' and Kenny's chapters in this volume have already pointed out the less-than-straightforward relationship between descriptive and substantive representation.

Childs and Webb (2012) highlight the importance of taking conservatism and conservative women seriously. What concerns them and what representative claims do conservative women make? The number of Conservative women MPs certainly increased after the 2010 General Election, but not by as much as it could have done if the party had adopted more thorough measures, such as all-women shortlists. There remains a strong antipathy in the party to using these stronger forms of selection.

Childs and Webb found that the Conservative Women's Organisation had limited resources but did articulate women's concerns, which fed into the policy process. Overall, the party under Cameron adopted a 'liberal feminist' position (Childs and Webb 2012: 230–231). Thus: 'The reconciliation of the potentially oppositional goals or equal opportunities in the public sphere and more traditional roles in the private sphere (and the ideologies upon which they are premised) manifests itself within the contemporary Conservative Party through the concept of choice' (Childs and Webb 2012: 230). Conservatives posited that women could choose how they wished to reconcile competing demands in their lives, but this position does not confront whether all women have the resources to make that choice a meaningful one.

Childs and Webb's survey of Conservative Party members found that women members tended to favour more state intervention in the economy. They were also 'more centrist, less post-materialist and more "One Nation"' (Childs and Webb 2012: 231). Conservative women members were also more sympathetic to feminist positions on 'equal opportunities, women's suitability for politics, and the impact of women's paid work on family life' than men (Childs and Webb 2012: 231).

Conclusion

After the 2024 election defeat, the Conservative Party finds itself pulled in different directions. The unity of the 2019 election victory has evaporated; Cameron's modernising prescriptions seem even further in the past. The Conservative Party entered 2024 in a state of profound confusion: a Prime Minister who claimed to believe in lower taxes instead raised them to record levels (Emmerson et al. 2023); the latest Conservative Home Secretary who promised to lower immigration looked on as net migration reached its highest-ever recorded level (Office for National Statistics 2023a); and a party that wanted to use Brexit freedoms to unleash dynamism and growth instead presided over the only Parliament since 1945 in which people's real incomes were lower at the end than at the start (Corlett and Try 2024).

It is therefore little wonder that internal dissent is increasing. The Conservatives are suffering from an identity crisis. Some of the causes are short term. Any governing party would have been severely tested by the challenges of managing the pandemic and its aftermath. Moreover, growth in other comparable European countries has not exactly been stellar of late. However, the party's predicament also finds its roots in longer-term changes in the electorate. The profile of Conservative support is changing. Should the Conservatives double-down on trying to win over former Labour voters and Brexiteers, or do they need to resurrect the Cameron ideas to appeal to graduates and Remainers? These questions are at the heart of debates for the Conservative Party in opposition.

We return at the end of this chapter to the three ideological orientations we outlined at the beginning. The Conservatives are pulled in one direction by those who want to emphasise more conservative themes about family, community and immigration. They pulled in another direction by the strong tendency to believe that Thatcher's prescription was correct and that the UK needs to return to competitiveness, free markets and lower taxes. Finally, there may be a pragmatic path through this tension or the Conservatives may be able to hold both tendencies together, but they have not found it yet.

Summary

- The Conservatives' period in office since 2010 has been particularly turbulent.
- The Conservatives have gone through several electoral and governing strategies in quick succession, resulting in ideological and policy confusion.
- The Conservative electorate is changing: this presents dilemmas and opportunities for the party in opposition.

Recommended and further reading

- Tim Bale is the most prominent scholar of the contemporary Conservative Party. His book *The Conservative Party: From Thatcher to Cameron* (2016) is a lively and accessible account of the party's move from opposition to government in the late 2000s. His later work *The Conservative Party after Brexit: Turmoil and Transformation* (2023) examines the impact of the 2016 referendum on the party's ideology, personnel and policies.

- Beech and Lee's *Conservative Governments in the Age of Brexit* (2023) brings together a stellar group of scholars to analyse different areas of policy and the Conservatives' impact.
- Beyond the centre, Convery's *The Territorial Conservative Party* (2016) looks at how the party adapted to devolution in Scotland and Wales. Sam Blaxland's *The Conservative Party in Wales, 1945–1997* (2024) provides a revisionist account of the party's evolution in the Welsh context.
- The definitive take on gender and the Conservative Party is Childs and Webb's *Sex, Gender and the Conservative Party* (2012). Berthezène and Gottlieb's *Rethinking Right-Wing Women: Gender and the Conservative Party, 1880s to the Present* (2017) provides an excellent account of the evolution of women's thinking about conservatism and right-wing politics over a long time period.

Chapter 7

The Labour Party

Karl Pike

What will this chapter tell me?

- This chapter will explain what the purpose of the Labour Party has been over time and how the present Labour Party – in power after 14 years of opposition – is seeking to realise its ideological goals.
- While it has lost more elections than it has won in the twentieth and twenty-first centuries, the UK Labour Party still has many policy legacies – from the National Health Service to equality legislation – and Labour has enjoyed consistent electoral success in parts of the UK, for example in Wales.
- The 2024 general election marked a historic win for Labour, with 411 seats (excluding the Speaker of the House of Commons) for Keir Starmer's party, albeit without a large increase in UK vote share (Labour won 34% of the vote, up from 32% in 2019). Labour's victory included becoming the largest party in Scotland at a Westminster election once again (where its vote share increased greatly), ending the period of dominance by the Scottish National Party.
- The chapter will explore in greater depth Labour's recent past, from the global financial crisis to the debates over Brexit – including the collapse of the so-called 'Red Wall' – and Labour's triumphant return to office.
- The leaderships of Ed Miliband and Jeremy Corbyn will be analysed and explained.
- By the end of the chapter, you will know how Labour has managed the last two decades of political change.
- The chapter will bring you right up to date with Keir Starmer's leadership and introduce the questions that are being asked about Labour in government – what is the government seeking to achieve, and can Labour bring about 'change'?

What do I need to know?

- You should know what the main political parties in British politics are and be familiar with the UK's constitutional arrangements.
- The Labour Party is the main centre-left party in the UK.
- Centre-left parties come in a variety of forms and draw on different ideological traditions. One of the major dilemmas for these parties is how to balance the state and the market.

Introduction

Since its founding at the beginning of the twentieth century, the British Labour Party has lost elections more often than won them. In 2024, Keir Starmer's Labour bucked that trend, with the Labour leader becoming the party's seventh prime minister. It marked the end of another long period in opposition for Labour; 14 years of Conservative rule that included five Conservative Prime Ministers (including the very brief tenure of Liz Truss) and great turmoil. It was not all doom and gloom for Labour during those 14 years. Welsh Labour has dominated politics in Wales throughout Labour's history (Davies 2024: 72), for example, and that broadly continued. While out of power in Westminster after 2010, Labour politicians have been in power in local government, including in London with the mayor Sadiq Khan, in West Yorkshire with the mayor Tracy Brabin, and in Greater Manchester with mayor Andy Burnham. But the overall story of the twentieth and twenty-first centuries has been this one: when the Conservative Party is talked about as one of the most successful political parties in the world, the unspoken, partnering claim is that the Labour Party often loses. Labour's victory in 2024 was historic, then, not only because the party won 411 seats, but because *any* Labour victory can be seen as historic, despite the significant periods in office that feature in this chapter.

Much discussion of the UK Labour Party, including in academic work, has revolved around the question of why Labour loses. Changes in society, for example class composition (Hobsbawm 1989), and changes in Labour's connection with the working class (owing to it appealing to middle-class voters) have all featured in debates (Evans and Tilley 2017). So too Labour's ideas: whether the party has been 'too left-wing' to win elections, or too similar to the Conservatives, thereby losing distinctiveness and any benefit to be had from a national mood for change. The party's leaders, and leading personalities, have also been much debated. We have seen all of this during Keir Starmer's time as Labour leader: as Leader of the Opposition, he was often criticised for not generating sufficient excitement for Labour, something that has continued to be called into question after the general election: did Labour win only because the Conservatives were so unpopular?

If much time has been spent discussing Labour in the electoral wilderness, the rest of it has been spent judging the party when it does manage to win office. As Jon Cruddas, the author and former Labour MP noted, while the party has struggled to end Conservative dominance, it has delivered some big changes when it has governed (Cruddas 2024: 241): the creation of a National Health Service, expansion of the welfare state, devolution in Scotland, Wales and Northern Ireland (the latter a consequence of another great achievement, the Good Friday Agreement), a national minimum wage, independence for the Bank of England and landmark equality legislation, to name a few.

Yet, plenty of people, including people in the Labour Party, have rued missed opportunities to do more when the party has held office. Cruddas is not untypical of many Labour people in thinking that New Labour – the period of Labour's history when it was led by Tony Blair and Gordon Brown, from 1994 to 2010 – could have achieved more than it did after winning a landslide victory in 1997 (Cruddas 2024: 198). For some on the political, sometimes Marxist-influenced left, the Labour Party is almost structurally designed to disappoint: it seeks to ameliorate, at best, some of the worser aspects of capitalism in Britain. It does not seek to fundamentally change the economic system, which for some people is the essence of socialism. For others, this all misses the point. Labour, as a party on the left that wants to win elections, has to get by within the constraints of the time.

Those constraints are real, so this argument goes, and multi-faceted. There are economic constraints, such as global economic conditions, or growth within the UK economy, that affect what Labour can do, and crucially how much it can spend on egalitarian policies – things like more generous welfare entitlements, or more comprehensive public services. And there are political constraints, including what mandate Labour has from the British people, and how popular its policies are. There are big expectations placed upon Conservative leaders to win elections. There are big expectations placed upon Labour leaders to win elections and deliver significant change, albeit in circumstances not of their own choosing. Starmer's Labour government is facing up to these familiar constraints, all the while promising 'change' to the British people. Labour's permanent conundrum is how to bring about radical change in a country it perceives as being fond of moderate politics.

What is Labour for?

Everyone within the Labour Party would agree that the party exists to make things 'fairer' for people. But this is an ambiguous statement. It does not tell us much about *what* Labour should prioritise in government, nor how it can bring about a fairer society. This ambiguity has been ever-present for Labour, throughout its history. Labour is, at least on paper, a democratic socialist party. When Tony Blair changed the party's constitution (more on that below), those words – a democratic socialist party – were inserted into it. It is also often referred to as a centre-left or social democratic party, along with other political parties elsewhere in Europe, such as the Sozialdemokratische Partei Deutschlands (German Social Democrats), the Swedish Social Democratic Party or the Parti Socialiste (French Socialist Party). For Labour, this ideology – whether people refer to it as democratic socialist or social democratic – has meant different things over the party's 125-year history. Today, some critics of the Labour Party would firmly reject that the party is socialist. They would accept that at most it is rather weakly social democratic.

The differences between the two can be explained simply and starkly: socialism is for a fundamentally different economic system, one where the power of capital, and the profit motive, is replaced with an economy that rewards the value of a person's labour (work) to that person, not a capitalist (property owner). It is an emancipatory doctrine. Social democracy, by contrast, is an ameliorative ideology – that means it seeks to modify the existing system, making it fairer for people in society, including workers, and less exploitative. For the rest of this chapter, I will for the most part refer to Labour's 'socialism'. That is not because Labour is, today, committed to overhauling the existing economic system – it is not. Instead, I use the term 'socialism' because, for many people in the Labour Party, that is the appropriate term to describe Labour's ideological tradition, particularly its past achievements.

The word 'socialism' goes in and out of fashion, however. For example, in 2020, Keir Starmer said he wanted to 'make the moral case for socialism' (Starmer 2020), but that phrase was rarely heard of again. So, what is the contemporary Labour Party's socialism? It still bears some resemblance to what experts have suggested is the core of socialist ideology: the importance of equality and the significance of relations between people as key to human flourishing (Freeden 1996: 425–426). With socialism, the key ingredient for people living a full and better life is the benefit of acting together – the 'social' bit of socialism, rather than an individual liberty as with some interpretations of liberalism (Freeden 1996: 461). Of course, this can lead to a variety of different socialisms. It can lend itself to a 'big state', in so far as socialists think the state – as one way of us acting collectively – can and should try to fix many social problems. But it can equally mean that socialists trust communities of people much more, empowering them – say, with resources – and trusting that they will act together to further the goals of everyone. Both of these ideas are present in today's Labour Party: an active state and empowering communities of people.

Labour's ideas over time

In the early to mid-twentieth century, Labour's socialism became, as with the other parties listed above, associated with public ownership (the nationalisation of major industries) and economic planning (the government having a major role in coordinating the economy). The party's constitution – the values and rules governing it – had within it the famous 'Clause IV', which said the party sought:

To secure for the workers by hand or by brain the full fruits of their industry and the most equitable distribution thereof that may be possible, upon the basis of the common ownership of the means of production, distribution, and exchange, and the best obtainable system of popular administration and control of each industry or service.

As Labour leader, Tony Blair revised Clause IV, removing the commitment to common ownership. However, Clause IV had ceased, in effect, before this time, and for some people within the Labour Party, long before this time. A previous Labour leader had tried – and failed – to do what Tony Blair did in 1995. Following Labour's defeat in the 1959 election, the then Labour leader Hugh Gaitskell suggested a revision of Clause IV, but lost out to internal opposition. Following Clement Attlee's pioneering Labour government, in office from 1945 to 1951 (after a landslide win in 1945, and a very narrow win in 1950), Labour did not win again until 1964 – and much of the debate about how Labour needed to move forward centred around nationalisation. Attlee's government nationalised a number of important industries, including electricity, gas and coal (Toye 2024: 61). Recent academic work exploring arguments *for* nationalisation has suggested some (or all) of the following three reasons: an economic problem the private sector cannot fix; a 'fundamental' part of the economy the private sector cannot sufficiently guide in the required direction; and 'values', including the place and role of workers (Gibbs et al. 2024: 3). These rationales remain part of the debate today.

Some further nationalisation followed in subsequent decades, in lower numbers, before the privatisation boom during the years of Margaret Thatcher's governments in the 1980s (Gibbs et al. 2024). Within Labour, there was a questioning of how necessary further nationalisations were following the postwar Attlee years – and in response to Thatcher's privatisations decades later. In a period of Labour's political thought known as 'revisionism', prominent Labour politicians and thinkers made the case that capitalism was completely different in the 1950s from what it had been during the interwar years and before. In short, they believed it was significantly better, even completely transformed, and that Labour's policies had played their part in making it so (Thompson 2006: 149–172). Macroeconomic levers associated with Keynesianism – things like state spending to prevent lasting economic downturns and a strategy to maintain 'full employment' – had, along with an expanded welfare state, shown that Labour's goals were achievable through a variety of economic policies, not only nationalisation. That did not mean 'socialism' had been achieved, however. The foremost revisionist thinker of the 1950s and 1960s, Anthony Crosland (Labour MP for Great Grimsby and Cabinet minister before his death in 1977 at the age of 58), said as much in his book *The Future of Socialism* (1956: 115):

Many liberal-minded people … have now concluded that 'Keynes-plus-modified-capitalism-plus-Welfare-State' works perfectly well. … Yet this is not socialism. True, it is not pure capitalism either. … To put the matter simply, we have won many important advances; but since we could still have more social equality, a more classless society, and less avoidable social distress, we cannot be described as a socialist country.

Note Crosland's reiteration of Labour's socialism: greater equality, tackling class divisions and advancing the social conditions of the people. The second half of the twentieth century saw Labour struggle to articulate exactly how to build upon the legacy of the postwar government. Most would have agreed with Crosland that great progress was made but with much more still to do. The question was *how* to make that further progress. When it came to economic policy, 'planning' – as I noted above, a somewhat ambiguous word to describe different kinds of state involvement in how the economy is run and should develop – made a return during Harold Wilson's first period as prime minister, starting in 1964 (Thompson 2006: 176–186). The Labour governments of the 1960s also introduced the first legislation aimed at preventing discrimination towards people from ethnic minorities – passing two Acts of Parliament, the Race Relations Act 1965 and 1968 (Brown 2018). As Labour and Britain entered the 1970s – the Conservatives being in power from 1970 to 1974 – the confidence of the 1950s that Britain's major economic ills had been solved evaporated. The Labour Party itself began to debate and then embrace proposals for large-scale ownership and control of private companies, nationalisation and more ambitious planning (Thompson 2006: 216–220). With Thatcher's election in 1979, the Labour Party turned in on itself, with increasing factionalism – that is, political groups and identities within a political party competing for control – and often vehement argument and disagreement.

After losing the 1979 election, Labour lost the 1983, 1987 and 1992 elections. High-profile Labour politicians (including Shirley Williams and Roy Jenkins) left the party to help form the Social Democratic Party (SDP), believing Labour to have moved too far to the left. Michael Foot, Labour leader from 1980 to 1983, did his best to hold together a party seemingly at war with itself. These were the 'wilderness years' for Labour, with Neil Kinnock – leader from 1983 to 1992 – working both to defeat 'hard left' factions within the party and to 'modernise' Labour's policies, including moving away from nationalisation and towards more market-friendly policies, and ending Labour's support for unilateral nuclear disarmament. Labour recovered electorally over time, and with John Smith as leader after Kinnock, looked to be in a good position to take on the Conservatives when the next election came. Smith's untimely death in 1994 meant Labour suddenly needed a new leader, and the choice was between two of the party's rising stars: Tony Blair or Gordon Brown. Brown chose to back Blair, and Blair became Labour's leader, easily defeating his competitors John Prescott and Margaret Beckett. The New Labour era had begun.

The New Labour legacy

When Tony Blair said goodbye to the Labour Party in a speech at the party's conference in 2006 – his last as party leader before passing on the leadership to Gordon Brown – he said there was only one Labour tradition that he did not like: losing. Blair won three consecutive elections as Labour leader – 1997, 2001 and 2005 – something no previous Labour leader had ever achieved. And the New Labour governments, with Blair as prime minister and Brown as chancellor, before becoming prime minister in 2007, pursued many policies that both built upon Labour's past and achieved egalitarian outcomes. The National Health Service saw huge investment, as did the education system. Child and pensioner poverty were significantly reduced. Britain took a number of steps forward in terms of equality. Civil partnerships for same-sex couples (the Conservative–Liberal Democrat coalition then went on to introduce equal marriage) were introduced. The Equality and Human Rights Commission (EHRC) was established, the age of consent was equalised, and a piece of homophobic legislation in educational settings – introduced during the Thatcher years, known as 'Section 28' – was scrapped

(Diamond 2021: 217–218). There were advances on gender equality, although Diamond noted that reforms to improve the rights of women in the workplace and the introduction of parental leave were arguably 'instrumental' in terms of seeking electoral support (Diamond 2021: 219) and perhaps some economic benefits. A National Minimum Wage was introduced – something since built upon by the Conservatives too. Devolution in Scotland, Wales and Northern Ireland fundamentally changed the governance of the UK.

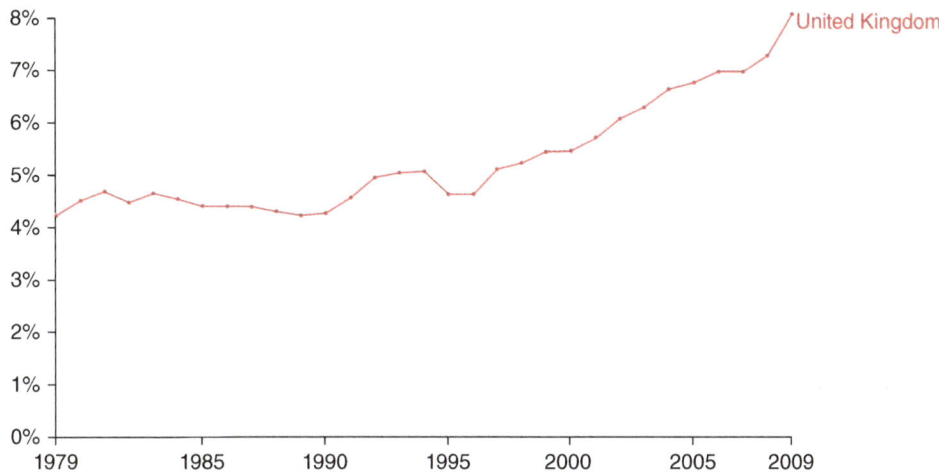

Figure 7.1   UK health spending as a percentage of GDP

Yet while few doubted New Labour achieved good things in office, the legacy of New Labour – one often viewed, in large part, as the legacy of Tony Blair – proved to be divisive (see Hindmoor and Pike, 2022). Blair's decision-making, on both foreign and domestic policy, was often in the spotlight: for example, the decision to join the US-led invasion of Iraq in 2003, and an increased push from Blair towards public service reform, including private sector involvement. On income inequality, while the increases seen during the Thatcher years had paused, it remained high. By the time New Labour left office in 2010, losing the 2010 election and being replaced by a Conservative coalition with the Liberal Democrats (with David Cameron as prime minister), Blair was becoming an increasingly isolated figure within Labour.

So began a lengthy period out of office for the Labour Party, but so too began a period of significant change for Labour: ideological, organisational and political (Pike 2024). 'Blairism' had come to be seen as further and further away from Labour's (albeit ambiguous) socialist or social democratic tradition. What had begun as Blair's version of ethical socialism soon morphed into what was known as the 'Third Way' within social democracy – considered by some scholars to be 'between neoliberalism and "old" social democracy … an approach that adapted Labour's traditional goals to the challenges posed by the new globalized world' (Goes 2024: 88). By the end of Blair's tenure, New Labour's ideology was increasingly drifting towards an amorphous 'centre', less about long-held 'ends' and more about specific 'means' that had come to dominate Blair's political thinking. The generation of Labour politicians who came after Blair and Brown, then, included some who were motivated to move on from New Labour, and from Blair's mistakes. Others were less sure. All of this involved significant political risk – were the Labour politicians that followed Blair trashing their own party and doing the Conservatives' work for them?

The austerity era

New Labour's period in office ended with the global financial crisis and its fallout. Bubbling up in 2007, and then exploding in 2008, the global financial crisis brought about the sudden collapse of some of the world's largest banks, leading to a 'credit crunch' – an absence of lending – and an economic slump around the world. Governments, including the UK Government, had to intervene in the financial markets, in some instances becoming owners or part-owners of banks: in effect, nationalising aspects of the banking system. The global financial crisis had many repercussions, but one became particularly important in Britain: how much the UK Government had needed to spend, and borrow, to bail out the financial system and seek to prevent a lasting economic depression. Looking back from the middle of the 2020s, we now know this was the first major shock to the global economy after a relatively benign macroeconomic period. Another came along in 2020 with the Covid-19 pandemic, and then an energy price shock following Russia's invasion of Ukraine in 2022. Figure 7.2 presents a measure of UK Government debt, in this case the UK's total level of debt as a percentage of GDP. The graph

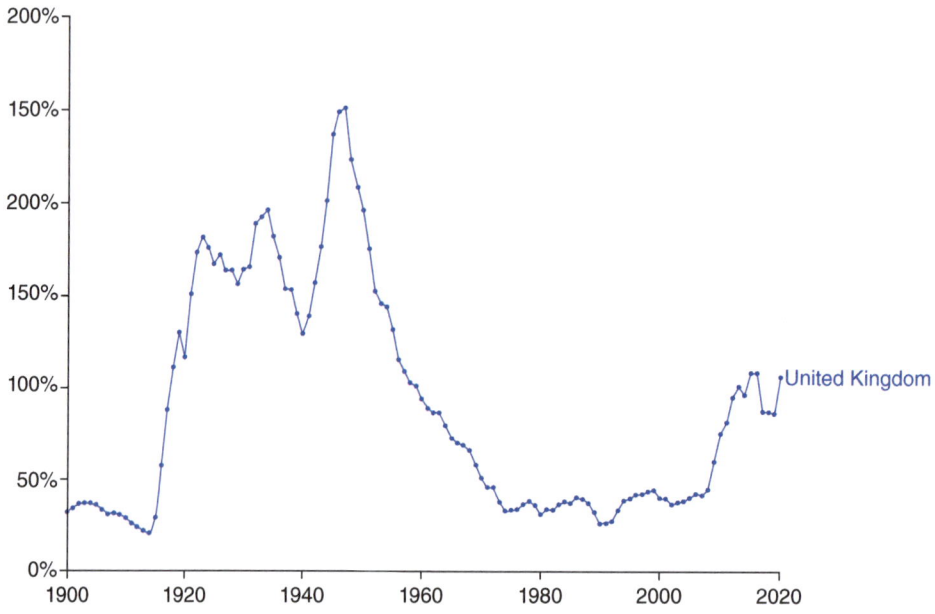

Figure 7.2   UK Government debt as a percentage of GDP

starts at the beginning of the twentieth century, and we can see the impact of two world wars, followed by a reduction in the debt as a percentage of GDP measure, before the impact of the global financial crisis can be seen on the right-hand side.

For many economists, the fact that debt would increase during an economic crisis, with the government borrowing more to try to prevent a prolonged slump, was unextraordinary. In addition, monetary policy pursued by central banks around the world to help prevent a lasting depression had resulted in very low interest rates, reducing the cost of borrowing. No one, meanwhile, envisaged government borrowing increasing forever. Rather, Gordon Brown's Labour government was committed to reducing borrowing when policymakers judged the economy had sufficiently recovered. The Conservative Party, in opposition and then in government after 2010, had a different interpretation. Labour's increases in public spending *before* the economic crisis were now used against Labour, as evidence that the party had been irresponsible. The Conservative Party skilfully positioned 'the deficit' – the gap between government receipts and spending – as the foremost political issue in British politics, and one requiring significant reductions in public spending: austerity.

The Labour Party was mindful of this political weakness that had emerged, but was simultaneously unwilling to accept responsibility for what was a global economic crisis.

Labour moved into opposition in 2010, having lost the general election. Following Gordon Brown's resignation as prime minister, a leadership contest was held to decide on the party's next leader. The candidates included Ed Balls, Diane Abbott and Andy Burnham, but it was really just a contest between two people: David and Ed Miliband, brothers, and who had both been cabinet ministers during Brown's time as prime minister. David Miliband had worked for Tony Blair before becoming an MP in 2001, while Ed Miliband had worked for Gordon Brown before becoming an MP in 2005. They therefore had political identities partly bestowed on them because of their respective career paths – David Miliband was considered the more 'Blairite', or centre-right, Labour politician, and Ed Miliband the 'Brownite', or more centre-left Labour politician. Ed Miliband won the race to be leader, by a very narrow margin, and aimed to change the Labour Party in ways partly motivated by a desire to move away from New Labour (Pike 2024).

In particular, Ed Miliband was motivated by tackling economic inequality – something that had increased significantly during the Thatcher years and had not been sufficiently addressed by New Labour. Miliband often railed against an economy that was too often rewarding those at the top and letting down those on lower incomes (Pike 2024). Yet he was also leading Labour at a time when the major criticism levelled at the party was having spent too much money. This placed him in a bind: how to move on from New Labour in some ways, but defend it in other ways? Miliband's popularity with the British people was always a concern too. While Labour did manage to lead the opinion polls for much of Miliband's tenure, David Cameron – the Conservative prime minister from 2010 to 2016 – consistently led Miliband in polling about who 'would make the best Prime Minister'. According to the polling company YouGov, in April 2015 – the month before the general election – Cameron was the preferred choice of 40% of people, with Miliband behind on 24–26% (YouGov 2015).

With Labour failing to overcome voters' hesitancy, the party lost the 2015 general election, with the Conservatives winning a surprise majority. Miliband promptly resigned as leader of the Labour Party. Amid the political upheaval of the Scottish independence referendum, which the cross-party 'No' campaign won, Labour experienced an electoral wipe-out in Scotland. Scottish Labour had struggled to assert its own identity over the years, while the UK party had struggled with the necessary political response to devolution, leading to concerns that Scottish Labour was not distinctive enough and not empowered to pursue its own political identity (Bennett et al. 2021; Brown Swan and Kenny 2024). In 2015, Labour went from having 41 MPs in Scotland to having one MP. Only in 2024 did Labour recover, amid negative news headlines for the Scottish National Party.

Corbynism

What came next after the 2015 defeat surprised pretty much everybody. The veteran, rebel backbench MP Jeremy Corbyn managed to persuade enough of his fellow Labour MPs to add him to the ballot paper for the leadership election that followed Miliband's resignation. While nobody, at that time, expected him to win, he did – despite the overwhelming majority of Labour MPs supporting another candidate, and a media environment that was highly sceptical (to say the least) that a Corbyn government was even possible. This proved something of a puzzle for many commentators and academics. Indeed, two political scientists judged that many academics simply did not understand Corbyn – or 'Corbynism' as the movement became known – and were insufficiently curious about why some people were very passionate about Corbyn's Labour and committed to his leadership (Maiguashca and Dean 2020). Taking issue with the characterisation of Corbyn's leadership as inept, 'hard left' and populist, Maiguashca and Dean (2020) told a different story of a leadership that had generated enthusiasm, offered policies that sat within a social democratic or socialist tradition and was not populist in the way figures like Donald Trump were.

Research in Focus

Myth

In seeking to understand how and why Jeremy Corbyn struck a chord with many Labour supporters after 2015, Maiguashca and Dean (2020) were treading familiar ground in the social sciences: How important are our *beliefs*? And how important in our decision-making are very strong beliefs? Within political science, *rationality*, and more specifically *rational choice theory*, has been used by scholars to understand why people make certain choices. The theory here is that people will act in the way most likely to attain their preferences – and in politics, that is typically winning elections to realise your political goals. That means, for example, making policy choices in politics because we think those choices could help us win and attain our preferences. But politics, like life, seems messier and more complex than that.

Not only do we act on the basis of our perception – how we *perceive* people and our environment – but we also ascribe meaning to things. A political party, for example, is not just an organisation than runs candidates for office. It is an institution with a whole host of stories and meanings attached, some historical, some cultural, some personal. Jeremy Corbyn's candidacy brought together a set of very powerful meanings for some people on the left, namely: saying what you believe; the importance of class; being part of a wider left movement happening around the world after the global financial crisis; and a repudiation of the Iraq

War. These comprised one collective 'myth' (Pike and Diamond 2021). Someone sceptical of Corbyn may have thought it was a bad choice to support him because they feared he would be unpopular with the public, and that Labour would lose. But others were conscious of very different meanings, because for many they spoke to some important things that had been wrong with politics for many years.

The concept of myth – the bringing together into one narrative a number of separate meanings – is underused in the social sciences. Thanks to scholars who have worked on the theory of myth (see Bottici 2007; and Midgley 2011), we can begin to understand its relevance to politics and why different groups of people invest so much importance in a particular political project or story.

One political theme was stressed more than any other during Corbyn's race to be Labour leader: the importance of being anti-austerity. Where Miliband was seen to compromise in the face of the prevailing narrative of Labour's alleged profligacy (spending too much money), Corbyn would not. The most 'left' political platform since Foot's 1983 programme (Cowley and Kavanagh 2018: 184), which was epitomised by the party manifestos produced during Corbyn's leadership, saw Labour commit once again to some public ownership and big increases in public spending. Tax rises were endorsed to pay for the increases in day-to-day spending – that is, things governments fund year after year – with borrowing to fund big investment ambitions. This was key to the then shadow chancellor John McDonnell, who, while embracing an anti-austerity strategy, also wanted to show that he took seriously Labour's sums adding up. They were still bold pledges, however, and open to critique.

Within Corbynism was also a variety of left traditions, including a renewed focus on class (Pike and Diamond 2021). Maiguashca and Dean (2020: 58–59) noted too the 'growing space … created – consciously and unconsciously – for the politics of race (or rather anti-racism) and feminism' that found political expression in and around the Corbyn project. Yet, as the same authors also noted (2020: 58–59), Corbyn's own reputation – and that of his 'project' – for anti-racism was fundamentally undermined by Labour's anti-semitism crisis. Jewish Labour politicians and members had received abuse when raising concerns about anti-semitism within the Labour Party. One MP, Luciana Berger, left the Labour Party, noting the lack of an adequate response from the leadership. After Corbyn's leadership of the party had ended, the Equality and Human Rights Commission (EHRC) concluded that during his tenure the leadership could have done more to tackle anti-semitism (EHRC 2020: 6). Jeremy Corbyn ultimately had the Labour whip removed after his response to the EHRC report – meaning he stopped being a Labour MP and was formally an independent MP – owing to his statement that the scale of anti-semitism within Labour had been 'overstated' (Elgot and Walker 2020). He was later also prevented from being a Labour candidate at the 2024 general election by the National Executive Committee, although he was re-elected in his constituency of Islington North as an independent, defeating the Labour candidate.

Labour broken by Brexit?

Corbyn's time as Labour leader – and therefore 'Corbynism overall' – was a tale of two very different general elections: a surprise in 2017, when Corbyn's Labour deprived the then Conservative prime minister Theresa May of a majority, and a heavy defeat in 2019, with Boris Johnson the triumphant Conservative prime minister taking seats that had been Labour for generations. An electoral and political analysis of Corbyn's Labour has to take into account both results – the surprise (though note, Labour still lost) and the big defeat. One particular issue stands out as the theme that dominated British politics between 2017 and 2019: Brexit. From the moment that Britain voted to leave the European Union in 2016 – famously, by 52% to 48% – Labour knew it faced some difficult political judgements. As David Cameron resigned as Conservative leader following the referendum result, Labour's MPs were demanding Corbyn also quit.

Corbyn lost a 'confidence' vote of the Parliamentary Labour Party after the Brexit referendum result – a test as to whether his parliamentary colleagues wanted him to continue or quit – by 172 votes to just 40 supporting him. However, pointing to his mandate from Labour Party members, Corbyn refused to quit (Asthana et al. 2016). A leadership contest followed, yet the candidate put up to challenge Corbyn – the then MP for Pontypridd, Owen Smith – did not come close to defeating him among Labour's members and supporters. What then followed was a period of renewed confidence for Jeremy Corbyn and his team. With a refreshed mandate from Labour's membership, he remained behind in the polls, but convinced by his anti-austerity message. When Theresa May called a surprise general election in 2017 – May had said she would not be calling one, and then promptly did – there was a widespread expectation among followers of British politics that May would win well. Instead, Corbyn's Labour confounded most expectations. As Cowley and Kavanagh (2018: 412) put it, 'Labour began the campaign staring down the barrel at one of its worst election performances in its history, but ended just a few thousand votes away from Downing Street'.

After 2017, while Corbyn and his team enjoyed having stunned the political world – and the leader took to the Pyramid Stage at Glastonbury to the sound of a crowd signing 'Oh Jeremy Corbyn' – things changed. Theresa May had tried to make the 2017 election about Brexit and giving her a mandate to deliver a particular kind of Brexit (however vague that agenda was at this time; see Convery's Chapter 6 on the Conservative Party for more details). Ironically, May made it even harder for herself to deliver that task, losing the small majority she inherited from David Cameron, and being reliant on the hard Brexit-supporting Democratic Unionist Party (DUP) of Northern Ireland for votes. This context dramatically reduced her chances of securing parliamentary support for compromises made with the European Union. All of this heightened the drama and tension of Brexit – and the need to spell out detailed policy positions.

Remain and Leave

Yet Labour was in a difficult position and found itself divided. There are two factors in explaining this. The first, and by far the most significant for the majority of Labour people, was the *electoral* challenge of Brexit. While the UK had voted to leave the European Union, by 52% to 48%, the story across the nations and regions was far from clear. Scotland had voted to remain in the EU, and the SNP adopted a pro-European position bolstered by what it saw as the democratic scandal of Scotland having to leave the EU against its will. What was Labour to make of that, as it sought some kind of recovery in Scotland? Within England and Wales, the story was of geographical splits and divides among different groups of voters. The best-known of these geographical and voter divides was Labour's so-called 'Red Wall' – constituencies that had traditionally voted Labour and were located from the Midlands and further northwards. These constituencies, or 'seats', included former coal-mining areas and had strong connections with Labour, not just in terms of voting, but in the shared meanings and identities fostered over decades, which arguably declined with New Labour, but remained important for people in the Labour Party.

However, many of these seats were also considered to be 'Leave' constituencies – areas that had voted to leave the EU. Labour, meanwhile, was a party that had backed 'Remain'. Labour Party members were overwhelmingly in support of being in the EU and supported another referendum – what became known as a 'People's Vote' (Bale, Webb and Poletti, 2020: 68). Most Labour MPs were 'Remain' and most Labour voters were 'Remain'. But the seats Labour needed to win had within them significant numbers of 'Labour Leave' voters. This did not mean that, because a constituency had supported Leave, and previously elected a Labour MP, Labour's voters in those areas were all 'Leavers'. Indeed, polling evidence suggested that 'Leave' voters were a minority of Labour's supporter base in Leave seats, with the remainder of Labour's support being 'Remain'. But that Leave minority was very significant, approaching or exceeding four in ten of Labour's voters in seats that had voted Leave (Curtice et al. 2021: 468–469). The dilemma was clear: if Labour opened up a clear, pro-European dividing line with the Conservatives, then they could have been punished in Labour seats that had voted Leave. Yet if they backed Brexit come what may, they could have lost the support of Remain voters.

The last point is connected to the second factor in explaining how Brexit divided Labour. The vast majority of the party's members and MPs had opposed Brexit during the referendum campaign because they were pro-European. They *believed* in remaining within the EU. Likewise, after the referendum, they *believed* in as close a relationship between the UK and the EU as possible, and then – in increasing number – backed a referendum to stop Brexit too. Jeremy Corbyn, however, had never been pro the EU, and neither had some of his close colleagues in politics. This, then, created an *ideological* divide between a leadership that was not very pro-EU and a parliamentary party and membership that was very clearly pro-EU.

In the end, the electoral dilemma and the ideological divide resulted in a Labour policy and strategy that risked pleasing nobody. Labour moved, gradually after 2017, towards a close relationship with the EU and then to supporting a referendum. However, mindful of losing Labour's Leave voters, the party did not say whether it would back 'Remain' or leaving with a new 'deal' in a future referendum. The party sat on the fence. Electorally, this was bad news for Labour, although there were no easy choices. From its voters in 2017, the party lost 'Leave and Remain supporters in equal measure', which meant an even greater proportion of its Leave voters (Ford et al. 2021: 539). In 'Red Wall' seats, the party suffered big losses. These were 'the product of a pincer movement – a Conservative advance from 2016 onwards, which combined with relative decline after 2017 to put many of these once-safe Labour seats in jeopardy' (Ford et al. 2021: 508). In the 2019 election, Labour only held on to half of the Leave voters who had supported the party in 2017 (Curtice et al. 2021: 469).

Yet, this was not the whole story. Research looking at the choices of ethnic minority voters showed that, while some Labour supporters from ethnic minorities had opted to vote 'Leave' in the EU referendum, these voters largely went on to vote Labour in the 2019 election, rather than for Boris Johnson's Conservative Party running on a hard Brexit platform (Martin and Sobolewska 2023: 568). On this point, the Conservative Party's 'reputation as the white ethnocentric party whose policies and narratives are directed against ethnic minorities clearly held them back' (Martin and Sobolewska 2023: 569).

Starmer's victory

The 2019 election result was an awful one for the Labour Party. The Conservatives won 43.6% of the vote to Labour's 32.2%, which was enough to secure the Conservatives 365 seats to Labour's 203 (Ford et al. 2021: 607). While politicians in the UK – like the rest of the world – were suddenly managing the pandemic crisis, by the autumn of 2021 the Conservatives, and Boris Johnson, were confident in their position (Swinford and Wright 2021). That did not last. Within a year Johnson had resigned, having lost the confidence of his party. Liz Truss became prime minister for one and a half months, amid economic and political chaos, and then resigned too. Rishi Sunak, inheriting a fractious party and an economy on the rocks, was also swiftly under pressure, experiencing poor opinion poll ratings. Through all of this, Keir Starmer led Labour. Elected in 2020 after Jeremy Corbyn's resignation triggered a leadership contest, Starmer easily defeated the other two candidates for the job – Rebecca Long-Bailey and Lisa Nandy. Labour has still not elected a woman to be the leader of the UK party in its history – itself a highly problematic fact for a party of equality.

Starmer endured a difficult start. Unable to introduce himself to the British public in the usual ways because of Covid restrictions (his leadership victory speech was video-recorded at home), Starmer struggled to define himself and encountered some significant setbacks. A by-election in Hartlepool – a seat Labour held – was lost to the Conservative Party in May 2021, and Starmer's leadership was subject to much critical commentary, often around his perceived lack of 'vision'. And yet, Starmer continued, and gradually asserted his authority over Labour. As Johnson became mired in scandals related to parties held in Downing Street during Covid restrictions, the polls changed and Labour posted a narrow lead. After the meltdown of Liz Truss' government, Labour's lead was consistent, and often over 20 points (YouGov 2024).

Yet, it is also true that Starmer's leadership embraced a 'safety first' strategy after posting polling leads over the Conservative Party. Labour, seemingly above all else, sought to prevent the Conservatives creating 'dividing lines', particularly on economic policy issues such as how much the government spends, or how much people are taxed to pay for the things the government spends money on. People can be forgiven for thinking that politics sometimes seems to go around in circles. After the post-2010 austerity politics gave way – temporarily – to a bigger state, post-Brexit politics, the middle of the 2020s has seen politics headed back towards familiar and recent territory: concerns over the amount of money the government spends and how to get the UK economy moving again. Keir Starmer's political challenge – alongside Rachel Reeves, who became Chancellor of the Exchequer in 2024 – is principally an economic one: how can the UK continue to find more money for under-pressure public services when economic growth is far from strong and when the Labour Party, following the Conservative Party, has been reluctant to talk to voters about increasing taxes?

Case Study 7.1

What drives Labour's economic policy?

Academics have debated how the Labour Party decides on its economic policies. There are many factors to consider. To win elections, political parties need enough voters to win a majority of seats in Parliament, and to do that, they must take into account what the public think about the economy. The relative strength of the UK economy is, of course, also affected by a number of factors, from the policies the UK and devolved governments pursue to global shocks, such as the global financial crisis, discussed earlier, or Russia's invasion of Ukraine and the effects on global energy markets. These things impact on people's household finances, and so how much they spend, how much businesses make, how much tax governments receive, and so on.

The connections between these factors and others have been analysed in different ways. According to Jacobs and Hindmoor (2024), Labour's economic policies have been guided more by the prevailing condition of the UK (and global) economy than by electoral considerations (voters) or ideological factors (e.g. people who believe in public ownership). In bad economic times, when Labour politicians see big, systemic problems, the party adopts bigger, more systemic policy measures. In better economic times, Labour redistributes the proceeds of growth (Jacobs and Hindmoor 2024). Engaging with this argument, Sloman (2024: 24) has suggested that an important factor – and 'constraint' – has been what he calls policy making 'within a fiscal register'; that is, economic policies needing to be paid for in ways that are judged (at the time) to be fiscally credible and responsible.

The word 'fiscal' is used to refer to policies and decisions that are about how governments bring money in and how they distribute money out. A shorthand for this in politics is 'tax and spend'. When you watch a politician being interviewed, that politician is often asked: 'how are you going to pay for that?' That is what Sloman means by 'fiscal register'. Economic policy making occurs within an environment that says if you're going to spend some money, you need to raise that money in a credible way. If their answer is not seen as credible, a politician will be concerned that this will be used by political opponents to criticise them, sow doubt in voters' minds over whether their sums add up, and potentially affect how financial markets view the UK Government.

Reflective questions

1   What do you think matters most when taking decisions about economic policy?
2   What 'constraints' on Labour Party politicians can you think of?

Some of the criticism levelled at Keir Starmer has revolved around his lack of 'radicalism', in particular his decision to walk away from commitments he made when he was running to be Labour leader to stick to some of the principles of 'Corbynism': higher taxes on the wealthy, for example, and some public ownership. That being said, Labour under Starmer has developed some distinctive policies, including more investment in green energy and technologies to help meet the country's climate commitments. Labour in government is seeking to implement its plans around strengthening workers' rights, devolving power from London and central government to local councils and communities (much of which is based on the report of a commission led by Gordon Brown), new race equality legislation, more teachers in schools in England, along with free breakfast clubs in primary schools, and planning reform to make building in Britain easier. On Brexit, Labour was intentionally quiet before the 2024 general election, noting it wanted a better deal with the EU, but not wanting to fundamentally change the arrangements in place. This area will be closely watched during the Labour government.

The question, then, is not about the presence or lack of policies. Labour has plenty of policies. The questions are rather about scale – just how ambitious is Starmer's Labour? – and about whether achieving Labour's historic goals of greater equality and strong public services to help bring about a fairer society are possible without taking on some of the harder questions: notably, choosing between lowering rates of taxation and investing in public services. The Labour Party is hoping that a growing economy, and more tax revenue as a result, prevents that from being its only choice.

Conclusion

The Labour Party followed 13 years in government led by Tony Blair and Gordon Brown with an even longer period out of office. Ed Miliband, and to an even greater extent Jeremy Corbyn, tried to win back power for Labour by showing how the party had *changed* after New Labour (Pike 2024). Yet, both leaders could not seize the political agenda away from the dominant themes of their respective leaderships: austerity during the Miliband years and Brexit during the Corbyn years. While Corbyn defied his sceptics in 2017 with a strong performance, in 2019 Labour went backwards again.

Under Keir Starmer's leadership, the party has won its first general election since 2005 and has a very large majority in the House of Commons. Consecutive Conservative Party crises – the scandals, Johnson's resignation, economic turmoil and Truss's resignation – certainly helped to put Labour in a better position to win office. But Keir Starmer's leadership played a role too, with Labour winning seats from the Conservatives across England and Wales and from the SNP in Scotland. The party did not hugely increase its vote share on 2019, but the context is a changing one, with more parties (the Liberal Democrats, Greens, Reform, Plaid Cymru) winning votes and seats and the SNP continuing to compete with Labour in Scotland. For Labour, ending another long period in opposition brought great joy. Entering office, facing a huge pile of problems and in the context of an economy that continues to under-perform, is when the really hard work begins.

Summary

- Labour's ideology – what it stands for and what it seeks to achieve – has been vague over its history. While all Labour politicians broadly seek a 'fairer' society, *how* to achieve that and *what outcomes* they have had in mind have changed over time.
- The party has lost more elections than it has won and has often faced long periods in opposition – the latest, ending in 2024, lasted 14 years. Yet it is also proud of its record when it has been in government. Indeed, the role of historic achievements in the party's history (e.g. the National Health Service) is important for understanding what Labour politicians prioritise.
- The New Labour years, with Tony Blair as prime minister (1997–2007) and Gordon Brown as prime minister (2007–2010), were both electorally successful and controversial. Blair's decision to join the United States in invading Iraq is enduringly controversial. And while New Labour hugely increased public spending in health and education, and reduced pensioner and child poverty, the New Labour governments have also been criticised for leaving the UK's economic model unchanged.
- The global financial crisis of 2008, and its aftermath, dramatically changed the political landscape for Labour. The party lost the 2010 election to the Conservatives and was attacked for having overspent in office. The 'austerity' years challenged Labour, and Jeremy Corbyn's rise can be partly explained by concerns within the Labour Party that it had not opposed austerity well enough, nor put forward a radical alternative.
- Jeremy Corbyn's surprise 2017 general election performance proved to be a short-lived moment of confidence for the Labour Party. As Brexit came to dominate British politics,

Labour struggled with a big dilemma: how to keep its mostly Remain supporters happy but not lose its Leave supporters? In the end, the party could not square that circle.

- Keir Starmer became Labour Party leader in 2020 and prime minister in 2024. Starmer's leadership of the Labour Party has not been without its challenges, and he has been subject to criticism on a number of points, from a lack of radicalism to his judgement on foreign policy, including the conflict in Gaza which began in 2023. With Labour returned to office, Starmer has become the party's seventh prime minister since the creation of the Labour Representation Committee in 1900. His Labour government faces huge challenges, particularly over how to fund spending increases for public services like the National Health Service.

Recommended and further reading

- For general histories of the Labour Party, read Cruddas, J. (2024) *A Century of Labour*. Cambridge: Polity Press, and Toye, R. (2024) *Age of Hope: Labour, 1945, and the Birth of Modern Britain*. London: Bloomsbury.
- For more on Ed Miliband's leadership, read Goes, E. (2016) *The Labour Party under Ed Miliband*. Manchester: Manchester University Press.
- For more on Jeremy Corbyn's leadership, read Maiguashca, B. and Dean, J. (2020) '"Lovely people but utterly deluded"? British political science's trouble with Corbynism', *British Politics*, 15: 48–68.
- For the role of New Labour and Keir Starmer's leadership, read Pike, K. (2024) *Getting Over New Labour*. Newcastle: Agenda.

Chapter 8

Elections and voting

Ailsa Henderson

What will this chapter tell me?

- This chapter examines the ways in which voters in the UK behave at different levels: in local, regional and UK elections. It also outlines the variety of voting systems in operation across the UK.

- It summarizes the various changes in terms of electoral boundaries and procedures for electoral registration in recent years.

- This chapter outlines some of the main theories political scientists have used to explain people's vote choices and shows how these might (and might not) shed light on UK voters.

- It suggests four ways in which our study of elections in the UK needs to change if we are going to capture the sub-state variations in political behaviour: acknowledge there are four electorates; look at different patterns of competition in different areas; recognise that people's vote choice in different areas is driven by different factors; and do not assume that elections beyond Westminster are treated as 'second order'.

What do I need to know?

- The UK's First-Past-the-Post electoral system for UK Parliament elections is only one of the many electoral systems operating in the UK.

- The devolved legislatures highlight the operation of different arenas for electoral competition in the UK, but variation precedes devolution. . Northern Ireland always had a different party system and Scottish and Welsh voting behaviour has been diverging from England since the 1970s.

- The field of political behaviour seeks to use surveys to test how people think about their vote and then formulate theories to help explain the patterns we see.

Introduction

The study of electoral behaviour requires an understanding of two related subjects: the institutions governing elections in the UK and theories of voting behaviour as they are applied to a UK context. Together, these provide us with the tools to understand why we see the patterns that we do in terms of voter engagement and voter behaviour. Institutions include the electoral system, the size and location of electoral constituencies, the rules for voter registration and casting ballots, as well the rules for calling elections, their timing and organisation.

The study of voting behaviour, by contrast, typically identifies general theories of voting based on assumptions about how individuals reach decisions, and then tests to see whether such theories apply in particular elections, or for particular types of people. Thus far, the study of British voting has tended to focus on Great Britain rather than the UK as a whole, the different party system and drivers of vote choice in Northern Ireland being so distinct that they are typically excluded. In addition, the study of British voting has tended to employ, understandably, England-dominated data, resulting in England-dominated explanations of vote choice. For much of the postwar period this approach mattered little given similarities in partisan preferences across the three British territories, but from the 1970s onwards, diverging political preferences and the arrival of devolution in the 1990s has meant that voters in Scotland, Wales and Northern Ireland are now navigating resolutely multi-level electoral worlds. As a result, any comprehensive study of voting in the UK must explore all four territories, must seek to determine whether English-driven explanations apply equally well across the state and must acknowledge multi-level realities.

A truly multi-level understanding requires not just knowledge of the different electoral systems in operation at different levels, but also the different demands the systems make of voters, the consequences of elections at different levels being held on the same day and the capacity for split-level partisanship or the ordered-ness of elections – terms we will all come to understand at the end of this chapter.

Electoral systems and electoral boundaries

For many people, their primary form of electoral engagement is casting a ballot in an election. How they do so, the choices available to them and the types of decisions they can make are structured by the electoral system. There are currently three electoral systems employed in UK elections. UK General Elections employ a Single Member Plurality (SMP) voter system, or First-Past-the-Post (FPTP), the strengths and weaknesses of which will be familiar to most students of politics. While they tend to generate majority governments, they typically do so on the basis of false majorities. Of the ten UK General Elections in the last 40 years, eight have resulted in majority governments, all of them false majorities; while the largest party won a majority of seats, this was not because they won a majority of votes. Until recently, the largest gap between voter preferences and results was in 2005, when Labour formed a government on the back of only 35% of the popular vote. In the 2024 UK General Election, Labour formed a majority government from only 34% of the popular vote.

There are multiple electoral systems employed throughout the UK. This includes the Mixed Member Proportional (MMP) system which, for now, is employed in devolved elections in Scotland and Wales (sometimes referred to as the Additional Member System (AMS). These vary in their proportionality, measured as the number of regional 'compensatory' seats compared to constituency seats. The higher the number of regional or compensatory seats relative to constituency seats, the greater the degree of proportionality in the result since these are designed as a corrective on the disproportional results generated in constituency contests. Since 1999 both devolved institutions have kept the same ratio of constituency to regional seats, 73:65 in the case of Scotland, 40:20 in Wales.

While more proportional than single member plurality, MMP systems can be criticised for creating two classes of representatives, with those representing the constituencies seen as 'core' representatives and others seen as 'extra' representatives (Curtice 2006). This is reinforced when commentators refer to 'first' and 'second' votes, assuming that voters prioritise decisions in constituency contests (in both temporal order and importance) over regional contests. In addition, if citizens vote for different parties on the constituency and regional ballots, and if parties choose only to field candidates on only one of these (as is typically the case with the Scottish Green Party), then the regional calculations do not correct for disproportional constituency results at all. When voters cast ballots for different parties, this is referred to as split-ticket voting. The alternative, backing the same party in both ballots, is known as straight-ticket voting. How much split-ticket voting do we typically see? In Scotland, it has increased from 22% in 1999 to 31% in 2021, having reached a high of 41% in 2011. In Wales, around one in five backed different parties in 1999, but by 2021 this had risen to almost one in three. This compares to around 22% in German Länder elections, which use the same electoral system (Gschwend et al. 2003).

The Single Transferable Vote (STV) is used to elect members of the Northern Ireland Assembly, as well as for local elections in Northern Ireland (since 1973) and Scotland (since 2007). While local councils in Wales are currently elected by SMP/FPTP, the Local Government and Elections (Wales) Act 2021 allows councils to change their electoral systems to STV if two-thirds of members support such a move. To date, no council has opted to switch to a different electoral system.

In STV elections voters rank candidates and can thus choose from across parties in their ranking. Candidates are then elected in rounds if they pass a threshold, with voters' second preferences redistributed once their first choice has been elected. The proportionality of STV systems depends on the number of representatives elected per district. In some applications an entire state is a single electoral district. In its UK formulation, however, district magnitude currently extends to no more than seven, and the rules allow for optional, rather than compulsory ranking, i.e. voters can rank as many or as few as they wish.

STV is portrayed as a helpful system for divided societies because it facilitates the emergence of moderate parties (Lijphart 1977) rather than those reflecting the poles of society, whether defined as constitutional preferences or an ethno-nationalist representation of interests. Others dispute such a claim, asserting that it is better at ensuring that distinct communities can reflect their preferences in a more consociational way, and in so doing serve as a tool for moderating debate (McGarry and O'Leary 2006a, 2006b, 2009): the debate, in a way, is about the capacity of the electoral system to generate moderate results (centripetal approach) or to facilitate the moderation of debate (consociational approach). After five devolved elections in Northern Ireland, Coakley and Fraenkel (2017) concluded that patterns of vote transfers suggested that the Social Democratic and Labour Party (SDLP) was acquiring lower preferences from Sinn Fein voters, suggesting that voters on the republican side were prioritising less moderate parties in their initial preferences. While the reverse was initially true on the unionist side, growing electoral support for less moderate parties across the nationalist–unionist divides (Sinn Fein, Democratic Unionist Party (DUP)) suggests that STV has not facilitated the emergence of moderate parties. As further proof, the Alliance Party of Northern Ireland's vote share has typically varied between five and eight percentage points, although it reached a high of 13.1 in the most recent (2022) devolved election.

The electoral boundaries for Westminster and other UK elections are generated by independent, non-partisan boundary commissions. Four commissions cover the four territories of the UK for Westminster elections, and a range of four other bodies for devolved and/or local boundaries. Wards are devised for local elections, and these become the building blocks for all other electoral boundaries. By virtue of the different electoral systems used for local elections, and the different sizes of councils, the wards themselves are of different sizes throughout the UK. Small single-member wards are used where local elections employ SMP. The single transferable vote, by contrast, leads to larger wards because each ward elects more than one representative. For Northern Ireland, Assembly elections have a district magnitude of six, while wards in local elections elect between five and seven members. Welsh councils have the option of moving to wards of between three and six members. Scottish wards used to vary between three- and four-member wards, but the Islands (Scotland) Act 2018 allowed for one- and two-member wards on wholly or mainly island wards, and the Scottish Elections (Reform) Act 2020 extended this to two- and five-member wards on the Scottish mainland.

Electoral timing: From simultaneous elections to the Fixed Term Parliament Act

The timing of elections can influence engagement and is therefore assumed to have an impact on the results themselves. Election timing includes the number of days over which elections take place, the days of the week on which they occur, whether there are electoral 'seasons', but also who wields power over electoral timing. Table 8.1 lists the national election days typically used across Europe.

Table 8.1   National election days in Europe

Day	Countries
Monday	Norway
Tuesday	Denmark
Wednesday	Netherlands
Thursday	UK
Friday	Ireland (often)
Saturday	Iceland, Latvia, Lithuania, Malta, Slovakia
Sunday	Austria, Belgium, Croatia, Estonia, Finland, France, Germany, Greece, Hungary, Italy (often), Luxembourg, Montenegro, Poland, Portugal, Slovenia, Spain (often), Sweden, Turkey

Elections in the UK have been held on Thursdays since 1965 – as it is a market day – although there have been occasional exceptions. The 1978 Hamilton by-election in Scotland, for example, was held on a Wednesday to avoid clashing with the opening of the Argentina World Cup, for which Scotland had (unusually) qualified. Within Europe, the UK is unique in its choice of Thursdays, with most other countries choosing a day on the weekend, typically Sundays. UK elections are all held on one-day periods, with polling stations open from 7 a.m. to 10 p.m. This compares to elections in the Czech Republic, for example, where elections can occur from Friday to Saturday afternoon, or in Switzerland, where they occur on a Saturday and Sunday.

In multi-level systems, the electoral timing for one level can have an effect on others. This is relevant for the cycles of popularity enjoyed by parties in government. If other elections are held during the 'honeymoon' period for parties, which typically occurs in the months following election, it can offer a boost to the governing party at other electoral levels. Mid-cycle elections, however, can offer a boost to opposition parties. One way to avoid such effects is to hold simultaneous elections, with elections for multiple areas or levels on the same day.

Simultaneous elections tend to boost voter engagement, particularly if legislative bodies with considerable power, or that people feel are important to their lives, hold their elections on the same day as lower salience elections. Local elections in all four territories are horizontally simultaneous within that territory: local authorities hold their elections on the same day. Whereas in Scotland, Wales and Northern Ireland all councils elect all members on the same day, in England council elections are held every two years, with a mix of whole-council elections and those where one-third or one-half of the council is elected at each democratic contest. While the elections are internally simultaneous (all within Wales are held on the same day), there is typically no coordination across the four territories about the timing of local elections.

For both parties and voters there are certain benefits to simultaneous elections, driven primary by the economy of scale. Media outlets pay more attention to simultaneous elections because they are happening throughout a single territory. Parties are able to balance the needs of national and local campaigns, relying primarily on the national campaign in safer wards/ authorities and dedicating resources to those where contests are closer. Admittedly this targeting of marginal seats and paying less attention to safe seats has consequences for turnout and other forms of engagement (Middleton 2021). Such a distribution would not be possible were elections for individual local authorities held on different days. Media and party attention is relevant because it facilitates a greater capacity for information to be distributed, for voters to translate this into knowledge and, thus, for meaningful political engagement.

There are some drawbacks to simultaneous elections. A reliance on the national campaign and a national focus can inhibit attention to local issues. This is not a drawback of simultaneous elections *per se* so much as a consequence of cost-saving measures by parties being made more possible in simultaneous elections. The drawbacks of simultaneous elections are more obvious when elections are held across levels where different electoral systems are used, for it increases the risk of voter error. In 2007, for example, the Scottish Parliament elections using the Additional Member System (AMS) were held on the same day as the local elections, which, for the first time, were using STV as their electoral system. The number of spoiled ballots in the Scottish Parliament election jumped from around 12,000 in 2003 to almost 86,000 in 2007, which was attributed to a mix of voter confusion about electoral systems (this was, after all, only the third AMS election) and the fact that in two of Scotland's eight regions key ballot instructions were either abbreviated or left off the regional ballot (Carman et al. 2008). A post-election evaluation, the Gould Report, recommended never scheduling local and devolved elections on the same day as a way to minimise voter confusion and they have been split ever since (Electoral Commission 2008).

For researchers, simultaneous elections allow a direct comparison of preferences across levels, enabling them to see whether individuals are split-partisans, voting for party A in one type of election but party B in another. If contests are held on the same day, it allows researchers to control for other features (domestic political developments, changing economic conditions, changing international security contexts) that might naturally cause voters to switch from party A to party B over time. At the start of devolution, elections for local and devolved elections were vertically simultaneous within and across Scotland and Wales. Some of this simultaneity was baked in. Despite holding their referendums on devolution one week apart, Scottish and Welsh devolved elections have been held on the same day thereafter because both institutions had regular, fixed, four-year, then five-year, cycles.

Box 8.1   Spoiled ballots

Spoiled ballots in elections can stem from accident or design. Voters can lack the knowledge to vote appropriately, putting an x outside the box, or employing an x where the numbered ranking of candidates is required. In 2019, for example, of the 4,258 spoiled ballots cast in Northern Ireland, 2,472 were rejected for being unmarked or marked in such a way that the voter's intentions were not certain, 1,610 were rejected for supporting more than one candidate (as would be required using STV), 175 (170 in Upper Bann) were rejected for allowing the voter to be identified and one was rejected for not being an official ballot (Electoral Office of Northern Ireland 2000). In the 2022 devolved elections in Northern Ireland, by contrast, there were 11,074 rejected ballots, 5,234 rejected for being unmarked, 2,801 for failing to indicate a first preference, 2,375 for indicating more than one first preference and 664 (571 in Belfast West) for identifying voters. These figures show that a considerable source of ballot rejection in Northern Ireland is using STV in a Westminster election, and improperly using STV in the Assembly election.

It is also the case that voters can spoil their ballots intentionally, to express a lack of support for any of the parties or candidates on offer. Before the 2010 election, for example, *The Guardian* offered advice on *how to* spoil a ballot (Barnett 2010).

Table 8.2   Spoiled ballots as a percentage of votes cast, 2015–2019

	England	Wales	Scotland	NI
2021/2022 devolved	--	0.18%	0.11%	1.30%
2019 UK General Election	0.37%	0.33%	0.25%	0.53%
2017 UK General Election	0.24%	0.18%	0.15%	0.37%
2016 devolved	--	0.63%	0.40%	0.12%
2015 UK General Election	0.35%	0.21%	0.13%	0.66%

Source: Electoral Commission results datasets

Electoral reform since 2010

Electoral institutions are not static. Changed practices can bring new electoral systems and new rules of who can engage with formal politics. There have been various examples of unsuccessful reform. This includes a referendum on changing the UK electoral system to the Alternative Vote (AV). Seen as a Liberal Democrat price of entering the 2010 coalition government, the referendum occurred on the same day as devolved elections in Scotland, Wales and Northern Ireland. Over two-thirds of voters (67.9%) opposed the change. Support was highest in Northern Ireland, where 43.7% of voters backed the new system, then in Scotland (36.4%) and Wales (34.6%). In England, support was highest in Greater London (39.5%) but considerably lower everywhere else, ranging from 28% in the North East, East and West Midlands to 31% in Yorkshire and the South West. Other abortive efforts at electoral reform included a move to a 600-person House of Commons, attempted in two boundary reviews that were either halted or not implemented. Some efforts to modernise electoral institutions were more successful. The third attempted boundary review returned plans for a 650-person House, with strict attention to quotas for constituency size (and thus moving from 40 to 32 constituencies in Wales and 59 to 57 in Scotland), alongside the innovation that boundary proposals would be automatically accepted by Parliament.

When the Conservatives and Liberal Democrats formed a coalition in 2010, they introduced a Fixed-term Parliaments Bill, which would set parliamentary elections on a regular five-year cycle, something that had been included in the Liberal Democrat (and Labour) manifesto but not the Conservative one (Labour 2010; Liberal Democrats 2010). Fixed terms remove from prime ministers the ability to call an election, and thus remove from the governing party a key advantage to hold elections on a cycle determined purely by maximizing their chances of re-election. Such an advantage obviously translates to a structural disadvantage to opposition parties, who are also faced with uncertainty over the timing of candidate selection or when to incur the costs of publishing commitments or purchasing advertising time. Flexibility delivers parliaments of unequal length. In the postwar period, government tenure has varied from eight months (February and October 1974) to the full five years (between the 1992 and 1997 elections).

The Fixed-term Parliament Act 2011 allowed elections to be called outside their regular five-year cycle if two-thirds of MPs voted for an election or if the Government lost a vote of no confidence and a new government had not formed within a fortnight. While the 2015 election was held on cycle, the next was not expected until spring 2020. Prime Minister Theresa May called an early election in 2017 to resolve the deadlock within Parliament over Brexit. This was then backed by the necessary two-thirds of MPs. The Conservative manifesto promised to repeal the Fixed-term Parliament Act. In that election, the Conservatives lost their majority and May's successor, Boris Johnson, proved no more able to identify a way forward on Brexit. Johnson therefore called an early election in 2019 to 'get Brexit done'. Again, the Conservative Party promised to repeal the Fixed-term Parliament Act. A returned Conservative majority followed through on this, attributing the Act – rather than Brexit – to the political deadlock frustrating Parliament since 2016.

At the UK level, the most recent instance of electoral reform is the requirement to provide voter identification (ID) when casting a ballot in English local elections (first applied in 2023) and in UK general elections (first applied in 2024), thanks to the Elections Act 2022/ Voter Identification Regulations 2022. Since responsibility for devolved elections rests with the devolved legislatures, the rule does not apply for Scottish and Welsh elections. Voter ID was already required for Northern Ireland Assembly elections, where voters can apply for an electoral identity card if they lack the requisite other forms of identification. Electoral Commission analysis of the 2023 experience showed that 14,000 voters were turned away at the polling station because they did not have the proper ID and 4% of non-voters attributed their lack of engagement to a lack of ID (Electoral Commission 2023). Research conducted around the time the changes were first mooted suggested that 7.5% of voters were without the appropriate ID (Electoral Commission 2015). Notwithstanding such concerns, the change was introduced so as to limit electoral fraud.

Electoral fraud can take many forms but there are four main categories: registration (by falsely registering oneself to vote or registering ghost voters at properties); voting (by voting when one shouldn't or *where* one shouldn't, and acts of coercion around postal ballots); nomination (by nominating a candidate when one isn't allowed and by standing as a candidate when one is disqualified from doing so); and campaigning (by disobeying electoral rules related to campaign finance, including not declaring or under-declaring campaign donations). The voter identification rules were introduced specifically to address a sub-set of voting fraud, personation: attempting to be someone else so as to vote (or to vote multiple times).

Table 8.3   Electoral fraud allegations by type, 2013–2023

	Campaigning	Voting	Nomination	Registration	Other
2023	71	13	9	6	1
2022	64	20	9	6	1
2021	52	25	10	11	1
2020	4	0	0	10	1
2019	54	24	12	10	1
2018	48	21	15	15	0
2017	49	31	7	11	2
2016	37	43	9	8	2
2015	56	26	10	8	1
2014	38	27	14	15	6
2013	54	13	8	18	6

Source: Electoral Commission

As Table 8.3 shows, most allegations of electoral fraud relate to campaigning, which includes campaign finance. Voting allegations vary between 13% of total allegations and a high of 43% in 2016. Whether these result in conviction, though, is another matter. What we find with electoral fraud is that the vast majority result in no action or are resolved locally. A very, very small proportion, typically less than 2% of instances, result in police investigations and low single digits result in conviction. In the last ten years, there have been a total of 32 convictions for electoral fraud. These vary by territory, by electoral level (local, devolved, UK) and by type of fraud. The most frequent is nomination-related fraud, including falsifying signatures on ballot papers, with charges for candidates or election agents for the Conservatives (2019, 2018(2), 2013), Labour (2019, 2018), the Greens (2019, 2018), the United Kingdom Independence Party (2014, 2013(2)) and the Scottish National Party (SNP) (2013). This compares to four convictions in ten years for personation (see Table 8.4). This background, and the risk of disenfranchising voters who lack the required identification, suggests that the change has been something of a sledgehammer to crack a nut.

Theories of voting behaviour

Studies of British voting in textbooks tend to focus on voting behaviour in UK elections rather than devolved elections, with a particular focus on support for the main parties operating on mainland Britain. Analyses typically seek to explain support for these parties with

Table 8.4   Electoral fraud allegations, charges and convictions

	Allegations	Convictions
2023 English local elections	342	1 candidacy
2022 English local elections	179	1 personation
		1 campaigning
2022 Scottish local elections	0	
2022 Welsh local elections	0	
2022 Northern Ireland Assembly elections	1	
2021 English local elections	272	2 personation
		1 nomination
2021 Scottish Parliament	2	
2021 Welsh Senedd	8	
2019 English local elections	370	2 false voting
		2 nomination
		1 attempted ballot tampering
Euro	21	4 nomination
		1 registration/false voting
2018 England local	204	4 nomination
2017 UK General Election	334	2 imprint
		1 personation

Note: Local in England includes local councils, Mayor of London, local mayoralty and Police and Crime Commissioner.

reference to wider theories of vote choice. These include sociological models, which suggest that the sociological characteristics of individuals lead them to support certain parties over others, or economic models, which suggest that individuals back parties that will further their own financial interests (so-called pocketbook voting) or the nation's economy (sociotropic voting). Notwithstanding the value of such explanations, they work better when we assume that these are not zero-sum, and that different voters are influenced by different types of factors and features, depending on a range of experiences. This includes the wider societal and political events as they were socialised as citizens, in childhood and early adulthood, but also how they see themselves as citizens, and the various groups (social, political, national) to which they feel closest. One way of combining these various features is in a 'funnel of causality'. It implies that there is no single factor that influences vote choice, but that there are many factors at play, some related to one's socio-economic status, to the identities one holds, but also to the things that vary from election to election, including one's assessment of the main issues or party leaders.

When voters feel closer to a particular party, or when they think of themselves as a supporter of that party, it is described as their partisan identification. If that party identification endures over multiple elections, it is described as partisan alignment. The process by which individuals, or groups of individuals, become detached from the usual parties they support is called partisan *de*alignment. If individuals or groups of voters find new parties to support, it is a process called partisan *re*alignment.

A separate body of work examines issues of electoral performance. We know that different voters are persuaded by different aspects of political actors. Some support a party because of its leader, because, for example, they believe that individual will make the best prime minister; others cast their ballot because of their local candidate, because they want a particular person to serve as their constituency MP. In addition, voters can cast a ballot for parties either because they believe that party has the best policies on a particular issue, or because they believe that the party has performed best or will perform best as a government.

On policy, debates in the literature distinguish between spatial or directional models. Do voters assess where they are on an issue, evaluate where all parties stand and then cast a ballot for the most proximate party (as they do in proximity spatial models) or do they view issues in a binary manner and work out which party broadly supports their preferred option? Policies related to tax lend themselves to proximity methods, while issues such as constitutional reform, including Brexit or Scottish independence, work more as directional issues. For evaluations of performance, voters can undertake retrospective or prospective (future-oriented) evaluations. These are issues where 'handling it well' matters more than the specifics of individual policy positions. Management of the economy is seen as a classic instance of a valence issue, and in recent years Labour's weakness at the ballot box has been attributed to the fact that voters did not trust them to manage the economy well. In 2019, the Conservative Party sought to make the management of Brexit, specifically 'Getting Brexit done', a valence issue. In Scotland, the SNP has for years suggested that standing up for Scotland is the valence issue against which voters should judge its record.

Separate from each of these is a series of voting theories that apply to multi-level polities. The most oft-cited is a theory of election orderedness, which distinguishes between first-order or more important elections and second-order or less important elections. Orderedness is seen to be influenced by electoral stakes, determined in part by the legislative competence of the institution, whether the election will result in the election of a government that decides policy over areas that affect voters' lives. In their original formulation, Reif and Schmitt (1980) distinguished between national or state-wide elections, which they termed first-order contests, and European or local contests, which they deemed to be second-order contests. While the distinction might seem artificial, Reif and Schmitt argued that turnout would be lower in second-order contests, voters would be more likely to cast a ballot for smaller or frivolous parties, and/or would make their voting decisions on the basis of first-order political events, thus turning second-order elections into mini-referendums on the performance of first-order governments. This research sits alongside what we know about electoral timing, namely that parties at other levels can be hindered or helped by the electoral cycle of national governing parties.

A second category of multi-level voting theories relates to balance, and the specific efforts of voters to ensure that there is partisan balance across the system as a whole. Originally stemming from national-level elections in the USA, where voters were seen to make different choices across Presidential, Congressional and Senate contests so as to give no one party total control over all the institutions of the executive and legislature, it has since been applied in multi-level contexts as a way of understanding why voters reach different voting decisions at the ballot box.

Finally, we know that political environments below the level of the state can serve as 'small worlds' for political engagement, instilling in voters a distinct sense of trust, efficacy and partisanship. When sub-state polities are powerful, when they control considerable areas of policy, and when they control key agents of socialisation, such as the education system, or if there are regionalised media environments, it can lead individuals to develop a split-level citizenship or partisanship, evaluating different parties based on separate performance at multi-levels. The knowledge requirements for this are high, for they require voters to identify the policy areas controlled by different institutions so as to identify the appropriate actors to blame and reward. Whether these conditions are present in the UK is something that we discuss below.

'British' voting behaviour

Analyses of British voting behaviour typically begin with the postwar pattern of class voting, in which working-class voters backed the Labour Party and middle-class voters backed the Conservatives. While this was true at an individual level, it was also the case that areas where a particular class of voters were present exerted a contextual effect on all. In this way, middle-class voters in working-class areas were also more likely to back the Labour Party, and vice versa.

Features that are currently described as important elements of British political life were often in fact either short lived or limited in scope. In the case of class voting, we have to remember that the electoral franchise was very different from what we know now. While the 1832 Reform Act extended suffrage beyond the fewer than 5,000 males able to vote in 1831 (of 2.6 million adults), the work of Chartists and the Reform League failed to achieve adult male suffrage in either the 1867 or 1884 Reform Acts, although piecemeal changes ensured more equal rules between towns and rural areas. Universal male suffrage was not achieved until the 1918 Representation of the People Act, thanks in part to political pressure bought by campaigners for female suffrage. When we speak of class voting in Britain, we therefore have to remember that much of the working class could not vote at all until the years after the First World War. Class voting reached its peak in the decades after the Second World War, where heightened class consciousness and the precarity of social and economic conditions combined with a growing engagement of the government to enter fields of social policy that had previous been left to the church. In this context, Labour advocated the advance of the social welfare state while the Conservatives emphasised the importance of social responsibility.

The decline of class voting in Britain is typically attributed to four sources. First, increasingly porous boundaries between classes relate both to social mobility and to the decreasing salience of class markers. Attributed to the decline of traditional industry and the rise of the services sector, rising educational attainment and economic mobility, this is partly a story of a shrinking working class in the UK and partly a blurring of the signals around class itself, which made the easy identification of which class a person is in rather more difficult. Second, as class has become more difficult to detect and/or less static, new sociological groups, including those around other identities, such as national groups, have become more important drivers of political preferences. Third, new issues facing governments and voters are less easy to plot on the economic left–right dimension. This includes attitudes to immigration, European integration, climate change as well as post-materialism, including citizen engagement or having a say. For example, one can oppose European integration from a typically right-wing, free-market approach, but one can also oppose it from a typically left-wing perspective, as a specific instance of a protectionist continental project that limits market access to developing countries. Likewise, one can be anti-EU membership because it fosters high levels of immigration, but one can also oppose EU membership because it depresses immigration from the rest of the world. Finally, party behaviour has also changed. The oft-employed example is New Labour's move to the centre, away from its socialist roots, which was exemplified by the party's debate over Clause IV in the party's constitution. This was not just a UK debate, but part of a wider shift exploring the third way, identifying advantages from both the right and left.

The other change to party behaviour here is the increasingly sophisticated targeting of voters based on data-driven campaigning technologies, which means that appeals to broad groups are no longer necessary. With greater information, parties can target specific streets or highly specific socio-economic groups defined by their shopping habits or online practices, to reach undecided voters or those who they believe might be persuaded to support the party.

While class as such might be a less obvious driver of vote choice, we know that features that often correlate with class retain an influence over voting. Both education and income, even once we control for other characteristics, such as age, ethnicity or religion, influence vote choice, with higher-income voters still backing the Conservatives, those on lower incomes voting Labour, and those with higher levels of education tending to back the Liberal Democrats.

In addition, while class identities might have decreased in salience, other identities, including national identities, remain influential, with English identifiers being far more likely to vote Reform or UKIP or Conservative, British identifiers in Scotland and Wales more likely to vote Conservative, and Welsh identifiers, particularly if they also speak Welsh, more likely to vote for Plaid Cymru. In Northern Ireland, there is a near perfect correlation between national identity and party preferences, with British identifiers backing the DUP and Ulster Unionist Party (UUP), Irish identifiers voting Sinn Fein or SDLP, and those with dual identities or describing themselves as 'Northern Irish' more likely to back Alliance.

Multi-level voting in a plurinational state

As the example of class voting shows, the relationships that the voting literature tells us to expect work slightly differently in different parts of the UK. This speaks to a wider issue, namely that the study of British voting has often underestimated the variation across the four parts of the UK (or at least the three parts of Britain) and the multi-level reality of both parties and voters. A truly multi-level analysis of voting in Britain requires four major corrections: there are four electorates, not one; party competition differs across the electorates; voting explanations are varied; and orderedness and primary political communities differ.

Four electorates not one

It is not uncommon to note that the four territories of the UK have different party systems and different party preferences. While all are multi-party systems, the number of parties contesting seats varies, as does the axis of party competition. The presence of nationalist parties in Scotland and Wales (SNP, Plaid Cymru) and an entirely different party system in Northern Ireland, with Irish and British nationalist parties and the Alliance, means that the dominant Conservative–Labour battle that dominates English coverage is not in fact animating electoral competition in the rest of the UK. In addition, political parties that in England are preferred by English (as opposed to British) national identifiers, such as UKIP or the Brexit Party or Reform, each have enjoyed lower levels of popularity outside England, and speak to a party system that is distinct by design not just default. The boundary between the English and Welsh party system is more porous, a reflection of the fact that there is greater population movement between England and Wales than between any other two parts of the United Kingdom. Figures 8.1–8.4 illustrate this point.

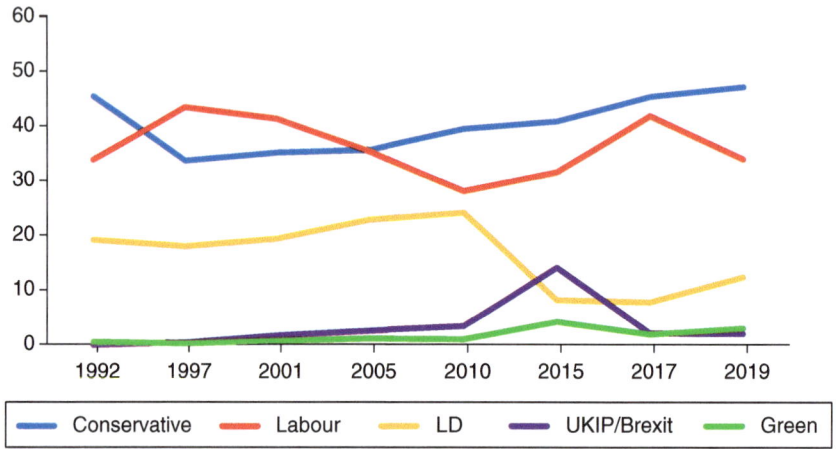

Figure 8.1   Electoral support in England, 1992–2019

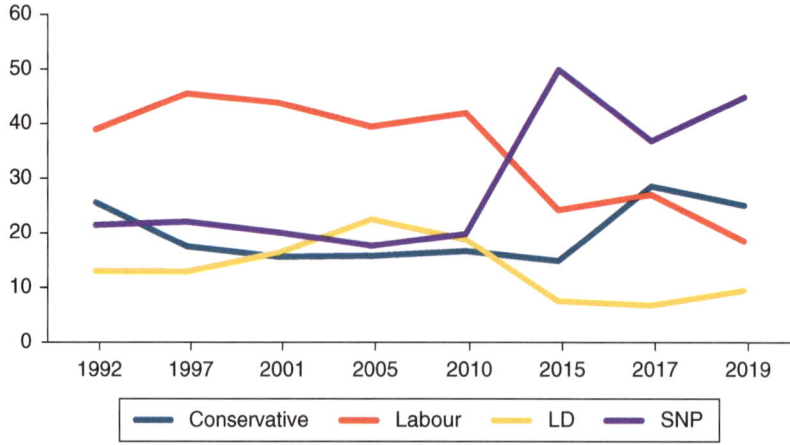

Figure 8.2   Electoral support in Scotland, 1992–2019

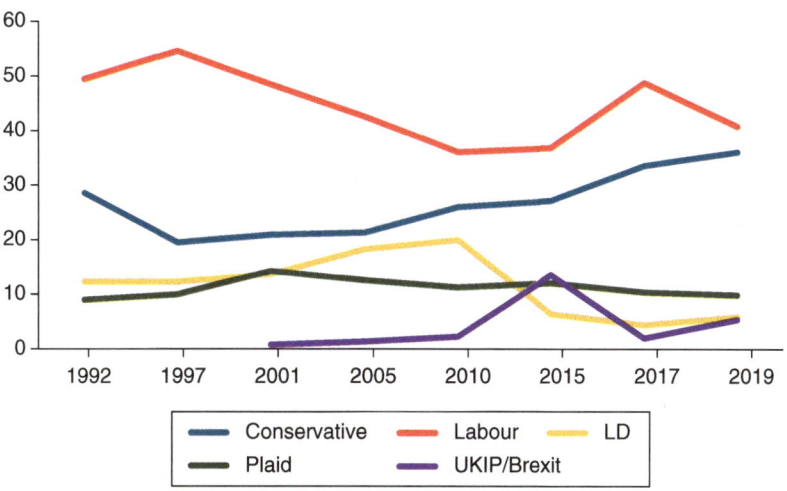

Figure 8.3   Electoral support in Wales, 1992–2019

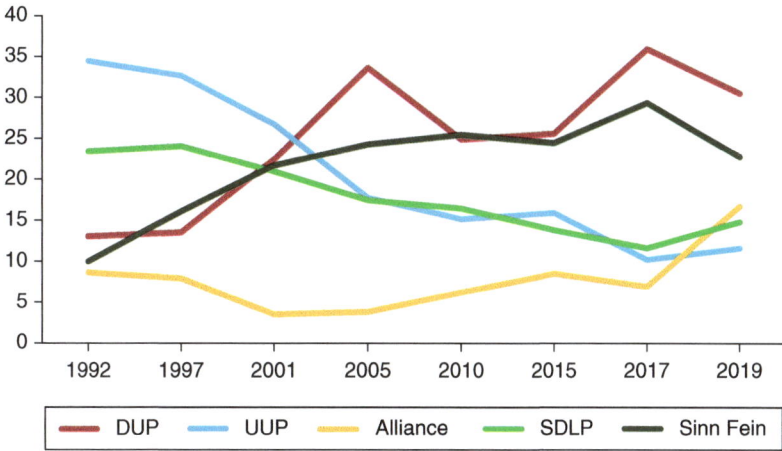

Figure 8.4   Electoral support in Northern Ireland, 1992–2019

In recent elections, a different party has earned the most votes and seats in each of the four parts of the UK: Conservatives in England, DUP in Northern Ireland, Welsh Labour in Wales and SNP in Scotland. But it is not just that the most popular parties in the four locations have been different, but that in each of them, the trends and patterns of party competition are different. We are used to talking about tumultuous elections in the UK, and the Labour majority in 1997 is one particular example. And yet if we look at Northern Ireland, 1997 looked pretty much like business as usual, with only a slight rise for Sinn Fein to distinguish it from 1992. In Wales, we see Labour dominance in each election since 1992, widening in 1997 but with a healthy Labour lead throughout the last 40 years, an unsurprising fact perhaps since Labour has won every election in Wales since 1922. Even in Scotland, we see a pattern of clear Labour dominance, followed by a period of SNP dominance after 2010. The 1997 election in Scotland looked much the same as had the one in 1992. This is important because the story often told about UK elections is an English story. It is perhaps not surprising given that England represents such a large proportion of the population, and thus the electorate, and thus seats. But it is worth pointing out that what is true for England, while obviously almost never true for Northern Ireland, is almost always not true for Scotland or Wales either. This is true for a range of issues – in the referendum to leave the European Union, British identifiers voted Remain in England, but voted Leave everywhere else.

Take, for example, the rise of UKIP and the recent performance of the Reform Party. There are many ways to measure the impact of a party on electoral politics. One is to ignore its electoral fortunes and focus on how it frames debate. In this we can say that UKIP had a transformative effect on British politics because, by focusing on standing up for English interests, opposing European integration and criticising mass migration, it encouraged the Conservative Party to adopt these views as well so as to avoid losing votes on their right flank. In this respect, UKIP's influence extends beyond its electoral successes, but it is also the case that this was, for most if its time, electorally, a negligible fringe party outside England and Wales, losing 100% of their deposits in Scotland and 70% of their deposits in Northern Ireland in 2015 (see Table 8.5).

Table 8.5   Electoral support for UKIP and Reform, 2015 and 2024

	UKIP	England	Scotland	Wales	Northern Ireland
2015 candidates	624/650	533	41	40	10
Deposits lost	80	32	41	0	7
2024 candidates	609/650	521	57	31	0
Deposits lost	32	22	10	0	NA

Differentiated party competition

Second, we must acknowledge the important variations in party message and tone across Britain. While constitutionally the Greens and Liberal Democrats are the most organisationally distinct across the UK, it is also the case that UK-wide Scottish and Welsh variants of parties hold different views on the Union, and hold different positions in party space in their domestic nations. These variations are caused by the (perceived) dominant values of the electorates in which they contest seats, but also the policies pursued by and electoral support for their main rivals. Labour offers a useful example. The Welsh Labour Party has been the party of government since devolution began, but has also won every Westminster election in Wales for over 100 years. It is perceived to be unquestionably Welsh in allegiance and identity, critical of different aspects of UK policy, including on transport, and actively campaigning for constitutional change, including the additional devolution of justice and policing to Wales. Its main rivals are the Conservatives in Wales.

By contrast, Scottish Labour is by some measures far more unionist in outlook than UK Labour. Its supporters are most likely to believe that there is only one nation, the British nation. By virtue of the fact that its main rivals are the SNP, its opposition centres more on the issues that divide these two parties (the constitution) rather than the considerable shared views on economic and social life. As a result, Labour and the Conservatives banded together in the 2014 referendum to campaign against constitutional change. Constitutional politics in Scotland has made bedfellows of two parties that, in a wider British context, are each other's main rivals.

UK Labour lies between these two poles. On the constitutional issue, UK Labour Party leaders were far more sympathetic to the holding of a second independence referendum in Scotland than were Scottish Labour leaders. The origins of these differences are a bit like fragment cultures: the nature of party competition encourages parties to emphasise or de-emphasise certain aspects of policy or understandings of the state, and as a result they come to occupy different positions on the political spectrum.

This fact is typically ignored in studies of voting behaviour in Great Britain. Expert surveys typically code British parties on a single position rather than with a single location for each part of the UK. This is more than an interesting point about nuance. It changes the decision-making calculus in different parts of the UK because parties aligned with different ingroups or outgroups are different in different parts of the state.

Differentiated voting explanations

If we put one and two together, it is no surprise that the drivers of voting decisions across the UK may vary from territory to territory. UK political scientists have typically shied away from generating different models of vote choice for different parts of the UK. The typical exclusion of Northern Ireland because of its difference has not led to a consistent effort to disaggregate within the island of Britain. This is important because the use of (understandably) England-dominated samples that lead to 'British' explanations of vote choice are rarely checked to see if they travel equally well outside England. While some explanations of vote choice are both English and British – and indeed throughout much of the twentieth century this was indeed the case – increasing partisan divergence should have prompted far greater efforts to identify different drivers of voting behaviour. Two examples prove useful.

First, the different Brexit results in the four UK territories (England and Wales for Leave, Scotland and Northern Ireland for Remain) did not lead to a series of papers examining territorial differentiation. Instead, British explanations about left-behind voters or the losers of globalisation were assumed to work equally well across the UK, and Scotland and Northern Ireland respondents, if they were included in the analysis at all, were captured by dummy variables that sought to absorb the different possible drivers of vote choice there. Each was treated as an aberrant black box, with little effort to uncover *why* this was the case. As a result, we know little of why the same types of voters, with similar views of globalisation and immigration in Scotland and Northern Ireland, opted to vote Remain.

Related to this, efforts to identify the role played by national identity highlighted the impact of British identity as a driver of Leave support. If we compare British identity to sub-state identity, and if we disaggregate across the four territories of the UK, what we see is that British identifiers voted Remain in England, but voted Leave in Scotland, Wales and Northern Ireland. This is important because England and Wales both voted Leave, and yet there were different patterns between Leave support and national identity. In part, it stems from the different baskets of values and the different understandings of the state held by British identifiers in England, Scotland, Wales and Northern Ireland. Efforts to analyse British voting should have as one of their core missions the duty to check whether British explanations apply equally across Britain.

Orderedness and primary political communities

Earlier we discussed the work of Reif and Schmitt (1980), which distinguishes between first- and second-order elections. In a UK context, this has been assumed to mean that Westminster contests will be first-order contests, while devolved and local elections will be second-order contests. Certainly, there is more evidence to suggest that local elections are second-order contests, but in devolved contests a growing body of work challenges this assumption (Jeffery and Hough 2009; Jeffery and Schakel 2013). We know that for some voters, particularly those with strong sub-state identities, interest in devolved elections is higher than for Westminster elections, devolved partisan preferences influence how they will later cast a ballot in UK elections, and debates internal to the territory, including about its constitutional future, exert a greater influence on vote choice than attitudes to reserved policy. This would seem to suggest that we might think of two first-order contests for some voters, particularly for those who would describe their sub-state nation or territory as their primary political community. The automatic assumption that Westminster contests are first-order and devolved are second-order is therefore something that should be routinely examined to determine whether it varies over time and across voters. The same sort of idea holds for debates about the centre and periphery, which seem to sit uneasily with the way devolved voters evaluate their political worlds. Devolved voters don't necessarily see themselves living at the periphery of British political debate, but at the centre of Scottish, Welsh and Northern Irish political worlds.

Does all of this suggest that the UK is an ideal context for multi-level voting? Not quite. Earlier we discussed the pre-existing conditions necessary for split-level partisanship, including a knowledge of what is devolved and reserved so that voters can undertake separate evaluations of blame and reward at different territorial scales. We have reason to believe that such conditions might be lacking in the UK. First, we know that knowledge of legislative competence is patchy across the UK. Voters in Scotland, Wales and Northern Ireland are more likely to be able to identify reserved areas than devolved ones. During the Covid pandemic, after a year of television broadcasts discussing the Scottish government's response to the health pandemic, one-third of the Scottish electorate did not know that health was devolved. But it is also the case that knowledge of devolution in England is low. In part, this is explained by the dual role of the UK Government as government of the whole of the UK and as government of England for policy areas that are devolved in Scotland, Wales or Northern Ireland. This dual role is typically hidden, rarely highlighted by government departments or government ministers (for an analysis of how this operated in Covid, see Henderson 2023). During elections, political parties willingly blur the lines between devolved and reserved competence, complaining about the SNP's management of education or Welsh Labour's management of health during Westminster contests when the electoral outcome will not influence the party deciding education or health policy in devolved areas. Broadcasters are little better, holding election debates with devolved politicians, none of whom is standing for election. As a result, we see a lot of cross-level contamination during UK electoral contests, all of which suggests that the UK is perhaps a challenging context for the development of split-level citizenship.

Case Study 8.1

Covid and elections

The Covid-19 pandemic affected many aspects of our daily lives in the UK and elections were no exception. Lockdowns, which began in March 2020, were still in place in various forms when English local elections were to have taken place on 7 May 2020. The Coronavirus Act delayed these elections until 6 May 2021, the same day as the elections in the devolved Scottish Parliament and Welsh Senedd. Different legislative competence meant that council by-elections had taken place in Scotland (UK Parliament 2020).

 The Scottish Election Study (SES) asked respondents both before and after the election how they felt about attending the polling station during the 2021 election. Before the election, 84% of respondents reported that they felt 'not anxious'. After the election, 98% reported that they'd felt safe visiting the polling station. When asked about the range of precautionary measures put in place, more than four in five reported that there were screens separating the poll workers from voters (85%), that hand sanitiser was readily available (88%) and that appropriate social distancing was maintained (93%) (Scottish Election Study (SES) 2021).

Research in Focus

The 2024 General Election

The 2024 General Election changed the electoral landscape in three ways. First, it delivered for the first time in more than a decade, a similar winning party in three parts of Britain, with Labour earning the most votes in Scotland, Wales and England, albeit with different parties in second place. Second, it was a volatile election, with large constituency-level swings in support not just from the Conservatives to Labour, as one might expect in an election in which Labour won, but also from the Conservatives to Reform. Such swings were akin to those seen in Scotland from Labour to the SNP in the 2015 UK General Election. Third, the election is noteworthy because, in the aggregate, Labour support increased by less than 2 per cent. As a result, 2024 offers a new example for the false majority literature. 2024 delivered a majority with the smallest percentage of votes, delivered the most disproportional in UK history, offered the smallest combined vote share for the top two parties and the second lowest turnout since the 19th century. Rather than an act of collective enthusiasm for Labour, 2024 is better understood as the total collapse of support for the Conservative Party and an indictment of First-Past-the-Post.

 This was also a difficult election to predict. New constituencies, and the loss of seats in both Scotland and Wales, made it difficult to track swings. A late census in Scotland in particular also meant that the level of demographic and socio-economic data typically available to analyse constituencies and their likely results was lacking. Perhaps for that reason the MRP models of constituency contests predicted a wide range of outcomes, with anticipated Labour seat totals in the high 300s to the low 500s.

(Continued)

Vote choice can be explained by anti-incumbency effects. This was an anti-incumbent election in a straightforward sense that the Conservative government was delivered something of a kicking to the tune of a 20-point drop in support. Explanations for a loss of support include the perception that they were divided, they had an unpopular leader and they'd lost the argument on handling the economy. But there is a multi-level story here too. Both Conservative (down 12 points) and SNP (down 15 points) support declined in Scotland, marking a shift away from the parties at the constitutional poles of the independence debate. In Northern Ireland it saw the DUP (down 9 points) replaced as the largest party by Sinn Fein. In Wales, Labour has won every UK election since 1922 so it comes as no surprise that it did so again, but against a pattern of rising support for Labour Welsh Labour saw a decrease in its fortunes against a surge from both Plaid (up 5) and Reform (up 12) though the electoral system translated that into a nine-seat gain. The Conservatives lost all 12 of their Welsh seats. Reform's rise was remarkable but also regionally varied, earning 15 per cent in England, 17 per cent in Wales, but only seven per cent in Scotland, a figure which would put them on track to win seats in the next devolved elections in 2026. Reform's performance could be attributed to dissatisfaction with the implementation of Brexit, but it is best understood as a sign of dissatisfaction with the Conservative Party, if not conservatism, much in the same way that declining SNP support should not be read as decreased support for independence.

The same winning party in Scotland, Wales and England masks territorial variation in gains and losses. Labour's fortunes rose most in Scotland were almost static in England and fell in Wales. SNP support decreased in Scotland but Plaid support rose in Wales. The only consistent result is the two-digit decrease in support for the Conservatives across Britain, suggesting that 2024 was the election that the Conservatives lost, rather than the election that Labour won.

Conclusion

Voting in the UK takes place in a resolutely multi-level world, marked by considerable diversity in the ward sizes, electoral systems and political parties available to parties. As devolved legislatures acquired the legislative competence to alter their electoral arrangements various initiatives of electoral reform have further differentiated the structure and rules under which elections take place across the UK. Different electoral contexts sit alongside different party systems and partisan preferences and for much of the past decade the four parts of the UK have preferred different political parties. While diversity might be one of the defining features of UK electoral behaviour, that diversity has less often occupied scholars. Recognising that the four different electorates make different choices – or sometimes make similar choices but for very different reasons – is a necessary step to understanding voting in the UK as a whole.

On the one hand, the 2024 UK General Election might seem to contradict this narrative of diversity. After all, voters in Scotland, Wales and England each provided greater electoral support to the Labour Party than other rivals. The partisan balance in each remains markedly different but it is also the case that the 2024 election highlighted the multi-level reality of UK electoral life. Parties leading devolved administrations faced criticism for their handling of devolved policy areas, even though a UK election would not remove them from office. UK broadcasters hosted debates with devolved politicians who were not running for office. Twenty-five years after devolution the political ecosystem has adapted unevenly to its multi-level reality. In this, the 2024 UK General Election was business as usual.

Summary

- UK voters operate in a multi-level political system in which competition, parties and calculations are different at different levels.
- UK political science is now catching up with the idea of a multi-level electorate but it can still be tempting to substitute English for British when studying elections.
- The multi-level UK is still poorly understood even by government departments.

Recommended and further reading

- Denver, D. and Johns, R. (2022) *Elections and Voters in Britain*. Basingstoke: Palgrave. This classic text is updated frequently by two of the UK's most accomplished psephologists and is sensitive to the multi-level context of voters.
- There are two long-running book series on UK elections: the *Britain Votes* series, the most recent of which is Tonge, J., Wilks-Heeg, S. and Thompson, L. (eds) (2020) *Britain Votes: The 2019 General Election*. Oxford: Oxford University Press; and *The British General Election of …* series, the most recent of which is Ford, R., Bale, T., Jennings, W. and Surridge, P. (eds.) (2021) *The British General Election of 2019*. Basingstoke: Palgrave Macmillan. Each contains an edited collection of chapters covering the main parties, territories and key themes, and each offers a detailed account of elections within the wider context of British voting.

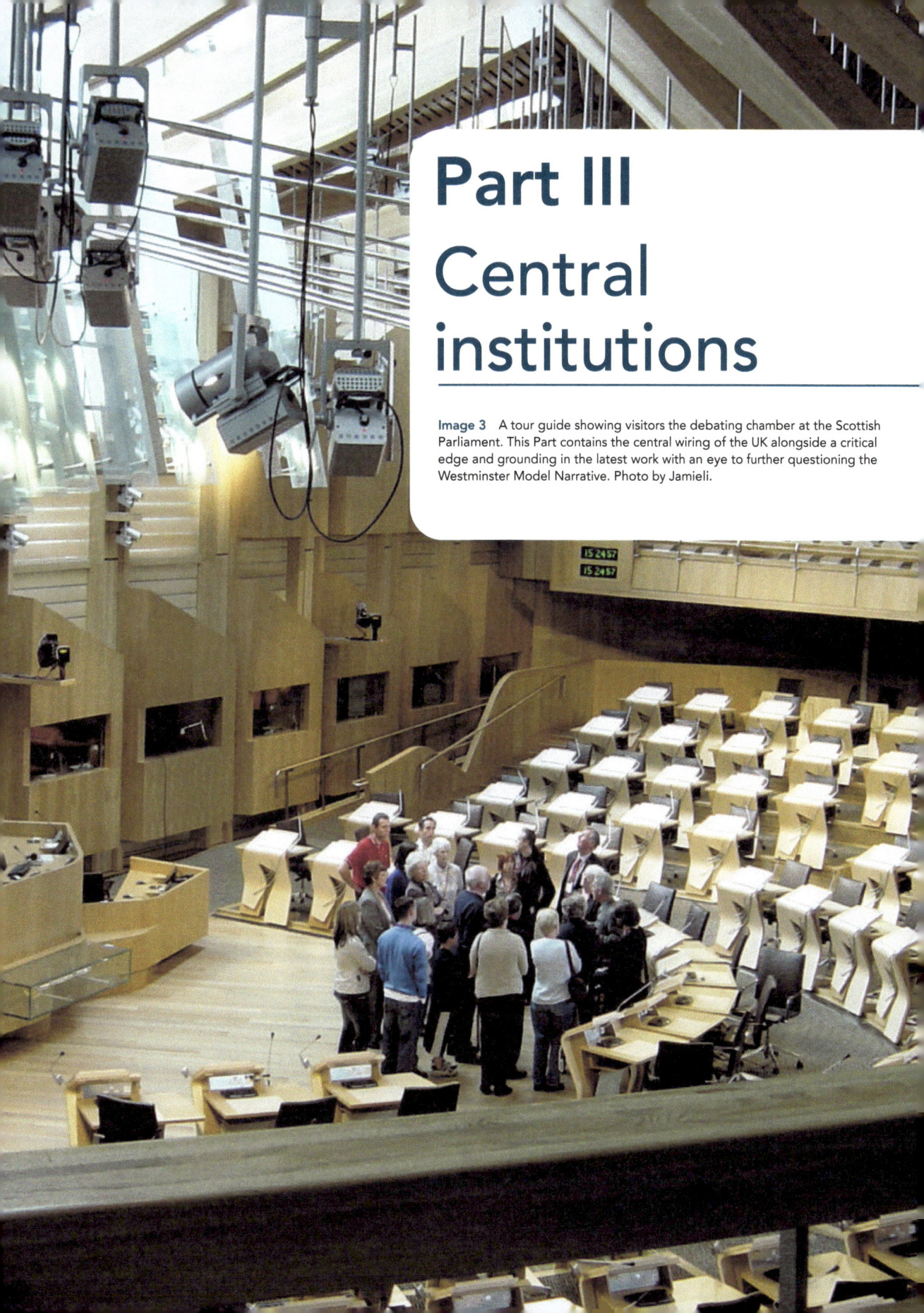

Part III
Central institutions

Image 3 A tour guide showing visitors the debating chamber at the Scottish Parliament. This Part contains the central wiring of the UK alongside a critical edge and grounding in the latest work with an eye to further questioning the Westminster Model Narrative. Photo by Jamieli.

Chapter 9
The UK constitution
Alan Convery and Asanga Welikala

What will this chapter tell me?

- This chapter outlines the key features of the UK constitution and how they have evolved in recent years. The UK's constitution is not contained in a single document and is drawn from several sources.
- Stable understandings of the UK's constitution have been replaced in recent years with much more debate and contestation. Parliamentary sovereignty remains the central organising principle at the heart of the constitution, but it is under pressure on several fronts (from devolution to conceptions of popular sovereignty during the implementation of Brexit).
- The UK no longer has its old constitutional order, but nor has it moved to a completely new or planned alternative. It finds itself somewhere between old and new understandings of its constitution.
- The biggest shake-ups of constitutional understandings occurred during the constitutional reforms of the Labour Governments (1997–2010) and the process of implementing Brexit from 2016. Several thorny questions about the nature of the constitution suddenly needed answers in short order. That process upset some delicate compromises and resulted in the constitution becoming a major political issue.
- Further constitutional reforms are likely to come through the elite consensus about the need for further regional devolution in England.

What do I need to know?

- Most countries have a foundational constitutional document, but the UK does not. Unlike other European countries, it also does not have a clear post-1945 break in its constitutional development.
- The UK is a multi-national state but different parts of the UK entered at different times, for different reasons and on different terms.
- The dominant organising perspective for the UK constitution in the twentieth century was the concept of parliamentary sovereignty – the idea that the UK Parliament possesses ultimate power and can make or unmake any law.

Introduction

Vernon Bogdanor (2009) likened the development of the UK's constitution to a slow simmering after the 1960s followed by a coming to a boil during the Labour Government's reforms in 1997–2010. The period after 2016 for the UK constitution may be likened to turning the temperature up even higher: a divisive referendum and the heat of political controversy tested the limits of devolution, sovereignty, secession and the rule of law itself. This chapter examines the origins and development of the UK's constitution. We try to show how contemporary debates reflect much deeper fissures in the UK's constitutional arrangements and why previously dormant abeyances have now taken on huge significance.

The traditional way to think about the UK's constitution involves the centrality of the idea of parliamentary sovereignty. We agree that it is a foundational element of the UK's arrangements.

However, we suggest that it needs to be more carefully unpacked by students of UK politics. Uncritical appeals to parliamentary sovereignty often mask more than they reveal and students need to be able to examine the unspoken assumptions behind its use. We conclude by suggesting that 'constitutional unsettlement' (Walker 2014) is probably here to stay.

The basic architecture

Before delving into debates about the nature of the UK constitution, it is useful to clarify the basic architecture of the UK state. Parliament is central to the UK state, government, and indeed (for many elites) the UK's sense of itself. Parliament in the UK exists in three parts: the House of Commons, the House of Lords and the monarch. Acts of Parliament, the highest form of law and the greatest source of new law in the UK, are agreements between all three of these parts. The Crown-in-Parliament therefore sits at the apex of the UK constitution (Figure 9.1).

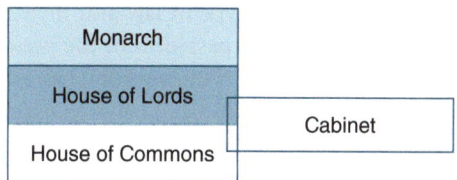

Figure 9.1   The core of the UK state

Another essential feature is the fusion of the legislature and the executive. Parliament and government are not the same thing. However, in the UK, the political executive (the government) is drawn from Parliament. To be a government minister (a member of the executive branch in the UK), you must be a member of either the House of Commons or the House of Lords. In the nineteenth century, Walter Bagehot famously referred to this as the 'efficient secret' of the UK constitution (Bagehot 1867). To be asked by the monarch to form a government means that you can command the confidence of the House of Commons. You can therefore pass legislation and get things done because you have a majority that enables you to do so. The cabinet is therefore the 'buckle', according to Bagehot, that joins authority between these two branches of government.

The UK is a constitutional monarchy. That means that the monarch is bound by conventions and defers in all matters to the elected government. That does not mean that monarchs are entirely without influence, but they leave the day-to-day running of the state to ministers. Their role is more symbolic and cultural.

The UK is also a union state (Keating 2021), rather than a unitary state. It is a plurinational entity that is made up of four distinct nations which joined at different times, by different means and on different terms. As Gamble (2006: 21) points out: 'The British state began as the English state, and the expansion of this state throughout the territorial space of Britain and Ireland created the United Kingdom.' However, the expansion of the English state was not a uniformly incorporating process. It did not entirely efface sub-state cultures or governing arrangements. Even before the introduction of devolution in 1999, therefore, the UK was not a pure unitary state.

One of the things that distinguishes the UK's constitutional arrangements is that some parts are 'very, very old' (Tomkins 2009: 244). They were not designed from scratch; rather, they have evolved over time. Democratic processes have gradually been grafted on to pre-democratic institutions. The core elements of what we now recognise as the modern UK state were in place by the beginning of the twentieth century, decades before the UK became a full democracy (Judge 1993: 26).

The gradual impact of all these developments served to establish the modern constitutional settlement as the twentieth century dawned, which can be summarised in the following terms. Constitutional monarchy was established by the abolition of certain of the monarch's royal prerogatives and the line of royal succession being decided not by custom but by Parliament. Parliament became a co-participant in the government of the state, sometimes as an inhibitor of executive power and a guardian of civil liberty, and at other times as a facilitator of the objectives of the state. The ultimate authority of the state reposed in and was exercised by the composite institution of the Crown-in-Parliament, and its will was legally expressed in the form of statutes. This was the highest type of law and the Crown-in-Parliament could make or unmake any law. Executive authority passed from the person of the Monarch to the office of the Crown, on behalf of which ministers drawn from, representative of and responsible to Parliament exercised that authority. The relationship between executive and legislature came to be governed by the principle of collective cabinet and individual ministerial responsibility to Parliament. Independent and impartial courts became the upholder of both the common law and the law made by Acts of Parliament, holding the government to legal account and protecting the rights of the individual.

It must be noted that the development of the UK state has not been a linear path towards democratic constitutional monarchy. It has arrived here via some randomness and contingency. Moreover, until at least the 1990s, political violence was a common feature of the UK state in relation to Northern Ireland.

Uncodified but not entirely unwritten

In most countries, there is a fundamental legal document called a 'constitution'. This document will typically set out the principles on which the state is founded, the structure of its government, the basic rules of governing, the territorial organisation of the state, and the rights of the people. There are of course many other principles, rules and practices concerning the use of public power that are not found in the constitution. But it is still broadly true to say that the legal document called the constitution is the starting place for gaining an understanding of the most fundamental political features of most countries.

The UK is an outlier in this regard. The UK does not have a single, legal document that is understood as stating the fundamental rules and principles of the state. This may lead some to conclude that the UK does not have a constitution. This is true in one sense, but is misleading in another. If the conclusion is to be taken as true, then we must take the concept of 'constitution' as something that must possess certain attributes before it can be described as such. Those attributes are that a constitution must be in the form of a single written document that establishes not just the basic rules of politics, but constitutes the state itself, and as such is prior to and supreme over all other institutions, offices, laws and practices of the state. Moreover, such a constitution is taken as the legal expression of a universal understanding of what a polity is, to mean a community of self-determining individuals possessed of liberty and reason, who agree terms of a social contract to achieve certain common purposes through government, but who retain their right to withdraw their consent to that arrangement if it violates their liberty beyond reason.

There is no doubt that this modern sense of the concept of 'constitution' is the most widespread understanding of that concept in the world today. This is because, in the modern period of world history (i.e. since the eighteenth century), most countries have undergone historical processes, such as revolutions or decolonisation, that have fundamentally reconstituted their political arrangements with a constitution in this sense. However, the upheavals, such as religious reformation, political revolution and civil war that shaped the UK took place at an earlier period in history, such that its constitution today retains characteristics of an older concept of 'constitution' that has been deliberately rejected in most other countries. So it is the case that, in the UK, that older idea of 'constitution', in which tradition and organicism play a greater part, continues to be a good way of describing what obtains in the present.

The early eighteenth-century statesman Henry St John, the first Viscount Bolingbroke, provided a famous definition of 'constitution' in 1734. He wrote:

> By constitution we mean ... that assemblage of laws, institutions, and customs, derived from certain fixed principles of reason, directed to certain fixed objects of public good, that compose the general system, according to which the community hath agreed to be governed. (Armitage 1997: 88)

This continues to have relevance today. Bolingbroke's method is descriptive and empirical. He takes the 'assemblage of laws, institutions, and customs' as they are. They are an accretion of social experience, the embodiment of a human community's responses to the evolving requirements of living together in a settled place. The authority and legitimacy of institutions and law do not rest upon the rational quality of political principles enshrined in a legal document at some founding moment of the polity, but because they have evolved within the political community since time immemorial. When, in this view, custom is advanced as the main basis of the community's governing arrangements, it suggests a culture in which the collective wisdom of social experience is taken seriously. Laws and institutions, developed incrementally according to customary habits, reflect the compromises that human beings make when they have to cooperate as a community, but at the same time preserve some measure of liberty for themselves.

Yet Bolingbroke's reference to reason, principles, objects and the public good implies that the form and content of law and institutions are always amenable to change by human agency, according to prudential need. We can use human reason – which is conditioned over time by changes in a society's perception of what is right, wrong, good, bad or reasonable – to assess existing arrangements, and to change them if there is good reason to do so. But the scope of constitutional change is defined by two crucial limitations. First, a society's government must be for its public good and society consents to government only on that basis. The reference to the common good has important normative implications for the idea of constitutional government in this conception. Government can only be constitutional (i.e. accepted not merely as legally valid but as morally legitimate) if it serves the common good as opposed to the private interests of rulers. It excludes from the category of constitutional government unlimited, authoritarian, corrupt and self-serving government, even if such government enjoys the support of the majority or promotes the liberty of the individual.

Second, and more impliedly, we might say that Bolingbroke's view of constitution is sceptical about radical experiments in political reconstitution based on this or that theory of the ideal political state, and it sees the political as a limited sphere and just one among many facets of human life. The constitution is never perfect – it cannot be so because it is a product of imperfect human beings – but through a combination of reason, experience and sentiment, a society may constantly strive for its improvement. Bolingbroke's 'general system' is composed of legal rules, political principles and moral sentiments, which implies that neither a written legal document nor sharp separations between the political and the social aspects of the community are essential to this understanding of a constitution.

There are several implications of this conception of constitution for our understanding of how the British constitution operates in practice. As there is no single written legal document called the constitution, the UK constitution's sources are many (discussed below). Those sources provide constitutional rules that are both legal and political in character. Some may be enforced by the courts, while the observance of others is entirely dependent on political actors. While certain formal laws (Acts of Parliament or statutes) do contain important constitutional rules, there is no clear distinction between what is a constitutional statute and what is not. Since there is no legal constitution enjoying a higher status among the laws of the country, a statute of a constitutional character as well as an ordinary statute is made and unmade in the same way by Parliament. Even an ordinary statute of a later date may be held by the courts to have impliedly repealed an earlier constitutional statute. The courts have no power to invalidate an Act of Parliament on the grounds that it is in breach of a higher law. All this gives the UK constitution a fluid and flexible character, in contrast to other countries where the legal constitution is often difficult to amend and amendment requires special legislative procedures.

If this traditional rather than modern conception is what describes the nature of the British constitution, which thus means that there is no single written legal document that authoritatively lays down fundamental rules and principles, where are we to find it? What are its sources?

Sources of the UK constitution

There are four main sources of legal and political rules that comprise the UK constitution. These are: custom, statute, conventions and case law.

The Royal Prerogative

These are the powers used by the executive that derive from ancient customs and the medieval constitution that still survive. Their origins lie in the time before constitutional monarchy, when the monarch was the actual ruler of the realm. Over time, the role of the monarch in government has become largely ceremonial, and the prerogative powers are exercised by ministers and, under their direction, by civil servants. Notwithstanding their ancient provenance, prerogative powers continue to be a significant source of legal powers for the executive in the contemporary constitution, recognised and controlled by the courts as part of the common law.

The conduct of foreign affairs, the command and control of the armed forces, the summoning, prorogation and dissolution of Parliament, the giving of royal assent to statutes and the appointment of the prime minister and other ministers are all significant examples of executive functions that are done under the authority of the prerogative (Hazell and Foot 2022).

However, areas of executive authority traditionally derived from the prerogative may and are increasingly governed by statute. For example, to better conform with human rights standards under the European Convention on Human Rights, the intelligence and security services were put on a statutory footing by the Security Service Act 1989 and the Intelligence Services Act 1994. In this way, the range of prerogative powers can be expected to gradually diminish as more statutory regulation is introduced, and it has been judicially noted that no new prerogatives will be recognised. However, while Parliament may at any time create new powers akin to prerogatives by statute, these would of course be statutory and not prerogative powers. More rarely, it appears that Parliament may, by repealing a statute in a particular form, also restore a function governed by prerogative that it had previously statutorily regulated. For example, the Fixed-term Parliaments Act 2011 statutorily regulated the previously prerogative-governed functions of summoning and dissolving Parliament. The Dissolution and Calling of Parliament Act 2022 repealed the Fixed-term Parliaments Act and restored the situation prior to 2011, whereby the dissolution and calling of Parliament is a royal prerogative exercised by the monarch on the advice of the prime minister.

Acts of the UK Parliament

Primary legislation of the Westminster Parliament, which prevails over all other types of law (such as the case law of the courts, statutes of devolved legislatures, regulations made by ministers, or bylaws of local authorities), contain many important rules of British constitutional law. These may be historic legislation (such as the Bill of Rights 1688 or the Acts of Union 1707) and many other more recent key pieces of legislation (such as those establishing devolution in Scotland, Wales and Northern Ireland, the Supreme Court, the domestic enforcement of the European Convention on Human Rights, and much more). The reason why statutes of the UK Parliament enjoy the status of legal supremacy is that they are more specifically Acts of the Crown-in-Parliament, which is the institutional complex at the apex of the British state composed of the Crown, the House of Lords and the House of Commons. Accordingly, primary legislation is positive law formally passed by both the House of Commons and the House of Lords and assented to by the monarch.

Constitutional conventions

Strictly speaking, constitutional conventions are less a source of the constitution than a set of practical understandings about how the key institutions of government can function smoothly to ensure peace, order and good government. They are political and not legal rules, and as such their observance is dependent on political actors agreeing that a convention exists and is binding upon their behaviour. The courts may recognise and even discuss the scope of a constitutional convention when the occasion arises, but they will not enforce a convention because it is a convention; it is not a law. Constitutional conventions nevertheless provide some of the most important constitutional rules, such as the rule that the King must appoint as Prime Minister the Member of the

House of Commons who is able to command the confidence of that House. Another important example is the Sewel convention, whereby the UK Parliament will not normally legislate in an area of devolved competence without the consent of the devolved legislature. Constitutional conventions are increasingly codified in official documents such as *The Cabinet Manual* (2011) and *The Ministerial Code* (2022) and sometimes even in primary legislation (e.g. the Scotland Act 2016 added a new subsection (8) to section 28 of the Scotland Act 1998 to put the Sewel convention on a statutory footing for Scotland). In either case, they remain only politically and not judicially enforceable.

Common law

Constitutional rules are also declared and recognised by the common law, which is the body of judicial decisions that interpret statutes, recognise customs and develop the law from precedent to precedent. Many civil and political liberties now recognised in international human rights law in the form of positive rights emerged from the common law. Similarly, the common law was also instrumental in establishing many principles of constitutional government and the rule of law that remains the mainstay of the modern constitution.

A final point can be mentioned in this section and that is the importance of the works of constitutional scholars from a variety of disciplines, including history, politics, sociology and economics, in addition to law, for understanding of the UK constitution. The absence of a single text, the long history, and the complexity of events and sources make the discovery of the UK constitution a difficult task, and in this context academic or popular works uncovering, explaining and interpreting the constitution assume a particular importance. The work of nineteenth-century scholars and journalists such as A.V. Dicey (who popularised the idea of 'parliamentary sovereignty') and Walter Bagehot (who distinguished between the dignified and the efficient institutions of the British system) were able to offer strikingly confident and insightful accounts of the core principles of the British constitution which continue to have relevance, even though in many other significant respects the constitution they were describing has changed beyond recognition (Bagehot 1867; Dicey 1887).

Parliamentary sovereignty and the UK constitution

The idea that Parliament can make or unmake any law and that there is no higher authority than Parliament is the core guiding principle of the UK constitution. All other laws and rules in the UK constitution are subordinate to laws passed by Parliament. Most other branches of the state also derive their own authority from Parliament. The executive in the UK is accountable to Parliament and must seek Parliament's authorisation to extend its powers or spend money. Ministers must use the powers granted to them as Parliament intended (Gordon 2015: 23–26). The centrality of Parliament and parliamentary sovereignty provide a lodestar and centre of gravity for the UK's constitutional order.

However, beyond its legal applications, the concept of parliamentary sovereignty also has strong cultural and symbolic significance in the UK. As Michael Gordon (2016: 341) points out, in the absence of a constitutional document, it becomes a 'key touchstone of domestic political debate'. The debates about Europe in the Conservative Party, for example, revolved in large measure around the need to defend parliamentary sovereignty against encroachment from the European Union. Beyond untrammelled law-making power, therefore, adherents to parliamentary sovereignty might also attach other meanings.

First, it has implications for what people might see as the purest or most proper form of legitimate government. Parliamentary sovereignty advocates often also talk about outside influence on Parliament (whether from the courts or the EU) as constraining the will of the people. That will finds its best expression, they argue, in the governing majority in Parliament. Putting obstacles in the way of the transmission of the will of the people into laws or policies via that majority is therefore seen as illegitimate or anti-democratic.

Second, defence of parliamentary sovereignty is also often associated with a preference for a strong executive (Loughlin and Tierney 2018). As Geddes points out elsewhere in this volume (Chapter 10), the executive tends to control parliamentary business and rarely loses votes in Parliament and, therefore, parliamentary sovereignty in theory often translates into executive sovereignty in practice. This is not necessarily a bad thing, especially if you believe that it demonstrates democracy in action. However, as Judge (1993: 6) argues: 'the distinguishing feature of the English (later British) state since the late thirteenth century, and the origins of Parliament itself, is the emphasis placed on *government* rather than Parliament'. Parliament has therefore developed more democratic features but there is a strong tendency to view it as means of legitimating executive control.

Finally, parliamentary sovereignty is also used to express a facet of British or English identity. The UK's distinctive constitutional traditions say something about nationhood. Part of being British or English is to be the inheritors of a certain way of doing things. It is a practical and flexible approach to government that can be contrasted with other more rigid and legalistic constitutional orders. For example, for Ben Wellings (2012), Euroscepticism is an expression of English nationalism rooted in a defence of parliamentary sovereignty (see also Wellings, in this volume).

How, then, do you change the UK's constitution? Other countries have specific mechanisms for altering fundamental constitutional rules. They often set a higher legislative bar for these changes or (in the case of Ireland, for example) require referendums. In the UK, there is no legal distinction between any Act of Parliament. The simplest way to change the constitution is therefore to pass an Act of Parliament. However, technically the Dangerous Dogs Act 1991 and the Northern Ireland Act 1998 have the same legal status. One might have wider-reaching significance, but both only require a simple majority in both Houses of Parliament (together with the assent of the monarch) to pass into law (see Geddes, in this volume). The Coalition Government introduced the Fixed-term Parliaments Act in 2011; the Conservative Government of Boris Johnson repealed its provisions by the Dissolution and Calling of Parliament Act in 2022 . Such a change might be thought to have constitutional significance, but it faced no greater scrutiny than a more everyday piece of legislation. There is therefore a lively argument about whether we accept that there is no distinction or whether in fact 'constitutional statutes' exist in the UK (Elliott and Thomas 2020: 59-60).

Pressures on parliamentary sovereignty

The concept of untrammelled parliamentary sovereignty is a useful starting point for understanding the development of the UK constitution. However, it is not uncontested and brings along with it some (often implicit) ideological baggage. It is not a neutral description of the UK constitution and we need to unpack it.

The first set of objections concerns the nature of the UK's union state itself, particularly the Act of Union with Scotland in 1707. Should that Act be taken to mean that the previously English concept of parliamentary sovereignty simply expanded and applied in its entirety to the new state that was created? There is an argument to be made for that interpretation. However, it is equally clear that interpretations of sovereignty have differed in the Scottish context (Keating 2021). One of the most famous examples is the case of *MacCormick v Lord Advocate* in the Court of Session in Edinburgh in 1953. The case asked whether the new monarch, Elizabeth, had the right to style herself 'Queen Elizabeth II' in Scotland. There had not been a previous Queen Elizabeth in Scotland. The judge in the case ruled against MacCormick but noted that: 'the principle of unlimited sovereignty of Parliament is a distinctively English principle and has no counterpart in Scottish constitutional law' (MacCormick 1999: 54).

There are, at the very least therefore, contrasting interpretations of the reach of parliamentary sovereignty in the constitution. The UK Government also arguably conceded the sovereignty of the people of Scotland in the matter of Scottish independence in 2014. In Northern Ireland, the Good Friday Agreement explicitly recognises the right of Northern Ireland to secede from the UK if most of its residents vote for it.

Another set of qualifications relates to whether in fact parliamentary sovereignty is a set of normative assumptions masquerading as an unquestioned legal concept. As Convery points out in the introduction to this volume (Chapter 1), in addition to being a constitutional concept, parliamentary sovereignty also empowers certain actors in UK Government. Adhering to a purist conception of parliamentary sovereignty means strong central government based at Westminster. For Loughlin and Tierney (2018: 1015), for example: 'a conception of sovereignty which is equated to the unlimited legislative authority of the Crown-in-Parliament and which rests on an inchoate appeal to the need for Westminster to hold on to untrammelled power is inadequate and must be jettisoned'. In contrast with political and judicial understandings of parliamentary sovereignty, most academic lawyers take a much more nuanced interpretation. There is, therefore, a gulf between how you will find it discussed in university and how you will find it discussed in the House of Commons.

Pressures on the 'old' constitution

In addition to these fundamental objections, the UK constitution was also coming under pressure from wider political changes in the latter half of the twentieth century. Vernon Bogdanor (2009) makes a distinction between what he calls the 'old' and the 'new' British constitution. The old constitution was a much more settled set of arrangements. In the 1950s, the notion of parliamentary sovereignty (notwithstanding the discussion above) was much less a point of debate. Two parties alternated in power and government was much more centralised at Westminster. That period also marked the high watermark for UK unionism: postwar unity and the establishment of new institutions like the National Health Service focused attention on a common Britishness (Edgerton 2018). The old constitution is sometimes summarised in the study of UK politics as the Westminster Model Narrative, as Convery discussed in the Introduction to this volume.

However, the old constitution started to come under pressure on multiple fronts. The rise of the Scottish National Party in Scotland and Plaid Cymru in Wales called into question the assumption that national pluralism could be adequately represented by the territorial secretaries of state at Westminster. Election results created pressure for devolved assemblies. The plans for a Scottish and Welsh Assembly failed in the 1970s, but they came into being in 1999. The Government in Northern Ireland, run by the Ulster Unionist Party, was perceived by Catholics and Republicans to be failing to adequately represent minorities. It was eventually dissolved in 1972, marking the start of decades of violence and instability (see Whitten, in this volume). Alongside votes for nationalist parties, the vote share of the two main parties was also declining. There was also an increasingly prominent critique of the UK's constitutional arrangements from those who argued that they were too majoritarian and placed too much power in the hands of the executive.

The other main point of pressure came from the UK's decision to join the European Community in 1973. Member States must both give direct effect to new European laws and regulations and accept that European law will have supremacy over all national laws. These undertakings posed some questions for the doctrine of parliamentary sovereignty. This debate was never definitively settled. As European integration deepened during the 1980s and 1990s, this unresolved tension became much more difficult for the Conservative Party to manage (see Convery's Chapter 6 in this volume).

The Labour Governments (1997–2010)

These issues were bubbling under the surface. However, constitutional change took centre stage after 1997. Having been in opposition for so long, the Labour Party gradually built up a long list of commitments for constitutional change when it entered office.

Box 9.1   Constitutional Changes under the Labour Governments (1997–2010)

Independence of Bank of England

Devolution in Scotland, Wales and Northern Ireland

Creation of London Mayor and Assembly

House of Lords reform (incomplete)

Freedom of Information Act (2000)

Political Parties, Elections and Referendums Act (2000)

Constitutional Reform Act (2005): reform of Lord Chancellor and creation of the Supreme Court

The Human Rights Act (1998)

The Human Rights Act (1998) means that UK citizens can try to enforce their rights in the European Convention on Human Rights in UK courts. If courts perceive that an Act of Parliament cannot be reconciled with these rights, then they can issue a declaration of incompatibility and ask Parliament to reconsider. Unlike constitutional courts in other countries, they cannot strike down laws that they think interfere with fundamental rights. There is thus a compromise between parliamentary sovereignty and the rule of law.

The Constitutional Reform Act (2005) removed the UK's highest court from the House of Lords and placed it in a new institution called the Supreme Court. It is in a refurbished building across the square from the Houses of Parliament. However, its powers are not comparable to the US Supreme Court and the place of judicial review in the UK constitution is becoming more controversial, particularly in the Conservative Party.

From a traditionalist standpoint, these reforms vandalised the old constitutional order and weakened the longstanding strengths of the UK system. From the reformers' side, there are two central critiques of the New Labour constitutional reforms. The first is that they were not as radical as they could have been. In the case of Freedom of Information, for example, there is evidence that the original intentions were watered down when Labour entered government (Marsh and Hall 2007). Moreover, the party failed to follow through on a promise to change the electoral system.

That links to the second critique that the reforms go with the grain of the old constitution and Westminster Model Narrative and are specifically designed not to interfere with its fundamental tenets. The basic architecture of the Westminster Model Narrative remained largely intact. For example, devolution was tacked onto existing arrangements and did not involve much change at the centre of government in Westminster. The New Labour Government emphatically did not want to move the system in a decisively federal direction that abolished parliamentary sovereignty. There were therefore a series of (sometimes substantial) changes but they did not add up to a coherent vision of where Labour wanted to see the constitution in, say, 10 years' time. A defender might say that the reforms dealt with practical problems as they arose and created bespoke solutions for them. Moreover, it appears that most of the reforms have stood the test of time and have not been unwound by subsequent Conservative governments. A critic might argue that the reforms were piecemeal, lacked an overall strategy and have left the constitution looking decidedly messy (with lots of unanswered questions).

Devolution: The 'Millennium Settlement'

The most significant set of New Labour reforms concerned the devolution of power to Scotland, Wales, Northern Ireland and London. Michael Keating labelled Labour's devolution reforms and the understandings about the constitution that built up around them as the 'Millennium Settlement' (Keating 2021).

One of the key features of devolution in the UK is that it is highly asymmetrical. Not only were different powers given to Scotland, Wales and Northern Ireland, but England (outside London) did not receive any devolution. Another key feature is that the system has not stood still. The powers of the Welsh Assembly (now the Welsh Parliament or Senedd), for example, were up for debate almost immediately after it was established (Scully and Wyn Jones 2011). The powers of the Scottish Parliament were also modified significantly by the Scotland Acts 2012 and 2016.

The interaction between parliamentary sovereignty and devolution has raised some fundamental questions about the UK's constitutional order. It hits at the heart of the critique of New Labour that they sought above all to preserve central elements of the old constitution or the Westminster Model Narrative. The Labour Government's answer to the conundrum was essentially to avoid the question. Thus, two seemingly contradictory things could be true at the same time. The Scots, Welsh and Northern Irish could imagine that sovereignty had been divided in the UK at the same time as English elites at Westminster could believe that nothing had fundamentally changed and parliamentary sovereignty was still intact. Sandford and Gormley-Heenan (2020) characterised this arrangement as 'Schrodinger's devolution'. In the same way that Schrodinger's cat might be both alive and dead, devolution can both divide and not divide sovereignty. Scholars sometimes refer to this as a 'constitutional abeyance': a dormant question that it is politically easier to leave untouched (Foley, 1989).

Other ways of working also gradually built up around devolution. One of the most important everyday mechanisms came to be known as the Sewel Convention. The UK Government wanted to create a mechanism whereby it could legislate on devolved matters with the permission of the devolved legislatures. The devolved legislatures could explicitly grant permission for the UK Government to do this by passing a legislative consent motion. These became known as Sewel motions, after Lord Sewel, a Labour minister, who mentioned this possibility in debates on the devolution legislation in 1998. The convention that the UK Government would 'not normally' legislate on devolved matters without the devolved legislatures' permission was also written down in the Scotland Act 2016. The devolved administrations thought that it was also strengthened and becoming a much more established part of the constitution through usage. It was a fudged compromise of the sort in which the UK excels: the UK Government retained its right to legislate on devolved matters without asking anyone's permission; however, in practice it did not do so. That situation pertained until the Brexit debates (see below).

Another fundamental (but overlooked) aspect of this Millennium Settlement was the fact that it was underpinned by EU membership. To borrow Peter Hennessy's phrase, EU law, regulations and expectations provided much of the 'hidden wiring' that made devolution work (Hennessy 1996). For example, there was no need before Brexit to think about something called the UK internal market because the whole of the UK was in the EU's single market. All parts of the UK had to comply with EU rules. There was thus no question of a product being available for sale in Glasgow and not in Basingstoke. EU rules thus acted as a brake on divergence among different parts of the UK. Policy areas such as agriculture ended up being devolved but mainly 'Europeanised'. The devolved administrations on paper had control over these areas but had to comply with EU rules, so there was no chance of radically different agricultural policies causing any friction within the UK. Even more seriously, in the case of Northern Ireland's devolution arrangements, the EU's single market and customs union played a vital role (see Whitten, in this volume).

The removal of EU membership thus had a destabilising effect on the UK's system of devolution, at best. The gaps that were plugged by EU laws and regulations needed to be filled, immediately politicising a series of thorny issues that hitherto existed in the background or were the subject of fudged compromises. The question of whether the UK Parliament required the devolved legislatures' permission to enact Brexit became part of a massive UK Supreme Court case: *Miller v Secretary of State for Exiting the European Union.*

Case Study 9.1

Miller v Secretary of State for Exiting the European Union

The Supreme Court dealt with two central questions in this case. The first was whether the UK Government could deploy its prerogative powers to initiate the formal process of exiting the European Union in terms of Article 50 of the Treaty on European Union (TEU), or whether primary legislation was required for this purpose. Second, if it was held that primary legislation was indeed required, whether the legislative consent of the devolved legislatures in Scotland, Wales and Northern Ireland was further required for that Act of the UK Parliament, in terms of the Sewel Convention. On the first question, the Supreme Court held by a majority of eight to three that the UK Government could not use the prerogative, but that the UK Parliament would have to authorise the exit process through legislation. If not exactly radical, this conclusion nevertheless required a fairly robust judicial reinterpretation of the role of the prerogative in the British constitution, as highlighted by the dissents. It rested on the grounds that the prerogative cannot be used to eliminate a source of UK law (which EU law has been since the European Communities Act 1972) or the removal of individual rights emanating from that source of law, without prior parliamentary sanction. The central foundation of this conclusion was the Court's powerful endorsement of the orthodox doctrine of parliamentary sovereignty as the basis of the UK constitution, in support of which it set out historical, doctrinal and normative arguments. Given this finding on the main question before it, it was perhaps unsurprising that on the second question the majority held that there was no requirement for the consent of the devolved legislatures for UK legislation authorising the initiation of the exit process from the EU. But the three dissenting judges also joined the majority in enabling the Court to hold unanimously that the Sewel Convention, despite its statutory footing, was judicially unenforceable and exclusively a creature of politics. If Parliament is supreme without qualification in terms of the dominant orthodoxy about the UK constitution, which purists had maintained for more than a century, then, of course, in both logic and law, no question of a requirement of consent of a subordinate legislature can arise, notwithstanding the existence of the clearest evidence of a constitutional convention that suggests otherwise.

The constitutional future of England

The place of England in this evolving constitutional settlement has received much more attention in recent years (Henderson and Wyn Jones 2021). The devolution reforms to Scotland, Wales and Northern Ireland in 1999 were not accompanied by an equivalent process in England. The northeast of England rejected plans for a regional assembly in a referendum in 2004. England therefore remained highly centralised.

Devolution in England is complicated because of its size. Any attempt to carve out a role for England as a whole in the UK's constitutional arrangements would mean a wholesale change in the UK constitution. Henderson and Wyn Jones (2021) identify three constraints that make it very difficult:

> The fusion of English and British functions built into the very architecture of the
> state means that to recognize England qua England in any serious way would
> necessitate a fundamental restructuring of the state itself: everything would have to

change (our first constraint). Even if public acquiescence could be secured for such a venture (the second constraint), any systematic attempt to separate out English and British institutions would ultimately still require a choice between rendering English institutions subservient to those of the UK, even if the former would be very much larger than the latter in terms of budget and staffing levels, or recognizing the brute fact of English numerical dominance, with predictable consequences across the rest of the state (our third constraint). (Henderson and Wyn Jones 2021: 170)

Politicians have therefore alighted on the solution of a revived form of English regionalism via combined authorities and metro mayors. The first such 'devolution deal' was signed between the government and the Greater Manchester Combined Authority in 2015. Devolution deals have since been signed with 21 other areas. In keeping with its approach to devolution, deals with different areas of England are asymmetrical and involve a different mix of powers and budgetary responsibilities. It is also very much a top-down process, where combinations of authorities have to apply to central government in order to receive powers and funding (Sandford 2016).

This process was started under the Conservatives, but both main parties are now committed to it as a means of spreading wealth and 'levelling up' outside the southeast of England. It is therefore an area of considerable movement and is likely to shape the constitutional future of England markedly in the next Parliament.

Key debate   Federalism and the UK constitution

The word 'federalism' is sometimes invoked in UK constitutional debates. There are suggestions that the UK should become more federal or that Scotland might get something called 'full federalism' in exchange for not voting for independence. There is sometimes confusion about the meaning of federalism, so it is helpful to pin down some definitions. One way of looking at it is: 'In a federal system of government, *sovereignty is shared and powers divided* between two or more levels of government, each of which enjoys a direct relationship with the people' (Hueglin and Fenna 2006: 32–33, emphasis added). Thus, a federation is a state in which: 'neither the federal nor the constituent units of government are *constitutionally subordinate to the other*; that is, each has sovereign powers derived not from another level of government but from a constitution that is *not unilaterally amendable by either level of government*; each is empowered to deal directly with its citizens in the exercise of its constitutionally assigned legislative, executive and taxing powers; and each is directly elected by its citizens' (Watts 2007: 240, emphasis added).

On this set of definitions, the UK is not a federal system of government. The devolved legislatures (and the new English regions) are very much constitutionally subordinate to the UK Parliament. Their powers are also unilaterally amendable by the UK Parliament, and the UK Parliament did indeed unilaterally amend them when it came to the implementation of Brexit.

We might say that federal systems display aspects of *self-rule* (what the sub-state governments can do themselves) and *shared rule* (processes of joint decision-making between the federal government and the sub-state governments). The UK system displays high levels of *self-rule* (devolved budgetary freedom, policy flexibility, no central interference), but very limited provisions for *shared rule* (no territorial second chamber, few formal mechanisms for intergovernmental relations, no courts to enforce agreements).

Conclusion

Having modified (or vandalised) its 'old' constitution and not adopting the idea of moving to an entirely 'new' one, the UK now finds itself constitutionally somewhere in the middle. It is not a federal state, but it does exhibit some federal features. Parliamentary sovereignty is still central, but it faces more challenges than ever before and co-exists alongside other sovereignty claims. A devolution compromise known as the 'Millennium Settlement' was upended by the process of implementing Brexit, but the basic relationship between the devolved legislatures and the UK Parliament remains intact. England remains a highly centralised country, but the experiments with English regionalism are now gathering pace and enjoy cross-party support.

While there is some appetite for making the system work better, none of the main parties has proposed a wholesale change to the UK's constitutional arrangements in favour of a neater or more explicitly federal system. As the Brexit process has demonstrated, having to find definitive answers to fudged compromises can be a fraught process and involves a great deal of political energy. Labour has promised to improve intergovernmental relations, but the overall strategy of muddling through seems to be the most likely outcome.

That leaves a series of open questions for students to contemplate about the tensions between parliamentary sovereignty and devolution, judicialisation and popular sovereignty claims. If constitutional issues settle back into the background after the heat of Brexit implementation, there will be even less pressure to find answers to dormant questions.

Summary

- Parliamentary sovereignty is still the key concept at the heart of the UK's constitution. However, it has never been uncontested and it now faces more practical and intellectual challenges.
- The UK's settled constitution came under pressure from the 1970s. It was modified extensively by Labour's ambitious reforms (1997–2010), but the understandings put in place under that 'Millennium Settlement' came under severe pressure in the heat of implementing Brexit, resulting in a rupture with previous narratives.
- The direction of travel appears to be further English devolution alongside some post-Brexit soothing of relationships and some tidying up here and there. There does not appear to be an appetite among the UK's elites for a radical shift in the basic architecture of the system.

Recommended and further reading

- Gordon, M. (2015) *Parliamentary Sovereignty in the UK Constitution*. Oxford: Hart Publishing. This is detailed and closely argued for a legal audience. However, it is worth taking the time to engage with it as students of politics. Dipping into even a few chapters will fill in some of the background on the state of debates in this area. Gordon defends a conception of parliamentary sovereignty at the heart of our understanding of the constitution.

- McHarg, A. (2018) 'Navigating without maps: Constitutional silence and the management of the Brexit crisis', *International Journal of Constitutional Law*, 16(3): 952–968. McHarg looks at the idea of 'silences' in the UK constitution and the gaps that needed to be filled in order to implement Brexit.
- Sandford, M. and Gormley-Heenan, C. (2020) '"Taking back control": The UK's constitutional narrative and Schrodinger's devolution', *Parliamentary Affairs*, 73(1): 108–126. Sandford and Gormley-Heenan use the metaphor of 'Schrodinger's Cat' to shed light on the UK constitution. They argue that Brexit has shattered one of the key features of devolution in the UK: the idea that devolution can mean different things to different actors.

Chapter 10

The UK Parliament

Marc Geddes

What will this chapter tell me?

- The core argument presented here is that Parliament is often misunderstood, especially in simplistic conclusions about its role in British politics. Academic research indicates a far more nuanced assessment of the institution, which this chapter will discuss.
- The chapter considers how different theoretical and analytical approaches in the study of representation apply to British politics, including territorial and constituency representation, descriptive and substantive representation, and political representation.
- It provides an overview of the different factors that affect Parliament's role in British politics and decision-making. While this will focus mostly on the legislative process, it also applies more broadly to how Parliament seeks to hold government and powerful interests accountable.
- It identifies the different tools and processes that MPs and peers use to hold government and powerful interests to account, including through parliamentary questions and debates in the chamber as well as through inquiries by committees.
- The chapter focuses on executive–legislative relationships, the UK Parliament's relationships with other institutions, how Parliament connects with the public and prospects for reform.

What do I need to know?

- There is a major difference between parliamentary and presidential systems of governing. Most European polities are parliamentary; many in the Americas are presidential. The UK fits this geographic pattern: it is a representative, parliamentary democracy.
- The key parts of any state are the government, parliament and judiciary (see Convery and Welikala, in this volume). They are not the same.
- As Sarah Childs (in this volume) outlines, the most influential model of representation in the UK system is trusteeship.
- The basic structure of the UK Parliament is bicameral: it is made up of two chambers, the House of Commons and House of Lords.

Introduction

The UK Parliament sits at the apex of representative and democratic politics, even as it exists alongside a range of other representative bodies and institutions, not least legislatures in Edinburgh (the Scottish Parliament), Cardiff (the Senedd Cymru) and Belfast (the Northern Ireland Assembly). Parliament is also closely related to executive politics, the judiciary, party politics, and more. In other words, while the main focus of this chapter is on the UK Parliament – specifically the House of Commons and House of Lords – it is impossible to study parliamentary politics without reference to a range of other institutions and actors. Indeed, one of the most important points in thinking about Parliament is that it is an institution entangled so deeply across British politics that David Judge (1993) argues that the UK is a 'parliamentary state'. This is in no small part due to the many roles and functions the institution performs in British politics, including – broadly – the representation of people, interests and ideas; the place where decisions are made, and rules and laws are passed; and, where governments and powerful interests are held to account for decisions that affect public life.

Parliament is a complex, multi-faceted and multi-layered institution. This complexity also translates into diverse approaches to studying the institution, which leads to different conclusions about the way that Parliament works – and 'should' work. This chapter seeks to engage with that diversity of research by examining some of the core functions and roles that Parliament seeks to fulfil in British politics and to bring out the normative underpinnings and ideas that research suggests about Parliament. These are important debates because they affect strategies that institutional actors may adopt to address declining trust in politics.

Representation ... of what?

The foundational and arguably most important function of a parliament is to represent; they are, after all, representative institutions that exist to bring different parts of the nation together. The UK is no different in that regard; indeed, early and medieval parliaments in England were used to bring together representatives from across the country to advise monarchs about their decisions (Judge 1993). The theoretical and analytical ideas of representation are covered elsewhere (see Childs, in this volume; Kenny, in this volume); here, it is worth dwelling on how such ideas are realised and applied in practice. Of course, the UK Parliament is only one of multiple representative bodies – alongside it are the legislatures in Scotland, Wales and Northern Ireland, as well as local councillors, mayors in cities and larger combined authorities, and elected police and crime commissioners. This indicates a complex landscape for applying representative ideals, and the UK Parliament plays only one part in British representative democracy.

Territorial representation through constituencies

Six-hundred and fifty Members of Parliament (MPs) are elected from across the UK via First-Past-the-Post (FPTP), the majoritarian electoral system where each MP represents a clearly defined geographic area – a constituency – in the House of Commons. The relationship between constituency and MP has been widely debated by representatives themselves and academic researchers alike (as discussed in Childs, in this volume). These debates can be particularly pronounced at particular moments, such as during the Brexit years (see Case Study 10.1 below; Russell and James 2023: 65–98). To date, there has been no solution, suggesting a lingering question about the role of an MP that has normative implications about the nature of representation in British politics.

Regardless of how MPs conceive the relationship with their constituency, it is clear from academic research that it plays a crucial role in MPs' work. Not only do MPs make significant efforts to be present in their constituencies through newsletters, campaigns or holding advice and drop-in 'surgeries', constituents also make significant demands on MPs through letter-writing or emails to voice their opinions or concerns, or to ask their MP to support them with various grievances (Norris 1997; Gay 2005; Crewe 2015: 83–109; Hardman 2018: 60–82). Indeed, academic research also demonstrates a growing shift in favour of greater 'localness' of representation. Data shows that constituents prefer their MPs to be rooted in their local area

(Campbell and Cowley 2014; Campbell and Lovenduski 2015; Campbell et al. 2019), which has led, first, to growing claims by MPs to emphasise their links to their constituency (McKay 2020), but also, second, to an increasing number of MPs to be actually born in the area that they represent (Cowley et al. 2022).

Given its importance, MPs weave their constituency into much of their parliamentary work, whether it is by mentioning the local area in their activities (Willumsen 2019) or by affecting how they hold government to account (Kellermann 2016; Geddes 2020: 46–48). It is rare for MPs to express concern for how much of their time is spent on constituency work, given voters' preferences for constituency service. However, one MP asked in 2015:

> Is it really our job to deal with immigration appeals, benefits disputes, Child Support Agency arguments, planning applications, school placements and the like? Is there not a risk that it diverts us from our true purpose of running the country and holding the government to account? (Gray 2015: n.p.)

It raises an interesting normative point about the role of an MP and the potential tensions between different functions that Parliament seeks to fulfil.

Representative work is affected by a range of factors, such as the MP's own background and characteristics (Childs and Cowley 2011; Durose et al. 2013) or their party affiliation. The chapter now turns attention directly to this issue.

Key debate   What is the role of an MP?

As there is no job description for MPs, questions about the role of an MP have never been settled (Wright 2010). This means that there is continuing debate about the purpose of MPs. Historically influential has been the study of Donald Searing (1994), who used large numbers of interviews with MPs to identify different roles that MPs can play in Parliament, such as 'policy advocates', 'ministerial aspirants', 'constituency members' or 'Parliament men' [sic]. However, his approach has not gone without criticism (Strøm 1997; Andeweg 2014). For example, Stephen Holden Bates (2021) is not only sceptical of how MPs themselves interpret their roles, but also argues that we need to more clearly distinguish beliefs and motivations with behaviours and wider structural contexts. Meanwhile, others have adopted insights from other disciplines to study MPs. For example, James Weinberg's (2020, 2021) research draws attention to the psychological character traits of MPs in understanding success in office. Elsewhere, scholars have adopted insights from social anthropology and sociology to undertake ethnographic studies of politicians in Parliament (Crewe 2005, 2015; Geddes 2020; Miller 2021).

What can we learn from all this research? It reinforces the view that there is no single or dominant approach of being an MP, and that they bring distinctive styles. Importantly, it highlights a range of different factors that might affect their behaviour, which different scholars focus on depending on the theoretical, analytical and methodological tradition of their research. This also means that it might be difficult to achieve a single job description for MPs.

Discussion questions

1   Is it possible to identify and write a 'job description' for an MP?
2   What factors are the most important in shaping the work of MPs?

Descriptive and substantive representation

How do the theoretical and analytical dynamics raised by Sarah Childs (in this volume) and others translate with respect to the UK Parliament? We can consider a range of factors that intersect with one another, including gender, ethnicity, disability, age, sexuality, educational background and/or previous occupations (see also other chapters on these dynamics in British politics). The House of Commons periodically publishes up-to-date statistics on some (but not all) of these characteristics, the most recent of which this chapter draws on (Cracknell and Tunnicliffe 2022; Cracknell and Baker 2024).

In Figures 10.1 and 10.2, we can see how some of the descriptive characteristics of MPs have changed over time and, in particular, that the diversity of MPs has been increasing. Nevertheless, Parliament's descriptive representation of the country at large is mixed: since the 2024 UK general election, 40% of MPs are women, while the general population is made up of approximately 51% women; ethnic minorities make up 14% of MPs, which is around about the proportion of the general population (Cracknell and Baker 2024: 42–48).[1] There are inter-party differences: for example, 46% of Labour MPs are women, while 24% of Conservative MPs are women. We therefore need not only to look at parliamentary representation overall, but to dig beneath the surface to explore impacts at candidate selection (Durose et al. 2013; Kenny 2013) and dynamics within parties (Childs 2004b; Childs and Webb 2012). For instance, the Labour Party's use of all-women shortlists has significantly increased the proportion of women elected to Parliament, which has since opened a debate about the legitimacy of quotas (Nugent and Krook 2016) and their possible extension to other groups (Labour Party 2018) (for a discussion, see Kenny, in this volume).

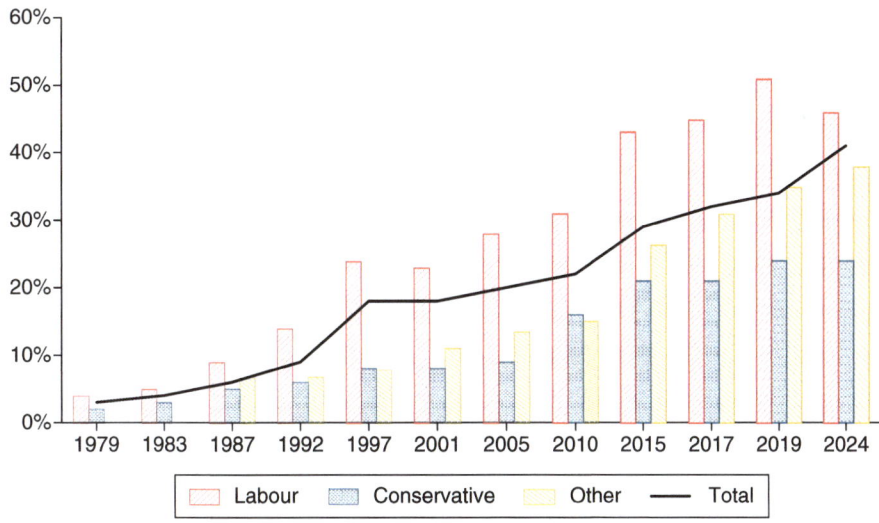

Figure 10.1   Share of women MPs elected to the House of Commons, 1979–2024

Source: Cracknell and Tunnicliffe (2022) and Cracknell and Baker (2024)

---

1 There are considerable difficulties in understanding descriptive representation of ethnic minorities because grouping them together under umbrella terms, such as BAME, masks considerable differences between groups (for a discussion, see Aspinall 2021 and Peace and Meer, in this volume).

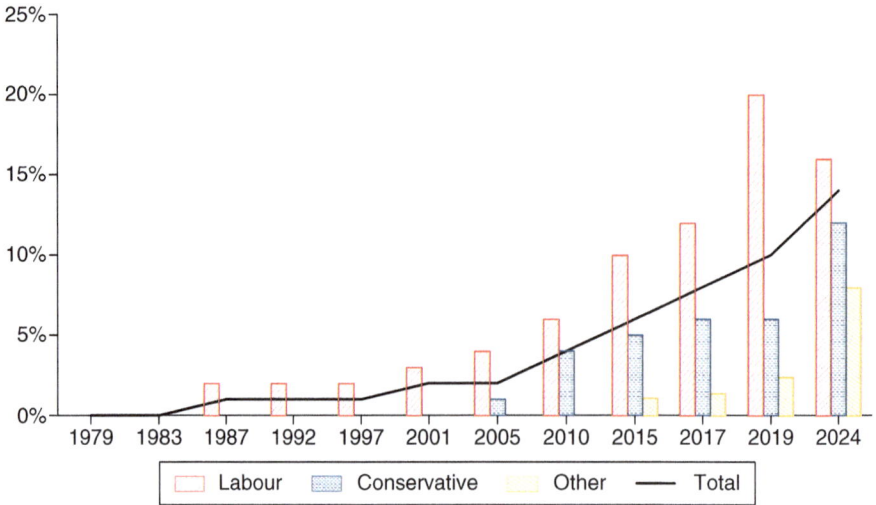

Figure 10.2   Share of ethnic minority MPs elected to the House of Commons, 1979–2024

Source: Cracknell and Tunnicliffe (2022) and Cracknell and Baker (2024)

Alongside gender and ethnicity, the educational and occupational backgrounds of MPs is worthy of consideration because of their link to social class. Figures show that 23% of MPs attended fee-paying schools and 90% graduated from university (20% attended Oxford or Cambridge) (Cracknell and Baker 2024: 46–47). This contrasts with the general public, in which 7% attend fee-paying schools and 19% hold an undergraduate degree or higher qualification (while less than 1% went to Oxford or Cambridge) (Social Mobility Commission and The Sutton Trust 2019; Cracknell and Baker 2024). Meanwhile, Figure 10.3 shows changes in occupation over

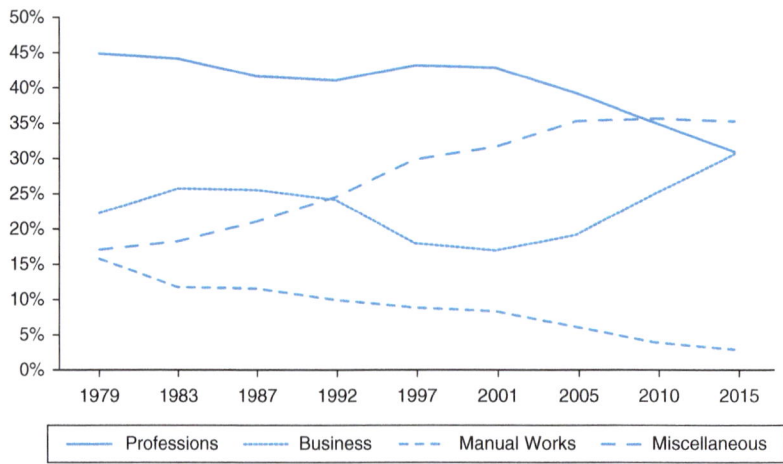

Figure 10.3   Occupation of MPs, 1979–2015

Source: Cracknell and Tunnicliffe (2022)

time for MPs before achieving elected office. It reveals that the proportion of manual workers has decreased considerably while 'miscellaneous' occupations, which includes those with
politically relevant backgrounds (e.g. political organisers, local councillors and journalists), has
increased. Recent research indicates the ongoing professionalisation of MPs (Allen and Cairney
2017; Allen 2018).

How does descriptive representation affect parliamentary work? Political scientists have
shown that: women MPs concentrate on different issues from men MPs (Catalano 2009); there
are gendered differences between interactions of men and women in parliamentary debates
(Hargrave and Langengen 2021); and, ethnic minority MPs ask more parliamentary questions
about problems and rights of minorities in the UK (Saalfeld and Bischof 2013). Different characteristics may also intersect to reinforce and heighten particular issues, such as disability and
gender (Evans and Reher 2022, 2023) or ethnicity and gender (Siow 2023a). As these findings
suggest, intersectionality is therefore an important consideration throughout analysis of parliamentary work. As discussed by others in this volume (e.g. Childs, Chapter 2; Kenny, Chapter
3), the relationship between descriptive and substantive representation is further complicated
by other constraints and factors that mediate how MPs behave. To echo other chapters in this
volume, then, there are nuanced and multi-faceted issues regarding the study of representation
and institutions.

One further important reason why descriptive representation matters is because it
is assumed to affect wider trust in politics and politicians. If MPs are not in touch with
the concerns of ordinary citizens and are perceived to be a different, elite class that is far
removed from the lives of the people that they seek to represent, then this can be damaging
for the legitimacy of Parliament (Patel et al. 2023). This is a theme to which we return in
the final section of this chapter.

Political representation through parties

Almost all MPs are elected as representatives of political parties, which is often the basis of
voting behaviour, even if the other considerations discussed above may also influence voting
behaviour. Given the majoritarian electoral system, however, the distribution of seats in Parliament is not proportional to the public vote (for a discussion of electoral systems and voting
behaviour, see Henderson, in this volume).

Figure 10.4 shows the breakdown of MPs in the House of Commons, which indicates the
outcome of the most recent general election at the time of writing (July 2024), and peers in
the House of Lords. From this, it is noticeable that the dynamics between the two Houses of
the UK Parliament are quite different. Political representation is distinctive in the House of
Lords, which includes not only political representatives but non-party aligned 'crossbench'
peers, who are usually appointed on the basis of their expertise (scientific, religious, ethical,
political, etc.) and a small number of bishops to represent the Church of England. In general, peers are appointed for life through life peerages, though a small number of hereditary
peers also sit in the House of Lords, while bishops sit in the House due to their position
in the ecclesiastical hierarchy (which results in discrimination against women and ethnic
minorities given the legacies of hereditary peerages following male lines) (Crewe 2005; for
a discussion, see Kelso 2006).

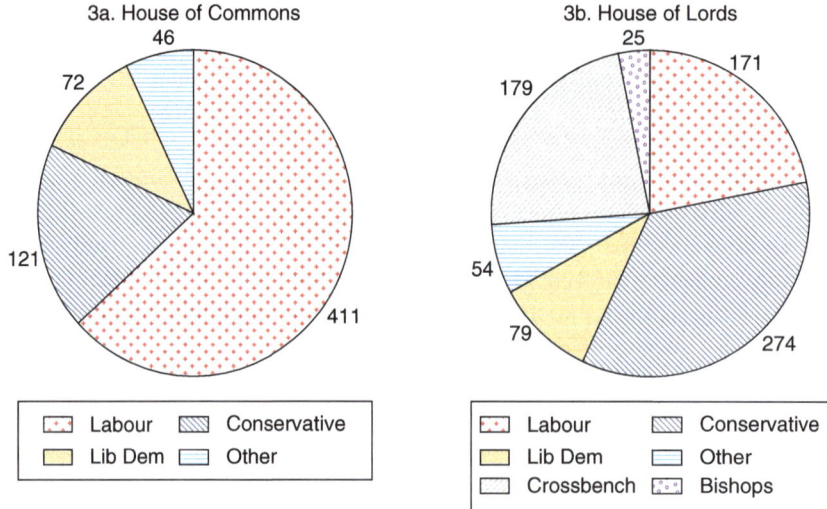

Figure 10.4 Distribution of seats in Parliament, July 2024

Source: Baker (2024); UK Parliament (2024a)

Parliamentary parties are organised distinctively, with their own factions and groups (see Convery, Chapters 6, and Pike, Chapter 7, in this volume). The Conservative Party, for instance, has the 1922 Committee, which is made up of all backbench Conservative MPs, to provide a channel of information between the leadership team of the Party with the wider parliamentary party (Norton 2023). Meanwhile, Labour has its Parliamentary Labour Party, or PLP. Both groups meet weekly when Parliament is sitting and have their own set of internal, party-focused committees and caucuses to represent political ideas and groups (e.g. the PLP has a separate caucus for women MPs; see Allen and Childs (2019) for an analysis). Most crucially, the government is formed and maintained on the basis of a majority that can be found in the House of Commons. Following the 2024 general election, the Labour Party formed the governmnet with a simple majority of 174 seats (this number may fluctuate owing to by-elections, suspensions and other factors). Single-party majority governments are the norm in the UK; since 1945, only three general elections (in February 1974, May 2010 and June 2017) led to a 'hung' Parliament with no majority for one party. The basis for governments comes from the House of Commons; as you can see from Figure 10.4, no party has a majority in the House of Lords.

Political parties underpin the vast majority of parliamentary work, which are the organisational vehicles through which parliamentary politics takes place. Given that, additionally, the government is drawn from Parliament – thereby fusing powers between the executive and legislature – it often means that government dominates parliamentary business. This has crucial ramification for how Parliament organises its business and how it fulfils its other functions. We turn to these issues now.

Organising parliamentary business and making law

Parliament remains the supreme legal authority across the country (i.e. the constitution continues to follow the doctrine of 'parliamentary sovereignty'; for a discussion, see Convery and

Welikala, in this volume). In other words, a crucial function or role of Parliament is to legislate, which is achieved through Acts of Parliament. These *primary* pieces of legislation have legal force across the UK (with some law-making powers devolved to representative institutions in Scotland, Wales and Northern Ireland). Primary legislation may also contain provisions for ministers to issue *secondary* or *delegated* legislation through statutory instruments (for more on different types of legislation, see Besly and Goldsmith (2023); on secondary legislation, see Hansard Society (2021)).

First reading	A bill may be introduced to either the House of Commons or the House of Lords. At this stage, the bill is published without a debate.
Second reading	The principles of the bill are debated in the chamber in which it was introduced. At the end, MPs or peers vote on whether the bill should proceed.
Committee stage	The bill will go to committee (sometimes 'committee of the whole House') for line-by-line scrutiny. Amendments can be tabled for (almost) any part of the bill, which will be voted on.
Report stage	The bill is considered by the House a further time. Amendments can be tabled at this stage, which will be voted on.
Third reading	A final debate on the bill, as amended by the House. The debate is on the bill as a whole, with a vote at the end to either pass or reject the bill.
Passage in the other House	After a bill has gone through all its stages in one House, it will then undertake all of the above stages again in the other House. It will then go back to where it started.
Consideration of amendments	At this stage the two Houses will consider amendments passed. The bill will go back and forth – 'ping pong' – until both Houses pass an identical bill.
Royal assent	Once a bill has been passed in both Houses, it may then be passed to the monarch for royal assent, formally signing off the legislation. It will then enter force.

Figure 10.5 Summary of the legislative process

Source: Adapted from Besly and Goldsmith (2023)

The legislative process is summarised in Figure 10.5. Parliamentary bills may start in either the House of Commons or the House of Lords (conventionally, non-controversial legislation begins in the upper chamber). The first substantive debate on legislation takes place at second reading, when the broad principles of a bill are debated by the whole House. Provided bills pass, they then move to committee stage, where MPs (or peers) undertake line-by-line scrutiny of the bill and where amendments can be tabled. Bills then return to the whole House for report stage, in which further amendments can be tabled and voted on. Finally, the bill, as amended and with no further opportunities to change the legislation, will be debated at third reading. So long as the bill passes this stage, it will then move to the other House where the same process takes place. Once it has completed its stage in the second chamber, the bill returns to the first House to consider amendments. Here, bills may 'ping pong' between the two Houses until both agree an identical bill. It can then, finally, be sent for royal assent to turn the legislation from a bill into an Act (for a detailed summary, see Besly and Goldsmith 2023).[2]

---

2 For assessments on other aspects of parliamentary involvement in legislation, such as pre- or post-legislative scrutiny see Smookler (2006) and Caygill (2019).

A key area of debate about the UK Parliament is the extent to which government dominates the legislative process. And at face value, it does indeed look like the government dominates parliamentary business: the vast majority of bills come from the executive; government decides how much time to allocate – or crucially to *not* allocate – to bills; accepted amendments are overwhelmingly from the government; and dissenting votes by government MPs have historically been very low (Norton 1975). Others take this argument yet further: not only does Parliament struggle to impact on the legislative process, it is 'peripheral' to policy making altogether (King and Crewe 2013: 361; see also Richardson and Jordan 1979), given the extent to which legislative proposals are designed outside Parliament by specialist policy makers in the civil service, by arm's-length bodies (ALBs) or enacted through Statutory Instruments. These perceptions and assessments of the weakness of the UK Parliament are often captured in public debates and by the media (Brady 2015; McTernan 2016; Jenkins 2021), as well as through comparative research (Martin and Vanberg 2011; Kreppel 2014), in which Parliament is labelled as 'reactive' or 'arena', among other things.

And yet, in-depth, mixed-methods academic research paints a far more nuanced picture about the influence of Parliament on legislation (and not only on legislation – see the sections below on accountability and cross-cutting themes, too) in at least two ways: the changing nature of party discipline and the informal means of influence.

Parliamentary influence on legislation

The last time that the government lost a vote specifically on legislation in the main chamber was in 1986, over Sunday trading laws.[3] Louise Thompson (2015: 52–58) has also shown that, between 2000 and 2012, the government was successful 99.9% of the time in amending legislation at committee stage while non-government amendments were only successful 0.6% of the time. Similarly, Meg Russell and co-authors have shown that, based on their dataset of over 4,000 amendments on 12 case study bills between 2005 and 2015, 94% of government amendments were successful while fewer than 1% of non-government amendments were agreed and not overturned (Russell et al. 2016: 292–293). However, these authors also point out that relying purely on voting outcomes is far too simplistic in assessing the influence of Parliament on legislation.

Detailed amendment analysis from the House of Commons suggests that the initial figures, above, are misleading and overstate government success for several reasons. First, many amendments by government do not provide substantive change but correct mistakes or clarify ambiguities. For example, in Russell et al.'s (2016) study, less than one-third of government amendments sought substantive policy changes to bills; meanwhile, three-quarters of non-government amendments were substantive. Second, many substantive amendments from government stem from parliamentary pressures made elsewhere, by a different actor, or at a different time in the legislative process (or indeed before or after the formal process). For example, Thompson (2015: 69–93) shows that amendments may

---

3 There have been other defeats since 1986; some more significant than others. For example, Opposition Day motions do not require government action, so aren't much of a 'defeat'. More significant defeats might include a 'humble address', requiring government to publish information, as happened several times since 2016.

be rejected at committee stage, but are then introduced later at report stage by government. Meg Russell and Daniel Gover (2017) also show that amendments may arise from select committee reports or other actors. Regardless of source, governments often prefer to introduce their own amendments in order to ensure that the text is drafted in a way that it is legally appropriate (Greenberg 2011). Third, non-government amendments are perhaps overstated because political parties may each table their own amendments, while the government only introduces one. Fourth, non-governments amendments are not always designed to change legislation but act as 'hooks' for debate. These are called 'probing' amendments and are common across the legislative process, including to signal opposing parties' intent if they were in government, and so on (Russell et al. 2016: 299–300). When taken together, the picture that emerges is that, while government frames the legislative process, parliamentary influence is far from negligible.[4]

Party discipline and dissent

As discussed previously, political parties are key organisational vehicles for parliamentary politics. Not only do they form the basis for governments, however, they also organise parliamentary business through their business managers or 'whips'. There is some coordination across parties through the 'usual channels', whereby the whips of the different parties meet to discuss, negotiate and agree parliamentary activities. Whips are essential to ensure the smooth running of Parliament.

Whips try to ensure party discipline by indicating to their MPs how they should vote. This is circulated through a document that is underlined once, twice or three times to indicate the importance of their attendance and vote (a one-line whip requests the attendance of MPs in votes, a two-line whip expects MPs to attend, while a three-line whip means attendance is essential). Additionally, whips also keep track of what their MPs do and persuade them to keep to the party line. They have various arsenals at their disposal to incentivise 'good behaviour': they can suggest a promotion or demotion; they have influence over which committees MPs may sit on; they can grant or block proxy votes (i.e. when voting for the MP is done on their behalf so the MP can miss it, e.g. for personal reasons); or, in the worst case, they allude to possible deselection and/or losing the party whip. Their 'dark arts' are assumed to be influential in keeping MPs toeing their party line, once again giving the impression of party and government dominance over Parliament. However, it is not quite so simple.

In the UK Parliament, party discipline has been traditionally very high. It arguably reached its zenith in the 1950s, when fewer than 10% of votes saw a dissenting vote from a government-side MP (Norton 1975). It contributed to the image of MPs as 'sheep' or 'lobby fodder', and is the basis of conclusions by early comparative research of the UK Parliament as a weak institution. However, things have changed considerably. Since the 1970s, in particular, MPs have begun to vote in ever greater numbers against their party whip, as demonstrated in Figure 10.6, and which has been documented in research by Philip Norton (1975, 1980) and Philip Cowley (2002, 2005).

---

4 Research on devolved parliaments in the UK also reveal a nuanced picture regarding their influence on legislation (Haughey 2023; Shephard and Cairney 2005).

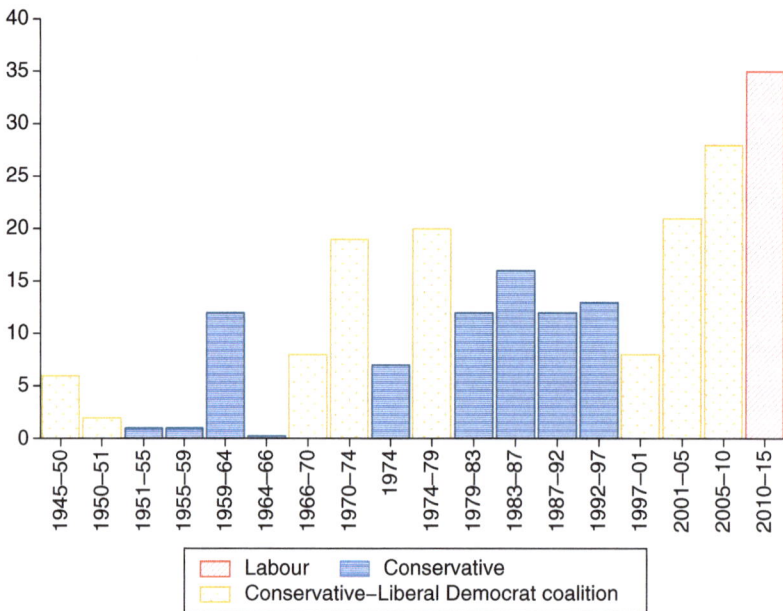

Figure 10.6   Percentage of divisions to see a government MP vote against the whip, 1945–2015

Source: Mortimore and Blick (2018: 324).

Case Study 10.1

Brexit and Parliament

The referendum result to leave the European Union in 2016 had a significant impact on Parliament, not least the intensive clashes between direct democracy (the referendum) and representative democracy (Parliament). Brexit raised questions not only about whether sovereignty had shifted from Parliament to the people (Blick and Salter 2021; S.G. White 2022), but also about dealing with internal divisions within both political parties: in the case of Labour, through the leadership of Jeremy Corbyn between 2015 and 2019; in the case of the Conservatives, through their different views on Brexit. And then a further challenge came from the outcome of the 2017 general election, in which no party had an overall and secure majority to form a government. It led to a 'perfect storm' (Russell 2021) and several years of debate and indecision.

The early Brexit period was characterised by dilemmas of representation and sovereignty. MPs had to directly confront how to represent the nation, i.e. on the basis of how their constituency voted or what the MP thought was right. Meanwhile, in the first of two high-profile court cases, the Supreme Court ruled in favour of Parliament to trigger Article 50 of the Treaty of European Union to allow for the departure of a member state, rather than the government. This eventually took place in 2017, followed shortly afterwards by a snap general election that resulted in the loss of the Conservative Party's already slim majority and a considerable cause of parliamentary instability. MPs used the weak position of the executive to empower Parliament in exceptional ways. First, Parliament secured a 'Meaningful Vote', which meant that any Brexit deal needed approval of Parliament. Second, MPs in the House of Commons extraordinarily 'took control' of the Order Paper (i.e. of parliamentary business), away from government in order (i) to give MPs the opportunity to hold 'indicative votes' on alternative Brexit outcomes and (ii) to legally instruct government to seek extensions on securing a Brexit deal.

The House of Commons, in particular, became a site for and against Brexit, with MPs seeking to capitalise on any parliamentary and procedural rules to get their way. The government's responses to the instability were often intransigence, including repeatedly putting a proposed deal to Parliament and, in the end, failed attempts to 'shut down' Parliament through an extended prorogation period in autumn 2019 at a key time during UK negotiations with the European Union. However, the failure of government to overcome the hurdles and obstacles presented by Parliament meant that, ultimately, a general election was sought in December 2019. For an assessment and detailed analysis of the 'parliamentary battles' over Brexit, see Meg Russell and Lisa James' (2023) extensive research.

Overall, the events between 2017 and 2019 broke records, precedents and conventions. And importantly, they suggest that Parliament cannot be taken for granted. In particular, it shows that the governing parties are reliant on the confidence of its MPs to sustain their executive position, and that the cohesion and discipline of MPs is not a given. It also demonstrates the rather complex constitutional positions of Parliament, government and judiciary, in which the legal supreme authority is still perceived to rest with Parliament. However, while the Brexit years were a show of strength for Parliament over the executive, it also did not enhance its reputation in the eyes of the public and continues to raise questions about the effectiveness of the institution to (i) make policy decisions and/or (ii) hold government to account.

Reflective questions

1   Was Parliament the source of the Brexit stalemate between 2016 and 2019?
2   What are the long-term consequences of Brexit for Parliament?

Party discipline is a fundamental aspect of efficient parliamentary work; without discipline and a reliable majority, it is impossible for governments to achieve, well, much. This was clearly observable during the Brexit years (see Case Study 10.1 and Martill, in this volume), in which both parties were hugely divided and where rebellions led to such stalemate that the Prime Minister at the time, Theresa May, felt unable to govern. This indicates that discipline is important, and also that it is misleading to suggest that MPs are 'lobby fodder'.

While Brexit may seem an anomaly, Figure 10.6 shows that the trend of rebelliousness by MPs has been growing for a long time. What causes MPs to rebel? And why do they do so more often now than in the past? According to Cowley's (2002) research, MPs are more likely to rebel, first, if their ideology or beliefs differ from the leadership and, second, if they have done so before – i.e. rebelling becomes a habit. Other research has suggested that voters prefer independently minded and rebellious MPs (Campbell et al. 2019), so some MPs may use dissent as a way to signal their independence from their party and/or their opposition to a particular policy (Slapin et al. 2018; Slapin and Kirkland 2020). Finally, it may also be explained due to the nature of political parties acting as 'broad churches', with different ideological wings, which has spread over time. This was especially pronounced during the Conservative–Liberal Democrat Coalition between 2010 and 2015, when the government had two 'wobbly wings', i.e. a wing of rebellious right-wing Conservatives and a wing of rebellious left-leaning Liberal Democrats (Cowley and Stuart 2012).

An important caveat to this discussion is that academic analysis relies on when an MP has voted against their party. What Figure 10.6 does not show, and what is even harder to research, is when MPs *threaten* to vote against their party. There are cases, usually documented in the media, when government responds to potential discontent by backbench MPs by making amendments to legislation or, in the worst case, not putting something to a vote because the whips do not believe the vote would pass. For example, in December 2022, the Department for Levelling Up, Housing and Communities announced changes to the government's Levelling Up and Regeneration Bill that watered down mandatory housebuilding targets. This outcome came as a result of critical amendments to the bill tabled a month earlier, supported by 60 Conservative MPs, and, with the prospect of defeat, forced the government to rethink its legislation (Brown 2022). Backbench MPs therefore seek to use their potential powers of dissension to negotiate for amendments and compromises. Some research has suggested that different MPs try to do this in different ways. For example, research on women MPs elected in 1997 suggests that, while these MPs were less likely to rebel (giving rise to the label 'Blair's babes'), they would fight harder behind the scenes in attempts to persuade government to change tack. In this respect, many women MPs thought rebellion was unproductive (Childs 2004a). This discussion suggests that governments need to be responsive to MPs and gauge their satisfaction with legislation and policy decisions; the support of its MPs cannot be taken for granted. And, given the rise in MPs' willingness to rebel, it is an ever-important issue. At the same time, the power of rebellions waxes and wanes according to different wider issues, such as the extent of disagreement and the willingness of removing the whip from MPs (such as under Boris Johnson in 2019) or the extent of the majority of the governing party (such as under Labour since 2024).

What about the House of Lords?

The focus of this section has, so far, been on the House of Commons and MPs' behaviour. The House of Lords, meanwhile, is comparatively understudied and less understood. In part, attention is drawn to the House of Commons because: it is seen as the 'primary' chamber with more powers and from which the majority of ministers, including the prime minister, are drawn; the House of Commons has democratic legitimacy that the House of Lords does not; the House of Lords does not vote against manifesto commitments, in what has become known as the Salisbury convention; and the Parliament Acts 1911 and 1949 allow the House of Commons to bypass the House of Lords if absolutely necessary (meaning that the Lords can only delay and frustrate) and prevent the upper house from amending 'Money Bills' (legislation that raises money through taxation or that spends public money). That said, the House of Commons uses its powers over the House of Lords sparingly; it has made use of the Parliament Acts since 1949 on only four occasions, the last of which was used to pass the Hunting Act 2004. This is despite a very active House of Lords, which, as shown in Figure 10.7, regularly defeats the government.

Research indicates that the House of Lords has become especially more active since the 1990s, when reforms were introduced to remove most hereditary peers, which have arguably enhanced peers' perceptions of their legitimacy as a chamber of appointed experts (Russell and Sciara 2008; Russell 2010, 2013). Not only has the House of Lords become more willing to amend legislation, but the government also does not seek to overturn those changes in many cases. This is, at least in part, because amendments by peers tend to be based on detailed scrutiny and are informed by expertise following an arguably more deliberative process (Parkinson 2007), and also in part because the government cannot necessarily afford to spend more resources, notably in terms of time, to fight the House of Lords. As a result, governments seek to be more responsive to concerns raised by peers and devote more resources for 'handling strategies' for the upper house. This is especially important because traditional whipping in the

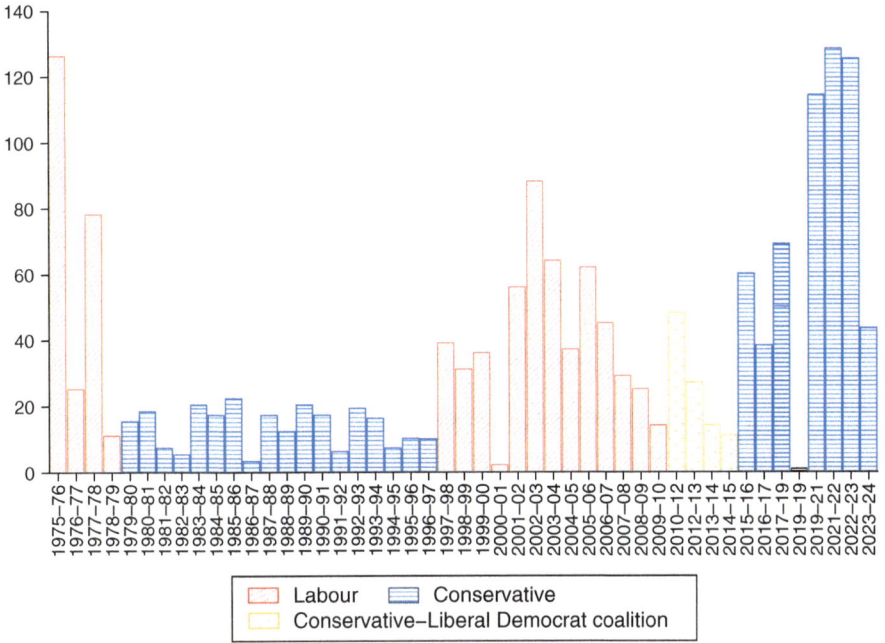

Figure 10.7 Government defeats in the House of Lords, 1975–2024

Source: UK Parliament (2024b)

House of Lords is weak – the incentives used for MPs do not carry the same force for peers (such as the prospect of promotion or demotion).

Where does all of this leave us? It suggests that Parliament's relationships with government are more complex than initial impressions or simplistic assessments may suggest. Government may indeed play the most important role in shaping legislation to its preferences, but this does not mean that Parliament is 'peripheral' or a 'rubber stamp'. It also highlights some of the methodological difficulties in trying to study the influence of Parliament; it is not necessarily easy to assess, even if some data is readily published by Parliament. Finally, it is only one role – albeit an important one – that Parliament plays. Its relationship with government is also shaped by attempts to hold it to account for broader policy decisions. We now turn to this theme.

Holding government and powerful interests to account

A basic structural feature of parliamentarism is that the legislature delegates most day-to-day executive decision-making to the government. However, at the same time, governments are held to account for their decisions in Parliament. Taken to its most fundamental level, this means that governments depend on their parliamentary majorities and must retain the confidence of the legislature to govern. The ultimate form of accountability, then, is the ability of Parliament to withdraw its confidence in government through a confidence vote. While the most recent vote of confidence took place in 2022 (which the government won), confidence votes are not common and the last vote which led to the defeat of the government took place in 1979, leading to a general election. That said, certain votes in Parliament can be labelled as confidence issues. For example, in 2003, Tony Blair's government made clear that the parliamentary debate and vote on military intervention in Iraq would be a confidence issues; if the government lost, Blair would resign.

While retaining the confidence of the House of Commons is a precondition for executives to govern with stability, it is not the main way through which accountability operates on a day-to-day basis. As covered in the previous section, MPs undertake detailed legislative scrutiny of bills. Furthermore, Parliament has several institutionalised mechanisms with which to oversee and scrutinise government decision-making: (i) through parliamentary questions (written and oral) and parliamentary debates, and (ii) through non-legislative committee work.

Parliamentary questions and debates

The best-known activity in Parliament is the weekly questions to the prime minister (PMQs). It is what members of the public think about when it comes to Parliament (Hansard Society 2014). First established in 1961, PMQs has become renowned across the world for the adversarial jousting between the prime minister and MPs. It has also garnered academic attention, with studies *inter alia* exploring the discursive styles of prime ministers and their willingness to answer questions (Bates et al. 2014; Lovenduski 2014b; Bevan and John 2016; Bull and Strawson 2020).

By comparison, parliamentary questions (PQs) in general are not as well studied in parliamentary research (Martin 2011), despite their prevalence in everyday parliamentary life, with around 40,000 questions asked in a typical parliamentary session. Parliamentary questions across both houses must be used 'to obtain information or to press for action' (Erskine May 2019: para 22.11). They can take written or oral form, i.e. they can be tabled with government ministers providing a written response, or they can be asked in the chamber. The Speaker of the House of Commons may also grant so-called Urgent Questions (UQs), which take precedence in parliamentary proceedings and require attendance of the relevant minister (or, in some cases, the prime minister). This mechanism also exists in the House of Lords, where they are known as Private Notice Questions. Since 2009, UQs have grown in frequency, improving the topicality of issues discussed in Parliament.

While up-to-date studies about the impact or effectiveness of PQs as an accountability tool, especially in the House of Lords, are sparse (Franklin and Norton 1993; Cole 1999), studies demonstrate that PQs are important for MPs to monitor their coalition partners in government (Martin and Whitaker 2019) and that MPs in marginal constituencies are more likely to table written questions (Kellermann 2016). Other scholarship, meanwhile, has sought to make use of the published data on PQs to examine the characteristics and behaviour of MPs in making use of PQs. This research has found that, among other things, descriptive representation translates into substantive representation of varying degrees in the case of gender (Bird 2005), ethnic minorities (Saalfeld and Bischof 2013) and religious minorities (Kolpinskaya 2017). It suggests that descriptive representation affects the accountability of government.

Complementing parliamentary questions are other mechanisms and instruments that MPs can – at least in theory – use for scrutiny and accountability. This includes Early Day Motions, which are non-debated motions that MPs can sign to demonstrate their support for a particular point of view. They can also be used to assess the 'mood' of the House on particular matters.

Another tool is through debate. In the main chamber of the House of Commons, government no longer has exclusive power to allocate business.[5] For 20 sitting days per session, opposition parties can determine parliamentary time for debates and motions of its choosing (of which 17 days are given to the official (main) opposition party and three days to the second largest opposition party). These debates have been used to highlight the priorities of non-governing parties and usually intend to provoke the executive. Indeed, between 2017 and 2024, Conservative governments whipped their MPs to abstain from non-binding opposition day motions, which are often worded in a partisan manner to embarrass them.[6] Meanwhile, the Backbench Business Committee, which was introduced in 2010 as part of a wider package of reforms to the House of Commons known as the Wright reforms (see Case Study 10.2), may allocate business on 35 sitting days per session (of which 27 days must be in the main chamber and the remainder in Westminster Hall – see below). This innovation was designed to give backbench MPs the opportunity to hold debates without control from frontbench politicians. Early assessments suggest that this has been an important mechanism to hold government to account (Foster 2015). Additionally, backbench MPs have an opportunity to consider Private Members' Bills on 13 sitting Fridays per session.

While control over parliamentary time has shifted away from government in several key ways (Norton 2017), Meg Russell and Daniel Gover (2021: 23–39) have identified shortcomings in how non-government business is allocated, not least that sessions vary in length and that the precise timings for when non-government business may take place still needs to be negotiated with the government. So, while Parliament may have gained some independence in terms of allocating its own time, Russell and Gover conclude that considerable further reforms are necessary.

In other forms of parliamentary debate, the impact on government can play a significant role. One particularly interesting change, especially since 2003, is the growing influence of the House of Commons in discussing and voting on military intervention. Following the aforementioned vote on military action over Iraq, Parliament has had debates and votes on military action in Libya in 2011 and in Syria in 2013 and (retrospectively) in 2018. These debates and votes are tabled by government, and some have suggested that a new convention has emerged that gives Parliament the final say on military action, especially given the 2013 vote, whereby a majority rejected proposed military involvement in Syria by the UK Government, but this remains contested (Strong 2015, 2022; Kaarbo and Kenealy 2016).

The various mechanisms outlined here indicate that the UK Parliament has several different instruments available to hold government accountable for its decisions. These mechanisms shape much of the parliamentary calendar and day-to-day life. However, the quantity of time available for accountability does not necessarily translate into quality scrutiny. Academic research continues to paint a mixed picture here, even if much more research is possible.

---

5 In parallel to the main chamber, debates in the House of Commons may take place in Westminster Hall, giving space to debate motions arising from petitions, motions put forward by MPs, motions allocated by the Backbench Business Committee, and to debate parliamentary reports from select committees.

6 It nevertheless raises the question of the added value and effectiveness of such votes if they are routinely ignored.

Select committees

Across both houses, small groups of cross-party MPs or peers come together in select committees to hold government to account. They have been variously praised and even labelled as the most important part of the accountability arsenal available to Parliament (Fisher 2015). Turning first to the House of Commons, the structure of present-day committees was introduced in 1979. It specifies that every ministerial department is shadowed by one select committee (e.g. the Health and Social Care Department is mirrored with a Health and Social Care Committee in the House of Commons). Additionally, there are some cross-cutting committees, such as the Environmental Audit Committee, which scrutinises environmental policy across the whole of government. The function of select committees is to 'examine the expenditure, administration and policy' of ministerial departments and their associated public bodies, as set out in House of Commons Standing Orders. One of the most recent additions includes the Women and Equalities Committee, which is not only an example of gendered institutional change (Childs 2023), but also a body that scrutinises equalities issues across government.

Select committees are made up of a small cross-party group of MPs that reflects the overall party balance in the House. Since the 2024 general election, select committees have a majority of Labour members, followed by a minority of Conservatives, and representation from a third party (such as the Liberal Democrats). Members are appointed following internal elections among their party colleagues. The party balance is also reflected in the distribution of chairs, which is largely decided through the usual channels. Chairs are responsible for the overall management and direction of committee work. They are elected to their position by secret ballot and by the whole House. The election procedures for members and chairs were introduced in 2010, following the Wright reforms (see Case Study 10.2).

Case Study 10.2

Select committees and the Wright reforms

The present-day structure of select committees has evolved over time, punctuated by various reforms. Departmental committees were first introduced on a systematic scale in 1979. Greater resources through the introduction of a Scrutiny Unit, additional payments for chairs to incentivise an alternative career, and hearings with the prime minister were introduced in 2002 (for an assessment, see Flinders 2007). And, in 2010, the Wright reforms were introduced to address the huge reputational damage to Parliament following the MPs' Expenses Scandal of 2009 – a scandal marked by outrage by the public and which led to resignations and even prison sentences (Kelso 2009; Crewe and Walker 2019; Flinders and Anderson 2022).

The Wright reforms are named after the chair of the House of Commons Reform Committee, Tony Wright. The committee's final report, *Rebuilding the House* (House of Commons Reform Committee 2009), recommended a package of reforms, including: (i) changes to the appointment procedures for committees from selection by political parties to election for members (within their party groups) and for chairs (by secret ballot by the whole House); (ii) improving the scheduling of government and non-government business through a new Backbench Business Committee; and (iii) strengthening public engagement initiatives. As analysed by Meg Russell (2011), the reforms were eventually introduced but faced many obstacles from the executive and political parties, who were not keen on relinquishing power.

How important were the Wright reforms? Some have argued that select committees have become more autonomous and influential (Fisher 2015). In particular, some qualitative research suggests that the legitimacy and prestige of committee membership has been enhanced, especially for chairs (Kelso 2016; Crewe and Sarra 2019; Geddes 2020: 60–76). However, other, more quantitative, research suggests that the reforms have not noticeably improved members' engagement with committee work (Bates et al. 2017) or addressed gendered divisions of labour, even if elections have improved the overall gender balance (O'Brien 2012; Goodwin et al. 2021). With respect to other reforms, David Foster (2015) suggests that the Backbench Business Committee has made a 'significant impact' in its early years; meanwhile, public engagement initiatives continue to become embedded in parliamentary work (but which predate the Wright reforms). According to the latest research, then, the jury is still out.

Reflective questions

1   How would you assess the impact of the Wright reforms on Parliament?
2   What other reforms are needed to strengthen democracy in the UK?

Given the appointment procedures for select committees, they are largely independent from government and the party machinery. Committees determine their own work agendas and decide which topics to investigate (even if these often react to the salience of political debates in the media). Topics can and have ranged from large international issues about fraud (e.g. from the House of Commons Digital, Culture, Media and Sport Committee's inquiry into fake news (2019)) to domestic social policy questions (e.g. the House of Commons Education Committee's inquiry into school performance of white working-class pupils (2021)). Committee investigations rely on written evidence submitted to them and committee hearings, which are analysed and published in reports with recommendations and conclusions. Most of these reports are published with cross-party agreement, which arguably lend reports significant credibility and persuasive power for action (White 2015). This is particularly important because committees do not have any formal powers to force government to accept any of their recommendations. Despite their formal lack of powers, however, academic research suggests that committees can be highly influential, with one study finding that around 40% of committee recommendations are accepted and implemented by government (Benton and Russell 2013; see also Hindmoor et al. 2009; White 2015).

In recent years, committees have broadened their scrutiny activities by holding one-off evidence sessions not only with ministers (and the prime minister through the Liaison Committee; see Kelso et al. 2016), but also with powerful interests, such as CEOs of major companies, which are often well attended and publicised across the media (Mellows-Facer et al. 2019; Prescott 2019). However, there are some questions about the power of committees to compel the attendance of witnesses, which have been tested in recent years by individuals refusing to attend (House of Commons Committee of Privileges 2021, 2022). It remains a live issue and serves as a reminder that committee influence is contingent on the willingness of actors, including government, to engage with select committee inquiries.

While research suggests that select committees in the House of Commons are vital for accountability, they arguably also play a wider role in parliamentary and public life. Although less well researched, select committees are mechanisms through which information and evidence can be brought before Parliament and into the public domain. Such evidence and information can come from a range of sources, including government and public bodies directly, as well as think tanks, trade unions, scientists, businesses and the general public (Geddes 2018). As such, select committee are also a tool for MPs to learn and build expertise, potentially professionalising the work of Parliament further. That said, research also suggests that membership attendance and turnover remains variable (Bates et al. 2017) and there is also a danger that, in focusing on learning about a policy, MPs may forget that their role is to scrutinise policy (Geddes 2020: 49–50, 144).

Select committees are a permanent and everyday feature of parliamentary life, both in the House of Commons and in the House of Lords. However, the discussion so far has largely focused on committees in the lower chamber because academic research on committees in the upper chamber are sparse. The committees in the House of Lords are structured slightly differently, according to cross-cutting government themes, and with some committees appointed on an *ad hoc* basis to address specific yet persistent policy challenges (these are known as 'special inquiry committees'). Committees in the House of Lords are perceived to be of high quality and are widely respected, not least because of the high number of experts that sit in the upper chamber. And yet, as Connolly et al. (2022) point out, these committees are 'institutions ignored'. This means that, aside from isolated assessments – often by peers themselves – it is hard to gauge their influence on parliamentary work.

Recurring themes in the study of Parliament

While three major themes of parliamentary work – representation, law-making and accountability – present significant overviews of the main activities in both the House of Commons and the House of Lords, it is obvious that they overlap and intersect but also don't quite holistically capture all parliamentary work. In this section, we will look at some wider themes, not least understanding the nature of the relationship between Parliament and government; the place of Parliament in wider political and public life; Parliament's place in the union; and explore challenges and possible reform.

The changing nature of executive–legislative relationships

One prominent theme in this chapter is the relationship between Parliament and government. Anthony King (1976), in a highly influential article, wrote that executive–legislative relationships need to be broken down. He identified three 'modes': first, an intra-party mode, which is about the interactions between government backbenchers and the government; second, an opposition mode, which is about the interactions between government parties and opposition parties; and third, a non-party mode, which is about work in committees or free votes. King went on to analyse these different modes, and suggested that – especially in the UK Parliament – the intra-party mode, about party discipline and dissent within the governing party, is the most consequential for influencing the executive's behaviour in Parliament. Meanwhile, the opposition mode tended to be more obstructionist, in which opposition parties sought to thwart the executive, and the non-party mode tended not to play a role given the focus on plenary debates with weak committees.

While King's article was highly instructive, the UK Parliament has changed in several important ways. Indeed, Meg Russell and Philip Cowley (2018) argue that King's argument needs updating. They point out that the intra-party and non-party modes have become stronger as a result of (i) changes to the party system (there are now more parties in Parliament), (ii) the growth of dissent (as discussed in previous sections of this chapter), and (iii) the greater accountability capacities introduced through select committees. Additionally, the opposition mode has shifted. Parties in Parliament are now more focused on reasoned debate and policy substance than the obstructive approach that they had adopted in the past. Finally, they argue that King overlooked bicameral relations, i.e. the importance of the House of Lords, which has changed significantly since the 1990s. Taken together, Russell and Cowley (2016: 134) have concluded that Parliament is an 'extremely influential' institution. This conclusion contrasts with much public policy and comparative parliamentary literatures.

Connecting Parliament with the public

Philip Norton (2017) has concluded that Parliament is going through both the 'best' and 'worst' of times: the best of times because of the expanding opportunities to rebalance relationships *vis-à-vis* the executive; the worst of times because trust in politics and in Parliament by the general public remain extremely low. The Hansard Society's *Audit of Political Engagement* (2019) found that the UK's systems of governing were at their lowest ebb in the 15-year history of the survey; more recently, the Institute for Public Policy Research (IPPR) found that only one in three trust Parliament to fulfil its core function of acting in the best interests of people across the UK (Patel et al. 2023: 8). While not new (e.g. see Dalton 2004; Hay 2007), it has become more pronounced in the mid- to late 2010s as dissatisfaction has grown and as new factors have emerged, such as a growth in political violence and threats against MPs (Matthews and Haughey 2024), often with considerable gendered dimensions (Esposito and Breeze 2022).

Parliament has actively sought to address public disengagement with politics by strengthening initiatives to connect with the public and promote greater public participation with politics. In particular, from 2004 onwards, the UK Parliament has increased its investments and developed a more outward-facing approach (Walker 2012). For example, it has led to a new Education Centre in a purpose-built facility at the UK Parliament, campaigns for improving public knowledge about politics (e.g. Parliament Week, usually held in the autumn for one week), integrating engagement activities in committee work (Walker et al. 2019), expanding social media accounts, investing in staff teams and resources devoted to engagement, developing the system and use of e-petitions (Leston-Bandeira 2019; cf. Matthews 2021), and more. While this work may not (yet?) have turned the tide on negative perceptions by the public of politics, Cristina Leston-Bandeira (2016) argues that it has changed the role of Parliament from a purely representative institution to a 'mediator parliament' that plays an important role in mediating between publics and elites.

Parliament's place in the union

Territorial representation and parliamentary politics in the UK are affected by the multi-level nature of the state. As covered in other chapters, devolution across the UK nations led to new representative institutions for, and shifted legislative competencies to, Scotland (the Scottish

Parliament), Wales (the Senedd Cymru) and Northern Ireland (the Northern Ireland Assembly). On the one hand, it has meant that the UK Parliament conventionally seeks not to ordinarily legislate on devolved matters. In cases where it does, it seeks 'legislative consent motions' (LCMs, also known as Sewel motions) from the relevant devolved legislatures. Historically, these have often been granted, but not always. In the case of refusal, the UK Government has sometimes made changes but, in others, enacted legislation anyway (Cairney and Keating 2004; Evans 2020). On the other hand, devolved parliaments have also pushed against the limits of their powers. In a case where a devolved legislature seeks to pass a bill that can have an adverse effect on the operation of reserved matters, the UK Parliament can make an order to 'veto' this bill. In January 2023, this happened for the first time since devolution was introduced to prevent the Scottish Parliament's Gender Recognition Reform (Scotland) Bill from reaching royal assent (Torrance and Pyper 2023).

Devolution has also raised the question of unequal patterns of representation inside the UK Parliament. MPs from Scotland, Wales and Northern Ireland have long played a significant role in substantively representing their nations in the UK Parliament (Sheldon 2022). Furthermore, it has also given MPs from devolved nations opportunities to vote on legislation that only affects England, something which English MPs cannot do in the case of devolved legislation. This problem – also known as the West Lothian Question (named after the constituency of the MP who repeatedly raised the issue in the 1970s) or English question – suggests unequal representation and power for MPs (Bogdanor 2010). For a time, the UK Parliament had introduced procedures to allow only English MPs to vote on English legislation (or English and Welsh MPs for legislation that affects England and Wales only), known as 'English Votes for English Laws', or EVEL (Gover and Kenny 2018). These procedures were abolished in 2021 in order to, according to the government, streamline the legislative process (BBC News 2021).

On the whole, inter-parliamentary relations are under-researched but, according to the limited research that does exist, these relations are 'extensive and dynamic' (A. Evans 2019: 110), with representatives and officials meeting both formally and informally on a range of matters (see also Hansard Society 2023). Given the tensions and impact caused by Brexit and the Covid-19 pandemic on policy making across the union (Kenny and Sheldon 2021; Morphet 2021), understanding these dynamics remain important for understanding representative democracy in the UK.

Research in Focus

The politics of bricks and mortar

Issues about physical space and the design of the Palace of Westminster have been thrown into sharp relief in recent years. Several reviews have indicated that the masonry is crumbling and that there are leaks, problems of damp, electrical failures, fire risks and asbestos. As a result, there are calls for a much-needed programme of the 'Restoration and Renewal' of Parliament (UK Parliament 2012; Joint Committtee on the Palace of Westminster 2016). There have been major debates within Parliament by MPs, peers and officials (Siebert 2023; Meakin and Siebert 2024) but, crucially, it has not been reflected in wider public debate. According to Flinders et al. (2019), this is a missed opportunity. Rather than re-imagining how politics is done, direction of travel has been to rebuild and restore the Palace brick for brick, with MPs and peers regularly delaying decisions about implementation due to the price tag – thus increasing the costs of R&R further and, more gravely, the danger of serious accident and failure.

Regardless of the future of R&R, focusing on the physical nature of Parliament offers a distinctive vantage point for analysing the process and conduct of politics. This is not just to identify the symbolic importance of buildings or architecture – even though, of course, symbols, ceremonies and rituals are crucially important (Waylen 2010; Rai and Johnson 2014; Rai 2015). Design and space also matter because they directly shape the nature of politics and political behaviour (Psarra et al. 2023). In particular, it draws attention to the unequal presence of different groups in British politics, historically as well as today, which returns to a core theme of this textbook to ask critical questions about who is included and excluded from decision-making in political and public life. For instance, Nirmal Puwar (2004, 2010) has shown how physical layouts and spaces have historically been used in Parliament to regulate behaviour and, especially, to enforce divisions between class, gender and race/ethnicity. Meanwhile, the parliamentary estate was also built at a time of limited interest in physical accessibility of its buildings. This means that the built environment can represent major barriers to participation for people with physical impairments – both for ordinary citizens wishing to get involved in politics, but also for people running for elected office and holding a position as MP (Evans and Reher 2022).

An unanswered question remains about how far the physical embodiment of politics in parliamentary buildings may be (causally) connected to wider parliamentary and political culture. While in theory we may be able to argue that the opposing benches in the UK Parliament reflect an adversarial culture in contrast to hemicycles in the devolved parliaments of Wales and Scotland, this has not been demonstrated empirically – yet. Moreover, other architectural elements that emphasise transparency, such as the use of glass, do not seem to be connected to higher levels of trust in politics and politicians.

Taken together, the 'politics of bricks and mortar' highlights several interconnected debates about public engagement with politics, the inclusion or exclusion of voices in parliamentary spaces, and the relationship between the built environment and political behaviour, and a fruitful avenue for future research.

Discussion questions

1   To what extent and in what ways does space and design shape British politics?
2   What is the best way forward in restoring and renewing the Palace of Westminster?

Challenges for Parliament and prospects for reform

British politics has been in flux over the past two decades. The UK Parliament has been central to a range of challenges for effective governance, including coalition politics between 2010 and 2015, with distinctive styles of bargaining in Parliament (Matthews and Flinders 2017); referendums that are in tension with the ideals of parliamentary sovereignty (Atkinson et al. 2020); dealing with the 'battles' of Brexit (Russell and James 2023); rewriting parliamentary procedures to hold government to account during a pandemic (Evans et al. 2021); and continuously dealing with scandals, whether it is the MPs' Expenses Scandal from 2009 (Crewe and Walker 2019; Flinders and Anderson 2022) or issues regarding integrity, bullying and (gendered and sexual) harassment (Raney and Collier 2022).

When placed in wider context of public distrust in politics, questions about the influence of Parliament on executive politics, and concerns over its physical environment (see the Research in Focus box above), it is fair to say that Parliament has been, and continues to be, under significant pressure. It has raised clear questions over shortcomings in Parliament, including: is the government too powerful *vis-à-vis* parliamentary business? Does the legislative process adequately achieve scrutiny? How might the public be more involved in parliamentary work to combat distrust? Should the UK retain an unelected upper house? Recently, there have been several contributions that have sought to address some of these questions. Some are technical and focus on improving aspects of the legislative process (Sargeant and Pannell 2022), while others take a broader position to recommend changes to how time is organised in Parliament (Russell and Gover 2021). More significantly, a range of commentators have recently published books to imply that Parliament needs wide-ranging reform, including from a former official from the House of Commons, Hannah White (2022), current Labour MP Chris Bryant (2023) and political journalist Ian Dunt (2023). Meanwhile, discussions about reforming the House of Lords have ebbed and flowed for over 100 years (Kelso 2006; Dorey 2023) with no political consensus. Furthermore, while there have been repeated calls for reform in recent years, it is also worth noting that political salience for reform has not been high. For example, the 2024 general election was dominated by debates about economic growth and public services, with limited attention and scrutiny in debate or in manifestos about potential reforms.

Conclusion

Overall, this chapter shows that Parliament is a complex and multi-faceted institution, with wide-ranging roles in British political and public life. While public and media perceptions usually have a simplistic view of Parliament's role and its ability to carry out those tasks effectively, this chapter has identified some of the nuances and subtleties when it comes to understanding parliamentary work. This does not mean that you must conclude that Parliament is necessarily influential in the legislative process or effective at holding the government to account. Rather, the aim of this chapter is to suggest (i) that you should be suspicious of simplistic statements about Parliament and (ii) that there is a range of different views about Parliament. It is now up to you to dig deeper and take the analysis further to make your own assessment about the effectiveness of Parliament in British politics.

Summary

- This chapter has sought to give you an overview of the main parliamentary activities in the UK Parliament and the role of the institution in wider political and public life.
- It has identified how theoretical and analytical concepts of representation have been applied in the UK's political system, specifically in the case of the UK Parliament.
- It has given a state-of-the-art review of the current research about Parliament's role in British politics, demonstrating complexity around parliamentary influence and its place in public life.

- It has given you a summary of the different ways in which MPs complement their law-making capacities through their scrutiny roles and the wide-ranging tools available to MPs and peers.

Recommended and further reading

- To understand the influence of Parliament on governance, see Russell, M. and Cowley, P. (2016) 'The policy power of the Westminster Parliament: The "parliamentary state" and the empirical evidence', *Governance*, 29(1): 121–137.
- To understand the significance of select committees in parliamentary life, consider the Special Issue released by *Parliamentary Affairs* in 2019 – volume 72, issue 4 – which includes a range of papers about their history and development, actors and roles, and the evolution of their activities.
- To explore intersectional challenges faced by some MPs, see this detailed case study: Evans, E. and Reher, S. (2023) 'Gender, disability and political representation: Understanding the experiences of disabled women', *European Journal of Politics and Gender*, 28 March, 1–18. E-pub ahead of print. https://doi.org/10.1332/25151082 3x16779382116831
- To delve deeper into a range of topics, research and issues regarding the UK Parliament, the most up-to-date academic introduction is: Leston-Bandeira, C. et al. (2024) *Exploring Parliament* (2nd edn). Oxford: Oxford University Press.
- For a technical summary and overview regarding how everything in Parliament works, the best go-to guide is: Besly, N. and Goldsmith, T. (2023) *How Parliament Works* (9th edn). Abingdon and New York: Routledge.

Chapter 11

The executive

Richard Parry

What will this chapter tell me?

- In the UK, the executive branch emanated from the Crown, the King, whose functions eventually passed to a politically accountable government, rather than emanating from the people and codified in a written constitution.
- The British way of politics is fluid and changeable. Its strength is flexibility and the possibility of parliamentary majorities enacting change without obstacle. Its weakness is the way that important changes can be enacted by the same legislative or executive power as even the most minor.
- Prime Ministers have the freedom to reshape the machinery of government without passing laws – and they frequently do – but the Treasury, the Home Office and the Cabinet Office stand out for their little-changing, controlling mentality.
- Failings at the heart of government led to the decisive end of the Conservative government in July 2024, but similar challenges of organisation and performance face Labour.

What do I need to know?

- The UK executive doubles as the central government for the whole of the UK (what in other countries would be called the 'federal' government) and as the government of England. The lines are often blurred.
- The UK executive is drawn entirely from Parliament: to be a government minister, you must be, in practice, a member of the House of Commons or the House of Lords.
- The range of functions carried out by the executive has grown in size and complexity over the course of the twentieth century.

Introduction

The executive branch of the state is formed by agencies of government that perform public tasks in a context of political accountability. In law, every public employee works for somebody and so has an employment position that defines their recruitment and rewards. In practice, they encounter a sociological pattern of doing the job in a certain way, which over the years crystallises into accepted working practices transmitted between generations. A public sector job has a rather different character from one in the private and self-employed sector. It may be more passive, have greater solidarity between workers, and imply a trade-off between public service and personal reward. But employment patterns everywhere have become more flexible and precarious. A 'career' is often an actual 'careering around' between multiple positions, income streams and employers. The concept of the 'gig economy' sums up many of these issues, not least that political action can be an impermanent performance with a shifting cast of characters who do not build up long-term knowledge and loyalty.

Like economists, political scientists set out narratives about the working of systems that may become myths – that is, idealised representations of how things work. For economists, these often relate to the free market and the pursuit of shareholder value. In the political sphere, the narratives tend to be about accountability and the securing of the democratic will through ministerial responsibility to an elected parliament. These convenient myths may not correspond to reality.

The UK lacks a written constitution – a basic law emerging from an idea of the sovereignty of the people that is harder to amend than ordinary laws and may be interpreted by a constitutional court. The political system, and particularly the body of unelected officials within it, relies on efficient, honest and public-spirited behaviour, and also some degree of organisational stability. But this stability has been lacking in recent years. The theme of this chapter is the breakdown of this normative structure of UK Government through variables such as politicisation, contractorisation, regulation, deconcentration and diversification.

Politicisation is the interpretation of every event and policy through the prism of political advantage. The American phrase 'in Washington, everything is political' applies to other capitals as well. Defensive rebuttal has always been a strong theme in the British system, reflecting the adversarial nature of law and Parliament. Scandals, sometimes involving assertive legal threats against isolated citizens, show the dangers of this mentality: the state-owned Post Office falsely accusing sub-postmasters of fraud (the Williams inquiry, already under way before the ITV drama series *Mr Bates vs the Post Office* in January 2024 struck a massive public chord), the administration of contaminated blood products (the Langstaff inquiry report in 2024) and the fire at Grenfell Tower in London in 2017 (the Moore-Bick inquiry report in 2024). The speed on political action has vastly increased – the system is not waiting on tomorrow's newspapers but on the next minute of social media posts. This is not conducive to good policy making, and produces empty claims of 'top priority', 'taking very seriously', 'robust procedures', 'new investment on the way' that lose meaning the more they are routinised.

Contractorisation is delivering public services through arm's length mechanisms, including the privatisation of government enterprises. The use of contractors by government is necessary – it can never construct facilities and operate services entirely through its own employees – but it has been much extended. Governments may seem to have the scale and spending power to get a good deal in these transactions, but it is not so simple. Contracts may be large and complex – capital projects, information technology systems, provision of workforce. Specifications of what is required may not be precise. Public managers may be reluctant to change contractors and may be happy to export the blame for failure. A contract may seem a convenient way of 'doing something', but it can become a road to dependency, in which familiar contractors are unduly favoured and the market for alternatives diminishes. Public services may become more expensive as a lack of suppliers forces prices up and public sector managers become accustomed to signing off on expensive bills. In some cases, such as social care, private suppliers need the volume of public purchases but find that the fees payable do not cover costs and attempt to cross-subsidise from other consumers.

Regulation. Public services have always been audited for financial propriety, and long-standing inspectorates of constabulary (police) or schools were high-prestige jobs staffed by ex-practitioners whose visits were high-tension experiences. But the attraction of the concept as a visible form of quality assurance has now been extended to health, social care and public administration. Essential industries that have moved into the private sector are typically subject to public regulation of their pricing, ownership and solvency. Elected politicians can also get caught up in codes about parliamentarians' outside interests and earnings. Written codes, such as the Ministerial Code, Civil Service Code and the Cabinet Manual (Cabinet Office 2011), and rules for public appointments are typically enforced by commissioners and advisers independent of government. But the enforcement and design of these procedures can never be removed from politics. What starts out as a guarantee of good policy, administration and service delivery can become a substitute for it (Sawers 2024).

Deconcentration includes 'devolution', a response to nationalist pressures outside England, and an ambivalent relationship of the centre with local government, which in the early twentieth century ran many developing public services. The trend under the post-1945 welfare state was in the other direction, to nationally uniform health, social security, transport and utility systems. Local authorities retained school education, social care and public housing, and as organisations they became bigger through reorganisation into larger units even as their discretion was restricted under the pressure of national politics. Meanwhile, new local legislatures in Scotland, Wales and Northern Ireland were formed in 1999 as a response to unique political circumstances in the three smaller nations of the UK. They have administrations running services for 2–5 million people, a natural scale for a workable span of coverage and responsibility. England attempts to run services for 60 million from a single centre of control and accountability.

Diversification. An awareness of biases in recruitment and lack of diversity has led to a greater codification of good practice and self-reflection on the ways tasks are done. Norms of behaviour for public sector workers are set sociologically. Even in the female-heavy teaching and nursing professions, 'leadership' was often a male characteristic. There was a lack of awareness of the risk of direct and indirect discrimination. As equality law became wider-ranging, public employers naturally wished to be in the lead on enforcement, and human resources operations (traditionally called 'establishments' or 'personnel' and now often 'people') expanded. But formalisation has its costs, and the growth of so-called 'woke' behaviour and language (best defined as a heightened awareness of the correct way of speaking about discriminated-against groups) further complicates the operationalisation of this concept.

Taken together, these five variables put pressure on traditional 'textbook' understandings of the way that executive power is exercised in the United Kingdom. A country of 'taken for granted' stability, celebrated as a model of good government for the world, has found it difficult to handle change in order to achieve good policy performance and meet the demands of citizens. That is the theme of this chapter.

The architecture of the UK public sector

Our firmest anchor to an understanding of the UK executive is through the employment position of those working in it. Effective state funding or control of nominally private or charitable organisations, and the use of contractors, may make it difficult for some workers to know what sector they are in, but we can categorise Crown service, other central government, local government and public corporations.

Crown service, initially military (the armed forces) and later civil (the Civil Service), expressed the way that executive power originated with the Crown (the King) and, in the democratic era, became accountable to *government ministers* appointed and dismissed by the Prime Minister (political heads of department are usually called *Secretaries of State* and sit in the *Cabinet*). From the mid-nineteenth century recruitment to the civil service became independent of politicians and, at higher levels, was through competitive examination in a process supervised by an independent Civil Service Commission. This led to the stratification of the services into 'classes' (administrative, executive, clerical, professional) with a pattern of grades within them that resembled military ranks and were held independently of the particular job an individual was doing. A key characteristic of the civil service – political impartiality and the ability to continue serving through a change of government – survives at all levels up to Permanent Secretary, but in recent years has been somewhat compromised by the use of staff on temporary secondments and political appointments.

Important reforms were made after the 1968 Fulton Commission recommended abolishing classes and set out a common route to the top. But in practice the 'fast stream' recruitment of graduates into an elite scheme, and central planning of career moves in the top two grades through what is now called the 'Senior Leadership Committee', maintains biases. Much political effort in recent years has been devoted to getting effective, competent, skilled and diverse civil service 'leaders' into the top jobs, with career-long devotion to the civil service seen as a less positive variable.

The concept of the 'public sector bargain' (Hood and Lodge 2006) explores the implicit 'deal' between politicians on the one hand and their officials on the other. The traditional 'bargain' has traded off the chance of high rewards against anonymity, security, respectful treatment and protection from criticism. The difficulty arises when the 'bargain' is an all too good one. The protections are valuable (in particular, a generous pension is worth a lot and redundancies are rare) but the marketable talent may not be all that great. Politicians who have had to hustle for their position and risk losing it to the whim of the electors or head of government may feel resentful of their officials.

Other central government includes staff that are not civil servants. Many work in so-called 'quangos' (quasi non-governmental organisations), which are run through government-appointed boards. In recent years, many educational establishments (schools organised as 'academies', sixth-form colleges and further education colleges) have moved to this sector from local government. But the largest group is the National Health Service, established in 1948 – 'state socialism' in a large and essential part of the economy, a universal service without direct user charges. To recruit medical professionals, various compromises had to be made: primary care physicians ('general practitioners') remained nominally self-employed, and senior hospital doctors were free to supply some of their services to the private sector. Medical earnings profiles favoured experience (including access to a government-funded pension scheme), leaving younger doctors tied exclusively to the NHS in a weak position in the economic market compared to their private sector contemporaries. The lack of integration between free health services and social care services with some charges impedes the best and most cost-effective care. With no economic mechanism to express demand for services except 'going private' and purchasing treatment, the NHS and every aspect of its activity became politicised.

Under the Labour governments of 1997–2010, many new hospitals were built though the contractorised mechanism of private finance (up-front construction and maintenance by the private sector in return for guaranteed long-term payments). This built on the experience of the 'Private Finance Initiative' of 1992, but the 'buy now, pay later' aspect was flawed. New types of contract kept staff happy: senior doctors could do more private work, and general practitioners were allowed to buy themselves out of 24/7 responsibility to patients. Alongside this, the vogue for planning and reorganisation continued, with hospitals forming business entities ('trusts'), contracting within the service and with private suppliers, and in 'partnership' models with local authorities supposedly relating health and social care – deconcentration themes that are hard to achieve in practice.

When spending slowed after 2010, what remained were even more complex reorganisations and political interventions. In England, purchasing by consortia of GPs became the norm. The Covid pandemic set back for years the ability to meet the demand for non-emergency attention. GPs proved unreachable and waiting lists for diagnosis and treatment moved in the wrong direction. The pressure felt by front-line staff expressed itself in the end of the traditional reluctance of organised doctors and nurses to behave like conventional trade unions. During 2023 and 2024 intermittent strikes followed the refusal by government to make health an exception to its general public sector pay policy. Politicians could not face up to the fact that running through public, political means a sector that represented 10–20% of the economy in all advanced societies might be beyond them.

Local government has been dominated by professional cadres – lawyers, teachers, accountants, social workers. The simplest way to organise local authorities is to leave them to raise revenue to pay for their services and run them under local political accountability. But the gap between the local tax base (property taxes on households and business) and spending demands (including some legal obligations to provide social care and housing) requires central grants, and these come with conditions and political manipulation. Local government direct employment, particularly in manual occupations, has declined in favour of contractorised approaches, and some authorities have been found to have discriminated against female employees, even with nominally equal pay, because of bonus schemes that favoured male-dominated occupations. The cost of rectifying this, and of unwise property and IT investments, tipped some English authorities in the 2020s into bankruptcy and handing their affairs over to central government commissioners.

Public corporations, free from day-to-day ministerial control but not influence, extended the public sector in the mid-twentieth century but then shrunk it through privatisation. These services are revenue-earning (energy bills, transport fares) and, if profitable, tempted governments from the 1980s to sell them off. In England, this process is virtually complete, with even the Royal Mail having been privatised while maintaining its obligation for postal delivery to every household. Electricity, gas and water privatisation was controversial as the new entities could pay dividends to shareholders and raise debt to do so; regulation limiting price rises and requiring investment was patchy, and the complicated financial structure of privatised water utilities in England attracted particular scrutiny. Workers were removed from the public sector and so in theory the state was no longer involved in industrial relations, but traditions of trade union organisation persisted. In practice, finances were often government-subsidised and so politicians were dragged into pay disputes, such as those with railway and postal workers in 2022–2023.

Organisations such as companies where all or most of the shares are publically held, and universities, might regard themselves as outside the public sector but have such a preponderance of state funding and control to make them classifiable as public. Official data on public employment exclude general medical practitioners and university staff, but in recent years the Office for National Statistics (ONS) has reflected political reality by classifying entities dependent on and controlled by government as being in the public sector. This brought in the Royal Bank of Scotland and Lloyds Banking Group after the financial crisis of 2008, leaving it after the majority of shares were sold.

Throughout the public sector, important common variables include pay review and good pensions. Pay review is based on the concept that the best way of valuing public employees, given that their tasks may be unique and not subject to market forces, is to benchmark them against private sector wages at comparable level of skills. But although pay review bodies are meant to be independent, they have to take account of government pay norms. Pension rights are an important part of remuneration, and those that are 'defined benefit' – i.e. linked to final earnings or, increasingly, career average earnings – are now largely confined to the public sector where they can be underwritten by the government.

Table 11.1 summarises the trajectory of public employment from its peak of over 30% of the workforce in the 1970s. Privatisations took it down to around 20%, where it has remained despite expansions in health and social care jobs. The civil service has drifted up recently, despite the automation of many processes, and it has sought to correct disparities; its senior grades were 47.9% female in 2023, up from 36.3% in 2013 (Office for National Statistics 2023b). The public sector has overall become more female (typified by the female general secretaries of the two main unions (Unite and Unison)) but the rapid generation of private sector jobs has become the dominant and norm-setting characteristic of the labour market.

Table 11.1 Public employment by organisational type, headcount (thousands)

	Civil service	Other central government	National Health Service	Local government	Trading Enterprises	Total public	% of labour force
1981	690	471	1,318	2,899	2,254	7,632	31.4
2001	518	663	1,249	2,778	372	5,580	20.1
2011	483	793	1,531	2,772	658	6,237	21.3
2023	522	1,186	1,962	2,002	194	5,866	17.7

Notes:
1 Schools organised as 'academies' move from local to other central government and employed 170,000 in 2011 and 507,000 in 2023.
2 University staff and general practitioners in the NHS are excluded from the public sector and would add about 2% to the 2001–2023 percentages.
3 On a consistent classification of organisations always in the public sector, ONS estimates the percentage as 18.5% in 2001, 18.6% in 2011 and 17.3% in 2023.

Sources: 1981 figures from Parry, R., in Massey, A., ed., *International Handbook of Civil Service Systems* (Cheltenham: Edward Elgar, 2011) Table 15.1; 2001–2023 figures from the Office for National Statistics, www.ons.gov.uk/employmentandlabourmarket/peopleinwork/publicsectorpersonnel/bulletins/publicsectoremployment/previous releases, March 2024, tables 2, 5 and 11

The course of political development until the 2010s

For decades after 1945, the basic mood around UK Government was one of celebration of the universal welfare state and the probity and dedication of public servants. Three Prime Ministers from 1964 to 1979, Harold Wilson, Edward Heath and James Callaghan, had once been civil servants. Over time there was a build-up of central capability. Heath set up a 'think tank', the Central Policy Review Staff (CPRS), with seconded civil servants. A new Civil Service Department was split from the Treasury in 1968 and its Permanent Secretary became Head of the Civil Service and sometimes a close policy adviser to the Prime Minister.

Prime Ministers have total freedom to reorganise government departments and changes are often opportunistic attempts to signal attention to an issue or resolve personnel problems in the Cabinet. Standing out as little-changed are the *Treasury*, jealously guarding its authority over finance, economics and public expenditure, the *Home Office* as the centre of 'control' functions, such as police, citizenship and immigration, and the *Cabinet Office* managing the policy process and official machine.

From the 1980s new initiatives and plans changed the character of the UK public sector and are summarised in Table 11.2. Margaret Thatcher, Britain's first female Prime Minister (1979–1990), was susceptible to conservative theories about state failure previously confined to the USA. Thatcher promoted perspectives that the civil service was a site of inefficiency and complacency. A 1980 BBC comedy series *Yes, Minister* (and later *Yes, Prime Minister*) made play with the self-serving actions of devious officials: the Permanent Secretary figure, 'Sir Humphrey' (Appleby), entered folklore as a negative role model. Thatcher's efficiency adviser, Sir Derek Rayner, had a background in the then-admired retailer Marks and Spencer, and conducted rapid 'Rayner reviews' of government operations. In 1981 Thatcher abolished the Civil Service Department; her other policies included the privatisation of utilities and compulsory competitive tendering of many local government services, such as rubbish collection and building maintenance. It marked the decisive move towards contractorisation at all levels of government.

Table 11.2   Major heart of government initiatives since the 1980s

1980	Thatcher government plans to cut civil service number from 730,000 to 630,000 over four years, achieved
1986	Compulsory competitive tendering (CCT) for some local government services starts movement to privatise under contract numerous government services
1988	'Executive agencies' under accountable chief executives launched in the civil service
1991	'Citizen's Charter' seeks to set better service standards by public providers
1992	Private Finance Initiative (PFI) launched to engage private investment in public projects; later called 'Public Private Partnerships' it was used by all parties to rebuild public infrastructure but was dropped as poor value in the 2010s
1996	Senior Civil Service created with individual contracts; pay, grading and recruitment for other grades delegated to departments (and now Scottish and Welsh Governments)
1999	White Paper *Modernising Government* sets trend for 'digital by default' use of IT, emphasis on diversity, equal opportunity and effective performance
2010	Constitutional Reform and Governance Act puts civil service on a statutory basis for the first time
2012	Civil Service Reform Plan leads to departmental boards with non-executive directors
2014	Prime Minister to have final word on permanent secretary appointments, Chief Executive Officer of the Civil Service appointed
2020	*Places for Growth* plan to locate half of senior civil servants outside London, part of the 'levelling-up' agenda

Much of the civil service was organised as 'executive agencies' from 1988, with accountable chief executives. For a while, 'agencification' seemed likely to become an important theme. It offered governments a chance to distance themselves from blame for failing policies in difficult areas (such as prisons and border control) and also raise money through fees, charges and trading activities. But it quickly became apparent that ministers could not avoid parliamentary scrutiny of agency activities and a theme of 'reconnecting' with parent departments took hold. The fact that staff continued to be civil servants in trade unions which resisted workforce fragmentation was a decisive point of detail.

Thatcher's successor, John Major (1990–1997), took privatisation and contractorisation further and left a personal stamp with his 'Citizen's Charter', an attempt to codify the rights of service users and give means of redress. In 1996, a centrally run 'Senior Civil Service' was established, leaving the organisation and pay of other grades to departments and agencies. Major left a managerial foundation for his Labour successor Tony Blair (1997–2007) and his Chancellor of the Exchequer, long-time rival and eventual unopposed successor Gordon Brown (2007–2010). Blair's style was much less respectful than his predecessors of Labour's trade union roots. New possibilities of information technology prompted dreams of both a better and a cheaper interaction of citizen and state. *Modernising Government* (Cabinet Office 1999) started the path towards 'digital by default' that gave the Treasury the opportunity of cutting running costs. Brown built up the Treasury's policy control capacity through successive spending reviews. Relations with Blair's growing policy staff were dysfunctional, but the two stuck together through years of economic growth and electoral success.

Labour's original territorial policy was of deconcentration, and Scottish and Welsh devolution was achieved in 1999. This was to be accompanied by a tier of elected regional government in England but the policy was abandoned after a heavy referendum defeat (by 78% to 22%) for it in the North East in 2004. Conservatives never became devolved ministers, and the administrations – run by Labour in Wales and from 2007 by the Scottish National Party in Scotland – had uneasy relations with the UK centre even before the Conservatives took control of it in 2010.

English local government became a mixture of single-tier and two-tier authorities, with a developing vogue for elected city or multi-authority mayors. The resource base of local authorities weakened: property taxation on businesses was taken over by the centre and the 'council tax' on residential property could not raise enough revenue. The centre no longer trusted elected local government and regional health authorities, and started relating directly to hospitals and schools. Blair's 'Delivery Unit' under Michael Barber set out detailed performance targets for hospitals and schools. The policy functions of the Department of Health and the central management of the National Health Service were fused. The scale of England-made micro-management by central politicians and the plausible officials who rose to the top by a 'can-do' mentality was wildly inappropriate, but those in the grip of a politicised approach were not deterred.

Summarising these trends, we can draw a map (Table 11.3) of what came to be called the 'core executive' of UK Government (Smith 1999). This is a series of networks. The Prime Minister is at the heart, working through the formal structures of the Cabinet and its committees, and civil servant Cabinet Secretary and Principal Private Secretary. Alongside this is a political and policy staff typically under a politically appointed Chief of Staff, and a communications teams running a 'grid' of coordinated policy announcements. They are located at, and known as, '10 Downing Street', the Prime Minister's official residence in London.

Number 10 staff all have cross-cutting links to opposite numbers in control departments (the Treasury running public spending and the Cabinet Office running the civil service) and spending departments (theoretically, but decreasingly, the policy makers in their areas, such as health, education and defence). The departments run large executive operations (e.g. tax collection, benefits payments and prisons), and through grants and regulation have much control of devolved and local government. As with all organisational maps, this is only the starting-point for understanding the reality – in this case, a highly politicised reality – of influence.

Table 11.3   UK core executive map

Prime Minister/10 Downing St.	Central control departments	Spending/executive departments
Ministers	Treasury	Subject area departments
Cabinet		
Cabinet Committees		
	Spending teams - - - - - - - - -➤	Principal Finance Officers
Chief of Staff - - - - - - - - - - - -➤	*Special advisers*	
	- - - - - - - - - - - - - - - - - -➤	*Special advisers*
Communications teams - - - - - - - - - - - - - -➤	Communications teams	
		Communications teams
- - - - - - - - - - - - - - - - - - - -	- - - - - - - - - - - - - - - - - -➤	
Permanent staff		
	Cabinet Office (independent) Civil Service Commission)	
Cabinet Secretary and Head of the Civil Service	- - - - - - - - - - - - - - - - - -➤	*Permanent Secretaries*
	Permanent Secretary of the Treasury	
	Civil Service Chief Operating Officer - - - - - - - -➤	*Heads of People*
Principal Private - - - - - - - - -➤ *Secretary*	*Private Secretaries*	
	- - - - - - - - - - - - - - - - - -➤	*Private Secretaries*
	Operational directorates and agencies	Operational directorates and agencies
	(through grants and funding rules)	
	devolved and local government	

The turbulent central executive politics of the 2010s and 2020s

Public sector politics in the UK after 2007 was driven by four 'hot' events. The first, the collapse of many financial institutions in 2008–2009, was well handled by Gordon Brown, who used state power to underwrite the fragile financial system, but he could not survive the general election of 2010, where a hung parliament produced Britain's first modern peacetime coalition. A dominant Conservative Party under Prime Minister David Cameron and Chancellor George Osborne attempted to bring the public finances under rapid control through deep cuts in public spending that their Liberal Democrat partners could not resist. More starkly than ever before, health spending and pension benefits were protected but local services and working-age bene-fits were not. Against the odds, the Conservatives won a slim overall majority in 2015.

The second hot event was David Cameron's self-inflicted referendum on leaving the Euro-pean Union ('Brexit'). Meant to resolve the issue by mobilising a cross-party majority against the long-troublesome Conservative 'Eurosceptics', this ploy not only failed to deliver the major-ity, but actually lost the vote in June 2016 by 51.9%. Cameron resigned immediately and the period before Brexit took place in January 2020 (with a transitional period delaying practical consequences until the end of December 2020) was turbulent. The tightening labour market after the end of free movement from the EU complicated public sector service delivery.

The third hot event, from March 2020 to early 2022, was the worldwide Covid pandemic, the most significant global event since the Second World War. It knocked to the floor the balance of public finances and introduced a wartime-like state control of economic and social life. Revelations to the Covid public inquiry in 2023–2024 showed deficiencies of decision-making at the centre, with the Cabinet Secretary messaging on 2 July 2020 'I've never seen a bunch of people less well-equipped to run a country'. Public sector debt bounced back to a size equivalent to the national economy (GDP). A temporary, emergency increase in public expenditure could be justified as fiscally acceptable, but also set up Liz Truss's disastrous attempt to spend her way to economic growth in September 2022 on the premise that if the politics were right the economics could take care of themselves.

The fourth hot event was the Russian invasion of Ukraine in February 2022 and its impact on world energy markets. This fuelled inflation both directly, through household energy bills, and indirectly through input and supply-chain costs of everything else. Inflation, in turn, was brought under control through the crude mechanism of higher interest rates, which among other things raised the cost of government borrowing (including that previously issued at rates of interest linked to inflation).

By the end of all this, the Conservatives had burned through three Prime Ministers (Theresa May, Boris Johnson and Liz Truss) before alighting on Rishi Sunak. May could not improve on her lacklustre performance in previous jobs; Johnson was an erratic and flawed personality who had come through eight years as Mayor of London but could not raise his game; and Truss came and went in 49 days, a rare example even in international terms of a failure of basic competence by a new leader.

Constitutional norms were also upset. In September 2019 the Johnson government prorogued (suspended) Parliament using an Order in Council issued by Queen Elizabeth, under the convention of accepting government advice. After petitions from members of the public for 'judicial review', an appeal court in Scotland and later the UK Supreme Court ruled that it was unlawful. Parliament immediately reassembled.

Several aspects of this case shocked the Johnson government – that the courts could review royal prerogative; that Scotland's separate judicial system, guaranteed in the Act of Union of 1707 and now under the jurisdiction of the Scottish Government, could pronounce on UK constitutional matters; and that the Supreme Court could overrule England's most senior judges, who had sided with the government. Further interventions by the judiciary, especially on human rights matters, continued to challenge government pretensions. In 2024, a new law declared Rwanda to be a safe country for immigrant deportations in order to overrule a finding by the Supreme Court that it was not.

The twenty-first century also brought important changes in the tools of communication and decision-making. Ironically, these brought back a written record that in the twentieth century had often been superseded in sensitive matters by telephone conversations and unrecorded meetings. Text-based commercial software preserved loosely worded conversations. Modern norms of social media both multiplied the range of contributors to public discourse and led to a uniform news agenda as traditional media monitored the trends of social traffic and chased after the leading stories.

Government manipulation of the agenda also became more adept. The Johnson government explored White House-style on-camera press briefings in 10 Downing Street, but press journalists preferred the cosy 'lobby' system where accredited political correspondents were given quotes and 'steers' by an unnamed (and multiple) 'Prime Minister's Official Spokesperson'. It became routine for policy changes to secure a triple impact through an 'exclusive' article or interview, a briefing on the purpose of the policy and the announcement itself. Under the guise of security, the timing and location of politicians' movements were often embargoed to the media until they happened. Journalists, knowing they could be disfavoured or excluded, connived in the system. With 'open government' a norm and the regulatory theme in play through calls for inquiries into almost anything, the practice of politics became febrile and exhausting.

The check on behaviour in the British system had always been the rather boring reputation of non-political officials for impartiality and competence, but from 1974 it became possible for ministers to bring in temporary officials who were not politically impartial, known as 'special advisers' or 'spads'. Often young and active within their political party – or a faction within it – from an early age, they were sometimes dismissed as never having had 'real jobs' outside politics (but fast-streamers may be no less unfamiliar with 'real life' and lack training in disciplines relevant to public policy). Using the special adviser mechanism to install a Chief of Staff at Number 10 started under Tony Blair in 1997 with Jonathan Powell, who, along with Press Secretary Alastair Campbell, was given power to issue instructions to permanent officials. That power was later dropped, but it scarcely constrained incumbents such as Theresa May's joint chiefs Nick Timothy and Fiona Hill, and most notoriously Boris Johnson's Dominic Cummings. Real-life personalities seemed to resemble the outrageous Malcolm Tucker of the TV series *The Thick of It* (2005–2012). By presiding over a network of 'spads' around Whitehall, they could bypass ministers but, in the end, they had no political resources beyond the Prime Minister whom they had accompanied into Number 10, and were forced out.

A further reinforcement of Number 10 was the institution of the post of Permanent Secretary at Downing Street, which was separate from the Cabinet Secretary. The first holder of this rank was Jeremy Heywood, a long-time 'consigliere' Private Secretary to a Conservative Chancellor and Labour Prime Minster, who eventually became Cabinet Secretary and Head of the Civil Service himself before dying in post in 2018 (Heywood 2021). The post, held by him for only months, propelled Simon Case to become a young Cabinet Secretary at Boris Johnson's behest in 2020. In adept civil service fashion, he avoided being sanctioned by the police over Covid lockdown behaviour, unlike past and future Prime Ministers Boris Johnson and Rishi Sunak.

Under David Cameron, ministers gained greater control over senior appointments, including the right to choose permanent secretaries from among the candidates considered appointable by the Civil Service Commission and to place them on fixed, five-year contracts. Cameron favoured outside consultants and job experience, and a 'Civil Service Reform Plan' in 2012 created departmental boards with non-executive directors (Diamond 2023).

The Cabinet continued to diminish as a real centre of decision, but events of 2017–2022 – the assertion by the House of Commons of control over the Brexit process, and the ouster of Boris Johnson by mass resignations from his government – provided contrary evidence to the much-discussed 'presidentialisation' of the Prime Minister role. The House of Commons has become more rebellious, and its committees a more searching check on government, but apart from that the 2017–2022 period may turn out to be an exception to the long-term concentration of power in Number 10.

Some of the turbulence can be put down to personality and general competence. Many academic commentators have studied the way that political leaders become locked into a structure and try to manage issues and political time (Byrne and Theakston 2019). Rory Stewart (2023) has given a vivid picture of the Prime Ministers he served from 2015 to 2019. Conservative absorption with internal party affairs followed its split on Brexit in 2016; 'respecting the result' of the referendum tugged the party towards an extreme version of the policy many had opposed, and ministers changed rapidly, to the detriment of policy making.

Registers of MPs' interests showed the earnings potential – from consultancy and paid speeches – of not being a minister. For politicians with name or face recognition and some wish for personal and family privacy, the rewards could be great. The only job better than Prime Minister was ex-Prime Minister after a quick exit as an MP. Post-office experiences varied. Tony Blair and Gordon Brown established charitable foundations and contributed to policy debates into their seventies. David Cameron attracted ignominy for consultancy and lobbying income from the alleged fraudster Lex Greenshill, but he dramatically reappeared as Foreign Secretary in 2023 after being appointed to the House of Lords. Theresa May served one further term as a backbencher. Boris Johnson left Parliament and reverted to his lucrative journalism and writing. Liz Truss, unapologetic about her populist-tinged policies, sought to rebuild her political position as an MP. Rishi Sunak, independently wealthy, was in at age 42 and out at 44 after calling a general election six months before he needed to.

An overarching theme of these developments is the importance of economics, and to some extent sociology, in supplementing what has been an unhelpful emphasis on law and public administration in securing policy performance. The Treasury remains under persistent criticism for its money-in/money-out focus. Approaches that keep the up-front cost off the public accounts are favoured. Rules of thumb about public finances – such as that public expenditure could not rise above 60% of national income (1970s) or public debt above 90% (2010s) without dire consequences – proved plain wrong. And standing over all of this is the idea of a 'contract' between government and citizens – that it is the duty of the state to provide well-working services in areas that are public responsibility and should be technically deliverable. The Covid pandemic caused backlogs in health and the courts system that were slow to be removed, and the feeling of 'downward spiral' (Bowers 2024), that standards would never again match reasonable expectations, became pervasive.

Research in Focus

The nature and functioning of the core executive

Academic debate has evolved from one over the power of the Prime Minister versus the Cabinet (1960s) to that of a 'core executive' where policy and politics intersect (1990s), leaving key decisions with 10 Downing Street or the Treasury (Smith 1999). The latest research focuses on personalities and settings. Rhodes (2022) has written of 'court politics', suggesting that the core executive has been superseded by a household executive defined by proximity and current favour (the concept originated with t'Hart, who delineated its components as 'think tank', 'sanctuary', 'arena' and 'ritual'). Ministers, permanent officials and special advisers interact and cope in an all-too-human way in what Rhodes (2011) calls 'everyday life in government', almost imprisoned by settings, roles and stories that may not add up.

There is an ambivalence between 'letting go' of government into deconcentrated networks and 'getting a grip' through central levers of control. Agencification did not work and Dommett and Flinders (2015) suggest that more generally the centre 'strikes back' through a beefed-up Cabinet Office through a Chief Executive (now called Chief Operating Officer)

(Continued)

of the Civil Service. Both deconcentration and control have been expressed by plans under the 'Places for Growth' programme of 2020 to move half of Senior Civil Service posts out of London, with the Cabinet Office having a second hub in Glasgow.

Physical proximity remains important when for historical reasons a cramped old house, 10 Downing Street, is both home and office for the Prime Minister. Domestic provision and support for the PM have been notoriously poor, but transport, communications and security have become more cocoon-like over the years. The British system at least keeps the Prime Minister grounded by requiring frequent attendance at Parliament and attention to a constituency whose residents generate personal issues for the PM's attention. But the basic artificiality of political life at the top persists.

During the Covid pandemic various gatherings – essentially social prolongations of meetings by officials who were authorised to be in the building because of their essential work – later incurred sanctions by the police (Gray 2022). The later Hallett inquiry revealed a 'blokish' atmosphere which bypassed the increasingly common bans on alcohol in workplaces. The evidence of Helen MacNamara, the most senior woman in Whitehall, was telling: she wrote of ego-contaminated 'grippy', 'macho and heroic' ways of working in which 'humanity and humility' were lacking and 'you have to be physically in the conversation to input' (MacNamara 2023). On 19 May 2020, she told her colleague Simon Case (as reported in his oral evidence to the Covid inquiry on 23 May 2024) 'this has been the most overtly sexist environment I have ever been asked to work in'. Distanced working led to a reliance on written messaging, and the regressive costs of transport and childcare made in-person meetings hard to reinstate even after the pandemic was over. Dominic Cummings became notorious because his aggressive personality meshed with a deep but erratic interest in the detail of policy and the obstacles to its implementation. Whatever the stated goals, biases between diversity were built in as like-looking and like-minded people sought one another out.

Research awareness of group behaviour is helping us to a much better understanding of the way that politics is often not a sacred space but rather a reproduction of everyday life with all the discriminations and biases that perpetuate patterns of power. In recent years, there has been a much better understanding of the dimensions of ethnicity, disability, sexual orientation and gender identity, especially through the notion of protected characteristics in the Equality Act 2010. Annesley and Gains (2010) noted how the disposition of the core executive is detrimental to women and traps them in organisational and housekeeping roles; Kroeber and Huffelman (2022) note that women face additional obstacles to getting on in government. For all their promise of new leadership, Keir Starmer, his Chancellor Rachel Reeves and Chief of Staff Sue Gray, a former senior civil servant who undertook the 'parties at Number 10' inquiry, have careers strongly embedded in the British institutions that produced these outcomes. Sue Gray's involuntary replacement by strategy chief Morgan McSweeney in October 2024 was the result of her failure to retain support within the two groups she was meant to reconcile, Whitehall officials and long-serving activist special advisers.

Case Study 11.1

Officials complaining about ministers

Two well-documented cases put into question our understanding of the norms between politicians and officials and the balance of their relationship. Ministers had expectations of civil servants – but what about expectations in the other direction? Much of the diversification agenda is about mutual respect, but how is this to be enforced when the power imbalance in a relationship is so clear, and indeed the word 'servant' is used? Pyper (2020), and contributions from practitioners in the same issue of *Public Money and Management* (Volume 40, issue 8, 2020), give a flavour of the issue.

Our cases are the complaints made against Alex Salmond, First Minister of Scotland, in 2017 and Dominic Raab, UK Deputy Prime Minister, in 2022. Both concerned alleged harassment against staff. In Salmond's case, a new Scottish Government procedure, issued three years after he had stepped down, was used by two officials to report alleged sexual harassment. The content of the complaints led to a referral to prosecutors (by senior officials, not the complainers) and criminal charges against Salmond of which he was acquitted (Clegg and Andrews 2021). Before his trial in 2020, Salmond had won a civil case against the Scottish Government on the grounds that prior contact between the complainants and the investigating officer rendered the findings of fact against him unlawful. The officer was 'Head of People' at the Scottish Government, who joined it after Salmond left office and so seemed suitable, but her supportive advice to the complainants could be characterised as lack of impartiality.

Salmond's case raised general questions. What do you do when the chief of the government is the alleged malefactor? What happens when alleged harassment moves into the sexual area? Does anything change when complainants may be special advisers who got to know their ministerial chief through party channels? And on what basis should retrospective complaints, not made at the time of the events but after the end of a tenure in office, be entertained?

A 2017 case involving a member of the Scottish Parliament had set a precedent that departing from office did not close the book on complaints (on the model of the regulation of professions such as law and medicine). The adversarial legal processes used by Salmond ran into the human relations approach around workplace issues – which might be seen as a masculine/feminine conflict. The parliamentary report (Scottish Parliament 2021) and a sensible independent appraisal by a lawyer (Dunlop 2021) showed the dangers of retrospective complaints and internal investigations – and Alex Salmond was able in some small measure to rebuild his political career outside the SNP in his new Alba Party. Salmond died suddenly in October 2024 while still pursuing a legal claim against the Scottish Government that the harassment procedure had ben devised conspiratorially to get at him personally.

Dominic Raab attracted complaints on more generalised suggestions of 'bullying' in his roles as Justice Secretary and Foreign Secretary. Raab himself asked for an investigation by an outside lawyer Adam Tolley and resigned after the report was issued. Ironically, the Tolley report said that Raab's behaviour had improved since the investigation started and that if he had behaved in that way previously there would have been no valid grounds for complaint (Tolley 2023: 173).

Tolley's findings built on a distinction between 'abrasive' and 'abusive' behaviour set out in Sue Owens' *Review of Arrangements for Tackling Bullying, Harassment and Misconduct in the Civil Service* and between 'one-off' and 'repeated' incidents in Laura Cox's report on *The Bullying and Harassment of House of Commons Staff* (both 2018). Although not exclusively a male phenomenon (Priti Patel's tenure as Home Secretary survived scrutiny of similar complaints), the issue is 'demanding but fair' behaviour that challenges subordinates to take criticism without flinching. Raab's response in articles and interviews (20 April 2023) was that 'activist, over-unionised' civil servants had a 'passive-aggressive-culture' of fragile sensibility that quickly went into complaining mode; and that there was 'cultural resistance' to some of his policies as part of a left-leaning 'blob' of dominant opinion.

Tolley's conclusions captured some of the nuances in the issue: 'the combination of explicit unconstructive criticism and frequent interrupting may have a cumulative effect as a firm on intimidating or insulting behaviour' (Tolley 2023: para 172); and the perception of cultural resistance 'was explicitly rejected by many, particularly in view of the obligation to give informed and impartial advice' (para 167). Most tellingly, Raab had stepped out of long-standing civil service norms: 'I did not detect any material lack of resilience in those who had made the complaints. Most of the individuals in question had many years of experience working closely with ministers' (para 133). In the familiar imagery, 'if you can't stand the heat get out of the kitchen', but not all kitchens and not all chefs are the same.

Conclusion

The UK executive has been beset by performance issues and failure to build new norms in line with the changing social and economic context. It is no longer run by a cadre of career-long officials – administrators and professionals – operating on agreed protocols with politicians. It reflects many themes of modern life – precariousness, the infinite capacity for information storage and transmission, the scope for productivity improvements. It will be expected to have the best employment practices and express the diversity and inclusivity of modern society. Above all, it will be expected to work in terms of the quality of both policy process and service delivery. There are only so many times when narratives of improvement fail before a destabilising lack of confidence sets in. The chaotic politics of the 2010s and 2020s have been a warning sign, and the Starmer government of 2024, rooted in caution and respectability, was given perhaps a last chance to reform process and improve performance alongside the press of current events.

Plans to fix institutions continue to emerge. The Institute for Government (2024) proposed merging Number 10 and the Cabinet Office into a 'Department of the Prime Minister and Government', with a separate 'Department for the Civil Service'. In 2023, former Conservative minister Francis Maude produced an official independent review of civil service governance that advocated an alternative rearrangement, with an 'Office of Prime Minister and Cabinet' and an 'Office of Budget and Management' eating into Treasury responsibilities, a civil service-critical and politician-friendly approach (Maude 2023, especially annex 3). It is the note of frustration about getting the heart of government to work efficiently and equitably that comes through the many years of reports and reviews. In 2024, as in 1997, an incoming Labour government sought to improve standards and performance while not departing from the managerial and organisational path of their Conservative predecessors.

The UK does not have a written constitution that separates branches and levels of government and gives them unchallenged powers in their own sphere. Faults at the centre are not hedged by other views, power bases, evidence and life experience. The limitations of contractorisation and regulation as a technocratic approach to public sector management have become apparent. Buying time before policy failure becomes apparent cannot be repeated indefinitely. Eventually the mask slips and the discrepancy between theory and practice stands revealed. In the nineteenth century Walter Bagehot famously spoke of the 'dignified' and 'efficient' parts of the constitution. Authority is attributed to quasi-theatrical institutions like the Crown, Parliament, the Cabinet and local authorities to conceal the exercise of real power held elsewhere. While we need to understand the formal institutions and processes of central government, the primary focus must be on practices and impacts, and their response to economic and social modernity.

Summary

- The United Kingdom, lacking a written constitution, runs its central government through a mixture of law and practice, with public administration best defined by the employment position of public sector workers.
- Themes of politicisation, contractorisation, regulation, deconcentration and diversification run through much recent policy.

- There is a general tension between a stated wish to deconcentrate and 'let go', and the reality of the centre 'striking back' in the search for political control and policy success. Regulation and contractorisation have not turned out to be short-cuts to good performance on public services.
- Relations between politicians and officials fractured at the heart of Conservative governments through hot events like Brexit and Covid and a febrile atmosphere in the 'court executive' at 10 Downing Street.
- The Starmer government of 2024 emphasises stability and good practice in its approach to governing, opening up a new era at the heart of the British state.

Recommended and further reading

- Operations at the heart of government have long had a mystique linked to an ideal of public service and democratic politics, and sustained by secrecy about what was actually going on. Academic textbooks fall out of date very quickly. Politicians' memoirs give their partial view, and rapid semi-academic accounts based on interviews (notably by Anthony Seldon and Tim Shipman) provide a valuable 'first draft of history' (the latest being Seldon and Newell (2023) and Shipman (2024)). Rhodes (2011) is based on earlier ethnographic research but gives the best flavour of life in Whitehall.
- Overall, the best place to begin may be the work of the Institute for Government, especially its report (2024) on the working of central government. Public inquiries, such as the war on Iraq 2009–2016 (chaired by John Chilcot) and the Covid pandemic in 2023–2024 (chaired by Heather Hallett), have opened up decision-making, the latter inquiry yielding an array of informal and over-candid messaging and compelling written and oral evidence by key players. The House of Commons Public Administration and Constitutional Affairs Committee, and the House of Lords Constitution Committee, undertake investigations of many Whitehall issues; their written evidence includes material from academics and their oral evidence sessions are probably the best way into the recent thoughts of politicians and civil servants.

Part IV
Beyond the centre

Image 4 Houses in Hotwells, Bristol. Territory is essential to understanding UK politics, and this Part offers chapters on each UK nation: England, Scotland, Wales and Northern Ireland. Photo by Matt Prosser. License: CC BY-SA 3.0.

Chapter 12

England

Ben Wellings

What will this chapter tell me?

- This chapter outlines the difference between England, Britain and the UK in policy and politics.
- It applies four different frameworks for understanding the place of England and Englishness in British politics: allegiance, governance, politicisation and post-Empire.
- It examines normative debates about the feasibility and desirability of England as a distinct political community.
- Finally, it unpacks the overlapping institutions and politics of Englishness and Britishness.

What do I need to know?

- The United Kingdom (UK) is a plurinational state that developed as the English state entered into treaties of union with its neighbouring island kingdoms and principalities, while creating colonies and markets overseas.
- England is the largest part of the United Kingdom, in terms of territory and population, with 56.5 million of the UK's 2021 population of 67 million.
- There is little consensus on what to call the phenomenon under analysis: English national identity, Englishness, English nationhood, English nationalism.
- English nationality developed within the context of the formation of the English and British states, but also during the expansion and contraction of the British Empire, and during membership of the European Union. This process of nation-formation is ongoing.
- There are no mainstream political parties that represent England as England in the way that other nations of the UK have party representation, in the way that the Scottish National Party, Plaid Cymru, or most of the parties in Northern Ireland represent their nations or political communities.
- The UK's political institutions are England's institutions. However, there are a growing number of mayors representing cities and regions across England, and England is represented in civil society organisations such as the Football Association or English Heritage.
- There are several adjacent concepts that are pertinent to the study of England and English politics, notably Unionism and Britishness, as well as aspects of conservative and radical political traditions.

Introduction: Englishness and English nationalism in British politics

This chapter describes and analyses the place of England in British politics. This is not as straightforward as it might at first seem. Scotland, Wales and the different communities in Northern Ireland all have political parties that seek to represent their interests as nations or distinct political communities. England has no such explicit representation. England's parties are 'British' parties, and England's political institutions are those of the United Kingdom (UK).

Given the demographic preponderance of England within the United Kingdom, and notwithstanding the embedding of devolution in other parts of the UK since the end of the 1990s, it remains hard to separate debates in British politics and even public policy from English concerns. This is compounded by the existence of the related concept of Britishness and the various forms of unionism that inform some expressions of nationalism in the UK's constituent nations. Add to this a normative dimension whereby Britishness is often portrayed as an inclusive form of collective identity, whereas Englishness is framed as narrow and exclusive. Throw in other intersections of identity politics – those known as 'English identifiers' tend to be older, less educated and drawn from lower socio-economic status groups than the rest of the UK population – and you can see a structural and political squeamishness about speaking for, or even about, England. Thus, England poses something of a paradox in British politics: it is both ubiquitous yet often absent in debates about policy, politics and the future of the plurinational United Kingdom. In this way, it is hidden in plain sight.

This implies taking the politics and politicisation of Englishness seriously as an object of enquiry. It means that we need to see England as an important, even foundational, element in British politics. The reason to use England as an analytical concept is that it opens up new ways of thinking that help students and researchers to understand the role that majority nationalisms play in the integration – or even disintegration – of plurinational polities.

Many of the themes that we need to consider when analysing England politically were touched upon by Gareth Southgate, the England men's football team manager from 2016 to 2024, when he wrote an open letter to the nation ahead of the Euro 2020 finals. 'For me, personally', he wrote, 'my sense of identity and values is closely tied to my family and particularly my granddad. He was a fierce patriot and a proud military man, who served during World War II. The idea of representing "Queen and country" has always been important to me. We do pageantry so well in Britain, and, growing up, things like the Queen's silver jubilee and royal weddings had an impact on me' (Southgate 2021).

Figure 12.1   The Prime Minister Rishi Sunak visits England's football training centre St George's Park where he announced EURO 28 would be coming to the UK and Ireland and met the England manager Gareth Southgate along with the England men's squad

Source: Simon Walker/ No 10 Downing Street

But his position as England manager and the politics of nationhood that focused on the national team and its players during that pandemic-delayed tournament had an inescapably political element:

> I understand that on this island, we have a desire to protect our values and traditions – as we should – but that shouldn't come at the expense of introspection and progress. … Why would you choose to insult somebody for something as ridiculous as the colour of their skin? *Why?* Unfortunately for those people that engage in that kind of behaviour, I have some bad news. You're on the losing side. It's clear to me that we are heading for a much more tolerant and understanding society, and I know our lads will be a big part of that. (Southgate 2021)

Southgate's words reflected on some important issues and assumptions that this chapter will help to decode and reveal. He touched upon institutions that were British rather than exclusively English (the Army and the Monarchy), talked about the tension between tradition and progress, and addressed the link between race, nationality and the future of collective belonging. He even made the common but erroneous conflation of England with an island; England is on an island, but isn't an island itself, having land borders with Scotland and Wales. Southgate was not the first – and won't be the last – to make such conflations between England and Britain. England forms the largest nation of Great Britain (that being a product of the unions of Wales and Scotland with England) and Northern Ireland (itself a rump of the union of Great Britain with Ireland), which together form the United Kingdom. Unpacking England from Great Britain and the United Kingdom, and the politics required to do this, will be the purpose of this chapter.

Analytical frameworks

The elision of England and Britain in our understanding of British politics needs to be addressed. This occlusion has implications for both politics and academic analyses. As Ailsa Henderson, Charlie Jeffery, Dan Wincott and Richard Wyn Jones argue:

> the complexities of a state with four component units become simplified into the study of 'British politics', [that creates] a process which has the effect of veiling the characteristics and impact of England, the biggest part of the United Kingdom, at the same time as marginalising engagement with other parts of the UK. (Henderson et al. 2017: 632)

The result of this effect is a 'triple effacement' that has marginalised Northern Ireland, pushed Scotland and Wales to the edges of most research and effaced England, meaning that 'we end up analysing the United Kingdom as a fictive country: Anglo-Britain' (Henderson et al. 2017: 632). Therefore, it is always important to ask about the limits and boundaries of politics and policies: do they apply to England alone, England and Wales, Great Britain, or the entirety of the United Kingdom?

Political science was late to engage with the emergence of Englishness as a political force, so much of the early analyses came from outside the discipline. Important in this regard was

Susan Condor's contribution from social psychology (2010); Gerald Newman's (1987), Linda Colley's (1992), Richard Weight's (2000), Robert Colls' (2002), Peter Mandler's (2006) and Jeremy Black's (2018) historical analyses; and sociological contributions by Krishan Kumar (2003), David McCrone and Frank Bechhoffer (2015), and Robin Mann and Steve Fenton (2017). It was only by the beginning of the 2010s that English nationalism – in the sense of a political programme allied to a sense of politicised Englishness – drew attention from political scientists and was characterised as 'the dog that finally barked' (Wyn Jones et al. 2012).

Michael Kenny has outlined a four-part framework for the analysis of political nationhood in England (Kenny 2016: 326–330). The first of these frames is to see the politicisation of English nationhood as a question of political allegiance: are you English or British, and as such how does this affect attitudes towards the continuation of the United Kingdom in its current form? This leads on to the second framework, which is to see the politicisation of English nationhood as an issue of constitutional reform in which a 'permissive consensus' on allegiance to the UK has come under strain and that some form of constitutional readjustment will resolve such tensions. The third framework involves a movement from a cultural to a political understanding of nationhood, a shift observable in many nationalist movements when an interest in vernacular culture leads to an alteration in consciousness that translates into the political realm. All three of these approaches see what we might therefore call English nationalism in very similar ways to Scottish secessionist nationalism and anticipate a rise in English consciousness that will tend towards demands for the disintegration of the UK. The fourth frame is that of the postcolonial, which usually refers to the effect of postwar immigration on English consciousness, although it should also include the revival of transnational allegiances and policy-transfer across the English-speaking countries of the Anglosphere (Kenny and Pearce 2018; Wellings and Mycock 2019; Legrand 2021), and for which the term 'post-imperialism' might be best. Both terms can be subsumed under the heading of post-Empire.

This framework gives us four ways of thinking about Englishness in British politics:

- Allegiance
- Governance
- Politicisation
- Post-Empire

These frameworks will be used to structure the analysis of Englishness, English identity and English nationalism that follows.

Allegiance: National identity and political allegiance in a plurinational polity

One of the key elements in understanding the politics of Englishness is to understand the extent to which Englishness and Britishness are merged. This merging is more pronounced than in other nations of the United Kingdom. This merging has relevance to the politics of allegiance and national identity in England. Disentangling Englishness from Britishness, and determining if and when this shift occurred and what its political implications might be, became the defining question of analyses of the politics of Englishness, in academia and politics itself

(Curtice 2018; Henderson and Wyn Jones 2021; Kenny 2024). Survey evidence drawn from the British Electoral Study (BES) and British Social Attitudes Survey (BSAS) shows a noticeable jump in those identifying as mostly or exclusively English after 1999 (Table 12.1).

Table 12.1   Trends in 'Moreno' national identity, England, 1997–2016 (British Electoral Study and British Social Attitudes Survey)

	BES		BSAS										
	1997	1999	2000	2001	2003	2007	2008	2009	2011	2013	2014	2015	2016
English not British	7	18	19	18	17	19	19	18	24	16	19	18	15
More English than British	17	14	14	13	20	14	16	16	13	12	14	10	11
Equally English and British	14	11	14	9	13	14	9	10	7	8	9	8	8
More British than English	9	14	12	11	10	12	7	12	9	12	9	12	12
British not English	9	14	12	11	10	12	7	12	9	12	9	12	12
Other/None		7	8	8	9	10	3	7	2	8	2	9	11
Don't know	0	0	0	0	0	0	0	0	0	0	0	0	0
n	2492	2718	1928	2761	4432	859	2558	1940	2448	2799	2087	3778	2525

Source: From Henderson and Wyn Jones (2021: 40). Printed with permission

The contemporary study of the politics of Englishness began in the mid-1990s, anticipating New Labour's devolution of power to some of the nations, provinces and cities of the United Kingdom, thus prompting new questions in survey research. The principle of devolution was endorsed by referendums in Scotland and Wales in 1997, and Northern Ireland and London in 1998. Yet England was conspicuous by its absence in this scheme of 'devolution-on-demand', which was designed to stem the rise in support for Scottish secessionism that the Conservative administration's unbending Unionism was seen to have exacerbated. At this moment in British politics there was no demand for political representation of England, nor did the question of how English or British an English person might feel have any apparent political implications.

It was this idea of 'absence' that characterised early considerations of the problem (or not) of English national identity in a plurinational polity. One of the arguments deployed against devolution in the 1997 general election was that granting Scotland and Wales new representative institutions would lead to a backlash in England, with the English demanding fairness in representation. Yet aside from some early grumbling from MPs associated with Eurosceptic right of the Conservative Party, this backlash did not immediately materialise.

The idea of England as an absence in British politics changed with the advent of the Conservative-led coalition government in 2010. This government was committed to the politics of austerity in response to the global financial crisis of 2008. New Labour, particularly under Gordon Brown, had been committed to the idea of Britain and Britishness to the exclusion of Englishness. This was seemingly not lost on the electorate, as it was in the early years of the 2010s, when researchers began to pick up on a shift in English attitudes (Skey 2012). Arthur Aughey characterised Englishness as an identity driven by a twin sense of 'anxiety and injustice' (Aughey 2010). The injustice element was linked to the workings of the devolution settlement. The anticipated backlash began to emerge in the 2010s as the Scottish National Party (SNP) consolidated its status as a party of government and began its long period of dominance in Scottish politics. The Scottish independence referendum of 2014, and the subsequent collapse of the Labour Party in Scotland throughout the rest of the decade, increased the salience and politicisation of Englishness. As David Cameron said when speaking about the victory for the No campaign in 2014:

> I have long believed that a crucial part missing from this national discussion is England. We have heard the voice of Scotland – and now the millions of voices of England must also be heard. The question of English votes for English laws – the so-called West Lothian Question – requires a decisive answer. (Cited in BBC News 2014)

The anxious aspect of Englishness picked up by Arthur Aughey (2010) was developed by Michael Kenny in his seminal contribution to the literature, *The Politics of English Nationhood* (2014). This collective anxiety was driven by the austerity-led decline in material conditions and status of many people in England. Kenny's account was more sympathetic than other analyses of this 'resurgence' in English nationalism, which had become closely linked with analyses of populism and even related ideologies like neo-fascism. Notable in this regard were Ford and Goodwin's *Revolt on the Right* (2014), and Eatwell and Goodwin's *National Populism* (2017).

Survey research on national identity, political allegiance and the politics of Englishness tended to show a noticeable move towards a politicised English identity and away from British identity in the late 1990s to 2014 (Curtice 2018; Henderson and Wyn Jones 2021).

Yet there was no consensus on the political implications of this identity shift. Some felt that its effects were minor (Curtice 2018), whereas others linked the shift to a transformation of British politics (Henderson and Wyn Jones 2021). Others still pointed out that the Labour Party had not won a general election in England from 2001 until 2024, and that the results of the 2019 and 2024 elections in particular suggested that the self-consciously English now had a key role to play in whoever was able to form government at Westminster (Denham and McKay 2023).

Nevertheless, in the wake of the Scottish and Brexit referendums of 2014 and 2016, it was clear that English-identifiers had become politically salient as Englishness became a vehicle for expressing political discontent. As Michael Keating argued, an English political identity emerged 'not in the form of separatist or even devolutionary demands, but as an ontological claim for recognition' (Keating 2021: 116). Moreover, this shift had some consequential outcomes, primarily the UK's withdrawal from the European Union, which some researchers saw as being 'made in England' (Henderson et al. 2017). However, discussion about the political and national allegiances of the English rested on some important assumptions about nationalism since academic attention turned to the issue in the late 1990s. The most important of these was that English nationalism could only really be nationalism if it looked and behaved something like contemporary Scottish secessionism. The idea underpinning the 'missing backlash' explanation for the absence of English nationalism in the 2000s was because England did not have explicit expression in a party whose *raison d'être* was to reform the relationship between state and nation, possibly to the point of secession. In the absence of English secessionism from the UK – which misunderstood the relationship between a majority nationalism and the state and overlooked growing calls to leave the EU – debate focused on what might be the best descriptor for whatever was animating an increasing number of people to identify as solely or mostly English at the expense of Britishness.

Such assumptions about the nature of politicised Englishness affected the early debate on the phenomenon of shifts in national identity in England and the political consequences that such changes might entail. The development of a sense of political grievance linked to Englishness contributed to the vote to leave the EU in parts of England that proved decisive for the overall vote across the UK (Henderson et al. 2017). It also suggested that although there was some evidence that this aggrieved Englishness directed some of its ire at the UK, the EU was much more of a target for popular resentment in England than the UK itself.

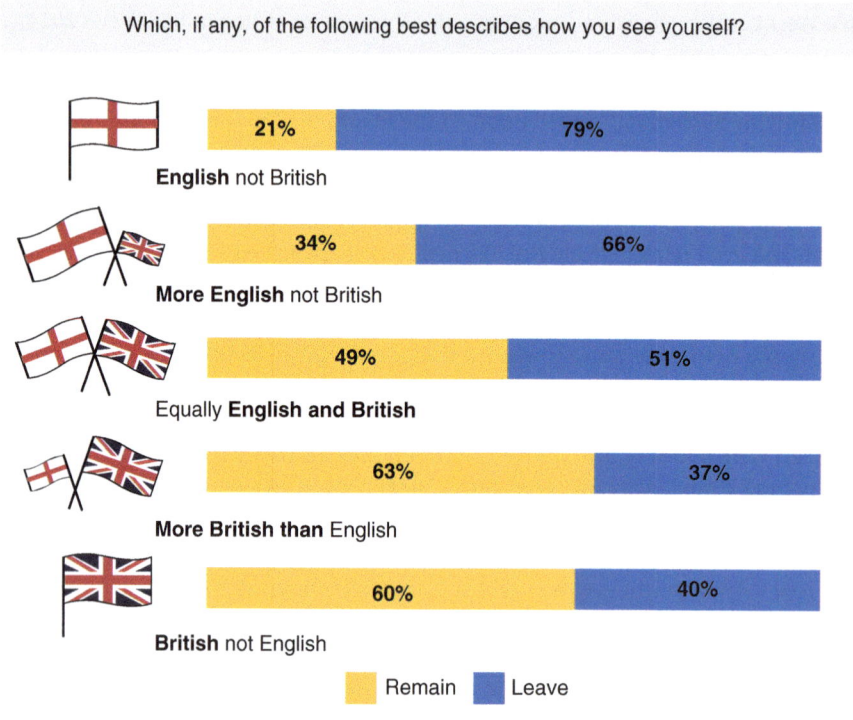

Which, if any, of the following best describes how you see yourself?

English not British — 21% Remain, 79% Leave

More English not British — 34% Remain, 66% Leave

Equally **English and British** — 49% Remain, 51% Leave

More British than English — 63% Remain, 37% Leave

British not English — 60% Remain, 40% Leave

Remain   Leave

Figure 12.2   National identity and Brexit voting

Source: Lord Ashcroft Polls (2016)

Thus when the opportunity arose in 2016 to express anger at 'the system', withdrawal from the EU rather than secession from the UK was the result.

These shifts forced a rethink about how to analyse nationalism in England. In particular, it showed how too much focus had been given to the purely UK aspects of the politics of English nationhood which could have looked to former Dominions for models of national identity development. This was itself a product of the waning place of Empire in national consciousness in Britain. This was a potential loss because the development of distinct forms of nationhood in the settler societies of former Dominions, as opposed to the independence movements of colonies, could add insight into the process of British disintegration that seemed to be occurring in the UK (Pedersen and Ward 2019; Ward 2023). In a mindset where instances of secessionist nationalism dominated the political and analytical imagination, the gradualism of nation-formation in English-speaking settler societies of the former Empire and Common-wealth went almost unnoticed in the political science literature. Henderson and Wyn Jones' analysis of the importance of such countries, as well as the USA, to the English self-conception was a notable exception (Henderson and Wyn Jones 2021: 90–100).

Again, developments outside political science suggested alternative analytical frameworks were available. Stuart Ward's interventions from the discipline of history were instructive in this regard. Ward suggested that rather than seeing the 'break-up of Britain' as the logical out-come of the growth of nationalism in all parts of the UK, the 'break-up of Greater Britain' – the idea that Britishness was a political identity founded on Empire loyalty – showed the ways in which new national identities might emerge from older polities, and those new national iden-tities' relationship to older forms of Britishness (Ward 2023).

Related to this 'imperial turn' in the analysis of Britishness and Englishness was a new empha-sis on the Anglosphere in British politics. This frame of analysis also examined the links between Britishness, Englishness and older forms of belonging related to the endurance and revival of ideas about Britain's traditional allies as the UK sought to leave the EU (Kenny and Pearce 2018; Wellings and Mycock 2019). The political strains and uncertainties attending the UK's with-drawal from the EU led to the revivification of older relationships that had seemingly fallen into a second tier of importance after the UK joined the EU. At times, former Dominions – in this case Canada – seemed to show the type of post-Brexit trade relationship that the UK could aspire to with the EU. At other times, former Dominions – in this case Australia and New Zealand – became the focus of immigration policy transfer, and politically driven free trade agreements (FTAs) designed to signal that there was economic life after Brexit. The USA was a major focus of such aspirations for Brexiteers, although both the Trump and Biden administrations were both sceptical of the UK for different reasons, and an FTA with the USA remained out of reach. Although distinct from questions of Englishness framed solely in a UK context, the focus on the Anglosphere revealed that questions of political allegiance and worldview in England extended beyond the UK, and even the EU, and shaped the political imagination in ways that reached back to enduring historical constructions of Englishness and Britishness (Wellings 2019).

Governance: England and the UK constitution

By the middle of the 2010s, it was clear that Englishness had become the vehicle for the expression of some sort of anti-systemic grievance. However, while it could be demonstrated that English identifiers existed, and that politically speaking they were not happy, it was not particularly clear what they wanted beyond this. This was especially the case when it came to governance.

This inchoate nature of English grievance affected the various schemes for addressing an emerging political Englishness. The idea of England has not been well developed in politi-cal thought. Explicit thinking about England only tends to occur in moments of constitu-tional tension in British politics. Walter Bagehot's *The English Constitution* (1867) stands out as the best-known example of this tension-driven theorising of England (although he conflated England, Britain and the UK). A.V. Dicey's anti-home rule treatises *England's Case Against Home Rule* (1887) also reflected the emergence of a specifically English perspective in times of a chal-lenge to Westminster sovereignty in other parts of the Union, in this case Ireland. The ferocity of responses to seemingly modest suggestions for constitutional reform – plans for home rule in

Ireland almost led to mutiny and civil war in the 1910s – suggest the importance of unionism and the sovereignty of Crown-in-Parliament for political conceptions of the English nation, thus blurring the boundaries of political Englishness with other parts of the UK where Westminster's sovereignty runs.

A similar phenomenon of gloomy prognoses for the future of England and the UK because of devolution were evident at the turn of the twenty-first century. Roger Scruton's *England: An Elegy* (2000) was the best-known of these titles, but progressives weighed in too. Billy Bragg's *The Progressive Patriot* (2007) sought to engage an otherwise largely disinterested progressive side of politics with the idea of England as a political community worth taking seriously. When English sentiment began to have noticeable political consequences, particularly after the Brexit referendum of 2016, the mood turned more sombre. Non-English writers led the charge with Fintan O'Toole's *Heroic Failure* (2018) and Gavin Esler's *How Britain Ends* (2022), picking up Scottish nationalist Tom Nairn's idea that English nationalism was the nationalism most likely to lead to the break-up of the UK – which in Nairn's view would be a good outcome (Nairn 2003 [1977]). Caroline Lucas, Greens co-leader in England and Wales, attempted to re-interpret political Englishness from an ecological place-based perspective after her retirement from Parliament (Lucas, 2024).

As a result of this historically weak articulation of England and its place in the UK, when schemes for modest forms of devolution were raised in the 1970s, England was present only as a theoretical abstraction. This absent presence came in the form of Labour MP Tam Dalyell's 'West Lothian Question' (WLQ). The Question asked whether, if power were devolved to an assembly in Scotland, could Scottish MPs at Westminster still vote on matters pertaining to England and the rest of the UK, and if so, how was this fair and legitimate?

The failure to establish a Scottish assembly in 1979 deferred this theoretical problem until the establishment of a Scottish Parliament and Welsh Assembly two decades later. In the intervening period, England remained a 'stateless nation', albeit a majority one in which the relationship between the English nation and the British state appeared unproblematic. It was this situation that led Richard Rose to famously claim that England was an idea rather than a political reality (Rose 1982: 4). But ideas matter in politics, and contexts change. The establishment of a Scottish Parliament and a Welsh Assembly (the Senedd) in 1999 raised the WLQ about England's place in the Union and the governance structures of a reformed UK with greater urgency than before.

Yet as Michael Keating has noted, although the so-called 'Millennium devolution settlement' was portrayed by its critics as a constitutional revolution, it had remarkably little effect on the perception of the UK at the centre of British politics (Keating 2021: 49). This left England as what Jim Gallagher called the 'ghost in the machine' of the British constitution (Gallagher 2018: 69). Initially, the post-devolution spectre of English nationhood stalking the land hardly troubled Britain's political class. As Derry Irvine, Lord Chancellor from 1997 to 2003, famously stated, the best way to answer the West Lothian Question was to stop asking it. Nevertheless, the idea grew that something ought to be done to address an obvious asymmetry in devolution and governance across the UK.

However, the response that emerged was more *ad hoc* devolution-on-demand, where a desire for regional assemblies appeared to be strongest. In London, the old Greater London Council (GLC), abolished under Margaret Thatcher's government in 1986, was re-established as the London Assembly in 1999. But in 2004, voters rejected a proposal for a North East Assembly in a local referendum. Thereafter, responses to the 'English question' were driven less by demand

and more about the logic of somehow fitting England, which was for historical reasons out-sized in administrative terms, into the post-devolution British constitution. During the 2010s, English voters seemed to want some form of devolved or strengthened local government, but consensus on what that might actually look like quickly broke down (Curtice 2018: 269). Metro mayors – notably in Greater Manchester – were extended across northern England and the Midlands, but were accepted unenthusiastically. This, however, is as far as the cross-party consensus goes and so the prospect of any other England-wide reforms seems remote even with Labour in power after 2024. The overall picture remains of an *ad hoc* approach to the post-devolution governance of England, an impression that was only reinforced by the responses to the Covid pandemic across the governance structures of England and the UK.

None of these constitutional reforms considered England as a whole as an appropriate governmental unit, it being considered too large for the UK's form of asymmetrical devolved governance. The only time an England-wide response occurred was the short-lived experiment of English Votes for English Laws (EVEL), which was established at Westminster by David Cameron's government in 2015 in an attempt to address the logic of the WLQ (Gover and Kenny 2018a).

Yet in a move that seemed to underscore the 'hyper-Unionism' (Kenny and Sheldon 2021: 3) of the Brexiteer wing of the Conservative party that flourished in the late 2010s, EVEL was abolished by the Johnson Government in 2021, signalling a return to a more traditionally unionist, although perhaps more rhetorically strident, form of English Conservatism within the Conservative Party.

Politicisation: Englishness and the party politics of nationhood

Alongside asymmetrical devolution, one of the other important structures that complicates analysis of England in British politics is the lack of an explicitly English political party. Here the analyst of England and Englishness in British politics might look with some envy on fellow students and researchers seeking to understand the politics of nationhood in other parts of the United Kingdom. These other nations have parties that claim to represent those nations' interests within the realm of British politics, at Westminster and in devolved parliaments and assemblies. The Scots have the Scottish National Party (SNP), the Welsh have Plaid Cymru (PC), the nationalist-Catholic community in Northern Ireland has Sinn Féin or the Social Democratic Labour Party (SDLP). Even the loyalist-Protestant community has parties that represent its interests to whichever party is in government at Westminster. All nations and communities have representation in devolved legislatures, even if this picture is complicated in the case of Northern Ireland when power-sharing agreements have broken down in the past. None of this is the case for England and the English. Again, England is conspicuous in its absence, but also hidden in plain sight. Although there are 'national' branches of the main British parties – such as Scottish Labour, the Scottish Conservatives – and 'national' campaigns during the Brexit referendum – 'Scotland in Europe' – there are no equivalents for England. In England's case, an implicit or explicit Britishness stands in for Englishness – the Labour Party, the Conservatives, Britain in Europe. Nevertheless, it is possible to discern stated or more usually unstated politics of Englishness among the major parties in England – the Conservatives, Labour, the Liberal Democrats and, during the 2010s, the UK Independence Party (UKIP) (Mycock and Hayton 2014; Denham and McKay 2023).

The Conservatives were often considered as a *de facto* English party, particularly from 1997 to 2017, when their representation in Scotland and Wales in the Westminster Parliament was either negligible or non-existent. (After 1997, it was often joked that there were more pandas in Edinburgh Zoo (two) than Conservatives MPs in Scotland.) At the ideational level, the party leadership flirted with English sentiment ahead of the 2015 general election, to promote fears of a Labour–SNP coalition. It returned to a more traditional form of pan-British unionism after 2016, even if the commitment to Northern Ireland was more ambivalent until the Windsor Framework was established in 2023, and the Unionism displayed towards Scotland was more confrontational towards the SNP government in Scotland under Johnson, Truss and Sunak than it was under May. Thus, political developments outside England enhanced the Englishness of the Conservative Party without that party having to do anything. This was also because the waning of the influence of the Ulster Unionist Party (UUP) in Northern Ireland meant that institutional links between the Conservatives and Ulster unionism weakened, and Scottish Conservatives were notably more progressive on social issues than even David Cameron-style Conservatives in the 2010s.

If the Conservatives were seemingly reluctant to openly embrace Englishness, at least at the level of party leadership, such a move was doubly difficult for the Labour Party. The Labour Party's roots are perhaps the most 'British' of all the major political parties (Robinson 2016, 378–387). In the same way that the Industrial Revolution was a 'British' phenomenon, with centres of industrial finance, extraction and production across the UK, the English-speaking world and beyond, the working class that grew with this economic development in the UK was heavily British in consciousness. Although the Scottish and Welsh branches of the party that emerged in 1900 to represent organised labour in Parliament were strongly in favour of Home Rule, the party that played such an important role in postwar reconstruction was strongly British in outlook (Edgerton 2018: 43). As its parliamentary influence grew after 1945, much of Labour's voting support came from the industrial regions in nations outside England – nations that found themselves on the wrong side of industrial decline from the 1960s. In the early twenty-first century, Gordon Brown's emphasis on Britishness as a form of inclusive belonging expressed the dominant view among the Labour leadership (Brown, 2005).

This meant that the politics of an emerging political Englishness in the 2010s was difficult for Labour leaders to navigate as they attempted to manage the dealignment of formerly Labour voters before and after the Brexit referendum (Mycock 2016). Both Ed Miliband (cited in Watt, 2012) and Jeremy Corbyn (Press Association, 2018) attempted to address Englishness. Corbyn was least predisposed to do so, and under his leadership all that was offered was to make St George's Day a Bank Holiday. Following Scottish Labour's electoral collapse in 2015, the Labour Party found itself in a similar situation to the Conservatives in 1997, although it retained significant representation from Wales. Even after the 2019 general election, when Labour losses in so-called 'Red Wall' seats in the Midlands and North of England contributed to a significant loss, Labour seemed unwilling or unable to address the issue of politicised Englishness to its political advantage. Given that much of its support also came from younger, tertiary educated professionals and minorities wary of nationalism, a cleavage exacerbated by the division over Brexit (Ford et al. 2021: 505), the Labour leadership had to tread carefully if seeking to mobilise English opinion (Starmer 2024), a point further underscored by the riots in England in the summer of 2024.

The party that had done the most explicit thinking about England's place in the UK was the Liberal Democrats (Lib Dems). The Lib Dems' federalism can trace its origins back to the Liberal Party's three attempts to solve the 'Irish Question' between 1885 and 1914, and the concomitant idea of 'home rule all round' that emerged with those efforts. Although a favourite rallying cry for members at party conferences, the federal option did not emerge from the bargaining process with the Conservatives during the period of coalition government in 2010–2015. So it seems that such an outcome will remain an issue for the party faithful alone. The Lib Dems will not be the route to England-level governance in the foreseeable future.

The party that perhaps best exemplifies the merging of England, Britain and the UK was the UK Independence Party (UKIP) and its successors in the guise of the Brexit Party and Reform UK. Although founded in 1992, UKIP's impact can be dated from the elections to the European Parliament in 2009, an institution which UKIP wanted to get the UK out of, but whose system of proportional representation allowed its MEPs a platform which Westminster's First-Past-the-Post system did not permit. Despite seeking the *UK*'s independence from the EU, UKIP's support was concentrated in England and Wales. It had less support in Scotland and almost none in Northern Ireland. Yet by threatening to take votes away on the right of politics, its historical impact on the Conservatives, and hence the decision to call a referendum on the UK's EU membership, cannot be understated. Aside from this, and despite its name, UKIP was a largely English phenomenon that saw the UK as the political vehicle for England's withdrawal from the EU (Tournier-Sol 2015).

Figure 12.3   UKIP leader Nigel Farage

Source: Creative Commons PDM 1.0

The concept that cuts across all these party positions and facilitates the merging of England and Britain, as well as Englishness and Britishness, is Unionism. Unionism means different things in different parts of the United Kingdom, as an examination of the issues driving Unionism in Northern Ireland (remaining out of the Republic of Ireland and in the UK) and England (keeping England and Scotland united) demonstrates. Although politicised in the nineteenth-century debates about home rule, Unionism also has ideological affinties with the 'Empire Loyalism' that linked the UK to its British populations in the colonies and dominions (Ward 2023). But as the institutional links that bound Unionists across the UK weaken, the Unionist rhetoric has increased. Michael Keating (2021) calls this phenomenon a 'neo-Unionism', whereas Kenny and Sheldon (2021: 3) refer to this as 'hyper-Unionism'. Keating makes the point that Unionists did not respond well to the new status quo represented by devolution. Indeed, after devolution, Unionism began to look and sound more like the nationalisms it opposed (Keating 2021: 193). When expressed in England, the language of Unionism leads to a merging of English and British symbolic repertoires, in which the institutions of the British state, including the Monarchy, come to stand for expressions of Englishness.

After Empire: Post-imperial and postcolonial Englishness

The fourth of Michael Kenny's frames for understanding the politics of English nationhood relates to the considerable volume of work written since the 1980s that deals with the issues of racism, multiculturalism and religious identities, and the relationship of Englishness and Britishness to each of these. It is in this area of analysis that questions of diversity and representation are most to the fore, although they are implicit in other areas of research and political activity focusing on changing identities and the structural issues driving such change. Note that the term 'post-imperial' used here refers to a temporal moment after the end of the British Empire as a historical episode, which may include the politics of nostalgia for the Empire and the UK's place in the global order that went with it (Melhuish 2023). The term differs from 'postcolonialism', which is a way of seeing the world that developed out of critiques of empire as an ongoing structure of global politics, and which also forms an important part of understanding identity politics in contemporary England.

In addition to salient contributions and important interventions from academic analysts such as Paul Gilroy (1987, 2006), Yasmin Alibhai-Brown (2000) and Bhikhu Parekh (2000), one politician stands out for his articulation of a racialised Englishness that was notable for being English rather than British: Enoch Powell. Powell's articulation of a post-imperial Englishness stands out for being perhaps the only attempt to define Englishness (through actions, speeches and poetry) rather than enact it in quotidian ways, as his followers on the right and far-right attempted to do, or Nigel Farage did in the twenty-first century. Powell's politics of Englishness thus form an instructive way to analyse racialised expressions of Englishness and Britishness.

During the 1960s, Powell's views on two important issues – immigration and entry to the European Economic Community (EEC) – hardened. These two issues, combined with his defence of the Union during the Troubles in Northern Ireland, coalesced to form his definition of England: a racially homogeneous nation built upon Crown-in-Parliament sovereignty. Powell – and his vision of England – are remembered for two moments of political iconoclasm. The first was the so-called 'Rivers of Blood' speech of 1968, in which Powell spoke out effectively against the political consensus on immigration from the (non-white) New Commonwealth. This gained him both political opprobrium in Parliament and wide public support (Crines et al. 2016). The second was his suggestion that, although still a Conservative MP at the time, he might have voted for Labour in the February 1974 general election to try to reverse the UK's entry into the European Economic Community (EEC) (Gifford and Wellings 2018: 272).

Powell's impact on the politics of nationhood in England during the 1970s cannot be understated. Although the issues of the UK's membership of the EEC appeared to be resolved with the 'Yes' vote in the 1975 referendum, Powell's view of England as a racially homogeneous nation whose democracy would be undermined by immigration from the former Empire energised the hard right and far right during a period of economic hardship in the 1970s. Powell's legacy in the Brexit referendum in 2016 was refracted through Nigel Farage and UKIP's endorsement of Powell's positions on immigration and membership of what was now the European Union (EU), although UKIP were much more pro-Anglosphere than Powell had been.

It was against this backdrop of racialised majority identities that recently arrived and second-generation migrants began to carve out identities that were distinct from, but negotiated within, Englishness, and especially Britishness, thereby altering the construction of both. In terms of the literature on this phenomenon, important in this regard was Paul Gilroy's *There Ain't No Black in the Union Jack* (1987), which took a well-known racist comment as a starting point for an analysis of race and national identity in Britain of the 1980s. The murder of Stephen Lawrence in 1993 served as a catalyst for a wide reaction against racism, to the extent that, reversing some of its previous and subsequent positions, the *Daily Mail* came down on the side of what was by now called 'multicultural Britain'.

Powell died in 1998, but the legacy of his articulation of a post-imperial Englishness outlived him. The publication of the Parekh Report on multiculturalism in 2000 appeared to put the seal on a pluralistic vision of British national identity that was part of New Labour's modernising project (Parekh 2000). This period of optimism was curtailed by the impact of the 2001 al Qaeda attacks on the USA, and the polarising effects of terrorism during the first decade of the twenty-first century, as conflicts in the Middle East spilled over into acts of terrorism in England. Paul Gilroy's notion of 'postcolonial melancholia' (2006) stands as an expression of this waning optimism.

It is important to note that the boundaries between Englishness and Britishness are particularly blurred in the postcolonial literature on national identity in the UK. There are two main reasons for this. The first is that as Englishness and whiteness were closely aligned from the 1970s, Englishness was seen more as an impermeable 'ethnic' identity, whereas Britishness appeared more capacious, an identity that – not without a long struggle – could be co-opted as an inclusive space for diverse identities (Alibhai-Brown 2000) reflecting an articulation of Empire-era Britishness different from the residual race patriotism of the Conservative right. The second was the close alignment of minorities with the Labour Party. The diversity of the UK Cabinet after 2019 was very much a surprise for those who had been observing identity politics in the UK. Since the beginning of postwar migration to the UK, the Labour Party had been the natural political home of migrants, even those who may have been more conservative in their values than the elements of the progressive electoral coalition (Ford and Soboloewska 2020: 70).

The postcolonial literature on Englishness is very much focused on the politics of race and how this intersects with English and British national identities. But if we examine Powell's career, we see that, in addition to India, Australia had a small but formative effect on his world view. Ideas of the importance of racial homogeneity to the functioning of representative democracy had been in operation in Australia since 1901. Furthermore, they had a liberal lineage in the writings of John Stuart Mill (Mill 1926: 363–364). Ideas of whiteness were formed across the Dominions, and in relation to developments in the USA, and thus understanding the lineages of race and nation in England should not overlook these important 'external' examples of racialised nationhood which contributed to important articulations of Englishness in the twentieth and twenty-first centuries (Wellings 2019).

These ideas and identities fed into the so-called 'culture wars' of the twenty-first century. There was nothing particularly new about such culture wars. Contestation over whose values should dominate in a polity were and are part of nation-formation and maintenance. The German *kulturkampf* in the 1880s that followed unification was one such historical example. Struggles over 'values', in this case religion, were foundational to political life in Northern Ireland. The issues over which such contestation played out in England in the twenty-first century were usually framed in the language of Britishness, even though they differed from issues in other parts of the UK. Unlike Wales, language played no explicit part in identity politics other than to link England with other English-speaking parts of the world at the expense of Europe. Contestation over religion was not between Catholic and Protestant as in Northern Ireland, but between radical Islam and non-believers in the wake of the terrorist attacks of 2005. Whereas in Scotland the salient political divide was between those in favour of or opposed to independence, in England this played out on the terrain of membership of the European Union, which in turn was refracted through attitudes towards immigration. The latter issue was not just about opposition to free movement of labour within the EU, but took in attitudes towards historic episodes, notably a growing awareness of Britain's role in the slave trade, which led to the dropping of a statue of Edward Coulston into the River Avon in 2020. The deportation of members of the 'Windrush generation' during the 2010s was the realisation of Powellite calls for 'repatriation' of Commonwealth immigrants, which in turn has its antecedents in the racialised politics of migration developed across the Dominions, such as the White Australia Policy during the 1900s. The racialised dimensions of Englishness and Britishness are historical and transnational in origin, meaning that debates about Englishness, race, religion and identity in the twenty-first century are inherently grounded in contested understandings of the past. Criticisms of 'woke', which developed in the USA, have even played out over the ingredients of National Trust scones.

Conclusions: Hidden in plain sight?

To aid analysis, this chapter has used four concepts to analyse England and the politics of Englishness in the UK and, while it was a member state, the EU: allegiance, governance, politicisation and post-Empire. Using these frameworks of analysis allows us to draw some conclusions about the politics of Englishness in the UK.

Allegiance: A sense of politicised Englishness distinct from Britishness became significant during the 1990s. It prompted questions about the political allegiance of these 'English identifiers' to the United Kingdom. These concerns mirrored the development of political nationalism in other parts of the UK. In reality, it was the allegiance of the English identifiers to England's other Union – the European Union – that was tested first, and which they chose to reject.

Governance: Explicit thinking about England only tends to occur in moments of constitutional tension in British politics. As devolution was granted 'on demand' in the late 1990s, it developed an asymmetrical character. England was too large to fit comfortably into this model, but there was little enthusiasm for regional devolution within England. England ended up with an *ad hoc* approach to governance, because this is what the political consensus could deliver. The pandemic responses of 2020–2021 highlighted the confusing and *ad hoc* relationship between England as an administrative unit and the UK Government.

Politicisation: Political parties, or at least their leadership, trod wearily around Englishness. Voting patterns altered across the UK in the twenty-first century, although whether in England this was cause or effect of a politicised Englishness remains debatable. However, a politicised Englishness certainly emerged in the 2010s, most notably as an expression of anti-systemic sentiments. As such, Englishness played a key role in the vote to leave the EU in 2016.

Post-imperial: The postwar politics of Englishness was first expressed in a coherent way by Enoch Powell and his resistance to New Commonwealth immigration and European integration, in addition to his defence of the Union in Northern Ireland. As a result, Englishness was often understood as an impermeable 'ethnic' identity, whereas Britishness appeared more capacious, an identity that – not without a long struggle – could be co-opted as an inclusive space for diverse identities.

Overall, one of the defining characteristics of Englishness is its merging with Britishness. This merging is transmitted through institutions of governance and political parties. It complicates questions of allegiance and leaves the identity of England and being English as fields of, at times unstated, political contestation. It means that the politics of England and Englishness in British politics is often hidden in plain sight.

Key debate   Is English nationalism good or bad?

This question depends a lot on the definition of nationalism used. Nationalism has a bad reputation for good reasons. But it has also been at the centre of resistance struggles that have been valorised across the political spectrum, such as the collapse of communism in Europe, the ending of Apartheid in South Africa or the Palestinian struggle. Our normative views on nationalism also tend to shape our perceptions of forms of collective belonging that link state and society. Positive views of such collective belonging tend to self-reference as patriotism, which is seen as good, and is contrasted with nationalism, which is seen as bad, as George Orwell argued in the 1930s. Is there really a distinction between the two?

Since the start of the twenty-first century, political parties and citizens in the UK have struggled to respond to the idea and implications of English nationalism. It has been a normative debate that has touched political cleavages of class, region, religion, age, education, race and ethnicity. Essentially, public debate characterises expressions of English nationhood as narrow and xenophobic, and expressions of other forms of belonging – usually Britishness or Europeanism – as open and cosmopolitan. Neither main political party has wanted to *explicitly* court English sentiment for political or electoral gain, outside the 2015 election.

(Continued)

The Conservatives (and UKIP/Brexit/Reform UK) rest heavily on an implicit Englishness in their understandings of the UK and its place in the world – they tend to say 'Britain' or 'the UK' when they mean 'England'. Labour is even more wary of political Englishness, even though some of its traditional support outside the tertiary-educated electorate in the big cities identifies as English more than British. The Lib Dems' idea of England tends to be subsumed into federal regions. This raises a series of questions about the value or otherwise of England and English nationalism:

1   Would English nationalism be more damaging to the Union than nationalism in other parts of the UK?
2   Why have political parties been wary of adopting an explicitly English form of politics?
3   Is England too big to be part of a federal or fully devolved UK?
4   Is a majority nationalism, such as England's, inherently xenophobic?

It is worth thinking about responses to these questions because this is how public debate about England and Englishness in British politics is framed.

Case Study 12.1

Emily Thornberry's 'Rochester' tweet

In November 2014, the Labour MP Emily Thornberry was forced to resign from her position as Shadow Attorney General for posting a tweet depicting a house in Rochester adorned with flags of St George. The tweet was accompanied by three words, 'Image from #Rochester', sparking allegations of snobbery.

Figure 12.4   Labour MP Emily Thornberry

Source: Richard Townshend, licensed under CC BY 3.0

Reflective question

1   Why do you think this three-word tweet might have led to her resignation from a senior
    position in the shadow cabinet?

In responding to this question and before 'phoning a friend' or asking the internet, break your thinking down based on further questions:

- What was the context in which the tweet was sent?
- What assumptions about England and Englishness are built into the selection of the image? In
  other words, what *doesn't* need to be said for people to 'get' what was meant?
- What kind of political cleavages of nationality, class, gender and geography help to explain
  the reaction to this tweet?

This episode became emblematic of the politics associated with, and in response to, an emerging
politicised Englishness. When you have finished thinking about and discussing the questions above,
research the responses to this and relate them to themes in the chapter above. Think about how
politicised Englishness has interacted with the big moments of British politics since 2014: the Scottish
independence referendum, Brexit and the Covid-19 pandemic. Ask friends, neighbours and relatives
if they feel English or British, or English and British, or something else. Warning: asking this question
can seriously ruin Christmas dinner! Nonetheless, it is a question worth asking to help us understand
the direction of British politics and the future of the United Kingdom.

Summary

- The elision of Englishness and Britishness occurs in UK politics and in the study of UK
  politics. Devolution and European integration have increased the focus on England and
  Englishness.
- There is a continuing sense of Englishness as a narrow form of national identity, resulting
  in a reluctance to talk about it among some politicians.
- There are no easy answers to the question of how to reform English governance.

Recommended and further reading

- Aughey, A. (2007) *The Politics of Englishness*. Manchester: Manchester University Press. A
  conservative view of emergent political Englishness during the first years of the twenty-
  first century.
- Denham, J. and McKay, L. (2023) 'The politics of England: National identities and
  Political Englishness', *The Political Quarterly*, https://doi.org/10.1111/1467-923X.13313.
  This article provides an overview of some of the drivers of English distinctiveness.
- Henderson, A. and Wyn Jones, R. (2021) *Englishness: The Political Force Transforming
  Britain*. Oxford: Oxford University Press. Chapter 2 provides quantitative analyses of the
  distinction and overlap between Englishness and Britishness and its political implications.

- Keating, M. (2021) *State and Nation in the United Kingdom: The Fractured Union*. Oxford: Oxford University Press. Chapter 7 analyses the link between unionism and nationalism in England and the UK.
- Kenny, M. (2024) *Fractured Union: Sovereignty, Politics and the Fight to Save the UK*. London: Hirst Publishers. Chapter 3 of this book is devoted to the politics of England in the UK since the referendum on Scottish independence in 2014.
- Kenny, M. (2014) *The Politics of English Nationhood*. Oxford: Oxford University Press. The definitive account of the politicisation of Englishness ahead of the referendums on Scottish independence (2014) and Brexit.
- Kumar, K. (2003) *The Making of English National Identity*. Cambridge: Cambridge University Press. A historical sociological account of the emergence of England and Englishness, especially its relationship to imperialism.
- Lucas, C. (2024) *Another England*: *How to Reclaim our National Story*. London: Penguin. An attempt to provide an alternative national narrative from England's highest-profile Green MP, 2010–2024.
- McCrone, D. (2023) 'The rise and rise of English nationalism?', *Political Quarterly*, 94(4): 602–613. Another way of understanding English from the perspective of political sociology
- Nairn, T. (1981) *The Break-up of Britain: Crisis and Neo-nationalism*. London: Verso. The classic text on nationalism in the United Kingdom, from a Scottish nationalist intellectual.
- Scruton, R. (2000) *England: An Elegy*. London: Pimlico. A Conservative account of the passing of a particular form of Englishness at the turn of the century, from a major conservative thinker.

Chapter 13
Scotland

Alan Convery and Ailsa Henderson

What do I need to know?

- Scotland is a distinct nation within the UK.
- Scotland existed as an independent state until 1707. It therefore has a much more strongly institutionalised sense of statehood than Wales and retained many of the trappings of an independent state even after the Act of Union.
- Separate institutions acted as civic carriers of a separate Scottish identity. The most important were the church and the legal and education systems.

What will this chapter tell me?

- Scotland voted to remain part of the UK in an independence referendum in 2014. However, the result demonstrated higher support for independence than had historically been the case (45%) and support for independence has hovered around this level in opinion polls ever since.
- The Scottish Parliament mainly took over the domestic policy functions of the Scottish Office before 1999. The UK Government has granted it further powers (particularly in relation to taxation and social security) since then.
- The independence referendum and Brexit were both electoral shocks that altered Scots' identity and political behaviour. Scots have gradually brought their political preference into line with their constitutional preference, depending on how they voted in 2014 and 2016.
- The Labour Party dominated Scottish politics at the end of the twentieth century but has been overtaken by the Scottish National Party. It has formed the Scottish Government since 2007.

Introduction

Scotland's independence referendum in 2014 was a major milestone. It re-emphasised the fact that Scotland was previously an independent state and that the UK Government explicitly recognised that it had the right to secede and become one again. This chapter explores Scotland's place in the UK and its distinctive character as a recognised political community and potential independent state. Although Scots voted to remain in the UK in 2014, the independence question has not gone away. There were further questions about Scotland's place in the UK after the 2016 EU membership referendum. Implementing Brexit disrupted some unspoken Scottish elite assumptions about devolution and the constitution. These questions remain unsettled and support for independence remains historically high, despite a dip in support for the Scottish National Party (SNP).

This chapter begins by outlining the context of the Scotland's place in the UK. The Act of Union in 1707 was an ambiguous document that left intact much Scottish autonomy (Kidd 2007). Distinctive Scottish institutions ensured the continuation of a sense of separate Scottish identity. That identity is based on civic, rather than ethnic, markers. The chapter then examines devolution and the sort of powers that were devolved to the Scottish Parliament under the 'Millennium Settlement' in 1999. The Scottish Parliament is, in comparative terms, a powerful sub-state legislature and it has gained more powers since 1999. Scottish governments have used these powers to diverge from England on important matters like healthcare and education, but the effects have been mixed.

The chapter then looks at Scottish identity and voting behaviour. The electoral shocks of the independence (2014) and EU (2016) referendums have had a big impact on electoral behaviour in Scotland. The Scottish party system has changed markedly since 1999 and includes branches of the main statewide parties and the SNP, which campaigns for Scottish independence.

Scotland's place in the UK

While Wales and Ireland/Northern Ireland entered the UK via conquest by the English state, Scotland joined voluntarily in 1707 via a treaty: the Act of Union. It possessed all the trappings of an independent state at this point and has retained many of them since. This agreement was an incorporating one in so far as it abolished the Scottish Parliament and did not envisage any sort of federal arrangements. However, it also left open many avenues for Scottish distinctiveness (Paterson 1994; Kidd 2007). The Scottish legal system remained separate and differs from the English system in important ways. The Scottish education system also imparted a sense of Scottishness, particularly through a distinctive approach to higher education (Scotland had four universities in 1707; England had only Oxford and Cambridge).

The Church of Scotland was also very important in maintaining a sense of difference. Scottish Presbyterianism rejected the English common prayer book and established a different pattern of worship and church governance. People's births, deaths and marriages were therefore imbued with a Scottish dimension that was passed on after 1707. There was also no state-sponsored attempt to extinguish Scottish identity. A common Britishness instead emerged mainly via the Protestant religion (Colley 1992) and latterly via the institutions of the welfare state (Edgerton 2018).

Between 1707 and 1999, this distinctive political culture was gradually given greater recognition by the UK state, culminating in the re-establishment of the Scottish Parliament. The post of Scottish Secretary was established in 1885. It was given cabinet status in 1926 and the functions of the Scottish Office gradually increased over the course of the twentieth century. As the state expanded, it did so with a distinctive Scottish dimension (Mitchell 2014). Eventually, most domestic policy in Scotland was overseen by the Secretary of State for Scotland, with junior ministers to assist. This system became known as administrative devolution (Mitchell 2003): recognition of territorial difference through the organs of the central state and without the creation of a separate Scottish legislature (see also Larner and Wyn Jones, in this volume on administrative devolution in Wales).

As a member of the UK cabinet, the Secretary of State for Scotland was appointed by the Prime Minister from their own party. While Scottish and English voting patterns remained broadly similar, the system worked reasonably well. However, as voting patterns diverged, it started to come under pressure. If Scotland started to lean towards Labour, but the Conservatives won a UK majority based on mainly English seats, then there would be a Conservative Secretary of State for Scotland. The rise of the Scottish National Party's vote share in the 1970s also began to worry the two main parties. Plans for devolution in the 1970s to Scotland and Wales were passed by Parliament, but failed because not enough Scottish or Welsh people voted for them in referendums in 1979.

The system then came under even greater pressure after 1979 and the Conservative Governments of Margaret Thatcher and John Major. The impression that Thatcher's governments were anti-Scottish became very difficult for the Conservative Party to deal with. Thatcher's economic policies were controversial and they had a disproportionate impact on areas of the UK with nationalised or heavy industries that were in decline. That affected some areas in the north of England, but it had a greater political impact in Scotland as some voters and elites felt that her policies were a direct attack on a separate political community. The combination of a strident leader implementing controversial policies in a context of declining Scottish Conservative support was lethal for the Conservative Party (Torrance 2009). It also provided the renewed impetus for discussions of devolution (Stewart 2009). The idea of a democratic deficit became more pronounced. Could the Secretary of State for Scotland continue to be appointed by a party whose support was declining?

Plans for devolution were drawn up by a group called the Scottish Constitutional Convention. It included the Labour Party, the Liberal Democrats, trade unions and various civil society organisations. It did not include the Conservatives or the Scottish National Party. The Scottish Parliament established in 1999 mostly reflected its recommendations. One of the key points for the architects of Scottish devolution was that a new Scottish Parliament should be different from Westminster. The UK Parliament was used as a bad template of a majoritarian, oppositional, executive-dominated legislature whose culture and procedures were to be avoided. Another key point was that the motivation for devolution in Scotland was in part to protect Scotland from unwanted policies from a future Conservative government at Westminster (Brown 2000).

Scotland and the Millennium Settlement

A majority of Scottish people voted in favour of establishing a Scottish Parliament with tax-varying powers in a referendum in September 1997. The Scotland Act 1998 was then passed by the Parliament at Westminster and the first elections to the new Scottish Parliament were held in May 1999. The Scottish Parliament is a 129-member unicameral legislature that uses the Mixed Member Proportional (MMP) electoral system. A similar system is used in Germany and New Zealand. The adoption of a proportional electoral system is one of the principal contrasts with the UK Parliament. It was in part designed to ensure that the SNP could not win a majority of seats on a minority of the vote (Convery and Lundberg 2020).

The core powers of the Scottish Parliament were mainly an inheritance from the old Scottish Office. The big-spending domestic portfolios (health, education, transport) and economic development were devolved, while matters of social security, pensions, defence, foreign policy and, crucially, the constitution were reserved at Westminster. In contrast to the original Welsh Assembly in 1999, the Scottish Parliament operated on a reserved powers model: that is, it was able to legislate on any area except those listed in Schedule 5 of the Scotland Act 1998. The overall system was therefore quite permissive. The UK Treasury transferred a block grant of money to Scotland each year and did not attach any strings about how it should be spent. There was also large scope for policy divergence if the Scottish Parliament chose to go in a different direction in domestic policy. In comparative terms, the Scottish Parliament is a fairly powerful sub-state legislature, certainly comparable to a German land or Canadian province.

However, as noted by Convery and Welikala (in this volume), devolution was mainly something that was done to the periphery of the UK. The central UK state hardly changed to accommodate the new devolved legislatures. The Secretary of State for Scotland remained a UK cabinet position, but was now more concerned with coordination than huge swathes of Scottish policy. There was no attempt to implement a federal system, nor was the House of Lords reformed to make it more of a territorial second chamber along the lines of the German Bundesrat or the Australian Senate. Intergovernmental relations (the relationship between the UK and the devolved administrations) remained informal and weakly institutionalised (McEwen et al. 2012).

The procedures of the Scottish Parliament were intended to mimic Scandinavian-style legislatures and be different from Westminster (Arter 2004). The Consultative Steering Group that advised on the standing orders envisaged parties working together and the government occasionally sharing power with the opposition and the people of Scotland (Brown 2000). It also wanted to ensure that the committees of the Parliament were a powerful check on government. However, much of the architecture and assumptions of the Scottish Parliament were also drawn from Westminster ideas (Mitchell 2009). The executive was drawn from Parliament and needed to command the confidence of Parliament; there would be a Scottish cabinet of senior ministers bound by collective responsibility and headed by a First Minister; and the permanent and neutral civil service that advised the previous Scottish Office was the same one that would now work for the new Scottish Executive.

There was from the outset, therefore, a tension between the idea of power-sharing and the idea of a government having the right to govern. This tension has given rise to debates about whether the Scottish Parliament has lived up to its founders' intentions or whether the differences from Westminster are exaggerated (Mitchell 2009; Cairney 2011. Critics point to First Minister's Questions resembling Prime Minister's Questions. This session, in particular, is criticised for encoding a masculine and performative mode of debate. They also note that although Scottish Parliament committees have the power to produce their own legislation, they rarely do so. The Scottish Parliament also rarely defeats the government, much like at Westminster. On the other hand, research shows that the Scottish Parliament does have a significant impact on government legislation (Shephard and Cairney 2005; MacGregor 2021). Moreover, the Scottish Parliament had 45% women's representation in 2021 and maintains a stricter policy of family-friendly working hours than Westminster.

In the first instance, the government in Scotland was known as the Scottish Executive. The SNP started using the term Scottish Government in 2007 and this change was officially recognised in the Scotland Act 2012. For the first two sessions of the Scottish Parliament (1999–2003 and 2003–2007), the government was a coalition between the Labour Party and the Liberal Democrats. The first government was rocked by the sudden death of First Minister Donald Dewar. Unlike in Wales, the Scottish Labour Party struggled to recover its footing thereafter.

In general, the devolved administrations have pursued a different policy agenda from the UK Government in relation to public services under governments of all parties. Under Labour, the Coalition and the Conservatives, English public services, such as health and education, have made use of market mechanisms to attempt to drive up standards. This approach has manifested itself in, for example, foundation hospitals and choice in the NHS and academy schools in education. The Scottish Government has rejected reforms like these in favour of more partnership working and coordination. In part, this choice reflects the fact that Scotland is simply a much smaller polity: it is easier to get all the key stakeholders in a room and talk to them than in bigger and more complex England (Cairney and Widfeldt 2015). However, it also reflects a choice about how best to approach governing in the twenty-first century. In some areas, the Scottish Government has pointed to success (for example, the Scottish Child Payment has begun to make an impact on poverty). However, in the case of school education, for instance, Scotland spends more per pupil than England and achieves worse results (Sibieta 2023).

In 2007, the SNP made strong progress in the election and secured 47 seats while Labour secured 46. The SNP were able to form a minority government and depended on negotiations with other parties to pass budgets and legislation. Alex Salmond became the first SNP First Minister of Scotland. The SNP Government knew that they lacked the votes in the Scottish Parliament to push for an independence referendum. Salmond's strategy was to demonstrate that the SNP could govern competently and use that as a springboard for the 2011 Scottish Parliament elections. The SNP Government abolished graduate contributions to university education in Scotland and scrapped NHS prescription charges.

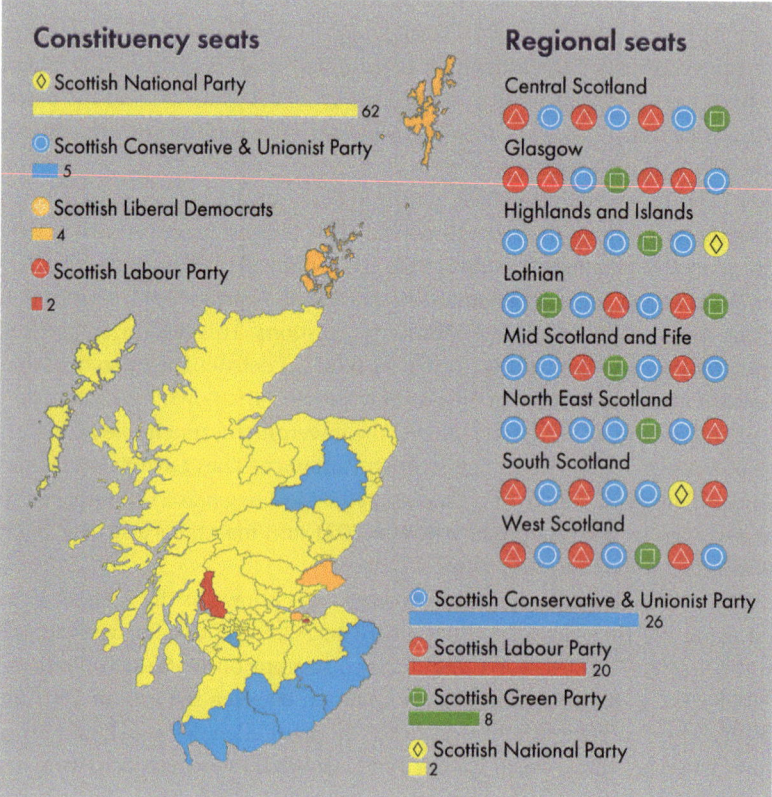

Figure 13.1   Scottish Parliament elections, 2021, constituencies and regional seats

Source: Scottish Parliament, 2021 election. Contains information licensed under the Scottish Parliament Copyright License

The SNP's biggest breakthrough came at the next elections in 2011. They won a majority of seats in the Scottish Parliament. The SNP's manifesto stated that they wanted to hold a referendum on Scottish independence. Alex Salmond therefore argued that there was a mandate to do so that should be respected by the UK Government. Because the constitution was specifically reserved to Westminster in Schedule 5 of the Scotland Act, the Scottish Government required the UK Parliament to temporarily devolve the power to hold a referendum. The UK Prime Minister at the time was David Cameron and he signed an agreement with the Scottish Government (known as the Edinburgh Agreement) promising to give the Scottish Parliament the power to hold a referendum and to abide by the result. The stage was therefore set for the 2014 Scottish independence referendum.

The politics of Scottish independence

The case for Scottish independence can be summarised in terms of democracy, prosperity and equality. The democratic case stems from the idea that Scots are different and they vote differently. The only way to ensure that Scotland gets the governments it votes for is therefore independence. There is always the chance that a Conservative government will be elected at the UK level, even if Scots vote decisively for other parties.

The prosperity case rests on the idea that the UK economy has been mismanaged and continually underperforms (Scottish Government 2023). It suffers from chronic lack of public and private investment, a preponderance of low-skill employment and weak productivity growth. The SNP argues that these problems were exacerbated under the economic policies of the Thatcher and Cameron governments. For Scotland to prosper economically, therefore, it needs to be untethered from the dead weight of the UK economic policy consensus. Instead, it needs to try to follow the path of other small and successful European economies that are much richer than the UK.

Relatedly, that economic prosperity will allow Scotland to become a much more equal country. The UK has the highest income inequality of any large European country (Resolution Foundation 2023). Independence supporters point instead to countries like Norway, Sweden and Denmark, which manage to combine higher growth with smaller gaps between rich and poor people. They also invest more in public services and generate better outcomes.

However, the case for independence has been complicated by Brexit. Much of the economics of independence presented to Scots in 2014 was predicated on the idea that both an independent Scotland and the rump of the UK would remain members of the European Union. As is the case in Ireland, EU membership solves a lot of otherwise knotty problems about borders, trade and cooperation. Both the UK and an independent Scotland would be subject to single market rules and there would be no hard economic border because both would also be members of the EU's customs union. Trade could continue in much the same way as before. However, if an independent Scotland is a member of the EU and England is not, there would need to be some sort of border (Hayward and McEwen 2022. The SNP still has to work through the implications of this problem in terms of the case for independence.

The economics of independence are also not straightforward and might involve some short-term costs. While it might be possible to change the trajectory of the Scottish economy in the medium to long term and make it more equal and productive, there are likely to be immediate fiscal challenges for an independent Scotland.

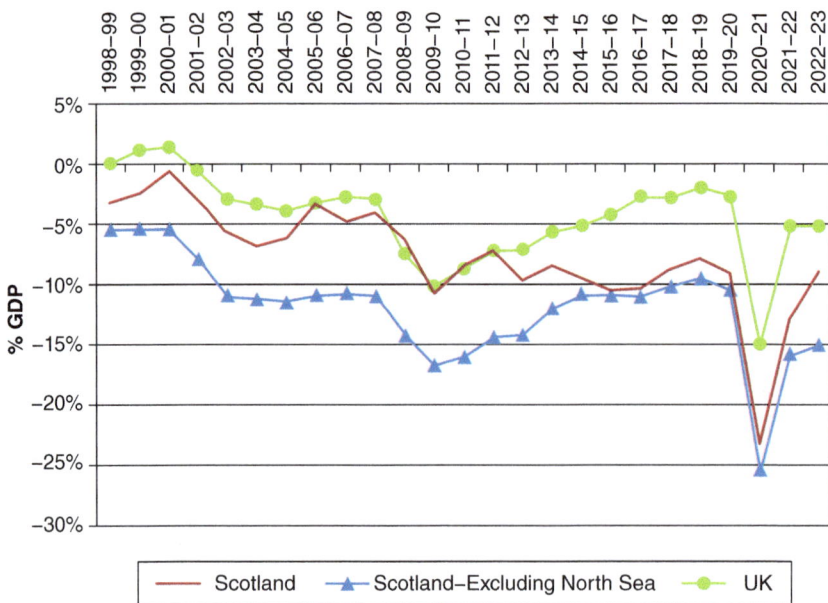

Figure 13.2 Net fiscal balance: Scotland and the UK, 1998–1999 to 2022–2023

Source: © Crown copyright 2023

Scotland's net fiscal balance (the difference between the taxes it raises and the money it spends) was £19.1 billion in 2022–2023 (9% of GDP) (Figure 13.2). This is not an unusual situation. Lots of countries run budget deficits. The UK as whole also runs a budget deficit and areas outside London have long tended to raise less money than is spent in them by the government. Independence would present Scotland with a different set of economic choices, but the starting point is that it would need to fund this difference through borrowing, cuts or (in the longer term) a more productive economy.

Explaining the result of the 2014 independence referendum

Scots voted against independence in 2014: 45% voted for and 55% voted against. However, the result was much closer than it appeared at the beginning of the campaign and much higher than the historical support for independence (which had hovered around one-third of the electorate before the referendum). How should we account for the result?

National identity played a key role in referendum choice. From the outset, those with a British identity or those who held their British identity as strongly as their Scottish identity were much less likely to be supportive of independence and further devolution. These people were also the least likely to have voted Yes in the referendum (Henderson et al. 2015). Voters who felt a strong sense of Scottish identity and little or no British identity were much more likely to have voted Yes (Henderson et al. 2022: 78).

The second key explanation for the result is people's evaluations of economic issues. No voters were not convinced that the economy would get any better within the union, but they were worried about the economic costs of independence. There is some evidence that voters with a higher appetite for risk were more likely to vote Yes (Liñeira and Henderson 2019). However, interestingly, economic evaluations had the most impact at the national level. Voters tended to base their referendum choice on whether they thought independence would be good for the economy overall, rather than the circumstances of their household (Henderson et al. 2022: 91). Overall, as Henderson et al. (2022: 91) conclude: 'many voters had a relatively optimistic picture of independence (at least relative to the Union); it was doubts about whether that picture would materialise that held Yes support back'.

The result reflected some socio-demographic divides. Broadly, the richer you were, the less likely you were to support independence. That also explains some of the geographic differences in the result: poorer Glasgow voted Yes, while comparatively wealthier Edinburgh voted No.

The Yes campaign focused on the case for independence, as described above, emphasising the opportunities for an independent Scotland to do things differently and create a more prosperous and equal society. The No campaign focused more on the negative effects of independence, but survey data suggests that Scots were not overly convinced by this strategy in deciding how to vote (Henderson et al. 2022). In the week before the referendum, the leaders of the three main UK parties came together to pledge 'The Vow'. They promised to maintain the Barnett formula in the event of a No vote and to devolve further powers to the Scottish Parliament. These powers were delivered in the Scotland Act 2016. The belief that more powers were coming to the Scottish Parliament anyway helped to boost No support (Henderson et al. 2022: 91).

Case Study 13.1

Political culture – are Scottish people more left-wing?

Scottish politicians from different parties (especially the SNP and Labour) have in the past claimed that Scottish people have different political values from people in the rest of the UK, particularly in England. They have used this perceived difference to argue for devolution or make the case for independence, for example. When scholars compare attitudes in different parts of the UK, they can identify differences. There are different patterns of national identities and people in Wales, Scotland and Northern Ireland vote for different political parties (some of whom only stand candidates in those regions). Scottish and Northern Irish attitudes towards the European Union exhibited longstanding differences from England and that was demonstrated forcefully in the results of the 2016 referendum (Henderson 2014b: 102–103).

However, beyond these behavioural manifestations of distinctiveness, do Scots have different fundamental *values* from voters in England or the rest of the UK? We might make the argument that Scotland has a distinct political culture if Scots believed different sorts of things about, for example, how much the state should intervene in the economy, how much the state should seek to equalise incomes between different groups, or whether two-parent families are best. On these issues of fundamental values, it is in fact difficult to find much of a difference between Scots and the rest of the UK. Scots are not more left-wing.

Nevertheless, that does not mean that this perception has no effect. Politicians' belief that Scottish people have more communitarian values has led them to argue for and implement different sorts of

(Continued)

policies in Scotland, from a more generous welfare state to free tuition for university students. In surveys, we can also see that rhetoric about Scottish people being different might feed into Scots' perceptions of other Scots. For example, the 2014 Future of England Survey asked questions about attitudes to same-sex marriage and immigration, and whether people thought that others in their part of the UK were more or less in favour of these policies. It found that: 'although Scottish attitudes are actually similar to those in England and Wales, Scots believe that they are more in favour of these policies than they actually are and the gap between actual attitudes and perceived attitudes is larger in Scotland than in any other part of Britain' (Henderson 2014b: 106).

Reflective questions

1   Are there distinct political cultures in different parts of the UK?
2   Why does the idea that Scots are more left-wing persist?

Voting behaviour

Scottish voters operate in a multi-level system. They vote in local government, Scottish Parliament and UK Parliament elections. They also used to vote in European Parliament elections. All three elections use different electoral systems: Single Transferable Vote (STV) in local government, Mixed Member Proportional (MMP) for the Scottish Parliament, and First-Past-the-Post for Westminster. Scottish voting behaviour began to diverge significantly from English voting behaviour from the 1970s (Miller 1981).

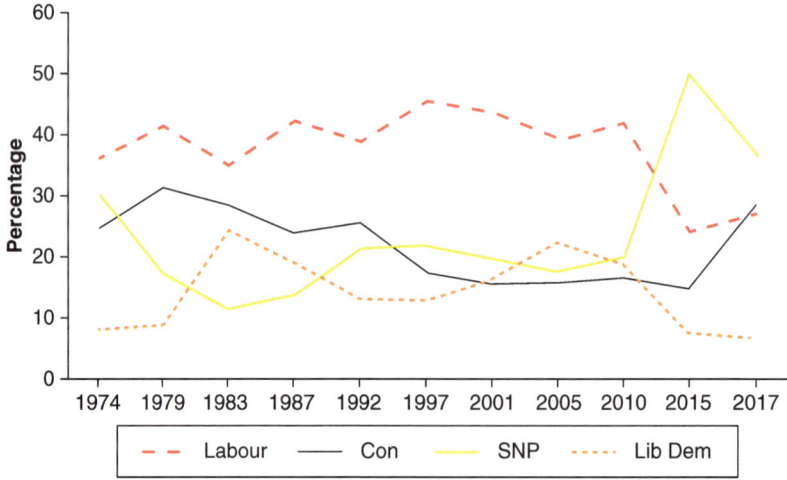

Figure 13.3   Scottish voting in UK elections

Source: Ailsa Henderson, Robert Johns, Christopher Carman, James Mitchell 'Political Behaviour in Scotland', in Keating, M. (ed.) *The Oxford Handbook of Scottish Politics*, p.225

The classic electoral divide is between voters on the left and right of the economic spectrum. That divide exists in Scotland but it also operates alongside a divide on the constitution: do you support or not support independence? It is that latter divide that has become hugely important since the 2014 Scottish independence referendum (Henderson et al. 2022).

The explanation for the rise of the SNP in the 2007 Scottish Parliament elections lies in its ability to project itself as a credible government and a party that was best placed to stand up for Scottish interests (Johns et al. 2010. These valence explanations, rather than a dramatic rise in support for independence as such, explain its electoral performance in 2011 when it gained a majority. After the 2014 referendum, however, voters began a process of sorting themselves into ideologically consistent containers, moving to the SNP if they were Yes supporters and had previousy backed other parties, and moving to pro-union parties from the SNP if they had voted No. The Brexit referendum further complicated matters, with the creation of constitutional tribes depending on how one felt about independence but also how one felt about Brexit, resulting in, for example, Yes Remainers, Yes Leavers, No Remainers and No Leavers. The partisan sorting was asymmetrical: Leave voters shifted to the Conservative Party, unless they were Yes voters, in which case they stayed with the SNP. By the time of the 2021 devolved election 90% of voters with a constitutional preference were backing a party that shared their constitutional views. The relative lack of electoral competition on the Yes side guaranteed strong SNP support, but also ensured that No support was divided across the Conservatives, Labour and Liberal Democrats.

Since the referendum, Scottish voters had tended to cast ballots in UK elections on the basis of their constitutional preferences in a way that reflected the post-referendum partisan sorting. The result was that elections were less about picking a party to govern for the UK than about sending a party to London to stand up for Scotland. The Conservative government was not particularly popular to start with, so it was difficult to detect decreases in approval throughout the Brexit nego-tiations, the elections in 2017 and 2019. What we saw instead was rising support for independence, though often short lived. Two factors help to explain the 2024 election result in Scotland. First, declining approval levels in England and rising support for UK Labour had a knock-on impact on the popularity of Conservatives and Labour in Scotland. Second, and related to this, voters prior-itised removing the Conservatives from office rather than sending a constitutional message. The result was not just a change in preferences but a change driven by different electoral priorities.

The 2024 election in Scotland can therefore be understood as a double incumbency disad-vantage, with declining electoral support for the UK incumbents and for the devolved incum-bents in favour of Labour. Indeed across the UK as a whole, Labour saw the largest increase in support in Scotland. SNP support had been declining since the 2021 election, attributable to concerns over competence (in particular the handling of education), changes in leadership, polarising policy choices including GRR and the Supreme Court case that appeared to block the path to any future independence referendum. The result was a slow leaking away of support for the SNP-led Scottish government, and for the party itself but not, it seems, independence, which remains stubbornly stuck at 45%. For this reason, the consistency between constitu-tional preferences and party preferences we saw after 2014, has started to return to normal. Instead, the old negative partisanship towards the Conservative Party in Scotland has been joined by a level of negative partisanship towards the SNP.

Scottish political parties

The SNP has been the dominant party in Scottish politics for the past 15 years. Their election success in 2007, 2011 and beyond followed a long period in which the Labour Party dominated

Scottish politics. When John Swinney took over from Humza Yousaf as First Minister in 2024, the SNP had been in government in Scotland for 17 years. At the time of the next Scottish Parliament elections in 2026, it will have been in power for longer than the Conservatives at the UK level in 1979–1997. It is a remarkable success story for a party that often struggled for relevance in the twentieth century, faced with the difficulties of the First-Past-the-Post UK electoral system and the lack of a separate Scottish Parliament.

We can categorise the SNP as a Stateless Nationalist or Regionalist Party (McAngus 2017). Its core purpose is to achieve Scottish independence and it only stands candidates in Scotland. In recent years, it has become one of the most successful examples of this type of party in Europe, regularly winning elections and forming the government in Scotland since 2007. The 'national' in Scottish National Party can be interpreted in different ways. Political scientists sometimes make a distinction between ethnic nationalism (based on cultural markers like language or ethnicity) and civic nationalism (based on citizenship, territory or institutions), although this binary is debatable. The SNP tries to place itself firmly in the latter category (Lynch 2013; van der Zwet 2015). The SNP emphasises the idea that everyone who lives in Scotland and wants to be Scottish counts as a Scot, regardless of their background. Scottish nationalism does not have a major language issue to deal with. The SNP in government has also emphasised a more supportive approach to asylum seekers and immigration in general. Its argument is that Scotland needs more immigration due to its population decline and therefore the party supports EU freedom of movement and a less restrictive immigration regime than the UK Government.

Although it was originally difficult to categorise ideologically, the SNP gradually settled in the latter half of the twentieth century into a party of the centre left (Mitchell et al. 2011). The party's vision for an independent Scotland in 2014 also emphasised a social democratic vision. Jackson (2014) identifies three significant (but sometimes competing) strands of the SNP's ideological vision. First, there is an analysis of the UK state as one which is sclerotic and unreformable. It contrasts with a Scottish commitment to a more modern and radical form of politics in the service of working people. Ridding Scotland of the dead hand of the UK state opens new possibilities.

Second, Jackson (2014: 52) argues that:

> for many nationalists the core of the case for Scottish independence ultimately reduces to the argument that Scots want to build a social democratic or socialist country while the English do not (the views of the Welsh and the Northern Irish are usually put to one side). On this account, Scottish statehood is not so much about the expression of a national identity as an instrumental device for the realisation of a more egalitarian society.

Thus, this is the much more civic and practical version of nationalism that is attached to a project, rather than the protection of a particular cultural or linguistic heritage.

Third, the SNP subscribes to a 'post-sovereign' view of Scotland's place in the world (Keating 2009). One view of sovereignty (sometimes associated with Conservatives who supported a harder vision of Brexit) emphasises the idea that it is something that states have or do not have. Modern SNP politicians, in contrast, tend to emphasise ideas of cooperation and interdependence (Jackson 2014: 55). An independent Scotland would retain the monarchy and the pound, and it would still have a close relationship with the other parts of the UK. It would also be a member of the European Union. Thus, the vision is for a Scotland that is enmeshed in different networks, pooling sovereignty to gain influence and maximise its advantages.

The new Scottish Parliament in 1999 presented the SNP with the opportunity to attract more support and to form the government in Scotland for the first time. It streamlined and professionalised its internal operations, creating the formal post of 'leader' for the first time, to ensure it could start to appear like a credible alternative government (Mitchell et al. 2011: 39). Since 2007, the SNP has also benefitted from two leaders who were perceived to be some of the most talented politicians of their generation in Alex Salmond and Nicola Sturgeon. The SNP used its period in government as a platform to emphasise its governing competence and appeal to voters beyond its traditional base. It changed the name of the Scottish Executive to the Scottish Government.

The party attracts support from those who support Scottish independence, as you would expect, but it would be wrong to assume that support for the SNP is based solely on the independence issue. It has also attracted support on the basis that it is perceived as a competent governing party, and this issue was one of the main explanations for it winning a majority of seats in the Scottish Parliament in 2011 (Johns et al. 2013).

The Scottish Labour Party is a branch of the UK-wide Labour Party. It enjoyed a period of dominance in Scottish politics between the mid-1980s and the mid-2000s. As the Scottish Conservative Party declined in popularity, Labour was the main beneficiary. However, competition with the SNP was a key theme running through the party's strategies from the late 1960s. The Scottish Labour Party has a separate original history, but latterly became much less autonomous and was integrated much more fully with the UK-wide party (Hassan and Shaw 2020). Although popular, it never reached the heights of dominance achieved and maintained by the Welsh Labour Party (see Larner and Wyn Jones, in this volume).

Scottish Labour's support for devolution was originally lukewarm. However, as the 1980s progressed, it began to see a Scottish Parliament as an important protection against UK Conservative governments that it saw as pursuing a damaging agenda for Scotland. Margaret Thatcher inadvertently helped to persuade the Scottish Labour Party that devolution was necessary and that it should campaign to shape it. It joined the Scottish Constitutional Convention in the late 1980s and drew up the plans for the Scottish Parliament in the 1990s in conjunction with other parties and civil society groups.

Scottish Labour were in government with the Scottish Liberal Democrats in Scotland for the first two terms of the Scottish Parliament. The death of the first First Minister Donald Dewar, a widely respected figure, in 2000, robbed the party of a capable leader and caused some instability. Henry McLeish served for a short time before he was succeeded by Jack McConnell in 2001. In government, Scottish Labour pursued an agenda that did not follow the prescriptions of New Labour at the UK level. It declined to implement more choice in education or health and did not create Scottish versions of foundation hospitals or city academies. Instead, it tried to work in partnership with public sector organisations and professional bodies. It also implemented free personal care for elderly people, a policy that caused some tension with the UK Labour Party because it was not adopted by the UK Government at the time (Hassan and Shaw 2012). During its time in government, Scottish Labour benefitted from economic growth and rising public sector budgets because of decisions made by the UK Labour Government under Chancellor Gordon Brown. It was therefore able to increase public expenditure in Scotland.

Even before its electoral decline in Scotland, there were suggestions that Scottish Labour were complacent and organisationally hollowed out (Hassan and Shaw 2012: 257–258). Scottish Labour lost narrowly to the SNP in 2007, when the latter was able to form a minority government. However, in 2011, the SNP campaigned on its record in government and won a majority. The decline in Scottish Labour since then has been more dramatic, particularly after the Scottish independence referendum in 2014. At the 2015 general election, Scottish Labour lost all but one of its UK MPs. Labour's period in opposition in Scotland has been marked by a constant leadership turnover and a series of organisational reforms to try to give the party more autonomy and make it appear more distinct from UK Labour. While the SNP had two leaders in 20 years, Labour ended up going through ten. It has tried to steal back the 'standing up for Scotland' mantle that was claimed by the SNP. Overall, the party has struggled with the balance between pursuing further autonomy and retaining influence in the central UK Labour Party (Brown Swan and Kenny 2024).

The Scottish Conservative Party is a branch of the UK-wide Conservative Party. It has a previous history as a separate political party (the Scottish Unionist Party) but merged more closely with the UK Conservatives in 1965. The party actually enjoyed considerable success in Scotland between the end of the First World War and the mid-1960s. However, as we have noted above, the 1980s and 1990s were particularly tough. There were no Scottish Conservative MPs elected at the 1997 general election. The party also opposed devolution and so had to perform a quick turnaround to serve in the new Scottish Parliament.

The party languished at around 18 seats for the first four Scottish Parliament elections. It was difficult for it to shake off its previous association with the Conservative governments of the 1980s and 1990s and its reluctance to support devolution (Convery 2016). However, the election of Ruth Davidson as leader in 2011 coincided with some other changes that provided an opening for the party to play to its strengths (Torrance 2020). The party was able to emphasise its credentials as the main unionist alternative to the SNP. It suggested that Scottish Labour were less dependable in this regard, and it hammered home its opposition to a second independence referendum.

Conclusion

Like the rest of the UK, Scottish politics has been through a few turbulent years. The most important electoral split that has emerged concerns the constitution: those for and against Scottish independence. That split has shaped voters' perceptions and much of Scottish political debate. It also helped the SNP to become the dominant party in Scotland at the Holyrood and Westminster levels.

Beyond party politics, there has also been a story of public policy divergence from the rest of the UK. In line with the pre-devolution pattern, Scotland approaches key policy areas differently and has used it tax powers to try to pursue a more progressive distribution. That in part reflects the identities of Labour and the SNP as centre-left political parties and the perception that Scottish political culture is more left-wing.

Summary

- Part of the story of Scottish devolution has been the decline of Scottish Labour and the rise of the Scottish National Party. This effect became even more pronounced after the 2014 independence referendum.

- There has been some notable policy divergence between Scotland and the rest of the UK since devolution, particularly in health, education and on tax policy.
- Support for independence has hovered at around 45% since 2014. The issue is therefore not going to go away entirely, even if the SNP's electoral fortunes decline.

Recommended and further reading

- Henderson, A., Johns, R., Larner, J. and Carman, C.J. (2022) *The Referendum that Changed a Nation: Scottish Voting Behaviour, 2014–2019*. Basingstoke: Palgrave. This is the definitive survey of the impact of the independence referendum on Scottish politics. It draws on original survey data and provides an excellent summary of how Scots think and vote.
- Keating, M. (2009) *The Independence of Scotland: Self-government and the Shifting Politics of Union*. Oxford: Oxford University Press. This book provides a comprehensive overview of the politics of Scottish independence and the options open to Scotland. It also argues that there has been a shift towards a 'post-sovereign' understanding of self-government.
- Kenny, M. and Mackay, F. (2020) 'Women, gender and politics in Scotland', in Keating, M. (ed.), *The Oxford Handbook of Scottish Politics*. Oxford: Oxford University Press, pp. 59–77. This chapter concludes that there has been uneven progress towards greater representation for women in Scottish politics and highlights how opportunities for change have run into institutional stickiness since devolution.

Chapter 14

Wales

Jac Larner and Richard Wyn Jones

What will this chapter tell me?

- This chapter examines Wales and its place in the UK, placing its development in context and noting the unique place of the Welsh language and culture.
- Wales is distinctive in having been long dominated by one party: the Welsh Labour Party. The chapter looks at the explanations for and consequences of this long period of dominance.
- The chapter also examines the evolution of Welsh devolution and the experience of devolved politics so far. The Welsh model of devolution has changed significantly since 1999 and more change is on the way.

What do I need to know?

- **Devolution**: The process of transferring powers from the UK Parliament to Wales. The National Assembly for Wales (now Senedd Cymru) was established in 1999, with powers gradually increasing over time.
- **Senedd Cymru (Welsh Parliament)**: The devolved legislature of Wales, based in Cardiff. It currently has 60 members (MSs) elected using a mixed electoral system, but is expanding to 96 members elected by a closed-list proportional representation electoral system.
- **Welsh Government**: The devolved government of Wales, led by the First Minister. It has responsibilities in areas such as health, education and economic development.
- **Political parties**: Key parties include Welsh Labour (dominant since devolution), Plaid Cymru, Welsh Conservatives and Welsh Liberal Democrats. Note the distinction between Welsh branches of UK-wide parties and Wales-only parties.
- **Electoral system**: The Senedd uses the Mixed Member Proportional (MMP) system, combining First-Past-the-Post constituency seats with proportional regional seats.
- **Reserved Powers Model**: Since 2017, the Welsh Parliament can legislate on any area not specifically 'reserved' to Westminster.
- **Fiscal devolution**: Wales has limited tax-raising powers, including control over some taxes and borrowing capabilities.
- **Historical context**: Understanding Wales's industrial past, particularly in mining, is crucial for grasping its political leanings.
- **Current issues**: Key debates include further devolution, potential independence, post-Brexit policies and economic development strategies.
- **Media landscape**: Wales has distinct Welsh-language and English-language media, influencing political discourse.

Introduction

Wales – according to some, England's first colony (Johnes 2019) – was conquered militarily in the thirteenth century and assimilated legally and administratively into England in the sixteenth century (Davies 1994). Unlike the other constituent parts of the state, namely England, Scotland and Northern Ireland, Wales is not represented on the state's Union flag. The country's cultural distinctiveness has eroded to a significant degree since the turn of the twentieth century as a result of the decline of the Welsh language and secularisation (Davies 1994). Nonetheless, politically speaking, Wales remains if not quite a place apart, then at least very distinctive – not only compared to the rest of the UK, but to the rest of the democratic world.

What makes Wales so distinctive is the pattern of vote choice among the Welsh electorate. Even if it is, as we shall see, an internally diverse country, in terms of voting behaviour, elections in Wales have long been dominated by one party. More specifically, for more than a century, Labour has emerged from *every* UK general election as the largest party in Wales in terms of both seats won and votes cast. This represents the longest period of democratic one-party electoral dominance anywhere (see Figure 14.1). More recently, Labour has been the largest party in terms of votes cast and seats won in every Senedd election since the Welsh Parliament was established – initially as the 'National Assembly for Wales' – in 1999. As if this record was not remarkable enough, Labour's (so-far) unbroken history of electoral dominance first established in 1922 followed directly from a period of Liberal Party dominance extending back to the extension of the (male) franchise by the Second Reform Act of 1867. In other words, since the dawn of anything that might be regarded as approximating democratic politics, Wales has only ever experienced one-party electoral domination.

In this chapter we seek to do two things. First, we explain why and how the same party keeps on winning elections in Wales for decade after decade. Second, we explore the ways in which one-party electoral dominance has shaped the form taken by devolved government in Wales. Relatedly, we also focus on the ways in which Labour's electoral dominance has influenced both the other political parties active in Wales and the internal dynamics of the Labour Party itself – not least, the relationship between 'Welsh Labour' and the British party centred on Westminster. As will become clear, while Wales is often overlooked by commentators, closer attention reveals a part of the UK with its own, unique political dynamics. Answering the analytical questions prompted by the Welsh case requires a different approach from the one normally utilised by scholars of British politics.

Voting behaviour: The socio-psychological basis of one-party dominance

In the democratic world, Wales stands as a remarkable anomaly. No other democracy in the world, whether liberal or illiberal, has witnessed a comparable period of electoral dominance by a single party at either the state or sub-state level. Figure 14.1 presents the electoral fortunes of Labour and the Conservatives in Westminster elections since 1900 – expressed in terms of voter share – in England, Scotland and Wales. Across all three countries, we can see the emergence of the Labour Party and its rapid ascent in vote share, coinciding with the extension of the franchise to all men and some women in 1918. In England, the Conservatives largely maintained their position as the dominant party, with only occasional interludes of Labour victory. Scotland, too, saw the Conservatives remain relatively successful until the late 1950s, after which Labour enjoyed a remarkable 60-year period of dominance, ended only by the rapid rise of the Scottish National Party. Wales, however, presents a strikingly different picture: the two lines representing Labour and Conservative vote shares never converge. On average, Labour's vote share in Wales is a full 10 points higher than in England.

The current period of Labour dominance in Wales is, remarkably, not without precedent. It emerged from the ashes of another seven-decade period of one-party rule by the Liberal

Party. Indeed, these two eras of political hegemony could be reframed as a singular, extended period of Conservative weakness and rejection in Wales. Since 1918, Conservative vote share in Wales trails England by a staggering 15 points (see also Wyn Jones et al. 2002). The last time the Conservatives claimed the mantle of largest party in Wales was during the General Election of 1859, under the guise of the Conservative and Peelite Party. This was an era when the total Welsh electorate numbered fewer than 5,000 men. It would not be an overstatement to assert that the Conservative Party has never won an election in Wales in the modern democratic era.

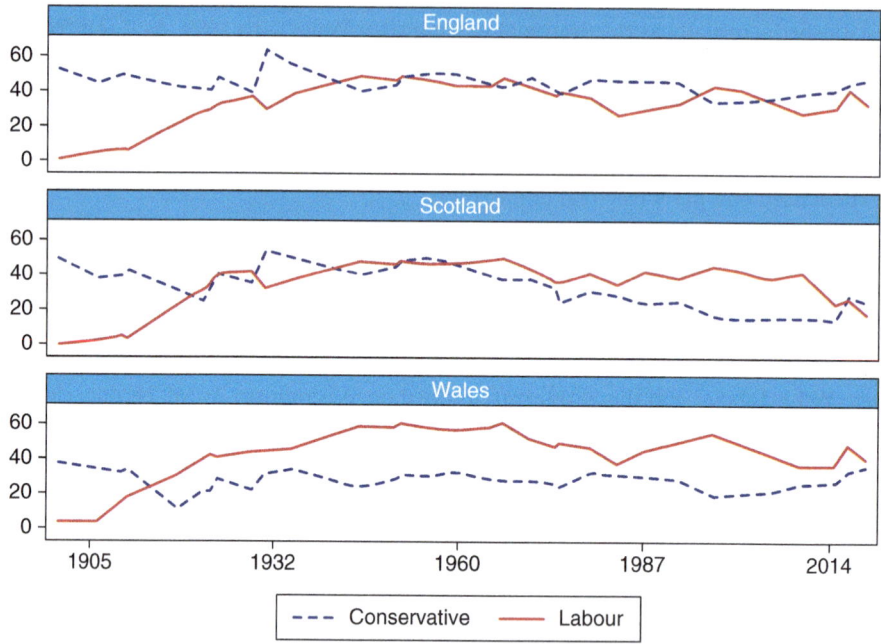

Figure 14.1   Vote share for Conservative and Labour parties at UK general elections in Britain

Source: House of Commons Library (2023) 'UK Election Statistics: 1918–2023: A century of elections' https://commonslibrary.parliament.uk/research-briefings/cbp-7529/

This enduring political distinctiveness of Wales remains a perplexing enigma. The border between Wales and England, arguably the oldest existing territorial division in Britain, closely follows the contours of Offa's Dyke – a structure built some 1,300 years ago by the Anglo-Saxon Mercian King Offa. Unlike in Scotland and what would come to be Northern Ireland, this border did not mark meaningful institutional separation between the two countries: there was no separate legal system, education system or religious divide for the best part of half a millennium. Yet it is a testament to the profound and lasting impact of history and culture that an eighth-century land excavation continues to mark differences in political opinions and behaviours well into the first quarter of the twenty-first century. This phenomenon presents a captivating puzzle for scholars of political behaviour in the United Kingdom.

Case Study 14.1

Y Gymraeg/The Welsh Language

Unlike the other constituent countries of the United Kingdom, a substantial proportion of Wales' population speak a language other than English: Cymraeg (Welsh). For most of Wales' history, Welsh was the main language for the vast majority of the population. However, substantial in-migration during the 1800s and early 1900s into Wales' industrial heartlands from England, Ireland and Europe saw a steady decrease in the percentage of speakers, from 50% in 1891 to 39% in 1921, to 19% in 1981. The decline of the language has had a substantial impact on Wales' political landscape, inspiring the foundation of Plaid Cymru as a political party (Wyn Jones 2024) as well as several substantial activist movements (King 2022).

The exact number of people who can speak Welsh now is surprisingly difficult to establish, with different sources producing considerably different estimates. For example, the 2021 Census estimates that 17.8% of the population speak Welsh, the Annual Population survey estimates 29.2% (using the same question), while the National Survey for Wales estimates 16–26%.

Whichever estimate is correct, survey data confirms a strong link between language ability and political attitudes, values and behaviour. For example, Welsh speakers are on average more left-wing economically and more socially liberal, more likely to vote Plaid Cymru, and were more supportive or remaining in the European Union of any group in the UK. There is even some evidence that the language has extended downstream effects. Welsh Election Study data from 2021 suggests that having a Welsh-speaking grandparent increases the likelihood of voting Labour and Plaid Cymru by three percentage points, and reduces the probability of voting Conservative by five percentage points, even if a person does not speak Welsh themselves.

Understanding vote choice

Analysing this extended period of political dominance is no straightforward task. Quality, regular survey data in Wales is a relatively recent development, leaving researchers to grapple with a paucity of empirical evidence for much of the period in question. Whereas many attempts have been made to analyse singular elections based on competence evaluations, often with great statistical success, on the basis of competence evaluations (e.g. Scully and Wyn Jones 2012; Scully 2013; Scully and Larner 2017) grappling with a century of single-party dominance requires an examination of longstanding elements of the political system that often extend far beyond the reach of existing survey data. Nevertheless, several pioneering works have attempted to make sense of these long-term political trends.

Several decades prior to devolution, Blondel's pioneering work *Voters, Parties and Leaders: The Social Fabric of British Politics* (1963) highlighted the distinctive patterns of electoral support in Wales, noting above-average levels of support for Labour among the 'lower and middle classes' and uniquely low levels of support for the Conservative Party among the 'middle class' (Blondel 1963: 62–64). Likewise, in their seminal analysis of British voting behaviour *Political Change in Britain*, Butler and Stokes (1969: 171) recognised that Wales was uniquely hostile to the Conservative Party. Butler and Stokes' answer to explaining voting in Britain was to introduce the socio-psychological model of political behaviour. The model in its original form first originated in the USA from scholars at the University of Michigan. The model argued that people identified psychologically with political parties, just as they might with their socio-economic class, religion or race (Campbell et al. 1960).

This identification with a political party was a long-term component of a political system, and that this identity had not only a direct influence on vote choice, but also an indirect influence on political attitudes associated with voting (Hutchings and Jefferson 2017: 22). According to this model, we begin to acquire this party identification early on in life, largely through parental transmission, and it is largely crystalised prior to adulthood through further processes of socialisation.

For Butler and Stokes (1969, 1970), the central social force which drove people to acquire their partisan 'self-image' was their class position, where party identity translates social class into support for either the Labour Party or the Conservative Party (Evans 2017: 178). This in turn built on earlier sociological work by Andersen and Davidson (1943), who argued that elections should be seen as 'democratic class struggle'. For Butler and Stokes, Wales' electoral distinctiveness was merely a function of its class milieu: a higher share of working-class voters than elsewhere given Wales' heavy industrial past and small professional middle class. Yet this explanation has always struggled to adequately explain voting patterns in Wales. First, even when controlling for social class, middle-class Labour support was unexpectedly high and Conservative support unexpectedly low – or as noted by geographer Kevin Cox in 1970, 'Levels of left-wing voting in Wales ... are highly underpredicted when regressed on social class measures' (Cox, 1970: 118). Second, it fails to account for the phenomena of class and partisan dealignment that have occurred in recent decades (Clarke et al. 2004; Fieldhouse et al. 2020). Third, it remains unable to account for the existence and success of an additional political party in Wales: Plaid Cymru. Using the existing British framework, it is unclear how class socialisation leads to a psychological attachment to a nationalist party.

As a result, scholars turned to other social identities and societal factors in order to explain this distinctiveness. Balsom et al. (1983) developed what became known as the 'Three Wales Model' to explain the distinctiveness of Welsh electoral behaviour. Welsh voting behaviour, they argued, was driven by three central cleavages in Welsh society: social class, national identity and language (Balsom et al. 1983, 1984; Scully and Wyn Jones 2012). Voters who identified as exclusively Welsh, or more Welsh than British, were substantially more likely to support the Labour Party. Voters who considered themselves to be British rather than Welsh were more likely to vote Conservative. Ability to speak Welsh (or one's family's ability to speak Welsh) was strongly correlated with support for Plaid Cymru.

Despite some notable challenges to this model (see Scully and Wyn Jones 2012, cf. Wyn Jones 2022), we argue that national identity remains essential for understanding the story of single-party dominance. Indeed, since Balsom and colleagues published their work, the proportion of people in Wales identifying with a national identity has increased: data from the 2021 Welsh Election Study suggests that 98% of respondents identified with either Welsh, British or English identity (compared to 68% for a social class). Theoretically, there are good reasons to suspect national identity plays a large role in behaviour and attitude persistence. First, national identity is typically acquired early in life through various socialisation processes, involving family, education systems and cultural institutions. This early internalisation contributes significantly to its durability and long-term influence on political orientations. Moreover, national identity is not a monolithic construct, but rather a complex amalgamation of other identities, including social class, language and values. This multi-faceted nature reinforces its pervasiveness in shaping political attitudes in Wales. While national identity can evolve over time, it generally remains relatively stable throughout most individuals' lives, providing a consistent framework for political decision-making and party affiliation (see also the Cutting-edge Research box in this chapter).

National identity in Wales is also notably more heterogeneous compared to other parts of the UK, reflecting a complex interplay of Welsh, British and English identities. Unlike Scotland or

England, where for a majority national identity tends to be more binary, Wales presents a more nuanced picture (see Figure 14.2). The presence of a significant English-born population (over a quarter of the electorate) introduces an additional layer of complexity. This demographic may identify as British, English, Welsh, or any combination thereof, creating a more diverse identity landscape. Furthermore, the strength of identity affiliation plays a crucial role. Individuals may feel strongly or weakly Welsh, British or English, leading to various combinations that impact political attitudes and behaviours. The rejection of certain identities is also significant. Some may embrace Welsh identity but reject Britishness, while others may identify as British but not Welsh, despite living in Wales. These choices often correlate with distinct political views and voting patterns. This heterogeneity also makes it easier to explain vote choice in statistical models that use survey data.

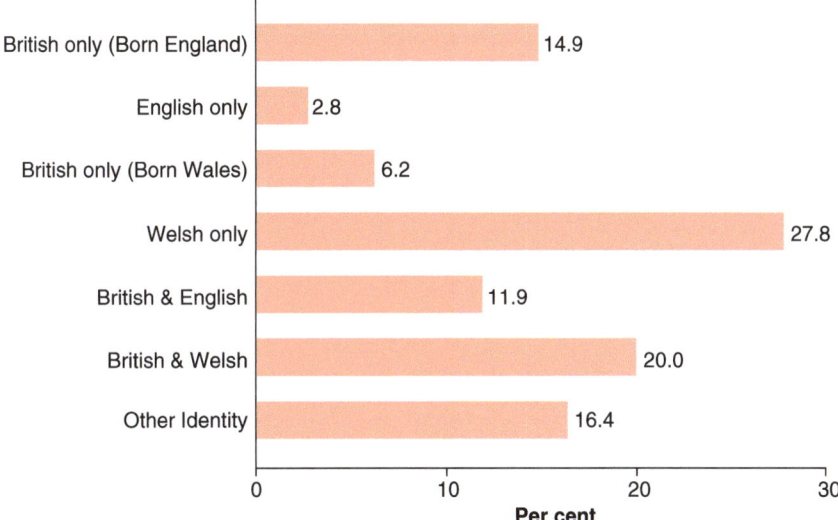

Figure 14.2   National identity in Wales, 2024

Source: Source is Wyn Jones, R., Larner, J., Poole E. G. and Griffiths, J. (2024) 2024 Welsh Election Study

The impact of national identity on political behaviour is particularly evident in voting patterns, where it often acts as a constraining factor, creating distinct 'blocs' of parties between which voters may alternate. This phenomenon is well illustrated in the Welsh political landscape, where significant voter movement is observed between Plaid Cymru and Labour in Senedd and Westminster elections, while transitions to the Conservatives are comparatively rare. For example, in the 2021 Senedd elections, 21% of 2019 Labour supporters voted for Plaid Cymru (compared to just 2% for the Conservatives). This pattern can be attributed to the alignment of these parties with different aspects of Welsh national identity, with Plaid Cymru and Labour often perceived as more congruent with Welsh interests, whereas the Conservatives are often seen as an 'English' party (Wyn Jones et al. 2002; Larner et al. 2023).

We can also see how national identity is associated with vote choice in the most recent UK General Election. As Figure 14.2 demonstrates, Plaid Cymru derive much of their support from those who feel very strongly Welsh but not at all British, while the Conservatives do very well among those who feel strongly British but not Welsh. Outside these groups, both parties have historically struggled to garner significant levels of support. This is the key to Labour's prolonged success. Unlike Plaid Cymru and the Conservatives, Labour in Wales can rely on support from across the national identity spectrum, positioning themselves both as a Welsh party standing up for Wales against Westminster, and also as a bulwark against Welsh 'nationalism'.

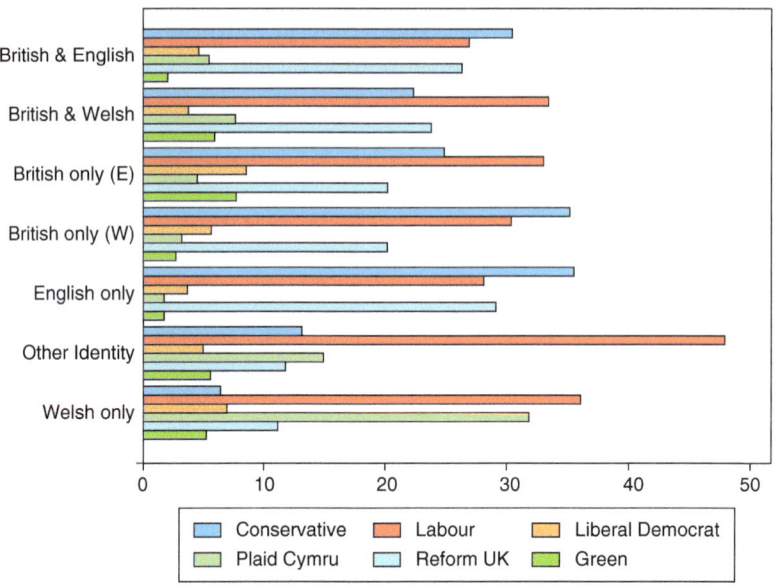

Figure 14.3   2024 vote choice by national identity

Key debate   National identity and values

A key argument in the socio-psychological model of voting is that our identities shape our political values, which in turn shape our political attitudes and behaviours. In Wales, this is certainly the case, with different national identity groups holding often substantially different sets of values (Campbell et al. 1960).

To illustrate this complexity, we examined the relationship between values and national identities in Wales, considering both left–right and libertarian–authoritarian scales. We differentiated between two national identity complexes: Welsh (those who can identify as Welsh and/or British) and English (those in Wales who can identify as English and/or British), separating Wales-born and England-born residents.

Our findings are striking. Those with a strong Welsh identity tend to lean more left politically than those without. Moreover, individuals who identify strongly as Welsh but not British exhibit particularly radical left-wing tendencies. This insight is crucial in understanding Labour's dominance and the Conservatives' comparative weakness in Wales. Importantly, the rejection of certain identities is as significant as the adoption of others. While some people in Wales who feel Welsh also identify as British, others choose not to. This distinction has been recognised as politically meaningful. For instance, during the 2016 referendum to leave the European Union, those feeling strongly Welsh but not strongly British had markedly different attitudes compared to those identifying as both strongly Welsh and strongly British.

In the Welsh context, it is essential to recognise which territorial identity is being rejected when someone adopts a solely British identity. This nuanced understanding of national identity – encompassing both chosen and rejected identities – is key to comprehending the intricacies of Welsh political behaviour and the broader dynamics of identity politics in Wales.

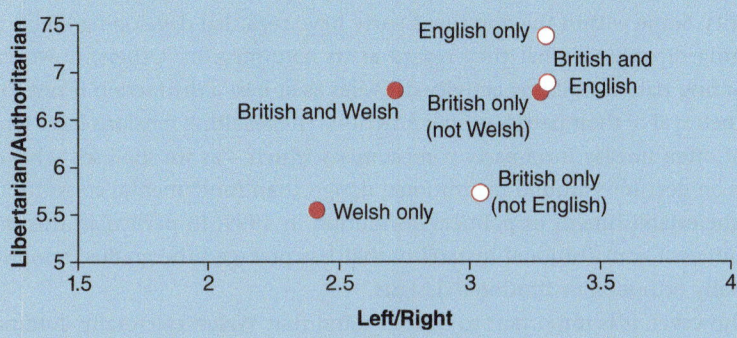

Figure 14.4   Identity politics in Wales, 2024

The impact of one-party dominance

Thus far, we have sought to explain why and how elections in Wales have produced such a distinctive history of very long-term democratic one-party dominance. In this section we consider some of the consequences of this. We do so by focusing on the evolution of devolution – that this is the ways in which Wales has gradually emerged as, first, a distinctive administrative and, subsequently, political space within the UK state. In addition, we consider the ways in which the dominance of the Labour Party in Wales has impacted on the other political parties active on the Welsh political stage, namely the Conservative Party and Plaid Cymru. Focusing on developments since the establishment of the Senedd, we also consider the relationship between 'Welsh Labour' and the wider British party in the light of Labour's distinctive – and uniquely successful – position in Wales.

One-party electoral dominance and constitutional development

As we have seen, voting behaviour in Wales has long been closely linked to patterns of national identity and related markers, for example language and – previously, at least – religion. For the past century, Welsh identity has been primarily associated with support for Labour, with Plaid

Cymru drawing its support from a sub-section of Welsh-identifying voters. The Conservative Party has relied on the support of those in Wales who identify as primarily or solely British.

This has two key implications for institutional developments in and for Wales. The first is that moves to build national institutions for Wales have overwhelmingly relied on the support of Wales' electorally dominant party. As a result, internal divisions and debates within that dominant party have in turn played a key role in determining both the direction and the pace of Wales' constitutional journey from what was, in essence, complete assimilation with England in the mid-nineteenth century through to the present day. Central to this dynamic has been the fact that even if the extent of their electoral dominance reflects the association between Welsh identity and vote choice, neither Labour nor, before them, the Liberal Party were solely or even primarily concerned with representing what might be termed the Welsh 'national interest'. Rather, Wales' electorally dominant parties have contained within them different currents. Some within the dominant party have regarded developing Welsh institutions as contributing directly to what they regard as its core mission. Others, however, have disagreed, regarding nation-building activity in Wales as at best a distraction if not, on occasion, an outright betrayal of their party's proper function. The resulting tensions have tended to lead to a series of often uneasy intra-party compromises which – as we shall see – have often had *more* impact on decisions around institutional design than fundamental constitutional principles. Since the establishment of political devolution in 1999, in particular, this has been the cause of significant constitutional instability that has presaged the gradual adoption of more constitutionally orthodox institutional designs.

Second, however, it is important to bear in mind that Wales' electorally dominant party is not the party that tends to win most elections in England. Given that England is by far the largest part of the state (currently home to around 85% of the total population), this has meant that opportunities for institutional development in Wales have tended to be confined to those relatively infrequent periods in which electoral preferences in both countries align. The significance of this point is underlined when we recall the fact that while the Conservative Party last emerged from a UK general election as Wales' largest party in thoroughly pre-democratic 1859, in the intervening period it has won most seats in England in 29 out of 40 general elections. Focusing on the period since 1922, when Labour first won most votes and seats in Wales, the Conservatives have won most seats in England in 21 out of 27 elections – only once in that period, namely in 2005, was a UK Labour government established without the backing of a majority of England MPs. Thus, we find that the most significant periods of constitutional development for Wales coincide with the relatively brief period of non-Conservative government at the UK level; that is, the various periods of Liberal rule prior to the First World War and the Labour governments of the post-Second World War era.

As we shall see, the only exceptions to this general pattern have occurred during those periods when the Conservative Party has actively sought to court the Welsh-identifying vote or are best characterised as tidying-up exercises. It should further be noted that the establishment of the National Assembly for Wales – now Senedd – in 1999 has meant that some constitutional development is possible in Wales without the involvement of Westminster and Whitehall. Nonetheless, any attempt to address the remaining major anomalies in devolved powers, for example, by devolving justice functions to Cardiff remains wholly reliant on action in London, thus ensuring that different patterns of vote choice among the Welsh and English electorates – as well as internal divisions within Labour – retain their significance for any potential future institutional developments.

Table 14.1   The evolution of devolution since 1918

1920	The Anglican Church (Church of England) **disestablished** in Wales with the enactment of the Welsh Church Act 1914 – a measure long supported by the Liberal Party and bitterly opposed by most Conservatives.
1944	The first '**Welsh Day**' debate held in the House of Commons – an annual discussion of Welsh affairs in the Commons chamber.
1948	The **Council for Wales and Monmouthshire** (later 'Council for Wales') established as an advisory body to the UK government – the result of compromise between Labour MPs who supported the establishment of a Secretary of State for Wales in the UK cabinet and those who opposed any form of devolution.
1950	**The Parliament for Wales Campaign** established to promote the establishment of a legislative Welsh parliament and associated devolved government. In 1955, Labour MP S.O. Davies introduced a private members' bill in the Commons aimed at establishing a Welsh parliament. Davies was one of a group of Labour MPs censured by their party for supporting the campaign.
1951	Post of **Minister of Welsh Affairs** established by Conservative UK Government – upgraded to the rank of **Minister of State** in 1954 – as part of a concerted effort by the Conservative Party to widen its appeal in Wales as well as exploit Labour's divisions on devolution.
1964	Incoming UK Labour Government establishes the post of **Secretary of State for Wales** and associated **Welsh Office**, the latter drawing together various UK government departmental offices for Wales mainly established in the pre-First World War era. Following its establishment, the Office becomes the focus for administrative devolution to Wales with more areas of responsibility transferred on a regular basis until the late 1990s.
1979	The **first devolution referendum** sees the UK Labour Government's plans for a Welsh Assembly embodied in the Wales Act 1978 rejected by an overwhelming 4:1 majority of the Welsh electorate. Opposition to the plans was spearheaded by a group of Welsh Labour MPs who regarded their own party's policy as anathema.
1980	The **Welsh Affairs Select Committee** established to provide (Westminster) parliamentary oversight of the work of the Welsh Office – regarded by some leading members of the previous year's successful No campaign as an alternative to devolution.
1997	The **second devolution referendum** sees the UK Labour Government's proposals for a Welsh Assembly narrowly approved by the Welsh electorate. The proposals largely mirrored those contained in the Wales Act 1978. The main difference was that the 1997 proposal was for a 60-member Assembly elected by a semi-proportional electoral system – the proposal rejected in the 1979 referendum was for a 72-seat Assembly elected on a First-Past-the-Post (or single-member plurality) basis.
1998	The **Government of Wales Act 1998** passed creating the National Assembly for Wales. The Assembly would have secondary law-making powers only, inheriting almost all the powers of the Wales Office and operating within the framework of primary legislation created in Westminster. It would be organised as single 'body corporate', i.e. there was to be no formal division of powers between the executive and legislature (although a cabinet structure was incorporated into the plans during the parliamentary passage of the legislation). The National Assembly would have no taxation powers but would rather rely on a 'block grant' from Westminster.
1999	First election to the National Assembly for Wales.
2000	Labour rebrands as 'Welsh Labour' and forms a coalition with the Welsh Liberal Democrats. As part of the coalition agreement, both parties agree to establish an independent commission to consider the powers and electoral arrangements of the National Assembly.
2003	The **Welsh Assembly Government** is established to signal a *de facto* division of powers between the executive and the legislature.
2004	Report of the all-party **Commission on the Powers and Electoral Arrangements of the National Assembly for Wales** (the Richard Commission) is published. It rejects the executive devolution model arguing that secondary legislative powers were inadequate and that the lack of formal separation between executive and legislature was confusing and undermined accountability. Instead, it advocated a formal division of powers between the executive and the legislature and a move to legislative devolution. It also argued that, at 60 members, the Assembly was too small to deal with enhanced powers and responsibilities and recommended a move to 80.

(Continued)

Table 14.1   (Continued)

2006	The **Government of Wales Act 2006** is passed. The result of another internal Labour Party compromise, the legislation formalised the division between executive (the Welsh Assembly Government) and the legislature (the National Assembly for Wales) while incorporating two different schemes of legislative empowerment: the first – a very tightly constrained scheme of legislative devolution – set out in Part 3 of the legislation, and the second more generous scheme set out in Part 4 to be unlocked following a further referendum vote. The Government rejected calls for more Assembly members.
2007	The new (Part 3) scheme of legislative empowerment is introduced – and rapidly becomes bogged down in delays in both Whitehall and Westminster.
2011	The **third devolution referendum** on 'further powers' sees a comfortable majority of those participating support a move to a different, more generous system of legislative empowerment as set out in Part 4 of the Government of Wales Act 2006.
2011	The Welsh Assembly Government is rebranded as the Welsh Government.
2014	**Wales Act 2014** passed by Conservative–Liberal Democrat coalition government devolving limited tax powers to Wales. Most significantly it allows the introduction of the Welsh variable rate of income tax bringing Wales into line with Scotland.
2014	The **Supreme Court** finds in favour of the Welsh Government's position in its ruling on the **Agricultural Sector (Wales) Bill** case brought by the UK Government implying that the scope of the legislative powers enjoyed by the National Assembly under the model of devolution are set out in Part 4 of the Government of Wales Act 2006 are more extensive than the UK legislators had imagined.
2017	**Wales Act 2017** passed changing the model of legislative devolution to a 'reserved powers' model similar to that enacted Scotland in 1999. This development is best understood as the UK Government's response to the 2014 Supreme Court judgment in that it more tightly delimited the legislative competence of the National Assembly. It should also be noted, however, that this was also a model devolution favoured by devolutionists in Wales on the basis that it introduced more clarity and certainty about the extent of devolved powers. The legislation also allows the National Assembly for the first time to determine its own size as well as the voting system used to elect its members (subject to the agreement of a two-thirds majority in the National Assembly).
2019	The report of the **Commission on Justice for Wales** (the Thomas Commission) recommends the full devolution of justice powers to Wales.
2020	The National Assembly for Wales is renamed **Senedd Cymru** (the Welsh parliament).
2024	The **Senedd Cymru (Members and Elections) Act** is passed increasing the size of the Senedd to 96 members to be elected via a closed list proportional electoral system with changes to be introduced in time for the next Senedd election scheduled for 2026.

Table 14.1 summarises the evolution of devolution in Wales since the end of the First World War. There are several points to note, the first is the general trajectory of institutional development from administrative devolution (whereby Wales is treated as an organisational unit for the administration of the state) through executive devolution (the transfer of executive powers from the Welsh Office to a democratically elected Assembly) to legislative devolution (the creation of a fully-fledged law-making parliament in Cardiff). In this way, Wales has moved from being (politically and administratively) part of England to being regarded as one of four component territories of the state enjoying a constitutional status broadly akin to that of Scotland and Northern Ireland.

Also striking is the sheer extent of the constitutional change that has taken place since the establishment of the-then National Assembly in 1999. Thus far, the operation of the Welsh Parliament has been underpinned by four different pieces of (Westminster) constitutional legislation for Wales from 1998, 2006, 2014 and 2017. Indicative of the degree of change experienced is that not only has Wales experienced a shift from executive to legislative devolution, but that the Senedd has experienced no less than three different forms of legislative devolution – the first in operation from 2007 to 2011, the second from 2011 to 2017, and a third since 2017. If continuity is one of the more striking characteristics of UK-level political institutions, for those interested in Wales, the story is rather one of almost constant development and change.

To understand why this is the case, we need to return to the impact of one-party electoral domination and recognise the extent to which it is intra-party compromises within the dominant Labour Party that have determined key decisions about the form that Welsh devolution might take. The result has been a series of what might be politely described as 'experimental' constitutional designs that have not only offended against some of the basic constitutional principles that we tend to associate with so-called Westminster Model democracies, but have also, relatedly, proven unwieldy and even unworkable in practice.

Take, for example, the executive devolution model embodied in the Wales Act 1978 and then implemented after the establishment of the National Assembly in 1999 on the basis of the previous year's Government of Wales Act. Executive devolution became established as Labour Party policy in the late 1960s as – in essence – a way of splitting the difference between those in the Labour Party (its MPs, in particular) who opposed devolution and others within the party who supported the establishment of a legislative parliament in Wales (Wyn Jones and Scully 2012). By proposing the transfer of the powers of Welsh Office ministers but not those of the Westminster Parliament to Cardiff, the concerns of MPs were at least partly assuaged, while devolutionists would be allowed to fulfil their ambition of securing a democratic body directly elected by the people of Wales. But while squaring the circle internally, when Labour's plans were implemented, it became almost immediately apparent that the lack of a clear separation of powers between legislature and executive was a recipe for confusion and an active barrier to genuine accountability. Similarly, coherent joined-up policy making proved nigh-on impossible when devolved government was forced to rely on a patchwork of secondary powers generated by Westminster legislation that was never drafted with the aim of facilitating the operation of a Welsh Assembly that had its own democratic mandate to govern.

In short, the move to a *de facto* and later formal division of powers as well as genuine legislative empowerment was driven in large measure by widespread frustration at the failings of the previous executive devolution scheme. The fact that there have subsequently been three different iterations of legislative devolution is again explained by the deficiencies of the first two versions, both of which were, again, the product of internal compromises within the dominant party and problematic in their different ways.

The net result of this instability is, paradoxically, a scheme of Welsh devolution that in constitutional terms is not only substantially stronger but also more constitutionally orthodox than was previously the case. Over time, the Welsh model of devolution has come to broadly approximate the Scottish model established in 1999. The key difference – and the remaining anomaly in the Welsh devolution dispensation – is that while justice functions have been devolved to both Scotland and (since 2010) Northern Ireland, Wales remains part of a single England and Wales system that is the jealously guarded preserve of the UK Government (Jones and Wyn Jones 2022). While the report of the Commission on Justice for Wales (2019), chaired by the former Lord Chief Justice of England and Wales, Lord Thomas, recommended that justice be devolved to Wales – a position that is supported by the Labour group in the Senedd – most Welsh Labour MPs are apparently resolutely opposed to this idea. It remains to be seen whether this becomes the latest site of intra-party compromises leading (eventually) to full devolution, or if this policy area remains an exception to the story of the evolution of devolution.

Political parties in the context of 'one-party dominance'

As well as the impact on constitutional developments, it is also worth considering how long-term one-party electoral dominance impacts the political parties themselves, shaping both Wales' dominant party and those parties seeking (largely unsuccessfully) to compete with it. Let us start with the former before we proceed to the main challengers, namely the Conservative Party and Plaid Cymru.

Labour in Wales and 'Welsh Labour'

Even if the longevity of Labour's electoral dominance in Wales means that it stands alone in democratic history, one-party dominance is not unique to Wales. The political science literature on 'party dominance' tends, however, to focus on those examples where long periods of electoral dominance serve to underpin long periods in government: parties such as Japan's Liberal Democratic Party and (previously, at least) Sweden's Social Democrats and Ireland's Fianna Fáil (e.g. Carty 2022). In this regard, Wales' dominant party represents an interestingly different case.

For most of Labour's 100-plus years of winning elections in Wales, the party has been in opposition in Westminster – between 1922 and 2022, Labour formed the UK Government for only 31 years. But since the establishment of the country's devolved institutions in 1999, it has simultaneously led every government in Wales itself (and at times in coalition with other parties). This has given rise to a series of complex and sometimes contradictory intra-party dynamics.

Writing in the early 1980s – that is, when Labour domination was a 'mere' six decades or so old – Iain McAllister and Anthony Mughan (1984) argued that the party's dominant position had the paradoxical effect of fostering organisational weakness. In those constituencies where Labour faced no serious electoral challenge, there was no reason to maintain a vibrant activist base or campaigning infrastructure. Thus, it was only in those parts of the country where elections were genuinely competitive that the party organisation could resist a tendency to atrophy.

Moreover, with Labour MPs from Wales more often than not occupying the opposition benches at Westminster, neither was there any reason to expect them to be associated with much by way of innovative thinking around issues of public policy. The significant roles played by Welsh Labour MPs such as Aneurin Bevan ('father' of the NHS) and James Griffiths in the post-Second World War Attlee Government, for example, suggests that this argument should not be overplayed. Nonetheless, it remains the case that Labour politicians from Wales have been better known for their loyalty than their creativity.

But the demands of being the permanent party of government – as has been the case for Labour at the Welsh level since 1999 – are clearly different. At the devolved level, executive ability, including a detailed interest in the implementation of public policy, is at a premium. The tension between the different demands of politics at different levels of government is only one of the ways in which post-devolution multi-level politics has impacted on Wales' dominant political force (Wyn Jones and Larner 2020). But thus far, at least, it has succeeded remarkably well in negotiating this potentially tricky terrain.

Much of this success can be attributed to the party's enthusiastic embrace of a self-consciously Welsh identity – through the 'Welsh Labour' brand – at the devolved level, especially in the aftermath of the first devolved election in 1999 when the party found itself strongly challenged by Plaid Cymru. This has involved differentiating the party in Wales from the wider British party, especially on those occasions when Labour is in power at the UK level. The 'Welsh

Labour' brand has been central to this (Wyn Jones and Larner 2020). In the face of Conservative or Conservative-led administrations in London, Welsh Labour has presented itself as 'standing up for Wales' – to quote an election slogan – championing the Welsh national interest against the central state. In this regard, Welsh Labour has adopted an approach that is very different from the one adopted by its Scottish equivalent; it has also proven to be a notably more successful one (Griffiths et al. 2023). The party's ability to maintain its unparalleled record of success in Wales will likely depend on its ability to continue to negotiate and reconcile competing, multi-level pressures: being the party of government in Wales while often a party in opposition in Westminster; being a party that is seen by many as a bearer of Welsh identity; but also being a party that supports a UK union that an increasing proportion of those who identify as Welsh regard as inimical to Welsh interests (Griffiths et al. 2023). It also remains to be seen if the party eventually starts having to pay the 'costs of governing' in the wake of its (so far) permanent role in the Welsh Government and becomes more susceptible to the 'time for a change' arguments that resonate elsewhere (Rose and Mackie 1983; Paldam 1986; Strøm 1990; Powell and Whitten, 1993). Hard though it may be for many in Wales to imagine, continued Labour electoral domination cannot simply be taken for granted.

The Welsh Conservatives

In many ways, the Welsh Conservatives present a mirror image to Welsh Labour: while so often the largest party in England and even, until the 1950s at least, Scotland, the Conservatives have never been returned as the largest party in Wales at a UK general election in Wales in the democratic era. As we have seen, part of the explanation for this situation is the extent to which Conservative voting in Wales is strongly associated with British, and not Welsh, identity. Indeed, not voting Conservative appears to be regarded by many as part and parcel of Welshness itself (Wyn Jones et al. 2002). In the pre-devolution era, this meant that Conservative strength in Wales was largely confined to more Anglicised areas, such as the larger urban areas, as well as the old borough towns (Heath and Taylor 1999). In the rest of Wales, Conservatives were often something of a curiosity, with the party regularly using Welsh constituencies to 'blood' new candidates before they moved on to more promising electoral terrain. Included among the former we find such subsequently prominent Tories as future UK Prime Minister Boris Johnson, future party leader Michael Howard and future Chancellor Geoffrey Howe.

Given that the Conservatives were able to form UK governments on a very regular basis without ever enjoying the support of the majority of Welsh MPs, there were relatively few incentives for the party to seek to address its chronic weakness in Wales. Attempts to do so, for example those in the mid-1950s, prompted by the unlikely figure of Enoch Powell, proved short-lived (Blaxland 2024). While Labour domination may have served to render the Conservatives an embattled if resilient minority in Wales itself, it had little impact on the party's overall fortunes beyond the country's borders. But the establishment of the National Assembly in Wales in 1999 was to create a wholly new set of dilemmas – and potential incentives – for the party.

In seeking to adjust to the reality of the establishment of Welsh democratic institutions – a development that the party had resolutely resisted – the Welsh Conservatives have adopted two contradictory positions. On the one hand, part of the party – in the ascendancy between around 2000 and 2016 – has sought to embrace devolution and a Welsh identity; on the other hand, another section – dominant since around 2016 – has remained deeply sceptical of devolution, emphasising its support for so-called 'muscular unionism'. In truth, neither approach has been notably more electorally successfully than the other. Focusing on the results of devolved elections, the high-water mark of the more devolution-friendly, self-consciously Welsh approach was marked in 2011, when the Conservatives achieved 25% of the constituency vote. In 2021, when the party's devo-scepticism was at its most marked, the Conservatives received 26.1% of constituency votes cast in that year's Senedd election. Moreover, it is hard to foresee any circumstances in which the Conservatives can hope to form part of any future Welsh Government. While the party may have briefly entertained hopes of forming a 'rainbow coalition' government in an unlikely partnership with both Plaid Cymru and the Liberal Democrats in 2007 (Osmond, 2007), the ideological chasm that currently divides the Conservatives from Plaid Cymru appears unbridgeable. Yet without some form of rapprochement between both parties – or, equally as hard to imagine, the formation of a pan-unionist alliance between the Conservatives and Labour – the Conservatives appear destined for permanent opposition status in the Senedd. If this remains the case, we might reasonably expect that the party's group in the Welsh Parliament becomes a place where ambitious young Welsh Conservative politicians are 'blooded' before they too move to the more promising terrain of the House of Commons.

Plaid Cymru

In 2025, Plaid Cymru (the name translates as 'party of Wales') celebrated the hundredth anniversary of its foundation. The party was established partly in response to the end of Liberal Party electoral domination in Wales – as noted, until that point, the Liberals had been closely associated with attempts to ensure the recognition of Wales within the UK state. Also influential was the radicalising effect of both the Irish Easter Rising and the First World War on younger Welsh nationalists. But while the fledgling party soon came to have a significant intellectual influence on Welsh life, it did not become a serious electoral force in Welsh life until its president, Gwynfor Evans, entered the House of Commons in 1966 in the wake of a by-election victory (McAllister 2001; Wyn Jones 2024). After this, Plaid Cymru replaced Labour (which had itself replaced the Liberals) as the main party of Welsh-speaking communities in the west and north of the country (Balsom et al. 1983). Beyond these areas, however, any electoral success experienced by the party was always fragile and short-lived.

One of the characteristics of one-party dominant political systems is that key political cleavages are found within the dominant party (cf. more competitive party systems where different parties represent opposite sides of those cleavages.) The result is that smaller parties often find themselves supporting 'their' side of salient political cleavages within the dominant party. This has certainly been the case for Plaid Cymru in the context of the evolution of devolution. It has regularly found itself allying with – and campaigning with – the most pro-devolution elements within Labour. This was the case prior to the establishment of the National Assembly for Wales in 1999 and has remained the case since then (Wyn Jones and Scully 2012).

Apart from a brief period in the aftermath of the party's success in the first devolved election, when some in the party may have hoped to replace Labour as Wales' largest party, Plaid Cymru has used its influence in the Welsh legislature to pull policies into closer alignment with its priorities. This has meant pulling social policy to the left (Plaid Cymru is formally committed to 'community socialism') while championing nation-building – the establishment and strengthening of 'national' institutions for Wales. This has been achieved via a series of different arrangements with Labour (note here the contrast with Scotland where a similar degree of cooperation between Labour and the Plaid Cymru sister party, the SNP, is unthinkable). These have included a formal coalition arrangement (2007–2011), an agreement that encompasses some but not all of the government's programme (2021–2024), as well as various one-off deals when Labour has required additional votes to carry votes on the Welsh Government's annual budget. In the terms of Müller and Strøm's now classic model of party behaviour, Plaid Cymru has continued to prioritise 'policy' over 'office' or 'votes' (Müller and Strøm 2010; and McAngus, 2014). But while the continuing structural reality of one-party electoral domination makes this choice almost inevitable – and while there is clearly significant scope for further nation-building within the confines of the current dispensation, most obviously through the devolution of the justice system – there are limits to this approach. Most obviously, it is far from clear how Plaid Cymru can hope to attain its ultimate ambition of Welsh independence without replacing Labour as Wales' largest party. Yet by supporting Labour as a junior partner, the danger is that it ends up shouldering the blame for the larger party's failings, rather being able to take electoral advantage of them. Here we find yet another example of the dilemmas that Labour's very long-term dominance generates for other political parties active in Wales.

Conclusion

Politics in Wales is highly distinctive, not only compared to politics in other parts of the UK state, but internationally. The country's extraordinary – indeed, unprecedented – history of one-party electoral dominance has in turn profoundly shaped institutional development in Wales ('the evolution of devolution') as it also moulds the behaviour of the other political parties active on the Welsh political stage.

Understanding this different political terrain makes different demands of analysts. While it is changing patterns of alignment in voting behaviour that tend to interest scholars of British electoral behaviour, for those focused on electoral behaviour in Wales they key question is rather how the same party keeps winning election after election for decade after decade? In this context, it is inherently implausible to assume that Labour's sustained success can be attributed to the virtues of any particular party leader, or the popularity of a given electoral programme. Not only have leaders and programmes changed, but those same leaders and programmes have generated very different levels of support in different parts of the state. It should come as no surprise, therefore, that fundamental issues of political sociology – how and why different social identities influence political behaviours – are at the heart of the academic literature on voting in Wales.

Conversely, if gradual, incremental change in the context of remarkable institutional stability is perhaps *the* key theme for those interested in the institutions of the UK state, the Senedd's relatively short life has been characterised by regular and fundamental changes in both institutional architecture and schemes of constitutional empowerment. Again, therefore, the Welsh experience raises different analytical questions requiring different approaches to answer them. Readers of this book will now be aware that the Welsh context is also very different from those in Scotland or Northern Ireland.

Finally, given that very long-term one-party electoral dominance is so unusual, it is reasonable to ask for how long this – the defining feature of democratic politics in Wales – can be maintained? We are political scientists not prophets and will therefore eschew predictions! It is worth noting, however, that for the first 75 years of Labour dominance, winning elections in Wales did not necessarily lead to the formation of Labour governments. Government formation at the UK level depended on electoral outcomes in other, more populous parts of the state, which meant, as we have seen, that Labour was in opposition for a large proportion of this period.

Things have changed, with Labour having now led every devolved government since the establishment of what is now known as the Senedd. In these circumstances, it is easy to assume that the party will inevitably lose popularity over time and eventually become more susceptible to what we have termed the 'time for a change' argument. Perhaps so, but this is not necessarily the case. There are certainly examples of other political parties that have remained dominant as both electoral and governing forces at the so-called regional level for many decades. Thus, except for a period between 1954 and 1958, Bavaria's Christian Social Union (CSU) has led the government of that German *länder* since its establishment in 1946. Only time will tell if Welsh Labour manages to match this record of success as a dominant party of government.

Summary

- The trajectory of Welsh politics has been substantially influenced by the dominance of the Labour Party. This dominance had big consequences for the sort of devolution offered to Wales in 1999 and its subsequent move towards more of a Scottish model.
- The Welsh language makes Welsh nationalism distinctive and exerts political consequences in terms of vote choice.
- The continuing dominance of the Labour Party is not assured, but they performed extremely well in the 2024 general election and the next Senedd elections are in 2026.

Recommended and further reading

- Wyn Jones, R. and Scully, R. (2012) *Wales Says Yes*, Cardiff: University of Wales Press. This book traces the emergence of Wales' complicated devolution settlement and how it led to the 2011 referendum on law-making powers.
- Griffiths, J., Wyn Jones, R. W., Poole, E. G., Larner, J. M., Henderson, A. and McMillan, F. (2023). 'Diverging electoral fortunes in Scotland and Wales: National identities, national interests, and voting behaviour'. *Regional & Federal Studies,* 33(4): 487–510. This article traces the ways that national identity has influenced vote choice in Wales (and Scotland) over time and how this relationship has changed.
- Balsom, D., Madgwick, P. J. and Van Mechelen, D. (1983) '"The Red and the Green: Patterns of Partisan Choice in Wales'. *British Journal of Political Science,* 13(3): 299–325. This is the foundational text of political behaviour in Wales introducing Wales-specific variables into the socio-psychological model of voting.

Chapter 15

Northern Ireland

Lisa Claire Whitten

What will this chapter tell me?

- Northern Ireland is often 'set apart' or treated differently in analyses of the United Kingdom (UK) and its politics; the reasons for this trend are valid. Shaped by a history of conflict, the party politics and governing institutions of Northern Ireland today are unlike those anywhere else in the UK.
- While understandable, the tendency to portray Northern Ireland as an exceptional case and/or to leave its particularities out of wider discussions about the political dynamics at play in the contemporary UK can also be problematic.
- The pivotal and contested position of Northern Ireland in the process of the UK's withdrawal from the European Union – Brexit – was, for example, exacerbated (if not actually caused) by a longstanding trend of overlooking and under-analysing the UK's most unique constituent part.
- To ensure Northern Ireland is not left out of the big picture of UK politics painted in this volume, this chapter does two main things: the first section briefly summarises its history and the second outlines the current structure of its government, party politics and recent electoral trends.
- Throughout, when explaining Northern Ireland particularities, the chapter notes how these interact with or differ from UK-wide political dynamics.

What do I need to know?

- Northern Ireland is the smallest constituent part of the United Kingdom and is located on the northeast corner of the island of Ireland.
- Northern Ireland was established in 1920 when the island of Ireland was partitioned into Northern Ireland and what became the Republic of Ireland.
- Political identities in Northern Ireland have traditionally been defined by opposing views of its constitutional status and preferences for its constitutional future. They are also very closely linked to religious identities.
- Politics has historically been divided between: unionists, who identify as British, come from a Protestant background and want Northern Ireland to remain part of the United Kingdom; and nationalists, who identify as Irish, come from a Catholic background and want Northern Ireland to unify with Ireland.
- From 1920 to 1972, there was a devolved government and parliament in Northern Ireland that was led exclusively by Protestant/unionist politicians. Systemic discrimination against Catholic/nationalist communities took place during this era.
- Responses to civil rights marches in the late 1960s ended in violence towards those protesting against discriminatory systems and practices that favoured Protestant/ unionists over Catholic/nationalists.
- From 1969 onwards, the security situation in Northern Ireland deteriorated such that British Army troops were deployed to prevent the further escalation of violence, but conflict continued. In 1972 the devolved government in Northern Ireland resigned and the institutions were dissolved the following year.
- What is now known as 'The Troubles' lasted for nearly three decades. This conflict was fought between extremist nationalist paramilitary groups – often referred to as

'Republican' – extremist unionist paramilitary groups – often referred to as 'loyalists' – and the British Army.

- After a long process of talks between the parties involved in the conflict, a peace agreement was signed in 1998 between the British Government, the Irish Government and most political parties in Northern Ireland.
- The Belfast 'Good Friday' Agreement of 1998 (1998 Agreement) laid down a series of innovative provisions for new devolved institutions in Northern Ireland for cooperation between the two jurisdictions on the island of Ireland and for relations between executive authorities across the whole of the British Isles.
- Northern Ireland today continues to be governed in line with the provisions of the 1998 Agreement and by the institutions it established. These have proved vulnerable to collapse, leading to prolonged periods without fully functioning government.
- Party politics and electoral behaviour in Northern Ireland reflect ongoing divisions between nationalist/Catholic and unionist/Protestant voting blocs. In recent years, however, support for political parties who align with neither traditional political identity has grown considerably.

Introduction

To understand the politics of Northern Ireland (NI) today it is necessary to have some knowledge of how they came to be. This first section of the chapter therefore provides a brief summary of NI history, from its establishment to its present-day. What follows is an inevitably partial account of the long and often-painful evolution of relations between the islands of Ireland and Great Britain, and the starring role Northern Ireland has played in the broader story.

A Unionist 'mini-state' and a troubling conflict: 1920–1998

Since it was created in 1921, Northern Ireland has been a place of constitution contestation. In the early decades of the twentieth century, destabilisation of the union between Great Britain and Ireland, which had existed since the Acts of Union of 1800, led to the creation of two new constitutional settlements on the island of Ireland: a devolved parliament under the authority of Westminster in Northern Ireland, and an independent Irish Free State south of the newly created land border (see Calvert 1968). Partition of the island of Ireland into Northern Ireland and what became the Republic of Ireland developed as a means of solving Great Britain's so-called 'Irish Question'. For Northern Ireland, however, the 'solution' of the 1920s did not ultimately last.

Amendments to electoral laws that applied in Northern Ireland straight after it was established meant that its governing architecture facilitated indefinite rule by the unionist, largely Protestant, majority at the expense of a nationalist, largely Catholic, minority. In the words of the first Prime Minister for Northern Ireland, it was 'a Protestant Parliament and Protestant State' (Craig 1934: 1095). Prolonged discrimination and intermittent clashes between members of the minority nationalist community and representatives of the NI state led to the outbreak of violence in the late 1960s following a series of civil rights protests.

After various interventions from Westminster, the first era of self-rule in Northern Ireland, and first experiment in UK devolution, ended with the suspension of the Stormont institutions in

March 1972, and their abolition the following year amid a seemingly inexorable slide into civil war. Over the next three decades lives in Northern Ireland were dominated by an internecine conflict between two communities defined by their opposing visions for its constitutional future – nationalists who sought a united Ireland and unionists committed to staying part of the UK.

An improvement from 1985 onwards in relations between the governments of Britain and Ireland, which effectively served as proxy representatives for unionist and nationalists respectively, paved the way for peace. A long and arduous process of inter-party talks – brokered by the two governments – eventually led to the signing of the Belfast 'Good Friday' Agreement on 10 April 1998 (the 1998 Agreement) (Northern Ireland Office 1998). With the inauguration of the 1998 Agreement, and the new institutions established under its terms, Northern Ireland entered a new era characterised by the absence of violent conflict and a fragile peace.

A constructively ambiguous Agreement: 1998

The 1998 Agreement has two parts: a political agreement between most NI political parties, known as the Multi-Party Agreement (MPA) and an international treaty between the British and Irish governments, known as the British–Irish Agreement (BIA), which act as 'guarantors' to the substance of the MPA.

Both parts of the 1998 Agreement begin with statements about the NI constitutional status. All signatories here recognised the present wish of the majority of the people of Northern Ireland was to remain in the UK but agreed that, if that wish changes, it is for 'the people of the island of Ireland alone' to 'bring about a united Ireland' by consent (Northern Ireland Office 1998: Article 1(i)–(iii)). The two guarantor governments also agreed: to exercise any sovereign power held in respect to Northern Ireland with 'rigorous impartiality' (ibid.: 1(v)); to allow people in Northern Ireland 'to identify themselves and be accepted as Irish or British, or both' regardless of its constitutional status (ibid.: Article 1(vi)); and to introduce legislation necessary to recognise the constitutional status of Northern Ireland in the event of any future change in it. This series of commitments are normally referred to collectively as the 'principle of consent'.

Based on the principle of consent, the 1998 Agreement set out an innovative system for multi-levelled government through the 'three strands' of the MPA. Strand One provided for the creation of new democratic institutions – the Northern Ireland Assembly and the Northern Ireland Executive – to which powers were devolved on the basis of a system for power-sharing between nationalists and unionists, underpinned by rights-based safeguards. Strand Two provided a North–South dimension through the North South Ministerial Council (NSMC) and North–South (N–S) Implementation Bodies to enable cooperation between the Irish Government and the NI Executive. Strand Three provided an East–West dimension through the creation of the British–Irish Council (BIC), to facilitate relations between Ireland, the UK, its devolved governments and its Crown Dependencies, and a bilateral, British–Irish Intergovernmental Conference (BIIC), to preserve and strengthen relations between the governments of the neighbouring states.

To implement what had been agreed, the Irish Government proposed to remove the territorial claim to Northern Ireland that was in the Irish Constitution at the time; this was approved by referendum. Following a concurrent referendum in Northern Ireland, the principal content of the MPA was transposed into UK law via the Northern Ireland Act 1998 (National Archives

1998). The Northern Ireland Act 1998 remains the primary statutory source for the government institutions and constitutional laws that are specific to Northern Ireland.

The 1998 Agreement (and thereby the 1998 Act) embrace 'constructive ambiguity' on those issues which were at the heart of The Troubles conflict. On national identity, people in Northern Ireland can choose to identify as British, Irish, or both, according to preference, and can hold citizenship accordingly. On the constitutional future, the 1998 Agreement represents a consensus on means but not ends. If ever there is a change in the constitutional status, it will be as a result of a democratic exercise on the part of the people of Northern Ireland and Ireland. In the meantime, the Strand Two and Strand Three dimensions of governance in/of Northern Ireland symbolise the multiplicity of national identities and constitutional aspirations traditionally associated with the place – the Britishness of unionists and the Irishness of nationalists.

Through its constructively ambiguous compromises the 1998 Agreement therefore enabled previously warring parties to agree to disagree and live together regardless. In this way, the 1998 Agreement did not solve the conflict in Northern Ireland but rather established a series of political principles and governing institutions by which it could be differently managed.

A fragile peace: 1998–2016

The first elections to the new Northern Ireland Assembly were held in June 1998. Its inaugural meeting took place in July of that year, but its full legislative powers were only formally devolved in December 1999. Since it was established, the operation of the 1998 Agreement governing architecture has had a staccato quality. In particular, its Strand One institutions have proved liable to collapse because of the capacity and propensity of one or other of the two largest political parties to withdraw support for the mandatory power-sharing government, which, in effect, puts the Northern Ireland Executive (and thereafter the NI Assembly) into abeyance.

Prior to 2016, the NI Assembly had collapsed on four separate occasions following related collapses of the NI Executive. Three of these suspensions were brief, but the most significant lasted nearly five years. Strand One institutions were not fully operational between October 2002 and May 2007 after the withdrawal of unionist politicians in protest over police raids on Sinn Féin offices during an investigation regarding intelligence gathering conducted on behalf of the Irish Republican Army (IRA) – the main Republican terrorist group active during the NI conflict – by the party's representatives in Stormont.

Northern Ireland devolution was re-established in 2007 after multi-party talks resulted in the signing of the *St Andrews Agreement* in October 2006 (Northern Ireland Office 2006). This agreement is the most significant of the numerous 'successor' agreements which build on the provisions of the 1998 Agreement, due to specific revisions it contains and because these were sufficient to bring the Democratic Unionist Party (DUP) onboard with power-sharing. Under the leadership of Ian Paisley Senior, the DUP had vociferously opposed the 1998 Agreement, but changes agreed in the *St Andrews Agreement*, primarily regarding procedures for nominating the First Minister (FM) and deputy First Minister (dFM), resulted in the party consenting to the structure of NI devolution for the first time (see Anthony 2008). The *St Andrews Agreement* also included a commitment from Sinn Féin to support the Police Service of Northern Ireland (PSNI). This was significant because of historic discrimination towards nationalists at the hands of the earlier NI police forces. Subsequent elections, held on 7 March 2007, saw the DUP returned as the largest unionist party and Sinn Féin as the largest nationalist party, and the two thus agreed to enter a power-sharing government together under the respective leaderships of FM Ian Paisley and dFM Martin McGuinness.

There have been various other 'successor' agreements, three of which were agreed since *St Andrews* and prior to 2016, which are worth briefly noting. The *Hillsborough Castle Agreement*, reached in February 2010 (Northern Ireland Office 2010), enabled the devolution of justice and policing to the NI institutions later that year. The *Stormont House Agreement*, reached in December 2014 (Northern Ireland Office 2014), made recommendations to deal with contested issues regarding flags, identity, culture and tradition, and set out a process for the resolution of legacy issues – meaning unsolved atrocities committed during The Troubles and compensation to victims and survivors of the same. Some proposals about the Irish language were also included. Difficulty implementing aspects of *Stormont House* led to more inter-party talks the following year, which resulted in the *A Fresh Start: the Stormont Agreement and Implementation Plan*, reached in November 2015 (Northern Ireland Office 2015). It made provisions for tackling paramilitarism alongside procedures for implementing its 2014 predecessor and included some measures to deal with more 'normal' policy problems, such as tax, welfare and financial stability.

The fact that these 'successor agreements' exist demonstrates the still-in-process nature of the hard-won peace that has been present in Northern Ireland since 1998. To function, its power-sharing system of government requires parties from opposite ends of its politics and history to cooperate, notwithstanding their differences. The arrangement has proved fragile. External shocks, such as the UK's decision to withdraw from the European Union, tend to exacerbate that pre-existing fragility.

The Brexit era: 2016–2024

As the only part of the UK to share a land border with another EU member state, Northern Ireland was always going to be the most visible physical canvas for the outworking of the UK's decision to leave the bloc. As the only part of the UK with a recent history of violent conflict over the legitimacy or otherwise of its borders and, consequentially, the only part of the UK with carefully constructed constitutional architecture that hinged on making those same borders less significant and more fluid, Northern Ireland was even more exposed to the effects of Brexit than its geography alone would suggest.

From early on in UK–EU negotiations, both parties had agreed that the 'unique circumstances' on the island of Ireland in the context of the UK's decision to withdraw from the EU – arising from the land border alongside the 1998 Agreement and the north–south cooperation it had facilitated – would require some sort of special accommodation. Notably, the NI devolved institutions were not operational for almost the full duration of UK–EU negotiation; internal political divisions over Brexit and its implications contributed to what proved to be a three-year hiatus in the NI devolved government from January 2017 to January 2020.

After several years of considerable Brexit-related political drama, the agreement (eventually) concluded between the UK and the EU on arrangements for Northern Ireland came in the form of a *Protocol on Ireland / Northern Ireland*, which is part of the EU–UK Withdrawal Agreement (European Commission 2020; and see Whitten 2023). Under its terms, Northern Ireland remains aligned with a specified selection of EU laws so as to continue to trade freely into the EU Single Market for goods, thereby avoiding the need for a physical hardening of the land border on the island of Ireland, which was, all sides agreed, to be avoided (Official Journal 2020). The corollary of the compromise embodied in the Protocol – read together with the relatively 'thin' nature of the EU–UK Trade and Cooperation Agreement – was that new checks, controls and restrictions would be applied on goods entering Northern Ireland from the rest of the UK. This proved controversial. Exacerbating established political divisions in Northern Ireland, and stoking longstanding fears, the effective creation of a so-called 'Irish Sea Border' was deemed an anathema by its unionists and loyalists, many of whom interpreted the new trading arrangements as a contravention of and threat to Northern Ireland's place in the UK. In February 2022, the largest unionist party, the DUP, resigned from the Northern Ireland Executive in protest against the Protocol, and thereby collapsed the devolved government.

Despite being agreed between the two sides, the Protocol also became a source of contestation in UK–EU relations. The UK accused the EU of being overly legalistic in its interpretation and the EU accused the UK of reneging on commitments it had signed up to. After a tumultuous first two years of implementation, in February 2023, the UK and the EU agreed a new set of conditions by which the Protocol – thereafter to be known as the *Windsor Framework* – would be interpreted and applied (The Prime Minister's Office 2023).

Under these new arrangements, EU laws continue to apply to producers and traders in Northern Ireland, although certain (primarily agri-food) goods coming from Great Britain to Northern Ireland and remaining there need not fully conform to all EU standards. Instead, some UK standards can apply, subject to conditions regarding trader authorisation, data sharing and labelling. As in the previous iteration of the Protocol, a selection of EU rights and equality directives still apply in Northern Ireland and are overseen by NI rights and equality bodies. Additionally, EU rules related to energy and electricity supplies, VAT and excise, and state aid also continue to apply in Northern Ireland, with the latter two areas being marginally narrower under the Windsor Framework than was the case under the original Protocol. The Windsor Framework revisions also included novel provisions for greater involvement of NI representatives in its implementation. These range from the creation of new working groups and stakeholder consultation mechanisms to the introduction of a so-called 'Stormont Brake', by which 30 members of the Northern Ireland Assembly (MLAs) from two parties in Stormont may notify the UK Government of their desire for a specific change or update to EU law that would ordinarily apply in Northern Ireland not to do so, subject to a case being made that the given change would have a lasting negative effect on the daily lives of its people.

Notwithstanding revisions to the Windsor Framework, the DUP maintained their boycott of the NI devolved institutions until the conclusion and publication, in February 2024, of a UK Command Paper setting out additional provisions and commitments agreed between the UK Government and the DUP regarding the current and future position of Northern Ireland in the UK internal market (Northern Ireland Office 2024). Among the substantive elements of this *Safeguarding the Union* Command Paper are: the establishment of new bodies intended to better monitor issues related to Northern Ireland and the UK internal market; new statutory requirements for UK Ministers to have regard for Northern Ireland when making laws related to the UK internal market; and further reassurances and provisions concerning easements on checks and controls applicable on goods moving from Great Britain to Northern Ireland, and vice versa.

Box 15.1   A quick recap of the history of Northern Ireland

The 1998 Agreement is still the basis on which Northern Ireland is governed. The power-sharing model of devolved government it set up requires cooperation between nationalist and unionist politicians. It has proved to be unstable and liable to collapse.

Since established, the power-sharing institutions have only been fully functioning for 60% of the time. This record is not conducive to good government or effective policy delivery.

Due to its geographic proximity to Ireland and history of conflict over the legitimacy or otherwise of borders, arrangements for Northern Ireland became central in the process of the UK's withdrawal from the EU.

The Protocol on Ireland/Northern Ireland, renamed the Windsor Framework, is an agreement between the EU and UK on arrangements necessary to address the 'unique circumstances' on the island of Ireland in the context of Brexit. It has been controversial and divisive in the politics of Northern Ireland.

In the post-Brexit era, under the Windsor Framework, Northern Ireland is the touching point between the two legal regimes and regulatory orders of the UK and the EU. This can prove advantageous or disadvantageous, it will likely be both to differing degrees and depending on context.

Manging this newly pivotal position effectively poses a challenge to the governing architecture and political culture of Northern Ireland that has, to date, been characterised by instability and division.

The contemporary politics of Northern Ireland

The politics and governing structures in each of the four constituent parts of the UK are unique. Of them all, however, those that operate in and are specific to Northern Ireland are the most unlike their counterparts in England, Scotland and Wales. Largely, this is due to the comparatively exceptional events and dynamics in NI history, as well as being a result of its geographic separation from the rest of the UK. While focused on the party politics, government structure and electoral trends in contemporary Northern Ireland, this section also notes how these compare to arrangements elsewhere in the UK.

The nature of party politics and political trends

Candidates in elections held in Northern Ireland, almost exclusively, represent political parties that do not stand anywhere else in the UK. Rather than falling on the more traditional spectrums of 'left versus right' on economic issues or 'conservative versus progressive' on social issues, the main political parties in Northern Ireland are styled and categorised according to their positions on the so-called 'constitutional question', i.e. whether or not Northern Ireland should be part of the United Kingdom or part of a United Ireland. Historically, the NI party political spectrum has therefore ranged from hard-line unionist parties to hard-line nationalist parties. There are also NI political parties which do not support either of the two traditional positions on the constitutional question. These parties tend to self-identify as 'neither' based on their explicit lack of preference on the politically dominant question of the constitutional status and future.

	Political Parties	
NATIONALIST	Sinn Féin	27
	SDLP	8
	Total	35
UNIONIST	DUP	25
	UUP	9
	TUV	1
	Independent	2
	Total	37
OTHER	Alliance	17
	People Before Profit	1
	Total	18

Figure 15.1 Political parties and designations in the Northern Ireland Assembly (from the 2022 election)

In the post-1998 chapter of NI politics, at least three major trends have shaped electoral outcomes across the decades: (1) a shift from moderate nationalist/unionist parties to their harder-line counterparts; (2) incremental decreases over time in the salience of both unionist and nationalist identities, but with a recent comparative strengthening in support for nationalists *vis-à-vis* unionists; and (3) an increase in the electoral significance of 'non-aligned' representatives, particularly in later years. Brief elaboration on each of these trends is warranted.

In 1998 the Social Democratic and Labour Party (SDLP) and the Ulster Unionist Party (UUP) dominated the NI political landscape. In the NI political party spectrum, the SDLP are a comparatively moderate nationalist party and the UUP are a comparatively moderate unionist party. After the inaugural election to the new Strand One institutions, the offices of FM and dFM were held by the UUP's David Trimble and the SDLP's Seamus Mallon, respectively. Marking a highpoint in both reputation and influence, the two parties' leaders were joint recipients of the Nobel Peace Prize in 1998, which was awarded 'for their efforts to find a peaceful solution to the conflict in Northern Ireland' (Nobel Prize 1998). From this point forward, however, the electoral strength of the UUP and the SDLP steadily declined.

In the 2003 NI Assembly election, the DUP overtook the UUP to become the largest unionist political party, and thereby became eligible to appoint a FM; in parallel, Sinn Féin overtook the SDLP to become the largest nationalist political party, and thereby became eligible to appoint a dFM. Notwithstanding a prolonged political impasse between the 2003 election and the (eventual) return of fully functioning devolved government in 2007, the shift away from the historically more moderate parties towards their harder-line counterparts proved decisive.

In every election since 1998, the number of MLAs returned for the SDLP has either declined or held; the same can be said of the number of MLAs consecutively returned for the UUP. By contrast, the electoral strength of the DUP increased steadily, reaching a zenith in the 2016 election (returning 38 MLAs) before dropping off in the 2017 election (largely due to a reduction in the size of the Assembly from 108 MLAs to 90 MLAs) but remaining comparatively strong. In the most recent 2022 election, however, support for the DUP noticeably declined as the party returned fewer MLAs than Sinn Féin, thereby paving the way for the latter to appoint the inaugural nationalist FM, Michelle O'Neill, when the institutions were restored in February 2024. Taking the long view, support for Sinn Féin increased between 1998 and 2007, from which point it has been relatively steady.

Up until 2017 the level of support for the non-aligned Alliance Party in Assembly elections had generally increased moderately over time. In the latest Assembly election of 2022, however, the party more than doubled the number of seats returned on the previous runout (from eight MLAs to 17 MLAs). A considerable uptick had been reflected in three electoral events of 2019: the NI local elections, the European Parliament elections and the UK general election. On each occasion, support for Alliance increased by significant margins. The recent increasing strength of the Alliance Party is mirrored in the apparent electoral salience of unionist and nationalist designations. As Table 15.1 indicates, these have been relatively stable since 1998, but with an emerging trend since around 2016, whereby the collective electoral strength of both unionists and nationalists has decreased just as the representation of those who identify as 'neither' has increased.

Table 15.1   NI Assembly elections 1998–2022, by designation (MLAs returned)

	1998	2003	2007	2011	2016	2017*	2022
Unionist	56 MLAs	59 MLAs	55 MLAs	55 MLAs	45 MLAs	40 MLAs	37 MLAs
Nationalist	42 MLAs	42 MLAs	44 MLAs	43 MLAs	40 MLAs	39 MLAs	35 MLAs
Neither	8 MLAs	7 MLAs	9 MLAs	9 MLAs	12 MLAs	11 MLAs	18 MLAs

Source: Compiled from Northern Ireland Elections data (see Northern Ireland Elections 2024)

*NI Assembly reduced in size from 108 to 90 in 2017

This broad pattern, as indicated in Table 15.2, is also reflected in UK general election results in Northern Ireland over time, notwithstanding that these are held according to the (less representative) 'First-Past-the-Post' voting system.

Table 15.2   NI Westminster elections 1997–2019, by designation (MPs returned)

	1997	2001	2005	2010	2015	2017	2019
Unionist	13 MPs	11 MPs	10 MPs	9 MPs	11 MPs	11 MPs	8 MPs
Nationalist	5 MPs	7 MPs	8 MPs	8 MPs	7 MPs	7 MPs	9 MPs
Neither	0 MPs	0 MPs	0 MPs	1 MP	0 MPs	0 MPs	1 MPs

Source: Compiled from Northern Ireland Elections data (see Norther Ireland Elections 2024)

While there has been a degree of ebb and flow in the ethno-nationalist breakdown of MPs elected to represent Northern Ireland since 1998, a long-established pattern of dominance on the part of political unionism infusing those voices with NI accents on the seats of Westminster has also, recently, begun to change. Whether or not the comparative strength of political nationalism and/or those in the 'non-aligned' category becomes embedded in future elections to both Westminster and Stormont remains to be seen.

The changing electoral demographics

Election results generally echo demographics. Due to the unique provision for a potential change in the constitutional position of Northern Ireland – from being part of the United Kingdom to being part of a United Ireland – on the basis of popular consent, media and academic analyses of the place are particularly prone to (sometimes deterministic) political demographic headcounts. It is not the intention here to *presume* a link between demographic changes, normally cited as evidence of the possibility or probability of a 'border poll' being held in the near future, and such an event taking place. At the same time, the unusually elevated significance in and for Northern Ireland of political demographic indicators, such as the percentage of the electorate that identify as either Catholic, Irish or nationalist *vis-à-vis* the percentage of the electorate that identify as either Protestant, British or unionist, cannot be ignored and ought not to be understated.

Based on opinion polling data, the proportion of people who do *not* identify as either unionist or nationalist has increased since 1998, such that this is now the largest demographic group when it comes to self-ascribed political identity. As Figure 15.2 demonstrates, this 'neither'

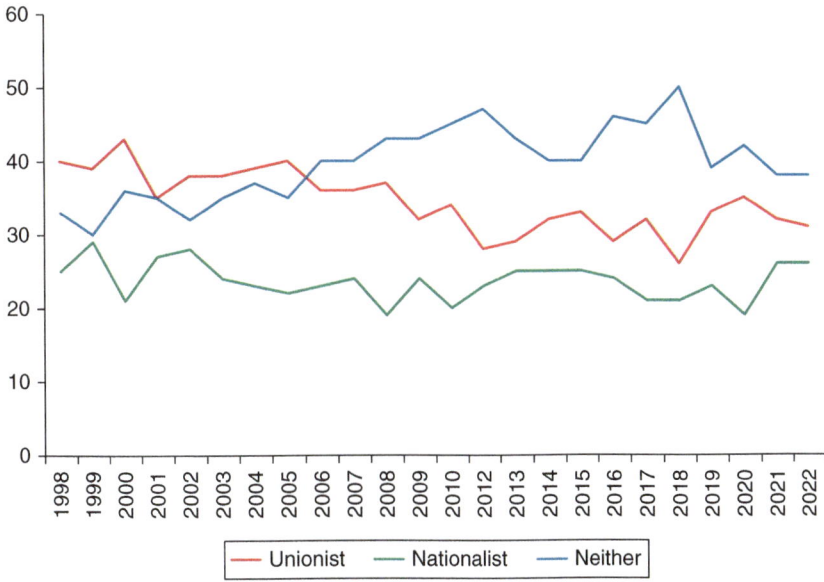

Figure 15.2 Political identities in Northern Ireland, 1998–2022

Source: Compiled from Northern Ireland Life and Times (NILT) survey data (see NILT 2024). Responses 'don't know' and 'other' are excluded. There is no data for 2011

grouping has overtaken 'unionists' historic role as the dominant political identity group in the NI population. Those who describe themselves as 'neither' would, of course, still be expected to vote in any future referendum on the constitutional future of Northern Ireland, should one ever be held. Which direction this 'non-constitutionally aligned' group would choose to follow – a United Ireland or the United Kingdom – is less clear. For this reason, the growing demographic significance of 'neithers' can also be said to make the outcome of any hypothetical future 'border poll' less certain. At the same time and on the same basis, it can be argued that this trends also reduces the likelihood of a Northern Ireland Secretary discerning that a majority of the population would vote for a United Ireland – which is the main statutory condition on which a decision to hold a border poll is to be taken – if given the opportunity.

Another important marker of political identity and constitutional preference in Northern Ireland is religion. As in the rest of the UK, the number of people practising religious faith has declined (albeit the NI rate of decline is comparatively slower) in recent decades. Still, the vast majority of the NI population (+80%) still clearly identify with one or other Christian denomination as the religion in which they were 'brought up'. Looking at relevant responses over time, it is clear that while the percentage of the population raised as Protestants is decreasing on 1998 figures, the percentage of the population raised as Catholics has remained relatively stable since the peace agreement was signed. With another caution regarding the importance of avoiding any overly deterministic conclusions from these trends, it is also worth noting that individuals in the Protestant faith are much more likely to support the UK, while individuals in the Catholic faith are much more likely to support or be open to a united Ireland in future.

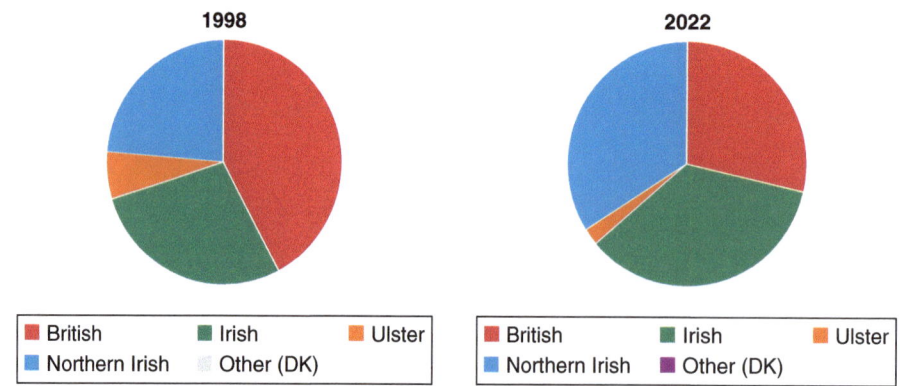

Figure 15.3   National identity in Northern Ireland in 1998 and in 2022

Source: Compiled from Northern Ireland Life and Times survey data (NILT 2024). Responses to 'Which of these best describes how you think of yourself?'

How people tend to describe their national identity in Northern Ireland has changed since 1998. Broadly, as Figure 15.3 indicates, the percentage of people who identify as 'British' has decreased, while the percentage of people who identify as either 'Irish' or 'Northern Irish' has increased. Perhaps unsurprisingly, given the change over time, the more recent data indicates that age is a significant factor in these trends, particularly as regards British versus Irish identities. Broadly, older individuals (those in the 55–64 and 65+ categories) are more likely to identify as British and less likely to identify as Irish, while younger people (those in the 18–24 and 25–34 categories) are more likely to identify as Irish and less likely to identify as British. Age is less of a determinative factor when it comes to the 'Northern Irish' identity, which has instead been growing in popularity since 1998 across the demographic board.

The structure of government

The institutions of government in Northern Ireland today and the rules by which they operate flow from the provisions and principles enshrined in the 1998 Agreement, as amended by its various 'successor' texts, and as implemented in domestic law, primarily via the Northern Ireland Act 1998. While the first 'strand' institutions – the NI Executive and NI Assembly – are undoubtedly the most significant in legislative and political terms, it is nonetheless important to view these against the backdrop of the interwoven and tripartite design of NI government. What follows is a summary of the key elements of each 1998 Agreement strand.

The 1998 Agreement: Strand One

Under the terms of the Northern Ireland Act 1998 the devolved institutions in Northern Ireland have competence in all matters that are not specifically excepted (under Schedule 2 of the Northern Ireland Act 1998) or reserved (under Schedule 3 of the Northern Ireland Act 1998). The Northern Ireland Executive can, however, legislate in relation to reserved matters, but only after permission to do so has been granted by the Northern Ireland Secretary (Northern Ireland Act 1998: s8(b)). Just like in Scotland and Wales, therefore, devolution in Northern Ireland today operates on the basis of what is called a 'reserved powers' model, meaning that all powers that are not explicitly excepted are devolved. But in the case of Northern Ireland, there is the additional category of powers which are 'reserved'; this is a legacy of the longer history of NI devolution (Figure 15.4).

The NI Executive is made up of ten ministers who are responsible for nine government departments (see Table 15.3). Unlike any other government system in the UK (where one party can govern alone subject to reaching the necessary majority threshold), the NI Executive *must* be a coalition government of at least two parties, representing unionists and nationalists respectively. Control of any 'Executive Committee' (equivalent to the Cabinet in other UK systems) is shared between the FM and the dFM in the department of The Executive Office. Although the FM is nominated from the largest party of the largest designation and the dFM is nominated from the largest party of the second largest designation, there is no difference in the powers available to either. To appoint seven of the other eight NI ministers, a system called 'd'Hondt' is used, whereby a mathematical formula that factors in the number of seats won by any given party in the most recent election dictates how many seats that party is able to choose in the new Executive. What this means is that the make-up of the NI Executive is proportionally representative of the electoral strength of political parties, provided they opt to enter government. There are separate requirements for the position of Minister for Justice, who must be elected by the NI Assembly on the basis of cross-community (for which, see below) support. This difference is in recognition of discriminatory practices in the history of the NI justice system.

At the beginning of each new mandate, the NI Executive is obliged to draft a Programme for Government (PfG) and an associated Budget for approval by the NI Assembly. Repeated delays in this process, due to instances of institutional collapse and party-political divisions, have meant that, as of the beginning of 2024, no PfG has ever been formally agreed and concluded for

NI no legislative competence

EXCEPTED POWERS
Parliament and the Crown
Defence
International Relations (excl. N/S coop)
Immigration
National Security and Terrorism
National Insurance
Inheritance Tax
Capital Gains Tax
Tobacco, Alcohol, Fuel duties
Supreme Court
Election Franchise
State Aid
Nuclear Energy
UK waters outside NI zone
Space
Antarctica

NI competence subject to UKG approval

RESERVED POWERS
Civil Aviation (not aerodromes)
Property of Government or Crown
Navigation (not inland waters/harbors)
Foreshore, seabed, submarine cables
Civil Defence
Explosives
Postal Services
Size of NI Assembly
Investigatory Powers
Import/Export controls
Financial Services
Intellectual Property
Competition Law
Human Genetics
Consumer Safety re Goods
Research Councils
Telecommunications
Units of Measurement

NI full legislative competence

DEVOLVED POWERS
Education
Housing, Communities, Local Government
Environment, Food and Rural Affairs
Health and Social Care
Culture and Sport
Justice and Policing
Social Security and Employment
Transport*
Business*
Energy*
Land Property Tax
Air Passenger Duty*
Corporation Tax

*indicates areas in which policy is partially devolved

Figure 15.4 Overview of excepted, reserved and devolved competencies in Northern Ireland

Northern Ireland by its government. Under the Northern Ireland Act 1998, read together with the NI *Ministerial Code* (Northern Ireland Executive Office 2024), which has a statutory basis in Northern Ireland unlike in the rest of the UK, decisions in the NI Executive are normally to be taken by consensus. However, if (as is often the case) consensus cannot be reached, a vote is taken. If three or more Executive Ministers indicate that the vote on a particular matter ought to be subject to cross-community support, it is required to achieve a relevant threshold (see below) among Executive Ministers.

Table 15.3   NI Departments and NI Ministers (as of February 2024)

Departments	Ministers	Political Parties
The Executive Office	Michelle O'Neill (FM)	Sinn Féin
	Emma Little-Pengelly (dFM)	DUP
Department of Justice	Naomi Long	Alliance Party
Department for the Economy	Conor Murphy	Sinn Féin
Department of Education	Paul Givan	DUP
Department of Finance	Caoimhe Archibald	Sinn Féin
Department for Communities	Gordon Lyons	DUP
Department of Health	Robin Swann	UUP
Department for Infrastructure	John O'Dowd	Sinn Féin
Department of Agriculture, Environment & Rural Affairs	Andrew Muir	Alliance Party

The NI Assembly has 90 seats for its members (or MLAs, short for members of the legislative assembly), representing 18 constituencies, to which five MLAs are elected via the proportional Single Transferrable Vote (STV) system every five years or as necessary, including due to NI Executive collapse. Reflecting the requirements of a mandatory power-sharing system, at the first session of each new NI Assembly, every MLA must 'designate' as either unionist, nationalist or 'other' (meaning those who do not proscribe to either category). This designation system underpins the operation of 'cross-community' voting in the NI Assembly, which is a threshold that must be reached for certain motions to pass. Cross-community consent can be achieved in two ways: either a motion will pass with overall majority support plus the support of the majority of nationalist and unionist MLAs (parallel consent); or it will pass with a 60% overall majority plus the support of 40% of nationalist and 40% of unionist MLAs (weighted consent). Ordinarily, votes in the NI Assembly are not required to meet the cross-community threshold. Instead, if 30 MLAs from two different parties sign a 'Petition of Concern' about a particular motion tabled for debate in the NI Assembly, then votes on that motion will need cross-community support to pass. Additionally, some votes require cross-community support as a matter of routine. These include: the election the Speaker, the appointment of the Minister for Justice (as mentioned) and the approval of the budget. The votes of MLAs who do not designate as either nationalist or unionist cannot contribute towards meeting the cross-community threshold. These 'non-aligned' members, such as those representing the Alliance Party, the Green Party or People Before Profit (see Figure 15.1), object to this system on the basis that their views on sensitive issues do not hold the same weight as their nationalist/unionist counterparts.

Case Study 15.1

Petition of Concern and minority safeguards

The context

Due to historic discrimination in the operation of the early period of NI government (1920–1972), the 1998 Agreement contained a range of safeguards designed to 'ensure that all sections of the community can participate and work together successfully' in the operation of the devolved institutions. One such safeguard is the Petition of Concern mechanism. This enables a minority group of MLAs to lodge a petition against any NI Assembly proposal indicating their collective concern about it and requiring the vote to gain cross-community support in order to pass.

The issue

Use of the Petition of Concern procedure has been very controversial due to the frequency with which it has been employed by NI parties to block legislative progress. It has been used by unionist representatives to block nationalist-supported initiatives, and by nationalist representatives to block unionist-supported initiatives, even when these are not related to the conflict or its legacy, for which the mechanism was designed.

The action

Requirements for use of the Petition of Concern have been amended at various points, most recently following the New Decade, New Approach agreement (Northern Ireland Office 2020), which provided the basis for the return of devolved government in January 2020 after a three-year break. Agreed changes include: a new 14-day consideration period between a valid petition being lodged and any vote on the matter concerned; the requirement of every petition to include a statement on the grounds and rationale behind its tabling; and a measure to ensure a petition can only be triggered by MLAs from two different parties (see Northern Ireland Office 2022).

The future

For much of the time since the most recent amendments were given effect (in February 2022) the NI institutions have not been fully operational, so the effect on the legislative capability and institutional stability in Northern Ireland are not yet fully clear.

Reflective questions

1   Are safeguards like the 'Petition of Concern' still necessary in Northern Ireland decades after the 1998 Agreement was signed?
2   Are non-aligned voters and representatives adequately represented in and protected by the current system?
3   Are other minority groups (i.e. minorities on the basis of race, ethnicity, sex, gender, etc.) adequately represented in and protected by the current system?

The 1998 Agreement: Strand Two

In the UK context, the institutions of Strand Two of the 1998 Agreement are constitutionally unconventional. The original text provided for the creation of a North–South Ministerial

Council (NSMC) to bring together the NI Executive and the Irish Government to 'develop consultation, cooperation, and action within the island of Ireland' in 'matters of mutual interest within the competence of the Administrations, North and South' (1998 Agreement, S2(1)). Additionally, Strand Two provided for six North–South (N–S) 'Implementation Bodies' to facilitate cooperation in dedicated areas and specified 12 areas where cooperation could take place, while also allowing for expansion.

In March 1999, two bilateral UK–Ireland treaties were concluded to establish the NSMC and N–S Implementation Bodies respectively (UK Government 2000a, 2000b). These treaties entered into force on 2 December 1999 and the inaugural meeting of the NSMC took place 11 days later (NSMC 1999). The international law underpinning of the Strand Two institutions is reflected in domestic law. There is an effective N–S carve out in the Northern Ireland Act 1998, whereby the otherwise excepted power to engage in international relations allows NI Ministers to engage in 'the exercise of legislative powers so far as required' to give effect to any agreement or arrangement entered into 'in a meeting of the North–South Ministerial Council' or in relation to the activities of any N–S Implementation Body (Northern Ireland Act 1998: Schedule 2 para 3). These provisions regarding N–S cooperation thus enable a sub-state entity – Northern Ireland – of a still relatively centralised (at least in theory) state – the UK – to enjoy law-making autonomy with another state – Ireland – within the limits of powers devolved to it but with guarantees in international law for its continuation. Viewed in this light, Strand Two of the 1998 Agreement invokes confederalism, a system of government that allows for separate states to share some powers and to take collective decisions – at least in theory.

Since established, the operation of the NSMC has been stymied by intermittent collapses and resultant hiatuses in the operation of the NI Executive. To demonstrate, the NSMC is theoretically to hold bilateral plenary meetings. However, by the beginning of 2024, only 26 had taken place rather than the 49 that could have been held if not for NI Executive collapses. Strand Two institutions are thus uniquely at the mercy of political will. Any realisation of the potential for N–S cooperation is contingent, first, on a functioning NI Executive and, second, on political leaders in Northern Ireland and in Ireland *wanting* to work together. It is notable in this regard that few major policy initiatives have been taken forward via the N–S institutions since they were set up. This is not to say, however, that N–S cooperation has not expanded over the same period. It has. This fact came to the fore in the Brexit process.

As part of the process of UK–EU negotiations, a joint 'mapping exercise' conducted by the two sides found that, in 2017, there were 142 areas of established N–S cooperation on the island of Ireland. Of these, 96 were underpinned by (in whole or in part) by EU law and policy frameworks. What this indicated was: (1) N–S cooperation had expanded since 1998, (2) joint UK and Ireland membership of the EU had facilitated this expansion, and (3) existing areas of N–S cooperation were therefore exposed to Brexit and its outworkings. These findings directly informed the substance of the legal text known first as the Protocol and latterly as the Windsor Framework.

To understand the current status and possible future of N–S cooperation it is instructive to compare those EU laws that continue to apply to Northern Ireland under the Windsor Framework (see section 1.4) and those EU laws that (pre-Brexit) underpinned areas of N–S cooperation identified during the UK–EU mapping exercise. Doing so reveals a three-way split: 35 areas of N–S cooperation of pre-Brexit N–S cooperation are fully covered; 33 are partially covered; and 28 are not covered by Windsor Framework applicable EU laws. What this means is that the Windsor Framework maintains *some* of the conditions necessary for continued N–S cooperation after

Brexit, but not all. Whether or not N–S cooperation continues will largely depend on the degree of divergence between UK rules and EU rules more generally, and on the willingness of those in power in both Ireland and Northern Ireland to overcome any consequential complexities.

Research in Focus

'Border polls' and deliberative democracy

The context

Uniquely, in both domestic law and international law, provisions exist for a change in the constitutional status of Northern Ireland from being part of the United Kingdom to being part of a United Ireland should a majority of the people of Northern Ireland and in Ireland vote in favour of bringing this about in referendums held for such purposes.

The issue

Section 1 of the Northern Ireland Act 1998 provides a legal basis for the NI Secretary of State to call a so-called 'border poll' on the constitutional future of Northern Ireland, based on their discernment of majority support in NI for constitutional change. There is, however, a distinct lack of detail, in the legislation or elsewhere, about, for example, what information ought to inform a NI Secretary decision; what preparations ought to take place in advance of any such vote(s); whether or not votes in NI and Ireland should be concurrent or consecutive; or whether or not the vote should be on an agreed form of a United Ireland or on the idea of pursuing one.

The research

In view of the lack of clarity over any potential future 'border poll', academics have been carrying out research into the possible forms that any referendums might take. A good example is the work of the Working Group on Unification Referendums on the Island of Ireland, which delivered a comprehensive report in 2021 of the many unanswered questions regarding potential unification and how these might be met (The Constitution Unit (UCL) 2021). Another body of related research looks at the role that forms of deliberative democracy, such as Citizens Assemblies, might play in any future process. Research by, for example, John Garry and Jamie Pow (2023) explore the potential of deliberative mini-publics to effectively contribute to democratic decision-making on highly contested issues, such as that of the constitutional future of Northern Ireland.

The 1998 Agreement: Strand Three

Strand Three of the 1998 Agreement has two dimensions: the interjurisdictional, manifesting in the British–Irish Council (BIC or the Council) and the intergovernmental, manifesting in the British–Irish Intergovernmental Conference (BIIC or the Conference).

Focusing first on the interjurisdictional dimension, the composition of the BIC is constitutionally and politically unconventional. Typically, its (in theory biannual) summit meetings are attended by senior representatives of the British Government and of the Irish Government, leaders of the UK devolved governments and senior representatives of the UK Crown Dependencies. The agreed aim of the Council is to 'exchange information, discuss, consult and use best endeavours to reach agreement on cooperation on matters of mutual interest within the competence of the relevant Administrations' (1998 Agreement, S3(5)). The Council is to normally operate by consensus and decisions taken are to be 'by agreement of all members participating' in the relevant policy or action (ibid.: (7)). This underlines the political and constitutional uniqueness of the BIC. At any given Council summit meeting, a spectrum of sovereignty is present: two internationally recognised state actors, one sub-state devolved institution with the exceptional capacity to enter agreements with fellow members (i.e. Northern Ireland), two additional sub-state devolved administrations, and three self-governing dependencies, which do not otherwise exercise powers in respect to international relations, relying instead on the UK Government to act on their behalf. Such variation of effective seniority among Member Administrations read alongside the egalitarian nature of the Council's operation is unusual, particularly in the specifically domestic UK setting.

Turning to the intergovernmental dimension of Strand Three, the Conference was set up under the 1998 Agreement with the intention that its meetings would be 'regular and frequent' and 'as required', with provision for either Summit (i.e. including the Prime Minister and Taoiseach) level or Ministerial level meetings, as appropriate (1998 Agreement, S3: (3) and (5)).

To date (February 2024), there have been 25 meetings of the BIIC. Of these, 18 occurred between 1999 and 2007 and seven have taken place since 2018. This bifurcated pattern of Conference meetings has several causes. Initially, a degree of momentum existed in both of the guarantor government systems to consolidate and cultivate the still fragile and long-awaited compromises inherent in the 1998 Agreement. After the collapse of the Strand One institutions in 2002, the Conference proved an important forum for bilateral coordination on the part of the UK and Ireland towards a shared aim of seeing them restored and ensuring NI governance continued to operate effectively in the interim. A prolonged hiatus between 2007 and 2018 could be said to reflect the effectiveness of the supplementary role played by joint EU membership as a means for enabling bilateral cooperation between the UK and Ireland. In the wake of the UK's EU referendum in 2016 and its pending formal withdrawal from the EU legal order and institutional architecture, the Conference resumed operation. Renewed activities of the BIIC in the last five years is indicative of the loss of formal and informal EU networks and contexts inhabited by the two guarantor governments during the period of mutual membership. With Brexit – in the words of Irish Foreign Minister Simon Coveney – the two sides would 'have to work to maintain the "habit of cooperation" that [they] have known over the past four decades working side by side in Brussels' and therefore 'existing bilateral mechanisms' would have to be used 'to greater effect' (Coveney 2018: n.p.). The recent frequency of BIIC meetings is an important outworking of such sentiment.

Comparing Northern Ireland

While the (reserved) model for devolution to Northern Ireland is not dissimilar to that of Scotland or Wales, the basis for and rules governing the governing institutions in Stormont differ from those in Holyrood and Cardiff in important ways. The mandatory power-sharing system, together with (Petition of Concern) safeguards built into the ordinary processes of law-making in Northern Ireland, are exceptional in the UK state. That the structure of its government flows from a bilateral international treaty – the 1998 Agreement – thereby granting it a basis outside the domain of domestic law, also sets it apart from arrangements elsewhere. Perhaps most unconventionally in the UK constitutional setting, the fact that devolution in Northern Ireland is just one strand of a tripartite, multi-levelled system of government incorporating an intergovernmental element (via Strand Three) and a quasi-confederal element (via Strand Two) underlines the extent of its differentiation from the otherwise predominant 'norms' associated with the territorial governance and politics of the UK.

Conclusion

On the brink of its post-Brexit era, Northern Ireland faces considerable challenges. It is now the touching point between the legal orders and regulatory regimes of the UK and EU, which are now on separate trajectories and potentially pulling in different directions in terms of policy aims and legal requirements. This position could prove economically beneficial or economically burdensome; it will likely be both, at different times and in different sectors. For a place with a history defined by constitutional contestation over the legitimacy or otherwise of the borders that define it, the Brexit-begotten refocus on those same borders is, at the very least, unhelpful for the still-in-process peace that still shapes NI politics. At the same time, the *slow* decrease in salience of the traditional political identities of unionism and nationalism and the rising electoral significance of those who identify as 'neither' may also indicate an increasing 'normalisation' of political debates and issues in Northern Ireland.

Perhaps unsurprisingly given that devolved government has only been fully functioning for 60% of the time since 1998, there is a long list of pressing and unresolved policy issues on the desks of NI Ministers, who (as of February 2024) are still very new in office. Whether or not the newest leaders of its power-sharing government can steer Northern Ireland into a more prosperous and peaceful future is not yet clear. Regardless, notwithstanding its particularities, what happens next in the politics of Northern Ireland will be important for the politics of the United Kingdom as a whole, so it may be worth paying attention.

Summary

- Northern Ireland's distinctive place in the UK is illustrated through its patterns of identity, politics and party system. It has tended to be viewed as a place apart from the rest of the UK.
- The 1998 Agreement is still the basis on which Northern Ireland is governed. The power-sharing model of devolved government it set up requires cooperation between Nationalist and Unionist politicians. It has proved to be unstable and liable to collapse.
- In the post-Brexit era, under the Windsor Framework, Northern Ireland is the touching point between the two legal regimes and regulatory orders of the UK and the EU. This could prove advantageous or disadvantageous; it will likely be both to differing degrees and depending on context.

Recommended and further reading

- Haughey, S. and Loughran, T. (2024) 'Public opinion and consociationalism in Northern Ireland: Towards the "end stage" of the power-sharing lifecycle?', *The British Journal of Politics and International Relations*, 26(1): 187–207. Using public opinion data, this article explores the effectiveness of the power-sharing government in Northern Ireland and considers whether or not the current system still enjoys popular support.
- Hayward, K. and Komarova, M. (2024) 'Has Brexit changed the Irish border question?', in Bell, D. and O'Dowd, L. (eds), *Northern Ireland beyond 100: The End of the Beginning or the Beginning of the End*. Cork: Cork University Press. This article considers the impact of Brexit on attitudes towards the Ireland–Northern Ireland land border and on the prospects for future changes in its status in the event of any 'border poll'.
- Murray, C. and Robb, N. (2023) 'From the Protocol to the Windsor Framework', *Northern Ireland Legal Quarterly*, 74(2): 395–415. Written in the aftermath of the UK and EU agreement on the Windsor Framework package of revisions to the original Protocol on Ireland–Northern Ireland, this article explains the substance and significance of the changes that were introduced and sets out some of their implications.
- Murray, C. and O'Donoghue, A. (2023) 'Unity in diversity? Constitutional identities, deliberative processes and a "border poll" in Ireland', *King's Law Journal*, 34(2): 340–368. Given the legal basis for a 'border poll' on the constitutional future of Northern Ireland to potentially be called in future, this article explores the possible use and role of deliberative democracy in any such process, it draws in particular on evidence from the use of citizens assemblies in Ireland.
- Pow, J. (2023) 'Beyond orange and green: The politics of Northern Ireland's 'neithers'', *Political Insight*, 14(3): 36–39. This article explores political and demographic data on the growing bloc of the Northern Ireland electorate who identify as 'neither' nationalist nor unionist.

Part V
Big issues

Image 5   Prime Minister Keir Starmer arrives in Washington, DC. This part spotlights crucial issues facing the UK, from our relationship with the EU, foreign policy more broadly, media and social media and making good public policy. Photo by Simon Dawson / No 10 Downing Street. License: CC BY 2.0.

Chapter 16

Public policy

Daniel Kenealy

What will this chapter tell me?

- This chapter examines what policy is, how it is made in the UK and how we might evaluate it. It draws on some of the major theories of policy change and shows how we can apply them to the UK case.
- Using recent case studies, this chapter shows how UK governments have tried (and sometimes failed) to grapple with major policy questions.
- It also examines the centre of government and the sort of actors who are involved in making policy in the UK. As policy has become more complex, coordination has become harder.

What do I need to know?

- The process of making public policy is far from the neat, rational, evidence-based process that we might imagine or hope it is. Decades of research on public policy suggests that policy is made under significant time, resource and cognitive constraints, which often leads to policy solutions that are deemed 'good enough' rather than ideal.
- Various theories and frameworks have been developed to study public policy – they usually focus on a particular element of policy making, such as agenda-setting, institutions, policy networks and communities, or implementation on the front line.
- Most policy is stable most of the time, characterised by continuity or at most incremental change, but sometimes critical moments can create windows of opportunity for more fundamental policy change. At such moments policy professionals need to be ready to capitalise on the moment to enact the change they prefer.

Introduction

Public policy affects all our lives in countless ways. Consider the scale of policy change in Britain's core public services since the Conservative–Liberal Democrat coalition government took office in 2010. In education, there has been a massive expansion in the number of academy schools in England, altering the balance of power between central and local government (Freedman 2022). The introduction of Universal Credit transformed the social security system (Timmins 2016). The National Health Service (NHS) was restructured and reorganised through the Health and Social Care Act 2012 (see Bramwell et al. 2023: 75–82), only for many of those changes to be dismantled a decade later through the Health and Care Act 2022 (King's Fund 2022). All of these are examples of public policy that have had a profound impact on the delivery of public services. And that is without mentioning the vast number of policy changes required by the UK's exit from the European Union (EU) – a decision that was driven largely by the question of *who should control policy* – and the pace and scale of policy development necessitated by Covid-19.

Beyond what *has been done* since 2010 – much of which has been controversial, such is the nature of public policy – there is much that *has not been done*. For example, many bemoan the uneven progress on climate policy, which has seen ambitious commitments and targets but inadequate policy delivery (Carter and Pearson 2024). Public policy is just as much about what is *not* said and done as about what *is*. Ultimately, we study public policy because we want to know why decisions that affect us are made. Why did the coalition government introduce an economic policy framework of austerity after 2010? Why did successive Conservative prime ministers support a policy of sending people seeking asylum in the UK to Rwanda to have their claims assessed there? Why did successive governments since 2009 commit to building a high-speed rail link between London and the north of England (HS2), only to incrementally scrap key parts of it? We also want to know how decisions are made – what are the processes through which policy is developed and who is involved?

Box 16.1   Policy instruments

Academic literature about public policy often talks about different ways through which policy is enacted. Lowi (1972) distinguished between four broad types of policy, each of which has different political implications and involves different trade-offs.

- Redistributive policy involves taking resources from one group and giving them to another group in society
- Distributive policy involves giving resources to a group in society without any clear sense that another group is paying
- Regulatory policy involves the use of penalties and incentives to influence behaviour
- Constituent policy involves representing the preferences and values of the public and can often be symbolic

Beyond those broad types, we can think about more specific *policy instruments*, including but not limited to (drawn from Cairney 2019a: 26–27):

- Changes to levels and types of taxation to encourage/discourage certain activities
- Increasing or decreasing public expenditure or public borrowing
- Introducing economic penalties for certain behaviours
- Means testing access to government services (e.g. based on income levels or need)
- Introducing conditions for access services (e.g. active job seeking to access benefits)
- Introducing charges or fees to access certain public services (e.g. prescription charges)
- Nudge effects designed to encourage decisions without forcing or prescribing them
- Legal penalties to punish certain behaviours (e.g. fines or prison sentences)
- Public education campaigns to raise awareness and influence behaviour
- Increasing or decreasing public funding for services
- Changing the organisation and machinery of government to focus on certain policies
- Creating markets or quasi-markets for public services (e.g. privatisation or partnerships)

To study or work in public policy is to engage with complexity. Even the term 'public policy' is difficult to define. One of the broadest, oft-cited definitions is this: 'whatever governments choose to do or not to do' (Dye 1972: 2). But even this, broad as it is, does not capture the activities of non-governmental organisations such as corporations, think tanks, academics, campaign groups – and more besides – all of which can be active participants in a broadly conceptualised policy process, from attempting to set the agenda for policy debate to trying to influence laws, regulations, budgets and various other outputs of the policy process (Box 16.1). This chapter will introduce some of the key issues in the study of public policy. After reading it, you will understand *some* of the most important concepts and ideas in the public policy literature. Furthermore, you will be able to use those concepts to help you think about why public policy develops in the way that it does and how alternative policy ideas can be advanced. There is no one, single way that policy gets made, and the specifics of any individual case will contain its own lessons. Using theories, concepts and frameworks can help us to understand some of the broader dynamics of how the policy process works and how we may better deliver policy change.

An important distinction can be drawn between *policy analysis*, which 'involves the use of research to address policy problems', and *policy studies*, which tries to understand how policymaking works (Cairney and Kippin 2023: 2). This chapter focuses on the latter. Starting from the image of the policy cycle, the chapter considers several key issues including: the policy agenda; the constraints facing policymakers when they make decisions; the role of institutions, often as a force of inertia and incrementalism; policy communities and networks; and policy implementation. In doing so, it offers insights from the vast public policy literature, with specific illustrative examples from the UK.

The policy cycle

Policy professionals and policy researchers have sometimes attempted to simplify the complexity of the policy process by describing it as a cycle (e.g. HM Treasury 2022: 15; see Figure 16.1). However, most academics reject the cycle because it oversimplifies. More critical and thoughtful practitioners point out that the cycle can only be a first step, 'a guide amid complexity' (Bridgman and Davis 2003: 98). Although the cycle does simplify, if we retain a critical view, it remains a useful starting point for thinking about different ways to 'cut into' the study of public policy. It identifies different elements of policymaking, such as agenda setting, decision-making and the formulation of policy, the legitimation of policy through discourse, narratives and engagement with stakeholders, the implementation of policy at street level and the evaluation of a policy's effectiveness, which are often studied discretely by researchers. However, we must bear three things in mind. First, there is not a single policy cycle. Numerous cycles operate simultaneously at different levels of government (national, devolved and local), in different policy areas (e.g. in health, education, transport) and at different rhythms (Sabatier 2007: 7). These cycles impact on each other with, for instance, developments in environmental policy – such as transitioning to Net Zero – having implications for transport, energy and housing policy.

Second, the policy process is not as rational and sequenced as the cycle implies. Consider the first two stages – agenda setting (defining the *problem*) and policy formulation (identifying the *solution*). History is littered with examples of solutions chasing problems, rather than vice versa (Béland and Howlett 2016). For example, the 'solution' of market approaches to NHS reform has characterised government policy under both Conservative and Labour governments since 1979 (Lewis 2020). During periods of Conservative government, it is typically presented as the solution to an inefficient, bloated public sector and during periods of Labour government as a solution to long hospital waiting times. The same 'solution' is repackaged and reframed as a solution to different problems, depending on who is in power. The policy world is full of ideas that, once developed, sit in a 'garbage can' of ideas (Cohen et al. 1972), waiting for the right problem to come along to which they can be offered up as the solution by policy

Figure 16.1   The policy cycle

entrepreneurs – individuals who attempt 'to transform policy ideas into policy innovations and, hence, disrupt status quo policy arrangements' (Mintrom 2019: 307).

Third, the cycle can imply that policymaking is a top-down process, where decision-makers at the top (or centre) set or respond to the agenda and formulate policy, which then gets passed down a chain to be implemented somewhere far from the centre. Decades of research on policy design (Hallsworth et al. 2011: 42–43; Slater 2022) emphasises the need to involve the implementers of policy in the design of policy if you want things to work in practice – perhaps even involving service users in 'co-production' (Osborne et al. 2016; Bandola-Gill et al. 2023). Other research reminds us that policy is often made at the point of implementation as street-level bureaucrats exercise discretion in deciding which targets set by the centre to prioritise and how (discussed below). In short, the policy cycle can help us to identify various components of public policy, but it cannot tell us much about what happens, such as why certain issues end up on the policy agenda while others do not, and why a particular decision is made. To explore such questions, we can use insights from policy theory. There are numerous theories, frameworks and approaches to the study of public policy and many of them can complement each other because they focus on different aspects of the policy system, for example institutions, policy networks or policy narratives. Looking at the same policy situation through multiple lenses is a useful way of grasping complexity (e.g. Allison and Zelikow 1999). We should resist the urge to latch on to one single theory or framework (Box 16.2).

> ## Box 16.2   Multiple lenses on devolution in England
>
> In November 2014, Chancellor George Osborne unveiled a significant package of devolved powers for the Greater Manchester city-region (Kenealy 2016). Similar devolution deals have subsequently been agreed with other areas of England, representing the most significant development in English governance and local government policy since the re-establishment of London-wide government structures in 2000 (see Beel et al. 2021). But this development looks different depending on which theory or concepts one uses for analysis. For example:
>
> - *Institutionalists* might explore how, following the abolition of metropolitan governance structures by the Thatcher government in 1986, Greater Manchester did more than any other city-region in England to maintain informal structures of cooperation and soft governance. Decisions taken in the mid-1980s helped set Greater Manchester down a different path from other city-regions, placing it in the vanguard for subsequent policy debates about city governance and regional growth in the 2000s.
> - An approach focused on *policy communities or networks* might explore how a diverse group of actors – local government officials, elected local politicians, business leaders, think tanks, academics, civil society actors – came to work together over decades, unified by the shared idea that Greater Manchester should have more autonomy to govern its affairs. These actors coordinated their work, commissioned research and developed policy ideas with a view to convincing the UK government to change the status quo. Policy entrepreneurs, such as the leader and chief executive of Manchester City Council, and particular policy brokers, such as Michael Heseltine and Jim O'Neill, who were able to frame the ideas well for a Conservative Chancellor, were vital to the process.
> - An approach focused on *discourse* and *policy narratives* might explore the same community or network of actors but focus explicitly on the way they developed an overarching narrative for their policy, one that came into alignment with the growth narratives of the coalition government that came to power in 2010.
> - An approach that focuses on political *windows of opportunity* might consider the importance of 2014 and George Osborne's political desire to focus on England after the attention paid to Scotland's independence referendum and his desire to try to secure more Conservative political power in the North by creating structures that might elect Conservative city-region Mayors in traditionally Labour areas.
>
> It should be apparent that these lenses are not mutually exclusive. Layering them on top of each other, much like lenses at an optician (Kenealy et al. 2022: 21), can help bring a complex reality into sharper focus. Choosing one lens will leave us squinting at an unfocused blur.

The policy agenda

One of the most important things to consider is the policy agenda, defined by Kingdon (1984: 3) as 'the list of subjects or problems to which government officials, and people outside of government closely associated with those officials, are paying some serious attention to at any given time'. The policy agenda is important because frustration at the failure of governments to tackle particular policy problems is often not because government is implementing *bad policy ideas*, but rather that they are not focusing on the problem at all.

Policymakers can only consider so many issues and the media can only elevate so many issues to the top of the news agenda. Often issues become crowded-out in a busy, chaotic policy agenda and most policy is stable most of the time because issues are typically not on the agenda. A strategy often employed to keep something 'off the agenda' is to present it as technical and mundane, keeping the issue in the shadows, away from public attention. Prior to the global financial crisis, for example, government policymakers who were happy for banks to generate more profits from speculative financial activities formed a cosy relationship with financial elites and lobbyists. Both were happy for the issue of banking regulation to remain in the shadows as a technical matter for expert regulators. Another approach is to define certain issues as 'private' matters – as things that government should not involve itself in. For example, the development of a coherent childcare policy was hindered for many years in part because it was seen as a private matter for families.

A distinction can be drawn between the institutional agenda and the systemic agenda. The institutional agenda can be thought of as the government of the day's agenda. It is made up of the problems that ministers and civil servants are actively paying attention to (Cobb and Elder 1972: 86). Governments enter office with a manifesto and they intermittently – through set-piece political events like Queen's/King's Speeches – set out the institutional policy agenda. Ministers and civil servants want to keep as much control of the overall policy agenda as possible – they have priorities, things they want to get done, and they do not want to get blown off course or distracted. However, beyond the institutional agenda is the broader, systemic agenda, which consists of 'all issues that are commonly perceived by members of the political community as meriting public attention' (Cobb and Elder 1972: 85). Those trying to influence the systemic agenda are ultimately seeking to affect the institutional agenda.

The agenda can be challenged, or shift, through several mechanisms. Crises or 'focusing events' – defined by Béland et al. (2018: 3) as events that elevate 'policy items from the unofficial or public agenda onto the government one' – can boost the salience of an issue in a way that demands a response from government (see Birkland 1997). In such moments, 'windows of opportunity' for policy change can open up for actors in the broader policy system, beyond government, to capitalise on. In such moments, governments may seek to delay a response, hoping an issue falls back down the agenda, for example, by convening a public inquiry that may take several years to conclude. Political strategy, effective communication and a degree of luck are among the factors determining whether a window of opportunity will be seized or not. For example, the global financial crisis of 2007–2008 opened a window of opportunity to significantly reform banking regulation in the UK. Regulatory bodies and political parties, particularly the Liberal Democrats, were successful in keeping the spotlight on the issue and outmanoeuvred the British Bankers' Association (the umbrella body representing the interests of banking and financial services), delivering policy change that, while flawed, went further than the banks wanted (Ganderson 2020).

Venue-shopping has also been identified as a way that groups outside government can try to shift the policy agenda. This happens when a policy actor who is unable to gain traction for their policy ideas in one space (or 'venue') looks for an alternative venue. This can involve shifting focus from government to Parliament, or to the Courts, or to another level of government. In the UK, the possibility of venue-shopping has increased because of devolution. A good example of this is tobacco policy, where policy actors who wanted smoking to be banned in public places shifted their focus from the UK level to the Scottish level, and then from the Scottish

Government to the Scottish Parliament (Cairney 2007). Scotland was the first part of the UK to introduce a smoking ban and the success in the Scottish policy venue focused attention on England by comparison, helping to get the policy enacted there too.

Ultimately, the policy agenda reflects the exercise of power. As Cairney (2019a: 8) explains: 'powerful groups often maintain their position by minimising attention to certain issues. Policy change requires attention from policymakers and other interested participants but such attention is a rare commodity.' The literature distinguishes three dimensions of power (for an overview, see Cairney 2019a: 46–68; for an application to the UK banking and finance industry, see Johal et al. 2014). The first focuses on observable moments of conflict or decision where power manifests itself in obtaining a preferred outcome. For example, the banking industry successfully lobbied against increased regulation or the taxation of bank profits or bankers' bonuses. The second looks at potential but unrealised conflict and 'non-decision making', which keeps issues off the agenda. For example, banks controlled the agenda of financial regulation behind closed doors via close relationships with relevant government officials. The third dimension of power is more structural in nature, captured by Lukes' (2005: 12) observation that power is 'most effective when least observable'. The third dimension focuses on how power can involve the creation of dominant ways of thinking about policy issues, which can come to frame political debate in a way that renders certain alternatives almost unthinkable. For example, critics of neoliberalism argue that its true power – as an ideology that privileges individualism over collectivism, markets over state planning, and that redefines citizens as consumers – is its anonymity and malleability (Monbiot and Hutchison 2024).

Over the longer term, agenda-setting has been researched using Punctuated Equilibrium Theory (PET). This research confirms that continuity, or incremental policy change, is the norm but that such 'equilibrium' situations can be 'punctuated' by periods of more rapid and significant policy change when attention is successfully shifted and the policy agenda is reframed (John et al. 2013).

Constrained decision-makers

Most policy theories accept that decision-makers operate under numerous constraints and understanding the nature of those constraints is important because it steers us towards a more realistic assessment of policymaking. In an ideal world, policymakers would take their time, consider all possible solutions to any given problem, weigh the pros and cons alongside other, competing priorities, and arrive at a rational decision. But such an ideal, comprehensively rational, world does not exist, and policymakers face significant constraints when developing and determining policy. Referring to various academic models of the policy process, a senior civil servant remarked: 'all the models that I've ever seen are great in theory but usually assume that you're going to stop for a month and examine everything. The world is rarely like that' (Hallsworth et al. 2011: 38). Instead, policymakers and organisations seek courses of action that are satisfactory, or 'good enough' (Simon 1976). Policymakers use shorts-cuts and rules of thumb, consulting a small number of trusted sources whose access is just as much – if not more – a function of their power and position within, and understanding of, the policy system as it is the quality of their knowledge and advice (see Cairney and Kwiatkowski 2017).

Beyond these time and resource constraints, policymakers face cognitive constraints – they are only human and are required to engage with complex evidence that specialist scientists, economists or doctors might struggle to understand. Take policymaking during Covid, for example: the government claimed to be 'following the evidence' and 'following the science', but in reality, they were following the advice of *their* scientists, who contributed to an advisory system that was not autonomous but was set up to answer questions posed by government, and led by advisers appointed by government (Jarman et al. 2022). Rather than a technical, rational process, policy-making is – as Lindblom (1959, 1979) identified decades ago – a process of 'muddling through'. Much of the frustration among researchers who bemoan the fact that government policy is not sufficiently 'evidence-based' is the result of misunderstanding the nature of government. The best we may hope for is more evidence-, or research-informed, policy, meaning that while evidence might sometimes be used to guide policymakers towards broad ideas and agendas, it will seldom be used to directly shape policy (Smith 2013). Evidence and research can be pumped into the policy system, but it must compete with values, ideologies and political considerations.

Time, resources and cognitive constraints – combined with the short-term thinking produced by the nature of electoral politics – hinders the development of longer-term policy of the sort that can help to prevent many of the societal problems and challenges that confront us. The UK has an ageing population and, in recent years, that population has become poorer and sicker (Raymond et al. 2021; Poku-Amanfo et al. 2024). Such trends make the case for a more preventative and joined-up approach to public policy more compelling (see Key debate box).

Key debate   Why isn't government policy more preventative?

For many decades, politicians have talked about the need to recalibrate public policy to shift away from the short-term management and mitigation of societal problems and towards a more proactive, preventative approach. Prevention covers a range of potential policies that are designed to intervene in people's lives to prevent subsequent bad outcomes (see Cairney and St Denny 2020).

One of the most important areas of public policy where prevention can indeed be better than cure is health. Much of the ill-health that the NHS has to deal with is preventable. However, developing a truly preventative policy would require significant changes to the way that government works. First, government would have to be more joined-up, with housing and social security, among other policy areas, aligned to preventing poverty-related health risks. Second, government would have to focus on the leading factors driving ill-health and design tax and regulatory policy in a way that reduces societal risks related to alcohol and tobacco, while also encouraging healthier diets. Such policy interventions would not be without challenge, especially from those who believe that government should intervene less in the lives of its citizens. Third, such policy change would be best driven by more empowered and better-funded local governments that can react better to local population health issues. Fourth, the NHS itself would need more resources to engage in preventative services, such as early detection screenings for cancer, cardiovascular disease and diabetes, for example (see Marshall et al. 2024).

Discussion questions

1   Thinking about this issue of preventative policy in the context of what you know about the policy process and the structure of government, what changes would you make to try to deliver a more preventative approach to public policy?
2   Connecting the issue to broader political discourse in the UK, how might you develop a political strategy to explain this to the electorate?

There are also institutional constraints specific to the UK policymaking system. The Westminster Model, and coverage of politics in the media, encourages us to focus on the prime minister and senior ministers sitting at the top of a massive machine called 'the government', pulling levers and making things happen. The reality is far different. Yes, the British state is highly centralised and displays power-hoarding tendencies (Marsh et al. 2003). However, the centre of government – especially the Prime Minister's Office/Downing Street – is underpowered, lacking the capacity to make and deliver policy across the whole range of government (Diamond 2013; Harris and Rutter 2014; Urban et al. 2024). The prime minister and their team in Downing Street can be more or less significant drivers of policy across government. However, the notion of a hierarchical system where prime ministers drive their policy preferences through Cabinet ministers, who in turn command their departments and civil servants, does not reflect reality. The dynamic is one of dependency and exchange between prime ministers and their ministers.

Prime ministers are assisted at the centre by the Prime Minister's Policy Unit, which functions as a source of ideas and can also serve an oversight role, with special advisers (SpAds) keeping an eye on the policy work of departments and ministries. Although the Policy Unit has been an important source of ideas at various times since the late 1970s, it cannot steer the policy agenda because it is dwarfed by government departments, where ministers are surrounded by their own SpAds who generate policy ideas, as well as civil servants who brief ministers and who have strong connections with policy networks beyond government (Diamond 2013: 174–175). Historical research about Thatcher's Policy Unit affirms the notion that although the Unit can be an important source of ideas, those ideas – especially if they are more radical – can run into the sand when they are processed through departments that often prefer more evolutionary, incremental policy changes (Davies et al. 2023). The Prime Minister's Office technically sits within the Cabinet Office but remains organisationally distinct. However, the Cabinet Office, 'founded to serve cabinet and its committees, has become bloated and unfocused' (Urban et al. 2024: 9). Most policy is developed within departments, not Downing Street or the Cabinet Office (Marsh et al. 2001: 249).

Institutions, inertia and incrementalism

Departments can be thought of as institutions and institutions are important to the policymaking process. Policy is made in institutional settings and if we want to understand why certain policies are enacted, and others are not, we must think about the characteristics of those institutional settings. Consider the UK Treasury as an example of a powerful institution that is also part of the core executive. It is clearly recognisable as an institution. It occupies a grand building in London and is headed by the powerful figure of the Chancellor. Unlike in many other countries, however, the Treasury is both a finance ministry and an economics ministry, which grants it a powerful role at the heart of government, its policy influence extending into the major public service delivery ministries that are responsible for education, health and social security, among others (see Deakin and Parry 2000; Thain 2004; Davis 2022). We can trace the historical evolution of the Treasury as a powerful institution at the heart of government, one that is often able to dominate the policy process, filling a power vacuum created by a comparatively weak Prime Minister's Office/Cabinet Office (Urban et al. 2024: 9–10). However, when policy scholars write about institutions, they mean more than bricks-and-mortar institutions and the formal structures of government. They are equally concerned with the rules, norms, practices and common understandings that are embedded within, and reproduced by, institutional settings (see Béland 2019).

Institutions can have a default policy outlook, or a policy orientation, meaning that, as collectives of individual policymakers, institutions can come to see problems in a certain way, making certain solutions more acceptable than others. Consider the Treasury again: a focus on the ideas embedded within the Treasury can take us a step beyond understanding *why* it is powerful and towards understanding *how* it may use its power to advance or hinder certain policy ideas. The 'Treasury view' (as it is sometimes called) consists of a commitment to 'the importance of spending control, free trade and the need to control inflation, support markets and enhance the supply side of the economy', which shapes how Treasury officials approach policy problems (Wilkes et al. 2024: 4; Dorey 2014: chapter 4, which details a range of other departmental cultures). As the UK emerges from a period of crisis, former Prime Minister Gordon Brown has called for the Treasury to commit to a growth strategy and not retreat into its comfort zone focused on balancing the books (Elliott 2024). In everyday political language, this captures the idea that institutional cultures, norms and outlooks are important to understanding the policy process. Indeed, one of the cutting-edge debates in public policy today is not about any particular policy area, but rather about whether the state can *reimagine* itself as a powerful actor that can work *in partnership* with the private sector and the third sector, setting broad strategic missions and putting the financial power of the state behind those missions through sustainable investment and public borrowing for long-term projects (see Research in Focus box).

Research in Focus

Innovation and public purpose

We are currently witnessing a shift in political discourse about the role of the state. In part, that has been driven by a mounting series of policy failures (e.g. banking regulation before the global financial crisis) and seemingly 'wicked' problems that are not being addressed at sufficient scale and scope by markets alone (e.g. climate change). Covid-19 was a reminder of the immense power of the state to shape our lives (Garrard 2022). The language of 'mission-driven government' is growing louder, as used by Keir Starmer, for example (Pannell 2024). There are important historical examples of governments setting broad missions that required solving a series of problems along the way. One example was the decision of the US government to put a man on the moon, the process of which harnessed the power of private and state actors and, along the way, produced a number of innovations that solved concrete problems, for example camera phones, foil blankets, baby formula and new forms of computing software (Mazzucato 2021).

A mission-driven approach to addressing the problems posed by climate change might similarly involve government setting a broad goal and then committing the public investment necessary to crowd-in private sector investment. That might involve a combination of grants, loans, investment schemes, outcome-oriented procurement and industrial strategy. However, doing this would involve rethinking how public and state financing *actually* works – in short,

(Continued)

not like a household credit card (see Berkeley et al. 2022) – and breaking fundamentally from austerity. The idea of mission-driven government is *not* about top-down micro-management or narrow government targets. It involves state *direction* but not state *management*. It is an approach that requires government to set a broad policy goal (the 'what' of public policy), while leaving open the precise developments that allow the goal to be attained (the 'how' of public policy).

But government cannot play this role if it does not appreciate the public and societal value that it can add. Hence the need for a paradigm shift. Whitehall would need to rebuild its capacity to manage and organise projects, shift from a model of power-hoarding to power-sharing, accept greater risk-taking and the possibility of some projects failing, and actively recruit a broader set of people and skills (Kaye 2022).

Discussion questions

1   How well is the Labour government elected in 2024 advancing its 'mission driven' approach to government?
2   What set of reforms would you introduce to Whitehall to more effectively pursue 'mission driven' government?

Taking the idea of institutions and institutionalism a step further, policy scholars often talk about policies themselves as types of institution, especially policies that involve creating large bureaucratic structures to administer them (e.g. health systems and social security systems). Over time, as people become used to these policy frameworks (so-called 'learning effects'), they become resistant to change. Historical institutionalists focus on the historical contingency involved in the establishment of such policy frameworks and the path dependencies that are created over time as more resources are committed to a policy (see Pierson 2000; Greener 2005). To fully understand the history of policies we must look back to 'critical junctures' – moments at which key decisions were made that led to the development of an institution or a policy framework (Capoccia and Kelemen 2007). The timing of these decisions, and the sequencing of events, can be crucial to determining how policy develops and can help us to understand why health, social security and education policy systems look so different across countries (Hacker 1998; Thelen 2004).

Take the NHS as an example. The integration of health and social care has been a long-standing policy priority in the UK (see Reed et al. 2021). The NHS is organised nationally but social care is largely organised through local government. A critical juncture that determined this structure can be identified in October 1945 when Minister of Health Nye Bevan's proposal for nationalising hospitals was pitted, in Cabinet, against Leader of the House of Commons Herbert Morrison's alternative proposal to organise the new health system through local government. Imagining the counterfactual, that Morrison's ideas had won the day, 'reminds us that things could have turned out differently, pointing to the importance of contingency and to causal relations' (Powell and Greener 2024). You start down a certain path and it makes it increasingly likely that you will continue down that path – a concept called 'path dependency' by institutionalists. This makes incremental policy change more likely than fundamental overhaul. Of course, the effect of many incremental changes over time can be significant – for example, the introduction of market-based mechanisms into the NHS under successive Conservative and Labour governments since 1979 (Lewis 2020). Scholars of institutionalism have developed their theories over time to explain how, between critical junctures, significant change can still occur through the combined effect of many smaller, incremental changes (see Mahoney and Thelen 2015).

Departments are the real engine of policymaking and ministers are vital to the policy process, although not all ministers approach their job in the same way. There have been several attempts to develop typologies of ministers, ranging from those who enter office with ambitious reform agendas to those who prefer to manage and administer departments quietly, avoiding crises and responding to policy issues as they arise (Norton 1988; Marsh et al. 2001: 133–141). Iain Duncan Smith, for example, took office as Secretary of State for Work and Pensions in 2010 and drove through significant reforms of the social security system both in terms of its administration – through the introduction of Universal Credit – and in terms of the principles underpinning it – through the more extensive use of conditionality and sanctioning, which was extended from what existed under the previous Labour government. Michael Gove was similarly dynamic in driving change across a range of educational issues during his tenure as Education Secretary between 2010 and 2014 (Finn 2015).

Ministers head government departments politically but the bureaucracy is headed by senior civil servants. Civil servants are a key source of policy advice to ministers. Ministers have to delegate and grant discretion to civil servants, especially policy-focused civil servants. Those civil servants will then do much of the work of policy development, which involves consulting outside groups, looking at options, doing research and producing written briefings for ministers, which will be reviewed for decision. Discretion enters the equation because civil servants can present advice in ways that steer their minister towards a certain decision. The minister retains the ultimate power of decision but, once a broad direction of travel has been established, civil servants in policy roles have significant scope to shape what happens next, refining policy proposals and designing the actual policy instruments that will be used. Page (2018) has studied how, for example, 'bill teams', made up of civil servants, turn policy ideas into draft legislation and how, through that process, they can shape what the precise policy and law ultimately looks like. This part of the policy process is not a simple translation of a policy idea into a law. It remains an opportunity for actors outside government to lobby and try to influence and change the policy in subtle but important ways.

Policy sub-systems, communities and networks

Civil servants have never enjoyed a monopoly on policy advice to ministers and recent decades have seen a diversification of the sources of policy advice flowing to ministers. The growth of SpAds across government has been notable (LSE GV314 Group and Page 2012: 715; Cabinet Office 2023: 2). However, a government department may have a small handful of SpAds at most, and their ability to make a large bureaucratic structure work to their demands is limited. More broadly, the development of 'policy advisory systems' has altered the landscape of policymaking (Craft and Halligan 2015, 2020; OECD 2017). Diamond (2020: 563) defines 'policy advisory systems' as 'the autonomous organisations that sustain government's "strategic knowledge infrastructure", such as advisory bodies, think tanks, policy labs, "what works" centres, political advisers, committees of inquiry'. Focusing on the Cameron years (2010–2016), Diamond (2023: 516) identified a change in the minister–civil servant relationship as ministers built up their policy capacity in an attempt to make themselves less dependent on their officials. Ministers increasingly 'drew on resources from outside the core executive', which had the effect of replacing 'the interpersonal and institutional resource dependency [between ministers and civil servants] with a "them and us" model' (ibid.).

Policy advisory systems are specific to particular areas of public policy. There is no single policy system and researchers tend to focus on policy sub-systems (e.g. education policy) or even sub-sub-systems (e.g. schools' policy). Much public policy is debated and developed within small, specialist policy communities that operate out of the public spotlight and with minimal involvement of ministers. As students of policy, the first thing we need to do is map the terrain of whatever policy we are interested in, asking: who are the key actors? What influence do they have on government? How have they come to hold that influence? These questions can guide us in establishing the terrain of whatever policy area we are interested in. It takes us beyond the realm of hierarchies, such as government ministries – bureaucracies that leave official records – and into the realm of networks, which are harder to trace but account for much of what happens in the real world of public policy.

The language of policy communities, and policy or issue networks, can be confusing. Sometimes the phrases are used interchangeably. We can think about a spectrum from tighter policy communities – characterised by a small and stable number of participants, frequent interaction, and a general agreement on the nature of the policy problem and how to solve it – to looser issue networks – characterised by a larger number of participants, with varying degrees of interaction between them, less stability in the network membership, and disagreement and differing outlooks about the nature of problems and the best solutions (Marsh and Rhodes 1992). Sometimes the language of 'insider' versus 'outsider' groups is used to distinguish those actors who are particularly close to government from those who try to influence policy via Parliament, the media or visible public campaigns, including protests. Ministers and civil servants tend 'to demand "responsible" behaviours from those to whom they will listen, such as think tanks, business lobbies, professions or expert academics. "Insider" groups have the ear of policymakers, while more strident, public and "extreme" voices are routinely discounted' (Dunleavy 2018: 119). Linking this distinction back to the earlier discussion of agenda-setting, insider groups are more focused on the institutional agenda, and outsider groups on the systemic agenda.

An important type of organisation often found within tight-knit policy communities and policy advisory systems are think tanks, which have become increasingly prominent on the UK policy landscape (Garnett and Lorenzoni 2021; Tchilingirian 2021). Think tanks may not always have direct, causal impacts on policy, but they can contribute to the broader policy discourse in ways that help political parties to clarify their agendas. For example, think tanks such as the Institute for Public Policy Research (IPPR) and Demos made important contributions to the broader policy discourse that Blair's New Labour adopted (Pautz 2011, 2012). Similarly, in the aftermath of the global financial crisis, think tanks helped to construct an austerity discourse that the Conservative party adopted (Pautz 2018). As an opposition MP, Iain Duncan Smith developed his ideas about welfare reform working through a think tank (the Centre for Social Justice) that he established, and with a variety of small charities focused on poverty reduction (see Haddon 2012). Once the political party they have influenced enters government, think tanks often step back as the Whitehall machinery develops concrete policies and laws. However, there has been a steady stream of think tank staff moving in and out of government, which strengthens the policy linkages and is a key characteristic of the newer style of policy advisory system.

Broader issue networks are also useful for civil servants and ministers because it helps them to organise the terrain of policy for which they are responsible. They can identify key stakeholders who ought to be consulted when making policy change, which might help them to avoid designing bad policy, or policy that will be resisted either by the groups it most directly impacts or the people required to implement the policy. Many government departments have insider groups and professional associations that are their key stakeholders. For example, although the Department of Health makes policy to try to improve the health care and public health of citizens, it is also making policy that will impact on the work of 1.4 million people, such as doctors and nurses, who work for the NHS. The same can be said for the Department of Education and teachers, or the Home Office and police officers. The professional associations that represent these groups are important actors on the policy landscape, although they often find themselves opposing government policies.

Broader issue networks are spaces of contestation and policy communities with different views about the same problem might exist within the same, loose network. A well-researched example from the history of UK public policy is tobacco policy (see Cairney 2007). For many decades, the broad issue network around tobacco policy was dominated by the tobacco manufacturers, pro-tobacco consumer groups, the union representing tobacco workers and the UK government department responsible for tobacco policy (the equivalent of what today is the Department for Business and Trade). This tight-knit policy community within the broader issue network was forged during the Second World War when tobacco advisory groups were established to ensure the supply of cigarettes. This community was able to form a 'policy monopoly', meaning a dominant image or frame on a particular policy issue, maintained by a structured interaction among the people and groups responsible for policymaking that limits access to the policy process (Baumgartner and Jones 2009: 7). Tobacco was framed as an economic issue, about jobs, taxes and exports, and as a matter of individual consumer choice, rather than as a public health issue. This policy monopoly and dominant image eventually shifted, but it took decades of work by health organisations such as the British Medical Association (BMA) and Action on Smoking and Health (ASH) to reframe tobacco as a public health issue (see Cairney 2019b).

The example of tobacco policy highlights that businesses are important players in public policy, although the reality of their power and influence is nuanced, ebbing and flowing in relation to other pressures. Take banking, for example. Before the global financial crisis, banks wielded significant influence over financial regulatory policy. However, post-crisis, political dynamics made it impossible for banks to resist reforms that they did not want, such as ringfencing and stricter regulatory frameworks (although individual banks did still manage to secure concessions) (Ganderson 2020). Following Brexit, the banking industry was unable to successfully lobby the Theresa May government for the 'soft' Brexit that they preferred, despite possessing formidable power. The translation of power into policy influence was constrained in that case by, among other things, the internal politics of the Conservative Party and structural changes in government which undermined the access points banking lobbyists had enjoyed in Whitehall. The banking industry typically lobbied through the Treasury, which pre-Brexit was an influential department in EU policy. However, Theresa May created a new department responsible for Brexit, one that banking lobbyists struggled to penetrate (James and Quaglia 2019). The case is a reminder of the importance of the sort of policy communities discussed above. In this case, that policy community was disrupted by institutional change.

Issue networks are populated by many other actors besides think tanks, professional associations and corporations. Take the issue of poverty, for example. Charities such as the Joseph Rowntree Foundation and the Child Poverty Action Group try to influence the policy agenda through a combination of producing research on the impact of existing policies, organising public campaigns, and appearing in the media and attempting to frame the broader policy discourse (the systemic agenda). Voluntary sector organisations, which help to deliver policy on the ground in communities, are also part of a broad policy landscape. Often, such organisations develop partnerships with the state and have to balance their criticism of existing policy with the need to maintain partnerships (see Milbourne and Cushman 2014). There are also a growing number of social movements, such as those organised around climate justice (e.g. Fridays for Future and Extinction Rebellion) or racial discrimination (e.g. Black Lives Matter), that try to shape the systemic agenda, often taking advantage of opportunities created by social media and adopting a more antagonistic approach to government (Doherty et al. 2016; Ishkanian 2022). Increasingly, these social movements are global networks that organise local protests.

Policy implementation and street-level bureaucracy

A final aspect of the policy system to consider is that of policy implementation at the 'street level'. It is a mistake to think that once a policy is written, and a law or a regulation is passed, that is the end of the story. The gap between policy design and delivery leaves space for discretion at the street level to deliver public policy. This is apparent, for example, in social security policy, where the discretion of individual welfare caseworkers can play an important role in shaping policy outcomes (Rice 2013). However, over time, as the 'primary concern of British social security policy has shifted from meeting the needs of the poor and vulnerable to cutting total spending', the ability of street-level bureaucrats in job centres has been curbed (Walker 2015: 60). As more targets are layered on to street-level bureaucrats, and fewer resources are available in a context of austerity and cuts to local government budgets, discretion ebbs away (e.g. Fuertes and Lindsay 2016; Greer et al. 2018; Johnson et al. 2023).

In parallel, courts have increasingly become a site where policies can be contested and amended (see Haddon 2021). Beyond high-profile cases – for example, that the government's proposals to send asylum seekers to Rwanda was initially unlawful – the process of challenging policy implementation through the judicial system is an important aspect of public policy. Advocacy groups – on behalf of social security claimants – have brought a series of court cases, producing judgments that, although not fundamentally altering Universal Credit, have made a substantive difference to its implementation (Hobson 2021: 36–37).

Policy implementation is particularly important in the UK because of a trend since the 1980s for more of the work of public policy to be done by quasi- or non-governmental organisations. What started with 'Next Steps' agencies, which placed the delivery of public policy at arm's length from their parent policy departments in Whitehall, has grown into a broader pattern of public–private partnerships and, increasingly, policy delivery that is outsourced, with private companies securing contracts to deliver public services (see Wilks 2013). This trajectory has expanded the gap between policy design (at the centre) and policy delivery (on the street). A former Whitehall permanent secretary has argued that this gap is increasingly problematic, with policymakers and policy designers typically having no experience of delivering public services (Slater 2022). The observation is not new: more than a decade ago the Institute for Government (Hallsworth et al. 2011: 43) observed that the structure of career progression, and what is valued in the civil service, puts a premium on smart policy briefs and good ideas on paper, rather than policy delivery on the ground. The obvious solution seems to be involving policy deliverers and implementers in the design of policy, but this does not seem to happen, despite decades of reports arguing that it should (e.g. National Audit Office 2001: 31; Sasse and Thomas 2022: 6).

So many of the 'blunders' of our government (King and Crewe 2013) seem to boil down to the disconnect between policy design and policy implementation. Examples cited by the Institute for Government include the Child Support Act (see McCarthy-Cotter 2018) and the introduction of single farm payments (House of Commons 2007). We can also consider the UK's Modern Slavery Act 2015, a hallmark of Theresa May's period in government as Home Secretary and then Prime Minister. Gardiner (2019: 1) has observed that, despite the introduction of policy (legislation), there has been 'no identifiable reduction in the prevalence of modern slavery in the UK, coupled with failures in the policing response and well-rehearsed criticisms in the quality of support provided to victims'. In part because of cuts to local government budgets, the implementation of the policy is inconsistent (Gardiner 2018). Taking public policy seriously, in terms of its delivery and its capacity to improve the lives of citizens, means paying attention to the implementation of policy and the gaps between intention (at the centre) and reality (on the ground).

This gap is mirrored in research on policy, much of which focuses on agenda-setting and decision-making, overlooking the ways in which policy is finalised through implementation. Nevertheless, a body of research confirms that people who work on the front line of public policy, the so-called 'street-level bureaucrats' (e.g. doctors, nurses, teachers, police officers, job centre workers, social workers, judges) possess discretion to shape public policy. Based on initial research in the USA, Lipsky (1980: 13–25) found that front-line public service workers were subjected to an immense range of often unclear requirements and targets laid down by laws and regulations designed by a central government. Among the sheer number of requirements placed upon them by a central government that often wants to simply deliver the public message that 'we have solved this problem', street-level bureaucrats have discretion about which priorities and targets they focus on, and how many of them they need to deliver to satisfy central government. Far from meeting every target and requirement, they use their discretion to establish routines to satisfy a proportion of central government objectives while preserving a degree of professional autonomy, which Lipsky argues is necessary to maintain morale (see also Zacka 2017). Research has found similar patterns of activity and behaviour in numerous countries, including the UK.

Summary

- Public policy affects all of our lives in countless ways – from the quality of the schools that children attend to the quality of health and social care we receive – and the process of making policy is complex and messy, with decision-makers facing significant constraints in terms of their cognitive abilities, time and resources.
- Given those constraints, most policy is stable most of the time, with changes arising from shifts in the policy agenda, focusing events, crises or critical junctures.
- Policies typically evolve incrementally and decisions taken in the past can create significant constraints. Once a policy framework has been set up, it can be quite costly and disruptive to move away from it.

- Policy is often made in small groups or communities that involve actors within government and actors outside government who work hard to establish and maintain privileged access to the policy process.
- Policy does not end when a law or a regulation is passed. The process of implementing policy at the street-level is an important part of the process and shapes much of the day-to-day experience of people who use public services.

Recommended and further reading

- The best general introductory text for the various theories, concepts and approaches to the academic study of public policy is Cairney (2019a), while Cairney and Kippin (2023) explore politics and policymaking in a British context.
- There have been some excellent insider accounts of government that include discussions of the policymaking process, including Barwell (2021) and Stewart (2023).
- King and Crewe (2013) remains an important and entertaining study of a range of policy blunders and failures.
- Diamond and Richardson (2023), which focuses on British policymaking after Brexit, includes articles covering a range of policy areas.
- The best think tank to follow to stay on top of the UK's policymaking process is the Institute for Government, while the UK in a Changing Europe is an academic think tank that provides research-based analysis of a range of policy issues facing the UK. Beyond them is a range of prominent think tanks on the UK policy landscape, some centre-right, others centre-left and others more centrist in policy orientation. Some have a specific policy focus, and others are more generalist. Some of the most prominent include the Institute for Public Policy Research, Policy Exchange, the Joseph Rowntree Foundation (on poverty), the Centre for Policy Studies, the Resolution Foundation, the King's Fund (on health policy), the Institute for Innovation and Public Purpose (on the role of the state and public finance), the Royal United Services Institute (on defence) and Chatham House (on foreign policy). Finally, although not a think tank, the Institute for Fiscal Studies is an excellent resource for economic analysis of UK government policy.

Chapter 17
Media and social media

Clare Llewellyn and Cristian Vaccari

What will this chapter tell me?

- This chapter surveys the media and social media landscape of the UK. As new media have evolved, parties and politicians have had to adapt to citizens' sources of news and the dynamics they create.
- The centrality of digital media for people's news consumption has forced all professional news organisations to adapt and change how they produce and distribute news so that it can be accessed by citizens.
- The rise of social media has allowed campaigns to experiment with new tools to reach their audiences, and regulation in the UK has so far failed to catch up with these changes.
- This chapter examines two of the key concepts in social media studies that are widely debated: echo chambers and polarisation.

What do I need to know?

- The media landscape in the UK was traditionally dominated by television and newspapers but the latter have gradually declined as people's main source of news.
- The First-Past-the-Post electoral system forces parties to campaign in both a national and highly localised manner for UK parliamentary elections.
- The BBC (British Broadcasting Corporation) is the UK's main public service broadcaster and it remains the most trusted and used source of news in the UK.

Introduction

On 19 November 2019, three weeks before an unprecedented December general election was due to be held, Prime Minister and Conservative Party leader Boris Johnson and Labour Party leader Jeremy Corbyn participated in the first live televised debate of the campaign, broadcast by ITV. Televised debates between party leaders or presidential candidates have become a staple of many Western democracies, following the lead of the United States, where they first took place in 1960, but they are still relatively rare in the United Kingdom, where they were inaugurated in the 2010 general election. The 2019 debate was highly anticipated due to the contentious atmosphere that had led to the election, which was called after Prime Minister Johnson had repeatedly failed to secure a parliamentary majority for the deal he had negotiated to exit the European Union. Moreover, the unusual timing of the campaign during the colder part of the year meant that many traditional electioneering activities on the doorstep and in public spaces became secondary to mediated forms of voter contact. Almost 7 million viewers, or one-third of the whole British television audience, tuned in to follow the debate. As is now customary, a lively parallel debate took place on social media, where many citizens nowadays follow and comment on live high-profile televised events (Vaccari et al. 2015). Political actors have learned the importance of engaging with and, if possible, shaping these conversations, and so both major parties – and the smaller ones whose leaders had not been included in this debate – took to social media to comment on the event. One of these parties, however, tried to exploit features of the system in a deceptive way that turned out to be counterproductive.

Fact-checking plays an important role in the British media system. Although the underlying premises, functioning mechanisms and operational practices of fact-checking are complex and may not always lead to unequivocal conclusions about what is true and what is false, these organisations are generally considered reputable by the public. In the UK, the main fact-checking organisations are FullFact, an independent charity, BBC Verify and Channel 4 News Fact Check. During the 2019 televised leaders' debate, their official social media accounts all posted live updates to establish the truthfulness of claims made by Boris Johnson and Jeremy Corbyn. However, during the debate, a seemingly new fact-checking organisation made its debut on Twitter (now X), a social media platform that in 2019 was used by 22% of British social media users (which in turn comprised 72% of the adult population; see OfCom 2020a), and played an important role during live public events such as the leaders' debate. The Twitter account was named 'factcheckUK' and posted many messages accusing the Labour leader of making inaccurate statements. If a user saw these posts in their newsfeed, they would be likely to think this was an independent fact-checking organisation. However, a closer look at the profile showed that it was the official Twitter account of the Conservative Campaign Headquarters, which had been rebranded to impersonate a fact-checking organisation for the occasion. Shortly after the debate, the account's name was changed back to 'CCHQ Press' and resumed its normal operations. Both Twitter and other fact-checking organisations heavily criticised the Conservatives for resorting to this tactic, which led to a barrage of negative news coverage in the aftermath of the debate.

The episode we have just described was made possible by a combination of features that characterise contemporary media ecosystems: in particular, the integration of traditional and digital media, a widespread concern for truth and falsehood in public debate, and the problematic behaviour of some political elites in exploiting the opportunities that result from this.

In this chapter, we discuss the key features of contemporary media systems and their implications for politics. First, we provide an overview of the key players in the British media environment and how their roles have evolved over time. We then discuss how campaigns are run in the UK and what their impact is on electoral outcomes. Next, we analyse the evolving role of social media and their key political implications. Finally, we address the ongoing controversy regarding the prevalence, spread and correction of misinformation and disinformation, including the potential for regulation, spurred on by concerns for this and other problematic aspects of online communication.

The UK's media environment

In 2023, the majority (74%) of the British public got its news online, including both websites and social media, while 52% relied on television and 14% on print newspapers. From a historical perspective, much has changed in just ten years: in 2013, 79% got their news on television, 74% online and 59% on print newspapers (Reuters Institute for the Study of Journalism 2023; see Figure 17.1). Behind these stark changes lies a process of generational change, as older citizens, who mainly rely on television and newspapers, are being replaced by younger citizens who mainly get their news on the internet (Andersen et al. 2021).

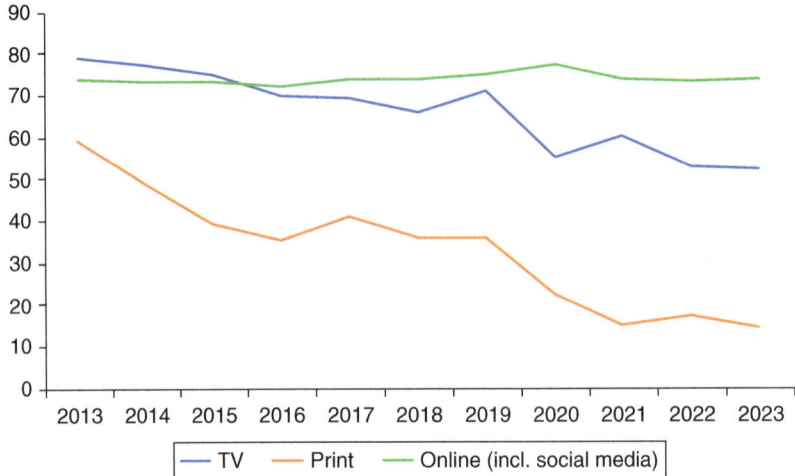

Figure 17.1   Most used sources of news in the UK, 2013–2023 (percentage of the population)

Source: Authors' elaboration of data from the Reuters Institute for the Study of Journalism (2023)

Another important change has occurred in how people access the internet: whereas in the past a personal computer was the main gateway to the web, nowadays smartphones, tablets and other mobile devices are much more relevant. Thus, in 2023, 89% of UK internet users went online using a smartphone, 46% with a tablet, 56% with a laptop and 27% with a desktop computer (OfCom 2024). In total, British internet users spend an average of six hours and two minutes online every day, evenly distributed between computers and tablets (three hours and five minutes per day) and smartphones (two hours and 57 minutes per day; We Are Social 2024).

The centrality of digital media for people's news consumption has forced all professional news organisations to adapt and change how they produce and distribute news so that it can be accessed by citizens. The five most widely used online news brands in 2023 showcase the diversity of professional news organisations in the UK (Reuters Institute for the Study of Journalism 2023):

- Public Service Media (PSM), the British Broadcasting Corporation (BBC), 45%
- the broadsheet newspaper *The Guardian*, 16%
- the tabloid newspaper *MailOnline* (i.e. the *Daily Mail*), 14%
- the commercial broadcaster *Sky News*, 12%
- regional and local newspapers online, 8%

We will now briefly discuss each of these types of news outlets.

The British Broadcasting Corporation (BBC) is one of the world's best-known Public Service Media (PSM). PSM are funded directly or indirectly by the State to pursue some public policy goals which commercial media are thought to be less well equipped to achieve, such as providing educational content, supplying costly high-quality content, promoting local culture and serving socially disadvantaged communities. The BBC was established in 1922 with the mission to 'inform, educate and entertain'. Funding for the BBC mainly comes from the licence fee, which the law requires any household watching or recording television programming to pay every year. The amount is formally set by the UK Government. In the 2022/23 financial year, roughly two-thirds of the BBC's income came from licence fees (BBC 2023). The BBC is a multimedia corporation that features nine UK-wide television services, ten radio services, eight television and radio services serving specific local audiences, and BBC Online, which includes its website and its on-demand service, BBC iPlayer. The BBC also owns the BBC World Service, which reaches more than 300 million weekly viewers around the world.

The BBC is by far the most trusted news brand in the UK, with 61% of the British public claiming to trust it (Reuters Institute for the Study of Journalism 2023), and there is evidence that the quality of its news content has positive effects on citizens' political knowledge (Soroka et al. 2013). However, controversies around its impartiality are a regular feature of UK public debate. For instance, in 2003 the Labour government commissioned a judicial inquiry to investigate the BBC's conduct after the suicide of David Kelly, a weapons expert and Ministry of Defence employee who had been named as the source of BBC reports that claimed the government had manipulated intelligence to make the case for the invasion of Iraq. The report, which criticised the BBC for its conduct, led to the resignation of its director-general, but also to continued criticism of the government in the press (Wring 2005). During the 2016 referendum that led to the UK's departure from the European Union, the BBC was accused of employing a misguided notion of 'balance', whereby expert opinion was given equal weight to partisan views without adequate scrutiny (Seaton, 2016; see also Hopkin and Rosamond 2018). At the same time, pro-Leave commentators emphasised the Corporation's supposedly elitist, metropolitan and internationalist bias in representing the debate around the referendum and the groups of voters who supported Brexit.

Commercial broadcasters, such as ITV, Channel 4 and Sky, have lower viewership ratings and are less popular for news than the BBC, but they still attract substantial audiences overall. Commercial broadcasters are licensed by the State and must comply with regulations to retain their licences. They are overseen by an independent regulator, the Office of Communications (usually referred to as OfCom), which is required by law to produce and update the so-called *Ofcom Broadcasting Code* (OfCom 2020b). The code applies to all television and radio broadcasters and mandates the standards that all their programmes must follow in various areas. Of the ten sections in the current Code, those on 'due impartiality and due accuracy' and on 'elections and referendums' are the most relevant to the production of political news (OfCom 2020b). Overall, the requirements provided in these provisions are rather strict and constrain commercial broadcasters so that their news coverage tends to be balanced between the main political parties and ideas at a given time. The result is what scholars of media and politics term *internal pluralism*, that is, a diversity of views represented in the coverage of a single media outlet (Hallin and Mancini 2004).

UK newspapers are commonly differentiated into 'broadsheets' and 'tabloids'. Broadsheets, such as *The Times*, *The Daily Telegraph*, *The Guardian* and *The Financial Times*, tend to provide more extensive and specialised coverage of public affairs and politics. Tabloids, such as *The Sun*, *Daily Mirror*, *Daily Mail*, *Daily Express* and *Daily Star*, tend to focus more on entertainment and lifestyle news, and cover politics in a more sensationalist fashion. Tabloid newspapers tend to have much higher circulation than broadsheet newspapers. Unlike broadcasting, the British press is entirely self-regulated. Partly due to a lack of regulation and partly due to commercial logics and traditions, British newspapers have traditionally covered politics in a rather slanted way, not only in terms of editorial positions, but also in how they report events and topics. Different newspapers usually present leaders, parties and issues in markedly different ways, and before elections most newspapers openly endorse a specific political party. Overall, the newspaper sector in the UK achieves *external pluralism*; that is, a wide range of views is available across the whole sector rather than within each publication (Hallin and Mancini 2004).

Over the past two decades, most newspapers, including the most widely read, have tended to support the Conservative Party. For instance, in the 2019 general election, the circulation of the newspapers which backed the Conservatives was five and a half times that of Labour-supporting titles and the tone of newspaper coverage was overly negative towards Labour and neutral towards the Conservatives (Wring and Ward 2020). In the 2024 general election, however, some titles switched their support to Labour and the overall balance in newspaper endorsements was more even. Newspapers do not necessarily lead their readers to vote for the parties they endorse, as publications reflect the preferences of their audiences as much as shape them. However, readers' political preferences are diverse. For instance, in the 2019 general election, 61% of *Guardian* readers who voted chose Labour (whom *The Guardian* endorsed), but 18% chose the Liberal Democrats and 9% the Conservatives. Among readers of the Conservative-supporting *Times*, 49% of voters chose the Conservatives, but 24% voted for the Lib Dems and 23% for Labour (calculations by the authors based on Fieldhouse et al. 2022). However, there is also some evidence that newspapers' endorsements contribute to shifting voting preferences above and beyond their readers' background political affiliations (Newton and Brynin 2001). This may be particularly likely when a newspaper switches its orientation from one election

| 1992 | 1997 | 2010 | 2019 |

Figure 17.2 Front pages of *The Sun* endorsing different party leaders in different elections. The 1992 front page features Neil Kinnock, the then Labour Party leader, whom *The Sun* relentlessly portrayed as a threat to the country's prosperity during the campaign. The 1997 front page announced *The Sun's* momentous endorsement of the new Labour leader Tony Blair, which as discussed above likely influenced a substantial number of readers. The 2010 front page shows *The Sun's* swinging back to supporting the Conservatives and their then leader David Cameron, portrayed with graphics and a slogan similar to Barack Obama's 2008 presidential campaign in the United States. The 2019 front page explicitly echoes the 1992 front page and repeats the theme that unless the endorsed candidate (Conservative leader Boris Johnson) won, the country would be plunged into darkness; it also highlights the importance of Brexit to the vote, after *The Sun* was one of the strongest advocates for leaving the European Union during the 2016 referendum

to the other, as many readers who may have chosen the newspaper at least in part due to its previous orientation find themselves exposed to arguments that differ from those they are used to. One famous such example was *The Sun*'s decision before the 1997 general election to break its tradition of supporting the Conservatives in favour of Tony Blair's New Labour (see Figure 17.2). A comparison of the changes in voting preferences over time among readers of *The Sun* and of three other newspapers that similarly switched their support from Conservative to Labour found that between 10% and 25% of those readers shifted to voting for Labour (Ladd and Lenz 2009). However, this was an exceptional case, and in general it is safe to assume that newspapers rarely have a direct influence on how most of their readers vote. Nevertheless, newspapers arguably maintain a substantial influence in shaping public debate and political culture, for instance by emphasising different problems, or aspects of those problems, at the expense of others and promoting particular narratives about current affairs.

Campaigns and elections

Although parties and politicians devote substantial efforts to engaging with voters at all times, election campaigns are when media and communication matter the most in politics. During campaigns, party strategists need to allocate scarce resources – mainly time, people and money – to achieve the most votes. To complicate matters further, the UK's First-Past-the-Post electoral system means that some votes are more important than others to elect Members of Parliament. Campaigns therefore concentrate their efforts in those constituencies where they have a realistic possibility of winning and the margin between their and the other leading parties' candidates is expected to be smaller. Moreover, campaigns in the UK tend to be short (25 working days according to the law), and 'snap' elections are often called at short notice by the Prime Minister, as was the case in 2024, which means parties have little time to prepare. Finally, there are no limits to how much money can be donated to parties or politicians, but the law stipulates spending limits for both parties and candidates during elections. A party that stood candidates in all constituencies in Great Britain could spend up to £34 million in the year prior to the 2024 general election.

In this complex context, campaign organisations usually divide the electorate into three broad groups: those who already support their party or candidate, often referred to as the 'base'; those who already support their opponents, or the 'opponents' base'; and those who are undecided, sometimes called 'swing voters'. As decades of voting behaviour research show, most voters do not radically change their minds during a relatively brief campaign, and strategists need to set realistic objectives for what they wish to achieve. In a nutshell, most campaigns' goals are to mobilise their base – ensuring they turn out to vote – and to persuade as many swing voters as possible to turn out and choose their party or candidate (Burton et al. 2015). However, campaigns sometimes also aim more or less explicitly to depress turnout among some groups of voters, by casting doubt on the qualities of other parties and candidates in the hope that their supporters, who are unlikely to switch sides, will decide not to cast their vote.

British parties and candidates rely on a variety of channels to contact voters during elections. Earned news coverage by professional media is a key avenue to reach the public, which is why parties and candidates devise complex strategies to create newsworthy content and attract journalists' attention. Strategies include, for instance, dedicating each day of the campaign to a specific theme, appearing in popular or unconventional settings, staging their appearances so they provide good visuals, speaking in short and catchy 'sound bites' that can be easily packaged into news content, and making controversial statements. However, earned news coverage comes with the disadvantage that political actors do not directly control its content, which, as seen before, can sometimes turn out to be negative for them. Thus, parties and candidates also rely on communication channels that they can control directly, whether by organising the labour of party members and volunteers or by paying for various types of campaign materials and advertisements. In the 2019 general election campaign, 69.7% of the electorate received at least one leaflet from one of the main parties, 22.5% was contacted at home by a canvasser, 7.9% was contacted via social media, 7.8% received an email or text message, 7.5% was approached in the street and 2.6% received a phone call (calculations by the authors based on Fieldhouse et al. 2022).

Personal campaign contacts can be quite helpful to remind people that there is an upcoming election and that they should vote. A study in the United States found that 7% of door-to-door visits by campaign volunteers result in an additional vote – i.e. they lead someone who would not have voted to turn out instead (Green and Gerber 2019). Another study based in the United Kingdom found that party leaflets boost turnout by 4.3% and canvassing has an additional effect of 0.6% (Townsley 2018). Although these numbers may look small, they can be crucial in constituencies where the margin between the two leading candidates is narrow. In the 2024 UK general election, nearly one in five seats (115 out of 650) was won by a margin of 5% or less. By comparison, 67 seats were won by such a margin in 2019, and 97 seats in 2017. (House of Commons Library 2024b).

While personal contacts can stimulate turnout among supporters, parties and candidates rely on advertisements to reach swing voters, some of whom may be open to changing their minds or wavering between two options. In Britain, however, similar to most other Western democracies, campaign advertising has historically been highly regulated. Paid advertising is allowed in newspapers – which, however, have seen a stark decline in their readership – but it is entirely banned on television and radio. Instead, parties are allowed free slots in Party Election Broadcasts (PEBs), which are made available by broadcasters and regulated by OfCom before each election. PEBs are also much longer than both commercial advertisements and political advertisements in the countries where they are commonly employed, such as the United States. Although they are a staple of British politics, PEBs' influence has arguably declined over time, particularly as audiences are migrating from broadcast television to digital media. In the 2019 general election, less than one-tenth of the television viewing audience tuned in for PEBs (Campbell 2019).

The rise of social media has allowed campaigners to experiment with new tools to reach their audiences, and regulation in the UK has so far failed to catch up with these changes. Most social media platforms enable parties, candidates and interest groups to easily place advertisements to target specific groups of voters identified based on location, demographic characteristics or interests manifested through their online activities. Social media also allow campaigns to 'A/B test' their messages, which means that they can assess the effects of different variations of the same message in real time by randomly assigning them to different subsets of their target audience. More troubling is the possibility of segmenting the target audience so precisely, and with messages only seen by very specific groups, that parties can potentially make contradictory promises to different voters without any of them, let alone the broader public, being able to spot the problem. Most importantly, in the UK context, political advertisements on social media are entirely unregulated, which means that parties and candidates can now direct substantial amounts of money to reach voters with the kinds of videos they are forbidden from airing on broadcast television – with the added benefits of the targeting and testing discussed above. Thus, parties' spending on digital advertising went from 24% to 43% of their total campaign budgets between the 2015 and

2017 general elections (Electoral Commission 2022). Although official data on the 2019 and 2024 elections is unavailable at the time of writing, estimates suggest that political spending on online advertisement may have grown by 50% from the previous cycle (2017–2019) (Electoral Reform Society 2020). It is highly likely that it will have grown further in 2024, when the total amount that parties could spend nearly doubled to account for inflation. For instance, news reports suggest that UK parties spent more than one million pounds in online advertisements during the first week of the 2024 General Election campaign (White, 2024), and about the same figure on Election Day of the same election (Waterson, 2024).

Although research on the effects of campaign advertising on social media is still in its infancy, the growth of this area of campaigning poses various normative problems. First, it is likely that it is putting pressure on the costs of running an effective campaign in the UK, which existing regulation was meant to constrain, thus potentially making parties and politicians more dependent on wealthy individuals and organisations for their funding and favouring larger parties and parties that cater to wealthy funders. Second, online political advertising is available not only to parties and candidates running for election, but also to outside groups who are interested in influencing public opinion. These 'non-party campaigners' must register with the Electoral Commission to legally run advertisements and must observe a spending limit of about £500,000 in a general election (Electoral Commission 2022), but they are free to use the same social media advertising tools as the parties and candidates in the election. In 2019, a record 61 of these organisations spent over £6 million, most of which was spent on online advertisements (The Constitution Unit (UCL) 2023). However, reports suggest that a variety of other groups buy advertisements on social media to influence elections, and there is not sufficient transparency on their identity, agenda and funding. From 2023 all campaigners must add 'imprints' showing who produced and paid for all their online materials during and outside elections. However, outside groups can adopt seemingly neutral names, such as 'Mainstream Network' or 'Britain's Future', and can sometimes present themselves as being run by members of the public to hide their connections with parties, interest groups or even foreign countries. One final problem with social media advertisements is that the main social media companies, such as Meta, tend to treat them as protected speech and thus leave them unchecked, even when they contain inaccurate information, contrary to how they treat content by other users (Kreiss and Mcgregor 2019).

Whether election campaigning, and campaigns more broadly, matter for electoral outcomes is a long-debated question in political science. Historically, research has suggested that, although voting intentions recorded by opinion polls, fluctuate during campaigns, most voters do not change their minds as a result of the campaign; rather, campaigns mainly serve to reinforce people's existing convictions and motivate them to turn out at the polls (Brady and Johnston 2006). A large study comprising 49 field experiments, in which researchers randomly assigned voters to being contacted by campaigners or exposed to advertisements to isolate the effects of these messages, showed that, on average, these effects are non-existent (Kalla and Broockman 2018). The authors found that campaign effects may be more likely to materialise when the opponent is unusually unpopular, when extra efforts are dedicated to precisely identifying persuadable voters and, at earlier stages of a campaign, when voters have not fully tuned in and may be more malleable. Still, these early-days effects tend to decay over time, as is the case in general for most political advertising (Hill et al. 2013). However, nowadays more voters than in the past tend to decide who to vote for later in the election (Willocq 2019) and these late-deciders tend to be more open to influence from the campaign (Johann et al. 2018). More broadly, voters have become less attached to specific parties and more open to choosing different options from one election to the next, partly in response to the different leaders, priorities and policies on offer. Electoral volatility, an indicator of change in voting outcomes from one election to the next, grew steadily in Britain from the 1960s to the 1990s, and in every General Election since 1992 more than 20% of voters chose a party they had not voted for in the previous election (Fieldhouse et al. 2023). This volatility provides opportunities for voters to be persuaded by campaigns, or to be convinced to vote when previously they may have abstained.

Although campaigns generally fail to *directly* persuade large numbers of voters, they can sometimes *indirectly* influence voters by shaping their perceptions of the issues the election hinges on. Most voters only consider a few topics when thinking about the election, and their propensity to turn out and to consider voting for different parties varies greatly depending on what these topics are. These priorities, in turn, can be shaped by campaign communication and news coverage of elections, an effect that researchers call *priming* (Iyengar and Kinder 1987). Importantly, different parties are deemed to be more credible in dealing with different problems, a phenomenon known as 'issue ownership' (Petrocik 1996). Issue ownership varies over time, based on parties' performance in government and ability to represent different groups (Green and Jennings 2017), but it is generally stable during a single election campaign. For instance, in the 2019 general election, the three most important issues for voters were Brexit, climate change and health, but when they were asked which party was best able to handle this issue, those who prioritised Brexit were much more likely to choose the Conservatives, while those who prioritised health were evenly split between Conservatives and Labour (calculations by the authors based on Fieldhouse et al. 2022). Because parties' electoral prospects change depending on the issues voters are thinking about at the time of the election, the key goal of most campaigns is not to convince their opponents' supporters to change their minds about which parties, candidates or policies are preferable, or even to convince the public that their party is a credible choice on issues where the electorate doubts its competence. Instead, the aim is to direct the focus of specific groups of voters towards certain topics on which their party or candidate already enjoys an advantage in the eyes of the electorate.

Politics, emotion and advertising

Our voting behaviour is often emotionally and socially driven; voters often vote against their self-interest (Graham et al. 2009). As voters behave in an emotional way, language can be altered to specifically trigger emotions. We respond to stories, metaphor and imagery. We know advertising campaigns use emotive content in traditional political advertising. Brader (2005) found that political adverts that used images and music that were specifically designed to evoke emotions led to observable differences in political behaviour, fear can stimulate a more persuasive state than any other emotion, mirroring public health research which found that fear changes behaviour more effectively. In contrast, Marcus et al. (2000) found that anxious citizens are more attentive and make more reasoned choices, whereas enthusiastic citizens rely on party predispositions. Emotional affect is a reaction to a stimulus which gives individuals energy and intensity and can promote political action. These reactions within a public can be difficult to control. In addition, historically, it has been argued that society should engage in rational intellectual political deliberation rather than be susceptible to emotion (Marcus et al. 2000).

Emotions are recognised as central to social and political life (Marcus 2010), and political decision-making is linked to emotion. Emotion can both encourage or limit participation in politics. Anger and love can be transformational in the political sphere. Social media is design to leverage emotional engagement. Users are likely to stay on a social media site longer, and see more adverts, if a variety of emotions are presented (Chowdhry 2016). Social media users react in an emotional way to posts through emotional affordances such as likes. They present themselves using personal branding and attempt to influence others by sharing content. Individuals may become less civil, and more emotional, within social media than they would be in person (Wahl-Jorgensen 2019).

Emotion serves as a powerful catalyst for political engagement and participation, motivating political action. Political adverts can be used to strategically leverage emotions to enhance political knowledge, reshape opinions and influence behaviour. Physiological arousal energises and enhances political participation (Marcus 2010; Karl 2021). Emotion can be intentionally manipulated to drive political actions and political adverts can be devised to establish connections between personal beliefs and campaign policies, thus employing this emotive framing to create political action (Wahl-Jorgensen 2019).

Digital disruption

The internet has given us the ability to access content, share information and form new connections. The model was created with the expectation of users that content is free at the point of access. The content providers must therefore make their revenue through paid-for advertising. Essentially, as we are not paying for it, we are the product. The specificity of this advertising, to whom and what adverts are shown, is determined by real-time bidding, where an automatic micro-auction occurs to buy each advertising space in front of our eyes. The choice to buy this space and what determines the adverts you see is based on your personal profile. Profiles are built on each of us, defined by our exhibited demographics, internet behaviour and similarity to other users. This is called micro-targeting. Not only is it used to identify the products that we may want to buy; political advertisers also use it to bid for the opportunity to influence your opinion and your vote.

There is a lack of regulation surrounding what is allowable in digital advertising, and regulation on internet activity in general. This is an area that is rapidly evolving; for example, in the UK context the Online Safety Act was published in 2023. It has a strong focus on the protection of children and the removal of illegal content, such as hate crime and sexual exploitation, rather than advertising *per se*. The communications regulator OfCom is now the regulator of online planforms and has the remit, along with the Advertising Standards Agency (ASA), to tackle misleading advertising and adverts that harm or offend their audience. The view on this bill is split. There are discussions on whether the bill damages freedom of speech (Coe 2022) or whether it does not go far enough and have the required legislative teeth (Trengove et al. 2022).

TikTok does not allow political advertising. It can be used in political campaigning, but it is not possible to use paid-for ads to extend the reach of political parties. Many countries have imposed restrictions on the use of TikTok, citing security concerns. In March 2023, the UK prohibited its use on the electronic devices of government ministers and employees. Nevertheless, during the 2024 general election campaign, all the political parties used the app to reach voters, utilising TikTok's performative short video style with content intended to grab people's attention and become viral (Moir 2023). According to Statista (Ceci 2024), TikTok users are generally younger than users of other social media sites, in March 2024, 76% of users were under 24 years of age. It suggest that political parties are engaging with young people in the place where they get their content.

Technology companies from the USA, such as Meta, Alphabet and X (formerly Twitter), are underpinned by Section 230 of the Communication Decency Act (Senate – Commerce, Science, and Transportation 1996). Section 230 states that: 'No provider or user of an interactive computer service shall be treated as the publisher or speaker of any information provided by another information provider.' It means that the technology companies are not treated as publishers of the content that is produced by users and cannot be held legally responsible for content on their sites. For example, when a fan racially abused three members of the England football team on Facebook, after they lost the 2020 European Championship final, it was the fan who was arrested and prosecuted, not Mark Zuckerberg, the owner of Facebook/Meta (*Guardian* 2021). Thus, Zuckerberg is not liable for the content users put on the Facebook site. Section 230 was put in place in 1996, when the internet comprised 258,000 websites, to allow the internet to grow and not to limit the number of content providers. In 1996 blogs had not been invented. By 2018, the internet contained 1.63 billion websites. Public discontent is growing at the lack of responsibility shown by the social media owners over the content put on their sites, but the volume of content produced, the adaptions of those who wish to disseminate manipulative content and the lack of consensus as to what is unacceptable content means that regulation is a not insignificant task and difficult to do in an automated way.

Social media are now an important source of information for the British public. It has been found that exposure to social media information can increase political knowledge, specifically knowing politically relevant facts and improving the identification of party-political positions on issues. This is likely to be a passive, incidental act rather than the result of an active search (Oeldorf-Hirsch 2017; Munger 2021). The effect differs according to the site, and whether it affects political knowledge and/or participation in politics also differs. For example, YouTube was shown to contribute to a reduction in political knowledge (Lee et al. 2022). Research into the effect on voters of political discussion in social media is contradictory, and often a product of research conducted on a specific social media site at a specific time. Studies have shown that politicians rarely talk about policies themselves, and when they do, it can yield lower engagement (Boulianne and Larsson 2023). People in general rarely discuss politics outside an election campaign. When they do engage in online political debate, they tend to be highly motivated, have an axe to grind, they may be younger than average (although not exclusively young), and are more likely to be men (Barberá and Rivero 2015; Jungherr 2016; Cram et al. 2017).

Two of the key concepts in social media studies that are widely debated are echo chambers and polarisation. An echo chamber, in social media, is where your own view is reflected to you in what you encounter without challenge. It can reinforce beliefs and create a false assumption of consensus. Polarisation is when the political conversation and political viewpoints move away from the centre and take increasingly extreme stances. It is seen as an effect of a fragmented news media, whether there is an increasing number of media options, social media algorithms show increasingly more extreme content to retain engagement on their specific platform. These are complex phenomena to study, it is difficult to identify the impact of social media as compared to the offline world, and to provide definitive and longitudinal evidence. Recent studies, undertaken at a very large scale in collaboration with social media giant Meta, found no evidence that Facebook and Instagram content affected polarisation, but they did find that the algorithms do lead to users seeing less content from moderate friends and more content from those who are like-minded, and that in the USA polarisation is much higher in conservative as oppose to liberal circles (González-Bailón et al. 2023; Guess et al. 2023a, 2023b; Nyhan et al. 2023). Furthermore, it has been shown that the echo chamber phenomenon is less prevalent in social media than in face-to-face conversations and on private messaging apps (Vaccari and Valeriani 2021).

Social media can improve political communication, allowing more people to discuss topics and have access to information and debate (Tucker et al. 2018), but political exchanges on social media over time have become increasingly negative and uncivil, which contributes to the rise in affective polarisation. People share information that supports their worldview and often do not check the source of the information. The spread of misinformation has been found to occur at comparable rates to mainstream media news stories (Tucker et al. 2018). There are pockets of the internet and social media which have allowed those with extreme views to find each other and share information. Sharing information and extreme views can confirm those opinions and strengthen individuals' perceptions that those views are correct.

Political communication in social media

In 2004, US presidential candidate Howard Dean said: 'Along comes this campaign to take back the country for ordinary human beings, and the best way you can do that is through the Net. We listen. We pay attention. If I give a speech and the blog people don't like it, next time I change the speech' (Shannon 2007). The quote highlights how political individuals can use social media to disseminate their messages and receive immediate feedback and reaction. Howard Dean shows us how social media was used at a very early stage in its evolution, before many of the platforms we currently know existed. Unfortunately for Dean, despite his early use of social media to craft and frame his message, he was undone when a viral meme – called the Dean Scream – damaged his credibility. During a speech he screamed 'yeah', which was broadcast again and again on news networks and talk shows. The example highlights how hard it is to control and manage one's media image in the digital age; once something is set free it is hard to get back.

Government can interact and communicate with the public in a wide variety of ways: through websites, chat, phones, apps and, increasingly, through social media, blogs, X (formerly Twitter), Facebook and Instagram. Social media promotes direct communication, either person to person or, in a broadcast mode, one to many (Mergel 2017). This type of communication can, of course, go two ways, not just from the government to the citizen but also citizen to government, which makes it more difficult to control and means it requires constant monitoring. Public conversation can be monitored, and can be used to determine public opinion. It provides the capacity to detect a social conversation that was impossible before. It allows real-time access to and input conversations that would have once happened in a way that could not be recorded, such as across garden fences or in the backrooms of pubs. Social media opinion does not equate to public opinion. Often studies are conducted on single platforms, and therefore are unrepresentative, only representing those on the platform studied (Tufekci 2014). It does not represent all viewpoints in the debate, and those with more moderate voices are less likely to post and engage (Neubaum and Kramer 2017). If a topic is being discussed on social media, it does not mean it has salience, as almost any topic that can be thought of will be discussed on social media due to the volume of the content. It does provide a reaction that is immediate and can be used to test and alter political messages. Every social media site has its own specific demographic profile, whether it is TikTok, Snapchat, Instagram, YouTube, Mumsnet or Reddit, and there are others who choose to avoid online political conversation entirely. Any understanding of the public gained from the political social media conversation are partial and can only represent the views of those who use the sites and those who participate in the debate. That said, social media reflects spontaneous, motivated behaviour that is very difficult to study elsewhere. Analysing social media narratives helps us to see where those highly motivated individuals position themselves in relation to the debate, what appears to provoke peaks in motivated activity and what the overall trends are in these vocal and active publics. Politicians pay attention to those who discuss politics on social media, which in turn, to some extent, shapes the conversation (Barberá et al. 2019). It also helps us to explore who sets the agenda and shapes conversations and how effective or ephemeral these narratives are.

In order to engage in political communication with voters, it is advisable for politicians and political parties to go where the people are, to communicate their messages where citizens get their information and have their own conversations. Individuals acquire political beliefs socially, through interactions with family, friends, colleagues and others, a process that is termed political socialisation (Heywood 2019). That circle of friends, for many, now spreads across the digital world. This world and social media do not exist in a vacuum. People often post when they are prompted to by real-world events, including what they see in other media. In turn, social media influences the content that appears in mainstream media, creating a media ecosystem. While citizens interact online in a social manner which may cause political socialisation and influence political beliefs and opinion, political elites and agents interact to obtain influence online and direct or frame the conversation in their favour to influence these beliefs.

Trust is very important. If the voters believe what they read and hear, and if citizens understand governmental decision-making, they are more like to accept it (Myeong and Ahn 2017). Political conversation can either be filtered through another media source or person, or direct, such as hearing a politician at a town hall or rally. This conversation is often filtered by the media. The rise of social media allows governmental actors to speak directly to citizens without the filter of the media. It means that control of the communication sphere has altered, because the political elites have a way to communicate directly with the masses. Individuals and grassroots have also gained access to this communication method. Journalists have adapted and use access to these conversations to create content, and stories are spread using this method. Social media is mainly used in broadcast mode (i.e. in one-to-many communications), to increase public awareness (Mergel 2017). Government transparency is increased as a biproduct. It can also be used to create a sense of community and to share knowledge at a more local level (Myeong and Ahn 2017).

When communication occurs via technological means, the perception of the information is influenced by the attitude individuals have towards the technology they are using. If you hear a message through Facebook, for example, your opinion is influenced by your opinion of Facebook as a medium, and your perception of information technology. The media that are used to spread the message influence how we interact with that message. The design of a social media platform affects what is expressed politically (Stockmann et al. 2020). The way that a social media platform is designed promotes certain communication affordances. There are two main designs for platforms: the town square and the social relationship. X (formerly Twitter) and Weibo are town square platforms; they are optimised for information sharing and therefore encourage political expression. WhatsApp, Facebook and WeChat optimise social connections, which can inhibit political expression. Platforms such as TikTok and Instagram encourage the consumption of images and video, often in a flow of connected messages which may not encourage the in-depth expression of political ideas.

How we choose to receive information alters how we view and trust the government. Publicly observable social media accounts are often used as they allow immediate communication with the public and real-time feedback. They can create a casual and a community feel, promoting trust in the person and empathy for the individual. If social media accounts are not managed 24 hours a day, they can lead to issues of non-communication – not answering comments that are made. When mistakes are made and posts are wrong this is quickly observed by the public. They are also easy to abuse when they are administered by teams, as many people will have access to passwords which mean they can login and post content, these passwords can be shared beyond the team allowing the accounts to be hacked and used by those not autorised. Mistakes can cause an impact that is impossible to remove. For example, on 24 May 2020, when Prime Minister Boris Johnson had backed his Chief of Staff Dominic Cummings in the latter's decision to travel to Durham during the Covid-19 lockdown, the Civil Service official Twitter account posted 'Arrogant and offensive. Can you imagine having to work with these truth twisters?' The post was quickly removed, but screen shots were taken and it is still often re-posted. We can reflect on the example presented earlier in the chapter, of the use of the publicly observable account of the Conservative Campaign Headquarters, which had been rebranded to impersonate a fact-checking organisation during the televised election debates in the 2019 general election campaign. It exemplifies how the flexibility of the medium allows political social media accounts to be presented in different ways for different objectives.

Brexit and the media frame

In the 2016 referendum on whether or not to leave the European Union, the Leave campaign had an issue in the debate, Brexit represented a change from the status quo, and a change is a risk because it is unknown. The term 'project fear' was first coined in the 2014 Scottish independence referendum, where it was adopted by those arguing for the Union. It was used again in the Brexit referendum by those who presented change as an economic risk. The 2015 Eurobarometer demonstrated that the British people knew less about the EU than any other member state (Hix 2015). It seemed that the EU was not an important issue to British voters. Economist/Ipsos Mori 2015 issue index found that 13% of respondents thought that Europe was the most important issue facing Britain (Ipsos 2015).

In 1978, during the Winter of Discontent, the Labour Party politician Denis Healey described political advertising as 'selling politics like soap-powder'. This was a response to a Conservative Party advertisement produced by Saatchi & Saatchi that showed a queue of people under the words 'unemployment office' and the phrase 'Labour isn't working'. The Labour Party were in power, and the upcoming election was likely to be fought on issues such as unemployment and the economy. Healey's argument was that those in the queue were not genuinely unemployed, as the advert presented. Healey's intervention and statement to the House of Commons ensured that the ad received more newspaper coverage and was more widely discussed. Saatchi & Saatchi stated that their role was to bring professionalisation to political communication. In 1979, the Conservative Party, led by Margaret Thatcher, won the general election. She had identified the need to apply a marketing approach to her version of the Conservative Party product. Policy was developed to appeal to voters and focus groups were used to see how voters responded to the presentation of ideas (Lees-Marshment 2001). The tactic has arguably impacted on the media strategy of politicians ever since.

In political communication, how you say something is important, not just what you are saying. Media campaigners want to define what the parameters of the debate are, to define what the important issues are and what should be discussed, and thereby shape the arguments in a way that presents a debate that will convince voters. There is an effort to present a dominant frame, which defines how information is to be communicated within a debate and what the parameters of that debate are. The Overton window is a way of describing political policies that are acceptable for debate. Political policies that fall within the window can be said to be acceptable, sensible or popular. These frames can influence citizens' confidence and trust in the ability of governments to enact policy (Kolpinskaya et al. 2019). Within a media frame, aspects of reality are selected and the frame projects what is important or salient. It can be used in debate to promote a problem, encourage a judgement and to recommend a solution (Entman 1993). The communications often contain and repeat keywords, stock phrases and stereotypes to increase this memorability.

To create content and increase engagement, social media campaigns encourage reaction to real-world events. These can be political events, such as debates or rallies, or they can be a response to news events or TV shows that discuss political topics. Journalists often use public reactions on social media to cover events. Politicians use social media to promote themselves and engage with the electorate. Often this is not to discuss key issues, but rather to react to what is happening in the world or to encourage participation in upcoming events.

Whilst leaving the EU was not an important issue to British voters in 2015 it was a topic of discussion within the Conservative Party. David Cameron wanted his party to 'stop banging on about Europe' and so committed to holding a referendum on membership of the European Union in the 2015 election manifesto (Bale 2023). There were three vocal groups during the campaign: two Leave groups called Vote Leave and Leave.EU, and the Remain group, Britain Stronger in Europe. The Vote Leave campaign wanted to frame the Brexit debate as a fight for sovereignty, as 'the voice of the people'. It framed the campaign as an antagonistic representation of the UK as 'us' and the EU as 'them'. It presented the debate as a crisis in immigration, sovereignty, the economy and public services. Brexit was framed around control of the four pillars of British freedoms: Trade (Global Britain), Laws (the European Court of Justice), Borders (Migration) and Money. It was framed as a move from ever-increasing integration and the supranational path of the EU towards a UK national path. It was framed as a rejection of the global elite, globalisation, neoliberalism and austerity. In this way, Vote Leave was able to present staying in the EU as a crisis.

The Leave campaign had a strong grassroots presence that dominated within social media from the start. Those who post political content on social media are generally highly motivated and feel their voices are not reflected in more mainstream media. The populist message motivated those who do not normally vote and felt unheard by the political system. Vote Leave presented a campaign that was well suited to social media. The Leave campaign was better able to control the frame and set the agenda (Usherwood and Wright 2017). Digital activism has a lower bar for inclusion, groups are loosely connected, and social media allows the exchange of ideas, opinions and associated content. During the EU referendum, much of the discussion was not about the EU, but about British sovereignty and globalisation. Social media allowed the expression of political opinion and enabled an active public, which was directed by campaigners. It has since been identified that pro-Brexit entrepreneurs were active in the debate, and that content that appeared to be posted by grassroots activists was in fact 'astroturf' content (Brändle et al. 2020), meaning this was fake grassroots content.

The Remain campaign, Britain Stronger in Europe, focused on controlling the mainstream media message rather than the social media space. It spent much of the campaign reacting to and trying to discredit the arguments produced by the Leave campaign. It used a variety of messages rather than a consistent, crafted message. While the Remain campaign used experts to provide evidence, the Leave campaign discredited those experts as being self-interested. Vote Leave was able to test out its arguments in social media and use social media's propensity for supporting reaction to provocations (Usherwood and Wright 2017). The Leave campaign comprised two campaign groups, which were able to give two different messages and target different groups of voters. The Leave campaign was more visible in social media throughout the campaign. The voters shared an anti-establishment position which motivated those who did not normally engage in political debate or vote (Llewellyn and Cram 2016).

Case Study 17.1

Disinformation in the Brexit referendum

One of the stand-out controversies of the referendum to leave the European Union was the message on the side of the Leave campaign bus that said, 'We send the EU £350 million a week let's fund our NHS instead Vote Leave'. Is this statement true?

The UK Office for National Statistics found the claim to be a 'clear misuse of official statistics', but can we say that it was fake news? 'Fake news' is a contested term and very hard to define. It has been used by right-wing populists to discredit professional news organisations. 'Fake news' comprises intentionally and unintentionally incorrect rumours and unsubstantiated information, and information that is designed to give a biased impression (Tucker et al. 2018). 'Disinformation' is where the intention of the information is to mislead. There are many reasons why disinformation is used, including to get clicks, to generate traffic and to sell things. We do not have the capacity to fact-check everything that we come across on the internet, so the strategy has the capacity to change our perceptions. If we see something often enough, it becomes background information and is almost true by assumption. This is known as the 'wall-paper effect'.

The £350 million claim was first made on Twitter by the Vote Leave campaign account on 11 October 2015. The claim had already been fact-checked by Channel 4 on 9 October 2015 and found to be inaccurate. But, in a study conducted by King's College shortly before the referendum, it was found that 42% of people who had seen the claim still believed it to be true (Duffy 2018).

Figure 17.3   Tweet from the Vote Leave campaign

Vote Leave was particularly effective in its use of social media, and it had more support across multiple platforms. The symbolic importance of the NHS means that it acts as a *de facto* national emblem, likely creating an amplifying effect and increasing the impact of the £350 million claim that

(Continued)

was disproportionate to its quantitative release. It is likely that the bus itself, and the wider media coverage of this issue, perpetuated the message, and once the claim had been set free it needed very little pushing on social media from the campaign itself. Efforts to debunk the claim backfired. In fact, the Britain Stronger in Europe campaign tweeted more often about the £350 million claim in its debunking effort than did Vote Leave in making the claim, and it was repeatedly referenced by Remain supporters in public debates. This may have been counterproductive; it has been suggested that repeating a false claim can actually increase its credibility even when it is being debunked (Schwarz et al. 2007). The Vote Leave campaign had a more efficient social media machine, reaching out into wider networks. Once released, this very potent message, harnessed to a highly salient national symbol, was kept alive through wider network spread and ultimately became a large part of the collective social media conversation.

Changing people minds is difficult. Moore, Hong and Cram (2021) undertook a study to examine the level of cognition involved in the acceptance or rejection of misinformation. They rated participants' beliefs and feelings about Brexit tweets while the participants were in a brain scanner. They found that people look for a reason not to update their worldview and identify specific content and sources that support their opinion. This is not reasoning, which is hard work for the brain; rather, it is reaction, which is not. Therefore, it is harder for our brain to consider information that is incompatible with our current worldview.

Reflective questions

1   How do you define disinformation? Was the £350 million statement an example of disinformation?
2   What can be done to limit our susceptibility to disinformation? How should the Remain camp have engaged with this debate?
3   How does your brain engage with information that is incompatible with your worldview?

Research in Focus

Active measures

In 2017, Twitter released a list of accounts to the US Senate that they believed were involved in Russian State manipulation of the 2016 US presidential election. They were believed to be from the Internet Research Agency, a known Russian 'troll factory'. In this case, trolls are humans who are employed to create content and manipulate opinion by spreading rumours, speculation and false information.

Active measures are approaches taken by Russian espionage and security agencies (Allen and Moore 2018). The aim is to spread disruptive information and to promote a feeling of instability and uncertainty. Trolls, hired trolls, bots, cyborgs, fake news websites, conspiracy theorists, politicians, media outlets and governments produce and amplify disinformation, many unwittingly. Those who do so intentionally use bots – accounts that are set up to automatically aggregate and re-publish content or to generate text – and hired trolls and cyborgs – accounts that exhibit both bot and troll behaviour. 'Astroturfers' are fake grassroots accounts, 'sock puppets' are false online personae and 'sleeper accounts' are accounts that discuss content that is currently useful but that can be activated at a later point to push a specific point of view.

These accounts amplify content, driving attention to present a false opinion or groundswell of opinion behind a cause. A 'Bot-legion' or 'Bot-swarm' is a large increase in activity by bots on a specific subject in a short time frame. It can lead to an 'amplification cascade', when a large amount of activity influences trending topics, being spread by non-bot accounts and being seen in multiple places. When we see ideas or opinions presented multiple times, it can lead to the 'wallpaper effect', discussed earlier, where information that is seen often is assumed to be true. The information in amplification cascades can be picked up by the media and presented as truth (M.O. Jones 2019).

The Russian troll accounts use a scatter-gun disinformation strategy that aim to disrupt and disorientate foreign regimes and to create a widespread sense of chaos and instability (White 2016). The attacks align with the foreign policy aims of the Kremlin. The list of accounts presented to the US Senate in 2017 were clearly designed to target the US election as most of the accounts masqueraded as US citizens. There was a suggestion of a wider strategy, because some of the accounts were fake German and Italian profiles.

There is also evidence of Brexit-related activity in the accounts (Llewellyn et al. 2019) because on the day of the Brexit referendum vote, there was a sharp increase in activity. The accounts were identified because of their tweeting about the US 2016 election, but there may be other Brexit-specific troll accounts that targeted the referendum that were never discovered. Why do these accounts take on a fake persona? Why do they look like the accounts of the people they are trying to influence? Because we are more likely to believe people whom we think are like us. As these accounts become part of existing networks and friendship groups, they can shift opinions from within.

Summary

- The most important sources of news for British citizens are the internet and social media, television and newspapers. The role of digital media has increased substantially over time, while print newspapers have seen their importance drastically decline. The BBC, a Public Service Media organisation, is the most used and trusted news organisation in the UK.
- UK broadcasters have to abide by strict regulations that ensure fairness in how they discuss public affairs, and so their news coverage of politics tends to be relatively balanced and impartial. By contrast, regulation of newspapers is minimal and their political coverage is more likely to implicitly or explicitly support specific parties and leaders.
- Election campaigns in the UK are relatively short and regulated by spending limits and the prohibition of paid-for televised advertising. Parties rely on different channels to persuade undecided voters and to mobilise their supporters, such as earned news media coverage, personal contacts by canvassers and advertising on social media, whose relevance has greatly increased over the past decade.
- In spite of all efforts by parties and candidates, most voters do not directly change their minds as a result of campaign communications. However, persuading a minority of undecided voters can sometimes be decisive in marginal constituencies, and voters have become more detached from parties over the past two decades, which has resulted in greater potential for electoral change as a result of campaigns.

- Emotion serves as a powerful catalyst for political engagement and participation, motivating political action. Political adverts can strategically leverage emotions to enhance political knowledge, reshape opinions and influence behaviour.
- Social media are now an important source of information for the British public. It has been found that exposure to social media information can increase political knowledge, specifically knowing politically relevant facts and improving the identification of a party-political stance on issues.
- Politicians pay attention to those who discuss politics on social media and to some extent shape this conversation. Social media allows them to speak directly to citizens without the filter of journalists. Individuals, grassroots activist groups and journalists have adapted to this medium, creating content, having conversations and gaining access to digital political influence.

Recommended and further reading

- Blumler, J.G. and Coleman, S. (2010) 'Political communication in freefall: The British case – and others?', *The International Journal of Press/Politics*, 15(2): 139–154. This paper is a thorough, critical assessment of key issues in contemporary media–politics relations in the UK.
- Chadwick, A., Vaccari, C. and O'Loughlin, B. (2018) 'Do tabloids poison the well of social media? Explaining democratically dysfunctional news sharing', *New Media & Society*, 20(11): 4255–4274. This article is a study of how disinformation in the UK flows from traditional to social media.
- Chadwick, A. (2017) *The Hybrid Media System: Politics and Power*. Oxford: Oxford University Press. This book offers a wide-ranging perspective on the key features of contemporary media systems.
- Dommett, K., Barclay, A. and Gibson, R. (2024) 'Just what is data-driven campaigning? A systematic review', *Information, Communication & Society*, 27: 1–22. This article provides a critical analysis of contemporary debates about the use of data in campaigns.
- Gaber, I. and Fisher, C. (2022) '"Strategic lying": The case of Brexit and the 2019 UK election', *The International Journal of Press/Politics*, 27: 460–477. This paper provides a critical analysis of the role of British political actors in spreading disinformation.
- Langer, A.I. and Gruber, J.B. (2021) 'Political agenda setting in the hybrid media system: Why legacy media still matter a great deal', *The International Journal of Press/Politics*, 26(2): 313–340. This article is a study of how different media contribute to setting the agenda of most important topics in the UK.
- Miller, M.L. and Vaccari, C. (2020) 'Digital threats to democracy: Comparative lessons and possible remedies', *The International Journal of Press/Politics*, 25(3): 333–356. This paper provides an overview of the key threats democracies face in the digital age.
- Persily, N., Tucker, J.A. and Tucker, J.A. (eds) (2020) *Social Media and Democracy: The State of the Field, Prospects for Reform*. Cambridge: Cambridge University Press. This book comprises a comprehensive collection of essays summarising the latest academic evidence on social media and democracy. It is available as open access via the publisher's website.

- Reuters Institute for the Study of Journalism (2024) *Reuters Digital News Report 2024*. Available at www.digitalnewsreport.org/. This one provides a comprehensive source of data on how citizens across the world get their news, and is updated every year.
- Van Aelst, P., Strömbäck, J., Aalberg, T., Esser, F., De Vreese, C., Matthes, J. ... and Stanyer, J. (2017) 'Political communication in a high-choice media environment: A challenge for democracy?', *Annals of the International Communication Association*, 41(1): 3–27. This article comprises a review of the state of the art of what we know about the key challenges contemporary media pose for democracy.
- Vaccari, C. and Valeriani, A. (2021) *Outside the Bubble: Social Media and Political Participation in Western Democracies*. Oxford: Oxford University Press. This book is a nine-country comparative analysis of how social media may enable citizens to engage with politics.
- Wring, D., Mortimore, R. and Atkinson, S. (eds) (2021) *Political Communication in Britain: Campaigning, Media and Polling in the 2019 General Election*. Berlin: Springer Nature. This book is a comprehensive collection of essays on the state of election campaigns in the UK.

Chapter 18

Brexit and beyond

Benjamin Martill

What will this chapter tell me?

- The UK's membership of the European Economic Community (EEC) and the European Union (EU) from 1973 to 2020 was notable for the UK's opposition to increasing supranational control, but also for its support of important initiatives, such as the Single Market Programme and the Common Security and Defence Policy (CSDP).
- Euroscepticism was initially a more powerful force on the left, but this changed during the 1990s, leading to growing opposition to the UK's EU membership in the Conservative Party.
- David Cameron's government promised an in/out referendum on UK membership if a majority Conservative government was elected, and when this happened in May 2015, Cameron renegotiated the terms of UK membership and put the agreement to a referendum, which he lost.
- Theresa May made the delivery of Brexit the cornerstone of her government but boxed herself in with strict 'red lines' which precluded many outcomes and failed to find sufficient support in Parliament to pass her agreement.
- Boris Johnson passed a revised Withdrawal Agreement with new arrangements for Northern Ireland in January 2020, after which the UK left the EU and entered a 'transition period' to allow for the negotiation of the Trade and Cooperation Agreement (TCA), ratified in December 2020.
- The UK–EU relationship declined precipitously after the Johnson government unilaterally opted not to introduce the required checks between Northern Ireland and the rest of the UK.
- The relationship gradually improved after the Russian invasion of Ukraine in February 2022 and the departure of Johnson in July of that year, with Rishi Sunak's negotiation of the Windsor Framework solving many of the disagreements in the Northern Ireland Protocol.

What do I need to know?

- The UK became a member of the European Economic Community (today's EU) in January 1973.
- David Cameron pledged an in/out referendum on UK membership in his Bloomberg Speech in January 2013.
- UK citizens voted by 51.9% on 23 June 2016 to leave the EU.
- Theresa May failed to pass the UK–EU Withdrawal Agreement on three occasions in early 2019.
- Boris Johnson passed a renegotiated Withdrawal Agreement in January 2020 and undertook negotiation of the Trade and Cooperation Agreement (TCA).

Introduction

On 31 January 2020 the United Kingdom (UK) left the European Union (EU), an organisation it had been a member of for just over 47 years, implementing the mandate established by the Leave vote on 23 June 2016. Formal withdrawal followed ratification of the Withdrawal Agreement, marking the end of a tortuous process of negotiations on the terms of exit, and was followed by a transition period until the end of 2020, during which the UK negotiated the Trade and Cooperation Agreement (TCA) covering the future relationship. The UK's exit – known colloquially as 'Brexit' – reflected deeper changes in UK politics since the 1970s as well as more proximate political developments in the years prior to the referendum. Brexit would also have seismic consequences for the UK politically, socially, economically and constitutionally, and would shape the process of European integration in important ways. For these reasons, no account of British or European politics in recent years can afford not to take seriously the processes reflected in – and set in train by – the referendum vote.

Brexit has received considerable scholarly attention, with hundreds of volumes in publication and doubtless hundreds more to come. This reflects not only the salience of Brexit and the level of interest globally in the UK's withdrawal, but also the impact of withdrawal itself, which left almost no stone unturned. Because the UK's EU ties had deepened over the decades, and because both sides believed Brexit had to bring about significant changes, no area of the UK polity or economy was left untouched by withdrawal. The breadth of coverage of existing research calls for selectivity in coverage for any introduction to the topic. This chapter offers an overview of Brexit and how it has affected British politics in the years since the referendum. It charts the UK's historical relationship with European integration before looking at the origins of the referendum pledge and the various factors influencing the Leave vote in June 2016. The chapter then follows the course of events as the UK prepared for withdrawal, negotiated (and then renegotiated) the Withdrawal Agreement, and concluded the talks on the TCA.

By the end up this chapter, you will understand the origins of European integration in Europe and the UK's place within this process both before and after accession. You will be able to identify some of the key dynamics which led David Cameron to commit to an in/out referendum on Britain's EU membership and you will come to know what the issues in the campaign were and which of the (many) factors ultimately contributed to the Leave victory. You will also understand how the UK government prepared to deliver Brexit and how it approached the negotiations, as well as the reasons why the UK approach did not live up to the expectations of many Brexit supporters. Finally, you will develop an understanding of the ways in which the politics of the negotiations came to shape the withdrawal process and how this subsequently brought about a harder Brexit outcome than many observers had initially anticipated.

The United Kingdom and European integration

European integration refers to the process through which the countries of (initially) Western Europe have agreed to pool their sovereignty in key areas since the 1950s, establishing in the process a highly centralised regional organisation – today's EU – to which they have delegated certain policy competencies. European integration has its origins in the late 1940s and early 1950s when priorities on the continent were focused on the simultaneous tasks of cementing peace on the continent, reconstructing the economy and constructing a bulwark against Soviet encroachment in Western Europe. By integrating economically, first through the European Coal and Steel Community (ECSC) in 1952 and then, more comprehensively, through the European Economic Community (EEC) in 1958, the original six countries party to European integration hoped to make war unthinkable between European countries while building up a stronger economic base in core industries.

The UK stood on the sidelines as these efforts played out, supportive of integration – Churchill famously argued in 1946 for a 'United States of Europe' – but not of the belief it was in the UK's best interests to join. The fact that most of the UK's trade at the time was concentrated within the Commonwealth was one of the main reasons given. Identity mattered too, especially the fact that the UK saw itself as a victor of the Second World War, lacking both the insecurities of states that had been occupied (like France) or the need for a new sense of self (like Germany). But changes in the international system – and the UK's place within it – in the 1950s and 1960s served to alter the calculus of British leaders *vis-à-vis* European integration. As the pace of decolonisation increased, trade became less focused on the UK's colonial ties, as newly independent states sought to diversify their international trade. The UK's material decline continued, with frequent balance-of-payments crises, such that the UK struggled to maintain its global credentials. The Suez Crisis of 1956, and the UK's humiliating climbdown in the face of US pressure, highlighted the limitations of unilateral action in a world dominated by continental superpowers, such as the USA and the USSR. Meanwhile, the continental European economies were growing rapidly, in part owing to their membership of the Common Market, while the UK's less centralised alternative – the European Free Trade Association (EFTA) – failed to bring about any such economic renaissance.

In the face of these trends, a cross-party consensus emerged regarding the value of British EEC accession, with the first application made by Conservative Prime Minister Harold Macmillan in 1963. The application was vetoed by French President Charles de Gaulle on the basis that British accession would be a 'Trojan horse' for American influence in the organisation. A subsequent application under Labour Prime Minister Harold Wilson in 1967 was also rejected by De Gaulle, and it was not until the President was ousted from power following the 1968 student protests in France that a more moderate government under Georges Pompidou consented to British accession after coming to power in 1969. The UK would thus accede to the EEC on 1 January 1973 under the premiership of the Conservative Ted Heath, albeit without having been present at the creation, and thus joining an organisation it had had little influence in the design of. While this was deemed the price of joining at the time, the UK's lack of influence over the project it had joined would create problems not just further down the line, but right from the get-go.

The first challenge to the UK's place in Europe came with the first change of government. When Harold Wilson returned to power in the February 1974 election, he committed to renegotiating the terms of the UK's membership and putting these to a referendum, which took place on 5 June 1975. Wilson styled himself as a leftist candidate in the party, and with high levels of Euroscepticism on the Labour left, criticism of Heath's European policy was an easy win while Labour was in opposition. The renegotiation was a success, partly because many of the UK's asks concerned distributional issues – i.e. monies the UK was owed – and partly because many of the identified problems were rectified in the meantime (Evans 2018). In the ensuing referendum, the Yes campaign backed continued membership on the basis it would bolster the UK's influence in the world, reduce the price of consumer goods and grow the economy, while the No campaign argued that membership detracted from the Commonwealth, promoted damaging subsidies and undermined British identity (Saunders 2018; Martill and Rogstad 2019). With the leadership of both parties and the majority of the press supporting Yes, the margin of victory was 67% in favour of staying in on a turnout of 64%, albeit with considerable territorial differentiation, with 58% Yes support in Scotland, 65% in Wales and 52% in Northern Ireland. Politically, the greatest share of Euroscepticism was to be found in the Labour Party and among nationalist movements, giving much of the 'No' campaign a leftist tinge.

The 1975 referendum cemented the elite consensus on European integration for the best part of two decades, although it fed into the narrative that the UK was an awkward partner (e.g. George 1990), as did the subsequent fight over the rebate by Margaret Thatcher at the Fontaine-bleau Summit in June 1984. Thatcher was successful in negotiating a rebate of 66% of the UK's contribution above its receipts, an undertaking which fed into political folklore regarding UK hard bargaining and Thatcher's own Euroscepticism (Martill and Staiger 2021). Thatcher's public airing of a more Eurosceptic line, associated with her 1988 Bruges speech, where she warned of the threat to UK sovereignty, reinforced this image. Thatcher had supported the Yes campaign in 1975 and was broadly supportive of the Single European Market, but not the extension of supranational control adopted for its implementation. The UK's ostensible awkwardness was also traced to similar critiques of the supranational elements of integration – such as direct elections to the European Parliament – and Britain's opposition to developments in EU foreign and security policy that might challenge the primacy of the Atlantic alliance (Ostermann 2015). It also came to be associated with the UK's practice, from the 1990s, of seeking opt-outs from particular aspects of integration, such as the euro and the Social Chapter in 1992, the Schengen acquis in 1997, and the Charter of Fundamental Rights and the Area of Freedom, Security and Justice in 2009 (Adler-Nissen 2014; Leruth et al. 2019; Martill 2021b).

Yet the UK's awkwardness was often overstated and likely persisted as a reputation because it was useful both to the other European member states, which could rely on the UK vetoing contentious proposals before they were forced to show their hand, and for UK elites keen to cultivate a reputation for taking the fight to Europe. In fact, the UK not only had an exemplary record on the implementation of EU directives and compliance with EU rules, but was well regarded in the club for its high regulatory standards and its constructive diplomatic activities. Popular depictions of the UK also underestimated its influence as one of the 'big three', able to get its way most of the time on issues it cared about. Indeed, the Single European Market programme of the late 1980s, the enlargement of the EU into Central and Eastern Europe, and the inception of the Common Security and Defence Policy (CSDP) in 1999 were all in part a product of British preferences and power, ironically helping to bring about many initiatives which would later become targets of the Leave campaign.

The UK's membership of the EEC/EU never translated into high levels of public identification with Europe, since the justification to accede was principally a pragmatic one, rather than any expression of a new 'European' future. Coupled with the failure of UK elites to justify the benefits of membership to the wider public, the resulting division between elite-level engagement and public apathy would make EU membership vulnerable to populist mobilisation strategies later on. Broader changes in the 1990s did not help the situation. The decline of traditional leftist parties post-Cold War ushered in an era of unprecedented globalisation and marketisation, which would concentrate wealth in the hands of the many, leaving others relatively worse off (Bickerton et al. 2015). State–society relations in this context began to fray, unmooring constituencies from implicit support for European integration and contributing to greater opposition to the European project (Hooghe and Marks 2009). The result was the decline of the 'permissive consensus', which had characterised questions of legitimacy in the EEC/EU for decades, and increasing politicisation of the European project (e.g. Follesdal and Hix 2006; Sternberg 2013).

The Maastricht Treaty, signed in 1992, proved a landmark moment for Conservative Euroscepticism, even though the UK did well out of Maastricht. As a powerful member state with a status quo bias, it secured opt-outs from the euro and the Social Chapter as the price of supporting the Treaty. Yet the rejection of the Treaty by Denmark led to calls from Thatcherite opponents that

John Major had not obtained enough concessions, forcing the Prime Minister to rely on a confidence motion in Parliament to ensure the Treaty's passage (Huber 1996). Maastricht not only crystallised the opposition of 'Thatcher's children' to European integration (Fontana and Parsons 2015), but also birthed proto-Eurosceptic organisations, such as the Anti-Federalist League, which would later become the UK Independence Party (UKIP). Maastricht was not a centralised power grab, as it is sometimes portrayed as. Member states wanted to cooperate in these new fields, in many cases precisely to halt centralisation via the Commission (Bickerton et al. 2015). But integration in new policy areas brought EU activities into domains that were closer to the heart of national sovereignty, such as defence and monetary policy, and where the potential for distributive conflicts was much higher (e.g. Hix 2018; Thompson 2017).

The referendum pledge

Conservative Euroscepticism festered in opposition after the May 1997 general election. With memories of Maastricht fresh in the minds of many MPs and with no engagement through EU structures as the party would have had in opposition, negative caricatures of the EU had little contact with the realities of day-to-day European politics. Labour's more pro-European position also helped make the EU a political issue. Even though Labour was pragmatically opposed to eurozone membership, this did not prevent the Conservatives fighting the 2001 general election on a 'Keep the Pound' platform. David Cameron was viewed as a moderate when elected leader in December 2005, but his campaign bore Eurosceptic elements too, notably his commitment to withdraw the Conservatives from the European People's Party (EPP) grouping in the European Parliament. In government with the Liberal Democrats, opposition to Europe in the Conservatives continued to mount, partially enabled by the government's ability to blame any diminution in its own Euroscepticism on its more Europhile coalition partners.

On 23 January 2013, in his Bloomberg speech, Cameron committed to the fateful in/out referendum that would come to define his premiership, announcing that he would seek to renegotiate the UK's membership of the EU if a majority Conservative government was elected in 2015. The renegotiated deal would be put to the British people in the form of an in/out referendum on EU membership. The renegotiation/referendum combination was designed as a form of hand-tying. By making the prospect of UK exit credible, Cameron hoped to obtain concessions from the EU – now fearful of the damage of a potential Brexit – he would not have been otherwise able to obtain. In turn, these concessions could then be used as the basis on which to win the subsequent referendum, thereby – it was hoped – removing the risk of Euroscepticism tearing the Conservatives apart. Because the referendum needed to be credible, and because Cameron wanted to avoid any impression that he was tipping the scales, he agreed to the pledge being enshrined in law and rejected franchise extensions for 16-year-olds and EU citizens, which might have influenced the outcome.

Several factors were responsible for Cameron's decision to commit to a referendum. One was Cameron's desire to put Tory factionalism to rest and get the party to – in his words – stop 'banging on about Europe', given the extent to which factionalism was undermining party cohesion and the ability to govern (Copsey and Haughton 2014). Linked to this was a belief that the mandate for UK membership, established in the 1975 referendum, was now wearing thin, such that an entire generation had not had their say over membership of a now very different Europe (Cameron 2019: 408). Another factor was the rise of UKIP and the threat its electoral success could pose to marginal Conservative seats. Even though UKIP's major success would be in the May 2014 European Parliament elections, it was assumed that the party could drain sufficient Tory support in marginal seats for Labour to sneak in. Another factor was Cameron's desire to place the UK's membership of the EU on more secure footing, to preclude the risk that the City of London might be threatened by the interests of the eurozone (Cameron 2019: 400), and to shift Europe in the direction of greater competitiveness and greater respect for national sovereignty (Martill 2022).

The Conservatives obtained a majority in the May 2015 general election, bringing about the first single-party Conservative government since 1997. The win came as a surprise, raising the question of whether Cameron had ever expected he would have to honour the promise of a referendum. Nonetheless, Cameron's victory triggered his pledge and fired the starting gun on the task of renegotiating the UK's existing relationship, which was formally launched in June 2015. European leaders reacted poorly to Cameron's approach, dealing as they were with the fallout from the 2014 annexation of Crimea, and disbelieving of the need for reform given the performance of the UK economy. Nevertheless, they engaged constructively to see what could be offered. For pragmatic reasons, Cameron kept his cards close to his chest, refusing to detail in advance what he was asking for so that he could tailor his demands to what the EU was prepared to offer (Kroll and Leuffen 2016). In his letter to European Council President Donald Tusk, Cameron (2015) outlined four 'baskets' of reforms: (1) economic governance, (2) increased competitiveness, (3) sovereignty and (4) migration (see Table 18.1). The final agreement, regarded as generous by insiders, introduced an 'emergency brake'

Table 18.1   Cameron's baskets of demands and the outcomes in the renegotiation

Basket	Aims	Outcomes
Economic governance	No discrimination between eurozone and non-eurozone members	Recognition EU has more than one currency
	Eurozone changes (e.g. Banking Union) should be voluntary for non-eurozone members	Commitment to non-discrimination for non-eurozone members
	Taxpayers in non-eurozone countries should not be liable for bailouts	Non-eurozone countries will not be responsible for bailouts
Increased competitiveness	Long-term commitment to boost competitiveness and productivity	Commitment to increased competitiveness and reduced regulatory burden
	Reduction of the burden of new regulations on business	
Sovereignty	Opt-out from the commitment to 'ever closer union' for the UK	UK is not committed to 'ever closer union'
	Enhanced role for national parliaments in EU decision-making	'Red card' system allowing a majority of national parliaments to overturn EU legislation
Migration	Reducing the flow of citizens into the UK	'Alert and safeguard' system to limit in-work benefits in emergency situations for four years (the 'emergency brake')
	Limits to free movement rights for new member states	
	Greater restrictions on in-work benefits	Child benefits indexed to the country where the child resides for new migrants

for countries facing unprecedented levels of migration, exempted the UK from 'ever closer union', a commitment to improved competitiveness in services, and introduced a 'red card' for national parliaments (Smith 2016). But it stopped short of affording Parliament a veto over the EU policymaking process or curbing the rights of EU citizens to free movement (Kroll and Leuffen 2016; Smith 2016).

Cameron's deal was viewed by the right-wing press and many Eurosceptics as a poor outcome (e.g. Hannan 2016b), and it did not figure much in the referendum campaign itself, although the government's own pamphlet – sent to every household – mounted a defence of the renegotiated agreement (HM Government 2016). The broader Remain campaign, comprising the official 'Britain Stronger In Europe' organisation alongside a multitude of party affiliated groupings, emphasised the threat of Brexit for jobs and the economy, the risk of rising prices, the threat to security and the risk of diminished status in the world (e.g. Menon and Salter 2016: 1307–1308; Rogstad and Martill 2022). The campaign was hampered by infighting and poor campaigning as well as the difficulty of articulating a positive message in defence of the status quo (Cameron 2019: 669). Such perceived negativity of the consequences of Brexit, seen in Figure 18.1, led to portrayals of the Remain campaign as 'Project Fear'. Cameron's ability to sell UK membership of the EU was undermined by his need to change gear after complaining about the Union, his inability to begin campaigning until after the renegotiation was in-hand, and the subtleties of selling a 'reformed EU' (Cameron 2019: 648).

Figure 18.1 A Liberal Democrat poster warning voters that leaving the EU would threaten jobs in the UK. Such scaremongering tactics lead the Remain campaign to be dubbed 'Project Fear'

Source: Liberal Democrats (2016)

The Leave campaign comprised the official Vote Leave campaign, Arron Banks' Leave.EU outfit, Nigel Farage's UKIP and cadres of Leave supporters from the mainstream parties (e.g. 'Conservatives for the UK', 'Green Leaves', 'Labour Leave'). The campaign claimed that the EU was undemocratic, that the nature of the EU had changed since the UK joined, that it was uncompetitive, that it cost UK citizens too much, and that it diminished the UK's role in the world (Menon and Salter 2016: 1310). By making an issue of the UK's contribution to the EU budget, itself dwarfed by the economic benefits of membership, the Leave campaign claimed withdrawal would bring about a windfall that could be spent on other areas, such as fixing pot-holes and – infamously – building new hospitals. The campaign benefited from the support of well-placed figures in the Tory Party, such as Boris Johnson and Michael Gove, who gave it credibility, as well as from the catchy slogans like 'take back control', which resonated with citizens (Menon and Salter 2016: 1310). More cynically, perhaps, it also benefited from deliberate misrepresentations of the EU itself (especially as regards enlargement, borders and the budget) (e.g. Mihai 2022) and from making promises based on overly optimistic readings of what Brexit would look like in practice (Glencross 2023). Observers accused Leave materials of 'dog whistle' racism through subtle emphases on migration, as seen in Figure 18.2.

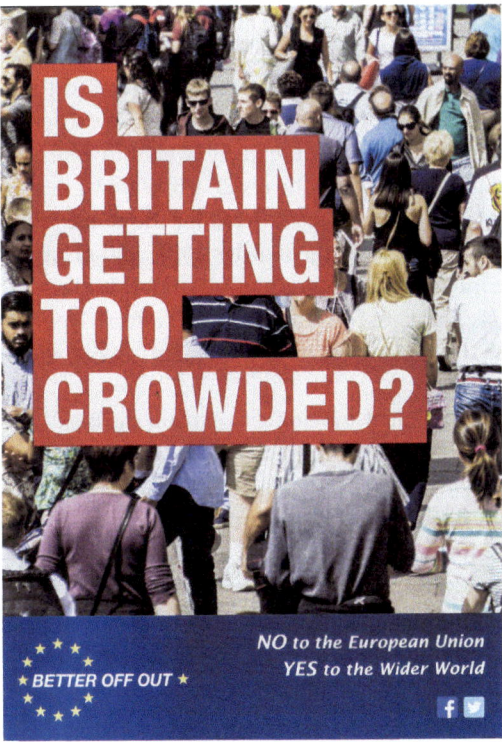

Figure 18.2 A campaign flyer from the Better Off Out campaign linking EU membership to migration. The close cropping of the picture presents a deliberately chaotic and stressful image of a crowded public space. The underlying assumption is that voters will associate this with migration without having to explicitly mention immigration, a form of 'dogwhistle' politics

Source: Better Off Out (2016)

The causes of Brexit

When the results were announced in the early hours of 24 June 2016, it became evident that Leave had clinched the vote, with 51.9% support for leaving the EU. The news sent shockwaves around the world (Adler-Nissen et al. 2017) but was especially seismic in its impact on British and European politics, since many had assumed that Remain would emerge victorious. Support for Brexit was highest in the rural parts of England and in the de-industrialised North of England, with peaks of support in many coastal areas, especially in the East of England. Remain support was concentrated in the more affluent parts of the UK, especially in cities and in the Home Counties surrounding London, with the capital voting overall strongly in favour of Remain. Without exception, all Scottish constituencies voted against Brexit, with a more mixed picture in Wales, which returned an overall Leave majority. In Northern Ireland, although the region voted Remain overall, voting was strongly influenced by political affiliation, with a majority for Leave among Unionists and a majority for Remain among nationalists.

Unsurprisingly – and not unproblematically – support for Brexit mapped onto a number of pre-existing socio-political divisions (Sobolewska and Ford 2020). Those in the lower income groups and without a higher degree were disproportionately likely to vote for Brexit than those who were more qualified and on higher incomes, reflecting the divergent ways in which European integration impacted on people's lives. Older voters were more likely to support Brexit, with an almost linear relationship between age and support for Leave, except for the oldest age bracket, which included many individuals who had experienced the 1940s and regarded the EU as a peace project. Politically, although support for Brexit existed among both Labour and Conservative supporters, the latter were more likely overall to vote Leave by a significant margin. On the categories of gender and race, the results broke down near-evenly, but finer-grained analyses have various intersectional effects, including the tendency for young women to be less Eurosceptic than men of the same age (Fowler 2023) and divergence within-and-between different minority and confessional communities in support for Brexit (Martin and Sobolewska 2023). The referendum also brought forth new forms of affective polarisation via the construction of 'Leaver' and 'Remainer' identities which operated outside traditional partisan affinities (Hobolt et al. 2021).

Many factors have been identified as helping to explain the Brexit vote. For some, the changing nature of the UK economy and the squeeze placed on incomes by austerity are significant factors underpinning the vote to leave (Hopkin 2017; Innes 2018; Rosamond 2019). For others, cultural factors are more important, including divisions between liberals and communitarian-minded citizens (Sobolewska and Ford 2020) and related masculinities and feminist positions (Achilleos-Sarll and Martill 2019). Attitudes towards race are also seen as a driver of the Brexit vote (Bhambra 2017; Virdee and McGeever 2018), as is a nostalgic yearning among many supporters for a return to an era when the UK was a major global/imperial player (Bell and Vucetic 2019; Dorling and Tomlinson 2019; Saunders 2020; Melhuish 2023). The emergence of populist modes of political communication and the success of anti-elite messaging combined with Euroscepticism is another prominent factor in the debate (Tournier-Sol 2015; Freeden 2017; Browning 2019). Some emphasise identity politics, both in terms of the dominance of English nationalism in the Leave campaign (Henderson et al. 2016; Wellings 2019) and the overall low levels of identification with the EU (Carl et al. 2019). Others have argued that immigration played a major role, with voters increasingly seeking to scapegoat non-nationals for domestic problems (Goodwin and Milazzo 2017). Changing patterns of media consumption, including the rise of social media echo chambers, and the private interests of media owners have also been linked to the success of the Leave campaign (Llewellyn et al. 2019). Others have blamed the EU system itself, not only in terms of recent major crises (e.g. Nugent 2018), but also its inflexibility in the face of variegated national economic interests (Thompson 2017; Bickerton 2019).

In practice, these factors are difficult to disentangle from one another, and the debates often boil down to questions of relative influence or the causal primacy of particular factors. This is part of a a more general methodological problem of how causality can be established in the social sciences, and not just an issue afflicting attempts to account for Brexit. Moreover, against the backdrop of broader changes in politics and society are more contingent factors that are seen as having influenced the vote. Individuals probably made a difference. The decisions of Boris Johnson and Michael Gove to back Leave lent the campaign credibility and recognisable faces. The charisma and personal appeal of Nigel Farage also helped Leave's message to resonate. On the left, the election of the Eurosceptic – though anti-Brexit – Jeremy Corbyn in September 2015 precluded a strong defence of EU membership from the opposition. Campaigning mattered too. Remain was racked by division and failed to land on an optimistic message which appealed to voters, while Leave engaged more actively in canvassing and campaigning (Menon and Salter 2016). Specific decisions taken by Cameron also made a difference, including the refusal to countenance extensions of the franchise, a proscription on EU leaders campaigning and the deliberate decision not to spell out what Brexit might look like.

Preparing for the negotiations

Regardless of its causes, the Brexit vote had immediate consequences for British politics. With his capital spent, Cameron resigned as prime minister, triggering a Conservative leadership election. Johnson and Gove found themselves out of the race rapidly, leaving Theresa May and Andrea Leadsom, the latter of whom withdrew after criticism that she had misrepresented her CV, leaving May unopposed. May was seen as a good compromise candidate by many, having remained loyal to Cameron and sided with Remain – albeit while keeping her head down in the campaign – but also being tough on law and order and seen as broadly Eurosceptic. Yet May's status as a Remainer left her vulnerable to criticism from the Tory right that she was not committed to the cause, while her coronation following Leadsom's withdrawal denied her a clear mandate of her own (Barwell 2021: 109). May's status as the second female prime minister after Margaret Thatcher was also much remarked on, with observers noting the new prime minister was held to different standards than her male colleagues, and that it was telling amid the chaos of Brexit that a woman was now relied upon to clean up the mess made by elite, white and male politicians (Hozić and True 2017).

May did indeed inherit a very difficult situation following the Brexit vote. What made things especially tricky was that there was no clear way forward spelled out by the referendum. A majority of citizens had voted for exit, but it was not clear what this would look like. In practice, leaving the EU could involve anything from the significant rupture of a 'no deal' Brexit to continued membership of the Single Market through the European Economic Area (EEA). Nor did the referendum offer any sense of what the process would be for delivering on the vote. The referendum was advisory, but established a strong political mandate, while a majority of MPs had opposed Brexit, setting the stage for conflict between Parliament and the government (Baldini et al. 2018; Russell 2021). The result's marginality, with a near 52/48 split, coupled with the salience of Leave/Remain as social identifiers, set the stage for increasing socio-political conflict during May's tenure. Meanwhile, the contrasting results in Scotland and Northern Ireland compared to England and Wales established competing mandates across different parts of the UK and would bring Westminster's Brexit policy into conflict with the devolved administrations (McHarg and Mitchell 2017; Keating 2022; McEwen and Murphy 2022). Finally, the Leave campaign also left deliberately vague the consequences of Brexit so as to appeal to as wide a range of supporters as possible, and made promises that would be up to the EU to offer, setting the stage for conflict between the mandate as expressed in the campaign and what could realistically be achieved amid myriad complex trade-offs.

The openness of the Brexit mandate was both a blessing and a curse, allowing May to interpret the 'will of the people' as she pleased, but affording her critics on both sides of the Brexit debate the same luxury. May was adamant that Brexit needed to be delivered and set this as the primary goal of her government, promising no re-entry through the 'back door'. Ending free movement was seen as essential, as was ensuring the UK could re-gain autonomy from EU institutions and avoid significant payments into the EU budget, and these strictures were incorporated into the 'red lines' articulated in the Lancaster House speech of January 2017 (HM Government 2017a). Within these confines, May hoped to maintain a close economic relationship, keeping the trading relationship as frictionless as possible. While May's Brexit designs seemed harder than many anticipated, in practice she was aiming for a bespoke deal that would provide a new basis for collaboration from outside (Figueira and Martill 2021). This was to be achieved through hard bargaining, leveraging the UK's market size and its importance to EU member states, and seeking to divide and rule between the EU27 (Martill and Staiger 2021).

May's Brexit designs were diametrically opposed to those of the EU27. Shocked by the Brexit vote, the EU had agreed early on that Brexit presented an existential threat to the Union. The UK's desire for a bespoke relationship was anathema to the EU because it would put the UK at a clear competitive advantage (Jurado et al. 2022). Because other member states and Eurosceptic parties were actively 'benchmarking' the Brexit process in order to ascertain how attractive such an outcome would be, there was a clear risk of contagion from affording the UK a generous deal (De Vries 2017; Beaumont 2019; van Kessel et al. 2020). To counter this, member states agreed to do all they could to maintain the integrity of the Single Market, preclude the UK from obtaining any competitive advantage and maintain unity among the 27 (Laffan and Telle 2023). Conduct of the negotiations was delegated to the Commission, via Task Force 50, led by Michel Barnier, a well-respected figure among European leaders who was able to directly intercede with heads of government and who engaged in a constant effort to maintain unity among the EU institutions and member states (Schuette 2021). With the EU opposed to any form of competitive advantage, May's 'red lines' effectively committed the UK to a harder Brexit than May's speech had implied, as shown in the graphic designed by Barnier's team (Figure 18.3). Moreover, the UK lacked leverage, being heavily dependent on access to the Single Market of 500 million consumers which the EU oversaw (Hix 2018). And EU member states – and firms – prioritised the integrity of the Single Market over access to the UK market (Gstöhl and Phinnemore 2021; Glencross 2023).

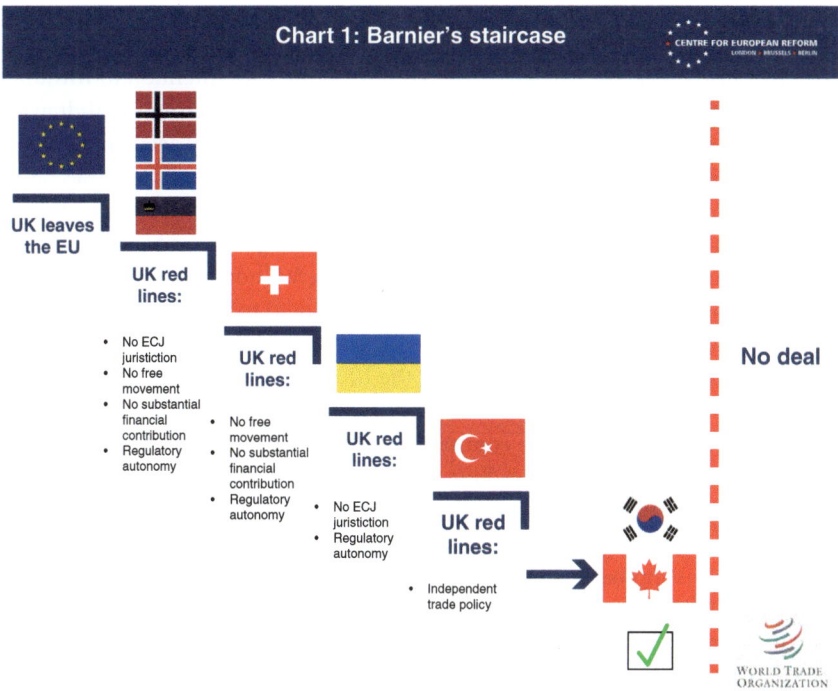

Figure 18.3 Slide designed by Task Force 50 to demonstrate the implications of the UK's 'red lines'

Source: Chart designed by Kate Mullineux, Centre for European Reform for 'Living next door to an elephant: Lessons for the UK from EFTA' by Aslak Berg, 29 April 2024

At home, too, the government's Brexit agenda ran into difficulties early-on. As a fiercely loyal Conservative (Heide and Worthy 2019; Dyson 2023), May hoped to deliver Brexit via Tory support, and thus did not seek to engage the political opposition or co-opt other parties into her designs on Brexit. May also sought to limit the ability of legislators to influence the Brexit vote, fearing initially challenge from Remain-supporting MPs (Timothy 2020). May's announcement that Article 50 would be triggered using the government's prerogative powers was successfully challenged in the High Court and then the Supreme Court by a coalition led by the fund-manager Gina Miller. The Court ruled that an Act of Parliament was required, but the resulting motion passed easily as both Labour and Conservative MPs were whipped in favour. An amendment seeking to tie the government to offering a 'meaningful vote' on the negotiated agreement was rejected, but marked the beginning of struggles by MPs to have their say on the outcome of the talks. There was also a significant territorial component to the *Miller* case. Asked to rule also on the status of the Sewel Convention – that Westminster did not legislate on devolved matters – the Court found the convention to be political and not legal, reducing the claim of the devolved regions to shape Brexit policy (Keating 2022; Martill 2023a). The *Miller* case overall set the tenor for forthcoming protracted battles between the executive and legislature, while highlighting at the same time how vituperative the rhetoric around Brexit had become, with Miller subjected to racist and sexist abuse and the judges identified as 'enemies of the people' (Rone 2023).

Negotiating the Withdrawal Agreement

The triggering of Article 50 on 29 March 2017 confirmed the UK's intention to withdraw from the EU and set the clock ticking on the two-year period within which the Withdrawal Agreement was to be negotiated. Fearing that the UK could hold the policy agenda hostage, the EU refused to enter negotiations until notification, which also suited May's purposes, as she was under pressure to trigger from pro-Brexit Conservatives. The talks were sequenced for legal and political reasons on the EU side, with the UK's outstanding obligations, citizens' rights, the Irish border and any transition arrangements to be agreed in the Withdrawal Agreement. This would have a non-binding Political Declaration appended, aiming to inform the negotiations on the future relationship, which would begin after the UK had formally exited. The logic of sequencing empowered the Commission by preventing the UK from using budgetary contributions or holding out on the Irish border in order to 'buy' access to the Single Market (Barnier 2021), but also made the negotiations more complicated and introduced difficult time asymmetries (Barwell 2021: 118). The Article 50 deadline also helped the Commission to keep the process moving along, precluding the UK from stalling and making the prospect of 'no deal' clear and credible to the UK side (Craig 2017).

As the negotiations approached in June 2017, May made the fateful decision to call a general election. Riding high in the polls, she hoped to increase her majority prior to the forthcoming talks and establish an electoral mandate of her own. But May proved a poor speaker on the campaign trail and her campaign began to lose momentum, while Jeremy Corbyn proved a surprisingly effective orator. Moreover, policy mis-steps on the part of the Conservatives, including the so-called 'dementia tax', undermined the core Tory vote, while Labour benefited from strategic ambiguity in their Brexit position (Heath and Goodwin 2017; Prosser 2018). In the end, the Conservatives emerged as the largest party but without a majority, forcing May into a confidence-and-supply agreement with the Democratic Unionist Party (DUP) to remain in power. May's 'loss' was less about her popularity than the unity of the opposition, but the effects on the government were seismic. Introducing the DUP into the mix made the government dependent on the representatives of one community in Northern Ireland with hard-line Brexit preferences. Meanwhile, Labour's strong performance gave the opposition an increasing incentive to trip the government up in order to force another election, making compromise more difficult. The election also contributed to the re-politicisation of Brexit debates, as Remain supporters claimed the result deprived May of a mandate for a hard Brexit, leading Leave supporters to counter-mobilise in order to 'save Brexit' (Martill 2021b).

Negotiations on the Withdrawal Agreement began in June 2017 and took place in successive 'rounds', giving each team the time to recuperate and engage with their respective stakeholders on relevant issues. Progress was slow in the initial months, with the Commission exasperated by UK efforts to make bilateral appeals to the member states and to seek to discuss issues reserved for the future relationship. Gradual progress was made on citizens' rights in the latter half of 2017, with both sides seeking similar protection for their citizens, and the main outstanding issues concerning the role of the Court of Justice of the European Union (CJEU) and the cut-off for EU citizens to arrive in the UK and receive settled status. The so-called 'divorce bill', which the Commission regarded as an existing UK legal requirement to cover agreed debts, was again simple in principle as a distributional issue, but complicated by growing politicisation in the UK – Johnson said the EU could 'go whistle' – and by Barnier's fears that the UK was dragging its feet on the issue so as to link the financial settlement to questions of market access (Barnier

2021: 78). Both Johnson, who was Foreign Secretary at the time, and David Davis, Secretary of State for Brexit, frequently articulated their own interpretations of what was being negotiated with the EU, undermining May's authority while simultaneously refusing to take responsibility for the outcome of the talks.

Research in Focus

Why did the UK struggle to negotiate?

Throughout the negotiations, May found that the UK did not have the power to alter the process the Commission had put in place, to gain significant concessions on withdrawal issues, or to move towards the 'bespoke model' at the heart of the British ask. With clear asymmetries in negotiating expertise, understanding of EU policies and processes, and in underlying bargaining power, the Commission was able to effectively set the agenda, with the UK ultimately acceding to many of these initial proposals (E. Jones 2019). Because London was not sure what it wanted out of Brexit, the UK was unable to design an effective strategy, while every potential outcome that could be negotiated with the Commission was unlikely to satisfy pro-Brexit constituencies (Schnapper 2021). The UK's hard bargaining strategy misconstrued what was at stake in the negotiations and fenced the UK in to harder designs which made eventual compromise more difficult, since it had already been precluded in principle (Larsén and Khorana 2020; Martill and Staiger 2021). The UK underestimated the EU's ability to hold the collective line in the talks (Jensen and Kelstrup 2019; Laffan 2019) and the extent to which this would prevent the UK engaging in 'divide-and-rule' tactics by appealing individually to the member states (Figueira and Martill 2021). And it failed to acknowledge the threat that Brexit – coupled with preferential treatment for the UK – represented for the EU's Single Market, along with the willingness of continental lobbies and the German government to assist the UK in obtaining a preferential agreement (Glencross 2023; Bale and Pike 2024).

The question of the Northern Ireland border proved most intractable. With the border between the Republic of Ireland and Northern Ireland set to become the EU's external border post-Brexit, arrangements would need to be put in place to prevent a return to the hard border of the past, inimical as it was to peace on the island of Ireland. In the absence of 'technical solutions' initially preferred by the UK, it was clear that some form of regulatory alignment was the only way of preventing a hard border, yet the Commission's insistence that 'cherry picking' be avoided and that the future relationship be negotiated *after* the Withdrawal Agreement made it difficult to specify what this would look like. The Joint Report of December 2017 set out a framework that would later come to be known as the backstop, detailing the provisions that would go into the Withdrawal Agreement, and amounting to a UK guarantee that arrangements would be put in place to prevent a hard border should this not be provided for by a close future relationship (HM Government 2017b). The backstop was problematic because it had to be indefinite (to provide guarantees) and it provoked particular ire among the government's allies in the DUP, who feared divergence from the rest of the UK. In response, the UK government pushed for an 'all-UK' backstop from the Commission, which regarded the proposals initially as a further effort to 'cherry pick', but later conceded on the issue.

Political problems associated with the backstop brought about a greater effort on the UK side to spell out what the future relationship might look like over the course of 2018. Elements of the new proposals were previewed in May's Mansion House speech on 2 March 2018, seen by her advisors as an opportunity to spell out the realities of post-Brexit trade-offs, especially regarding the need for continued alignment in some areas (Barwell 2021: 274). In July, May sequestered the Cabinet at the prime ministers' private residence in Chequers for a summit meeting on the future relationship proposals. These envisioned a form of customs' union, branded a 'facilitated customs partnership', alignment with EU rules on goods via a 'common rulebook' and committed the UK to non-regression on environmental standards and harmon-isation with rules on state-aid (Barwell 2021: 281). The Chequers proposals received the assent of the Cabinet, but prompted the resignation of Davis shortly after, with Johnson also following him out of the door. By highlighting how much May was willing to compromise on her own 'red lines', Chequers was the moment the pro-Brexit right broke with the government (Grey 2021: 128). Nor was the EU keen on the arrangements, with Barnier claiming they would afford the UK a competitive advantage (Barnier 2021: 157–163) and member states publicly rejecting the proposals at the Salzburg Summit in September. The combination of internal and external opposition to the proposals showed just how wide the gap that May was attempting to bridge was in practice (Schnapper 2021).

In November, the Withdrawal Agreement was finalised, with the European Council approv-ing the text on 25 November, paving the way for ratification on the UK side. By this point, the protracted back-and-forth between Parliament and the executive – facilitated by the govern-ment's lack of an overall majority (Russell 2021; Baldini et al. 2022) – had undermined the gov-ernment's ability to offer a last-minute take-it-or-leave-it vote on the agreement (Martill 2021a). With concerted opposition from the Tory right following Chequers, the first meaningful vote was pushed back to January so as to buy the whips more time. When the first vote was held on 15 January 2019, May's deal was rejected by an unprecedented 202–432. Surviving the ensu-ing confidence vote, May opened up talks with the Labour opposition, before seeking a way forward among Conservatives when these negotiations failed. Supporting the so-called Brady Amendment, May whipped the party to back a motion requesting that she attempt to re-open negotiations on the backstop, returning to Brussels in late January to do so but receiving only 'clarifications' instead of substantive change. At this point, both sides in the increasingly polar-ised debate were convinced they would get their favoured option (no Brexit, or no deal) if they rejected May's agreement (Heinkelmann-Wild et al. 2020; Quinn et al. 2024). The next vote on 12 March failed 242–391 and brought about scrabbling among opposition legislators to pre-clude a 'no deal' Brexit and a subsequent appeal from May for an extension to Article 50, which was granted by the Council. At the third attempt on 29 March, the government lost 286–344, and marked the final occasion May would seek approval for her deal.

Negotiating the Trade and Cooperation Agreement

The three-time failure of May's agreement to pass the Commons occasioned a protracted polit-ical crisis in the UK. The European Council granted a further extension until October 2019, allowing the UK more time to ratify the agreement. But with May's authority spent and with deadlock among legislative factions, no clear way forward presented itself. In May, the Conserv-ative Party polled an unprecedented 8.8% in the European Parliament elections, which the UK had not been expected to take part in, with the Brexit Party obtaining the greatest share of the vote (30.5%), followed by the anti-Brexit Liberal Democrats (19.6%) (Cutts et al. 2019; Martill 2020). May announced her resignation as prime minister and Conservative leader on 24 May 2019, pending a leadership contest to choose her successor. The campaign, which took place over June and July, was a contest aimed at the largely pro-Brexit Party membership and focused largely on the willingness of candidates to undertake a 'no deal' Brexit, which had become the favoured outcome of party members during the negotiations (Kettell and Kerr 2020). On 22 July, Johnson was announced as the winner by a 2:1 margin over Jeremy Hunt, becoming prime minister two days later.

Having campaigned on the basis of getting a better deal from the EU than his predecessor, Johnson set about seeking a renegotiation of the Withdrawal Agreement with the EU. The Commission opposed re-opening the negotiations, but a high-level meeting between Johnson and the Irish Taoiseach Leo Varadkar paved the way for agreement on revised arrangements through what would become the Northern Ireland Protocol. Returning to an idea considered (and rejected) by his predecessor, Johnson consented to arrangements whereby Northern Ireland would remain de facto in the EU Single Market but de jure within the UK legal system, with checks conducted in the Irish Sea. The Protocol precluded the need for the backstop by settling Northern Ireland's future status, amounting essentially to a 'front-stop' (Grey 2021: 185). In addition, Johnson amended the language of the Political Declaration, removing mention of a level playing field and making more references to UK sovereignty (Owen 2019). In late October, Johnson placed the agreement before Parliament, obtaining a majority but failing to obtain agreement on the necessary timeframe. Blaming Parliamentarians for stymying Brexit, Johnson called a fresh general election for 12 December. Standing on the 'Get Brexit Done' platform, Johnson obtained an 80-seat majority by successfully uniting Brexit supporters, while Remainers divided among the various opposition parties (Cutts et al. 2020).

Aided by Johnson's sizeable majority, the Withdrawal Agreement and Political Declaration were passed in January 2020, with the UK formally leaving the EU on 31 January and entering a transition period until the end of the calendar year. The transition period was designed to smooth the impact of withdrawal and give the opportunity for both sides to negotiate arrangements for the future relationship. Whereas May had imagined a close relationship in her Chequers Plan, the Johnson government sought a more distant arrangement built around a Free Trade Agreement (FTA) similar to the one the EU had with Canada. Unlike Canada, the UK's agreement would cover more areas, reflecting the denser ties between the UK and the EU, and would need to have more safeguards, reflecting the UK's geographical proximity to the EU market (Usherwood 2021). Negotiations on what would become the TCA began in February 2020 following the Commission's publication of its mandate and would cover various areas, including information sharing, goods trade, fisheries, energy, governance and dispute resolution. At the onset of the negotiations, the UK announced that it would deviate from the Political Declaration in several respects, removing both the commitment to maintain a level playing field and the aim of negotiating an agreement on foreign and security policy from the table, both of which contributed to increasing distrust between both sides (Martill and Mesarovich 2024).

The terms of the TCA were negotiated over the course of 2020, against the backdrop of declining political relationships and the spread of Covid. Infections within both teams forced negotiations online, which made the timeframe for the talks even more challenging. While much of the public focus lay in the distributive elements, such as fisheries, the greatest sticking points arose in relation to the level playing field and governance arrangements, with the UK seeking minimal restrictions on its freedom of manoeuvre and separate frameworks for dispute resolution and no role for the Court of Justice. Johnson ramped up the hard bargaining of his predecessor, undermining trust and making the talks more difficult. The Internal Market Bill (IMB), published in September, contained clauses that would undermine the Northern Ireland Protocol. Interpreted by the Commission as an effort to unpick the Withdrawal Agreement, the IMB served to further unite the member states against the UK and contributed to growing distrust (Wille and Martill 2023). Towards the end of the negotiations, the UK engaged in repeated threats to walk away, leaving the table at one point, only to return after the EU had 'acknowledged' British concerns. These actions obtained no meaningful concessions and were viewed by the Commission as intended entirely for the domestic audience in the UK. Compromise on governance issues as well as the UK's removal of the problematic clauses in the IMB paved the way for agreement, which was reached at the last minute on 24 December against the backdrop of a Covid surge and the closure of the border with France.

The TCA came into effect provisionally on 1 January 2021, pending the approval of the European Parliament, which was granted on 28 April. The agreement provides for free trade in goods, with no tariffs or quotas on either side, although it falls short of the 'frictionless trade' promised by successive Conservative leaders. It also provides for continuing cooperation on cyber-security and information sharing, and for judicial and police cooperation. The agreement on fisheries sees a gradual reduction in the catch allowed by EU member states in UK waters. The TCA contains a level playing field commitment designed to ensure that the UK cannot undercut European standards, with a non-regression clause, and although evolutionary mechanisms were rejected, both sides can take countermeasures where standards are raised unilaterally. In terms of governance arrangements, the TCA provides for a Partnership Council to implement the agreement and complex mechanisms for dispute resolution involving independent arbitration and the potential to suspend elements of the agreement. The agreement does not cover trade in services, including financial services, nor does it cover areas such as data adequacy, which are separate decisions taken by the Commission. Participation in the Horizon and Erasmus programmes for researchers and students were notable omissions, although the UK has subsequently re-joined the Horizon programme. Cooperation on foreign and security policy was another notable omission, and cooperation in this area has instead been built-up informally since 2021 (Martill and Mesarovich 2024). While both sides lauded the agreement, observers noted that it was a thin deal compared to what had gone before (Wachowiak and Zuleeg 2022), that it distributionally favoured EU designs and interests (Usherwood 2021) and that it laid the ground for considerable potential divergence (Collins 2021).

The coming-into-force of the TCA ended the formal Brexit negotiations and established a degree of certainty over what withdrawal looked like. Yet the implementation of the agreement involved a protracted process on both sides, with policymakers accustoming themselves to new arrangements and learning new practices. Areas outside the agreement remained the subject of speculation over what arrangements might be possible in the future. Meanwhile, the government's refusal to implement the checks required under the Protocol, which were unilaterally extended in March 2021, established long-running diplomatic issues leading to further negotiations and, eventually, infringement proceedings against the UK. Johnson's fall from power amid the 'Partygate' scandal in the UK presented an opportunity for a reset. While Liz Truss was not in power long enough to preside over significantly improved relations, she helped establish a more positive tone which was continued by her own successor, Rishi Sunak.

Sunak's background diplomacy resulted in the Windsor Framework, adopted in March 2023, which established a more workable situation for managing the regulatory border in the Irish Sea and which led to improvements in the UK–EU political relationship as well as a ramping up of security cooperation (Martill 2023b). The election of a Labour government under Keir Starmer in the 4 July 2024 general election has further improved the cross-Channel political relationship and is expecred to bring about further cooperation on key matters, including security. And yet Starmer is keen not to revisit the fundamentals of Brexit, given the impossibility of squaring market access with the UK's red lines and the risk of being accused of seeking to reverse Brexit. And while the TCA will be reviewed in 2026, the EU regard this as an opportunity to assess any implementation issues, rather than to substantially alter what Brexit looks like.

Key debate   Brexit

What were the main causes of Brexit? As discussed in this chapter, many different factors have been identified by scholars. These include the rise of new political movements (Osuna et al. 2021), populist modes of political mobilisation (Freeden 2017), distrust of politicians, disaffection with the political mainstream, changes in the UK political economy (Hopkin 2017), the impact of globalisation, the impact of the 2008 financial crisis and the eurozone crisis (Thompson 2017), rising intra-European migration (Goodwin and Milazzo 2017), changing patterns of media consumption (Llewellyn et al. 2019), nostalgia for empire (Bell and Vucetic 2019), hegemonic masculinities (Achilleos-Sarll and Martill 2019; Galpin 2022), underlying patterns of identity (Carl et al. 2019), and many other interrelated factors. Identifying which factors mattered most is difficult, given that many of these factors are themselves related to one another.

Why did we end up with a 'hard' Brexit? Some scholars have suggested that the answer lies in the UK political system and the factional politics of the Conservative Party, with outbidding for the soul of the party leading to increasingly radical positions among Brexit supporters over time (Heinkelmann-Wild et al. 2020; Russell 2021; Quinn et al. 2024). Others argue that the outcome was always likely to be a hard(er) Brexit given the UK's own 'red lines' and their incompatibility with models for the post-Brexit relationship deemed acceptable to the EU27 (Grey 2021; Glencross 2023). Scholars focusing on the UK's negotiating strategy have argued that harder designs for Brexit grew out of efforts to reinforce the credibility of Britain's claim it was prepared to walk away from the table (Martill 2022).

How has Brexit altered the UK's political system? The picture here is a highly mixed one, as charted by scholars working on Brexit and the UK constitution (Baldini et al. 2018; Bogdanor 2019). On the one hand, Brexit has seemingly altered many things, introducing elements of direct democracy, shifting the positions of the major parties, undermining norms of confidence in party leaders, challenging the devolved status quo, bringing about non-majority government, shaping norms of parliamentary procedure, and precipitating a severe crisis in executive–legislative relations (Eeckhout 2018; Russell 2021). On the other hand, many of these changes are rooted in the specific circumstances of the Brexit vote and the politics of the May government after the 2017 general election – a 'perfect storm' for Parliament (Russell 2021). Since 2019 we have seen a normalisation of executive–legislative relations, a recalibration of the party system, the return of majority government and little appetite for new referendums (Baldini et al. 2022).

(Continued)

Has Brexit made Scottish independence more likely? Since a majority of Scottish voters opted to Remain, and Brexit was very much a product of English discourses (Henderson et al. 2016), it is often argued that Scotland has been dragged out of Europe against its will (McHarg and Mitchell 2017). Brexit challenged the status quo in other respects, from the judgement on the Sewel Convention's 'political' status to the rise of 'muscular unionism' in Westminster (Sandford 2023b). The SNP-led Scottish Government embraced a strong anti-Brexit position and lobbied for a separate voice in the process as well as distinct arrangements for Scotland *vis-à-vis* the EU, but had little influence over withdrawal (Keating 2022; McEwen and Murphy 2022). Brexit and Boris Johnson have both been helpful to the independence cause, and support for independence rose just above 50% for the first time following the 2016 referendum. Although support for independence has declined slightly since, it has been largely unaffected by recent SNP misfortunes. But the prospects for independence are weakened by the difficulties of re-joining the EU while the UK is still on the outside and by the UK government's continuing refusal to countenance a second independence referendum (so-called IndyRef2) (Martill 2023a).

How has Brexit altered Britain's place in the world? Although the referendum was never really about foreign and security policy, the UK's withdrawal from the EU meant that foreign relations would inevitably shift away from Europe (Hadfield and Whitman 2023). Far from becoming more 'global', Brexit has undermined the UK's standing in world politics and made the country less relevant for other actors, including the United States and the Commonwealth, on whose behalf many Brexiteers recommended withdrawal (Oppermann et al. 2020). Successive governments have used the rhetoric of Global Britain to signal a new direction in foreign policy, and while this was a symbolic move under the May government, the Johnson government implemented more substantive changes, including cuts to UK aid and the severing of security ties with the EU (Martill 2023b). Since the Russian invasion of Ukraine in February 2022, informal UK–EU cooperation has been stepped up, with both sides increasingly coming to recognise their shared interests and values (Hill 2023).

Reflective questions

1   What were the most significant determinants of the Leave vote in the 2016 referendum?
2   In what ways did issues with the referendum mandate shape the Brexit process?
3   What assumptions about the EU led Britain to approach the negotiations in the way it did?
4   How significantly has Brexit impacted on the Westminster system?

Conclusion

This chapter has examined the causes and consequences of the 2016 Brexit referendum. Specifically, it has looked at the following aspects of Brexit:

- The UK's historical relationship with the project of European integration and the UK's status as both an awkward partner and an at-times constructive member state.
- The changing nature of European integration and the context of rising Euroscepticism within which David Cameron committed to an in/out referendum.
- What Cameron obtained in his renegotiation and the issues arising in the subsequent referendum debate.

- The result of the referendum and how this broke down along different socio-economic faultlines, as well some of the potential explanations for the victory of the Leave campaign.
- How the Leave vote changed UK politics and society and how the May government set about preparing to deliver Brexit, including its goals, its negotiating strategy and its key limitations.
- The negotiation of the Withdrawal Agreement and the fraught politics of the period, culminating in the stalemate of early 2019 and the failure of May's agreement.
- The Johnson government's renegotiation of parts of the deal and its highly performative bargaining style in negotiating the TCA in the talks on the future relationship.

Key terms

- **European Union (EU)** – a highly centralised political union of 27 member states, established after the signing of the Maastricht Treaty in 1992.
- **European Economic Community (EEC)** – the precursor to today's European Union, founded by France, Italy, West Germany, Belgium, Netherlands and Luxembourg in 1957.
- **European Coal and Steel Community (ECSC)** – the progenitor of the EEC which pooled control of national coal and steel industries, founded in 1951 between 'the six' original EEC members.
- **European Free Trade Association (EFTA)** – an organisation designed to lower trade barriers between members which was promoted by the UK as an alternative to EEC membership in the early 1960s.
- **European Economic Area (EEA)** – an arrangement whereby members of EFTA can participate in the EU Single European Market as long as they implement the required regulations.
- **Single European Market** – the internal market of the EU constructed from the late 1980s through the establishment of common EU-level regulations and built around the 'four freedoms' (people, goods, services, capital).
- **Customs Union** – the abolition of goods borders within the EEC/EU which has provided frictionless goods trade since 1968 and the corresponding common external tariff.
- **Area of Freedom, Security and Justice** – an EU policy domain dealing with police and judicial cooperation, migration and fundamental rights which evolved out of the Justice and Home Affairs 'pillar' of the Maastricht Treaty.
- **Schengen Area** – a border-free area in which only limited and temporary cross-border checks take place, originally agreed outside the EU framework in 1985 and incorporated in 1999.
- **Article 50** – the section of the Treaty on European Union spelling out the process through which a member state can leave the EU and which provides for an extendable two-year time-period for the negotiation of a Withdrawal Agreement.
- **Cliff-edge** – a phrase describing the end of the Article 50 period, after which the UK would default to a 'no deal' scenario in the absence of an agreement being reached.
- **Hard/Soft Brexit** – metaphors used to describe whether the outcome of the Brexit process would see the UK adopt a close (soft) or distant (hard) relationship with the EU.

- **Sequencing** – the division of the Brexit negotiations into two distinct phases covering withdrawal issues first, followed by later talks on the future relationship.
- **No Deal** – an outcome in which no negotiated relationship would be agreed for either phase of the negotiations, in which eventuality the UK would fall back on World Trade Organization rules.
- **Withdrawal Agreement** – a treaty agreed between the UK and the EU in order to settle the terms of UK withdrawal, covering citizens' rights, the Irish border and outstanding financial obligations.
- **Political Declaration** – a non-binding statement of principles appended to the Withdrawal Agreement, the aim of which is to set out the broad contours of the negotiations on the future relationship.
- **Meaningful Vote** – a campaign in the UK for Parliament to be offered a vote on the Withdrawal Agreement in a manner and timing that would not force the hand of legislators.
- **Transition Period** – a negotiated arrangement through which the UK would formally leave the EU but continue to abide by EU rules and access policies and programmes pending the negotiation of the agreement on the future relationship.
- **Trade and Cooperation Agreement (TCA)** – the legal agreement resulting from the talks on the future relationship between the UK and the EU which provides for the removal of tariffs and quotas on goods between both markets as well as cooperation in a host of other domains.

Recommended and further reading

- Barnier, M. (2021) *My Secret Brexit Diary: A Glorious Illusion*. Trans. Mackay, R. London: Polity Press.
- De Rynck, S. (2023) *Inside the Deal: How the EU Got Brexit Done*. London: Agenda.
- Grey, C. (2021) *Brexit Unfolded: How No One Got What They Wanted (and Why They Were Never Going To)*. London: Biteback.
- Hill, C. (2019) *The Future of British Foreign Policy: Security and Diplomacy in a World after Brexit*. Cambridge: Polity Press.
- Laffan, B. and Telle, S. (2023) *The EU's Response to Brexit: United and Effective*. Basingstoke: Palgrave Macmillan.
- Russell, M. and James, L. (2023) *The Parliamentary Battle over Brexit*. Oxford: Oxford University Press.
- Shipman, T. (2024) *No Way Out: Brexit: From the Backstop to Boris*. London: William Collins.
- Sobolewska, M. and Ford, R. (2020) *Brexitland: Identity, Diversity and the Reshaping of British Politics*. Cambridge: Cambridge University Press.

Chapter 19

UK foreign policy making

Victoria Honeyman

What will this chapter tell me?

- This chapter examines the prevailing approaches to foreign policy making in the UK since 1997. It looks at the pressures the UK faces and how it has managed its relative decline in terms of influence.
- It looks at the UK's relationship with the USA, a cornerstone of its foreign policy, and considers how the relationship has evolved and affects how the UK sees itself.
- The chapter also looks at Britain's approach to the former colonies of the British Empire and the Anglosphere. The transition from Empire to Commonwealth was a difficult one for the UK to manage and the role of the Commonwealth in foreign policy is still debated.
- Finally, the chapter examines the key foreign policy challenges the UK is facing, particularly in relation to threats, NATO and the UK's permanent UN Security Council seat.

What do I need to know?

- Having been the pre-eminent economic and diplomatic power at the beginning of the twentieth century, the UK has had to manage its decline over the course of the twenty-first century.
- Debates about the UK's foreign-policy role reflect wider debates about the UK's place is the world and its self-image – what sort of country should the UK be?
- The UK is sometimes seen as somewhere between Europe and the USA (geographically and intellectually). This tension plays out in its approach to foreign policy.

Introduction

No policy is as important to a nation as its foreign policy. Without strong borders and a stable economy, internal reform and growth is almost impossible. Fear of the actions of other states forces money, time and effort to be diverted from social or economic development to military development and defence spending. A continual state of war, or the threat of war, is hugely damaging for sovereign nations, so foreign policy is key to the success of all other policies.

The motivating factors informing foreign policy making in Britain have evolved and morphed over time, although there is some academic discussion over whether the way in which British foreign policy is made has changed over time or whether the 'change' is simply one of presentation or emphasis. While pragmatism and Britain's best interests have traditionally been the priority in foreign policy making, that does not mean other issues are entirely forgotten or overlooked. Nor does it always make policy making inevitable or predictable. During the days of the British Empire, the needs and wants of Britain were, inevitably, central to foreign policy making. Indeed, not only were they central, they were often exclusive, with the needs and wants of the colonised nations and their people barely featuring in discussion or decision making. That is not usual for empires, but as Britain moved away from its Empire during the postwar years, the demands of the British state could no longer be prioritised over wider considerations. Not only were the newly independent nations able to exercise some control over their own affairs (although this varied from nation to nation, and changed over time), the larger forces in global politics could not be ignored. The United States had rapidly overtaken the UK as the predominant nation on earth in the first half of the twentieth century, and their views were often dominant in the thinking of the UK government in foreign policy.

However, the US is not the only nation which has pushed itself into a prominent position. Other nations have also developed quickly, surpassing the economic strength of the UK. Britain retains its place in the top ten economic nations in the world as of 2023 and occupies some memberships which are the envy of others. It a prominent member of NATO, a nation which holds nuclear weapons, a member of the G7 and a prominent member of countless financial international organisations. Perhaps the jewel in the crown of the UK's international memberships is their permanent seat on the UN Security Council alongside the US, China, Russia and France. As a P5 member (the name given to the five permanent members of the UN Security Council), the UK also retains a veto on the UN Security Council, making it one of the most powerful nations on earth. One organisation which Britain has removed itself from is the European Union. While the effects of that are still being felt, the EU as an organisation remains a key 'unit' in global politics, having 27 current members, including Germany and France. Without the UK as a member moulding policy, particularly foreign policy, the organisation will undoubtedly move in directions which are, on occasion, at odds with the UK. This chapter will not focus on the EU (see Martill, in this volume), but its presence in policy making in the UK, even foreign policy where the EU organisation is not considered to be a key player, is considerable and should not be overlooked. The UK has, in the last 100 years, had to adapt to a very different international landscape, where its needs and wants cannot simply be achieved without thought to the needs and wants of others.

Inevitably, the key concerns of the UK often relate to the policies and actions of other nations, but there are other considerations, both in terms of problems and priorities. Currently, many of the biggest global problems are impossible to solve without cooperation. Environmental damage, energy security and the preservation of human rights are constantly under attack but the solution to these issues cannot be determined by one single nations, nor can it be achieved without considerable cost. Developed nations, including the UK, are now engaged in protracted discussions with less developed nations over who will bear the responsibility and cost of damage already inflicted and what the future will look like for millions of people. The days of simply ignoring the needs of nations are gone and now the UK is looking to find itself a new role as global champion on these issues.

At the heart of all of these debates are the motivations of the UK. While pragmatism was king, have more ideological concerns really never featured in foreign policy making? Was the move to a more ideological dimension under Blair real or mere marketing for electoral purposes? Where do the needs of ordinary people, whether they be in the UK or around the world, feature in the high politics world of British foreign policy making? This chapter will consider the motivations behind foreign policy making over the last 40 years before moving on to a discussion of the US–UK special relationship in British foreign policy making, Britain's relationship with some of its former colonies, before briefly considering some of the key issues facing the British.

Who 'makes' foreign policy and what are their priorities?

Every Prime Minister runs their government in a different style and, unlike some other policy areas, foreign policy tends to be made somewhere between the Foreign Office and Downing

Street. For some Prime Ministers, their interest in foreign policy only piques during a crisis. That means the Foreign Secretary has a considerable amount of leeway, if they choose to exercise it. For example, the government of Theresa May was so consumed by Brexit negotiations, intra-party disputes and the management (or mis-management) of policy through the House of Commons that the Foreign Secretary, Boris Johnson, had a considerable amount of freedom in his brief. However, he rarely exercised it, instead being viewed as the leader of the Brexiteers. For other Prime Ministers, they find themselves consumed by foreign policy, either because of events or because of their own interest in the policy area. For Blair, he seems to have fallen into the latter category, perhaps surprisingly. His time as a backbench MP gave no hint of an interest in foreign policy, and he did not occupy a shadow role in the area. However, his first term in office suggests that foreign policy became not only his area of interest but also his preoccupation.

The Blair era was something of a watershed moment for British foreign policy making, not simply because of Blair's foreign policy action or even the monumental world events which took place during his tenure. Traditionally, foreign policy making had taken a more pragmatic approach to world events. During the Cold War, the overwhelming ideological consideration of importance to the British government was whether another nation was following a capitalist or communist worldview. With the end of the Cold War, the collapse of the USSR and the reunification of Germany, a period of international reflection began, with organisations such as NATO considering their purpose in this brave new world. Sanders and Houghton (2017) noted that John Mearsheimer, prominent and well respected American political scientist, had predicted that NATO would miss the Cold War. In some ways, it did, but as they make clear 'what Mearsheimer and others missed is the extraordinary capacity of organisations to continue to exist even when their *raison d'être* – in this case, defeating the Soviet Union and global communism – has long gone (Sanders and Houghton 2017: 296). Blair's election in 1997 heralded in the UK a recognition of the changing world and that change was reflected in the messaging the new government produced on foreign policy. Pragmatism was no longer king, with 'ethical dimensions to foreign policy' being heralded as a new, more humanitarian approach to global affairs. However, what this practically meant was more problematic than the production of the slogan. This approach was labelled 'Liberal Interventionism' following Blair's speech to the Chicago Economics Club in 1999, where he explained his reasoning for intervening in conflicts not generally considered to involve the UK's national interests (Blair 1999).

Robin Cook's speech at the Foreign Office in the first week of the Blair government's term of office offered up no answers to these questions, but it did suggest a change in the priorities of foreign policy making (Cook 1997). The press heralded this as Britain's adoption of an ideological foreign policy, something which was both unlikely and impractical, but the Blair government's correction of this interpretation was underwhelming, allowing the misunderstanding to remain largely unchallenged. The period of electioneering which had preceded the 1997 election win was intense, with the party engaging in an all-out campaign to win against a fractured and split Conservative Party. The Labour Party sought to portray their competitors as corrupt, immoral and out of touch after 18 years in office. As part of their portrayal of the Conservative Party, and by focusing on human rights as a 'new' priority in foreign policy making, the previous Conservative government could again be presented as immoral and uncaring. Douglas Hurd suggested that the 'ethical dimensions' approach to policy was driven by a lack of experience (Gaskarth 2013a: 198). As Gaskarth noted, 'as with the previous Conservative administration, the new Labour government was accused of allowing the defence industry to corrupt domestic politics' (2013b: 104).

While in office, human rights were often discussed as a cause of action, for example in Kosovo, Sierra Leone, and latterly in Iraq. The validity of these claims is not clear, but it demonstrates how the issue of human rights was, by the late 1990s and early 2000s, a valid justification for foreign policy making and even military action overseas. At the same time, funding for overseas development assistance (ODA) was increased, with the government aiming for a target of 0.7% of gross national income (GNI). This was accompanied by the creation of a new Department for International Development (DFID) and a Secretary of State, demonstrating the high priority being given to this policy area (DFID n.d.). The changes were explained in humanitarian terms, providing an altruistic justification for the changes rather than a focus on the pragmatic benefits of the policy. It is unconvincing to suggest that pragmatic reasons did not continue to guide foreign policy making, but at least in terms of the messaging, human rights were considered a value worth defending. This approach officially continued under the Brown government, although foreign policy tended to be a less pressing concern during his short tenure in Downing Street. As with Blair, overseas development assistance maintained a high priority position in the Brown government, demonstrating again the change in approach in engagement with the wider world.

With the arrival of David Cameron in Downing Street, it might be expected that the prioritisation of human rights, at least in terms of the public justification of policy, might be changed to reflect a more 'experienced' approach, as suggested by Geoffrey Howe, or a less 'socialist' approach, as outlined by Tony Lloyd in Gaskarth's work on interpreting ethical foreign policy (Gaskarth 2013a: 199–200). However, that was not the case. With William Hague as Foreign Secretary, both Cameron and Hague introduced 'Liberal Conservatism', their response to Blair's agenda of 'Liberal Interventionism'. The content was similar, although not identical, and reflected the post-Iraq priorities of the UK, coupled with a commitment to taking action in defence of issues such as human rights, when it was deemed necessary by the British government. The same approach was adopted by the Cameron coalition government between 2010 and 2015, where foreign policy was dominated by the Conservatives. This justification was used when action was taken in Libya and Syria, but both conflicts also reflected a much longer-standing reason for Britain taking action – support for the US. The Cameron government continued to privilege the key relationship in UK foreign policy – the 'special relationship' with the United States.

Brexit led to the demise of the Cameron government and the new May government was entirely preoccupied with the issue. While foreign policy became even more reactive than previously, the May government remained committed initially to the upholding of human rights and the need to potentially use force to ensure them. However, there was limited overseas military action while May was in office, partly because of the Brexit issue and partly because of the short duration of the government. However, in early 2017 May announced that 'the days of Britain and America intervening in sovereign countries in an attempt to remake the world in our own image are over' (May 2017). It publicly declared the end of Blair's Liberal Interventionism doctrine and Cameron's Liberal Conservatism.

Key debate   Overseas development aid

Overseas development aid (ODA), and specifically the motives behind donor nations, has become an area of increasing research over the last five to ten years. While the focus has traditionally been on what ODA funding is invested in, the assumption has often been made that the donor nations are motivated either by some sense of altruism or are buying favour in developing nations. While both of these motivations may be at play, the reasons behind donation and the level of that donation vary hugely from nation to nation and help, at least partially, to explain the varying levels of funding from different developing nations. The UK's ODA policy is an interesting and complex case study due to the changing motivations, messaging and structure of aid distribution.

Writing in 2002, Thérien argued that the political position of a party impacted on their views on foreign aid policy, and therefore their policy decisions. He stated that:

> the Left has traditionally contended that the definition of aid should be restrictive, so as to avoid an overblown representation of the developed countries' generosity. The Right has been inclined towards a broader definition that might include the widest possible range of donor practices. (Thérien 2002: 451)

Tingley (2010) developed this theory further by arguing that those parties and individuals on the left of the political divide would support increased aid spending, while those on the right would want to reduce it and provide more oversight to it. Thérien and Tingley did not focus on one specific nation but provided a more general hypothesis.

Honeyman (2019) applied the work of Thérien and Tingley, and Breuning's (1995) work on the different labels used to categorise aid donor motivations, to the UK government. Synthesising their different approaches added greater understanding to the motivations of the UK government and how it changed over time. Honeyman demonstrated that the motivations of the Blair government evolved during its time in office, while the Cameron government acted in a way which confirmed the work of Tingley (Honeyman 2019).

The Johnson government cut the level of ODA spending by the UK in June 2020 from 0.7% to 0.5% GNI, highlighting the different policy aims between and within the two main political parties in the UK. By describing the UK as 'the giant cashpoint in the sky', Johnson demonstrated how ODA is viewed by those on the right wing of UK politics – that is, it was giving away money with no return (Honeyman and Lightfoot 2020). James Pritchett (2023) has written on the Johnson government and its approach to overseas development assistance in light of the impact of Covid and Brexit on the structuring of development policy and wider UK foreign policy. At the time writing, ODA spending in the UK remains at 0.5%.

Reflective questions

1 Why do developed nations commit to overseas development aid? What are their motivations?
2 What might we have expected the Cameron government's policy on ODA to be? Did they act as expected? Why?
3 What would be the potential benefits and costs to the UK of the Johnson government cutting ODA spending?

US–UK special relationship

The reasons why the relationship between the UK and the US is considered 'special' have little to do with the states themselves. A good working relationship certainly makes things easier for the UK and the US, and excellent chemistry between a President and a Prime Minister can really bring benefits, but even the worst relationship cannot (or has not to date) completely derailed the relationship. At worst, it has caused it to cool, as demonstrated during the leaderships of Eden and Eisenhower or Heath and Nixon. The relationship itself is built on a long history of cooperation, which creates trust between the nations, but, most importantly, it is based on shared ideals and values, and a shared view of what the world should look like and the position of the UK and the US within that world. The aim of a liberal, democratic, Western-focused, capitalist world (however loosely these terms are defined) is the basis of one of the strongest and longest-lasting relationships in international politics.

The aims of the UK and the US are not identical, but where there has been divergence, the relationship has tended to compartmentalise those issues to isolate them. An example of this was when photographs of the Manchester Arena bombing in 2017 were published in the *New York Times* before their official release in the UK (BBC News 2017). This incident could have been hugely problematic, potentially undermining the sacred trust between the nations over intelligence-gathering information, but it was quickly resolved and dismissed without either side being chastised publicly. The defence and intelligence links between the UK and the US are now so deeply ingrained in the governing systems of the two nations that to untangle them would be difficult. It reflects the deep level of trust between the two nations, where they are willing to share intelligence information with each other that they do not share with other nations and are willing to work together freely on sensitive policy areas. That does not mean that they are fully integrated, that they always work together effectively or that they share all their information. To suggest that would be foolish. However, the trust between the two nations is clear to see in their intelligence-sharing and defence cooperation.

The Thatcher–Reagan years are often identified as being the high point of the UK–US special relationship. Indeed, an aide of Thatcher once described the leaders as being 'political soulmates' (Abdullah 2013). While the relationship between these two individuals, as well as that between the two nations, was certainly close during this period, it is not the only high point in this international relationship. Often, the relationship is closest when there is a Conservative Prime Minister in Downing Street. While the explanations for this are not necessarily conclusive, the closer ideological positioning of a Conservative leader to the US political sphere certainly seems to play a role.

In the early years of the Blair premiership, the relationship with the US was certainly close. Blair and Clinton worked closely together during the Kosovo war, but also cooperated over other foreign policy initiatives, primarily Operation Desert Fox in 1998 and the Good Friday Agreement in 1998. The arrival of George W. Bush in the White House was greeted with some caution in the UK, as it was expected that the relationship between a Labour Prime Minister and a Republican President would be more difficult and testing. Initially, the relationship seemed cordial but not particularly close. All of that changed in 2001 with the attacks on the World Trade Center. Blair decisively backed the US very quickly after the 9/11 terrorist attacks, placing the UK as the strongest supporter of the United States. As action in Afghanistan was suggested and then planned for, the UK stood squarely with its international ally, working alongside other nations to support the invasion and then taking on the management of the volatile Helmand province in the south of the country. As action in Iraq began to appear more likely, again the UK stood by its international ally, something which caused considerable political upset in the UK and cost Blair a great deal of political capital. Indeed, his political reputation never recovered from the hammer blows which accompanied this decision. The war in Iraq tested the UK–US special relationship, but at no point did the relationship look like it would be destroyed or even fundamentally undermined.

The arrival of President Obama in the White House in 2008 signalled a shift change in the UK–US relationship. Gordon Brown had taken over as Prime Minister in 2007 but was, in many ways, a continuation of the previous administration, at least in the view of the Obama administration. With Cameron's election in 2010, a new era of cooperation might have been expected. However, the relationship between Cameron and Obama was not particularly close, reflecting both the aftermath of the Iraq War and the accusations of the overly close relationship between Bush and Blair, but also Obama's focus on the Indo-Pacific region.

When Donald Trump became President in 2016, it was explosive for the special relationship. Indeed, it was explosive for all the existing relationships the US had. Trump and Theresa May, who had succeeded Cameron as Conservative Prime Minister, had nothing in common and Trump's very combative style certainly made relations difficult between the two nations. May was also preoccupied with the impact of Brexit and the arrangements for the UK leaving the European Union, meaning her primary focus was not the special relationship. Indeed, Trump's time in office was marked by very little direct foreign intervention, allowing the special relationship to continue in a more regularised if less obvious way. One exception was the leaking of an email written by the UK ambassador to the US, Kim Darroch, in which the ambassador criticised Trump. The resulting furore led to Darroch resigning his post (Siddique 2023). It might have been expected that Johnson, a more ebullient individual, who became Prime Minister in 2019, would have found it easier to deal with Trump than the more formal May, but the relationship did not improve in any perceivable respect, and the UK was essentially marking time until a new President, Joe Biden, was elected in 2022 (Toosi 2022).

While the relationships between Biden and, in turn, Johnson, Truss and Sunak were certainly not as explosive as when Trump was in the White House, they were not particularly close either. Partly this was due to the number of UK Prime Ministers which Biden had to deal with. Although relations between the UK and the US regarding defence and the security services continued, as always, in regularised fashion, in terms of governmental relations, the relationship could best be characterised as cordial and functional. While the relationship between the two nations will remain close, the new Labour government will be keen to see the outcome of the 2024 Presidential election. A Harris win would allow the new government to build a strong relationship with a new but positively perceived President, while another Trump term would be greeted privately with some considerable concern based on his last period in office and his previous relations with UK Prime Ministers. Whether they be friendly or frosty, the defence and security services will continue to compartmentalise their relationship to ensure their co-operation can continue regardless of the political relationship between Prime Minister and President – as it has always been since the early days of the special relationship.

Relations with the Commonwealth and the Anglosphere

By the dying days of the twentieth century, the British Empire was gone, but it has cast a very long shadow on modern Britain and the former colonies. The relationship between the UK and its former colonies varies from nation to nation, but each exists within the prism of the UK's behaviour as coloniser. Some former colonial nations have managed to rehabilitate their relationship with the UK, while others continue to have poor relations with the UK. Often the defining feature of the relationship, and the basis of its success or failure, is the economic development of the former colony – the more economically important the nation, the more important it often is to the UK. The changing power dynamics can be extremely difficult for both nations to deal with. While the UK may tend to view itself as the senior partnership in many relationships with former colonies, that is not always an accurate current picture. Relationships need to reflect the new realities of economic dominance by former colonies and all relationships need to reflect the independence of those nations, both in terms of sovereignty and in policy terms, where they cannot be 'told' what to do. Perhaps the most obvious example is the relationship between the UK and India. India's rapid economic development has changed the relationship between it and the UK, from one where the UK felt it dominated to one which the UK appears uncertain how to manage. As India has economically overtaken the UK, the old certainties in the relationship have fallen away. That changing dynamic can often put the UK government in an uncomfortable position, situated between the historical version of Britain, which is often perpetuated in the press, and the modern-day realities of global politics (Scott 2017).

The British Empire was made up of a patchwork of different nations. Some were old nations with historic borders, while others were created by the UK (and other European nations) for political convenience. Each had its own cultural, religious and geographical features, and the powerful groups within the nations varied, as did their relationship with the UK. The peace and stability of each nation also varied, with some being very peaceful and some verging on civil war, which meant that the British methods of control differed from nation to nation. Often the decisions made relating to a colony were influenced by the ethnic make-up of the nation. Those nations with either a white majority or, perhaps more importantly, a white-dominated government tended to be treated more favourably than those with black majorities and black governing groups and parties. Cecil Rhodes once stated: 'You are an Englishman and have subsequently drawn the greatest prize in the lottery of life' (cited in Greene 2020). Of course, the subtext did not simply relate to Englishmen, but to the benefits of being white, particularly at a time when the largest Empire on earth was ruled by a white nation. Colonies such as Australia, Canada, New Zealand and South Africa (ruled by the white minority) were treated differently from other colonies. These four nations were decolonised at the turn of the twentieth century and given the authority to rule themselves. They were also admitted to a prototype Commonwealth. The impression given was that these colonies could be trusted to rule themselves, while others could not, and the inescapable conclusion was that that decision was reached, in part, because these nations were predominantly white and their governments were led by white individuals and parties.

While the early decolonisation of 'white' Empire states might be considered historic, it has a modern-day consequence with the rise of the 'Anglosphere'. This term is used to describe Australia, Canada, New Zealand and South Africa, alongside the UK, and the particular kind of relationship they share. Based on similar ideological positions globally, the nations are referred to as a grouping which maintains a close relationship, something that the UK government is attempting to build on with the signing of agreements such as AUKUS (a trilateral security partnership between Australia, the UK and the USA) and the Comprehensive and Progressive Trans-Pacific Partnership (CPTPP). The CPTPP has 12 members: the UK, Australia, New Zealand, Canada, Singapore, Malaysia, Japan, Brunei Darussalam, Vietnam, Chile, Peru and Mexico (Webb 2024). While the Anglosphere is currently not fully developed, these emerging relationships and new agreements suggest that the UK will strengthen its ties with Australia, New Zealand, Canada and South Africa going forward (e.g. Mycock and Wellings 2017).

Key global concerns

The end of the Cold War signalled a sea-change in global politics and international relations. The old enemy, the Soviet Union (and Russia before that), was welcomed back to the international community with open arms, and while concerns remained over communist strongholds (notably China, but also North Korea and Cuba primarily), the expectation was that a new world was beckoning. Unfortunately, that optimism was misplaced, and within the space of three decades, Russia has once again become a cause for concern in many Western nations. Beyond international relations with individual states, a number of larger issues require global cooperation and action, something which is almost impossible to achieve. Top of that list is action on climate change and its associated issues, such as deforestation, the effects of rising sea levels and global emissions. The knock-on effect of changes in the climate have created issues and disasters of their own. Whether it is the movement of people, driven from their homes by environment disasters, increasing economic pressure and civil war, the changes in global demographics are causing people to move, and that movement is being used by some to generate hate and violence against vulnerable groups. The remainder of this section will briefly consider some of the big challenges that the international community is trying to tackle, unfortunately with little tangible success.

Sovereign threats

The end of the Cold War heralded a restart in the relationship between many Western nations, including the UK, and Russia. However, as with many 'fresh starts', the memories of the recent past loomed large and the different priorities and interpretations of Russia and Western nations like the UK continued to cause periodic issues in the relationship. Russia's immediate neighbours, particularly Ukraine but also Georgia and other Eastern European states, live in the shadow of Russia and fear drives much of their foreign policy making, particularly that related to international organisations. Many former Warsaw Pact countries are now members of NATO (and the EU), which provide them with the defence of collective security (the Warsaw Pact was an organisation with some similarities to NATO but made up of nations under the influence of the Soviet Union). The war in Kosovo, and Russia's subsequent failure to recognise Kosovo as an independent state, demonstrated the gap between the stances of nations such as the UK and Russia. The old spheres of influence had not disappeared and the leadership of Putin has only amplified this. His expansionist foreign policy and 'Greater Russia' approach has not only made several nations on the border of Russia nervous (including Georgia and Finland) but has been of concern to the wider international community for several years (Hill 2022).

Case Study 19.1

The domestic impacts of the Iraq War

The war in Iraq was a watershed moment for British foreign policy. Controversial at the time, the war itself has arguably become more contentious as time has passed. The Iraq War caused a number of seismic shifts in foreign policy making, although not all of them have remained intact and many have been eroded over time. The most obvious impact of the war was an undermining of trust in the Parliament, government and politicians. Trust was already low in 2002, but the notion of a government sending troops to war, potentially under questionable or dishonest circumstances and against the will of a significant number of people within the UK (as demonstrated by the large public demonstrations objecting to Britain going to war in Iraq), was unsettling for large sections of the British public.

One domestic impact of the war was a growing concern over how policy is made. The tradition of Cabinet government, where decisions are reached in Cabinet and all members agree to them publicly regardless of any private reservations, is the official mechanism of decision-making in the UK. However, in practice, making decisions in this way is impractical. Different Prime Ministers have different methods of reaching decisions. Some, such as John Major, focused on small groups of key individuals to make decisions. Others, such as Thatcher and Blair, reached decisions in a very small group with only a handful of individuals, who were not necessarily members of the Cabinet. It led to accusations of presidentialism and sofa-politics. The Iraq War can be considered an example of presidentialism, where the views of the leader (in the case of the UK, the Prime Minister) are dominant and the opinions of the Cabinet were barely considered. During the build-up to the Iraq war the cabinet was largely tasked with deciding the more practical elements of the invasion rather than discussing the principle of war.

Another impact of the war was a change (at least in the short term) in the mechanism of declaring war and how a government takes Britain to war. Prior to the Iraq War, the prerogative for going to war lay with the Prime Minister (on behalf of the Monarch). However, the contentious nature of the war meant that the Blair government was keen to have 'Parliamentary buy-in' for the decision, heralding a change in Parliamentary tradition. The rules did not change – no Prime Minister needs to bring their decision to go to war to the Houses of Parliament. However, for a number of years, Prime Ministers did bring decision-making over military action to Parliament, sometimes with mixed results, because it provided an opportunity to give a thorough airing of different viewpoints and created the impression of collective responsibility across Parliament (Strong 2015). In reality, as First-Past-the-Post voting leads to majority governments, the potential for defeat is relatively low and, therefore, the impression of consensus and collectivity may be misleading.

Another change among the British public was the visibility of self-interest in foreign policy, particularly in the Middle East. The Iraq War made the public more aware of the vested interests at play in the Middle East, as different power groups and longstanding rivalries in the region became visible in a way that many had not seen before. This was demonstrated in the wider public debates and scepticism which surrounded UK action in Syria and Libya, and in other disputes and wars in which the UK was not directly involved, including the military action in Israel in 2024.

Reflective questions

1   What have been the long-term impacts of the Iraq War on the UK?
2   Does the Iraq War make Britain going to war somewhere else in the Middle East more or less likely? Why?

NATO

The status quo, established during the Cold War, separated Europe and Russia into two separate blocs – the NATO nations and the Warsaw Pact countries. Inevitably, not all nations in Europe joined either organisation, but the battle lines were drawn and the blocs provided collective security for their members, real or imagined. With the end of the Cold War and EU expansion, the issue of NATO membership became a hot topic in former Warsaw Pact countries. Although there is no automatic need for any state to become a NATO member, some nations, such as Poland and Romania, joined the organisation (Poland in 1999 and Romania in 2004), while others have continued to opt out. The reasons for non-membership are diverse. However, some members believed that their membership of NATO would potentially be viewed as an aggressive act by Moscow and therefore felt it was in their best interests to remain outside of the organisation. This was the position in which Finland and Sweden, both EU members, found themselves. Their membership of NATO, something which was often discussed, was indefinitely delayed over concerns about perceptions of this act in Russia (Taylor and Klimentov 2023).

The Russian invasion of Ukraine in 2023 changed the landscape. Ukraine, as a non-NATO state, was obviously not covered by the organisation's collective security pact, but with a war so close to so many NATO members, and concerns over where Russia might go next if it overran Ukraine, the traditional wisdom of keeping Russia relatively content in order to avoid conflict, and ignoring aggression wherever possible (which was largely the default position after the annexation of Crimea in 2014), faltered. Finland and Sweden both applied for NATO membership, and discussions about the future of Ukraine within the NATO alliance or as an autonomous sovereign nation began in earnest.

Beyond the immediate questions over the outcome of the Ukrainian war and the potential of NATO membership for Ukraine and Georgia, bigger questions also need answering. For the UK and its allies, concerns exist over the relationship between Putin and China's President Xi Jinping, and how Russia and China might cooperate in the future. It is becoming clear that NATO is not likely to be enough of a deterrent to prevent invasion in other nations beyond Ukraine, such as Taiwan or South Korea. For the UK, containment of Russia and ultimately China is important if almost impossible to achieve, but the peace brought by concessions appears to have little permanency.

The UN Security Council and collective decision-making

The UN Security Council is a group of 15 nations which determine the priorities and actions of the United Nations. This is done through UN Security Council discussing and the production of UN resolutions – statements which indicate the views of the council and what action they would prefer taken to resolve issues and disputes. The Security Council had five permanent members and ten rotating members (these change every two years and the nations are selected by the UN General Assembly). Russia occupies one of the five permanent seats on the United Nations Security Council (UNSC) alongside the UK, the USA, France and China. These seats are highly prized, offering these five nations the ability to shape, and importantly to veto, UN Security Council directives and shape (or ignore) global incidents such as invasions, terrorist attacks or threats of war and the United Nations' response to them. The power these seats hold is immeasurable and no member would willingly sacrifice their seat. There has been comment from successive UK governments about extending the number of permanent seats on the UNSC, with suggestions that the existing five could be joined by Germany, Japan, Brazil, India and possibly South Africa (or another African nation, such as Nigeria). The reasoning behind proposals for enlargement has been to support a reappraisal of the role of the UNSC in light of the new global realities, recognising that the existing five permanent members reflect the postwar settlement and exclude huge swathes of the world from leadership positions within the UN. Another motivating factor for the UK government, which is less publicly discussed, is the goodwill that such calls bring, as the UK can cast itself as the supporter of nations across the world. Interestingly, and perhaps obviously, these calls for an extension of the permanent seats at the UNSC are often made during, or just before, a UK government visit to one of the nations which is likely be the beneficiary of a new permanent seat (Wintour 2023). These statements can be made in complete safety by the UK government, because any changes in the composition of the UNSC (including the extension of the number of seats or the replacement of existing members) requires the support of all five permanent members, something which is extremely unlikely because China and Russia would not agree to this change and would therefore veto any resolutions on this issue. Both China and Russia have expressed concerns over the extension of the UNSC, in part because enlargement will exacerbate difficulties in terms of decision-making. Therefore, nations such as the UK are able to make empty promises that they cannot deliver on and still generate goodwill across the world by appearing to be progressive and inclusive in global governance.

The need for the five permanent members of the UNSC to agree unanimously on action (or at least not veto policy decisions) is difficult to achieve in practice. Putting aside the more divisive issues which will inevitably create division (such as those related to Israel, or concerning nations within the spheres of influence of both Russia and China, and any action motivated by ideals such as human rights, where the five permanent members are likely to have different viewpoints), even more straightforward issues can become complex. Attacks on different parts of the world tend to be viewed differently in the five permanent member states. Even those attacks on sovereign nations, where it would be expected that there would be more unity in condemnation, can be complicated, depending on the states involved and the action required to resolve the situation. For example, the war in Ukraine has stretch the UN Security Council to breaking point, because Russia is the aggressor. As a permanent member with the ability to veto any policy making, the UN Security Council finds itself virtually paralysed in the face of the invasion. Similar situations have arisen when other member states have taken action (including the war in Iraq in 2003) or when the nation where action has taken place is within the 'sphere of influence' of a member state. While the UN Security Council decision-making process is fragile and often contentious, there is little real appetite to change it and no agreement on what any potential change might look like in practice. Therefore, for the moment at least, the five permanent members remain in place with no extension likely in the short to medium term.

Conclusion

British foreign policy has traditionally been driven by self-interest. That is not to say that other considerations have not played their role in decision-making, or that the British government has pursued its foreign policy making in a way markedly different from other nations. Indeed, pragmatism and self-interest are the basis of the majority of foreign policy making globally, and that is a justifiable position for many nations to take. Any national government is responsible to its electorate and its interests, so making decisions based on the best interests (or at least the perceived best interests) of the electorate and the nation more generally is entirely justifiable. Opinions may differ on what is in the best interests of the nation. Accepted wisdom suggests that, as the external face of a nation, the national interest is easier to determine than domestic policy, and thus allows the political parties to unite on policy rather than to disagree. That view does not always hold true, however, as has been shown by the war in Iraq, debates over bombing campaigns in Syria and British action in Afghanistan, and questions over the use of overseas development aid have shown.

The move by the Blair government to introduce ideological elements to foreign policy making is therefore debatable. While the messaging associated with ODA focused on morality and the alleviation of poverty, the policy changes could be seen in a more self-interested light, where the real benefactor was the UK. Inevitably, this messaging, whether it was accurate or misleading, painted the UK in a charitable and altruistic light. Foreign policy can often be perceived in different ways, with some interpretations focusing on the positive reasons for action being taken and others focusing on the self-interested motivations. The prominence given to different factors can lead to differing interpretations of individual events or conflicts. Therefore, determining whether the Blair government acted in a more altruistic way, with 'ethical dimensions' at the core of their thinking is debatable and there is no clear answer. While some foreign policy decisions made by Blair look fairly similar in type to what had gone before, the action of the British in Kosovo appears to be an anomaly. Kosovo was a nation in which the British (and the US) had very limited interest. Without longstanding interest in the nation, and with the inevitable risk that any action would aggravate the Russian government and potentially start a wider conflict, the action appears motiveless if a concern for human rights is dismissed as being the real motivation for action. In the absence of other explanations, the action of the UK in Kosovo does appear to have been driven by concerns over human rights, something which is largely anomalous in British foreign policy making.

Overseas development assistance is another area where motivations can seem to be mixed. Inevitably, the giving of aid to developing nations can be considered an altruistic policy. Seemingly, when money is given to other nations (or money is spent 'beyond the water's edge'), self-interest can seem difficult to establish. However, ODA has many pragmatic benefits for a donor nation. For a former empire state like the UK, the rehabilitation of their international image, and a defence against any calls for reparations are obvious reasons for giving aid. Building new trade links and fostering good relations to enable more cooperation with emerging markets are also very good reasons for increasing ODA spending. However, the fact that there are pragmatic reasons for increasing and sustaining aid funding does not necessarily suggest that altruism did not play a part in the creation of the 0.7% ODA target by the Labour government, or its continuation by Cameron and the Conservative government. The rise to 0.7% of GNI spend was certainly a change from previous policy under the Thatcher and Major governments, but that does not mean that the pursuit of that spending target was driven by purely altruistic or purely selfish reasoning. Instead, a mix of the two motivations seems more likely over the time period.

The mixture of altruistic reasons and more self-interested reasons for foreign policy making appears to have been a longstanding feature of British foreign policy, something which was continued in a slightly different format by the Blair government and those which followed it. By flagging up more ideologically or morally driven foreign policy motives, governments were able to reap some reward internationally, being identified as a good global partner in various policy areas, not least ODA funding. However, Britain has never pursued an ideological foreign policy or one focused primarily or solely on human rights. Pragmatism remains king. With the demise of the Cameron government in 2016, even discussion of human rights as a policy making priority has tended to be more muted, signalling perhaps a return to the status quo. This can be seen in policy areas such as the UK's departure from Afghanistan and the reduction of the ODA spending target to 0.5% of GNI.

At the time of writing, the two biggest foreign policy worries for the UK government (putting aside the repercussions of Brexit, which are large and wide-ranging) is the war in Ukraine and violence in Israel. Both are politically sensitive and the UK finds itself in a global environment where its views and action, while important, are not the primary focus of those involved. In both conflicts, the actions of the US are key, with the UK playing an important supporting role. This is the reality of British foreign policy making in the twenty-first century. The UK is still an important nation, its policies still carry weight and it matters what the UK does. However, it is not a superpower and in the coming years the focus of international attention will be the global powerhouse nations – the US, China, the EU, and potentially nations such as India and Brazil. The UK is already adapting to that new reality, but it may mean that even more foreign policy decisions are made as a consequence of decisions made in Washington, Beijing or Brussels. That is not a situation in which the UK government would want to find itself, but it is increasingly the reality that is facing Westminster and Whitehall. The UK–US special relationship is likely to maintain its importance in the future, and may even become more important to the UK if her international voice reduces further.

Summary

- There are debates about ethical ideas in foreign policy, but UK policy in this area has probably been marked by pragmatism and practical considerations more than ethics. The UK has had to make do with what foreign policy choices were possible for a declining power.
- Foreign policy is made at the very top of government by the key actors, including the Prime Minister and the Secretary of State for Foreign, Commonwealth and Development Affairs.
- An uncertain international environment (including a more multi-polar world and more influence and competition from emerging nations) means that the UK's influence may diminish. The importance of the UK–US relationship in UK foreign policy is likely, however, to remain a constant.

Recommended and further reading

- Dee, M. and Smith, K.E. (2017) 'UK diplomacy at the UN after Brexit: Challenges and opportunities', *British Journal of Politics and International Relations*, 19(3): 527–542. This article examines the prospects for the UK's diplomacy at the United Nations after Brexit. The UK's position is under pressure, but Brexit may present some opportunities for the UK to exploit. Cooperation with the EU is likely to remain a key component of UK foreign policy at the UN, whatever the formal relationship.
- Honeyman, V. (2019) 'New Labour's overseas development aid policy – charity of self-interest?', *Contemporary British History*, 33(3): 313–335. This article examines the origins

of the UK's international aid diplomacy. The target for aid became a useful symbol for the government in many different ways.

- Oliver, T. and Williams, M.J. (2016) 'Special relationships in flux: Brexit and the future of the US–EU and US–UK relationships', *International Affairs*, 92(3): 547–567. The US–UK relationship has been a cornerstone of UK foreign policy, and there is much commentary that emphasises the usefulness of the UK to the US in promoting US views in Europe. This article examines the prospects for a post-Brexit role for the UK and the continued nature of the alliance.

- Wenzelburger, G. and Boller, F. (2020) 'Bomb or build? How party ideologies affect the balance of foreign aid and defence spending', *British Journal of Politics and International Relations*, 22(1): 3–23. Do left-wing parties in power tend to spend more on foreign aid and less on defence? These authors crunch the data and suggest that the answer is yes.

Chapter 20

UK politics and the end of empire

Harshan Kumarasingham

What will this chapter tell me?

- This chapter examines the legacy of empire for UK politics and society.
- It gives a brief overview of the late development and dissolution of that empire, noting the uneven effects of colonisation and decolonisation.
- It shows how the empire marked the society and governance of the UK's colonies and the UK itself. It discusses how the 'Westminster' mode of governing was used and adapted elsewhere.
- It suggests that a particular adaptation of that form of governance can be seen in Asia via what the author terms 'Eastminster'.
- One of the most enduring legacies of the empire can be seen in immigration to the UK and the changes in its society after 1945.

What do I need to know?

- The British Empire reached its peak in the early twentieth century. The concerns of empire were at the heart of British politics for decades. The story of politics since then has been about dismantling that empire and trying to work out what that would mean for the UK.
- Imperial legacies are the subject of fierce debate and involve big questions of race, exploitation and societal norms.
- The symbols of empire appear in every part of UK life, from the Foreign Office in Whitehall to universities and museums.
- While the formal Empire is no more, critical legacies of it remain for the United Kingdom and the world in the twenty-first century. The UK's institutions, foreign policy, demography, geostrategic thinking, economic interests, cultural preoccupations and identity are indelibly entwined with the British Empire and Commonwealth.

Introduction

In May 1941 the British Parliament was bombed by the Germans, which reduced the House of Commons to ashes. The decision was taken to rebuild the famed and emblematic parliamentary chamber just as it had been. Yet, there would a critical difference. The chamber would be restored from materials and ornaments sourced and gifted from the British Empire and Commonwealth. The doors to the chamber, the Speaker's Chair and bar to the House, among other items, all came from every part of the Empire. The British Parliament was therefore literally built from empire. However, more than masonry and decor, Westminster and Whitehall are the places that debated and determined the British Empire, and conversely British politics and policy operated for much of history with imperial matters at the top of the agenda. Decisions at Downing Street impacted on Nova Scotia and New Delhi as much as they did the United Kingdom. At its height, Britain had responsibility for the lives of almost half a billion people across every continent. The British Empire made British politics into world politics. While the formal Empire is no more, critical legacies of it remain for the United Kingdom and world in the twenty-first century.

The UK's institutions, foreign policy, demography, geostrategic thinking, economic inter-ests, cultural preoccupations and identity are indelibly entwined with the British Empire and Commonwealth. This chapter aims to show select ways in which the late British Empire and its dissolution were, and are, critical for British politics, and vice versa, in order to see the very real and pervasive influence that empire continues to hold on the politics and history of the United Kingdom. 'Britain' is also a term used here as much as 'United Kingdom' since it speaks not only to the framing of Britain from 1707 as an amalgamation of conscious imperial ambition (Colley 1992), but also the deep cultural and historical resonance of the word and Britishness at home and in the Empire (Ward 2023). In a similar vein, as Tom Devine (2003: 353) has noted, the Empire 'was always described as "the British Empire", never the "English Empire" due to its union-wide contribution and meaning'.

Case Study 20.1

Slavery and empire

Empires were the norm in world history and existed well before the advent of the nation-state. By their nature, they went beyond a single polity and instead ranged across communities and political units, and imposed hierarchies and distinctions over those they ruled (Burbank and Cooper 2010). The British Empire was the greatest and biggest example of empire in history. During the Napoleonic Wars, the modern Empire essentially took shape, when it expanded to become the most dispersed in the world, with new colonies taken in the Caribbean, Europe, Asia and West and Southern Africa, to add to its existing ones in places like India, North America and Oceania. It would now control over one-fifth of the world's population.

Slavery had been a major element of colonialism across the world and was an important aspect of the conflict with France. All empires engaged in its practice and the British Empire was no exception. However, the scale and power of the British Empire meant that what it did had more influence globally than any other. Therefore, British Acts that legislated for the ending of the slave trade in 1807 and, from 1 August 1834, the abolition of slavery across the British Empire constituted major developments that hastened the global end of the cruel practice. However, the laws passed at Westminster and petitions to end slavery that preceded it, did not lead to a dramatic change in the lives of those who had been enslaved. Most slaves carried on as 'apprentices' with chains, floggings and forced labour remaining part of their existence. Not a penny of compensation would reach them. Instead, dukes, barons, the Anglican Church and over 100 Members of Parliament were among those who would be recompensed in return for giving up their holdings. The family of long-serving Liberal prime minister William Gladstone, for example, would receive £14 million in today's money for the slaves owned in Demerara. It would not be until 2015 that the Treasury, through British taxpayers, had paid off those massive loans required to compensate British slave owners. This would be the price needed to convince those with vested interests across the British and political establishment to give up the slave trade (Taylor 2021).

Reflective questions

1 How should the UK deal with the legacy of its involvement in the slave trade?
2 Did the way in which the British Empire ended the slave trade justify the means it used to do it?

The imperial context

In 1945, as Britain proclaimed victory in the Second World War, it could also boast an empire that covered approximately a quarter of the world's population and landmass. Indeed, Winston Churchill's mournful claim that Britain was 'alone' in 1940 after the fall of France to face the growing spectre of Nazi Germany and its allies masked the fact that London commanded the resources and armies of the British Empire, with places such as India providing over 2 million troops and New Zealand suffering a greater proportion of its population in casualties than any other on the British side, in addition to the enormous contributions across the empire from places that stretched from Antigua to Zanzibar. The UK, therefore, was not at any point *alone* in its war effort. The United Kingdom's allies and enemies were fully aware of this too. The British Empire ensured that it had an influence on world politics like few others in history. The opposite corollary was also true, that without the empire, the United Kingdom's significance would have been marginal. Continuously, since at least the Napoleonic Wars till its dismemberment almost two centuries later, the British Empire enabled the UK to stand high abroad and sit securely at home. As such, the control, capacity and benefit of the British Empire was of the highest concern of British politics for almost three centuries, regardless of party. This realisation was deep. Lord Curzon, who had been at the centre of British and imperial politics at the height of empire in the early twentieth century, for example, remarked of the country's possessions in South Asia: 'as long as we rule India, we are the greatest power in the world. If we lost it, we shall straight away drop to a third-rate power' (Mansergh 1982: 54). Curzon, like most people in Parliament a century ago, would have been aghast by the eventual reality of losing not just the British Raj, but all the rest too.

Every continent had a British presence, including Antarctica. The United Kingdom also had major spheres of influence that went beyond its formal Empire, including in the Middle East, East Asia and South America. However, not all Britain's territorial possessions and overseas interests were treated the same or run uniformly. Instead, much as the British Constitution is uncodified and fuelled by both expedience and eccentricity, so too was the late Empire. British imperialism in fact had often been led not by the state itself, but by what we would today describe as venture capitalists. Rapacious trading corporations, sometimes referred to as 'company-states', which had armed powers and monopolistic rights, such as the Hudson's Bay Company in North America, the Royal Niger Company in West Africa and the East India Company in Asia, spearheaded the conquest, control and exploitation of vast regions and resources across the world in the quest for enormous profit, before formal state-sponsored British colonialism took up the baton (Stern 2023) – although the assumption of colonial rule by the UK state did not mean the end of financial motives. Outside the colonies, in the so-called 'Informal Empire', where there was not explicit control, 'financial imperialism' was also rampant. This was especially so in China and Argentina up to the end of the First World War. In China's case, it was due to crippling debts and loans owed to the UK, and for Argentina it was the overwhelming dominance of British imports and investments. In both cases, their scope for economic action mirrored colonial arrangements, not independent ones. The UK's motives in having an empire, whatever its type, was significantly driven by the cause of financial gain (Kohli 2020).

A critical part of empire were the areas of British settlement, which were often referred to collectively as the 'White Dominions'. Theses settler states comprised the modern countries of Canada, Australia, New Zealand and South Africa. The settler populations saw themselves as being at the core of the British race, and consequently as partners, not victims, in the imperial project. The local indigenous populations had little sway or say in the affairs of their home-lands. Instead, the settlers exercised locally their own specific brand of imperialism to assert dominance. They were aided by the fact that, increasingly, the White Dominions had near full political autonomy in their internal affairs and often acted in their own interest on the world stage. From the late nineteenth century, this was reflected by the fact that leaders of the set-tler colonies would meet for imperial conferences in London in one of the first real examples of cross-continental summitry. Major common concerns of the Empire were always on the agenda, which included distinct imperial ambitions, for example, of Australia and New Zealand in the Pacific, or fears over non-European migration, and military priorities that these 'kith and kin' allies expected Britain to help with in order defend *their* corners of the Empire.

While Britain was acknowledged by the White Dominions as the leader, it resembled a 'first among equals' relationship rather than one of servility (Darwin 2009). Politically, it translated into having systems of government that consciously mirrored the UK's, but with crucial differ-ences. Aware of how the American colonies broke away, the British expanded what was termed 'responsible government' where, in large measure, policies and leaders were determined not by London, but by the local electorates and legislatures. These 'Settler Westminsters' followed many of the conventions and principles of the original, such as having a strong concentration of executive power in a prime minister and a cabinet drawn from, and responsible to, parlia-ment, not London. Even the British Monarch's representative in the Dominion, the Gover-nor-General, rarely intervened in local politics, unlike in the rest of the colonial Empire. These institutional arrangements articulated a unique autonomy, which had long been the existing practice. It was formalised in the 1926 Balfour Declaration, which applied to all of settler states, including the United Kingdom itself:

> They are autonomous Communities within the British Empire, equal in status, in no
> way subordinate one to another in any aspect of their domestic or external affairs,
> though united by a common allegiance to the Crown, and freely associated as
> members of the British Commonwealth of Nations. (Imperial Conference, 1926)

This thinking would form the basis of the Statute of Westminster 1931, which gave legislative force to these realities and additionally stated that the UK ceased to have the ability to legislate for the Dominions without their express consent. As the French-Canadian prime minister Sir Wilfrid Laurier said almost a quarter century before, in 1907, at the Imperial Conference in London, it had been 'agreed that we have passed the state when the term "Colony" could be applied' to the select White settler-led countries of the British Empire (Wheare 1960: 8). That more subservient relationship and term was reserved for the non-Europeans.

Most colonial subjects of the British Empire could claim no such privileges of political autonomy enjoyed by the White settlers. Instead, the benevolence of the ruler was deemed to be all that was necessary. As such, their experience was starkly different. It was a conscious part of the imperial ideology of the British Empire to show who was fit for government, and who was not (Armitage 2000). The non-settler areas therefore engaged more strongly in the politics of anti-colonialism. There was also a long history of local political formations built upon the advocacy for self-government *within* the British Empire. Initially, political organisa-tions such as the Indian National Congress or the African National Congress, founded in 1885 and 1912 respectively, sought relatively modest aims that pushed for an improvement of their rights in the hope of equivalence with those of the settlers and the Dominions. These parties were generally made up of educated, professional and elite locals who were well attuned to the language and norms of Westminster politics. As it became evident that their objectives to improve the rights of their communities were being effectively ignored or the gains mediocre, they either transformed or were superseded by organisations that were impatient with gradualist politics. The change or replacement of these parties saw a more radical programme that included complete independence and sometimes open disobedience of colonial rule. Their message found greater appeal and participation from the masses, who bore the brunt of colonialism. Figures like Kwame Nkrumah, the future post-independence prime minister of Ghana, were adept at eclipsing the old guard, galvanising the crowds towards the anti-colonial movement, and compelling colonial officials to parley with them as the coming force. In fact, Nkrumah, who had been detained for his role in strikes and mass protests in the Gold Coast, would literally go straight from prison to parliament in February 1951. The British Governor, Sir Charles Arden-Clarke, released Nkrumah from incarceration and invited him to become the main political leader in the Legislative Assembly in recognition of Nkrumah's party's electoral performance earlier that year, and the *realpolitik* of where the coming power lay.

For everyday colonial subjects there were daily reminders of the disparity in rights and subordinate status as compared to the colonial officials. While the colonial presence in terms of the 'men on the spot' was small, their influence was deep, and their rule felt. At the beginning of the twentieth century, when the British Empire was at its height, the number of Britons living and ruling over 400 million people in what would become the modern states of India, Pakistan, Bangladesh and Burma (Myanmar) hovered at around 155,000 only. This was just a fifth of the size of the population of Glasgow (Gilmour 2018: 11–12). Yet a Briton in the Indian Civil Service or Colonial Service might find themselves as a district officer being the effective autocrat over millions of people in an area larger than Scotland. They would also be expected to exercise the powers of a judge, policeman, landlord, and even religious and social leader, whom the local population had to contend with as the personal manifestation of British power and authority. This, unsurprisingly, led to abuse.

British officer Reginald Dyer commanded his troops to consciously commit cruelty and death in April 1919 against an unarmed peaceful gathering of Indians in Amritsar. They were protesting against the draconian laws newly given to colonial authorities to arrest anti-colonial activists and limit civil liberties. Dyer had earlier forced Indians to crawl when passing the spot where an English woman had been assaulted. The one passage way to where the non-violent protestors convened at the Jallianwala Barg was blocked by Dyer's troops, who were ordered to fire into the heart of the crowd without warning, pause or mercy. No chance for escape or negotiation was possible. While no conclusive figure can be given on the casualties, it is estimated that up to 1,000 people died, including very young children, and thousands more were wounded. Dyer and his supporters had wished to impress the might of British rule and showed a callous indifference to justice and Indian lives. The episode highlighted for many, not just in India, the harsh reality of British colonialism. The non-violent protestors gathered in 1919 were not fermenting a rebellion, but their example inspired many that saw revolt as the only way. While censured by the House of Commons (but not in the House of Lords) and reprimanded by a Commission of Inquiry, the imperialist paper *The Morning Post* called Dyer 'The Man Who Saved India' and raised a huge sum for him via public subscription, after he was compelled to leave the Army. In 1920, in a parliamentary debate on the lessons of Amritsar, Edwin Montagu, the Secretary of State for India, asked the House of Commons a question that resonated across the wider British Empire and drove deep into the validity of the UK's imperial purpose:

Are you going to keep your hold upon India by terrorism, racial humiliation and subordination, and frightfulness, or are you going to rest it upon the goodwill, and the growing goodwill, of the people of your Indian Empire? (Wagner 2019: 237–242)

Politics and empire after 1945

Right up until the 1960s, senior Cabinet posts in British politics were associated with the British Empire. The Colonial Secretary, for example, carried significant power and profile. Giants of British politics, such as Lord John Russell, Joe Chamberlain, Winston Churchill, Andrew Bonar Law, Jimmy Thomas and Ian Macleod, held that post. Two future prime ministers, Anthony Eden and Clement Attlee, served as Secretary of State for Dominion Affairs. Commonwealth Secretary was an office held by noted foreign affairs experts Philip Noel-Baker and Alec Douglas-Home, while the office of Secretary of State for India was held by political heavyweights such as Lord Salisbury, Lord Hartington, John Morely, Austen Chamberlain and Lord Birkenhead. Imperial postings were much sought after too. Politicians as diverse as Stafford Cripps, Rab Butler and Enoch Powell dreamed of being Viceroy of India. It was very common in the nineteenth and early twentieth centuries for politicians to make their careers in the Empire. However, even in the 1960s, a serving Chief Whip, Speaker of the House of Commons and General Secretary of the Labour Party jumped straight from these posts to be the Governors-General of the West Indies, Australia and Mauritius respectively, while as late as the 1990s, Bermuda, Gibraltar and Hong Kong had Governors who had not long before served as Ministers under Margaret Thatcher.

After the end of the Napoleonic Wars in 1815, Britain would control over one-fifth of the world's population. Yet, the Colonial Office never matched this enlargement. In the early nineteenth century, it never had more than 20 staff, and even a century later, when the Empire was at its height, it remained one of the smallest departments in Whitehall, with just 113 members of staff in 1903. It eventually ceased being a separate department of state in 1966 and was subsumed into the Foreign Office in 1968. Even so, both Labour and the Conservatives, when in government, had hoped to build a grand new Colonial Office building after 1945, since they believed the sun had not yet set on Britain's colonial empire (Hyam 2010). The Office found in its polling in 1948 that most respondents in the UK could not name a single British colony, although one man thought Lincolnshire was one, and 3% of respondents believed that the USA still belonged to the British Empire. However, this level of ignorance masked a deep embeddedness of empire in public activity. Education, sports, media, arts, food, film, music, theatre, literature and ceremony had close ties to the British Empire, as did cultural and intellectual institutions such as the BBC, universities, museums, galleries and social organisations at all levels of society. As a leading cultural historian has argued, empire 'came to infuse and be propagated by every organ of British life in the period' (MacKenzie 1984: 2), and even after the British Empire began to disintegrate and colonies became independent sovereign nations its legacy remained in the consciousness of the British people (MacKenzie 1984: 2). Indeed, it has been argued that the British Empire helps us to understand the British domestically, through social structures and preoccupations, and outwardly, as a means to explore the UK's view of the world (Cannadine 2001).

While imperial affairs had been at the heart of British politics for centuries, it was essentially from the end of the Second World War that British Cabinets dealt actively with the reality of managing the *gradual* ending of the British Empire instead of preserving, let alone expanding, it.

The Labour Government of Clement Attlee, elected by a landslide in 1945, committed towards the end of its manifesto *Let Us Face the Future*, that if it gained power it would promote 'the advancement of India to responsible self-government, and the planned progress of our Colonial Dependencies' (The Labour Party 1945). It was not explicit what this meant in practice. Nonetheless, it was welcome news to freedom movements in the colonies since it contrasted with Winston Churchill proclaiming publicly a few years earlier in 1942 that he had not 'become the King's First Minister in order to preside over the liquidation of the British Empire' (Louis, 1998). Yet Churchill, who would return to Downing Street as prime minister in 1951, would indeed seriously have to do just that, as would his successors. The Attlee Government's shepherding of Indian and Pakistani independence in 1947 was seen as one of its greatest successes, despite the violence, loss and crises that the partition of the Indian Empire brought (Khan 2007). To many, including on the subcontinent, the pain of division was overshadowed by the joy of gaining freedom, which only a few years earlier seemed impossible. The fall of British Raj broke the dam of empire and released waves of similar declarations of independence that would continue for decades.

Nonetheless, all British governments from 1945 to the end of the twentieth century, including Attlee's, did not envisage an immediate and wholescale dissolution of the British Empire. Rather, UK governments sought to manage the decolonisation process *and* harness the remaining Empire for their own benefit, including its use to reach and influence the rest of the world. Remembering that the British Empire made the United Kingdom a world power, policy makers were ever ready to see the risks that its end would have for the UK's global standing. British governments brutally put down rebellions. Notoriously, Britain's colonial regime resorted to torture against followers of the anti-colonial Mau Mau uprising in Kenya in the early 1950s in order to maintain control of East Africa. The 1956 Suez crisis was another attempt to robustly assert British power, but would instead become an early and stark reminder of the limitations of British power in the postwar era. While Egypt was not a formal colony, it had effectively been one, with a deep imperial presence since 1882. Gamal Abdel Nasser's audacious nationalisation of the Suez Canal in 1956 from Anglo-French control led to the Eden Government launching an invasion, with the French and Israelis, in reaction. Eden and many others across the political and official spectrum saw that Nasser's action threatened the UK's economic and military interests given that Suez was a critical trade and geostrategic asset. While there was initial military success, the Americans and certain Commonwealth countries were not supportive. American disapproval in particular put pressure on sterling, which in turn compelled a humiliating climbdown, and later Eden's resignation after less than two years as prime minister. The politics of the event caused huge divisions in Parliament, the Cabinet, the media and with the UK's allies.

Eden's successors tried to be more careful when it came to the Empire, but were still drawn into colonial conflicts in regions as diverse as Southeast Asia, East and Southern Africa, the Middle East and the South Atlantic. These divisive and costly encounters drew substantial political energy in the UK. The encounters in Aden, Cyprus, the Falklands and especially Rhodesia/Zimbabwe produced marked political tensions and substantial public protests. The UK was also facing the reality that the Empire was not as profitable, politically or economically, as it had once been. Harold Macmillan even tasked the Civil Service in the wake of Suez in 1957 to prepare an 'Audit of Empire' to literally see what costs would be incurred if the remaining colonies were given independence and to produce an estimated timetable for self-government. In the 1960s, Harold Wilson's Labour Government would look at the country's considerable defence commitments around the Empire with the aim to reduce, and in some cases withdraw, the UK's military presence altogether, due to the expenditure and realities of Britain's diminished position in the world.

Global Westminster and Eastminster

The Westminster Model is the world's most famous parliamentary type. The reason for this is indelibly linked to the British Empire and the cultural and political digestion of the ideas, institutions and traditions of Westminster across the Empire. Without Empire, the British Constitution would arguably be known only to specialists and practitioners rather than being a globally pervasive and significant phenomenon in political culture and ideas (Kumarasingham 2023). However, the Westminster Model, for all its appeal and intellectual circulation, was not a system that was temporally or institutionally uniform, let alone easily exportable. Famously unwritten (or at least uncodified), the Westminster Model, and the constitution behind it, was in practice characterised by its ambiguity and its manner of 'muddling through', as Peter Hennessy (1996) put it, the events and changes in the United Kingdom's history. The institutions of state, such as Crown, Cabinet, Commons and Lords, transformed constantly, even if their names did not. The might of the British Empire contributed to the Westminster Model being the most sought-after system of government in the world. Even President Woodrow Wilson, who had taught Politics at Princeton University before entering the White House, hoped to reform America's system of government with lessons from Westminster, a model he greatly admired.

While every part of the Empire also craved the Westminster model for their own regions, there was a real reluctance from British political leaders and civil servants to grant the UK's political system to lands beyond the United Kingdom. A feeling existed that resembled that of Charles Dickens's pompous character Mr Podsnap, who informed a European visitor: 'We Englishmen are Very proud of Our Constitution, Sir. It Was Bestowed Upon Us By Providence. No Other Country is so Favoured as This Country.' Even places as near to Britain as Ireland or as traditionally loyal as New Zealand were deemed by many politicians as incapable of functioning under the British Constitution and its associated political system, while it was deemed impossible for places like Malta or Malaya. Nonetheless, the political classes of the British Empire, whether in the settler or non-settler parts, were unquestionably shaped by the practices and traditions of Westminster as well as the very real experience of living under local colonial government. This latter condition is critical when considering that for most of the Empire little to no democracy in the modern sense existed. Instead, British colonial officials, usually headed by a London-appointed Governor, exercised formidable executive power locally. Legally, and often practically, the Governor was able to override the wishes of the legislature, which were often filled by those whom he had selected (there were no female governors), and to govern unburdened by the constraints seen at Westminster. As such, political aspirations and realities were moulded by both the closeness of colonial autocracy and the distant democratic principle at the imperial metropole. Yet, despite having to be guided by an unwritten constitution and the very different colonial experience, the Westminster Model was taken up in an extraordinary way.

Naturally, the White Dominions were the areas that experienced the first modern experimentations with the Westminster Model abroad, as they identified historically as being part of the British race. The loyalty of settler communities towards Britishness did not dampen in any way their quest to wrest more control over their own affairs. They all saw the adoption of

Westminster's model of responsible government as essential to that objective since it would shield the glare of London's eye. Building on the recommendations of the 1839 Durham Report (which brought together upper and lower Canada), and the 1867 confederation that created a united Dominion from Britain's North American provinces, Canada became the first to experience responsible government) The Crown's Representative in Ottawa largely retreated from politics and executive power. Instead, local politicians and their bicameral federal legislature – the lower chamber would even be named after the House of Commons – took effective control of the Dominion's affairs without needing recourse to London. Canada's example would be followed by Australia, South Africa, New Zealand and, eventually, Ireland. These White-Settler Westminsters swiftly embraced their political autonomy, especially when that enabled, by virtue of not having imperial interference, an easier dominance of indigenous peoples. Westminster's forms and conventions were readily adapted and transplanted, with consciously identifiable features of the original. Writing in the 1980s, Arend Lijphart, the political scientist and comparativist, even described New Zealand's unwritten constitution and executive-dominant style as the 'purest' and most 'perfect example' of the Westminster Model (Kumarasingham 2010: 37).

Although significant political changes have taken place across the 'Old Dominions', it is worth noting that Canada, Australia and New Zealand still share with the United Kingdom, and other independent Realms in the Caribbean and Pacific, the same Head of State. Their parliamentary systems also still conspicuously abide by many of the norms and conventions of Westminster. There are, however, key differences. Australia and Canada have been federal states for over a century, well before devolution arrived in the UK. Quebec has asymmetric powers in the Canadian Federation and, relatedly, French-Canadians have protected rights in the Canadian Constitution. Australia has an upper house, which resembles the American Senate more than the House of Lords, while New Zealand broke away from the bicameral mould when it abolished its upper house in 1951. More consequentially, New Zealand established a proportional representation electoral system in 1996, which has ushered in a greater frequency of coalition governments. All three states deal with their own regional legacies of empire. This is especially the case regarding the accommodation and rights of indigenous people. Māori have had special representation in New Zealand since 1867, whereas it took another century for Australia to finally extend the franchise, which had been explicitly denied to them in the founding 1901 constitution, to indigenous Australians in 1962. All indigenous people in these countries have been toiling to gain not just equality, but also restoration of their lands and traditional rights prior to British colonisation.

British political scientists and constitutional scholars seldom – then or now – took the opportunity to study this astonishing and diverse articulation and interpretation of the Westminster model or how it was utilised and introduced in many former colonies. Nonetheless, it is imperative to examine this process and to study its manifestations in different contexts in order to better undestand the ambigious and ill-defined system of government (Kumarasingham 2013). While some important work has been completed on the adoption of the Westminster system in the former settler states in comparison with the UK (Rhodes et al. 2009; Strangio et al. 2013; Galligan and Brenton 2015), little has been done to appreciate the non-British-settlement regions, such as in Asia where the Westminster Model also fertilised the soil of lands afar. *Eastminster* is a conceptual tool that can be used not only to investigate how the Westminster system influenced and was reinterpreted beyond the UK and the 'old' 'settler' Dominions, but also to gain greater insights on Westminster's institutions and traditions by seeing them from a comparative perspective by states that reimagined Westminster for their own contexts. This is possible because 'the Westminster system is based on convention and ambiguity and not rigid rules and clarity', which means that it can 'be adopted and manipulated' in different settings and meanings (Kumarasingham 2016: 1-3). Eastminsters consciously had 'clear institutional and political resemblances to Britain's system, but with cultural and constitutional deviations from Westminster' (ibid.). Eastminster is also a distinctive variety of Westminster from that found in the settler states (Kumarasingham 2016). There are five key 'deviations', which are listed inTable 20.1 and discussed in the Cutting-edge Research box. These deviations outline the critical ways in which countries in the non-settler Westminster world diverged from the traditional cases in the White Dominions and the UK itself in the crucial early state-building years following independence from British rule.

Research in Focus

Eastminster and Westminster

Table 20.1   Westminster versus Eastminster

Westminster	Eastminster
1 Settler States	1 Asian Raj
2 Ceremonial Head of State	2 Interfering Head of State
3 Prime Ministerial and Cabinet Executive	3 Selective Dictatorship
4 Majoritarian System	4 Minority Rights
5 Reliance on Conventions and Flexibility	5 Colonial Continuities and Invented Conventions

1   *Asian Raj*: While those who spearheaded the modern states of Australia, Canada, New Zealand and South Africa were White settlers, many of whom thought of themselves as British, their equivalents in the Eastminster systems were conspicuously non-European and non-settler. Nonetheless, this small elite group, the Asian Raj, were very often educated in the prestigious universities in the UK taking subjects like history, law and politics. At the very least, they also spent considerable time in the local setting, studying and participating in British colonial politics. These tendencies of the local elite meant that they were well acquainted intellectually and culturally with the norms of Westminster, even if they were in opposition to it. Thus, an elite oligarchy, often with family and cultural ties, and which resembled the politics of England in the age before mass democracy, tended to dominate.

2   *Interfering Head of State*: While Britons are used to the Monarch, as the Head of State, staying out of active politics and who invariably leaves the exercise of the royal prerogatives like dissolving parliament or selecting the prime minister to the elected politicians, in *Eastminster* the position saw a more assertive one that spoke to earlier times in history when British monarchs exercised substantial power. It also more closely resembled the executive powers of the Crown, as practised during colonialism, when Viceroys and Governors wielded the sort of powers British monarchs had not used since

(Continued)

medieval times. This was a powerful legacy of the colonial experience, which saw local successors as Heads of State play a robust and critical part in politics just as much, if not more, than the prime minister as Head of Government.

3   *Selective Dictatorship*: Elections and democracy, as understood in the UK context, were far from the norm under colonialism. Political leaders in the colonial world often emerge by other means, such as through their proximity to the British, their social standing among their community, or authority over a freedom movement. Fully democratic mandates from the electorate were not possible under colonialism, and thus were not a prerequisite for assuming power. Instead, a highly personalised transfer of power occurred from the British to the local leadership that enabled a swift assumption of the reins of government. The famous concertation of power found in the Westminster executive therefore took accelerated and more pronounced meaning in the Eastminster foundation as democratic institutions had yet to be truly tried and tested, thanks to colonialism. It gave a 'selective' quality to what Lord Hailsham would later describe as the 'elective dictatorship' of British governments once elected in Westminster (Hailsham, 1976). This characteristic was further enhanced by the propensity of freedom movements to be driven by one party, which meant, on independence, that a single political organisation dominated the system without official or meaningful opposition.

4   *Minority Rights*: Historically, and institutionally speaking, Westminster makes little distinction regarding the population. There are few special rights for particular groups because the national electorate is one in which voters generally have equal status, regardless of background. It is also why majoritarian electoral systems like First-Past-the-Post are favoured. Since the mid-twentieth century, voters have usually been treated the same regardless of region, class, religion, sex, language or ethnicity. In the colonial empire, however, even the British had to recognise the very real diversity of the subject population. Indeed, they had always tried to justify colonial rule as being a regime where they benevolently protected the rights of all groups in their charge. For many, this accounted for nothing more than 'divide and rule', by favouring some communities and characteristics over others. As such, the question of rights and representation was a critical one. However, the majoritarian-favouring Westminster Model could not adequately accommodate the vast demographic variety found in the British Empire, especially where the 'artificial' borders of colonialism often rendered natural community alignment unlikely. In Eastminsters, majoritarianism created serious political problems for minority groups who struggled to find a voice and protection in the new regimes.

5   *Colonial Continuities and Invented Conventions*: All freedom movements in the British Empire campaigned in various ways for the reform of powers used against them, including detention for political protest. 'Emergency Rule' was frequently used by the colonial government to stymie, if not suspend, even the limited rights available to colonial subjects, especially if they fought against colonialism. It represented a powerful example and legacy. In fact, all new states that emerged from British rule would keep some colonial era laws on their legislative books. It was very common that some of the harshest colonial laws were retained or renamed, but essentially used for the same purpose: as a tool against the opponents of the rulers. It could mean party-political adversaries, but also employed against certain races, classes, religions, languages, regions or sexualities. In addition, as so much of Westminster is governed by convention and traditions, rather than laws and rules,

there was considerable scope for the reinterpretation of British political norms in these settings. This proved valuable in giving new leaders more opportunity to shape the system in their vision without having to change the constitution or political system. The British Empire, therefore, left powerful colonial continuities in the governance of the new states. While Westminster's lack of rigidity gave it ample chances to reinvent itself, through conventions and practices, in the Eastminsters, with critical consequences that are still being felt (Kumarasingham 2016: 1–35).

The Cutting-edge Research box gives a limited picture of the collective political legacies of the Westminster Model in the British Empire, but also, through Eastminster, allows certain reflections on both the export of the model and what it says about the original in the UK. The 'White Dominions' are no longer called that, and nor do they culturally identify with Westminster and the UK as they once did. Yet their politics and institutions recognisably remain familiar to Westminster's. Outside the former settler world, all the countries that were once part of the British Empire have changed their institutions, and sometimes their constitutions and regime type as well, since gaining independence, and some no longer conform to typologies of the British parliamentary model. However, all the states that were once part of the British Empire unquestionably have indelible legacies of the Westminster Model in their governance and understanding of politics.

Modern issues and debates on empire

Surprisingly, perhaps, the British Empire did not abruptly collapse and nor was there a complete break between coloniser and colonised at independence. The fall of the British Raj in August 1947 triggered a remarkable change unique in international and imperial politics: the transition from Empire to Commonwealth. The 'British Commonwealth', as it was termed in 1945, had been the preserve of the White Dominions as the self-selected leaders of the Empire, with their consequent higher status and autonomy. British India had been the most important part of the Empire and its division and independence was seen as a harbinger of the UK's own decline as well as the White Commonwealth's. Jawaharlal Nehru and Mohammad Ali Jinnah, the respective leaders of the newly independent states of India and Pakistan, decided to join the Commonwealth, despite the misgivings of many of their citizens, who wanted nothing more to do with their erstwhile ruler and any organisation that promoted it. There was considerable disquiet among some of the existing Commonwealth leaders, too, who worried that, due to race and political differences, it would be undesirable, if not impossible, for these South Asians to be full members of this club born of empire.

Despite these hurdles, the South Asian and British leaders believed that there were still advantages to be found from being together, with so many ties in trade, defence, education, culture, institutions, laws and the migration of people and ideas. In 1949, India declared its intention to become a republic. All Commonwealth members hitherto were realms, which meant having the British Monarch as the Head of State. This condition was too much for

Ireland. India, however, showed that it wanted to be a republic *and* stay in the Commonwealth. Its desire was granted as a way to demonstrate the UK's understanding of postwar realities as well as its aim to retain connections and influence globally. The decisions taken in 1949 enabled a new and modern multi-racial Commonwealth to emerge (and the subsequent dropping of the title 'British Commonwealth') since it would no longer be an organisation linked by blood and constitution. Instead, states from around the world could join despite huge differences in politics, institutions, development and policies, while nonetheless sharing a common background in empire and belief in cooperation. The rhetoric rarely matched the reality, but the Commonwealth showed a different path in postcolonial relations, especially when compared to the conflict-ridden and heavy-handed experience that characterised the ending of other European Empires in the post-1945 period. This is not to say the end of Britain's empire was seamless and without violence. Clearly not. However, there was, through the Commonwealth, a forum for debate and dialogue, such as over the vexed issue of apartheid in South Africa. The White-led independent state had been forced to leave the organisation in 1961 due to its racial policies, but once Black majority rule came in 1994, Nelson Mandela led his country to rejoin the Commonwealth as he knew the efforts so many members had helped to make this change in South Africa happen. However, other cases abound, from Fiji to Uganda, Pakistan to Nigeria, where efforts to bring about change in the direction of democracy and rights has not worked out. The organisation does not belong to the UK – indeed, during the apartheid era, for example, London was at times on the wrong side from most Commonwealth members – but there is an underlying sense of soft power and community among the more than 50 independent states representing every corner of the globe and full of multiple types of human diversity, which shows an improbable legacy of Empire.

The changing face of the Commonwealth also reflected the changing face of the UK itself. There had been widespread emigration, sometimes coerced, from the UK to the Empire. Millions left the British Isles in the nineteenth and twentieth centuries (remembering that until 1922 this included all of Ireland) and found homes across the British Empire, especially in the settler states. The number of Scots alone who emigrated to Canada between 1901 and 1930 was 440,000, while in 2006 there were 1.3 million British citizens living in Australia (Harper and Constantine 2014: 13 and 339). The Empire also caused massive demographic changes in the colonies themselves. Places like Trinidad, Fiji, Hong Kong, Singapore, Malaysia, Kenya and South Africa saw migrants arrive, often from far away, due to imperial management. This is in addition to the wide-ranging consequences of British settlers moving to and taking root in all corners of the Empire, sometimes in the wilful displacement of the indigenous people. The UK itself witnessed dramatic changes after 1945 as a result of immigration. The SS *Empire Windrush* brought around 500 people from Jamaica when it docked in the Port of Tilbury in June 1948. These migrants from the colonial empire were not refugees or asylum seekers, but instead were exercising their legal right to move across the Empire, thanks especially to the new British Nationality Act, passed that same year, which formalised a right which had existed in theory for all British subjects. It has been described as 'we're here because you were there' (Patel 2021). *Windrush* would become shorthand for Caribbean migration, and in 2018 a scandal hit, which saw the threat and actual deportation of some of that generation, who had migrated legally to the UK but were labelled 'illegal immigrants' due to not holding contemporary documents, which had not been necessary in 1948. Various legislative acts, such as the Commonwealth Immigrants Acts of 1962 and 1968 or the British Nationality

Act 1981, moved swiftly to close the right to enter the UK, even for those who held British papers (Patel 2021). Nonetheless, the make-up of contemporary Britain has determinedly been changed thanks to the British Empire, which has made the UK one of the most multicultural states in the world. The path to that status, however, has been a challenging one and at times incurred vitriolic resistance, such as Enoch Powell's infamous 'Rivers of Blood' speech in 1968, in which he decried the evils that 'coloured' immigration would bring to the UK. Such examples speak to the struggle of immigrants from the former Empire to be accepted in society. All these reactions raise important questions about the UK's identity and attitudes (Schofield 2013).

While today's politicians do not seek an empire, unlike their predecessors, there are still many who think that empire gave, and continues to give, the UK a special status of influence in the modern world. The fall of the British Empire compelled an extensive reduction in the UK's global reach, which also raised questions about the unity of the UK and the point of Britishness (Ward 2023). During the Brexit campaign, and after the referendum result to leave the European Union in June 2016, there were several who wanted what was termed 'Empire 2.0', which sought to revive and use the Commonwealth with its millions of people across the world as a target for the UK's goods and interests as a bigger and better replacement of the European Union Single Market. It was an attempt to revive and renew Britain's place in the world and they saw the former empire as the natural place to do it. Such thinking failed to recognise that the Commonwealth is not the same as the Empire. The Commonwealth cannot be directed, and, more critically, member states had moved on from thinking of London as the centre of the world. However, the discussion did spark considerable debate about the Empire in the modern UK. Statues, books, art, names, culture, education, institutions, media and politics itself came to be reflected through the lens of empire, and many did not like what they saw. Others would see an opportunity for 'Global Britain' once more to take up its place at the top table (Ward and Rasch 2019).

Conclusion

The British Empire was what made the United Kingdom a world power. Its rise and fall matched the fortunes of the UK. In terms of politics, the Empire had been at the centre of government and identity of the United Kingdom up until at least the late twentieth century. The UK's place in the world cannot be studied without knowing of its Empire. Nor can British politics be confined to the Palace of Westminster. British politics instead reached all corners of the globe and the influence of Westminster as an imperial institution cannot be underemphasised. This is because, at the very least, it provided the sanction and instruction to build an empire and eventually was the means of its dismantling. Empire meant that the UK influenced the politics and lives of millions of people abroad, and the consequences are still being felt. Crucial elements of world politics, such as borders, migrants, governance, institutions, laws and rights, have imperial roots. Policy makers realised the value that empire brought to the UK and were determined to keep that benefit for as long as possible. Westminster became a global brand due to empire, and the reach and example of its derivative forms are testament to it being a unique phenomenon of export government. The British Empire still weighs heavily on the politics of the United Kingdom and beyond.

Summary

- Understanding UK politics in the twentieth century involves understanding imperial politics. The two were indelibly linked. Understanding UK politics in the twenty-first century cannot avoid confronting the legacies of empire, which are both explicit and implicit.
- The UK exported its 'Westminster' system of government across the world, but it developed a different character depending on where it went. In particular, we can detect a form of 'Eastminster' governance in Asia.
- The dismantling of the Empire paralleled the UK's retreat from major global influence. It is therefore intertwined with questions of the UK's self-image, foreign policy role and place in the world.
- Debates about the UK's imperial legacy, and what it should do about it, are now much more regular features of UK politics.

Recommended and further reading

- Kumarasingham, H. (2023) 'Constitution and Empire', in Cane, P. and Kumarasingham, H. (eds.), *The Cambridge Constitutional History of the United Kingdom* (Vol. II). Cambridge: Cambridge University Press, pp. 496–528. This chapter provides an accessible overview of the ways in which the UK constitution was affected by empire, and vice versa. Neglecting the imperial influence risks losing sight of some of the key features of UK constitutional politics.
- Patel, I.S. (2021) *We're Here Because You Were There: Immigration and the End of Empire*. London: Verso. This book explores the origins of more restrictive UK Government immigration policy, defining citizenship along more racialised lines and setting up the circumstances for the Windrush scandal later.
- Saunders, R. (2020) 'Brexit and Empire: "Global Britain" and the myth of imperial nostalgia', *Journal of Imperial and Commonwealth History*, 48(6): 1140–1174. In this article, Saunders questions the idea of 'Empire 2.0' and suggests that viewing Brexit as a form of imperial nostalgia is too simplistic and requires further interrogation.

References

Abdullah, H. (2013) 'Thatcher and Reagan: "Political soulmates"', *CNN*, 9 April. Available at: https://edition.cnn.com/2013/04/08/politics/thatcher-reagan/index.html (accessed 4 March 2024).

Achilleos-Sarll, C. and Martill, B. (2019) 'Toxic masculinity: Militarism, deal-making and the performance of Brexit', in Dustin, M., Ferreira, N. and Millns, S. (eds), *Gender and Queer Perspectives on Brexit*. Basingstoke: Palgrave Macmillan.

Adam, S., Delestre, I., Emmerson, C., Johnson, P., Joyce, R., Stockton, I., Waters, T., Xu, X. and Zaranko, B. (2022) 'IFS Green Budget 2022: Mini-Budget response', *Institute for Fiscal Studies*, 23 September. Available at: https://ifs.org.uk/articles/mini-budget-response

Adler, D. and Ansell, B. (2020) 'Housing and populism', *West European Politics*, 43(2): 344–365. https://doi.org/10.1080/01402382.2019.1615322.

Adler-Nissen, R. (2014) *Opting Out of the European Union: Diplomacy, Sovereignty and European Integration*. Oxford: Oxford University Press.

Adler-Nissen, R., Galpin, C. and Rosamond, B. (2017) 'Performing Brexit: How a post-Brexit world is imagined outside the United Kingdom', *British Journal of Politics and International Relations*, 19(3): 573–591.

Akhtar, P. (2013) *British Muslim Politics: Examining Pakistani Biraderi Networks*. Basingstoke: Palgrave Macmillan.

Akhtar, P. and Peace, T. (2019) 'Ethnic minorities in British politics: Candidate selection and clan politics in the Labour Party', *Journal of Ethnic and Migration Studies*, 45(11): 1902–1918. doi: 10.1080/1369183X.2018.1443804

Akram, S. (2024) 'Dear British politics—where is the race and racism?', *British Politics*, 19(1): 1–24.

Alibhai-Brown, Y. (2000) *Who Do We Think We Are? Imagining the New Britain*. London: Allen Lane.

Allen, P. (2018) *The Political Class: Why It Matters Who Our Politicians Are*. Oxford: Oxford University Press.

Allen, P. and Cairney, P. (2017) 'What do we mean when we talk about the 'political class'?', *Political Studies Review*, 15(1): 18–27.

Allen, P. and Childs, S. (2019) 'The grit in the oyster? Women's parliamentary organizations and the substantive representation of women', *Political Studies*, 67(3): 618–638.

Allen, T.S. and Moore, A.J., (2018) "Voctory without Casualties: Russian's Information Operations" Parameters, 48(1) USAWC Press.

Allison, G. and Zelikow, P. (1999) *Essence of Decision: Explaining the Cuban Missile Crisis* (2nd edn). London: Pearson.

Alton, A., Atherton, S., Burnside, R., Campbell, A., Hudson, N., McIver, I. and Robinson, E (2021) *Election 2021: Constituencies and Regional Seats*. Edinburgh: Scottish Parliament. Available at: https://digitalpublications.parliament.scot/ResearchBriefings/Report/2021/5/11/591dc3c7-d994-4bbd-8120-767e9e781a67#Introduction

Andersen, K., Ohme, J., Bjarnøe, C., Bordacconi, M.J., Albæk, E. and De Vreese, C.H. (2021) *Generational Gaps in Political Media Use and Civic Engagement: From Baby Boomers to Generation Z*. Abingdon: Taylor & Francis.

Anderson, D. and Davidson, P.E. (1943) *Ballots and the Democratic Class Struggle: A Study in the Background of Political Education*. Paolo Alto, CA: Stanford University Press.

Andeweg, R. (2014) 'Roles in legislatures', in Martin, S., Saalfeld, T. and Strøm. K. (eds), *The Oxford Handbook of Legislative Studies*. Oxford: Oxford University Press, pp. 267–285.

Annesley, C. and Gains, F. (2010) 'The core executive: Gender, power and change', *Political Studies*, 58(5): 909–929.

Anthony, G. (2008) 'The St Andrews Agreement and the Northern Ireland Assembly', *European Public Law*, 14(2): 151–164.

Anwar, M. (1973) 'Pakistani participation in the 1972 Rochdale by-election', *Journal of Ethnic and Migration Studies*, 2(4): 418–423.

Anwar, M. (1975) 'Asian participation in the October 1974 General Election', *Journal of Ethnic and Migration Studies*, 4(3): 376–383.

Anwar, M. (2001) 'The participation of ethnic minorities in British politics', *Journal of Ethnic and Migration Studies*, 27(3): 533–549.

APPG on Women in Parliament (2023) *Open House: Where Next for Gender Equality in Parliament?* London: The Fawcett Society. Available at: www.fawcettsociety.org.uk/open-house-where-next-for-gender-equality-in-parliament (accessed 22 February 2024).

Appleby-Donald, K., Bartlett, R., Cairns, R., Cowley, G., Hurst, J., Jardine, A., Millar, K. et al. (2023) 'Scottish Parliament Statistics 2021–2022', SP 485. Edinburgh: The Scottish Parliament. Available at: https://digitalpublications.parliament.scot/ResearchBriefings/Report/2023/11/28/aaa2ad63-b6ae-4ae4-9e49-e2c4593316d7

Armitage, D. (2000) *The Ideological Origins of the British Empire*. Cambridge: Cambridge University Press.

Armitage, R. (ed.) (1997) *Bolingbroke: Political Writings*. Cambridge: Cambridge University Press.

Arter, D. (2004) *The Scottish Parliament: A Scandinavian-Style Assembly?* London: Routledge.

Ashe, J. (2019) *Political Candidate Selection: Who Wins, Who Loses, and Under-Representation in the UK*. London: Routledge.

Aspinall, P.J. (2021) 'BAME (black, Asian and minority ethnic): The "new normal" in collective terminology', *Journal of Epidemiology and Community Health*, 75(2): 107–107.

Asthana, A., Syal, R. and Elgot, J. (2016) 'Labour MPs prepare for leadership contest after Corbyn loses confidence vote', *The Guardian*, 28 June. Available at: www.theguardian.com/politics/2016/jun/28/jeremy-corbyn-loses-labour-mps-confidence-vote (accessed 12 March 2024).

Atkinson, L., Blick, A. and Qvortrup, M. (2020) *The Referendum in Britain: A History*. Oxford: Oxford University Press.

Aughey A. (2007) *The Politics of Englishness*. Manchester: Manchester University Press.

Aughey, A. (2010) 'Anxiety and injustice: The anatomy of Englishness', *Nations and Nationalism*, 16(3): 506–524.

Ayres, S., Flinders, M. and Sandford, M. (2017) 'Territory, power and statecraft: Understanding English devolution', *Regional Studies*, 52(6): 853–864.

Back, L., Keith, M., Shukra, K. and Solomos, J. (2022) *The Unfinished Politics of Race: Histories of Political Participation, Migration, and Multiculturalism*. Cambridge: Cambridge University Press.

Bagehot, W. (1867) *The English Constitution*. Oxford: Oxford University Press.

Baker, C. (2024) *General Election 2024 Results*. London: House of Commons Library. Available at: https://commonslibrary.parliament.uk/research-briefings/cbp-10009/ (accessed 8 July 2024).

Baldini, G., Bressanelli, E. and Massetti, E. (2018) 'Who is in control? Brexit and the Westminster Model', *The Political Quarterly*, 89(4): 537–544.

Baldini, G., Bressanelli, E. and Massetti, E. (2022) 'Back to the Westminster Model? The Brexit process and the UK political system', *International Political Science Review*, 43(3): 329–344.

Bale, T. (2012) *The Conservatives since 1945*. Oxford: Oxford University Press.

Bale, T. (2014) 'Introduction', in Bale, T. (ed.), *Margaret Thatcher*. London: Routledge.

Bale, T. (2016) *The Conservative Party: From Thatcher to Cameron* (2nd edn). Cambridge: Polity Press.

Bale, T. (2018) 'Who leads and who follows? The symbiotic relationship between UKIP and the Conservatives – and populism and Euroscepticism'. *Politics*, 38(3), 263–277

Bale, T. (2019) 'Conservative Party members do not support May's Brexit compromise', *UK in a Changing Europe*, Analysis, 4 January. Available at: https://ukandeu.ac.uk/conservative-party-members-do-not-support-mays-brexit-compromise/

Bale, T. (2022) *Brexit: An Accident Waiting to Happen? Why David Cameron Called the 2016 Referendum – And Why He Lost It*. Kindle Scribe Edition.

Bale, T. (2023) *The Conservative Party after Brexit: Turmoil and Transformation*. Cambridge: Polity Press.

Bale, T. and Pike, K. (2024) 'Hopes will be dashed: Brexit and the "Merkel myth"', *Journal of European Integration*, 46(2): 135–153.

Bale, T., Cheung, A., Cowley, P., Menon, A. and Wager, A. (2020) 'Mind the values gap: The social and economic values of MPs, party members and voters', *The UK in a Changing Europe*, June. Available at: https://ukandeu.ac.uk/wp-content/uploads/2020/06/Mind-the-values-gap.pdf

Bale, T., Webb, P. and Poletti, M. (2020) *Footsoldiers*. Abingdon: Routledge.

Balsom, D., Madgwick, P. and Van Mechelen, D. (1984) 'The political consequences of Welsh identity'. *Ethnic and Racial Studies*, 7(1), 160–181. https://doi.org/10.1080/01419870.1984.9993439

Balsom, D., Madgwick, P.J. and Van Mechelen, D. (1983) 'The Red and the Green: Patterns of Partisan Choice in Wales'. *British Journal of Political Science*, 13(3): 299–325. doi:10.1017/S0007123400003288

Bandola-Gill, J., Arthur, M. and Leng, R.I. (2023) 'What is co-production? Conceptualising and understanding co-production of knowledge and policy across different theoretical perspectives', *Evidence & Policy*, 19(2): 275–298.

Barberá, P. and Rivero, G. (2015) 'Understanding the political representativeness of Twitter users', *Social Science Computer Review*, 33(6): 712–729. https://doi.org/10.1177/0894439314558836

Barberá, P., Casas, A., Nagler, J., Egan, P.J., Bonneau, R., Jost, J.T. and Tucker, J.A. (2019) 'Who leads? Who follows? Measuring issue attention and agenda setting by legislators and the mass public using social media data', *American Political Science Review*, 113(4): 883–901. doi:10.1017/S0003055419000352

Barnett, L. (2010) 'General election 2010: How to spoil your ballot', *The Guardian*, 6 May. Available at: www.theguardian.com/politics/2010/may/06/general-election-2010-spoil-ballot

Barnier, M. (2021) *My Secret Brexit Diary: A Glorious Illusion*. Trans. Mackay, R. Cambridge: Polity Press.

Barwell, G. (2021) *Chief of Staff: Notes from Downing Street*. London: Atlantic Books.

Bates, S., Goodwin, M. and McKay, S. (2017) 'Do UK MPs engage more with select committees since the Wright Reforms? An interrupted time series analysis, 1979–2016', *Parliamentary Affairs*, 70(4): 780–800.

Bates, S., Kerr, P., Byrne, C. and Stanley, L. (2014) 'Questions to the Prime Minister: A comparative study of PMQs from Thatcher to Cameron', *Parliamentary Affairs*, 67(2): 253–280.

Bates, S.H. (2021) 'Re-structuring parliamentary roles', *International Journal of Parliamentary Studies*, 1(1): 22–46.

Baumgartner, F.R. and Jones, B.D. (2009) *Agendas and Instability in American Politics* (2nd edn). Chicago: University of Chicago Press.

BBC (British Broadcasting Corporation) (2023) *BBC Group Annual Report and Accounts 2022/23*. London: BBC. Available at: www.bbc.co.uk/aboutthebbc/documents/ara-2022-23.pdf

BBC News (2013) 'The Great British Class Calculator', *BBC News [Magazine]*. Available at: www.bbc.co.uk/news/magazine-22000973

BBC News (2014) 'In full: David Cameron statement on the UK's future', *BBC News*, 19 September. Available at: www.bbc.com/news/uk-politics-29271765 (accessed 14 November 2023).

BBC News (2017) 'Manchester attack: Police not sharing information with US', *BBC News*, 25 May. Available at: www.bbc.co.uk/news/uk-politics-40040210 (accessed 4 March 2024).

BBC News (2018) 'New domestic abuse law "could change Scotland"', *BBC News*, 1 February. Available at: www.bbc.co.uk/news/uk-scotland-42890990 (accessed 22 February 2024).

BBC News (2021) 'Commons scraps English votes for English laws', *BBC News*, 13 July. Available at: www.bbc.com/news/uk-politics-57828406 (accessed 4 October 2023).

BBC News (2024) 'Warning gender quotas could face legal challenge', *BBC News*, 7 June. Available at: www.bbc.com/news/articles/c2eel1y10j6o (accessed 12 June 2024).

Beaumont, P. (2019) 'Brexit and EU legitimation: Unwitting martyr for the cause?', *New Perspectives*, 27(3): 15–36.

Beckwith, K. (2005) 'A common language of gender?', *Politics & Gender*, 1(1): 128–137.

Beech, M. (2011) 'A tale of two liberalisms', in Lee, S. and Beech, M. (eds), *The Cameron–Clegg Government*. Basingstoke: Palgrave Macmillan.

Beech, M. and Lee, S. (eds) (2023) *Conservative Governments in the Age of Brexit*. London: Palgrave Macmillan.

Beel, D., Jones, M., and Jones, I.R. (2021) *City Regions and Devolution in the UK: The Politics of Representation*. Bristol: Policy Press.

Béland, D. (2019) *How Ideas and Institutions Shape the Politics of Public Policy*. Cambridge: Cambridge University Press.

Béland, D. and Howlett, M. (2016) 'The role and impact of the multiple-streams approach in comparative policy analysis', *Journal of Comparative Policy Analysis*, 18(3): 221–227.

Béland, D., Howlett, M. and Mukherjee, I. (2018) 'Instrument constituencies and public policy-making: An introduction', *Policy & Society*, 37(1): 1–13.

Belknap, E. and Kenny, M. (2023) 'The first but not the last': Women's descriptive and substantive representation in the 2021 Scottish Parliament election', *British Politics*, 25 November. E-pub ahead of print. https://doi.org/10.1057/s41293-023-00246-x

Bell, D. and Vucetic, S. (2019) 'Brexit, CANZUK, and the legacy of empire', *British Journal of Politics and International Relations*, 21(2): 367–382.

Bell, S. and Hindmoor, A. (2012) *Rethinking Governance*. Cambridge: Cambridge University Press.

Bennett, S., Moon, D.S., Pearce, N. and Whiting, S. (2021) 'Labouring under a delusion? Scotland's national questions and the crisis of the Scottish Labour Party', *Territory, Politics, Governance*, 9(5): 656–674.

Benton, M. and Russell, M. (2013) 'Assessing the impact of Parliamentary Oversight Committees: The select committees in the British House of Commons', *Parliamentary Affairs*, 66(4): 772–797.

Berkeley, A., Ryan-Collins, J., Tye, R., Voldsgaard, A. and Wilson, N. (2022) 'The self-financing state: An institutional analysis of government expenditure, revenue collection, and debt issuance operations in the United Kingdom', *UCL Institute for Innovation and Public Policy*, Working Paper, IIPP WP-2022-08. Available at: www.ucl.ac.uk/bartlett/public-purpose/publications/2022/may/self-financing-state-institutional-analysis

Berthezène, C. and Gottlieb, J. (eds) (2017) *Rethinking Right-Wing Women: Gender and the Conservative Party, 1880s to the Present*. Manchester: Manchester University Press.

Besly, N. and Goldsmith, T. (2023) *How Parliament Works* (9th edn). Abingdon and New York: Routledge.

Best, R.E. (2011) 'The declining electoral relevance of traditional cleavage groups', *European Political Science Review*, 3(2): 279–300. https://doi.org/10.1017/S1755773910000366.

Better Off Out (2016) 'Is Britain getting too crowded?' Referendum communication. LSE Britain and Europe Archive. Available at: https://lse-atom.arkivum.net/uklse-dl1er010020010152-uklse-dl1-er01-002-001-0152-0001-pdf (accessed 27 June 2024).

Bevan, S. and John, P. (2016) 'Policy representation by party leaders and followers: What drives UK Prime Minister's Questions?', *Government and Opposition*, 51(1): 59–83.

Bevir, M. and Rhodes, R.A.W. (2003) *Interpreting British Governance*. London: Routledge.

Bhambra, G.K. (2017) 'Locating Brexit in the pragmatics of race, citizenship and Empire', in Outhwaite, W. (ed.), *Brexit: Sociological Responses*. London: Anthem Press, pp. 91–100.

Bickerton, C.J. (2019) 'The limits of differentiation: Capitalist diversity and labour mobility as drivers of Brexit', *Comparative European Politics*, 17(2): 231–245.

Bickerton, C.J., Hodson, D. and Puetter, U. (2015) 'The new intergovernmentalism: European integration in the post-Maastricht era', *Journal of Common Market Studies*, 53(4): 703–722.

Bird, K. (2005) 'Gendering parliamentary questions', *The British Journal of Politics and International Relations*, 7(3): 353–370.

Birkland, T. (1997) *After Disaster: Agenda Setting, Public Policy and Focusing Events*. Washington, DC: Georgetown University Press.

Bjarnegård, E. and Murray, R. (2018) 'Revisiting forms of representation by critically examining men. *Politics & Gender*, 14(2): 265–270.

Black, J. (2018) *English Nationalism: A Short History*. London: Hurst & Company.

Blair, T. (1999) 'Doctrine of the International Community', speech delivered at the Chicago Economics Club, 22 April. Available at: www.britishpoliticalspeech.org/speech-archive.htm?speech=279 (accessed 23 February 2024).

Blaxland, S. (2024) *The Conservative Party in Wales, 1945–1997*. Cardiff: University of Wales Press.

Blick, A. and Jones, G. (2010) *Premiership*. Exeter: Imprint.

Blick, A. and Salter, B. (2021) 'Divided culture and constitutional tensions: Brexit and the collision of direct and representative democracy', *Parliamentary Affairs*, 74(3): 617–638.

Bloemraad, I. and Schönwälder, K. (2013) 'Immigrant and ethnic minority representation in Europe: Conceptual challenges and theoretical approaches', *West European Politics*, 36(3): 564–579.

Blondel, J. (1963) *Voters, Parti, and Leaders: The Social Fabric of British Politics*. Harmondsworth: Penguin.

Blumler, J.G. and Coleman, S. (2010) 'Political communication in freefall: The British case – and others?', *The International Journal of Press/Politics*, 15(2): 139–154.

Blyth, M. (2013) *Austerity: The History of a Dangerous Idea*. Oxford: Oxford University Press.

Bochel, J. and Denver, D. (1983) 'Candidate selection in the Labour Party: What the selectors seek' *British Journal of Political Science*, 13(1), 45–69.

Bogdanor, V. (1999) *Devolution in the United Kingdom*. Oxford: Oxford University Press.

Bogdanor, V. (2009) *The New British Constitution*. Oxford: Hart Publishing.

Bogdanor, V. (2010) 'The West Lothian Question', *Parliamentary Affairs*, 63(1): 156–172.

Bogdanor, V. (2019) *Beyond Brexit: Towards a British Constitution*. London: I.B. Tauris.

Bolet, D. (2021) 'Drinking alone: Local socio-cultural degradation and radical right support – the case of British pub closures', *Comparative Political Studies*, 54(9): 1653–1692. https://doi.org/10.1177/0010414021997158.

Bottici, C. (2007) *A Philosophy of Political Myth*. Cambridge: Cambridge University Press.

Boulianne, S. and Larsson, A.O. (2023) 'Engagement with candidate posts on Twitter, Instagram, and Facebook during the 2019 election', *New Media & Society*, 25(1): 119–140. https://doi.org/10.1177/14614448211009504

Bourdieu, P. (1984) *Distinction: A Social Critique of the Judgement of Taste*. Cambridge, MA: Harvard University Press.

Bourdieu, P. (1986) 'The forms of capital', in Richardson, J.G. (ed.), *Handbook of Theory and Research for the Sociology of Education*. New York: Greenwood Press, pp. 241–258.

Bowers, J. (2024) *Downward Spiral: Collapsing Public Standards and How to Restore Them*. Manchester: Manchester University Press.

Bradbury, J. and Mitchell, J. (2001) 'Devolution: New politics for old?', *Parliamentary Affairs*, 54: 257–275.

Brader, T. (2005) 'Campaigning for hearts and minds', in *Campaigning for Hearts and Minds*. Chicago: University of Chicago Press.

Brady, G. (2015) 'Parliament is weak and ineffective – it needs to change', *The Spectator*, 20 March. Available at: www.spectator.co.uk/article/parliament-is-weak-and-ineffective-it-needs-to-change/ (accessed 4 October 2023).

Brady, H.E. and Johnston, R. (eds) (2006) *Capturing Campaign Effects*. Ann Arbor, MI: University of Michigan Press.

Bragg, B. (2007) *The Progressive Patriot: A Search for Belonging*. London: Penguin Books.

Bramwell, D., Checkland, K., Shields, J. and Allen, P. (2023) *Community Nursing Services in England: An Historical Policy Analysis*. Basingstoke: Palgrave.

Brändle, V.K., Galpin, C. and Trenz, H.J. (2022) 'Brexit as "politics of division": Social media campaigning after the referendum', *Social Movement Studies*, 21(1–2): 234–253.

Breuning, M. (1995) 'Words and deeds: Foreign assistance rhetoric and policy behaviour in the Netherlands, Belgium and the United Kingdom', *International Studies Quarterly*, 39(2): 235–254.

Bridgman, P. and Davis, G. (2003) 'What use is a policy cycle? Plenty, if the aim is clear', *Australian Journal of Public Administration*, 62(3): 98–102.

Brine, S. (2019) 'Ministers reflect', *Institute for Government interview*. Available at: www.instituteforgovernment.org.uk/ministers-reflect/steve-brine

Brown Swan, C. and Kenny, M. (2024) '"We can't afford to be a branch office": The territorial dynamics of the British Labour Party, 2015–2019', *Parliamentary Affairs*, 77(1): 109–128.

Brown, A. (2000) 'Designing the Scottish Parliament', *Parliamentary Affairs*, 53(3): 542–556.

Brown, C. (2022) 'Gove to water down local housing targets following backbench pressure', *Housing Today*, 6 December. www.housingtoday.co.uk/news/gove-to-water-down-local-housing-targets-following-backbench-pressure/5120779.article (accessed 8 July 2024).

Brown, G. (2005) 'Britain rediscovered', *Prospect Magazine*, 16 April. Available at: www.prospectmagazine.co.uk/essays/56771/britain-rediscovered (accessed 28 November 2023).

Brown, J. (2018) *An Early History of British Race Relations Legislation*. London: House of Commons Library.

Browning, C.S. (2019) 'Brexit populism and fantasies of fulfilment', *Cambridge Review of International Affairs*, 32(3): 222–244.

Bryant, C. (2023) *Code of Conduct: Why We Need to Fix Parliament – and How to Do It*. London: Bloomsbury.

Bukodi, E., Evans, G., Goldthorpe, J.H. and Hepplewhite, M. (2024) 'The changing class and educational composition of the UK political elite since 1945: Implications for representation', *British Politics*, March. https://doi.org/10.1057/s41293-024-00253-6.

Bull, P. and Strawson, W. (2020) 'Can't answer? Won't answer? An analysis of equivocal responses by Theresa May in Prime Minister's Questions', *Parliamentary Affairs*, 73(2): 429–449.

Burbank, J. and Cooper, F. (2010) *Empires in World History – Power and the Politics of Difference*. Oxford and Princeton, NJ: Princeton University Press.

Burman, M. and Johnson, J. (2015) 'High hopes? The gender equality duty and its impact on responses to gender-based violence', *Policy & Politics*, 43(1): 45–60.

Burton, M., Miller, W. and Shea, D. (2015) *Campaign Craft: The Strategies, Tactics, and Art of Political Campaign Management* (5th edn). New York: Praeger.

Butler, C., Campbell, R. and Hudson, J. (2021) 'Political recruitment under pressure, again: MPs and candidates in the 2019 general election', in Ford, R., Bale, T., Jennings, W. and Surridge, P. (eds), *The British General Election of 2019*. Basingstoke: Palgrave Macmillan, pp. 387–420.

Butler, C., Miori, M. and Ford R. (2024) 'Inside the "secret garden": Candidate selection at the 2019 UK general election', *The British Journal of Politics & International Relations*, 19 September. E-pub ahead of print: https://doi.org/10.1177/13691481241270519

Butler, D. and Stokes, D. (1969) *Political Change in Britain*. Harmondsworth: Penguin.

Byrne C. and Theakston K. (2019) 'Understanding the power of the Prime Minister: Structure and agency in models of prime ministerial power', *British Politics*, 14(4): 329–346.

Cabinet Office (1999) *Modernising Government*, Cm 4310, London: The Stationery Office.

Cabinet Office (2011) *The Cabinet Manual*. London: HM Government.

Cabinet Office (2022) *The Ministerial Code*. London: HM Government.

Cabinet Office (2023) *Annual report on special advisers 2023*. London: HMSO. Available at https://assets.publishing.service.gov.uk/media/64e36fba3309b700121c9bc1/2023-06-20_-_SpAd_Annual_Report_2023_v3.docx.pdf.

Cairney, P. (2007) 'A "multiple lenses" approach to policy change: The case of tobacco policy in the UK', *British Politics*, 2(1): 45–68.

Cairney, P. (2011) *The Scottish Political System since Devolution*. Exeter: Imprint Academic.

Cairney, P. (2019a) *Understanding Public Policy: Theories and Issues* (2nd edn). London: Bloomsbury Press.

Cairney, P. (2019b) 'The transformation of UK tobacco control', in t'Hart, P. and Compton, M. (eds), *Great Policy Successes*. Oxford: Oxford University Press, Chapter 5 (pp. 84–103).

Cairney, P. and Keating, M. (2004) 'Sewel motions in the Scottish Parliament', *Scottish Affairs*, 47(1) (First Series): 115–134.

Cairney, P. and Kippin, S. (2023) *Politics and Policy Making in the UK*. Bristol: Policy Press.

Cairney, P. and Kwiatkowski, R. (2017) 'How to communicate effectively with policymakers: Combine insights from psychology and policy studies', *Palgrave Communications*, 3, article 37.

Cairney, P. and St Denny, E. (2020) *Why Isn't Government Policy More Preventive?* Oxford: Oxford University Press.

Cairney, P. and Widfeldt, A. (2015) 'Is Scotland a Westminster-style majoritarian democracy or a Scandinavian-style consensus democracy? A comparison of Scotland, the UK and Sweden', *Regional & Federal Studies*, 25(1): 1–18.

Calvert, H. (1968) *Constitutional Law in Northern Ireland: A Study in Regional Government*. London: Stevens.

Cameron, D. (2005) 'Full text of David Cameron's speech', *The Guardian*, 16 December. Available at: www.theguardian.com/politics/2005/dec/16/conservatives.liberaldemocrats (accessed 22 February 2024).

Cameron, D. (2015) 'Prime Minister's letter to President of the European Council Donald Tusk', 10 November. London: HM Government. Available at: www.gov.uk/government/publications/eu-reform-pms-letter-to-president-of-the-european-council-donald-tusk (accessed 27 June 2024).

Cameron, D. (2019) *For the Record*. London: HarperCollins.

Campbell, A., Converse, P., Miller, W. and Stokes, D. (1960) 'The American Voter'. Chicago: University of Chicago Press.

Campbell, J. (2001) *Margaret Thatcher. Volume I: The Grocer's Daughter*. London: Pimlico.

Campbell, J. (2003) *Margaret Thatcher. Volume II: The Iron Lady*. London: Pimlico.

Campbell, R. and Childs, S. (2013) 'The impact imperative: Here come the women :-)', *Political Studies Review*, 11(2): 182–189.

Campbell, R. and Cowley, P. (2014) 'What voters want: Reactions to candidate characteristics in a survey experiment', *Political Studies*, 62(2): 745–765.

Campbell, R. and Lovenduski, J. (2015) 'What should MPs do? Public and parliamentarians' views compared', *Parliamentary Affairs*, 68(4): 690–708.

Campbell, R. and Shorrocks, R (2021) 'Finally rising with the tide? Gender and the vote in the 2019 British Elections', *Journal of Elections, Public Opinion and Parties*, 31(4): 488–507. https://doi.org/10.1080/17457289.2021.1968412

Campbell, R., Cowley, P., Vivyan, N. and Wagner, M. (2019) 'Legislator dissent as a valence signal', *British Journal of Political Science*, 49(1): 105–128.

Campbell, V. (2019) 'Party election broadcasts... actually?', in Jackson, D., Thorsen, E., Lilleker, D. and Weidhase, N. (eds), *UK Election Analysis 2019: Media, Voters and the Campaign*. Bournemouth: Centre for Comparative Politics and Media Research. Available at: https://eprints.bournemouth.ac.uk/33165/13/UKElectionAnalysis2019_Jackson-Thorsen-Lilleker-and-Weidhase_v1.pdf

Cannadine, D. (2001) *Ornamentalism – How the British Saw Their Empire*. London: Allen Lane.

Capoccia, G. and Kelemen, D. (2007) 'The study of critical junctures: Theory, narrative, and counterfactuals in historical institutionalism', *World Politics*, 59(3): 341–369.

Carl, N., Dennison, J. and Evans, G. (2019) 'European but not European enough: An explanation for Brexit', *European Union Politics*, 20(2): 282–304.

Carman, C., Mitchell, J., & Johns, R. (2008). The unfortunate natural experiment in ballot design: the Scottish Parliamentary Elections of 2007. *Electoral Studies*, 27(3), 442–459.

Carnes, N. and Lupu, N. (2016) 'Do voters dislike working-class candidates? Voter biases and the descriptive underrepresentation of the working class', *American Political Science Review*, 110(4): 832–44. https://doi.org/10.1017/S0003055416000551.

Carrascal-Incera, A., McCann, P., Ortega-Argilés, R. et al. (2020) 'UK interregional inequality in a historical and international comparative context', *National Institute Economic Review*, 253: R4–R17.

Carter, N. and Pearson, M. (2024) 'From green crap to net zero: Conservative climate policy, 2015–2022', *British Politics*, 19(1): 154–174.

Carty, K.R. (2022). 'Into the void: the collapse of Irish party democracy', *Irish Political Studies*, 37(2), 303–325. https://doi.org/10.1080/07907184.2022.2043082

Carver, T. (1996) *Gender Is Not a Synonym for Women*. Boulder, CO: Lynne Rienner.

Catalano, A. (2009) 'Women acting for women? An analysis of gender and debate participation in the British House of Commons 2005–2007', *Politics & Gender*, 5(1): 45–68.

Ceci, L. (2024) TikTok: distribution of global audiences 2024, by age and gender. Statistic https://www.statista.com/statistics/1299771/tiktok-global-user-age-distribution/

Celis, K. (2008) 'Gendering Representation' in G. Goertz and A. Mazur (eds), *Politics, Gender and Concepts*. Cambridge: Cambridge University Press.

Celis, K. and S. Childs, S. (2020) *Feminist Democratic Representation*. Oxford: Oxford University Press.

Celis, K., Childs, S., Kantola, J. and Krook, M.L. (2008) 'Rethinking women's substantive representation', *Representation*, 44(2): 99–110.

Chadwick, A. (2017) *The Hybrid Media System: Politics and Power*. Oxford: Oxford University Press.

Chadwick, A., Vaccari, C. and O'Loughlin, B. (2018) 'Do tabloids poison the well of social media? Explaining democratically dysfunctional news sharing', *New Media & Society*, 20(11): 4255–4274.

Chaney, P. (2006) 'Critical mass, deliberation and the substantive representation of women: Evidence from the UK's devolution programme), *Political Studies*, 54: 691–714.

Chaney, P. (2015) 'Manifesto discourse and the substantive representation of ethnic minorities: Analysis of UK state-wide and meso elections, 1964–2011', *Parliamentary Affairs*, 68(1): 154–181.

Chappell, L. (2006) 'Comparing political institutions: Revealing the gendered "logic of appropriateness"', *Politics & Gender*, 2(2): 223–235.

Childs, S. (2004a) 'A feminised style of politics? Women MPs in the House of Commons', *The British Journal of Politics & International Relations*, 6(1): 3–19.

Childs, S. (2004b) *New Labour's Women MPs: Women Representing Women*. London: Routledge.

Childs, S. (2016) *The Good Parliament*. Bristol: University of Bristol. Available at: https://commonslibrary.parliament.uk/research-briefings/cdp-2016-0201/ (accessed 22 February 2024).

Childs, S. (2023) 'Feminist institutional change: The case of the UK Women and Equalities Committee', *Parliamentary Affairs*, 76(3): 507–531.

Childs, S. and Cowley, P. (2011) 'The politics of local presence: Is there a case for descriptive representation?', *Political Studies*, 59(1): 1–19.

Childs, S. and Evans, E. (2012) 'Out of the hands of the parties: Women's legislative recruitment at Westminster', *The Political Quarterly*, 83(4): 742–748.

Childs, S. and Kenny, M. (2025) 'Gender and parliaments', in Bernardes, C. and Crewe, E. (eds), *Elgar Encyclopaedia of Parliamentary Studies*. Cheltenham: Edward Elgar.

Childs, S. and Krook, M.L. (2008) 'Critical mass theory and women's political representation', *Political Studies*, 56(3): 725–736.

Childs, S. and Lovenduski, J. (2013) 'Political representation', in Waylen, G., Celis, K., Kantola, J. and Weldon, S.L. (eds), *The Oxford Handbook of Gender and Politics*. Oxford: Oxford University Press, pp. 489–513.

Childs, S. and Palmieri, S. (2023) 'Gender sensitive parliaments: Feminizing formal political institutions', in Sawer, M., Banaszak, L.A., True, J. and Kantola, J. (eds), *Handbook of Feminist Governance*. Cheltenham: Edward Elgar.

Childs, S. and Webb, P. (2012) *Sex, Gender and the Conservative Party*. Basingstoke: Palgrave Macmillan.

Chowdhry, A. (2016) 'Facebook emoji "reactions": Are there ulterior motives?', *Forbes*, 29 February. Available at: www.forbes.com/sites/amitchowdhry/2016/02/29/facebook-reactions/#5c920fe31a62

Churchill Archives Centre (n.d.) *Uphill All the Way: A Century of Women in Parliament*. Available at: https://archives.chu.cam.ac.uk/online-resources/online-exhibitions/uphill-all-way/ (accessed 22 February 2024).

Clarke, G. (2018) 'UK development policy and domestic politics 1997–2016', *Third World Quarterly*, 39 (1): 18–34.

Clarke, H.D., Whitely, P., Sanders, D. and Stewart, M. (2004) *Political choice in Britain*. Oxford: Oxford University Press.

Clarke, K. (2016) *Kind of Blue*. London: HarperCollins.

Clegg, D. and Andrews, K. (2021) *Break-Up: How Nicola Sturgeon and Alex Salmond Went to War*. London: Biteback Publishing.

Cobb, R. and Elder, C. (1972) *Participation in American Politics: The Dynamics of Agenda-Building*. Boston, MA: Allyn & Bacon.

Coe, P. (2022) 'The Draft Online Safety Bill and the regulation of hate speech: Have we opened Pandora's box?', *Journal of Media Law*, 14(1): 50–75. doi: 10.1080/17577632.2022.2083870

Cohen, M., March, J. and Olsen, J. (1972) 'A garbage can model of organizational choice', *Administrative Science Quarterly*, 17(1): 1–25.

Cohn, C. (2013) *Women & Wars*. Cambridge: Polity Press.

Colantone, I. and Stanig, P. (2018) 'The trade origins of economic nationalism: Import competition and voting behavior in Western Europe', *American Journal of Political Science*, 62(4): 936–953. https://doi.org/10.1111/ajps.12358.

Cole, M. (1999) 'Accountability and quasi-government: The role of parliamentary questions', *The Journal of Legislative Studies*, 5(1): 77–101.

Colley, L. (1992) *Britons: Forging the Nation, 1707–1837*. London: Pimlico and New Haven, CT: Yale University Press.

Collignon, S. and Rüdig, W. (2021) 'Increasing the cost of female representation? The gendered effects of harassment, abuse and intimidation towards parliamentary candidates', *Journal of Elections, Public Opinion and Parties*, 31(4): 429–449.

Collins, D. (2021) 'Standing the test of time: The level playing field and rebalancing mechanism in the UK–EU Trade and Cooperation Agreement (TCA)', *Journal of International Dispute Settlement*, 12(4): 617–636.

Colls, R. (2002) *Identity of England*. Oxford: Oxford University Press.

Condor, S. (2010) 'Devolution and national identity. The rules of English (dis)engagement', *Nations and Nationalism*, 16(3): 525–543.

Connolly, J., Flinders, M., Judge, D., Torrance, M. and Tudor, P. (2022) 'Institutions ignored: A history of select committee scrutiny in the House of Lords, 1968–2021', *Parliamentary History*, 41(3): 463–490.

Convery, A. (2016) *The Territorial Conservative Party: Devolution and Party Change in Scotland and Wales*. Manchester: Manchester University Press.

Convery, A. and Lundberg, T.C. (2020) 'Rational choice meets the new politics: Choosing the Scottish Parliament's electoral system', *Government and Opposition*, 55(1): 114–129.

Cook, R. (1997) 'Robin Cook's speech on ethical foreign policy', *The Guardian*, 12 May. Available at: www.theguardian.com/world/1997/may/12/indonesia.ethicalforeignpolicy (accessed 23 February 2024).

Copsey, N. and Haughton, T. (2014) 'Farewell Britannia? "Issue capture" and the politics of David Cameron's 2013 EU referendum pledge', *Journal of Common Market Studies*, 52(S1): 74–89.

Corlett, A. And Try, L. (2024) *Hard Times: Assessing Household Incomes since 2010*. London: Resolution Foundation.

Coveney, S. (2018) 'An Tánaiste speech: British–Irish relations: Past, present, and future', *simoncoveny.ie*, 31 January. Available: https://simoncoveney.ie/2018/01/31/tanaiste-speech-british_irish-relations-past-present-future/ (accessed 19 December 2023).

Cowley, P. (1996) 'How did he do that? The second round of the 1990 Conservative leadership election', *British Elections and Parties Yearbook*, 6(1): 198–216.

Cowley, P. (2002) *Revolts and Rebellions: Parliamentary Voting Under Blair*. London: Politico's Publishing.

Cowley, P. (2005) *The Rebels: How Blair Mislaid His Majority*. London: Politico's Publishing.

Cowley, P. and Childs, S. (2003) 'Too spineless to rebel? New Labour's women MPs', *British Journal of Political Science*, 33(3): 345–365.

Cowley, P. and Kavanagh, D. (2018) *The British General Election of 2017*. Basingstoke: Palgrave Macmillan.

Cowley, P. and Stuart, M. (2012) 'A coalition with two wobbly wings: Backbench dissent in the House of Commons', *Political Insight*, 3(1): 8–11.

Cowley, P., Gandy, R.J. and Foster, S. (2022) 'Increasingly local: The regional roots of British Members of Parliament, 2010–2019', *The Journal of Legislative Studies*, 30(3): 253–64.

Cox, K.R. (1970) 'Geography, social context, and voting behavior in Wales, 1861–1951', in E. Allardt and S. M. Lipset (eds), *Mass Politics: Studies in Political Sociology*. London: Collier-MacMillian.

Cox, L. (2018), *The Bullying and Harassment of House of Commons Staff: Independent Inquiry Report*. Available at: www.parliament.uk/globalassets/documents/Conduct-in-Parliament/dame-laura-cox-independent-inquiry-report.pdf

Cracknell, R., and Tunnicliffe, R. (2022) *Social Background of MPs 1979–2019*. Research Briefing, 15 February. London: House of Commons Library. Available at: https://commonslibrary.parliament.uk/research-briefings/cbp-7483/

Craft, J. and Halligan, J. (2015) 'Assessing thirty years of Westminster policy advisory system experience', *Policy Sciences*, 50(1): 47–62.

Craft, J. and Halligan, J. (2020) *Advising Governments in the Westminster Tradition: Policy Advisory Systems in Australia, Britain, Canada and New Zealand*. Cambridge: Cambridge University Press.

Craig, P. (2017) 'The process: Brexit and the anatomy of Article 50', in Fabbrini, F. (ed.), *The Law and Politics of Brexit*. Oxford: Oxford University Press, pp. 49–70.

Craig, Sir J. (1934) 'Unionist Party' *Northern Ireland House of Commons*. 1934, April 22. Vol. XVI, Cols. 109–195.

Craig, Sir J. (1934) 'Unionist Party', *Northern Ireland House of Commons*, 22 April. Vol. XVI, Cols. 1091–1095.

Cram, L., Llewellyn, C., Hill, R. and Magdy, W. (2017) 'UK general election 2017: A Twitter analysis', *Accessibility Forum* 2024, 7 June. Available as an arXiv preprint at: arXiv:1706.02271.

Cree, V., Clapton, G., and Smith, M. (eds) (2016) *Revisiting Moral Panics*. Bristol: Policy Press.

Crewe, E. (2005) *Lords of Parliament: Manners, Rituals and Politics*. Manchester: Manchester University Press.

Crewe, E. (2015) *The House of Commons: An Anthropology of MPs at Work*. London: Bloomsbury Academic.

Crewe, E. and Sarra, N. (2019) 'Chairing UK select committees: Walking between friends and foes', *Parliamentary Affairs*, 72(4): 841–859.

Crewe, E. and Walker, A. (2019) *An Extraordinary Scandal: The Westminster Expenses Crisis and Why it Still Matters*. London: Haus Publishing.

Crines, A; Heppell, T.; and Hill, M. (2016) 'Enoch Powell's "Rivers of Blood" Speech: a rhetorical political analysis', *British Politics*, 11, 1: 72–94.

Crosland, A. (1956) *The Future of Socialism*. London: Jonathan Cape.

Crowson, N. (2007) *The Conservative Party and European Integration since 1945*. Abingdon: Routledge.

Cruddas, J. (2024) *A Century of Labour*. Cambridge: Polity Press.

Curtice, J. (2006) 'Forecasting and evaluating the consequences of electoral change: Scotland and Wales', *Acta Politica*, 41: 300–314.

Curtice, J. (2018) 'How do people in England want to be governed?', in Kenny, M., McLean, I. and Paun, A. (eds), *Governing England: English Identity and Institutions in a Changing United Kingdom*. Oxford: Oxford University Press for the British Academy.

Curtice, J., Fisher, S. and English, P. (2021) 'The geography of a Brexit election: How constituency context and the electoral system shaped the outcome', in Ford, R., Bale, T., Jennings, W. and Surridge, P., *The British General Election of 2019*. Basingstoke: Palgrave Macmillan, pp. 461–494.

Cutts, D., Goodwin, M., Heath, O. and Milazzo, C. (2019) 'Resurgent Remain and a rebooted revolt on the Right: Exploring the 2019 European Parliament elections in the United Kingdom', *The Political Quarterly*, 90(3): 496–514.

Cutts, D., Goodwin, M., Heath, O. and Surridge, P. (2020) 'Brexit, the 2019 General Election and the realignment of British politics', *The Political Quarterly*, 91(1): 7–23.

Dahlerup, D. (1988) 'From a small to a large minority: Women in Scandinavian politics', *Scandinavian Political Studies*, 11(4): 275–298.

Dahlerup, D. (2006) 'The story of the theory of critical mass', *Politics & Gender*, 2(4): 511–522.

Dalton, R.J. (2004) *Democratic Challenges, Democratic Choices: The Erosion of Political Support in Advanced Industrial Democracies*. Oxford: Oxford University Press.

Dancygier, R. (2018) 'Beyond numbers: Inclusion types, candidate types, and descriptive representation', in Belton K. and Helbling, M. (eds), *American Political Science Association's Organized Section on Migration and Citizenship*, 6(1): 28–34. Available at: https://connect.apsanet.org/s43/wp-content/uploads/sites/13/2018/02/Migration-and-Citizenship-Newsletter-Issue-6.1-1.pdf

Darwin, J. (2009) *The Empire Project – The Rise and Fall of the British World-System 1830–1970*. Cambridge: Cambridge University Press.

Davies, A., Freeman, J. and Pemberton, H. (2023) 'Thatcher's policy unit and the "neoliberal vision"', *Journal of British Studies*, 62(1): 77–103.

Davies, J. (1994) *A History of Wales*. London: Penguin.

Davies, N. (2024) 'The language of priorities: Aneurin Bevan, Welsh labour and the politics of the past', *The British Journal of Politics and International Relations*, 26(1), 62–78.

Davis, A. (2022) *Bankruptcy, Bubbles and Bailouts: The Inside History of the Treasury since 1976*. Manchester: Manchester University Press.

De Rynck, S. (2023) *Inside the Deal: How the EU Got Brexit Done*. London: Agenda.

De Vries, C.E. (2017) 'Benchmarking Brexit: How the British decision to leave shapes EU public opinion', *Journal of Common Market Studies*, 55(S1): 38–53.

Deakin, N. (ed.) (1965) *Colour and the British Electorate, 1964*. London: Frederick A. Praeger.

Deakin, N. and Bourne, J. (1970) 'Powell, the minorities, and the 1970 election', *The Political Quarterly*, 41(4): 399–415.

Deakin, N. and Parry, R. (2000) *The Treasury and Social Policy: The Contest for Control of Welfare Strategy*. Basingstoke: Palgrave Macmillan.

Dee, M. and Smith, K.E. (2017) 'UK diplomacy at the UN after Brexit: Challenges and opportunities', *British Journal of Politics and International Relations*, 19(3): 527–542.

Denham, A. and Dorey, P. (2006) 'A tale of two speeches? The Conservative leadership election of 2005', *The Political Quarterly*, 77(1): 35–46.

Denham, J. and McKay, L. (2023) 'The politics of England: National identities and Political Englishness', *The Political Quarterly*, https://doi.org/10.1111/1467-923X.13313

Denver, D. (2020) 'The results: How Britain voted', *Parliamentary Affairs*, 73 (Supplement_1): 7–28. https://doi.org/10.1093/pa/gsaa037

Denver, D. and Garnett, M. (2021) *British General Elections since 1964: Diversity, Dealignment, and Disillusion* (2nd edn). Oxford: Oxford University Press. https://doi.org/10.1093/oso/9780198844952.001.0001

Denver, D. and Johns, R. (2022) *Elections and Voters in Britain*. Basingstoke: Palgrave.

Devine, T.M. (2003) *Scotland's Empire – The Origins of the Global Diaspora*. London: Allen Lane.

DFID (Department for International Development) (n.d.) 'About Us', *Gov.uk* [website]. Available at: www.gov.uk/government/organisations/department-for-international-development/about (accessed 4 March 2024).

Diamond, P. (2023) 'Core executive politics in the Camera era, 2010–2016: The dynamics of Whitehall reform', *Government & Opposition*, 58(3): 516–534.

Diamond, P. and Richardson, J. (eds) (2023) 'Special issue: British policymaking after Brexit', *Journal of European Public Policy*, 30(11).

Diamond, P. (2013) *Governing Britain: Power, Politics and the Prime Minister*. London: I.B. Tauris.

Diamond, P. (2020) 'Polycentric governance and policy advice: Lessons from Whitehall policy advisory systems', *Policy & Politics*, 48(4): 563–581.

Diamond, P. (2021) *The British Labour Party in Opposition and Power 1979–2019*. Abingdon: Routledge.

Dicey, A.V. (1887) *England's Case Against Home Rule*. London: John Murray.

Dinas, E. (2013) 'Opening "openness to change": Political events and the increased sensitivity of young adults', *Political Research Quarterly*, 66(4): 868–882. https://doi.org/10.1177/1065912913475874

Disch, L. (2011) 'Toward a mobilization conception of democratic representation', *American Political Science Review*, 105(1): 100–114.

Doherty, B., Hayes, G. and Rootes, C. (2016) 'Social Movement Studies in Britain: No longer the poor relation?', in Fillieule, O. and Accornero. G. (eds), *Social Movement Studies in Europe: The State of the Art*. New York/Oxford: Berghahn Books, Chapter 11 (pp. 191–213).

Dommett, K. and Flinders, M. (2015) 'The centre strikes back: Meta-governance, delegation and the core executive in the United Kingdom 2010–14', *Public Administration*, 93(1): 1–16.

Dommett, K., Barclay, A. and Gibson, R. (2024) 'Just what is data-driven campaigning? A systematic review', *Information, Communication & Society*, 27: 1–22.

Dorey, P. (1993) 'One step at a time: The Conservative Government's approach to the reform of Industrial Relations since 1979', *The Political Quarterly*, 64(1): 24–36.

Dorey, P. (2007) 'A new direction or another false dawn? David Cameron and the crisis of British Conservatism', *British Politics*, 2: 137–166.

Dorey, P. (2014) *Policy Making in Britain* (2nd edn). London: Sage.

Dorey, P. (2023) 'Elected or selected? The continuing constitutional conundrum of House of Lords reform', *The Political Quarterly*, 94(3): 402–411.

Dorling, D. and Tomlinson, S. (2019) *Rule Britannia: Brexit and the End of Empire*. London: Biteback.

Dovi, S. (2002) 'Preferable descriptive representatives: Will just any woman, Black, or Latino do?', *American Political Science Review*, 96(4): 729–743.

Dovi, S. (2007) *The Good Representative*. Oxford: Blackwell Publishing.

Dovi, S. (2010) 'Measuring representation: Rethinking the role of exclusion', paper presented at the American Political Science Association Annual Meeting, Washington, DC, 2–5 September.

Drever, F., Doran, T. and Whitehead, M. (2004) 'Exploring the relation between class, gender, and self-rated general health using the new socioeconomic classification: A study using data from the 2001 Census', *Journal of Epidemiology & Community Health*, 58(7): 590–596. https://doi.org/10.1136/jech.2003.013383.

Dudley, G. and Gamble, A. (2023) 'Brexit and UK policy-making: An overview', *Journal of European Public Policy*, 30(11): 2573–2597.

Duffy, B. (2018) 'Why leavers still believe the £350m claim: Emotion trumps facts where the EU is concerned', *UK in a Changing Europe*, 2 November. Available at: https://ukandeu.ac.uk/why-leavers-still-believe-the-350m-claim-emotion-trumps-facts-where-the-eu-is-concerned/

Dunleavy, P. (2018) 'The interest group process', in Dunleavy, P., Park, A. and Taylor, R. (eds.), *The UK's Changing Democracy: The 2018 Democratic Audit*. London: LSE Press, Chapter 3.2 (pp. 112–121).

Dunleavy, P. and Rhodes, R.A.W. (1990) *Prime Minister, Cabinet and Core Executive*. Basingstoke: Palgrave.

Dunlop, L. (2021) *Review of the Scottish Government Procedure for Handling Harassment Complaints Involving Current and Former Ministers*. Edinburgh: Scottish Parliament. Available at: www.gov.scot/publications/review-of-the-scottish-government-procedure-for-handling-harassment-complaints-involving-current-or-former-ministers/

Dunt, I. (2023) *How Westminster Works . . . and Why It Doesn't*. London: W&N.

Durose, C., Richardson, L., Combs, R., Eason, C. and Gains, F. (2013) '"Acceptable difference": Diversity, representation and pathways to UK politics', *Parliamentary Affairs*, 66(2): 246–267.

Dye, T. (1972) *Understanding Public Policy*. Englewood-Cliffs, NJ: Prentice-Hall.

Dyson, S.B. (2023) 'Theresa May and Brexit: Leadership style and performance', *British Politics*. Advance online article ahead of print. https://doi.org/10.1057/s41293-023-00230-5

Eagle, M. and Lovenduski, J. (1998) *High Time or High Tide for Labour Women?* London: Fabian Society.

Eatwell, R. and Goodwin, M. (2017) *National Populism: The Revolt Against Liberal Democracy*. London: Pelican Books.

Edgerton, D. (2018) *The Rise and Fall of the British Nation: A Twentieth Century History*. London: Penguin.

Eeckhout, P. (2018) 'The Emperor has no clothes: Brexit and the UK constitution', in Martill, B. and Staiger, U. (eds), *Brexit and Beyond: Rethinking the Futures of Europe*. London: UCL Press.

Electoral Commission (2008) *Scottish Elections 2007: The Independent Review of the Scottish Parliamentary and Local Government Elections 3 May 2007*. The Gould Report, 23 October 2007. Available at: www.electoralcommission.org.uk/sites/default/files/electoral_commission_pdf_file/Scottish-Election-Report-A-Final-For-Web.pdf

Electoral Commission (2015) https://www.electoralcommission.org.uk/sites/default/files/pdf_file/Proof-of-identity-scheme-updated-March-2016.pdf

Electoral Commission (2022) *Know Who Is Paying for Online Political Ads*. Available at: www.electoralcommission.org.uk/voting-and-elections/campaigning-election/online-campaigning/know-who-paying-online-political-ads

Electoral Commission (2023) https://www.electoralcommission.org.uk/research-reports-and-data/our-reports-and-data-past-elections-and-referendums/voter-id-may-2023-local-elections-england-interim-analysis

Electoral Office of Northern Ireland (2020) 'UK Parliamentary Election 2019: Summary of rejected ballot paper statements'. Available at: www.eoni.org.uk/getmedia/1c3a8e33-443a-4d9e-9660-130b86d602cb/UK-Parliamentary-Election-2019-Summary-of-Rejected-Ballot-Paper-Statements

Electoral Reform Society (2020) 'Democracy in the dark: Digital campaigning in the 2019 general election and beyond'. Available at: www.electoral-reform.org.uk/latest-news-and-research/publications/democracy-in-the-dark-digital-campaigning-in-the-2019-general-election-and-beyond/

El-Enany, N. (2020) *(B)ordering Britain: Law, Race and Empire*. Manchester: Manchester University Press.

Elgot, J. and Walker, P. (2020) 'Labour suspends Jeremy Corbyn over EHRC report comments', *The Guardian*, 29 October. Available at: www.theguardian.com/politics/2020/oct/29/labour-suspends-jeremy-corbyn-over-ehrc-report-comments (accessed 12 March 2024).

Elliott, F. and Hanning, J. (2012) *Cameron: Practically a Conservative*. London: Fourth Estate.

Elliott, L. (2013) 'Boris Johnson urges Osborne to drop "hair shirt" agenda for UK economy', *The Guardian*, 25 January. Available at: www.theguardian.com/business/2013/jan/25/boris-johnson-criticises-osborne-austerity

Elliott, L. (2024) 'Gordon Brown: UK has to get on war footing for economic growth', *The Guardian*, 10 March. Available at: www.theguardian.com/business/2024/mar/10/gordon-brown-uk-war-footing-economic-growth-treasury

Elliott, M. (2017) 'The Supreme Court's judgment in *Miller*: In search of constitutional principle', *Comparative Law Journal*, 76(1): 257–257.

Elliott, M. (2020) 'Constitutional adjudication and constitutional politics in the United Kingdom: The *Miller II* case in legal and political context', *European Constitutional Law Review*, 16(4): 625–646.

Elliott, M. and Thomas, R. (2020) *Public Law* (4th edn). Oxford: Oxford University Press.

Emmerson, C., Johnson, P. and Zaranko, B. (2023) 'IFS Green Budget 2023: This will be the biggest tax-raising Parliament on record', *Institute for Fiscal Studies*, 29 September. Available at: Available at https://ifs.org.uk/articles/will-be-biggest-tax-raising-parliament-record

English, P. (2019) 'Visibly restricted: Public opinion and the representation of immigrant origin communities across Great Britain', *Ethnic and Racial Studies*, 42(9): 1437–1466.

English, P. (2022) 'High rejection, low selection: How "punitive parties" shape ethnic minority representation', *Party Politics*, 28(2): 294–305.

Entman, R.M. (1993) 'Framing: Toward clarification of a fractured paradigm', *Journal of Communication*, 43(4): 51–58.

Equality and Human Rights Commission (EHRC) (2020) *Investigation into Antisemitism in the Labour Party, Report October 2020*. London: EHRC. Available at: www.equalityhumanrights.com/sites/default/files/investigation-into-antisemitism-in-the-labour-party.pdf

Erskine May (2019) *Erskine May's Treatise on the Law, Privileges, Proceedings and Usage of Parliament* (25th ed.). London: LexisNexis. Available at: https://erskinemay.parliament.uk (accessed 22 August 2019).

Esler, G. (2022) *How Britain Ends: English Nationalism and the Rebirth of Four Nations*. London: Head of Zeus.

Esposito, E. and Breeze, R. (2022) 'Gender and politics in a digitalised world: Investigating online hostility against UK female MPs', *Discourse & Society*, 33(3): 303–323.

European Commission (2017) 'Slide presented by Michel Barnier, European Commission Chief Negotiator, to the Heads of State and Government at the European Council (Article 50) on 15 December 2017'. Available at: https://commission.europa.eu/publications/slide-presented-michel-barnier-european-commission-chief-negotiator-heads-state-and-government_en (accessed 20 September 2024).

European Commission (2020) *The EU–UK Withdrawal Agreement*. Agreed on 17 October 2019, entered into force on 1 February 2020. Brussels: European Commission. Available at: https://commission.europa.eu/strategy-and-policy/relations-united-kingdom/eu-uk-withdrawal-agreement_en

Evans, A. (2018) 'Planning for Brexit: The case of the 1975 referendum', *The Political Quarterly*, 89(1): 127–133.

Evans, A. (2019) 'Inter-parliamentary relations in the United Kingdom: Devolution's undiscovered country?', *Parliaments, Estates and Representation*, 39(1): 98–112.

Evans, A. (2020) 'A tale as old as (devolved) time? Sewel, Stormont and the Legislative Consent Convention', *The Political Quarterly*, 91(1): 165–172.

Evans, E. and Reher, S. (2022) 'Disability and political representation: Analysing the obstacles to elected office in the UK', *International Political Science Review*, 43(5): 697–712.

Evans, E. and Reher, S. (2023) 'Gender, disability and political representation: Understanding the experiences of disabled women', *European Journal of Politics and Gender*, 28 March, 1–18. E-pub ahead of print. https://doi.org/10.1332/251510823x16779382116831

Evans, E. and Reher, S. (2024) *Disability and Political Representation*. Oxford: Oxford University Press.

Evans, E.J. (2019) *Thatcher and Thatcherism*. London: Routledge.

Evans, G. (1992) 'Testing the validity of the Goldthorpe Class Schema', *European Sociological Review*, 8(3): 211–232. https://doi.org/10.1093/oxfordjournals.esr.a036638

Evans, G. (2017) 'Social class and voting', in Arzheimer, K., Evans, J. and Lewis-Beck, M.S. (eds), *The SAGE Handbook of Electoral Behaviour* (Vol. 2). London: SAGE, pp. 177–198.

Evans, G. and Hepplewhite, M. (2022) 'Class and educational inequality in electoral participation', in Giugni, M. and Grasso, M. (eds), *The Oxford Handbook of Political Participation*. Oxford University Press, pp. 578–597. https://doi.org/10.1093/oxfordhb/9780198861126.013.34

Evans, G. and Menon, A. (2017) *Brexit and British Politics*. Cambridge: Polity.

Evans, G. and Tilley, J. (2017) *The New Politics of Class: The Political Exclusion of the British Working Class*. Oxford: Oxford University Press.

Evans, P., Salmon Percival, C., Silk, P. and White, H. (eds) (2021) *Parliaments and the Pandemic*. London: Study of Parliament Group. Available at: https://studyofparliamentgroup.org/study-of-parliament-group-papers/ (accessed 11 November 2022).

Ewing, K. (2017) 'Brexit and parliamentary sovereignty', *Modern Law Review*, 80(1): 685–721.

Eyles, A., Elliot Major, L. and Machin, S. (2022) *Social Mobility – Past, Present and Future*. London: The Sutton Trust. Available at: www.suttontrust.com/our-research/social-mobility-past-present-and-future/

Fakim, N. and Macaulay, C. (2020) '"Don't call me BAME": Why some people are rejecting the term', *BBC News*, 30 June. Available at: www.bbc.co.uk/news/uk-53194376

Fall, K. (2021) *The Gatekeeper: Life at the Heart of No.10*. London: HQ.

Fetzer, T. (2019) 'Did austerity cause Brexit?', *American Economic Review*, 109(11): 3849–3886.

Fieldhouse, E., Evans, G., Green, J., Mellon, J., Prosser, C. and Bailey, J. (2023) 'Volatility, realignment, and electoral shocks: Brexit and the UK General Election of 2019', *PS: Political Science & Politics*, 56: 537–545.

Fieldhouse, E., Green, J., Evans, G., Mellon, J., Prosser, C., de Geus, R. and Bailey, J. (2022) *British Election Study, 2019: Post-Election Random Probability Survey* [data collection]. UK Data Service. SN: 8875, doi: 10.5255/UKDA-SN-8875-1

Fieldhouse, E., Green, J., Evans, G., Mellon, J., Prosser, C., Schmitt, H. and van der Eijk, C. (2020) *Electoral Shocks: The Volatile Voter in a Turbulent World*. Oxford: Oxford University Press. https://doi.org/10.1093/oso/9780198800583.001.0001

Figueira, F. and Martill, B. (2021) 'Bounded rationality and the Brexit negotiations: Why Britain failed to understand the EU', *Journal of European Public Policy*, 28(12): 1871–1889.

Finn, M. (ed.) (2015) *The Gove Legacy: Education in Britain after the Coalition*. Basingstoke: Palgrave.

Fisher, L. (2015) 'The growing power and autonomy of House of Commons select committees: Causes and effects', *The Political Quarterly*, 86(3): 419–426.

Fisher, S., Heath, A., Sanders, D. and Sobolewska, M. (2015) 'Candidate ethnicity and vote choice in Britain', *British Journal of Political Science*, 45(4): 883–905.

Flinders M. (2010) *Democratic Drift: Majoritarian Modification and Democratic Anomie in the United Kingdom*. Oxford: Oxford University Press.

Flinders, M. (2007) 'Analysing reform: The House of Commons, 2001–5', *Political Studies*, 55(1): 174–200.

Flinders, M. and Anderson, A. (2022) 'MPs' expenses: The legacy of a scandal 10 years on', *British Politics*, 17(2): 119–143.

Flinders, M. and Kelso, A. (2011) 'Mind the gap: Political analysis, public expectations and the parliamentary decline thesis', *British Journal of Politics and International Relations*, 13(2): 249–268.

Flinders, M., Judge, D., Rhodes, R.A.W. and Vatter, A. (2021) '"Stretched but not snapped": A response to Russell and Serban on retiring the "Westminster Model"', *Government and Opposition*, 57(2): 353–369.

Flinders, M., Meakin, A. and Anderson, A. (2019) 'The restoration and renewal of the Palace of Westminster: Avoiding the trap and realising the promise', *The Political Quarterly*, 90(3): 488–495.

Flinders, M., Weinberg A., Weinberg J., Geddes M. and Kwiatkowski R. (2020) 'Governing under pressure? The mental wellbeing of politicians', *Parliamentary Affairs*, 73(2): 253–273.

Foley, M. (1989) *The Silence of Constitutions: Gaps, 'Abeyances' and Political Temperament in the Maintenance of Government*. Routledge.

Follesdal, A. and Hix, S. (2006) 'Why there is a democratic deficit in the EU: A response to Majone and Moravcsik', *Journal of Common Market Studies*, 44(3): 533–562.

Fontana, C. and Parsons, C. (2015) '"One woman's prejudice": Did Margaret Thatcher cause Britain's anti-Europeanism?', *Journal of Common Market Studies*, 53(1): 89–105.

Ford, M. and Goodwin, M. (2014) *Revolt on the Right: Explaining Support for the Radical Right in Britain*. London: Routledge.

Ford, R., Bale, T., Jennings, W. and Surridge, P. (eds) (2021) *The British General Election of 2019*. Basingstoke: Palgrave Macmillan.

Foster, D.H. (2015) 'Going "where angels fear to tread": How effective was the Backbench Business Committee in the 2010–2012 parliamentary session?', *Parliamentary Affairs*, 68(1): 116–134.

Fowler, C. (2023) 'Gender-age gaps in Euroscepticism and vote choice at the United Kingdom's 2016 referendum on EU membership', *British Journal of Politics and International Relations*, 25(4): 595–616.

Franklin, M. and Norton, P. (1993) *Parliamentary Questions*. Oxford: Clarendon Press.

Freeden, M. (1996) *Ideologies and Political Theory: A Conceptual Approach*. Oxford: Oxford University Press.

Freeden, M. (2017) 'After the Brexit referendum: Revisiting populism as an ideology', *Journal of Political Ideologies*, 22(1): 1–11.

Freedman, S. (2022) 'The Gove reforms a decade on: What worked, what didn't, what next?', *Institute for Government* analysis paper, 9 February. Available at: www.instituteforgovernment.org.uk/publication/gove-school-reforms

Fuertes, V. and Lindsay, C. (2016) 'Personalization and street-level practice in activation: The case of the UK's work programme', *Public Administration*, 94(2): 526–541.

Furlong, J. and Jennings, W. (2024) *The Changing Electoral Map of England and Wales*. Oxford: Oxford University Press.

Gaber, I. and Fisher, C. (2022) 'Strategic lying': The case of Brexit and the 2019 UK election', *The International Journal of Press/Politics*, 27: 460–477.

Galandini, S. and Fieldhouse, E. (2019) 'Discussants that mobilise: Ethnicity, political discussion networks and voter turnout in Britain', *Electoral Studies*, 57: 163–173.

Gallagher, J. (2018) 'The Ghost in the Machine? The Government of England', in Kenny, McLean and Paun (eds), *Governing England. English Identity and Institutions in a Changing United Kingdom*. Proceedings of the British Academy 217. Oxford: Oxford University Press.

Gallagher, J. 2018. 'The Ghost in the Machine? The Government of England', in Kenny, McLean and Paun (eds), *Governing England. English Identity and Institutions in a Changing United Kingdom*. Proceedings of the British Academy 217. Oxford: Oxford University Press.

Galligan, B. and Brenton, S. (eds.) (2015) *Constitutional Conventions in Westminster Systems: Controversies, Challenges and Changes*. Cambridge: Cambridge University Press.

Galpin, C. (2022) 'Contesting Brexit masculinities: Pro-European activists and feminist EU Citizenship', *Journal of Common Market Studies*, 60(2): 301–318.

Gamble, A. (1974) *The Conservative Nation*. London: Routledge.

Gamble, A. (1990) 'Theories of British politics', *Political Studies*, 38(3): 404–420.

Gamble, A. (2006) 'The constitutional revolution in the United Kingdom', *Publius*, 36(1): 19–35.

Ganderson, J. (2020) 'To change banks of bankers? Systemic political (in)action and post-crisis banking reform in the UK and the Netherlands', *Business & Politics*, 22(1): 196–223.

Garbaye, R. (2005) *Getting into Local Power: The Politics of Ethnic Minorities in British and French Cities*. Oxford: Blackwell.

Gardiner, A. (2018) 'An idea whose time has come? Modern slavery, multiple streams approach and multilayer policy implementation', *Journal of Human Rights Practice*, 10(3): 461–481.

Gardiner, A. (2019) 'Modern slavery: Addressing the gap between policy and practice', *University of Nottingham Rights Lab*, research briefing. Available at: www.nottingham.ac.uk/research/beacons-of-excellence/rights-lab/resources/reports-and-briefings/2019/may/briefing-%E2%80%93-modern-slavery-policy-and-practice.pdf

Garnett, M. (2012) 'Michael Howard, 2003–5', in Heppell, T. (ed.), *Leaders of the Opposition*. London: Palgrave Macmillan.

Garnett, M. and Lorenzoni, V. (2021) 'British think tanks in the time of Brexit', in Abelson D.E. and Rastrick, C.J. (eds.), *Handbook on Think Tanks in Public Policy*. Cheltenham: Edward Elgar.

Garrard, G. (2022) *The Return of the State: And Why It Is Essential for Our Health, Wealth, and Happiness*. New Haven, CT: Yale University Press.

Garry, J. and Pow, J. (2023) 'What happens when mini-publics are held in a deeply divided place? Evidence from Northern Ireland', *Political Science & Politics*, 56(4): 572–578.

Gaskarth, J. (2013a) 'Interpreting ethical foreign policy: Traditions and dilemmas for policy makers', *British Journal of Politics and International Relations*, 15(2): 192–209.

Gaskarth, J. (2013b) *British Foreign Policy*. Cambridge: Polity Press.

Gay, O. (2005) 'MPs go back to their constituencies', *The Political Quarterly*, 76(1): 57–66.

Geddes, A. (1993) 'Asian and Afro-Caribbean representation in elected local government in England and Wales', *Journal of Ethnic and Migration Studies*, 20(1): 43–57.

Geddes, M. (2018) 'Committee hearings of the UK Parliament: Who gives evidence and does this matter?', *Parliamentary Affairs*, 71(2): 283–304.

Geddes, M. (2020) *Dramas at Westminster: Select Committees and the Quest for Accountability*. Manchester: Manchester University Press.

George, S. (1990) *An Awkward Partner: Britain in the European Community*. Oxford: Oxford University Press.

Gest, J. (2016) *The New Minority: White Working-Class Politics in an Age of Immigration and Inequality*. Oxford: Oxford University Press.

Gibbs, E., McCartney, G. and Phillips, J. (2024) 'The fundamentals of public ownership: Learning from UK historical experience and recent Scottish policy', *The Political Quarterly*, 19 February, 1–10.

Gidron, N. and Hall, P.A. (2017) 'The politics of social status: Economic and cultural roots of the populist right', *The British Journal of Sociology*, 68(S1): S57–S84. https://doi.org/10.1111/1468-4446.12319.

Gifford, C. and Wellings, B. (2018) 'Referendums and European integration: The case of the United Kingdom', in Leruth, B., Startin, N. and Usherwood, S. (eds), *The Routledge Handbook of Euroscepticism*. Abingdon: Routledge.

Gilmour, D. (2018) *The British in India: Three Centuries of Ambition and Experience*. London: Allen Lane.

Gilroy, P. (1987) *There Ain't No Black in the Union Jack: The Cultural Politics of Race and Nation*. London and New York: Routledge.

Gilroy, P. (2006) *Postcolonial Melancholia*. New York: Columbia University Press.

Girvan, B. (1994) *The Right in the Twentieth Century: Conservatism and Democracy*. London: Pinter.

Glencross, A. (2023) 'The origins of "cakeism": The British think tank debate over repatriating sovereignty and its impact on the UK's Brexit strategy', *Journal of European Public Policy*, 30(6): 995–1012.

Goes, E. (2024) *Social Democracy*. Newcastle: Agenda.

González-Bailón, S., Lazer, D., Barberá, P., Zhang, M., Allcott, H., Brown, T., Crespo-Tenorio, A., Freelon, D., Gentzkow, M., Guess, A.M. and Iyengar, S. (2023) 'Asymmetric ideological segregation in exposure to political news on Facebook', *Science*, 381(6656): 392–398.

Goodwin, M. and Milazzo, C. (2015) *UKIP: Inside the Campaign to Redraw the Map of British Politics*. Oxford: Oxford University Press.

Goodwin, M. and Milazzo, C. (2017) 'Taking back control? Investigating the role of immigration in the 2016 vote for Brexit', *British Journal of Politics and International Relations*, 19(3): 450–464.

Goodwin, M., Holden Bates, S. and McKay, S. (2021) 'Electing to do women's work? Gendered divisions of labor in U.K. select committees, 1979–2016', *Politics & Gender*, 17(4): 607–639.

Gordon, M. (2015) *Parliamentary Sovereignty in the UK Constitution*. Oxford: Hart Publishing.

Gordon, M. (2016) 'The UK's sovereignty situation: Brexit, bewilderment and beyond...', *King's Law Journal*, 27(3): 333–343.

Gordon, M. (2019) *Parliamentary Sovereignty and the UK Constitution*. Oxford: Hart Publishing.

Gov.uk (2022) *A Guide to the Online Safety Bill*. Available at: www.gov.uk/guidance/a-guide-to-the-online-safety-bill

Gover, D. and Kenny, M. (2018) 'Answering the West Lothian Question? A critical assessment of 'English Votes for English Laws' in the UK Parliament', *Parliamentary Affairs*, 71(4): 760–782.

Graham, J., Haidt, J. and Nosek, B.A. (2009) 'Liberals and Conservatives rely on different sets of moral foundations', *Journal of Personality and Social Psychology*, 96(5): 1029.

Grasso, M.T., Farrall, S., Gray, E., Hay, C. and Jennings, W. (2019) 'Thatcher's children, Blair's babies, political socialization and trickle-down value change: An age, period and cohort analysis', *British Journal of Political Science*, 49(1): 17–36. https://doi.org/10.1017/S0007123416000375

Gray, J. (2015) 'What is an MP for?', *PoliticsHome*, www.politicshome.com/news/uk/social-affairs/politics/house/60356/james-gray-what-mp

Gray, S. (2022) *Final Report on Investigation into Alleged Gatherings on Government Premises During Covid Restrictions*. Available at: www.gov.uk/government/publications/findings-of-the-second-permanent-secretarys-investigation-into-alleged-gatherings-on-government-premises-during-covid-restrictions

Green, D.P. and Gerber, A.S. (2019) *Get Out the Vote: How to Increase Voter Turnout*. Washington, DC: Brookings Institution Press.

Green, E.H.H. (2002) *Ideologies of Conservatism*. Oxford: Oxford University Press.

Green, J. and Jennings, W. (2017) *The Politics of Competence: Parties, Public Opinion and Voters*. Cambridge: Cambridge University Press.

Greenberg, D. (2011) *Laying Down the Law: A Discussion of the People, Processes and Problems that Shape Acts of Parliament*. London: Sweet & Maxwell.

Greene, R.A. (2020) 'Who is Cecil Rhodes and why are UK demonstrators protesting at his statue?', *CNN*, 10 June. Available at: https://edition.cnn.com/2020/06/09/uk/cecil-rhodes-protest-oxford-intl/index.html (accessed 19 February 2024).

Greener, I. (2005) 'The potential of path dependence in political studies', *Politics*, 25(1): 62–72.

Greening, J. (2023) 'Westminster is rife with "entitlement syndrome": During Covid it cost lives', *The Guardian*, 7 November. Available at: www.theguardian.com/commentisfree/2023/nov/07/westminster-is-rife-with-entitlement-syndrome-during-covid-it-cost-lives

Greer, I., Schulte, L. and Symon, G. (2018) 'Creaming and parking in marketized employment services: An Anglo-German comparison', *Human Relations*, 71(11): 1427–1453.

Grey, C. (2021) *Brexit Unfolded: How No One Got What They Wanted (and Why They Were Never Going To)*. London: Biteback.

Griffiths, J., Wyn Jones, R., Poole, E.G., Larner, J.M., Henderson, A. and McMillan, F. (2023) 'Diverging electoral fortunes in Scotland and Wales: National identities, national interests, and voting behavior', *Regional & Federal Studies*, 33(4): 487–510.

Gschwend, T., Johnston, R. and Pattie, C (2003) 'Split-ticket patterns in mixed-member proportional election systems: Estimates and analyses of their spatial variation at the German Federal Election 1998', *British Journal of Political Science*, 33: 109–127.

Gstöhl, S. and Phinnemore, D. (2021) 'The future EU–UK partnership: A historical institutionalist perspective', *Journal of European Integration*, 43(1): 99–115.

Guardian (2017) 'From Lloyd George to Brexit: 10 of the best books on British Politics'. Available at: https://www.theguardian.com/books/2017/oct/09/ten-best-books-british-politics (accessed 20 September 2024)

Guardian (2021) 'Man jailed for racially abusing Rashford, Sancho and Saka after Euro 2020 final', *The Guardian*, 3 November. Available at: www.theguardian.com/football/2021/nov/03/football-fan-jailed-for-racially-abusing-rashford-sancho-and-saka-after-final-euro-2020

Guess, A.M., Malhotra, N., Pan, J., Barberá, P., Allcott, H., Brown, T., Crespo-Tenorio, A., Dimmery, D., Freelon, D., Gentzkow, M. and González-Bailón, S. (2023a) 'How do social media feed algorithms affect attitudes and behavior in an election campaign?', *Science*, 381(6656): 398–404.

Guess, A.M., Malhotra, N., Pan, J., Barberá, P., Allcott, H., Brown, T., Crespo-Tenorio, A., Dimmery, D., Freelon, D., Gentzkow, M. and González-Bailón, S. (2023b) 'Reshares on social media amplify political news but do not detectably affect beliefs or opinions', *Science*, 381(6656): 404–408.

Hacker, J.S. (1998) 'The historical logic of national health insurance: Structure and sequence in the development of British, Canadian, and U.S. medical policy', *Studies in American Political Development*, 12(Spring): 57–130.

Haddon, C. (2012) 'Making policy in opposition: Lessons for effective government', *Institute for Government* research report. Available at: www.instituteforgovernment.org.uk/publication/report/making-policy-opposition

Haddon, C. (2021) 'Judicial review and policy making: The role of legal advice in government', *Institute for Government* analysis paper. Available at: www.instituteforgovernment.org.uk/sites/default/files/publications/judicial-review.pdf

Hadfield, A. and Whitman, R.G. (2023) 'The diplomacy of "Global Britain": Settling, safeguarding and seeking status', *International Politics*. Advance online article ahead of print. https://doi.org/10.1057/s41311-023-00489-x.

Hailsham, Q. (1976) *Elective Dictatorship*. London.

Hall, M. (2011) *Political Traditions and UK Politics*. Basingstoke: Palgrave.

Hallin, D.C. and Mancini, P. (2004) *Comparing Media Systems: Three Models of Media and Politics*. Cambridge: Cambridge University Press.

Hallsworth, M., Parker, S. and Rutter, J. (2011) 'Policy making in the real world: Evidence and analysis', *Institute for Government* research report. Available at: www.instituteforgovernment.org.uk/publication/report/policy-making-real-world

Hamilton, L. (2014) *Freedom Is Power: Liberty through Political Representation*. Cambridge: Cambridge University Press.

Hannan, D. (2016a) *What Next: How to Get the Best from Brexit*. London: Head of Zeus.

Hannan, D. (2016b) *A Doomed Marriage: Why Britain Should Leave the EU*. London: Notting Hill Editions.

Hansard Society (2014) *Tuned In or Turned Off? Public Attitudes to Prime Minister's Questions*. London: Hansard Society.

Hansard Society (2019) *Audit of Political Engagement 16: The 2019 Report*. London: Hansard Society.

Hansard Society (2021) *Delegated Legislation: The Problems with the Process*. London: Hansard Society.

Hansard Society (2023) *A New Structure for Interparliamentary Relations in a Devolved Great Britain and Northern Ireland*. London: Hansard Society.

Hardman, I. (2018) *Why We Get the Wrong Politicians*. London: Atlantic Books.

Hargrave, L. and Langengen, T. (2021) 'The gendered debate: Do men and women communicate differently in the House of Commons?', *Politics & Gender*, 17(4): 580–606.

Harper, M. and Constantine, S. (2014) *Migration and Empire*. Oxford: Oxford University Press.

Harris, J. and Rutter, J. (2014) 'Centre forward: Effective support for the Prime Minister at the centre of government. *Institute for Government* research report. Available at: www.instituteforgovernment.org.uk/publication/report/centre-forward

Hassan, G. and Shaw, E. (2012) *The Strange Death of Labour Scotland*. Edinburgh: Edinburgh University Press.

Hassan, G. and Shaw, E. (2020) 'The Scottish Labour Party', in Keating, M. (ed.), *The Oxford Handbook of Scottish Politics*. Oxford: Oxford University Press.

Haughey, S. and Loughran, T. (2024) 'Public opinion and consociationalism in Northern Ireland: Towards the "end stage" of the power-sharing lifecycle?', *The British Journal of Politics and International Relations*, 26(1): 187–207.

Hay, C. (2007) *Why We Hate Politics*. London: Polity Press.

Hayton, R. (2012) *Reconstructing Conservatism? The Conservative Party in Opposition, 1997–2010*. Manchester: Manchester University Press.

Hayton, R. (2018) 'British Conservatism after the vote for Brexit: The ideological legacy of David Cameron', *British Journal of Politics and International Relations*, 20(1): 223–238.

Hayton, R. (2021) 'Conservative Party statecraft and the Johnson Government', *The Political Quarterly*, 92(3): 412–419.

Hayward, K. and Komarova, M. (2024) 'Has Brexit changed the Irish border question?', in Bell, D. and O'Dowd, L. (eds), *Northern Ireland beyond 100: The End of the Beginning or the Beginning of the End*. Cork: Cork University Press.

Hayward, K. and McEwen, N. (2022) *An EU border across Britain: Scotland's borders after independence*. London: UK in a Changing Europe. Available at: https://ukandeu.ac.uk/reports/an-eu-border-across-britain-scotlands-borders-after-independence/

Hazell, R. and Foot, T. (2022) *Executive Power: The Prerogative, Past, Present, and Future*. Oxford: Hart.

Heath, A., Fisher, S., Rosenblatt, G. et al. (2013) *The Political Integration of Ethnic Minorities in Britain*. Oxford: Oxford University Press.

Heath, O. (2015) 'Policy representation, social representation and class voting in Britain', *British Journal of Political Science*, 45(1): 173–193. https://doi.org/10.1017/S0007123413000318

Heath, O. (2018) 'Policy alienation, social alienation and working-class abstention in Britain, 1964–2010', *British Journal of Political Science*, 48(4): 1053–1073. https://doi.org/10.1017/S0007123416000272

Heath, O. and Goodwin, M. (2017) 'The 2017 General Election, Brexit and the return to two-party politics: An aggregate-level analysis of the result', *The Political Quarterly*, 88(3): 345–358.

Heide, M. and Worthy, B. (2019) 'Secrecy and leadership: The case of Theresa May's Brexit negotiations', *Public Integrity*, 21(6): 582–594.

Heinkelmann-Wild, T., Kriegmair, L., Rittberger, B. and Zangl, B. (2020) 'Divided they fail: The politics of wedge issues and Brexit', *Journal of European Public Policy*, 27(5): 723–741.

Henderson, A (2023) *Devolution and the UK's response to COVID-19*. Expert witness report for the UK Covid-19 Inquiry https://covid19.public-inquiry.uk/wp-content/uploads/2023/10/09184423/INQ000269372.pdf

Henderson, A. (2014a) 'Scotland', in Cowley, P. and Ford, R. (eds) (2015), *Sex, Lies and the Ballot Box*. London: Biteback.

Henderson, A. (2014b) 'The myth of meritocratic Scotland: Political cultures in the UK', in Cowley, P. and Ford, R. (eds), *Sex, Lies and the Ballot Box*. London: Biteback.

Henderson, A. and Wyn Jones, R. (2021) *Englishness: The Political Force Transforming Britain*. Oxford: Oxford University Press.

Henderson, A. and Wyn Jones, R. (2023) *The Ambivalent Union: Findings from the State of the Nation Survey*. London: Institute for Public Policy Research (IPPR). Available at: https://ippr-org.files.svdcdn.com/production/Downloads/the-ambivalent-union-sept23.pdf

Henderson, A., Jeffery, C. and Lineira, R. (2015) 'National identity or national interest? Scottish, English and Welsh Attitudes to the Constitutional Debate', *The Political Quarterly*, 38(2): 265–274.

Henderson, A., Jeffery, C., Liñeira, R., Scully, R., Wincott, D. and Jones, R.W. (2016) 'England, Englishness and Brexit', *The Political Quarterly*, 87(2): 187–199.

Henderson, A., Jeffery, C., Wincott, D. and Wyn Jones, R. (2017) 'How Brexit was made in England', *British Journal of Politics and International Relations*, 19(4): 631–646.

Henderson, A., Johns, R., Larner, J. and Carman, C. (2022) *The Referendum that Changed a Nation: Scottish Voting Behaviour, 2014–2019*. London: Palgrave.

Henderson, A., McMillan, F., Larner, J., Johns, R., Carman, C. and Hanretty, C. (2021) *The 2021 Scottish Election Study*. UK Data Archive.

Henderson, A., Poole, E.G., Wyn Jones, R., Wincott, D., Larner, J. and Jeffery, C. (2021) 'Analysing vote-choice in a multinational state: National identity and territorial differentiation in the 2016 Brexit vote', *Regional Studies*, 55(9): 1502–1516.

Hennessy, P. (1996) *Muddling Through: Power, Politics and the Quality of Government in Postwar Britain*. London: Indigo.

Heppell, T. (2002) 'The ideological composition of the Parliamentary Conservative Party 1992–1997', *British Journal of Politics and International Relations*, 4(2): 299–324.

Heppell, T. and Hill, M. (2008) 'The Conservative Party leadership election of 1997: An analysis of the voting motivations of Conservative parliamentarians', *British Politics*, 3(1): 63–91.

Heppell, T. and Hill, M. (2010) 'The voting motivations of Conservative parliamentarians in the Conservative Party leadership election of 2001', *Politics*, 30(1): 36–51.

Hewitt, P. and Mattinson, D. (1989) *Women's Votes: The Key to Winning*. London: Fabian Society.

Heywood, A. (2019) *Politics*. London: Macmillan International Higher Education.

Heywood, S. (2021) *What Does Jeremy Think? Jeremy Heywood and the Making of Modern Britain*. London: William Collins.

Hill, A. (2022) 'Deep-rooted Russian fear of the West has fuelled Putin's invasion of Ukraine', *The Conversation*, 3 March. Available at: https://theconversation.com/deep-rooted-russian-fear-of-the-west-has-fuelled-putins-invasion-of-ukraine-178351 (accessed on 4 March 2024).

Hill, C. (2019) *The Future of British Foreign Policy: Security and Diplomacy in a World after Brexit.* Cambridge: Polity Press.

Hill, C. (2023) 'Debating Britain's role in the world: From decolonisation to Brexit', *International Politics*. Advance online article ahead of print. https://doi.org/10.1057/s41311-023-00454-8

Hill, M. (2013) 'Arrogant posh boys? The social composition of the Parliamentary Conservative Party and the effect of Cameron's "A" list', *The Political Quarterly*, 84(1): 80–89

Hill, S.J., Lo, J., Vavreck, L. and Zaller, J. (2013) 'How quickly we forget: The duration of persuasion effects from mass communication', *Political Communication*, 30: 521–547.

Hindmoor, A. and Pike, K. (2022) 'Past, present and future: Tony Blair and the political legacy of New Labour', in Yeowell, N. (ed.), *Rethinking Labour's Past*. London: I.B. Tauris, pp. 249–265.

Hindmoor, A., Larkin, P. and Kennon, A. (2009) 'Assessing the influence of select committees in the UK: The Education and Skills Committee, 1997–2005', *The Journal of Legislative Studies*, 15(1): 71–89.

Hix, S. (2015) 'Brits know less about the EU than anyone else', *LSE European Politics and Policy (EUROPP)* [Blog], 27 November. Available at: http://blogs.lse.ac.uk/europpblog/2015/11/27/brits-know-less-about-the-eu-than-anyone-else/

Hix, S. (2018) 'Brexit: Where is the EU–UK relationship heading?', *Journal of Common Market Studies*, 56(S1): 11–27.

HM Government (2016) 'Why the Government believes that voting to remain in the European Union is the best decision for the UK'. London: HMSO. Available at: https://assets.publishing.service.gov.uk/government/uploads/system/uploads/attachment_data/file/515068/why-the-government-believes-that-voting-to-remain-in-the-european-union-is-the-best-decision-for-the-uk.pdf.

HM Government (2017a) 'The Government's negotiating objectives for exiting the EU: PM speech', 17 January. London: HMSO. Available at: www.gov.uk/government/speeches/the-governments-negotiating-objectives-for-exiting-the-eu-pm-speech.

HM Government (2017b) 'Joint report from the negotiators of the European Union and the United Kingdom Government', 8 December. London: HMSO. Available at: https://assets.publishing.service.gov.uk/government/uploads/system/uploads/attachment_data/file/665869/Joint_report_on_progress_during_phase_1_of_negotiations_under_Article_50_TEU_on_the_United_Kingdom_s_orderly_withdrawal_from_the_European_Union.pdf.

HM Treasury (2022) *The Green Book (2022)*. London: HMSO. www.gov.uk/government/publications/the-green-book-appraisal-and-evaluation-in-central-government

Hobolt, S., Leeper, T.J. and Tilley, J. (2021) 'Divided by the vote: Affective polarization in the wake of the Brexit Referendum', *British Journal of Political Science*, 51(4): 1476–1493.

Hobsbawm, E. (1989) *Politics for a Rational Left*. London: Verso.

Hobson, F. (2021) 'Universal credit: Ten years of changes to benefit claims and payments', *House of Commons Library* research briefing, No. 9109. Available at: https://researchbriefings.files.parliament.uk/documents/CBP-9109/CBP-9109.pdf

Honeyman, V. (2019) 'New Labour's overseas development and aid policy – charity or self-interest?', *Contemporary British History*, 33(3): 313–335.

Honeyman, V. and Lightfoot, S. (2020) 'The giant cash point in the sky: The DfID/FCO merger and its implications for Global Britain', *Political Insight*, 11(3): 30–31.

Hood, C. and Lodge, M. (2006) *The Politics of Public Service Bargains: Reward, Competency, Loyalty and Blame*. Oxford: Oxford University Press.

Hooghe, L. and Marks, G. (2009) 'A postfunctionalist theory of European Integration: From permissive consensus to constraining dissensus', *British Journal of Political Science*, 39(1): 1–23.

Hopkin, J. (2017) 'When Polanyi met Farage: Market fundamentalism, economic nationalism, and Britain's exit from the European Union', *British Journal of Politics and International Relations*, 19(3): 465–478.

Hopkin, J. and Rosamond, B. (2018) 'Post-truth politics, bullshit and bad ideas: "Deficit fetishism" in the UK', *New Political Economy*, 23(6): 641–655.

House of Commons (2007) 'The rural payments agency and the implementation of the Single Payment Scheme', House of Commons Environment, Food and Rural Affairs Committee, Third

Report of Session 2006–07, Vol. I, HC 107–I. London: HMSO. Available at: https://publications. parliament.uk/pa/cm200607/cmselect/cmenvfru/107/107i.pdf

House of Commons (2022) 'The experiences of minority ethnic and migrant people in Northern Ireland', Second Report of Session 2021–22. House of Commons Northern Ireland Affairs Committee. Available at: https://committees.parliament.uk/publications/9166/documents/159683/default/

House of Commons (2023) *Ethnic Diversity in Politics and Public Life*. House of Commons Library. 2 October 2023. Available at https://researchbriefings.files.parliament.uk/documents/SN01156/ SN01156.pdf

House of Commons Committee of Privileges (2021) 'Select committees and contempts: Clarifying and strengthening powers to call for persons, papers and records', First Report of Session 2019–21. London: HMSO.

House of Commons Committee of Privileges (2022) 'Select committees and contempts: Review of consultation on Committee proposals', First Report of Session 2022–23. London: HMSO.

House of Commons Digital, Culture, Media and Sport Committee (2019) 'Disinformation and "Fake News": Final Report', Eighth Report of Session 2017–19. London: HMSO.

House of Commons Education Committee (2021) 'The forgotten: How white working-class pupils have been let down, and how to change it', First Report of Session 2021–22. London: HMSO.

House of Commons Library (2019) *Political Disengagement in the UK: Who is Disengaged?* Briefing Paper. Available at: https://commonslibrary.parliament.uk/research-briefings/cbp7501/

House of Commons Library (2024a) *Women in Politics and Public Life*. Available at: https://commonslibrary. parliament.uk/research-briefings/sn01250/ (accessed 13 June 2024).

House of Commons Library (2024b) *General Election 2024: Marginality*. Available at: https://commons library.parliament.uk/2024-general-election-marginality/ (accessed 8 December 2024).

House of Commons Reform Committee (2009) *Rebuilding the House*. Final Report of Session 2008–09. London: HMSO.

House of Commons Women and Equalities Committee (2022) *Equality in the Heart of Democracy: A Gender Sensitive House of Commons*. HC 131. London: HMSO.

Howe, D. (2022) 'NI Assembly Election 2022 Results', *Equality Commission for Northern Ireland* [Blog], 9 May. Available at: www.equalityni.org/Blog/Articles/May-2022/Assembly-Election-2022-Results

Hozić, A.A. and True, J. (2017) 'Brexit as a scandal: Gender and global Trumpism', *Review of International Political Economy*, 24(2): 270–287.

Huber, J.D. (1996) 'The vote of confidence in parliamentary democracies', *American Political Science Review*, 90(2): 269–282.

Hueglin, T.O. and Fenna, A. (2006) *Comparative Federalism: A Systematic Inquiry*. Toronto: University of Toronto Press.

Hughes, M.M. (2011) 'Intersectionality, quotas, and minority women's political representation worldwide', *American Political Science Review*, 105(3): 604–620.

Hughes, M.M., Paxton, P., Clayton, A.B. and Zetterberg, P. (2019) 'Global gender quota adoption, implementation, and reform', *Comparative Politics*, 51(2): 219–238.

Hutchings, V. and Jefferson, H. (2017) 'The sociological approach and the social-psychological approach', in Fisher, J., Fieldhouse, E., Franklin, M.N., Gibson, R., Cantijoch, M. and Wlezien, C. (eds) *The Routledge Handbook of Elections, Voting Behavior and Public Opinion*. Abingdon: Routledge.

Hyam, R. (2010) *Understanding the British Empire*. Cambridge: Cambridge University Press.

Inglehart, R. (2015) *The Silent Revolution: Changing Values and Political Styles among Western Publics*. Princeton, NJ: Princeton University Press.

Inglehart, R.F. and Norris, P. (2016) 'Trump, Brexit, and the rise of populism: Economic have-nots and cultural backlash', SSRN Scholarly Paper ID 2818659. Rochester, NY: Social Science Research Network. https://doi.org/10.2139/ssrn.2818659.

Innes, A. (2018) 'The new crisis of ungovernability', in Martill, B. and Staiger, U. (eds), *Brexit and Beyond: Rethinking the Futures of Europe*. London: UCL Press, pp. 138–145.

Institute for Government (2024) *Power with Purpose: Final Report of the Commission on the Centre of Government*. London: Institute for Government.

Institute for Public Policy Research (IPPR) (2019) *Divided and Connected: State of the North 2010 Report*. London: IPPR. Available at: www.ippr.org/articles/state-of-the-north-2019

Inter-Parliamentary Union (2012) *Plan of Action for Gender-Sensitive Parliaments*. Geneva: IPU. Available at: www.ipu.org/resources/publications/reference/2016-07/plan-action-gender-sensitive-parliaments (accessed 22 February 2024).

Ipsos (2015) Economist/Ipsos June 2015 Issues Index. Avaliable at https://www.ipsos.com/en-uk/economistipsos-june-2015-issues-index (accessed 11 October 2024).

Ishkanian, A. (2022) 'Social movements and social policy: New research horizons', *Journal of Social Policy*, 51(3): 582–595.

Iyengar, S. and Kinder, D.R. (1987) *News That Matters: Television and American Opinion*. Chicago: University of Chicago Press.

Jackson, B. (2014) 'The political thought of Scottish Nationalism', *The Political Quarterly*, 85(1): 50–56.

Jackson, B. and Saunders, R. (eds) (2012) *Making Thatcher's Britain*. Cambridge: Cambridge University Press.

Jacobs, M. and Hindmoor, A. (2024) 'Labour, left and right: On party positioning and policy reasoning', *The British Journal of Politics and International Relations*, 26(1): 3–21.

James, S. and Quaglia, L. (2019) 'Brexit, the City and the contingent power of finance', *New Political Economy*, 24(2): 258–271.

Jamieson, K.H. (1995) *Beyond the Double Bind: Women and Leadership*. New York: Oxford University Press.

Jarman, H., Rozenblum, S., Falkenbach, M., Rockwell, O. and Greer, S.L. (2022) 'Role of scientific advice in COVID-19 policy', *British Medical Journal*, 378: e070572.

Jeffery, C. and Hough, D. (2009). Understanding post-devolution elections in Scotland and Wales in comparative perspective. *Party Politics*, 15(2): 219–240.

Jeffery, C. and Schakel, A.H. (2013). Towards a regional political science. *Regional Studies*, 47(3): 299–302.

Jeffery, D., Heppell, T. and Roe-Crines, A. (2020) 'The Conservative Party leadership election of 2019: An analysis of the voting motivations of Conservative parliamentarians', *Parliamentary Affairs*, 75(1): 113–134.

Jeffery, D., Heppell, T., Roe-Crines, A. and Butler, C. (2023) 'Trusting Truss: Conservative MPs' voting preferences in the (first) British Conservative Party leadership election of 2022', *Representation*, 59(4): 555–572.

Jenkins, S. (2021) 'Weak, crumbling and falling apart – Parliament is a lot like Boris Johnson', *The Guardian*, 17 December. Available at: www.theguardian.com/commentisfree/2021/dec/17/parliament-boris-johnson-democracy (accessed 4 October 2023).

Jennings, W. and Stoker, G. (2017) 'Tilting towards the cosmopolitan axis? Political change in England at the 2017 General Election', *The Political Quarterly*, 88(3): 359–369.

Jensen, M.D. and Kelstrup, J.D. (2019) 'House united, House divided: Explaining the EU's unity in the Brexit negotiations', *Journal of Common Market Studies*, 57(S1): 28–39.

Johal, S., Moran, M. and Williams, K. (2014) 'Power, politics, and the City of London after the great financial crisis', *Government & Opposition*, 49(3): 400–425.

Johann, D., Königslöw, K.K., Kritzinger, S. and Thomas, K. (2018) 'Intra-campaign changes in voting preferences: The impact of media and party communication', *Political Communication*, 35: 261–286.

John, P., Bertelli, A., Jennings, W. and Bevan, S. (2013) *Policy Agendas in British Politics*. Basingstoke: Palgrave Macmillan.

Johnes M. (2019) *Wales: England's Colony?* Cardigan: Parthian Books.

Johns, R., Mitchell, J. and Carman, C. (2013) 'Constitution or competence? The SNP's re-election in 2011', *Political Studies*, 61(1): 158–178.

Johns, R., Mitchell, J., Denver, D. and Pattie, C. (2010), *Voting for a Scottish Government: The Scottish Parliament Elections of 2007*. Manchester: Manchester University Press.

Johnson, M., Martínez Lucio, M., Grimshaw, D. and Watt, L. (2023) 'Swimming against the tide? Street-level bureaucrats and the limits to inclusive active labour market programmes in the UK', *Human Relations*, 76(5): 689–714.

Joint Committee on the Palace of Westminster (2016) 'Restoration and renewal of the Palace of Westminster', First Report of Session 2016–17. London: House of Lords; House of Commons.

Joly, D. and Wadia, K. (2017) *Muslim Women and Power*. London: Springer.

Jones, E. (2019) 'The negotiations: Hampered by the UK's weak strategy', *European Journal of Legal Studies*, 11(S2): 23–58.

Jones, M.O. (2019) 'The Gulf information war| Propaganda, fake news, and fake trends: The weaponization of Twitter bots in the Gulf crisis', *International Journal of Communication*, 13: 27.

Jones, R. and Wyn Jones, R. (2022) *The Criminal Justice System in Wales: On the Jagged Edge*. Cardiff: University of Wales Press.

Judge, D. (1993) *The Parliamentary State*. London: SAGE.

Judge, D. (1999) *Representation*. London: Routledge.

Jungherr, A. (2016) 'Twitter use in election campaigns: A systematic literature review', *Journal of Information Technology & Politics*, 13(1): 72–91. doi: 10.1080/19331681.2015.1132401

Jurado, I., León, S. and Walter, S. (2022) 'Brexit dilemmas: Shaping postwithdrawal relations with a leaving state', *International Organization*, 76(2): 273–304.

Kaarbo, J. and Kenealy, D. (2016) 'No, Prime Minister: Explaining the House of Commons' vote on intervention in Syria', *European Security*, 25(1): 28–48.

Kage, R., Rosenbluth, F. and Tanaka, S. (2019) 'What explains low female political representation?', *Politics & Gender*, 15(2): 285–309.

Kalla, J.L. and Broockman, D.E. (2018) 'The minimal persuasive effects of campaign contact in general elections: Evidence from 49 field experiments', *American Political Science Review*, 112: 148–166.

Kanter, R.M. (1977) *Men and Women of the Corporation*. New York: Basic Books.

Karl, K.L. (2021) 'Motivating participation through political ads: Comparing the effects of physiology and self-reported emotion', *Political Behavior*, 43(2): 687–710.

Katwala, S. and Rutter, J. (2024) *Ethnic and Gender Diversity in the Next Parliament*. London: British Future. Available at: www.britishfuture.org/wp-content/uploads/2024/06/Diversity-of-parliament-briefing.British-Future-June-2024.pdf

Kaye, S. (2022) 'Reimagining Whitehall: An essay', *Reform*. Available at: https://reform.uk/publications/reimagining-whitehall-an-essay/

Keating, M. (2009) *The Independence of Scotland: Self-Government and the Shifting Politics of Union*. Oxford: Oxford University Press.

Keating, M. (2021) *State and Nation in the United Kingdom: The Fractured Union*. Oxford: Oxford University Press.

Keating, M. (2022) 'Taking back control? Brexit and the territorial constitution of the United Kingdom', *Journal of European Public Policy*, 29(4): 491–509.

Keating, M. and Cairney, P. (2020) 'Scotland has its own political class…just like Westminster', *Centre on Constitutional Change* [Blog], 23 January. Available at: www.centreonconstitutionalchange.ac.uk/news-and-opinion/scotland-has-its-own-political-class

Kellermann, M. (2016) 'Electoral vulnerability, constituency focus, and parliamentary questions in the House of Commons', *The British Journal of Politics and International Relations*, 18(1): 90–106.

Kelso, A. (2006) 'Reforming the House of Lords: Navigating representation, democracy and legitimacy at Westminster', *Parliamentary Affairs*, 59(4): 563–581.

Kelso, A. (2009) 'Parliament on its knees: MPs' expenses and the crisis of transparency at Westminster', *The Political Quarterly*, 80(3): 329–338.

Kelso, A. (2016) 'Political leadership in Parliament: The role of select committee chairs in the UK House of Commons', *Politics and Governance*, 4(2): 115–126.

Kelso, A., Bennister, M. and Larkin, P. (2016) 'The shifting landscape of prime ministerial accountability to parliament: An analysis of Liaison Committee scrutiny sessions', *The British Journal of Politics and International Relations*, 18(3): 740–754.

Kenealy, D. (2016) 'A tale of one city? The "Devo Manc" deal and its implications for English devolution', *The Political Quarterly*, 87(4): 572–581.

Kenealy, D., Hadfield, A. and Corbett, R. (eds.) (2022) *The European Union: How Does it Work?* (6th edn). Oxford: Oxford University Press.

Kenny M. and Pearce, N. (2018) *Shadows of Empire: The Anglosphere in British Politics*. Cambridge: Polity Press.

Kenny, D. and Casey, C. (2021) 'The resilience of executive dominance in Westminster systems', *Public Law*, 2(1): 335–374.

Kenny, M. (2013) *Gender and Political Recruitment: Theorizing Institutional Change*. Basingstoke: Palgrave Macmillan.

Kenny, M. (2014) *The Politics of English Nationhood*. Oxford: Oxford University Press.

Kenny, M. (2016) 'The "politicisation" of Englishness: Towards a framework for political analysis', *Political Studies Review*, 14(3): 325–334.

Kenny, M. (2024) *Fractured Union: Sovereignty, Politics and the Fight to Save the UK*. London: Hirst Publishers.

Kenny, M. and Mackay, F. (2014) 'When is contagion not very contagious? Dynamics of women's political representation in Scotland', *Parliamentary Affairs*, 67(4): 866–886.

Kenny, M. and Mackay, F. (2017) 'Feminist and gendered approaches', in Lowndes, V., Marsh, D. and Stoker, G. (eds), *Theory and Methods in Political Science* (4th edn). Basingstoke: Palgrave.

Kenny, M. and Mackay, F. (2020) 'Women, gender and politics in Scotland', in Keating, M. (ed.), *The Oxford Handbook of Scottish Politics*. Oxford: Oxford University Press, pp. 59–77.

Kenny, M. and Sheldon, J. (2021) 'When planets collide: The British Conservative Party and the discordant goals of delivering Brexit and preserving the domestic Union, 2016–2019', *Political Studies*, 69(4): 965–984.

Kerr, P. and Hayton, R. (2015) 'Whatever happened to Conservative Party modernisation?', *British Politics*, 10(2): 114–130.

Kerr, P. and Kettell, S. (2006) 'In defence of British politics: The past, present and future of the discipline', *British Politics*, 1(1): 3–25.

Kettell, S. and Kerr, P. (2020) 'From eating cake to crashing out: Constructing the myth of a no-deal Brexit', *Comparative European Politics*, 18(4): 590–608.

Khan, Y. (2007) *The Great Partition: The Making of India and Pakistan*. New Haven, CT: Yale University Press.

Kidd, C. (2007) *Union and Unionisms*. Basingstoke: Palgrave.

King, A. (1975) 'Overload: Problems of governing in the 1970s', *Political Studies*, 23(2–3): 284–296.

King, A. (1976) 'Modes of executive–legislative relations: Great Britain, France, and West Germany', *Legislative Studies Quarterly*, 1(1): 11–36.

King, A. (2007) *The British Constitution*. Oxford: Oxford University Press.

King, A. and Crewe, I. (2013) *The Blunders of Our Governments*. London: Oneworld.

King, R. (2022) *Brittle with Relics: A History of Wales, 1962–97*. London: Faber & Faber.

King's Fund (2022) 'The Health and Care Act: Six key questions', *The King's Fund* long read. Available at: www.kingsfund.org.uk/insight-and-analysis/long-reads/health-and-care-act-key-questions

Kingdon, J. (1984) *Agendas, Alternatives and Public Policies*. New York: HarperCollins.

Kirk-Wade, E. (2023) 'Constituency data: Socio-economic status, 2021 Census', House of Commons Library. Available at: https://commonslibrary.parliament.uk/find-the-socio-economic-status-of-people-living-in-england-and-wales-by-constituency/

Kohli, A. (2020) *Imperialism and the Developing World: How Britain and the United States Shaped the Global Periphery*. Oxford: Oxford University Press.

Kolpinskaya, E. (2017) 'Substantive religious representation in the UK Parliament: Examining parliamentary questions for written answers, 1997–2012', *Parliamentary Affairs*, 70(1): 111–131.

Kolpinskaya, E., Katz, G., Banducci, S., Stevens, D. and Coan, T. (2019) 'Mandates matter: How decisive victories enhance expectations about government performance', *Journal of Elections, Public Opinion and Parties*, 30(4): 504–523. doi: 10.1080/17457289.2019.1599004

Kreiss, D. and Mcgregor, S.C. (2019) 'The "arbiters of what our voters see": Facebook and Google's struggle with policy, process, and enforcement around political advertising', *Political Communication*, 36: 499–522.

Kreppel, A. (2014) 'Typologies and classifications', in Martin, S., Saalfeld, T. and Strøm, K. (eds), *The Oxford Handbook of Legislative Studies*. Oxford: Oxford University Press, pp. 82–100.

Available at: www.oxfordhandbooks.com/view/10.1093/oxfordhb/9780199653010.001.0001/oxfordhb-9780199653010 (accessed 19 June 2019).

Kroeber, C. and Huffelman, J. (2022) 'It's a long way to the top: Women's ministerial career paths', *Politics and Gender*, 18(3): 741–767.

Kroll, D.A. and Leuffen, D. (2016) 'Ties that bind, can also strangle: The Brexit threat and the hardships of reforming the EU', *Journal of European Public Policy*, 23(9): 1311–1320.

Kumar, K. (2003) *The Making of English National Identity*. Cambridge: Cambridge University Press.

Kumarasingham, H. (2010) *Onward with Executive Power: Lessons from New Zealand 1947–57*. Wellington, NZ: Institute of Policy Studies/Victoria University of Wellington.

Kumarasingham, H. (2013) 'Exporting executive accountability? Westminster legacies of executive power', *Parliamentary Affairs*, 66(3): 579–596.

Kumarasingham, H. (2016) 'Eastminster – decolonisation and state-building in British Asia', in Kumarasingham, H. (ed.), *Constitution-Making in Asia: Decolonisation and State-Building in the Aftermath of the British Empire*. London: Routledge, pp. 1–35.

Kumarasingham, H. (2023) 'Constitution and Empire', in Cane, P. and Kumarasingham, H. (eds), *The Cambridge Constitutional History of the United Kingdom* (Vol. II). Cambridge: Cambridge University Press, pp. 496–528.

Kwarteng, K., Patel, P., Raab, D., Skidmore, C. and Truss, E. (2012) *Britannia Unchained*. Basingstoke: Palgrave.

Kymlicka, W. (1995) *Multicultural Citizenship*. Oxford: Oxford University Press.

Labour (2010) Manifesto https://manifesto.deryn.co.uk/wp-content/uploads/2021/04/TheLabourPartyManifesto-2010.pdf

Labour Party (2018) *Democracy Review*. London: Labour Party.

Ladd, J.M. and Lenz, G.S. (2009) 'Exploiting a rare communication shift to document the persuasive power of the news media', *American Journal of Political Science*, 53(2): 394–410.

Laffan, B. (2019) 'How the EU27 came to be'. *Journal of Common Market Studies*, 57(S1): 13–27.

Laffan, B. and Telle, S. (2023) *The EU's Response to Brexit: United and Effective*. Basingstoke: Palgrave Macmillan.

Langer, A.I. and Gruber, J.B. (2021) 'Political agenda setting in the hybrid media system: Why legacy media still matter a great deal', *The International Journal of Press/Politics*, 26(2): 313–340.

Langstaff www.infectedbloodinquiry.org.uk

Laniyonu, A. (2018) 'Police, politics and participation: The effect of police exposure on political participation in the United Kingdom', *The British Journal of Criminology*, 58(5): 1232–1253.

Larner, J., Wyn Jones, R., Poole, E., Surridge, P. and Wincott, D. (2023) Incumbency and identity: The 2021 Senedd election. *Parliamentary Affairs* 76 (4): 857–878.

Larsén, M.F. and Khorana, S. (2020) 'Negotiating Brexit: A clash of approaches?', *Comparative European Politics*, 18(5): 858–877.

Laswell, H. (1936) *Politics: Who Gets What, When, How*. New York: Whittlesey House.

Le Lohé, M.J. (1975) 'Participation in elections by Asians in Bradford', in Crewe, I. (ed.), *The Politics of Race*. London: Routledge.

Le Lohé, M.J. (1983) 'Voter discrimination against Asian and Black candidates in the 1983 General Election', *Journal of Ethnic and Migration Studies*, 11(1–2): 101–108.

Le Lohé, M.J. and Goldman, A.R. (1969) 'Race in local politics: The Rochdale Central Ward election of 1968', *Race & Class*, 10(4): 435–447.

Lee, S., Nanz, A. and Heiss, R. (2022) 'Platform-dependent effects of incidental exposure to political news on political knowledge and political participation', *Computers in Human Behavior*, 127. https://doi.org/10.1016/j.chb.2021.107048

Lees-Marshment, J. (2001) *Political Marketing and British Political Parties: The Party's Just Begun*. Manchester: Manchester University Press.

Legislation.gov.uk (1998) *Northern Ireland Act 1998*, c. 47. London: HMSO. Available at: www.legislation.gov.uk/ukpga/1998/47/contents (accessed 29 February 2024).

Legrand, T. (2021) *The Architecture of Policy Transfer, Ideas, Institutions and Networks in Transnational Policy Making*. Cham, Switzerland: Springer International.

Leruth, B., Gänzle, S. and Trondal, J. (2019) 'Differentiated integration and disintegration in the EU after Brexit: Risks versus opportunities', *Journal of Common Market Studies*, 57(6): 1383–1394.

Leston-Bandeira, C. (2016) 'Why symbolic representation frames parliamentary public engagement', *The British Journal of Politics and International Relations*, 18(2): 498–516.

Leston-Bandeira, C. (2019) 'Parliamentary petitions and public engagement: An empirical analysis of the role of e-petitions', *Policy & Politics*, 47(3): 415–436.

Leston-Bandeira, C. et al. (2024) *Exploring Parliament* (2nd edn). Oxford: Oxford University Press. [In press]

Lewis, J. (2020) 'Government and NHS reform since the 1980s: The role of the market *vis-à-vis* the state, and of political ideas about the "direction of travel"', *LSE Department of Social Policy*, Working Paper 05-20. Available at: www.lse.ac.uk/social-policy/Assets/Documents/PDF/working-paper-series/05-20-Jane-Lewis.pdf

Liberal Democrats (2010) *Change that Works for You*. Liberal Democrat Manifesto. London: Liberal Democrats.

Liberal Democrats (2016) 'Love jobs? Love Europe'. Referendum communication. *LSE Britain and Europe Archive*. Available at: https://lse-atom.arkivum.net/uklse-dl1er010020010126-uklse-dl1-er01-002-001-0126-0001-pdf (accessed 27 June 2024).

Lijphart, A. (1977). *Democracy in Plural Societies: A Comparative Exploration*. New Haven, CT: Yale University Press.

Lijphart, A. (1999) *Patterns of Democracy*. New Haven, CT: Yale University Press.

Lindblom, C. (1959) 'The science of muddling through', *Public Administration Review*, 19(2): 79–88.

Lindblom, C. (1979) 'Still muddling, not yet through', *Public Administration Review*, 39(6): 517–525.

Liñeira, R. and Henderson, A. (2019) 'Risk attitudes and independence vote choice', *Political Behavior*. Online first at: www.springerprofessional.de/en/risk-attitudes-and-independence-vote-choice/17032814

Lipset, S.M. and Rokkan, S. (1967) *Party Systems and Voter Alignments: Cross-National Perspectives*. New York: Free Press.

Lipsky, M. (1980) *Street-Level Bureaucracy*. New York: Russell Sage Foundation.

Llewellyn, C. and Cram, L. (2016) 'The results are in, and the UK will #Brexit: What did social media tell us about the UK's EU referendum', Article No. 122, *European Futures* [Blog], 27 June.

Llewellyn, C., Cram, L., Hill, R.L. and Favero, A. (2019) 'For whom the bell trolls: Shifting troll behaviour in the Twitter Brexit debate', *JCMS: Journal of Common Market Studies*, 57(5): 1148–1164.

Lord Ashcroft Polls (2016) How the United Kingdom Voted on Thursday... and Why. Available at: https://lordashcroftpolls.com/2016/06/how-the-united-kingdom-voted-and-why/ (accessed 5 October 2024).

Loughlin, M. and Tierney, S. (2018) 'The shibboleth of sovereignty', *Modern Law Review*, 81(6): 98–1016.

Lovenduski J. (ed.) (2005b) *State Feminism and Political Representation*. Cambridge: Cambridge University Press.

Lovenduski, J. (2005a) *Feminizing Politics*. Cambridge: Polity Press.

Lovenduski, J. (2014a) 'The institutionalisation of sexism in politics', *Political Insight*, 5(2): 16–19.

Lovenduski, J. (2014b) 'Prime Minister's Questions as political ritual at Westminster', in Rai, S.M. and Johnson, R. (eds), *Democracy in Practice: Ceremony and Ritual in Parliament*. Basingstoke: Palgrave Macmillan, pp. 132–162.

Lovenduski, J. (2019) 'Feminist reflections on representative democracy', *The Political Quarterly*, 90(S1): 18–35.

Lovenduski, J. and Guadagnini, M. (2010) 'Political representation', in McBride, D. and Mazur, A. (eds), *The Politics of State Feminism*. Philadelphia, PA: Temple University Press, pp. 164–192.

Lovenduski, J. and Norris, P. (2003) 'Westminster women: The politics of presence', *Political Studies*, 51(1): 84–102.

Lowi, T. (1972) 'Four systems of policy, politics, and choice', *Public Administration Review*, 32(4): 298–310.

LSE GV314 Group and Page, E. (2012) 'New life at the top: Special advisers in government', *Parliamentary Affairs*, 65(4): 715–32.

Lucas, C. (2024) *Another England: How to Reclaim our National Story*. London: Penguin.

Lukes, S. (2005) *Power: A Radical View* (2nd edn). Basingstoke: Palgrave.

Lynch, P. (2013) *SNP: The History of the Scottish National Party* (2nd edn). Cardiff: Welsh Academic Press.

Lynch, P. (2015) 'Conservative modernisation and European integration: From silence to salience and schism', *British Politics*, 10(2): 185–203.

Lynch, P. and Whitaker, R. (2013) 'Where there is discord, can they bring harmony: Managing intra-party dissent on European integration in the Conservative Party', *British Journal of Politics and International Relations*, 15(3): 317–339.

MacCormick, N. (1999) *Questioning Sovereignty*. Oxford: Oxford University Press.

MacCormick, N. (1999) *Questioning Sovereignty: Law, State, and Nation in the European Commonwealth*. Oxford: Oxford University Press.

MacGregor, S. (2021) 'Does government dominate the legislative process?', unpublished PhD thesis. University of Stirling.

Mackay, F. (2004) 'Gender and political representation in the UK: The state of the "discipline"', *The British Journal of Politics & International Relations*, 6(1): 99–120.

Mackay, F. (2008) '"Thick" conceptions of substantive representation: Women, gender and political institutions', *Representation*, 44(2): 125–139.

Mackay, F. (2010) 'Gendering constitutional change and policy outcomes: Substantive representation and domestic violence policy in Scotland', *Policy & Politics*, 38(3): 369–388.

Mackay, F. (2014) 'Nested newness, institutional innovation and the gendered limits of change', *Politics & Gender*, 10(4): 549–571.

Mackay, F. and McAllister, L. (2012) 'Feminising British politics: Six lessons from devolution in Scotland and Wales', *The Political Quarterly*, 83(4): 730–734.

Mackay, F., Meehan, E., Donaghy, T.B. and Brown, A. (2002) 'Women and constitutional change in Scotland, Wales and Northern Ireland', *Australasian Parliamentary Review*, 17(2): 35–54.

Mackay, F., Myers, F. and Brown, A. (2003) 'Towards a new politics? Women and the constitutional change in Scotland', in Dobrowolsky, A. and Hart, V. (eds), *Women Making Constitutions: New Politics and Comparative Perspectives*. Basingstoke: Palgrave, pp. 84–98.

MacKenzie, J.M. (1984) *Propaganda and Empire: The Manipulation of British Public Opinion, 1880–1960*. Manchester: Manchester University Press.

MacNamara, H. (2023) Witness Statement. Available at: https://covid19.public-inquiry.uk/documents/inq000273841-witness-statement-of-helen-macnamara-dated-09-10-2023/

Mahoney, J. and Thelen, K. (eds) (2015) *Advances in Comparative-Historical Analysis*. Cambridge: Cambridge University Press.

Maiguashca, B. and Dean, J. (2020) '"Lovely people but utterly deluded"? British political science's trouble with Corbynism', *British Politics*, 15: 48–68.

Major, J. (1993) 'Mr Major's speech to the Carlton Club', 3 February. Available at: https://johnmajorarchive.org.uk/1993/02/03/mr-majors-speech-to-the-carlton-club-3-february-1993/

Mandler, P. (2006) *The English National Character: The History of an Idea from Edmund Burke to Tony Blair*. New Haven, CT: Yale University Press.

Mann, R. and Fenton, S. (2017) *Nation, Class and Resentment: The Politics of National Identity in England, Scotland and Wales*. Basingstoke: Palgrave.

Mansbridge, J. (1999) 'Should Blacks represent Blacks and women represent women? A contingent "yes"', *The Journal of Politics*, 61(3): 628–657.

Mansbridge, J. (2019) 'Recursive representation', in Castiglione, D. and Pollak, J. (eds), *Creating Political Presence: The New Politics of Democratic Representation*. Chicago: University of Chicago Press, pp. 298–338.

Mansergh, N. (1982) *The Commonwealth Experience* (2 volumes). London: Macmillan.

Marcus, G.E. (2010) *Sentimental Citizen: Emotion in Democratic Politics*. University Park, PA: Penn State University Press.

Marcus, G.E., Neuman, W.R. and MacKuen, M. (2000) *Affective Intelligence and Political Judgment*. Chicago: University of Chicago Press.

Marsh, D. and Hall, A. (2007) 'The British political tradition: Explaining the fate of New Labour's constitutional reform agenda', *British Politics*, 2(2).

Marsh, D. and Rhodes, R.A.W. (1992) 'Policy communities and issue networks: Beyond typology', in Marsh, D. and Rhodes, R.A.W. (eds), *Policy Networks in British Government*. Oxford: Oxford University Press, Chapter 11 (pp. 249–268).

Marsh, D., Richards, D. and Smith, M. (2001) *Changing Patterns of Governance in the United Kingdom*. Basingstoke: Palgrave.

Marsh, D., Richards, D. and Smith, M. (2003) 'Unequal plurality: Towards an asymmetric power model of British Politics', *Government and Opposition*, 38(3): 306–332.

Marshall, L., Briggs, A. and Bibby, J. (2024) 'How can the next government take prevention from rhetoric to reality?', *The Health Foundation* long read. Available at: www.health.org.uk/publications/long-reads/how-can-the-next-government-take-prevention-from-rhetoric-to-reality

Martill, B. (2020) 'The 2019 European Parliament election in the UK', *Italian Political Science Review*, 50(3): 368–381.

Martill, B. (2021a) 'Deal or no deal: Theresa May's Withdrawal Agreement and the politics of (non-)ratification', *Journal of Common Market Studies*, 59(6): 1607–1622.

Martill, B. (2021b) 'Unity over diversity? The politics of differentiated integration after Brexit', *Journal of European Integration*, 43(8): 973–988.

Martill, B. (2022) 'Prisoners of their own device: Brexit as a failed negotiating strategy', *British Journal of Politics and International Relations*, 24(4): 582–597.

Martill, B. (2023a) 'Negotiating secession: Brexit lessons for Scottish independence', *British Politics*, 18(3): 364–383.

Martill, B. (2023b) 'Withdrawal symptoms: Party factions, political change and British foreign policy post-Brexit', *Journal of European Public Policy*, 30(11): 2468–2491.

Martill, B. and Mesarovich, A. (2024) 'Foreign policy as compensation: Why Brexit became a foreign and security policy issue', *International Studies Quarterly*. Advance online article ahead of print.

Martill, B. and Rogstad, A. (2019) 'The end of consensus? Folk theory and the politics of foreign policy in the Brexit referendum', *Global Affairs*, 5(4–5): 347–367.

Martill, B. and Staiger, U. (2021) 'Negotiating Brexit: The cultural sources of British hard bargaining', *Journal of Common Market Studies*, 59(2): 261–277.

Martin, L.W. and Vanberg, G. (2011) *Parliaments and Coalitions: The Role of Legislative Institutions in Multiparty Governance*. Oxford: Oxford University Press.

Martin, N. (2017) 'Are British Muslims alienated from mainstream politics by Islamophobia and British foreign policy?', *Ethnicities*, 17(3): 350–370.

Martin, N. and Khan, O. (2019) *Ethnic Minorities at the 2017 British General Election*. London: Runnymede Trust. Available at: www.runnymedetrust.org/publications/ethnic-minorities-at-the-2017-british-general-election

Martin, N.S. (2016) 'Do ethnic minority candidates mobilise ethnic minority voters? Evidence from the 2010 UK General Election', *Parliamentary Affairs*, 69(1): 159–180.

Martin, N.S. (2019) 'Ethnic minority voters in the UK 2015 general election: A breakthrough for the Conservative Party?', *Electoral Studies*, 57: 174–185.

Martin, N.S. and Blinder, S. (2021) 'Biases at the ballot box: How multiple forms of voter discrimination impede the descriptive and substantive representation of ethnic minority groups', *Political Behavior*, 43: 1487–1510.

Martin, N.S. and Sobolewska, M. (2023) 'The end of the ethnic bloc vote? Ethnic minority Leavers after the Brexit Referendum', *PS: Political Science & Politics*, 56(4): 566–571. https://doi.org/10.1017/S1049096523000288

Martin, S. (2011) 'Parliamentary questions, the behaviour of legislators, and the function of legislatures: An introduction', *The Journal of Legislative Studies*, 17(3): 259–270.

Martin, S. and Whitaker, R. (2019) 'Beyond committees: parliamentary oversight of coalition government in Britain', *West European Politics*, 42(7): 1464–1486.

Marx, K. and Engels, F. (1948) *The Communist Manifesto*. London: Lawrence & Wishart.

Matland, R.E. and Studlar, D.T. (1996) 'The contagion of women candidates in single-member district and proportional representation electoral systems: Canada and Norway', *Journal of Politics*, 58(3): 707–733.

Matthews, F. (2013) *Complexity, Fragmentation and Uncertainty: Government Capacity in an Evolving State*. Oxford: Oxford University Press.

Matthews, F. (2021) 'The value of "between-election" political participation: Do parliamentary e-petitions matter to political elites?', *The British Journal of Politics and International Relations*, 23(3): 410–429.

Matthews, F. and Flinders, M. (2017) 'Patterns of democracy: Coalition governance and majoritarian modification in the United Kingdom, 2010–2015', *British Politics*, 12(2): 157–182.

Matthews, N. and Haughey, S. (2024) 'The security of politicians: Towards a research agenda', *Parliamentary Affairs*, 17 July. https://doi.org/10.1093/pa/gsae015

Maude of Horsham, Lord (Francis) (2023) *Independent Review of Governance and Accountability in the Civil Service*. London: HMSO. Available at: www.gov.uk/government/publications/review-of-governance-and-accountability/independent-review-of-governance-and-accountability-in-the-civil-service/the-rt-hon-lord-maude-of-horsham-html

May, T. (2017) 'Prime Minister's speech to the Republican Party Conference 2017', 26 January. Available at: www.gov.uk/government/speeches/prime-ministers-speech-to-the-republican-party-conference-2017 (accessed 4 March 2024).

Mazzucato, M. (2021) *Mission Economy: A Moonshot Guide to Changing Capitalism*. London: Allen Lane.

McAllister, I. and Mughan, A. (1984) 'The fate of the language: Determinants of bilingualism in Wales', *Ethnic and Racial Studies*, 7(3): 321–341. https://doi.org/10.1080/01419870.1984.9993448

McAllister, I. and Studlar, D.T. (2000) 'Conservative Euroscepticism and the Referendum Party in the 1997 British general election', *Party Politics*, 6(3): 359–371.

McAllister, L. (2001) Plaid Cymru: The emergence of a political party. Cardiff: Seven Books.

McAngus, C. (2013). 'Office and policy at the expense of votes: Plaid Cymru and the One Wales Government', *Regional & Federal Studies*, 24(2), 209–227. https://doi.org/10.1080/13597566.2013.859579

McAngus, C. (2017) 'Do stateless-nationalist-regionalist parties differ from other party types? Comparing organisational reform processes in Plaid Cymru and the Scottish National Party', *British Politics*, 12(1): 20–41.

McAnulla, S. (2006) *British Politics: A Critical Introduction*. London: Continuum.

McCabe, L. (2024) 'An intersectional analysis of contestations within women's movements: The case of Scottish domestic abuse policymaking', *Policy & Politics*, 52(3): 521–545.

McCarthy-Cotter, L. (2018) *The 1991 Child Support Act: Failure Foreseeable and Foreseen*. Basingstoke: Palgrave.

McCrone D. and Bechhofer, F. (2015) *Understanding National Identity*. Cambridge: Cambridge University Press.

McCrone, D. (2023) 'The rise and rise of English nationalism?', *Political Quarterly*, 94(4): 602–613.

McEwen, N. and Murphy, M.C. (2022) 'Brexit and the Union: Territorial voice, exit and re-entry strategies in Scotland and Northern Ireland after EU exit', *International Political Science Review*, 43(3): 374–389.

McEwen, N., Swenden, W. and Bolleyer, N. (2012) 'Intergovernmental relations in the UK: Continuity in a time of change?', *British Journal of Politics and International Relations*, 14(2): 323–343.

McGarry, J. and O'Leary, B. (2006a) 'Consociational theory, Northern Ireland's conflict, and its agreement', *Government and Opposition*, 41(1): 43–63.

McGarry, J. and O'Leary, B. (2006b) 'Consociational theory, Northern Ireland's conflict, and its agreement', *Government and Opposition*, 41(2): 249–77.

McGarry, J. and O'Leary, B. (2009) 'Must pluri-national federations fail?', *Ethnopolitics*, 8(1): 5–25.

McHarg, A. (2018) 'Navigating without maps: Constitutional silence and the management of the Brexit crisis', *International Journal of Constitutional Law*, 16(3): 952–968.

McHarg, A. and Mitchell, J. (2017) 'Brexit and Scotland', *British Journal of Politics and International Relations*, 19(3): 512–526.

McKay, L. (2020) 'Does constituency focus improve attitudes to MPs? A test for the UK', *The Journal of Legislative Studies*, 26(1): 1–26.

Mcneil, A. and Haberstroh, C. (2022) 'Intergenerational social mobility and the Brexit vote: How social origins and destinations divide Britain', *European Journal of Political Research*, April. https://doi.org/10.1111/1475-6765.12526

McTernan, J. (2016) 'Parliament's fury at Philip Green is just grandstanding from powerless MPs', *The Telegraph*, 25 July. Available at: www.telegraph.co.uk/news/2016/07/25/so-what-if-mps-are-furious-with-philip-green-theres-nothing-they/ (accessed 9 September 2018).

Meakin, A. and Siebert, S. (2024) 'Custodians of the Palace of Westminster (Custodians)', *Parliamentary Affairs*, 77(2): 240–261. https://doi.org/10.1093/pa/gsad001

Meer, N. (2019) 'The Bristol School of Multiculturalism, and the political sociology of identity', *Ethnicities*, 19(6): 91–98.

Meer, N. (2022) *The Cruel Optimism of Racial Justice*. Bristol: Policy Press.

Meer, N. and Nayak, A. (2013) 'Race ends where? Race, racism and contemporary sociology', *Sociology*, 49(6): NP3–NP20.

Melhuish, F. (2023) 'Powellite nostalgia and racialised nationalist narratives: Connecting Global Britain and Little England', *British Journal of Politics and International Relations*, 26(2). https://doi.org/10.1177/13691481231162489

Mellows-Facer, A., Challender, C. and Evans, P. (2019) 'Select committees: Agents of change', *Parliamentary Affairs*, 72(4): 903–922.

Menon, A. and Salter, J.-P. (2016) 'Brexit: Initial reflections', *International Affairs*, 92(6): 1297–1318.

Mergel, I. (2017) 'Social media communication modes in government', in Chen, Y.-C. and Ahn, M. (eds), *The Routledge Handbook on Information Technology in Government*. Abingdon: Routledge, Chapter 11 (pp. 168–179).

Messina, A. (1989) *Race and party competition in Britain*. Oxford: Clarendon Press.

Middleton, A. (2021) *Communicating and Strategising Leadership in British Elections: Follow the Leaders?* London: Springer.

Midgley, M. (2011) *The Myths We Live By*. Abingdon: Routledge.

Mihai, M. (2022) 'Foundational moments, representative claims and the ecology of social ignorance', *Political Studies*, 70(4): 962–982.

Milbourne, L. and Cushman, M. (2014) 'Complying, transforming, or resisting in the new austerity? Realigning social welfare and independent action among English voluntary organisations', *Journal of Social Policy*, 44(3): 463–485.

Mill, J.S. (1926) *Utilitarianism, Liberty and Representative Government*. London, J.M. Dent & Sons.

Miller, C.M. (2021) *Gendering the Everyday in the UK House of Commons: Beneath the Spectacle*. London: Springer Nature.

Miller, M.L. and Vaccari, C. (2020) 'Digital threats to democracy: Comparative lessons and possible remedies', *The International Journal of Press/Politics*, 25(3): 333–356.

Miller, W. (1981) *The End of British Politics?* Oxford: Oxford University Press.

Mills, C. (2013) 'The Great British Class Fiasco', *Oxford Sociology* [Blog], 11 April. Available at: http://oxfordsociology.blogspot.com/2013/04/the-great-british-class-fiasco.html.

Mintrom, M. (2019) 'So you want to be a policy entrepreneur?', *Policy Design and Practice*, 2(4): 307–323.

Mitchell, J. (2003) *Governing Scotland: The Invention of Administrative Devolution*. Basingstoke: Palgrave.

Mitchell, J. (2009) *Devolution in the UK*. Manchester: Manchester University Press.

Mitchell, J. (2014) *The Scottish Question*. Oxford: Oxford University Press.

Mitchell, J., Bennie, L. and Johns, R. (2011) *The Scottish National Party: Transition to Power*. Oxford: Oxford University Press.

Moir, A. (2023) 'The use of TikTok for political campaigning in Canada: The case of Jagmeet Singh', *Social Media + Society*, 9(1). https://doi.org/10.1177/20563051231157604

Monbiot, G. and Hutchison, P. (2024) *The Invisible Doctrine: The Secret History of Neoliberalism (& How It Came to Control Your Life)*. London: Penguin.

Montoya, C.M., Bejarano, C., Brown, N.E. and Gerson, S.A. (2022) 'The intersectional dynamics of descriptive representation', *Politics & Gender*, 18(2): 483–512.

Moore, A., Hong, S. and Cram, L. (2021) 'Trust in information, political identity and the brain: An interdisciplinary fMRI study', *Philosophical Transactions of the Royal Society B*, 376(1822): 20200140.

Moore, J. (2022) 'Raab's opera slur towards Angela Rayner is a perfect example of Tory snobbery', *The Independent*, 30 June. Available at: www.independent.co.uk/voices/dominic-raab-opera-angela-rayner-glyndebourne-pmqs-b2112885.html

Moore-Bick www.grenfelltowerinquiry.org.uk

Morphet, J. (2021) *The Impact of COVID-19 on Devolution: Recentralising the British State beyond Brexit?* Bristol: Bristol University Press.

Mortimore, R. and Blick, A. (eds) (2018) *Butler's British Political Facts*. London: Palgrave Macmillan.

Mudde, C. (2004) 'The populist Zeitgeist', *Government and Opposition*, 39(4): 541–563. https://doi.org/10.1111/j.1477-7053.2004.00135.x

Mudde, C. and Rovira Kaltwasser, C. (2017) 'Vox populi or vox masculini? Populism and gender in Northern Europe and South America', *Patterns of Prejudice*, 49(1–2): 16–36.

Müller, W.C. and Strøm, K. (eds) (1999) *Policy, Office, or Votes?: How Political Parties in Western Europe Make Hard Decisions*. Cambridge: Cambridge University Press.

Munger K. (2021) 'Don't @ Me: Experimentally reducing partisan incivility on Twitter', *Journal of Experimental Political Science*, 8(2): 102–116. doi:10.1017/XPS.2020.14

Murray, C. and O'Donoghue, A. (2023) 'Unity in diversity? Constitutional identities, deliberative processes and a "border poll" in Ireland', *King's Law Journal*, 34(2): 340–368.

Murray, C. and Robb, N. (2023) 'From the Protocol to the Windsor Framework', *Northern Ireland Legal Quarterly*, 74(2): 395–415.

Murray, R. (2024) 'The substantive representation of men: Intersectionality, masculinities, and men's interests', *European Journal of Political Research*, 8 May. Online first. https://doi.org/10.1111/1475-6765.12684

Mycock, A. (2016) 'The politics of England', *The Political Quarterly*, 87(4): 534–545. https://doi.org/10.1111/1467-923X.12283

Mycock, A. and Hayton, R. (2014) 'The party politics of Englishness', *British Journal of Politics and International Relations*, 16(2): 251–272.

Mycock, A. and Wellings, B. (2017) 'The Anglosphere: Past, present and future', *British Academy Review*, 31. Available at: www.thebritishacademy.ac.uk/publishing/review/31/anglosphere-past-present-and-future/ (accessed 4 March 2024).

Myeong, S.H. and Ahn, M.J. (2017) 'E-government and citizen trust in government: The role of citizen characteristics and citizen trust in government', in Chen, Y.-C. and Ahn, M.J. (eds), *Routledge Handbook on Information Technology in Government*. Abingdon: Routledge, Chapter 10 (pp. 153–167).

Nairn, T. (1981) *The Break-up of Britain: Crisis and Neo-nationalism*. London: Verso.

Nairn, T. (2003 [1977]) *The Break-up of Britain: Crisis and Neo-nationalism*. London: Verso.

National Audit Office (NAO) (2001) *Modern Policy-making: Ensuring Policies Deliver Value for Money*. London: NAO. Available at: www.nao.org.uk/reports/modern-policy-making-ensuring-policies-deliver-value-for-money/

Neubaum, G. and Krämer, N.C. (2017) 'Monitoring the opinion of the crowd: Psychological mechanisms underlying public opinion perceptions on social media', *Media Psychology*, 20(3): 502–531.

Newman, G. (1987) *The Rise of English Nationalism: A Cultural History, 1740–1830*. London: Weidenfeld & Nicolson.

Newton, K. and Brynin, M. (2001) 'The national press and party voting in the UK', *Political Studies*, 49(2): 265–285.

Nobel Prize (1998) 'The Nobel Peace Prize 1998' *nobelprize.org* Available: https://www.nobelprize.org/prizes/peace/1998/summary/ (accessed 10 January 2024).

Nobel Prize (1998) 'The Nobel Peace Prize 1998', *nobelprize.org*. Available at: www.nobelprize.org/prizes/peace/1998/summary/ (accessed 10 January 2024).

Norris, P. (1996) 'Women politicians: Transforming Westminster?', *Parliamentary Affairs*, 49(1): 89–102.

Norris, P. (1997) 'The puzzle of constituency service', *The Journal of Legislative Studies*, 3(2): 29–49.

Norris, P. and Lovenduski, J. (1995) *Political Recruitment: Gender, Race and Class in the British Parliament*. Cambridge: Cambridge University Press.

Northern Ireland Elections (2024) 'Who won what when and where?' Available at: www.ark.ac.uk/elections/ (accessed 20 June 2024).

Northern Ireland Executive Office (2024) *Ministerial Code*. Belfast: Northern Ireland Executive Office. Available at: www.northernireland.gov.uk/topics/your-executive/ministerial-code (accessed 29 February 2024).

Northern Ireland Life and Times (NILT) (2024) 'Northern Ireland Life and Times Survey (NILT)'. Available at: www.ark.ac.uk/ARK/nilt (accessed 20 June 2024).

Northern Ireland Office (1998) *The Belfast Agreement*, 10 April 1998. Policy paper. Available at: www.gov.uk/government/publications/the-belfast-agreement (accessed 20 February 2023).

Northern Ireland Office (2006) *St Andrews Agreement, October* 2006, 16 July. Available at: www.gov.uk/government/publications/the-st-andrews-agreement-october-2006 (accessed 20 February 2023).

Northern Ireland Office (2010) *Hillsborough Castle Agreement*, 5 February. Available at: www.gov.uk/government/publications/hillsborough-castle-agreement (accessed 20 February 2023).

Northern Ireland Office (2014) *Stormont House Agreement*, 23 December. Available at: www.gov.uk/government/publications/the-stormont-house-agreement (accessed 20 February 2023).

Northern Ireland Office (2015) *A Fresh Start: The Stormont Agreement and Implementation Plan*, 17 November. Available at: www.gov.uk/government/news/a-fresh-start-for-northern-ireland (accessed 20 February 2023).

Northern Ireland Office (2020) *New Decade, New Approach*. Available at: https://assets.publishing.service.gov.uk/media/5e178b56ed915d3b06f2b795/2020-01-08_a_new_decade__a_new_approach.pdf

Northern Ireland Office (2022) *The Fourth Report on the Use of the Petition of Concern Mechanism in the Northern Ireland Assembly*, Command Paper 599. Available at: https://assets.publishing.service.gov.uk/government/uploads/system/uploads/attachment_data/file/1054277/PoC_report_4.pdf (accessed 2 March 2024).

Northern Ireland Office (2024) *Safeguarding the Union*. Policy Paper, 31 January. Available at: www.gov.uk/government/publications/safeguarding-the-union (accessed 2 March 2024).

Norton, P. (1975) *Dissension in the House of Commons, 1945–74*. London: Macmillan.

Norton, P. (1980) *Dissension in the House of Commons, 1974–1979*. Oxford: Clarendon Press.

Norton, P. (1988) 'Prime ministerial power', *Social Studies Review*, 3(2): 108–115.

Norton, P. (2017) 'Speaking for Parliament', *Parliamentary Affairs*, 70(2): 191–206.

Norton, P. (2019) 'Is the House of Commons too powerful? The 2019 Bingham Lecture in Constitutional Studies, University of Oxford', *Parliamentary Affairs*, 72(4): 996–1013.

Norton, P. (2023) *The 1922 Committee: Power Behind the Scenes*. Manchester: Manchester University Press.

NSMC (North South Ministerial Council) (1999) 'Inaugural Plenary Joint Communiqué: North/South Ministerial Council, Armagh, 13 December 1999', NSMC. Available at: www.northsouthministerialcouncil.org/publications/inaugural-plenary-joint-communique-13-december-1999 (accessed 1 March 2024).

Nugent, M.K. and Krook, M.L. (2016) 'All-women shortlists: Myths and realities', *Parliamentary Affairs*, 69(1): 115–135.

Nugent, N. (2018) 'Brexit: Yet another crisis for the EU', in Martill, B. and Staiger, U. (eds), *Brexit and Beyond: Rethinking the Futures of Europe*. London: UCL Press, pp. 54–62.

Nyhan, B., Settle, J., Thorson, E., Wojcieszak, M., Barberá, P., Chen, A.Y., Allcott, H., Brown, T., Crespo-Tenorio, A., Dimmery, D. and Freelon, D. (2023) 'Like-minded sources on Facebook are prevalent but not polarizing', *Nature*, 620(7972): 137–144.

O'Brien, D.Z. (2012) 'Gender and select committee elections in the British House of Commons', *Politics & Gender*, 8(2): 178–204.

O'Hara, K. (2011) *Conservatism*. London: Reaktion Books.

O'Neill, B. (2023) 'We need to talk about Just Stop Oil's class privilege', *The Spectator*, 23 May. Available at: www.spectator.co.uk/article/we-need-to-talk-about-just-stop-oils-class-privilege/

O'Toole, F. (2018) *Heroic Failure: Brexit and the Politics of Pain*. London: Head of Zeus.

OECD (Organisation for Economic Cooperation and Development) (2017) *Policy Advisory Systems: Supporting Good Governance and Sound Public Decision-making*. Paris: OECD. Available at: www.oecd.org/governance/policy-advisory-systems-9789264283664-en.htm

Oeldorf-Hirsch, A. (2018) 'The role of engagement in learning from active and incidental news exposure on social media', *Mass Communication and Society*, 21(2): 225–247. doi: 10.1080/15205436.2017.1384022

OfCom (UK Office for Communications) (2020a) *Media Literacy Tracker 2019*. London: OfCom. Available at: www.ofcom.org.uk/__data/assets/pdf_file/0028/196372/adults-media-use-and-attitudes-2020-data-tables.pdf

OfCom (UK Office for Communications) (2020b) *The OfCom Broadcasting Code (with the Cross-promotion Code and the On Demand Programme Service Rules)*. London: OfCom. Available at: www.ofcom.org.uk/tv-radio-and-on-demand/broadcast-codes/broadcast-code

OfCom (UK Office for Communications) (2024) *Adults' Media Use and Attitudes Report 2024*. London: OfCom. Available at: www.ofcom.org.uk/research-and-data/media-literacy-research/adults/adults-media-use-and-attitudes

Office for National Statistics (ONS) (2021) *Population Estimates for the UK, England, Wales, Scotland and Northern Ireland: mid-2021*. London: ONS. Available at: www.ons.gov.uk/peoplepopulationandcommunity/populationandmigration/populationestimates/bulletins/annualmidyearpopulationestimates/mid2021 (accessed 2 December 2023).

Office for National Statistics (ONS) (2023a) *Long-Term International Migration, Provisional: Year Ending June 2023*. London: ONS. Available at: www.ons.gov.uk/peoplepopulationandcommunity/populationandmigration/internationalmigration/bulletins/longterminternationalmigrationprovisional/yearendingjune2023

Office for National Statistics (ONS) (2023b) *Civil Service Statistics 2023*. London: ONS.

Office for National Statistics (ONS) (2024) *Public Sector Employment, UK: March 2024: Estimates of People Employed in the Public and Private Sectors in the UK*. London: ONS. Available at: www.ons.gov.uk/employmentandlabourmarket/peopleinwork/publicsectorpersonnel/bulletins/publicsectoremployment/march2024

Official Journal (2020) *Agreement on the Withdrawal of the United Kingdom of Great Britain and Northern Ireland from the European Union and the European Atomic Energy Community*. L29, 31 January, pp. 7–187. Available at: www.legislation.gov.uk/eut/withdrawal-agreement/contents (accessed 14 April 2023).

Oliver, T. and Williams, M.J. (2016) 'Special relationships in flux: Brexit and the future of the US–EU and US–UK relationships', *International Affairs*, 92(3): 547–567.

Omi, M. (2001) 'The changing meaning of race', in Smelser, N., Wilson, W.J. and Mitchell, F. (eds), *America Becoming: Racial Trends and Their Consequences* (Vol. 1). Washington, DC: National Academy Press, Chapter 8 (pp. 243–263).

Oppermann, K., Beasley, R.K. and Kaarbo, J. (2020) 'British foreign policy after Brexit: Losing Europe and finding a role', *International Relations*, 34(2): 133–156.

Osborne, S.P., Radnor, Z. and Strokosch, K. (2016) 'Co-production and the co-creation of value in public services: A suitable case for treatment?', *Public Management Review*, 18(5): 639–653.

Osmond, J. (2007) *Crossing the Rubicon: Coalition Politics Welsh Style*. Cardiff: Institute of Welsh Affairs.

Ostermann, F. (2015) 'The end of ambivalence and the triumph of pragmatism? Franco-British defence cooperation and European and Atlantic defence policy traditions', *International Relations*, 29(3): 334–347.

Osuna, J.J.O., Kiefer, M. and Katsouyanni, K.G. (2021) 'Place matters: Analyzing the roots of political distrust and Brexit narratives at a local level', *Governance*, 34(4): 1019–1038.

Owen, J. (2019) 'Brexit deal: Political declaration on future UK–EU relationship', *Institute for Government* explainer, 22 November 2018. Available at: www.instituteforgovernment.org.uk/article/explainer/brexit-deal-political-declaration-future-uk-eu-relationship.

Owen, S. (2018) *Review of Arrangements for Tackling Bullying, Harassment and Misconduct in the Civil Service*. London: Civil Service HR www.gov.uk/government/publications/bullying-harassment-and-misconduct-review

Page, E.C. (2018) 'Whatever governments choose to do or not to do', in Colebatch, H.K. and Hoppe, R. (eds.), *Handbook on Policy, Process and Governing*. Cheltenham: Edward Elgar, Chapter 2 (pp. 16–31).

Paldam, M. (1986) 'The distribution of election results and the two explanations of the cost of ruling', *European Journal of Political Economy*, 2(1): 5–24.

Pannell, J. (2024) 'Mission-driven government: What has Labour committed to?', *Institute for Government explainer*. Available at: www.instituteforgovernment.org.uk/explainer/mission-driven-government-labour

Parekh, B. (2000) *Rethinking Multiculturalism: Cultural Diversity and Political Theory*. Cambridge, MA: Harvard University Press.

Parkinson, J. (2007) 'The House of Lords: A deliberative democratic defence', *The Political Quarterly*, 78(3): 374–381.

Parry, R. (2011) 'The United Kingdom civil service: A devolving system', in Massey, A. (ed.), *International Handbook of Civil Service Systems*. Cheltenham: Edward Elgar, Chapter 15 (pp. 347–368).

Patel, I.S. (2021) *We're Here Because You Were There: Immigration and the End of Empire*. London: Verso.

Patel, P., Swift, R. and Quilter-Pinner, H. (2023) *Talking Politics: Building Support for Democratic Reform*. London: Institute for Public Policy Research.

Paterson, L. (1994) *The Autonomy of Modern Scotland*. Edinburgh: Edinburgh University Press.

Pautz, H. (2011) 'New Labour in government: Think tanks and social policy reform, 1997–2001', *British Politics*, 6(2): 187–209.

Pautz, H. (2012) *Think Tanks, Social Democracy, and Social Policy*. Basingstoke: Palgrave.

Pautz, H. (2018) 'Think tanks, Tories and the austerity discourse coalition', *Policy & Society*, 37(2): 155–169.

Pedersen, C. and Ward, S. (eds) (2019) *The Break-up of Greater Britain*. Manchester: Manchester University Press.

Perrigo, S. (1996) 'Women and change in the Labour Party 1979–1995', *Parliamentary Affairs*, 49(1): 116–129.

Perry, K.H. (2015) *London is the Place for Me: Black Britons, Citizenship and the Politics of Race*. Oxford: Oxford University Press.

Persily, N., Tucker, J.A. and Tucker, J.A. (eds) (2020) *Social Media and Democracy: The State of the Field, Prospects for Reform*. Cambridge: Cambridge University Press.

Petrocik, J.R. (1996) 'Issue ownership in presidential elections, with a 1980 case study', *American Journal of Political Science*, 40(3): 825–850.

Pevalin, D. and Rose, D. (2002) 'The National Statistics Socio-Economic Classification: Unifying official and sociological approaches to the conceptualisation and measurement of social class in the United Kingdom', *Sociétés Contemporaines*, 45–46(1): 75–106. https://doi.org/10.3917/soco.045.0075.

Phillips, A. (1995) *The Politics of Presence*. Oxford: Oxford University Press.

Phillips, A. (1998) 'Democracy and representation: Or, why should it matter who our representatives are?,' in Phillips, A. (ed.), *Feminism and Politics*. Oxford: Oxford University Press.

Pierson, P. (2000) 'Increasing returns, path dependence, and the study of politics', *American Political Science Review*, 94(2): 251–267.

Pike, K. (2024) *Getting Over New Labour*. Newcastle: Agenda.

Pike, K. and Diamond, P. (2021) 'Myth and meaning: "Corbynism" and the interpretation of political leadership', *British Journal of Politics and International Relations*, 23(4): 663–679.

Pitkin, H.F. (1967) *The Concept of Representation*. Berkeley, CA: University of California Press.

Poku-Amanfo, E., O'Halloran, J. and Thomas, C. (2024) 'Health places, prosperous lives', *Institute for Public Policy Research* discussion paper. Available at: https://ippr-org.files.svdcdn.com/production/Downloads/Healthy_places_prosperous_lives_Jan24.pdf

Pow, J. (2023) 'Beyond orange and green: The politics of Northern Ireland's 'neithers', *Political Insight*, 14(3): 36–39.

Powell, G.B. and Whitten, G.D. (1993). A cross-national analysis of economic voting: Taking account of the political context. *American Journal of Political Science*, 37(2), 391–414. https://doi.org/10.2307/2111378

Powell, M. and Greener, I. (2024) 'It's a wonderful NHS? A counterfactual perspective on the creation of the British National Health Service', *Social Policy & Administration*, 9 August. Online first. https://doi.org/10.1111/spol.12999

Prescott, C. (2019) 'Select committees: Understanding and regulating the emergence of the "topical inquiry"', *Parliamentary Affairs*, 72(4): 879–902.

Press Association (2018) Corbyn to announce four new bank holidays in St George's Day speech', *The Guardian*, 23 April 2028. Available at: https://www.theguardian.com/politics/2018/apr/23/labour-promises-four-more-bank-holidays-if-it-wins-general-election, accessed 5 October 2024.

Press Association (2018) Corbyn to announce four new bank holidays in St George's Day speech', *The Guardian*, 23 April. Available at: https://www.theguardian.com/politics/2018/apr/23/labour-promises-four-more-bank-holidays-if-it-wins-general-election (accessed 5 October 2024).

Pritchett, J. (2023) 'Foreign policy and international development from Cameron to Johnson', in Lee, S. and Beech, M. (eds), *Conservative Governments in the Age of Brexit*. Basingstoke: Palgrave Macmillan, pp. 231–253.

Prosser, C. (2018) 'The strange death of multi-party Britain: The UK General Election of 2017', *West European Politics*, 41(5): 1226–1236.

Psarra, S., Steiger, U. and Sternberg, C. (2023) *Parliament Buildings: The Architecture of Politics in Europe*. London: UCL Press.

Puwar, N. (2004) *Space Invaders: Race, Gender and Bodies Out of Place*. Oxford: Berg Publishers.

Puwar, N. (2010) 'The archi-texture of Parliament: Flâneur as method in Westminster', *The Journal of Legislative Studies*, 16(3): 298–312.

Pyper, R. (2020) 'Debate: The British Civil Service: Contextualisng challenges', *Public Money and Management*, 40(8): 555–557.

Quinn, T., Allen, N. and Bartle, J. (2024) 'Why was there a hard Brexit? The British legislative party system, divided majorities and the incentives for factionalism', *Political Studies*, 72(1): 227–248.

Rai, S.M. (2015) 'Political performance: A framework for analysing democratic politics', *Political Studies*, 63(5): 1179–1197.

Rai, S.M. and Johnson, R. (eds) (2014) *Democracy in Practice: Ceremony and Ritual in Parliament*. Basingstoke: Palgrave Macmillan.

Ramsden, J. (1998) *An Appetite for Power*. London: HarperCollins.

Raney, T. and Collier, C.N. (2022) 'Privilege and gendered violence in the Canadian and British Houses of Commons: A feminist institutionalist analysis', *Parliamentary Affairs*, 75(2): 382–399.

Raymond, A. et al. (2021) 'Our ageing population: How ageing affects health and care need in England', *The Health Foundation* policy report. Available at: www.health.org.uk/publications/our-ageing-population

Reed, S., Oung, C., Davies, J., Dayan, M. and Scobie, S. (2021) 'Integrating health and social care: A comparison of policy and progress across the four countries of the UK', *The Nuffield Trust* policy report. Available at: www.nuffieldtrust.org.uk/research/integrating-health-and-social-care-a-comparison-of-policy-and-progress-across-the-four-countries-of-the-uk

Reif, K. and Schmitt, H. (1980) 'Nine second-order national elections–a conceptual framework for the analysis of European Election results', *European Journal of Political Research*, 8(1): 3–44.

Rennwald, L. (2020) *Social Democratic Parties and the Working Class: New Voting Patterns*. London: Palgrave Macmillan.

Resolution Foundation (2023) *Ending Stagnation: A New Economic Strategy for Britain*. London: Resolution Foundation.

Reuters Institute for the Study of Journalism (2023) *Reuters Digital News Report 2023: United Kingdom*. Available at: https://reutersinstitute.politics.ox.ac.uk/digital-news-report/2023/united-kingdom

Reuters Institute for the Study of Journalism (2024) *Reuters Digital News Report 2024*. Available at www.digitalnewsreport.org/

Rhodes, R.A.W, Wanna, J. and Weller, P. (2009) *Comparing Westminster*. Oxford: Oxford University Press.

Rhodes, R.A.W. (2011) *Everyday Life in British Government*. Oxford: Oxford University Press.

Rhodes, R.A.W. (2022) 'Court politics in an age of austerity: David Cameron's court 2010–2016', in Kolltveit, K. and Shaw, R. (eds), *Core Executives in a Comparative Perspective*. London: Palgrave Macmillan.

Rhodes, R.A.W. and Bevir, M. (2003) *Interpreting British Governance*. London: Routledge.

Rice, D. (2013) 'Street-level bureaucrats and the welfare state: Toward a micro-institutionalist theory of policy implementation', *Administration & Society*, 45(9): 1038–1062.

Richards, D. (2014) 'A crisis of expectations', in Richards, D., Smith, M. and Hay, C. (eds), *Institutional Crisis in Twenty-first Century Britain*. Basingstoke: Palgrave.

Richards, D. and Smith, M. (2002) *Governance and Public Policy in the UK*. Oxford: Oxford University Press.

Richardson, J.J. and Jordan, G.A. (1979) *Governing under Pressure: The Policy Process in a Post-Parliamentary Democracy*. Oxford: Martin Robertson.

Robinson, E. (2016) 'Radical nostalgia, progressive patriotism and Labour's 'English problem', *Political Studies Review*, 14(3): 378–387.

Rogstad, A. and Martill, B. (2022) 'How to be Great (Britain)? Discourses of greatness in the United Kingdom's referendums on Europe', *European Review of International Studies*, 9(2): 210–239.

Rone, J. (2023) '"Enemies of the people"? Diverging discourses on sovereignty in media coverage of Brexit', *British Politics*, 18(4): 519–537.

Rosamond, B. (2019) 'Brexit and the politics of UK growth models', *New Political Economy*, 24(3): 408–421.

Rose, E.J.B. and Deakin, N. (1969) *Colour and Citizenship: A Report on British Race Relations*. London: Oxford University Press.

Rose, R. (1982) *Understanding the United Kingdom: The Territorial Dimension in Government*. Hoboken, NJ: Prentice Hall Press.

Rose, R. and Mackie, T. (1983) Incumbency in government: asset or liability?, in H. Daalder and P. Mair (eds) *Western European Party Systems: Continuity and Change*. Beverly Hills, CA: Sage Publications.

Russell, M. (2010) 'A stronger second chamber? Assessing the impact of House of Lords reform in 1999 and the lessons for bicameralism', *Political Studies*, 58(5): 866–885.

Russell, M. (2011) '"Never allow a crisis go to waste": The Wright Committee Reforms to strengthen the House of Commons', *Parliamentary Affairs*, 64(4): 612–633.

Russell, M. (2013) *The Contemporary House of Lords: Westminster Bicameralism Revived*. Oxford: Oxford University Press.

Russell, M. (2021) 'Brexit and Parliament: The anatomy of a perfect storm', *Parliamentary Affairs*, 74(2): 443–463.

Russell, M. and Cowley, P. (2016) 'The policy power of the Westminster Parliament: The "parliamentary state" and the empirical evidence', *Governance*, 29(1): 121–137.

Russell, M. and Cowley, P. (2018) 'Modes of UK executive–legislative relations revisited', *The Political Quarterly*, 89(1): 18–28.

Russell, M. and Gover, D. (2017) *Legislation at Westminster: Parliamentary Actors and Influence in the Making of British Law*. Oxford: Oxford University Press.

Russell, M. and Gover, D. (2021) *Taking Back Control: Why the House of Commons Should Govern Its Own Time*. London: The Constitution Unit, UCL.

Russell, M. and James, L. (2023) *The Parliamentary Battle over Brexit*. Oxford: Oxford University Press.

Russell, M. and Sciara, M. (2008) 'The policy impact of defeats in the House of Lords', *The British Journal of Politics and International Relations*, 10(4): 571–589.

Russell, M. and Serban, R. (2021) 'The muddle of the "Westminster Model": A concept stretched beyond repair', *Government and Opposition*, 56(4): 744–764.

Russell, M., Gover, D. and Wollter, K. (2016) 'Does the executive dominate the Westminster legislative process? Six reasons for doubt', *Parliamentary Affairs*, 69(2): 286–308.

Saalfeld, T. and Bischof, D. (2013) 'Minority-ethnic MPs and the substantive representation of minority interests in the House of Commons, 2005–2011', *Parliamentary Affairs*, 66(2): 305–328.

Sabatier, P. (2007) 'The need for better theories', in Sabatier, P. (ed.), *Theories of the Policy Process* (2nd edn). Boulder, CO: Westview Press, Chapter 1 (pp. 3–20).

Saggar, S. (2013) 'Bending without breaking the mould: Race and political representation in the United Kingdom', *Patterns of Prejudice*, 47(1): 69–93.

Saggar, S. (ed.) (2004) *Race and British Electoral Politics* (2nd edn). Abingdon: Routledge.

Saggar, S. and Geddes, A. (2000) 'Negative and positive racialisation: Re-examining ethnic minority political representation in the UK', *Journal of Ethnic and Migration Studies*, 26(1): 25–44.

Sanders, A. and Shorrocks, R. (2019) 'All in this together? Austerity and the gender–age gap in the 2015 and 2017 British general elections', *British Journal of Politics and International Relations*, 21(4): 667–668.

Sanders, D. and Houghton, D.P. (2017) *Losing an Empire, Finding a Role: British Foreign Policy since 1945* (2nd edn). Basingstoke: Palgrave.

Sandford, M. (2016) 'Signing up to devolution: The prevalence of contract over governance in English devolution policy', *Regional & Federal Studies*, 27(1): 63–82.

Sandford, M. (2023a) *Devolution to Local Government in England: Research Briefing*. London: House of Commons. Available at: https://researchbriefings.files.parliament.uk/documents/SN07029/SN07029.pdf

Sandford, M. (2023b) '"Muscular unionism": The British political tradition strikes back?', *Political Studies*, 72(3). Advance online article ahead of print. https://doi.org/10.1177/00323217231176474

Sandford, M. and Gormley-Heenan, C. (2020) '"Taking back control": The UK's constitutional narrative and Schrodinger's devolution', *Parliamentary Affairs*, 73(1): 108–126.

Sargeant, J. and Pannell. J. (2022) *The Legislative Process: How to Empower Parliament*. London and Cambridge: Institute for Government; Cambridge: Bennett Institute for Public Policy.

Sasse, T. and Thomas, A. (2022) 'Better policy making', *Institute for Government* policy report. Available at: www.instituteforgovernment.org.uk/publication/better-policy-making

Saunders, R. (2018) *Yes to Europe! The 1975 Referendum and Seventies Britain*. Cambridge: Cambridge University Press.

Saunders, R. (2020) 'Brexit and Empire: "Global Britain" and the myth of imperial nostalgia', *Journal of Imperial and Commonwealth History*, 48(6): 1140–1174.

Savage, M. (2015) *Social Class in the 21st Century*. London: Pelican.

Savage, M., Devine, F., Cunningham, N., Taylor, M., Li, Y., Hjellbrekke, J., Le Roux, B., Friedman, S. and Miles, A. (2013) 'A new model of social class? Findings from the BBC's Great British Class Survey Experiment', *Sociology*, 47(2): 219–50. https://doi.org/10.1177/0038038513481128

Saward, M. (2006) 'The representative claim', *Contemporary Political Theory* 5(3): 297–318.

Saward, M. (2010) *The Representative Claim*. Oxford: Oxford University Press.

Saward, M. (2021) *Democratic Design*. Oxford: Oxford University Press.

Sawers, J. (2024) *Downward Spiral: Collapsing Public Standards and How to Restore Them*. Manchester: Manchester University Press.

Schlozman, K.L., Brady, H.E. and Verba, S. (2020) *Unequal and Unrepresented: Political Inequality and the People's Voice in the New Gilded Age*. Princeton, NJ: Princeton University Press.

Schnapper, P. (2021) 'Theresa May, the Brexit negotiations and the two-level game, 2017–2019', *Journal of Contemporary European Studies*, 29(3): 368–379.

Schofield, C. (2013) *Enoch Powell and the Making of Postcolonial Britain*. Cambridge: Cambridge University Press.

Schuette, L.A. (2021) 'Forging unity: European Commission leadership in the Brexit negotiations', *Journal of Common Market Studies*, 59(5): 1142–1159.

Schwarz, N., Sanna, L.J., Skurnik, I. and Yoon, C. (2007) 'Metacognitive experiences and the intricacies of setting people straight: Implications for debiasing and public information campaigns', *Advances in Experimental Social Psychology*, 39: 127–161.

Scott, D. (2017) 'The rise of India: UK perspectives', *International Affairs*, 93(1): 165–188.

Scott, J.W. (1986) 'Gender: A useful category of historical analysis', *American Historical Review*, 91(5): 1053–1075.

Scottish Executive (2000) *National Strategy to Address Domestic Abuse in Scotland*, Edinburgh: Scottish Executive.

Scottish Government (2016) *Equally Safe: Scotland's Strategy for Preventing and Eradicating Violence Against Women and Girls*. Edinburgh: Scottish Government.

Scottish Government (2023) *Government Expenditure and Revenue: Scotland, 2022–23*. Edinburgh: Scottish Government. Available at: https://www.gov.scot/publications/government-expenditure-revenue-scotland-2022-23

Scottish Parliament (2021) *Report of the Committee on the Scottish Government Handling of Harassment Complaints. First Report* (SP 997, session 5), 23 March. Edinburgh: Scottish Parliament. Available at: https://digitalpublications.parliament.scot/Committees/Report/SGHHC/2021/3/23/3dc69e08-899e-4d55-aa77-83f08cc4a815#5b561795-53af-4544-971b-5508882c5715.dita

Scottish Parliament (2023) *A Parliament for All: Report of the Parliament's Gender-Sensitive Audit*. Edinburgh: Scottish Parliament. Available at: www.parliament.scot/about/news/news-listing/a-parliament-for-all-reforms (accessed 22 February 2024).

Scruton, R. (2000) *England: An Elegy*. London: Pimlico.

Scully, R. and Larner, J. (2017) 'A Successful Defence: the 2016 National Assembly for Wales Election', *Parliamentary Affairs*, 70(3): 507–529, https://doi.org/10.1093/pa/gsw033

Scully, R. And Wyn Jones, R. (2011) *Wales Says Yes*. Cardiff: Cardiff University Press.

Scully, R. and Wyn Jones, R. (2012) 'Still Three Wales? Social Location and Electoral Behaviour in Contemporary Wales', *Electoral Studies*, 31(4): 656–667.

Scully, R. (2013) 'More Scottish than Welsh? Explaining the outcomes of the 2011 devolved elections', *Regional & Federal Studies*, 23(5): 591–612.10.1080/13597566.2013.810147

Searing, D.D. (1994) *Westminster's World: Understanding Political Roles*. Cambridge, MA: Harvard University Press.

Seaton, J. (2016) 'Brexit and the media', *The Political Quarterly*, 87(3): 333–337.

Seawright, D. (2011) *The British Conservative Party and One Nation Politics*. London: Ashgate.

Seldon, A. (2019) *May at 10*. London: Biteback.

Seldon, A. and Ball, S. (1994) *The Conservative Century*. Oxford: Oxford University Press.

Seldon, A. and Newell, R. (2023) *Johnson at No 10: The Inside Story*. London: Atlantic Books.

Senate - Commerce, Science, and Transportation (1996) Communications Decency Act of 1995. 104th Congress (1995-1996) https://www.congress.gov/bill/104th-congress/senate-bill/314

Severs, E., Celis, K. and Erzeel, S. (2016) 'Power, privilege and disadvantage: Intersectionality theory and political representation', *Politics*, 36(4): 346–354.

Shannon, M. M, (2007) 'Shaking hands, kissing babies, and . . . blogging? The Internet and technology seek to influence politics as usual', *Communications of the ACM,* 50(9): 21–24.

Sheldon, J. (2022) 'Standing up for the nations? Devolution and the changing territorial role of backbench MPs with constituencies in Northern Ireland, Scotland and Wales, 1992–2019', *Parliamentary Affairs*, 75(4): 791–812.

Shephard, M. and Cairney, P. (2005) 'The impact of the Scottish Parliament in amending executive legislation', *Political Studies*, 53(2): 303–319.

Shepherd-Robinson, L. and Lovenduski, J. (2002) *Women and Candidate Selection in British Political Parties*. London: Fawcett.

Shipman, T. (2017) *All Out War: The Full Story of Brexit*. London: William Collins.

Shipman, T. (2018) *Fallout*. London: William Collins.

Shipman, T. (2024) *No Way Out: From the Backstop to Boris*. London: William Collins.

Short, C. (1996) 'Women and the Labour Party', *Parliamentary Affairs*, 49(1): 17–25.

Shukra, K. (1998) *The Changing Pattern of Black Politics in Britain*. London: Pluto Press.

Sibieta, L. (2023) 'Growing gap in school spending per pupil between Scotland and the rest of the UK', *Institute for Fiscal Studies*, 21 April. Available at: https://ifs.org.uk/news/growing-gap-school-spending-pupil-between-scotland-and-rest-uk

Siddique, H. (2023) 'Ministers accused of cover-up over claims former UK ambassador leaked intelligence', *The Guardian*, 31 May. Available at: www.theguardian.com/uk-news/2023/may/31/ministers-accused-of-cover-up-over-claims-former-uk-ambassador-leaked-intelligence (accessed 26 February 2024).

Siebert, S. (2023) 'Buildings and institutional change: Stepping stones or stumbling blocks?', *British Journal of Management*, 35(1): 281–294. https://doi.org/10.1111/1467-8551.12711

Simon, H. (1976) *Administrative Behavior* (3rd edn). London: Macmillan.

Siow, O. (2023a) 'Needles in a haystack: An intersectional analysis of the descriptive, constitutive and substantive representation of minoritized women', *European Journal of Politics & Gender*, 6(3): 328–358.

Siow, O. (2023b) 'What constitutes substantive representation, and where should we evaluate it?', *Political Studies Review*, 21(3): 532–538.

Skey, M. (2012) '"Sod them, I'm English!" The changing status of the "majority" English in post-devolution Britain', *Ethnicities*, 12(1): 106–125.

Slapin, J.B. and Kirkland, J.H. (2020) 'The sound of rebellion: Voting dissent and legislative speech in the UK House of Commons', *Legislative Studies Quarterly*, 45(2): 153–176.

Slapin, J.B., Kirkland, J.H., Lazzaro, J.A. Leslie, P.A. and O'Grady, T. (2018) 'Ideology, grandstanding, and strategic party disloyalty in the British Parliament', *American Political Science Review*, 112(1): 15–30.

Slater, J. (2022) 'Fixing Whitehall's broken policy machine', *King's College London Policy Institute* research report. Available at: www.kcl.ac.uk/policy-institute/assets/fixing-whitehalls-broken-policy-machine.pdf

Sloman, P. (2024) 'Labour, more or less? Policy reasoning in a fiscal register', *The British Journal of Politics and International Relations*, 26(1): 22–38.

Smith, J. (2016) 'David Cameron's EU renegotiation and referendum pledge: A case of *déjà vu*?', *British Politics*, 11(3): 324–346.

Smith, K. (2013) *Beyond Evidence-based Policy in Public Health*. Basingstoke: Palgrave.

Smith, M.J. (1999) *The Core Executive in Britain*. London: Palgrave Macmillan.

Smooth, W. (2011) 'Standing for women? Which women? The substantive representation of women's interests and the research imperative of intersectionality', *Politics & Gender*, 7(3): 436–441.

Sobolewska, M. (2013) 'Party strategies and the descriptive representation of ethnic minorities: The 2010 British General Election', *West European Politics*, 36(3): 615–633.

Sobolewska, M. and Barclay, A. (2021) *The Democratic Participation of Ethnic Minority and Immigrant Voters in the UK*. York: Joseph Rowntree Foundation. Available at: www.jrrt.org.uk/wp-content/uploads/2021/11/The_Democratic_Participation_of_Ethnic_Minority_and_Immigrant_Voters_in_the_UK.pdf

Sobolewska, M. and Begum, N. (2020) *Ethnic Minority Representation in UK Local Government*. Manchester: University of Manchester. https://documents.manchester.ac.uk/DocuInfo.aspx?DocID=49921

Sobolewska, M. and Ford, R. (2020) *Brexitland: Identity, Diversity and the Reshaping of British Politics*. Cambridge: Cambridge University Press.

Sobolewska, M., McKee, R. and Campbell, R. (2018) 'Explaining motivation to represent: How does descriptive representation lead to substantive representation of racial and ethnic minorities?', *West European Politics*, 41(6): 1237–1261.

Social Mobility Commission (SMC) (2021) *Simplifying How Employers Measure Socio-Economic Background*. London: Social Mobility Commission. Available at: www.gov.uk/government/publications/understanding-a-workforces-socio-economic-background-for-change/simplifying-how-employers-measure-socio-economic-background-an-accompanying-report-to-new-guidance

Social Mobility Commission and The Sutton Trust (2019) *Elitism in Britain 2019*. London: Social Mobility Commission.

Soroka, S., Andrew, B., Aalberg, T., Iyengar, S., Curran, J., Coen, S., ... and Tiffen, R. (2013) 'Auntie knows best? Public broadcasters and current affairs knowledge', *British Journal of Political Science*, 43(4): 719–739.

Southgate, G. (2021) 'Dear England', *The Players' Tribune*, 8 June. Available at: https://www.theplayerstribune.com/posts/dear-england-gareth-southgate-euros-soccer (accessed 5 October 2024).

Spiers, M. and Le Lohé, M.J. (1964) 'Pakistanis in the Bradford municipal election of 1963', *Political Studies*, 12(1): 85–92.

Squires, J. (1999) *Gender in Political Theory*. Cambridge: Polity.

Starmer, K. (2020) 'Labour can win again if we make the moral case for socialism', *The Guardian*, 15 January. Available at: www.theguardian.com/commentisfree/2020/jan/15/labour-socialism-values-election-economic-model (accessed 28 February 2024).

Starmer, K. (2024) 'Labour is now the true party of English patriotism', *The Daily Telegraph*, 20 April. Available at: www.telegraph.co.uk/news/2024/04/20/labour-is-now-the-true-party-of-english-patriotism/ (accessed 21 April 2024).

Stegmaier, M. et al. (2013) 'Standing for Parliament: Do Black, Asian and minority ethnic candidates pay extra?', *Parliamentary Affairs*, 66(2): 268–285.

Stern, P.J. (2023) *Empire, Incorporated: The Corporation that Built British Colonialism*. Cambridge, MA and London: Harvard University Press.

Sternberg, C.S. (2013) *The Struggle for EU Legitimacy: Public Contestation, 1950–2005*. Basingstoke: Palgrave Macmillan.

Stewart, D. (2009) *The Path to Devolution and Change: A Political History of Scotland under Margaret Thatcher*. London: I.B. Tauris.

Stewart, R. (2023) *Politics on the Edge: A Memoir from Within*. London: Jonathan Cape.

Stirbu, D., Larner, J. and McAllister, L. (2018) 'Gender representation in Wales: New approaches to candidate selection in UK's devolved legislatures and beyond', in Cordero, G. and Coller, X. (eds), *Democratizing Candidate Selection: New Methods, Old Receipts?* Basingstoke: Palgrave Macmillan, pp. 201–230.

Stockmann, D., Luo, T. and Shen, M. (2020) 'Designing authoritarian deliberation: How social media platforms influence political talk in China', *Democratization*, 27(2): 243–264.

Strangio, P., t'Hart, P. and Walter, J. (eds) (2013) *Understanding Prime Ministerial Performance: Comparative Perspectives*. Oxford: Oxford University Press.

Strom, K. (1990) 'A behavioral theory of competitive political parties', *American Journal of Political Science*, 34(2): 565–598. https://doi.org/10.2307/2111461

Strøm, K. (1997) 'Rules, reasons and routines: Legislative roles in parliamentary democracies', *The Journal of Legislative Studies*, 3(1): 155–174.

Strong, J. (2015) 'Why Parliament now decides on war: Tracing the growth of parliamentary prerogative through Syria, Libya and Iraq', *British Journal of Politics and International Relations*, 17(4): 604–622.

Strong, J. (2022) 'Did Theresa May kill the war powers convention? Comparing Parliamentary debates on UK intervention in Syria in 2013 and 2018', *Parliamentary Affairs*, 75(2): 400–419.

Swinford, S. and Wright, O. (2021) 'Boris Johnson eyes another decade in power', *The Times*, 11 September. Available at: www.thetimes.co.uk/article/boris-johnson-eyes-another-decade-in-power-jp0chz9xl

Taylor, A. and Klimentov, M. (2023) 'Why Finland – and not Sweden – in in NATO', *The Washington Post*, 4 April. Available at: www.washingtonpost.com/world/2023/04/04/finland-sweden-nato-membership/ (accessed 4 March 2024).

Taylor, M. (2021) *The Interest: How the British Establishment Resisted the Abolition of Slavery*. London: The Bodley Head.

Tchilingirian, J. (2021) '"Network intellectuals" and "Networked intellectuals": Relational approaches to the study of British think tanks', in Abelson, D.E. and Rastrick, C.J. (eds), *Handbook on Think Tanks in Public Policy*. Cheltenham: Edward Elgar, Chapter 1 (pp. 2–15).

Thain, C. (2004) 'Treasury rules, OK? The further evolution of a British institution', *British Journal of Politics & International Relations*, 6(1): 121–128.

The Cabinet Office (2011) *The Cabinet Manual: A Guide to the Laws, Conventions, and Rules on the Operation of Government*. London: The Cabinet Office.

The Constitution Unit (UCL) (2021) 'Working Group in Unification Referendums on the Island of Ireland: Final Report', May. London: The Constitution Unit, UCL. Available at: www.ucl.ac.uk/constitution-unit/sites/constitution-unit/files/working_group_final_report.pdf (accessed 20 June 2024).

The Constitution Unit (UCL) (2023) 'Election spending limits: We're going to spend, spend, spend (or are we)?', *The Constitution Unit Blog*, 5 October. London: UCL. Available at: https://constitution-unit.com/2023/10/05/election-spending-limits-were-going-to-spend-spend-spend-or-are-we/

The Executive Office (2024) 'Ministerial Code' *Northern Ireland Executive* Available: https://www.northernireland.gov.uk/topics/your-executive/ministerial-code (accessed 29 February 2024) para. 2.12.

The Labour Party (1945) *Let Us Face the Future: A Declaration of Labour Policy for the Consideration of the Nation*. London: The Labour Party. Available at: https://history.hanover.edu/courses/excerpts/111lab.html

The Ministerial Code (2022). *The Cabinet Office.*

The Prime Minister's Office (2023) *The Windsor Framework*. Policy paper, 27 February. Available at: www.gov.uk/government/publications/the-windsor-framework

The Prime Minister's Office (2023) *The Windsor Framework*. Policy paper, 27 February. Available at: www.gov.uk/government/publications/the-windsor-framework

Thelen, K. (2004) *How Institutions Evolve: The Political Economy of Skills in Germany, Britain, the United States, and Japan*. Cambridge: Cambridge University Press.

Thérien, J. (2002) 'Debating foreign aid: Right versus left', *Third World Quarterly*, 23(3): 449–466.

Thomas, G., Morgan, L. and Wilkes, J. (2021) 'Election 2021: How diverse is the sixth Senedd?', *Senedd Cymru* [Blog], 11 May. Available at: https://research.senedd.wales/research-articles/election-2021-how-diverse-is-the-sixth-senedd/

Thompson, H. (2009) 'The Thatcherite economic legacy', in Farrall, S. and Hay, C. (eds), *The Legacy of Thatcherism: Assessing and Exploring Thatcherite Social and Economic Policies*. Oxford: Oxford University Press.

Thompson, H. (2017) 'Inevitability and contingency: The political economy of Brexit', *British Journal of Politics and International Relations*, 19(3): 434–449.

Thompson, L. (2015) *Making British Law: Committees in Action*. Basingstoke: Palgrave Macmillan.

Thompson, N. (2006) *Political Economy and the Labour Party* (2nd edn). Abingdon: Routledge.

Thomson, J. (2018) 'Resisting gendered change: Feminist institutionalism and critical actors', *International Political Science Review*, 39(2): 178–191.

Thomson, J. (2019) *Abortion Law and Political Institutions: Explaining Policy Resistance*. Basingstoke: Palgrave Macmillan.

Thomson, J. (2022) 'A "United" Kingdom? The 1967 Abortion Act and Northern Ireland', in Bloomer, F. and Campbell, E. (eds), *Decriminalizing Abortion in Northern Ireland: Legislation and Protest*. London: Bloomsbury Academic, pp. 43–54.

Timmins, N. (2016) 'Universal Credit: From disaster to recovery?', *Institute for Government* research report. Available at: www.instituteforgovernment.org.uk/publication/report/universal-credit-disaster-recovery

Timothy, N. (2020) *Remaking One Nation: The Future of Conservatism*. Cambridge: Polity Press.

Tingley, D. (2010) 'Donors and domestic politics: Political influences on foreign aid effort', *The Quarterly Review of Economics and Finance*, 50(1): 40–49.

Tolley, A. (2023) *Investigation Report to the Prime Minister: Report of Formal Complaints about the Conduct of the Rt Honourable Dominic Raab MP, Deputy Prime Minister, Lord Chancellor and Secretary of State for Justice*. Policy paper, 21 April. Available at: www.gov.uk/government/publications/investigation-report-to-the-prime-minister

Tomkins, A. (2009) 'Constitutionalism' in Flinders, M., Gamble, A., Hay, C. And Kenny, M. (eds), *The Oxford Handbook of British Politics*. Oxford: Oxford University Press.

Tomkins, A. (2009) 'The constitution', in Flinders, M. et al. (eds), *The Oxford Handbook of British Politics*. Oxford: Oxford University Press.

Tonge, J., Wilks-Heeg, S. and Thompson, L. (eds) (2020) *Britain Votes: The 2019 General Election*. Oxford: Oxford University Press.

Toosi, N. (2022) 'US on Johnson's departure: "OK, bye"', *Politico*, 7 July. Available at: www.politico.com/news/2022/07/07/biden-on-johnsons-departure-who-00044584 (accessed 4 March 2024).

Tormey, S. (2015) *The End of Representative Politics*. Cambridge: Polity Press.

Torrance, D. (2009) *'We in Scotland': Thatcherism in a Cold Climate*. Edinburgh: Birlinn.

Torrance, D. (ed.) (2020) *Ruth Davidson's Conservatives: The Scottish Tory Party, 2011–19*. Edinburgh: Edinburgh University Press.

Torrance, D. and Pyper, D. (2023) 'The Secretary of State's veto and the Gender Recognition Reform (Scotland) Bill', Briefing paper, 17 January. London: House of Commons Library. Available at: https://commonslibrary.parliament.uk/research-briefings/cbp-9705/ (accessed 4 October 2023).

Tournier-Sol, K. (2015) 'Reworking the Eurosceptic and Conservative traditions into a populist narrative: UKIP's winning formula?', *Journal of Common Market Studies*, 53(1): 140–156.

Townsley, J. (2018) 'Is it worth door-knocking? Evidence from a United Kingdom-based Get Out The Vote (GOTV) field experiment on the effect of party leaflets and canvass visits on voter turnout', *Political Science Research and Methods*, First view: 3 October: 1–15. https://doi.org/10.1017/psrm.2018.39

Toye, R. (2024) *Age of Hope: Labour, 1945, and the Birth of Modern Britain*. London: Bloomsbury.

Trengove, M., Kazim, E., Almeida, D., Hilliard, A., Zannone, S. and Lomas, E. (2022) 'A critical review of the Online Safety Bill', *Patterns*, 3(8).

Trentini, M. (2022) 'Political attitudes, participation and union membership in the UK', *Industrial Relations Journal*, 53(1): 19–34. https://doi.org/10.1111/irj.12352.

Tucker, J.A., Guess, A., Barberá, P., Vaccari, C., Siegel, A., Sanovich, S., Stukal, D. and Nyhan, B. (2018) 'Social media, political polarization, and political disinformation: A review of the scientific literature', *SSRN Electronic Journal*, 21 March. http://dx.doi.org/10.2139/ssrn.3144139

Tufekci, Z. (2014) 'Big questions for social media big data: Representativeness, validity and other methodological pitfalls', in Proceedings of the International AAAI Conference on Web and Social Media, 8(1): 505–514.

UK Government (2000a) *Agreement between the Government of the United Kingdom of Great Britain and Northern Ireland and the Government of Ireland establishing a North/South Ministerial Council*. Treaty Series No. 53. Available at: https://treaties.fcdo.gov.uk/data/Library2/pdf/2000-TS0053.pdf (accessed 29 February 2024).

UK Government (2000b) *Agreement between the Government of the United Kingdom of Great Britain and Northern Ireland and the Government of Ireland establishing Implementation Bodies*. Treaty Series No. 51. Available at: https://treaties.fcdo.gov.uk/data/Library2/pdf/2000-TS0051.pdf (accessed 29 February 2024).

UK Government (2000c) *Agreement between the Government of the United Kingdom of Great Britain and Northern Ireland and the Government of Ireland (British-Irish Agreement)*. Treaty Series No. 50. Cm 4292. London: HMSO.

UK Parliament (2012) *Restoration and Renewal of the Palace of Westminster: Pre-feasibility Study and Preliminary Strategic Business Case*. London: UK Parliament.

UK Parliament (2018) *UK Gender-Sensitive Parliament Audit 2018*. London: UK Parliament.

UK Parliament (2020) 'Written evidence from Dr Alistair Clark and Professor Toby S. James (TEC 13)', 4 November. London: UK Parliament. Available at: https://committees.parliament.uk/writtenevidence/15072/pdf

UK Parliament (2024a) *Lords membership – MPs and Lords – UK Parliament*. London: UK Parliament. Available at: https://members.parliament.uk/parties/Lords (accessed 8 July 2024).

UK Parliament (2024b) *Government Defeats in the House of Lords*. London: UK Parliament. Available at: www.parliament.uk/about/faqs/house-of-lords-faqs/lords-govtdefeats/ (accessed 5 July 2024).

Urban, J., Thomas, A. and Clyne, R. (2024) 'Power with purpose: Final report of the Commission on the Centre of Government', *Institute for Government* research report. Available at: www.instituteforgovernment.org.uk/publication/power-with-purpose-centre-commission

Urbinati, N. (2006) *Representative Democracy*. Chicago: University of Chicago Press.

Usherwood, S. (2021) '"Our European friends and partners"? Negotiating the Trade and Cooperation Agreement', *Journal of Common Market Studies*, 59(S1): 115–123.

Usherwood, S. and Wright, K.A. (2017) 'Sticks and stones: Comparing Twitter campaigning strategies in the European Union referendum', *British Journal of Politics and International Relations*, 19(2): 371–388.

Vaccari, C. and Valeriani, A. (2021) *Outside the Bubble: Social Media and Political Participation in Western Democracies*. Oxford: Oxford University Press.

Vaccari, C., Chadwick, A. and O'Loughlin, B. (2015) 'Dual screening the political: Media events, social media, and citizen engagement', *Journal of Communication*, 65(6): 1041–1061.

Van Aelst, P., Strömbäck, J., Aalberg, T., Esser, F., De Vreese, C., Matthes, J. ... and Stanyer, J. (2017) 'Political communication in a high-choice media environment: A challenge for democracy?', *Annals of the International Communication Association*, 41(1): 3–27.

van der Zwet, A. (2015) 'Operationalising national identity: The cases of the Scottish National Party and Frisian National Party', *Nations and Nationalism*, 21(1): 62–82.

van Kessel, S., Chelotti, N., Drake, H., Roch, J. and Rodi, P. (2020) 'Eager to leave? Populist radical right parties' responses to the UK's Brexit vote', *British Journal of Politics and International Relations*, 22(1): 65–84.

Ventre, L. (2023) 'David Pitt', *UncoverED*, 24 June. Edinburgh: University of Edinburgh. Available at: www.ed.ac.uk/global/uncovered/1930/david-pitt

Virdee, S. and McGeever, B. (2018) 'Racism, crisis, Brexit', *Ethnic and Racial Studies*, 41(10): 1802–1819.

Vivyan, N., Wagner, M., Glinitzer, K. and Eberl, J.-M. (2020) 'Do humble beginnings help? How politician class roots shape voter evaluations', *Electoral Studies*, 63(February). https://doi.org/10.1016/j.electstud.2019.102093.

Wachowiak, J. and Zuleeg, F. (2022) 'Brexit and the Trade and Cooperation Agreement: Implications for internal and external EU differentiation', *The International Spectator*, 57(1): 142–159.

Wagner, K. (2019) *Amritsar 1919: An Empire of Fear and the Making of a Massacre*. New Haven, CT: Yale University Press.

Wahl-Jorgensen, K. (2019) *Emotions, Media and Politics*. Chichester: John Wiley & Sons.

Walker, A. (2012). 'A People's Parliament?', *Parliamentary Affairs*, 65:1, 270–280.

Walker, A., Jurczak, N., Bochel, C. and Leston-Bandeira, C. (2019) 'How public engagement became a core part of the House of Commons select committees', *Parliamentary Affairs*, 72(4): 965–986.

Walker, C. (2015) 'Discretionary payments in social assistance', in Hupe, P., Hill, M. and Buffat, A. (eds), *Understanding Street-level Bureaucracy*. Bristol: Policy Press, Chapter 3 (pp. 45–60).

Walker, N. (2014) 'Our Constitutional Unsettlement', *Public Law*, 529–548.

Walker, P. (2024) 'Voter ID rule may have stopped 400,000 taking part in UK election, poll suggests'. *The Guardian*, 8 July. https://www.theguardian.com/politics/article/2024/jul/08/voter-id-rule-may-have-stopped-400000-taking-part-in-uk-election-poll-suggests

Ward, J. (2020) 'Reasserting the centre: The Brexit Doctrine and the imperative mandate in British politics', *Parliamentary Affairs*, 74(4): 890–910.

Ward, S. (2023) *United Kingdom: A Global History of the End of Britain*. Cambridge: Cambridge University Press.

Ward, S. and Rasch, A. (eds) (2019) *Embers of Empire in Brexit Britain*. London: Bloomsbury.

Warren, M. (2019) 'How representation enables democratic citizenship', in Castiglione, D. and Pollak, J. (eds), *Creating Political Presence*. Chicago: University of Chicago Press, pp. 39–60.

Waterson, J. (2024) 'UK political parties on track to spend £1m on election day online ads'. *The Guardian*, available at https://www.theguardian.com/politics/article/2024/jul/04/uk-political-parties-election-day-advertising

Watt, N. (2012) 'Ed Miliband uses diamond jubilee buzz to talk up Englishness', *The Guardian*, 7 June. Available at: https://www.theguardian.com/politics/2012/jun/07/ed-miliband-diamond-jubilee-englishness (accessed 5 October 2024).

Watts, R. (2007) *The Federal Idea and Its Contemporary Relevance*. Kingston: Institute of Intergovernmental Relations, Queen's University.

Waylen, G. (2010) 'Researching ritual and the symbolic in parliaments: An institutionalist perspective', *The Journal of Legislative Studies*, 16(3): 352–365.

We Are Social (2024) *Digital 2024: The United Kingdom*. Available at: https://wearesocial.com/uk/blog/2024/01/digital-2024/

Weale, A. (2018) *The Will of the People: A Modern Myth*. Cambridge: Polity Press.

Webb, D. (2024) 'The Comprehensive and Progressive Agreement for Trans-Pacific Partnership (CPTPP)', research briefing, 19 January. London: House of Commons Library. Available at: https://commonslibrary.parliament.uk/research-briefings/cbp-9121/ (accessed 19 February 2024).

Weber, M. (2010) 'The distribution of power within the community: Classes, stände, parties' [Trans. Waters, D., Waters, W., Hahnke, E., Lippke, M., Ludwig-Glück, E., Mai, D., Ritzi-Messner, N., Veldhoen, C. and Fassnacht, L.], *Journal of Classical Sociology*, 10(2): 137–152. https://doi.org/10.1177/1468795X10361546

Weight, R. (2002) *Patriots: National Identity in Britain, 1940–2000*. London: Macmillan.

Weinberg, J. (2020) *Who Enters Politics and Why? Basic Human Values in the UK Parliament*. Bristol: Bristol University Press.

Weinberg, J. (2021) 'Who wants to be a politician? Basic human values and candidate emergence in the United Kingdom', *British Journal of Political Science*, 51(4): 1565–1581.

Weldon, S.L. (2002) 'Beyond bodies: Institutional sources of representation for women in democratic policymaking', *Journal of Politics*, 64(4): 132–154.

Wellings, B. (2012) *Euroscepticism and English Nationalism: Losing the Peace*. Oxford: Peter Lang.

Wellings, B. (2019) *English Nationalism, Brexit and the Anglosphere: Wider Still and Wider*. Manchester: Manchester University Press.

Wellings, B. and Mycock, A. (2019) *The Anglosphere: Continuity, Dissonance and Location*. Oxford: Oxford University Press for the British Academy.

Welsh Parliament (2021) *Senedd Election 2021: Research Briefing*. Cardiff: Welsh Parliament.

Wenzelburger, G. and Boller, F. (2020) 'Bomb or build? How party ideologies affect the balance of foreign aid and defence spending', *British Journal of Politics and International Relations*, 22(1): 3–23.

Wheare, K.C. (1960) *The Constitutional Structure of the Commonwealth*. Oxford: Clarendon Press.

White, H. (2015) *Select Committees Under Scrutiny: The Impact of Parliamentary Committee Inquiries on Government*. London: Institute for Government.

White, H. (2022) *Held in Contempt: What's Wrong with the House of Commons?* Manchester: Manchester University Press.

White, J. (2016) 'Dismiss, distort, distract, and dismay: Continuity and change in Russian disinformation', Institute for European Studies Policy Brief 13. Brussels: Vrije Universiteit.

White, J. (2024) 'Exclusive: UK political parties spend £1 million on online ads in first week of campaign'. *Tortoise*. Available at https://www.tortoisemedia.com/2024/06/03/exclusive-uk-political-parties-spend-1-million-on-online-ads-in-first-week-of-campaign/

White, S.G. (2022) 'The referendum in the UK's constitution: From parliamentary to popular sovereignty?', *Parliamentary Affairs*, 75(2): 263–280.

Whitten, L. C. (2023) *Brexit and the Northern Ireland Constitution*. London: Oxford University Press.

Whitten, L.C. (2023a) 'Brexit and Strand Three of the 1998 Agreement: The three faces of East–West', *The Political Quarterly*, 94(1): 122–132.

Whitten, L.C. (2023b) *Brexit and the Northern Ireland Constitution*. London: Oxford University Press.

Wilkes, G., Bartrum, O. and Clyne, R. (2024) 'Treasury "orthodoxy": What is it? And is it a problem for government?', *Institute for Government* research report. Available at: www.instituteforgovernment.org.uk/publication/treasury-orthodoxy

Wilks, S. (2013) *The Political Power of the Business Corporation*. Cheltenham: Edward Elgar.

Wille, T. and Martill, B. (2023) 'Trust and calculation in international negotiations: How trust was lost after Brexit', *International Affairs*, 99(6): 2405–2422.

Williams www.postofficehorizoninquiry.org.uk

Williams, M. (1998) *Voice, Trust, and Memory: The Failings of Liberal Representation*. Princeton, NJ: Princeton University Press.

Willocq, S. (2019) 'Explaining time of vote decision: The socio-structural, attitudinal, and contextual determinants of late deciding', *Political Studies Review*, 17: 53–64.

Willumsen, D.M. (2019) 'So far away from me? The effect of geographical distance on representation', *West European Politics*, 42(3): 645–669.

Wintour, P. (2015) 'One million minority ethnic votes helped Tories to No 10, think tank finds', *The Guardian*, 24 May. Available at: www.theguardian.com/politics/2015/may/24/one-million-minority-ethnic-votes-helped-tories-no-10

Wood, A.J. (2020) *Despotism on Demand: How Power Operates in the Flexible Workplace*. Ithaca, NY: ILR Press.

Wright, E.O. (1997) *Classes*. Verso Classics. London: Verso.

Wright, T. (2010) 'What are MPs for?', *The Political Quarterly*, 81(3): 298–308.

Wring, D. (2005) 'Politics and the media: The Hutton Inquiry, the public relations state, and crisis at the BBC', *Parliamentary Affairs*, 58(2): 380–393.

Wring, D. and Ward, S. (2020) 'From bad to worse? The media and the 2019 election campaign', *Parliamentary Affairs*, 73: 272–287.

Wring, D., Mortimore, R. and Atkinson, S. (eds) (2021) *Political Communication in Britain: Campaigning, Media and Polling in the 2019 General Election*. Berlin: Springer Nature.

Wyn Jones, R. (2022) 'Understanding a century of Labour dominance: Social science and the puzzle of voting behaviour in Wales', *Transactions of the Honourable Society of Cymmrodorion*, 28: 25–45.

Wyn Jones, R. (2024) *Putting Wales First: The Political Thought of Plaid Cymru Volume 1*. Cardiff: University of Wales Press.

Wyn Jones, R. and Larner, J. (2020) 'Progressive home rule?' *IPPR Progressive Review*, 27: 235–245. https://doi.org/10.1111/newe.12221

Wyn Jones, R., Lodge, G., Henderson A. and Wincott, D. (2012) *The Dog That Finally Barked. The Emergence of England as a Political Community*. London: Institute for Public Policy Research.

Wyn Jones, R., Lodge, G., Henderson A. and Wincott, D. (2012) *The Dog That Finally Barked. The Emergence of England as a Political Community*. London: Institute for Public Policy Research.

Wyn Jones, R., Scully, R., & Trystan, D. (2002). Why do the Conservatives always do (even) worse in Wales? *British Elections & Parties Review*, 12(1), 229–245. https://doi.org/10.1080/13689880208413079

YouGov (2015) 'Leaders – Perceptions', *YouGov*. Available at: https://ygo-assets-websites-editorial-emea.yougov.net/documents/YG-Archives-Pol-Trackers-Leaders-Perceptions-220415.pdf

YouGov (2024) 'Voting Intention Tracker', *YouGov*. Available at: https://yougov.co.uk/topics/politics/trackers/voting-intention

Young, I.M. (2002) *Inclusion and Democracy*. New York: Oxford University Press.

Young, M.D. (1994) *The Rise of the Meritocracy*. New Brunswick, NJ: Transaction Publishers.

Yousaf, H. (2024) 'Humza Yousaf's resignation speech in full', *BBC News*, 29 April. Available at: www.bbc.co.uk/news/uk-scotland-68921671

Zacka, B. (2017) *When the State Meets the Street: Public Service and Moral Agency*. Cambridge, MA: Belknap Press of Harvard University Press.

Index

Page numbers followed by "f" indicate figures; those followed by "t" indicate tables.